Poverty: A Global Review

Poverty: A Global Review
Handbook on International Poverty Research

Edited by Else Øyen, S. M. Miller,
and Syed Abdus Samad

SCANDINAVIAN UNIVERSITY PRESS
Oslo – Stockholm – Copenhagen – Boston

Scandinavian University Press (Universitetsforlaget AS)
P.O. Box 2959 Tøyen, N-0608 Oslo, Norway
Fax +47 22 57 53 53

Stockholm office
SCUP, Scandinavian University Press
P.O. Box 3255, S-103 65 Stockholm, Sweden
Fax +46 8 20 99 82

Copenhagen office
Scandinavian University Press AS
P.O. Box 54, DK-1002 København K, Denmark
Fax +45 33 32 05 70

Boston office
Scandinavian University Press North America
875 Massachusetts Ave., Ste. 84, Cambridge MA 02139, USA
Fax +1 617 354 6875

© Scandinavian University Press (Universitetsforlaget AS), Oslo
1996

ISBN 82-00-22649-2

Published with grants from UNESCO and Deutsche Gesellschaft für
Technische Zusammenarbeit (GTZ)

All rights reserved. No part of this publication may be reproduced,
stored in a retrieval system, or transmitted, in any form or by any
means, electronic, mechanical, photocopying, recording, or
otherwise, without the prior permission of Scandinavian University
Press. Enquiries should be sent to the Rights Department,
Scandinavian University Press, Oslo, at the address above.

Design: Astrid Elisabeth Jørgensen
Cover illustration: © Creastock/BAVARIA (Sjøberg Bildebyrå, Oslo)
Typeset in 10 on 11 point Times New Roman by
Paston Press Ltd, Loddon, Norfolk, UK
Printed by HS-Trykk a.s., Oslo, Norway

Contents

Foreword by Gro Harlem Brundtland vii
Preface ix

Part I: *Poverty and Poverty Research* 1
1 Poverty Research Rethought *Else Øyen* 3
2 Drawing Together Some Regional Perspectives on Poverty *Francis Wilson* 18
3 The Present Situation in Poverty Research *Syed Abdus Samad* 33
4 Concepts of Poverty *Mojca Novak* 47

Part II: *The Asian Region* 63
5 South Asia: An Overview *K. Tudor Silva and K. Athukorala* 65
6 Korea: Poverty in a Tiger Country *Hakchung Choo, Soon-Il Bark, and Suk Bum Yoon* 86
7 India: Tradition for Poverty Research *Bhaskar Dutta* 100
8 South-East Asia: Beyond the Economic Approach *Luzviminda B. Valencia* 123
9 China: Poverty in a Socialist Market Economy *Ruizhen Yan and Wang Yuan* 145
10 New Zealand: A Search for a National Poverty Line *Charles Waldegrave and Paul Frater* 160

Part III: *The African Region* 187
11 Egypt: Comparing Poverty Measures *Karima Korayem* 189

12 Anglophone West Africa: Poverty Without Research
   Dayo Akeredolu-Ale   210
13 South Africa: Poverty Under Duress
   Francis Wilson   227

Part IV: *The Western Region*   249
14 The European Community: Diverse Images of Poverty
   Jürgen Kohl   251
15 Greece, Turkey, and Cyprus: Poverty Research in a
   Policy Vacuum   *Maria Petmesidou*   287
16 The Nordic Countries: Poverty in a Welfare State
   *Björn Halleröd, Matti Heikkilä, Mikko Mäntysaari,
   Veli-Matti Ritakallio, and Charlott Nyman*   325
17 Russia and the Baltics: Poverty and Poverty
   Research in a Changing World
   Alastair McAuley   354
18 Former Czechoslovakia, Hungary, and Former
   Yugoslavia: Poverty in Transitional Economies
   Mojca Novak   385
19 Poland: Missing Link to Policy   *Ludmila Dziewiêcka-
   Bokun, Ewa Toczyska, and Witold Toczyski*   409
20 Israel: Resistance of Poverty to Change
   Rivka W. Bar-Yosef   429
21 North America: Poverty Amidst Plenty
   Ramesh Mishra   453

Part V: *The Latin American Region*   495
22 Latin America: Poverty as a Challenge for Government
   and Society   *Laura Golbert and Gabriel Kessler*   497
23 Brazil: Poverty Under Inflation   *Sonia Rocha*   517
24 Mexico: Poverty as Politics and Academic Disciplines
   Agustín Escobar Latapí   539

Part VI: *An Overview*   567
25 The Great Chain of Poverty Explanations
   S. M. Miller   569

About the Contributors   587
Index   597

Foreword

Gro Harlem Brundtland
Prime Minister of Norway

Life at the edge of existence. This predicament is shared by the equivalent of the populations of the USA, Europe, and Russia, and the number is increasing every year. Poverty is still the gravest insult to human dignity. Poverty is the scar on humanity's face. Poverty is prevalent despite decades of international efforts to eradicate it.

Our inability so far to beat poverty haunts our common political record. Our history of dealing with poverty is an epic of protracted stalemates, indifference, bureaucracy, and empty rhetoric. People and countries of goodwill have made serious efforts, only to suffocate in the quagmire of inefficiency, institutional rivalry, and inconsistent follow-up.

One hundred years ago, Norway was among the poorest countries in Europe. Its present society is shaped by generations of people who have made workable compromises between capital and labour within the framework of representative democracy. There is no other way to equity, prosperity, and social justice than empowering people (men and women), allowing democracy to work, harnessing market forces, taxing surpluses, and redistributing the proceeds.

We know a lot about the effects of poverty, how it is linked to environmental decline, how it squanders human resources, how it undermines the developing potential of countries. We know a great deal about the causes of poverty. In country after country we see the link between low rates of school enrolment and poverty, between insufficient basic health services and poverty, between the absence of credit opportunities and the presence of poverty, and between gender discrimination and poverty.

In the past, we have adopted work programmes and plans of action, even priority programmes, which have been acted on with a conspicuous lack of dynamism. The blame lies not only with the lack of generosity of developed countries that like to assume the mantle of donorship. The poor countries too are responsible. Priorities must be set and acted upon. Investment in people and affirmative action to the benefit of the poor are needed. Countries that do not put their own people first will pay dearly and lag even further behind.

We need constantly to remind ourselves and to expand our knowledge about the root causes of poverty and about its effects. That is why I welcome this book and recommend it. Its subject is compelling. How we respond to knowledge about poverty will determine how we enter the twenty-first century and the prospects for a more just, more equitable, world.

There is enough food in the world to feed the hungry, but they do not have access to it. There is enough knowledge in this world to educate everybody. Knowledge is an infinite resource, but the means of its dissemination are lacking, owing to a lack of political priorities.

My colleague from India said the following in the London Guildhall one year ago: "No great industrialist is going to come and look after the primary health centers of my country. No multinational company is going to run our primary schools." The market alone will not provide prosperity, equity, or social justice. Equal opportunity is created; it does not happen by means of trickle-down theories or monetary policies. In the course of history, there are examples of equal opportunities being taken where they were not given. We have the choice to give.

Preface

The Comparative Research Programme on Poverty (CROP) was launched by the International Social Science Council (ISSC) in 1992, in close collaboration with UNESCO's Sector for Social and Human Sciences.

The aim of CROP is to build a solid foundation of empirical and theoretical knowledge on poverty causes and poverty manifestations in developed and developing countries. The ultimate goal of such knowledge is to move to a broader and deeper understanding of the dynamics of poverty upon which future programmes for poverty eradication can be built.

As part of this aim, and in collaboration with ISSC and UNESCO, CROP organized an international scientific symposium to discuss the current status of research on poverty in different regions of the world. The papers for the symposium were prepared by scholars well-known for their work on poverty and representing different disciplines. The papers survey the ground that has been covered by research in the past and identify the gaps that exist which need to be filled by future research. In this way, the book fills an important need and should be an invaluable reference document both for policy-makers and poverty researchers alike.

The book is thus CROP's contribution to the International Year for the Eradication of Poverty (1996) proclaimed by the United Nations.

Funds for the project were provided by UNESCO, Deutsche Gesellschaft für Technische Zusammenarbeit (GTZ), ISSC, Centre for Health and Social Policy Studies of the University of Bergen, Norway, CROP, and the corps of authors who wrote their contributions to the book without any other compensation than the academic pleasure and altruistic satisfaction of collaborating with like-minded colleagues on an important project.

The CROP Secretariat and Centre for Health and Social Policy Studies coordinated the project and organized the scientific symposium in Paris where all the authors met to discuss their contributions to the book.

We are deeply grateful to the many people who made this book come true, whether on the funding, the organizing or the scientific side. Without the concerted efforts of the many actors involved in producing this volume, the book would never have appeared.

We would like to quote the greeting in Maori offered by the New Zealand participant at the symposium in Paris which very aptly summarizes our feeling: "Whakamoemiti kite Atua mo nga manaakitanga me nga awhina kia matou. Nga rangatira ma tena koutou, tena koutou, tena koutou katoa." (I thank the source and spirit of life for the many ways we have been blessed and protected in coming to this gathering. I greet you all as elders and chiefs.)

With this greeting, we invite the readers of this book who are concerned with the scourge of poverty and who are committed to its eradication.

ELSE ØYEN   S. M. MILLER   SYED ABDUS SAMAD

Part I
Poverty and Poverty Research

Chapter 1

Poverty Research Rethought

Else Øyen

This book started out as a traditional state-of-the-art review of poverty research in different regions of the world. By all accounts it can still be classified as such. But along the way, slowly and unintentionally, it has also become a document of the shortcomings of poverty research, and a demonstration of the lack of philosophy behind poverty measures and their accompanying concepts and theories. National poverty studies pose their own questions. The comparative aspect brings out other questions, such as why researchers in developing countries are using nonsensical poverty measures formulated in developed countries for another time and another context, and why so many of us are locked into a poverty paradigm that seems to take us nowhere, either as researchers or as policy makers.

The framework of the book

The Comparative Research Programme on Poverty (CROP) has as its major aim the facilitation of comparative studies of poverty in developed and developing countries, and the creation of an international arena where different disciplines can meet and discuss poverty research. This book has sprung out of an urgent need to know where poverty research stands in different regions of the world, to link discourses that have not been set in the same context before, and to broaden the intellectual discussion of poverty. The book provides a baseline for ongoing and future research, which will save researchers precious time and energy when engaging in poverty research in a new region. The book can also be seen as a cornucopia of ideas and reflections on poverty, poverty research, and poverty strategies.

This is the first time an international overview of poverty research, including both developed and developing countries, has been published. Poverty research has been more or less confined within national borders, because poverty has been considered to be a national problem that should find its remedies within a national context.

Poverty is at the same time culture-bound and universal. The purpose of the book is to bring out both aspects. It is hoped that this will spur the sorting process whereby the culture-bound causes and manifestations of poverty can be identified and marked as different from those causes and manifestations of poverty that seem to be universal, in the sense that they are part of a basic poverty-producing process, independent of the culture where poverty is found. Such a sorting process is a necessary step towards a better theoretical understanding of the poverty phenomenon. Bringing together the uses of poverty concepts and poverty thinking from different cultures will help further this long overdue sorting process, which must take place on the micro, meso, and macro level.

The book is also written to give support to all those poverty researchers who are weighed down by the conflicts surrounding their area of research, by the constant uneasiness of working in a field where neither the concepts and the methodologies, nor the theories are precise enough to be useful working tools, by the concern for an overwhelming poverty, and by the lack of an up-to-date infrastructure for doing research. It is not an unreasonable hypothesis that poverty researchers feel more frustrated and lonely than do researchers in most other fields. It takes courage to live with the complexity of a poverty definition and the lack of an adequate theoretical framework. Almost all the contributions to this book bear witness to the struggle to overcome the present poverty of poverty research. It takes courage to break down stereotypes of poverty when communicating research results to policy-makers who already have their embodied images of poverty. It takes courage to insist on an academic approach to poverty understanding when the call for action is closing in. The book is an attempt to show poverty researchers that they are not on their own with all these problems.

As a means of increasing the descriptive power and getting some order into the diversity of the many regional presentations, the authors were asked to follow a set of common guidelines for their contributions. The topics to be discussed were (a) the poverty concepts used in the different regions, including both the mainstream concepts and the more atypical or local variants, (b) hypotheses relating to causes and effects of poverty, whether stated explicitly or used implicitly, (c) theoretical frameworks for the studies reported, or, on a less ambitious level, identification of theoretical fragments used in poverty studies, (d) data sources available for poverty studies in the region, (e) major results drawn out from the studies, and (f) the author's own evaluation of the present state of affairs on poverty research in the region. As it turned out, not all the authors followed these guidelines – partly because the nature of the social sciences produces a much less disciplined brood of scientists than in other sciences; partly because poverty research in many parts of the world cannot be fully presented within a strict set of guidelines. The weak theoretical foundation of poverty research makes it difficult for most of the researchers to identify and use a coherent framework in poverty studies. The lessened demand of theory "fragments" or dominant hypotheses was not enough to yield a more ample harvest. The richness and diversity of poverty research set into a larger context come into bloom in the authors' own descriptions of the state of the art in their region.

The selection of regions covered in the review is somewhat arbitrary. On the one hand, it was important to cover major areas and a diversity of cultures. On the other hand, it was clear that not all countries could be included, and in some of the larger countries not all approaches to poverty research could be covered. The final selection of papers was made with a view to regional representation and criteria of quality.

In a volume this size, with many contributions that have to follow different paths in their presentations, a need arises for a guiding hand through the maze. Three different scholars were each asked to write a chapter based on their reading of the regional presentations, not summarizing but drawing out some more general observations. The authors come from South Africa, Bangladesh, and Slovenia, and their professional background can best be labelled social scientist, economist, and sociologist (although, when people engage in poverty research for a while, the disciplinary background tends to fade when concepts and methodologies from other fields are put to use). From each their corner of the world, they have read across national boundaries and disciplinary enclaves, bringing the many details into a new kind of order and, as it turns out, presenting us with quite different readings, emphases, and omissions. The three are the test cases of what can be learned from a book of this nature.

Doing comparative research

Doing comparative studies in the social sciences involves a whole set of methodological and theoretical problems of their own, which run as an undercurrent in all comparisons, irrespective of the field of research (Øyen 1990). Doing comparative studies on poverty adds some extra problems. Therefore, the regional reviews in this book are not meant to represent any rigorous attempt at comparison. But, by linking the reviews together, a new instrument is created that will foster thinking in comparative terms.

During the past twenty years or so, several attempts have been made to compare the extent and intensity of poverty on a global level. This has mainly been done (a) by international organizations using a few selected indicators to measure poverty on the national level, so as to rank countries according to their level of poverty, and (b) by social scientists using economic micro data, correcting for cultural differences. The former has been widely published in the media, while the latter has been hidden in professional journals. Some poverty studies covering a wider range of variables have been comparative in scope, but the comparisons have included only a limited number of countries, and comparisons between developed and developing countries have been avoided. Although new data banks are emerging that will help speed up international comparisons in the future, so far the lack of infrastructure will leave most developing countries out of such comparisons.

Common to all these approaches is the search for a measuring stick whereby poverty in one place or time can be compared with that of another place or time. The major criticism of these instruments concerns the limited kind of poverty being measured and the methodological problems encountered (Ruggles 1990; Streeten 1995).

Underlying the idea of doing comparative studies that include both developed and developing countries is a set of assumptions about the nature of poverty that are not always made clear (Øyen 1992):

- Can we, for example, assume that poverty is inherent in all societies, irrespective of their different social, economic, and political structures? If this is the case, the discussion has to distinguish between causes of poverty as inherent and manifestations of poverty as inherent.
- Causes of poverty can best be described as a set of (often invisible) causal elements woven into a dynamic process that produces the observable manifestations of poverty. Can certain causal elements be identified in all countries and cultures, in spite of the differences in manifestations of poverty?
- Since poverty always operates within a social context (even under natural catastrophes), it can be asked whether it is the

causal elements or the manifestations that are most influenced by the social context. Or, put in a different way, and taking the assumption about the universality of poverty into consideration, are the causes likely to be less culture-bound than the manifestations?
- Can the observable differences in manifestations of poverty be assumed to be merely a matter of degree of the extent and intensity of poverty, rather than entirely different poverty phenomena? If this is so, the contours of a model of poverty developing in consecutive stages is implied; a model, it should be added, that is often implied in development policies. If, on the other hand, poverty manifestations are expressions of different poverty phenomena, on what dimensions do the manifestations differ? And what are the likely implications for the proxies of poverty used in comparative measurements of poverty?
- The same causal processes of poverty can lead to different manifestations of poverty, and different causes of poverty can lead to the same manifestations of poverty. How can these two observations be linked theoretically and produce comparative insights?

With such questions in mind, and the knowledge of a weak theoretical foundation for poverty research, it can be argued that the time is not yet ripe for rigorous comparisons in poverty research.

In a somewhat different context it has been argued that comparative studies are at an intermediate stage where much can be learned simply by laying out the facts of similarities and differences (Smeeding et al. 1990). Another direction might be to shift the focus from comparisons of variables to comparisons of the processes producing poverty, i.e. intensifying research on causal processes more than on manifestations. That would be in line with Galtung when he argues that the way forward in creating comparative social science involves "a certain artisinal intellectual competence, with such elementary skills as care with definitions, ability to construct fruitful typologies, understanding of what inference means, knowing how to anchor the theory on the empirical end; yet tempering all this with theoretical pluralism, epistemological eclecticism, a spirit of tolerance" (1990:101).

The order is tall, but it matches the urgency to increase the scientific knowledge base and the need for a more global understanding of a wide range of poverty phenomena.

Philosophy of poverty research

It used to be a dogma of research that production of knowledge had its own value, independently of the use to which such knowledge was put. The nuclear bomb rocked this dogma, and the dogma is being further challenged by recent penetrations into the secrets of the genetic world. But in poverty research the dogma has not been questioned. It has been more or less taken for granted that the more we know about poverty, the easier it will be to alleviate it. Although this is certainly true, it must also be acknowledged that poverty research is nestled within a field of deep conflict, and that policies for the poor are not necessarily intended to eradicate poverty. This situation calls for a set of questions on the philosophy of poverty research, which may not be as relevant for other kinds of social research. It starts with the very simple question: Why are we doing poverty research?

The major part of research on poverty, for example, is concentrated on measuring the extent of poverty, as clearly documented in this volume. The tradition is long and well established, and it shows itself in a range of different measures, mainly based on the income and/or cost of living of the individual and the household. The research literature abounds with criticism of the different measures and their shortcomings, and much effort is invested in overcoming the faults of the different measurements in order to increase their validity and reliability. It is well documented throughout this volume that the choice of one poverty measurement instead of another leads to quite different results. Efforts are also invested in finding alternative measurements and to accommodate the fact that much poverty is located in the informal economy and on the periphery of major societal institutions. Built into these efforts is the so far unresolved issue of how to define poverty in an adequate manner.

On the one hand, it is in the nature of research to pursue the intricacies of measuring and to develop and refine measuring tools. On the other hand, underlying the research on measurements must be some kind of belief that it matters to know exactly how many people are poor, and how poor they are.

But how does it matter? For whom is it important to know how many people are poor? Does the knowledge of an exact number have an impact on poverty alleviation? Does this knowledge have more of an impact on poverty alleviation than other kinds of poverty research? Is the information on the number of poor people always used for the benefit of the poor? Who is asking for numbers rather than a broader picture of poverty? Why is it functional to present poverty as a set of numbers collected over time? And who are the actual users of those head-count numbers that researchers have struggled to come up with? Such questions are seldom asked. It is more or less taken for granted that the more precisely the numbers can be stated, the better equipped interested parties will be to combat poverty.

The numbers give a picture of poverty in a country or a region, and, however inadequate a picture they present, they are a better estimate than popular pictures of the extent of poverty. But who are the receivers of such a picture, and for what purposes is the picture used?

The United Nations Development Programme (UNDP), for example, has developed a worldwide and very simple Human Development Index, which ranks the different countries on their performance in providing for their people. The index is published widely and is consciously used as an embarrassment in order to press for an improvement in human conditions, both nationally and internationally (UNDP 1995). Social movements, benevolent societies, non-governmental organizations (NGOs), pressure groups, political parties, and engaged individuals are among those who actively use the numbers as a means of putting pressure on authorities to obtain better living conditions for the poor; while international organizations and donor countries have been subjected to the tyranny of numbers by national governments hoping to increase foreign aid through the visible presentation of high poverty rates in their countries.

Of course, information can always be used two ways. Unacceptable numbers of poor people can be portrayed both as a demonstration of unworthy poverty conditions and as a demonstration of a spreading moral ill.

The most ready users, however, are the policy makers and bureaucrats who need to reduce the complex issue of poverty to a few manageable variables. According to the rules of the game, the poor deserving help have to be identified so as to ensure some kind of "fair" allocation of resources. For this purpose those in charge need a distribution of the entire population on the relevant variable(s) in order to set a cut-off point between deserving and non-deserving people. Part of poverty research has gone into identifying such cut-off points, thereby also legitimizing a given distinction between deserving and non-deserving poor. Where the cut-off points are defined through a basket-of-goods method, such research can also be used to legitimize the extent of those transfers in cash or kind that are released at the cut-off point.

When the cut-off points become institutionalized and accepted by political authorities as official poverty lines, the duality of poverty alleviation becomes visible. On the one side, certain groups of the most deprived people are being helped. On the other side, the same people are seldom being helped enough to overcome poverty; while those people who are just above the poverty line sink back into increased relative poverty because they do not benefit from the transfers made to those below the poverty line. Thereby, data on the depth of poverty actually invite a cementation of poverty.

How much difference do a few million poor persons more or less make in the global picture of poverty? At the UN Summit on Social Development in Copenhagen in 1995, for example, would the national leaders have been more forceful, and committed their governments more strongly to concrete actions towards poverty alleviation, had they known there were x million more poor people in the world than hitherto known? Not likely. Is the monitoring of poverty figures and comparisons with other countries useful knowledge for poverty alleviation in countries where the majority of the people are poor? Can the figures release resources where there are none? Or are figures on poverty in poor countries mainly useful for external purposes?

Although it is important to ask for whom and for what purposes the figures are produced, this is by no means an encouragement to abandon research on measurements. Data on the development of poverty over time, for example, are an important instrument both for monitoring poverty and for exploring distributional effects and co-variation with other phenomena related to the poverty-producing process. Up-to-date data are necessary to ensure that the poor and the intensity of poverty are kept visible to the public eye, but it may still be wise to put somewhat less energy into sheer measurement research, and instead turn to issues that yield more in poverty understanding.

It may also be wise to let questions of a philosophical nature occupy a larger space in all kinds of poverty research, in order to open up for a better understanding of the academic content of poverty research. Intense conflicts surround the field of poverty studies, and poverty research has not yet found its form, either methodologically or theoretically. Studies weave their way between demands for basic research and demands for applied research, with the former calling for strict adherence to scientific standards for research, and the latter calling for short-cuts and speedy delivery of results. At the same time, researchers weave their way among a whole set of ethical issues that run as an undercurrent between the relatively affluent researchers and the poor people being studied. Ethical issues also arise between the researchers and the many parties interested in the outcome of the research and its political implications for the distribution and redistribution of material and non-material resources in a society (Øyen 1995).

The need for a new paradigm

In poverty research the poor are in focus. That may be one of the few contexts in which they are at the centre of attention. The poor are being studied as individuals, as families and households, as part of poor communities, neighbourhoods, and regions, as a product of larger poverty-creating structures, as victims and criminal actors, as minority cultures and producers of their own culture, as creators of survival strategies and bearers of an informal economy, as an economic burden on the larger society, and as a necessary element in the macro economy, to mention just some of the angles into poverty research. The picture is diversified, and the contents of this volume offer both generalized knowledge of the poverty phenomenon as well as culture-specific knowledge.

However, an interesting observation is that, in the bulk of the research literature, the poor and poverty are treated as a phenomenon that can be understood in isolation from society at large. True enough, major economic and social structures are pushed forward in explanations of poverty. But they tend to become anonymous, because the causal relationships are too diffuse to pin down the exact causes of the extent, intensity, and sustainability of specific kinds of poverty in specific kinds of context or location. But this is not the point here.

The point is that, in most poverty studies, the poor are studied in an isolated context. The fact that they are also living in symbiosis with the rest of the society is more or less ignored. The poor are mainly treated as an excluded group, living in a painful relationship with society at large. It seems as if the attitude of the majority society has rubbed off on the researchers' choice of poverty understanding.

If we are to advance further in poverty understanding, as researchers and policy makers, there is an urgent need to develop a more realistic paradigm where the focus is shifted to the non-poor part of the population. The non-poor and their role in creating and sustaining poverty are as interesting an object for research on poverty as are the poor. The non-poor, for example, have images of the poor and poverty that influence their behaviour and decision-making. We know very little about those images, except as portrayed in popular stereotypes. The non-poor have created a legal framework around poverty that must have profound, and mainly unknown, consequences for the poor (Mameli 1995). The non-poor have created political, educational, and social institutions to further mainstream interests that do not cater for the needs of the poor. The non-poor have spent resources to build up a physical infrastructure to help transport, industry, trade, and tourism, most of which is of no use to the poor.

It is no exaggeration to maintain the existence of two different worlds, that of the poor and that of the non-poor (with a grey zone of less poor people between the two). The discussion on the "culture of poverty" may be an adequate way to describe the reactions of the poor to the world they live in, just as we can describe the "culture of the elite" as the elite's reactions to its surroundings. But it is inadequate to describe the interrelationship between the two worlds, and how these two worlds are tied together in a way that may be more beneficial to the non-poor than to the poor.

The most cited of these relationships is the dominant discussion of the poor as an economic burden on the non-poor. A relationship much less observed is the need for a certain amount of poverty in a society, in order to secure the smooth functioning of the economy of the non-poor population. Gans (1973) was the first social scientist to point out how functional poverty can be to the non-poor society. According to him, poverty forces people to engage in certain activities because no other options are available. This in turn frees the non-poor from engaging in those kinds of activities. The poor, for example, perform the dirty and menial jobs that the non-poor shy away from. These are jobs that also provide low incomes. The poor are more likely to buy second-hand goods and food of low quality, thereby prolonging the products' economic usefulness. The poor are more likely to make use of second- or third-rate doctors, teachers, and lawyers, whom the non-poor shy away from, thereby prolonging their professional usefulness. The use of poor people as a mobile, unorganized, and low-income workforce, working as migrant and temporary workers, is among the more well-known and acknowledged positive functions of poverty for the non-poor society. The pressure towards downwards wage demands formed by the availability of cheap labour, is likewise a well-known advantage for the wealthier part of society.

Gans (1973) also saw the poor as functional for the non-poor in the political relationship between the two worlds. The political powerlessness of the poor makes them an easier target for absorbing economic and social change such as the reconstruction of city centres and industrialization. The poor also serve as symbolic constituencies and whipping boys for different political groups, without actually participating in politics or being asked about their preferences. On the more symbolic level, the sorting of the population into poor and non-poor stresses the norms of the non-poor population and helps guarantee their superior status.

The threats the poor pose towards the non-poor have obviously been in focus, whereas the threats of the non-poor to the poor have been less focused. But studies from many countries show that the urban poor, for example, experience an added vulnerability beyond their actual poverty, because they are exposed to a set of risks stemming from the majority society. Health risks arise from the spatial juxtaposition of industrial pollution, high traffic density, lack of sanitary installations, and a generally fragile infrastructure in the areas where the poor live and work (Wratten 1995: 26). Poor people often experience the state in negative ways: as an oppressive bureaucracy that attempts to regulate their activities without understanding their needs, as corrupt policemen, or as planners who make plans without an understanding of how the poor live and survive (ibid.). As a result, poor people prefer to avoid contact with official representatives of the majority society, thereby marginalizing themselves further. Although such situations may not always be the "responsibility" of one party, they are still a demonstration of the non-poor world having an impact on the world of the poor and on the intensity of poverty.

Whereas Gans has implied that a certain amount of poverty is functional for the non-poor society, the relationship between the two worlds can also be analysed within two different and interrelated frameworks, those of ignorance and of conflict (bearing in mind that, although the dichotomy between the two worlds is useful for analytical purposes, the reality of the actual world is more complex).

Within the analytical framework of ignorance the non-poor world knows little about the world of the poor, and there is little contact between the two. Physically the two worlds are kept apart through differential land use and ghettoization. Socially the two worlds are kept apart through differential participation in the labour market, the economy, and social and cultural institutions. Mentally the two worlds are kept apart through stereotyping and false images built by tradition and the media.

The strong emphasis on individual failures as causes of poverty is part of an image building that frees the non-poor from guilt and responsibility. Such an image also helps to keep the distance between the two worlds. The new concept of social exclusion, coined in Western Europe, stresses the need for new images of causal explanations. But social exclusion refers to a much wider range of disadvantaged groups than the poor, including problems stemming from family instability, the decline of class solidarity based on unions, youth problems, unsuccessful immigration, and weak social networks. This proliferation of the concept is due to a situation where politics and interest groups have taken over the concept and use it for their own internal purposes (Silver 1995). The introduction of the concept of social exclusion means at the same time that the concept of poverty becomes watered down, and that the complexity of social exclusion in the wider sense, defies a meaningful discussion of causal factors. It remains to be seen whether the new concept fares better than the old concept of relative deprivation, and whether it is powerful enough to change the images of the non-poor.

De Swaan (1988) links the continuation of poverty to the lack of a "social consciousness" among the non-poor. A social consciousness exists when the non-poor develop an awareness of the interdependence of all social groups, realize that they bear some of the responsibility for the fate of the poor, and believe that means are available to overcome poverty (ibid.: 253). He argues that developing a social consciousness among the non-poor is a necessary prerequisite in poverty alleviation.

The separation of the two worlds makes for few confrontations, meeting places, and corrections of false images. Decision makers continue to make decisions on the basis of incorrect information, and the role of the state continues expanding in favour of the non-poor world. The real world of the poor stays invisible, because the non-poor world has no need for more precise information. Decisions concerning poverty are based on such incomplete and misleading data as the non-poor would never accept in their own world, either in business or in politics. The present state of incomplete data and narrow definitions in poverty research may also be seen in this context.

Within the analytical framework of conflict, the non-poor may not have much more accurate knowledge about the world of the poor. As a matter of fact, the lesser the capital of precise knowledge about the counterpart, the higher the potential for conflict.

A starting point within the framework of conflict is a definition of poverty as an individual lack of resources. Resources are defined in a wide sense and include economic, social, political, and psychological resources. Access to clean water, as well as basic education, the opportunity to vote, a guarantee of a basic income, and freedom from hunger and epidemics are all considered as resources. Without these resources, an individual is considered to be poor. If alleviation, or even eradication, of poverty is to be efficient within this definition, a comprehensive transfer of resources to the poor is a necessary means.

A likely hypothesis is that the greater the resources incorporated in a transfer, the higher the potential for conflict between the two worlds. The conflicts are not confined to the economic sphere, but reach into the symbolic and social sphere as well.

Poverty is part of a socially and symbolically created hierarchy in which the poor have been allocated the role of underdog. The longer poverty has existed, the more established the hierarchy has become. *All* transfers of resources to poor people challenge the balance of such a hierarchy. A successful poverty alleviation programme increases the social position of the poor in the hierarchy, thereby changing the relative position of others. Even limited transfers can contribute to shifts in the present balance.

Because the elite in the non-poor world is the most likely to be heard when voicing an opinion, it is easy to believe that the influential part of the population has the most to lose when the hierarchy is challenged. But the "elite" in the world of the poor, i.e. those who are almost poor and just above the other poor people, also react strongly. If the poverty alleviation programmes are successful, the poorest group moves upwards in the hierarchy, thereby threatening the somewhat better position of the almost poor and depriving them of an underdog. Many of the conflicts in the world of the poor are centred around the change in balance brought about through even meagre poverty alleviation programmes.

In general, internal transfers, i.e. transfers from non-poor to poor within the same nation or region, are likely to have the largest conflict potential, in particular in countries where poverty is widespread and there is a need for several kinds of resources to be included in the transfers. But external transfers, too, i.e. transfers from other countries and from international organizations, have a large conflict potential. Although the non-poor do not have to contribute financially, the utility of the poor for the non-poor world, as described by Gans, will diminish.

The analytical framework of conflict can be extended by

including other issues. It is, for example, likely that the conflict potential brought about by transfers will increase with the juxtaposition of other conflicts, thereby also changing the priority given to the resources considered most important in the poverty definition. Where ethnic and political conflicts are woven into the world of poverty, the conflict potential is likely to increase until a transfer of political resources has also taken place. Where pressure on land use is the issue, the conflict potential may be the same in mega-cities where land is scarce as in open agricultural plains where land is plentiful, but inaccessible to the poor, but the concrete conflicts are likely to take different forms.

The long shadows of poverty

If poverty research is to advance further, there has to be room for both the global search for an understanding of poverty and the fact that poverty is existential for those who have to live in poverty. Poor people must meet their poverty face to face twenty-four hours a day, every day, all the year around. The way they dress, the way they talk, the way they prepare food, the way they fill their children with hope or hopelessness – all reflect the iron laws of poverty. For the majority there will never be an escape, whatever they may tell their children. But still, the variety of survival strategies is amazing.

Contributions from the literary sphere surpass the social sciences in their detailed descriptions of the lives of the poor. The social sciences surpass the literary sphere in their analysis of the iron laws of poverty. The future challenge for poverty research lies in linking the universal with the particular, and in tying the micro perspective to the macro perspective. For this purpose the contributions of many different disciplines are needed, with their diversity of paradigms and methodological approaches. So far we have only scratched the surface in explaining the causes and manifestations of poverty. Testable hypotheses brought out in different cultural contexts are a necessary step forward towards new theory formation. New ways of cooperation between the disciplines are another necessary step forward.

Much of poverty research has been parochial, insofar as it has been anchored in culture-specific perceptions of values and human life. Western thought has dominated and almost monopolized poverty thinking. Comparative studies are one way of rectifying the situation and bringing in conceptual thinking that may lead to new theory formation.

Poverty is going to be with us for a long time to come. In spite of a wide range of poverty alleviation programmes, poverty casts long shadows over most societies. Even when programmes are proved inadequate, they still continue, mainly for lack of alternatives based on sound data and theoretical understanding. Poverty must be one of those few areas where the medicine is prescribed before the malady is known.

REFERENCES

De Swaan, Abram (1988) *In Care of the State. Health Care, Education and Welfare in Europe and the USA in the Modern Era.* Oxford: Polity Press.

Galtung, Johan (1990) "Theory formation in social research", in Else Øyen (ed.), *Comparative Methodology. Theory and Practice in International Social Research*. London: Sage.

Gans, Herbert (1973) "The positive functions of poverty". *American Journal of Sociology*, 78(2).

Mameli, Antonella (1995) "The ideological implications of law and poverty: A social history of legal aid". Paper presented at the CROP/ISSL seminar on Law, Power and Poverty, Oñati, Spain, May. Publication forthcoming.

Øyen, Else, (ed.) (1990) *Comparative Methodology. Theory and Practice in International Social Research*. London: Sage.

Øyen, Else (1992) "Some basic issues in comparative poverty research". *International Social Science Journal*, 134.

Øyen, Else (1995) "Ethics of asymmetrical relationships evolving from doing comparative studies in poverty research". Bangalore (to be published 1996).

Robertson, Roland (1992) *Globalization. Social Theory and Global Culture.* London: Sage.

Ruggles, Patricia (1990) *Drawing the Line. Alternative Poverty Measures and Their Implications for Public Policy.* Washington, DC: The Urban Institute Press.

Silver, Hilary (1995) "Reconceptualizing social disadvantage: Three paradigms of social exclusion", in Gerry Rodgers, Charles Gore, and José B. Figueiredo (eds), *Social Exclusion: Rhetoric, reality, responses*. Geneva: International Labour Organization.

Smeeding, T. M., M. O'Higgins, and L. Rainwater (eds) (1990) *Poverty, Inequality and Income.* Washington, DC: The Urban Institute Press.

Streeten, Paul (1995) "Human development: the debate about the index". *International Social Science Journal*, 143, March: 25–38.

UNDP (1995) *Human Development Report 1995.* New York: United Nations Development Programme.

Wratten, Ellen (1995) "Conceptualizing urban poverty". *Environment and Urbanization*, 7(1): 11–36.

Chapter 2

Drawing Together Some Regional Perspectives on Poverty

Francis Wilson

We can begin with a recognition of different types of political economy within which poverty, as described in this volume, is currently to be found. At least five categories (which are not mutually exclusive) can be identified. These do not include every type of political economy in which serious poverty exists, but they help to identify some significant distinctions.[1]

- Political economies where, given the population living there, there are *inadequate internal resources* to sustain life for the vast majority above a basic poverty level. Such places include mountain China and much, it would seem, of rural India. In Africa, Rwanda for example would fall into the same category.
- Political economies where poverty seems to be largely a result of a particular *pattern of growth* or where, to put it another way, a reshaping of the growth path might well enable significant reductions of poverty to take place. Such places include Malaysia (where important reshaping has already occurred), South Africa, and much of Latin America.
- Areas where manifest *failure of the state*, for one reason or another, is forcing a return to the drawing board and a rethink, from scratch, of new strategies. This is true not only of Eastern Europe, including Russia, but also of such countries as Nigeria and a number of others in Africa.
- Countries where there is a rediscovery of poverty combined with serious attempts to *modify*, perhaps to salvage, the *welfare state* in an environment where new categories of people are finding themselves marginalized and in effect excluded from the mainstream of the political economy. Examples are Canada and much of Western Europe.
- Finally there are those countries such as the United States, the United Kingdom, and, surprisingly, New Zealand where (in

Figure 2.1 Countries with low, medium and high GNP per capita, vs. countries with a hostile, neutral and supportive political environment towards poverty, combined with a rural/urban dimension.

GNP/cap. Political environment	Low (1)	Medium (2)	High (3)
Hostile	rural / urban	rural / urban	rural / urban
Neutral	rural / urban	rural / urban	rural / urban
Supportive	rural / urban	rural / urban	rural / urban

the mid-1990s) it is difficult to avoid the conclusion that there is a *new assault on the poor* combined with active steps, ideological as well as practical, to dismantle social measures originally designed to protect citizens from the worst ravages of poverty.

There are, of course, other ways of categorizing poverty in different societies or countries. One distinction might simply be in terms of average income or GNP/capita as listed in the annual *World Development Report*. The analysis of poverty in Mozambique, say, is quite different from what is required in Switzerland. Another breakdown could be in terms of countries where poverty is primarily rural (e.g. in India) compared with those where much of it is urban, as in Western Europe. A third relevant distinction relates to the political environment within which poverty occurs. Not all countries could be deemed as supportive in their public policy of the poor as, say, Israel or the Nordic countries. A particularly clear example of public hostility to the poor was apartheid in South Africa, where many of the policies in the years before 1990 were best analysed as a direct assault on the poor (see, for example, Wilson and Ramphele 1989: ch. 11). Combining these three sets of distinctions it is possible to construct a two-way table to provide for a somewhat more systematic categorization of poverty than the more intuitive preliminary list drawn from the limited number of examples provided in this book.

Using the tables from the *World Development Report*, it is immediately possible to divide countries according to whether average GNP/capita is low, medium, or high and also according to whether the majority of the population live in rural or in urban areas. Categorization in terms of socio-political environment is more controversial and yet it is surely a relevant consideration. It is perhaps best to leave it to research workers in specific countries to make their own assessments in the light of their detailed knowledge of the situation. But once these assessments have been made it would then be possible to categorize poverty in different countries by these three criteria. Other criteria that might be used in creating other illuminating categories include the size of countries (in terms of total population) as well as the degree of inequality, as measured by the Gini coefficient, which however is not always available. As comparative studies on poverty in different parts of the world continue to expand so will it become clearer which set of criteria are most useful in creating categories that enable illuminating comparisons and contrasts to be made. For now it is sufficient to note the various possibilities as a starting place for future work.

It is clear from the chapters in Parts II–IV that the focus on poverty provides an important window onto the economic realities of our time. However, it is salutary to note the extent to which researchers into poverty agree that their work has been "long on measurements, but short on explanations and theories".[2] Indeed, there are times when one is tempted to see the search for yet more facts to measure an ever more precise definition of poverty as a form of displacement activity by academics, whose concern to reduce the poverty they find is outweighed only by their powerlessness to do anything effective about it.

It is true that poverty research, when one compares the relatively little attention paid to causes and strategies, is characterized by a strong emphasis on facts and definitions. Nevertheless, the advances made in various parts of the world, particularly over the past thirty years, in refining the definitions and measuring the extent of poverty are enormously important, as may be seen when one compares areas where there has been no research with those where a good deal is known. It is interesting to trace the process whereby countries, starting at very different dates, became more conscious of the poverty in their midst as more research was undertaken and published. In some countries poverty research can be traced back as much as two centuries (see, for example, Eden 1797), if not longer, whereas in others the very existence of poverty was being denied as recently as the

1980s. But it is striking to note the resurgence (in some countries the inauguration) of poverty studies in the 1980s. Although it is tempting to dismiss too much fact finding as mere collection of information and lacking in analytical rigour, it is important to recognize that the basic process of mapping the terrain of poverty and of attempting to measure the changes over time is fundamental to any analysis of causes and to any systematic attempt to reduce or eliminate the problem.

Thus, we must pay particular attention to the search by research workers in different parts of the world for definitions of poverty that make possible precise measurement and comparison over both space and time. But it is just here that we run into two major difficulties: the first relates to the arbitrariness of (i.e. the degree of normative judgement required in) even the most absolute of poverty lines; the second is due to the growing consensus that there is no single definition of poverty capable of serving all purposes. Poverty, it is generally agreed, is a "multifaceted and complex human condition". This conclusion for South-East Asia[3] is echoed around the world from Greece, to New Zealand, to South Africa. But the search for greater clarity continues and the Nordic distinction between direct (i.e. outcomes focusing on living conditions) and indirect (i.e. considering household or individual resources) measures of poverty may be helpful.[4] From the United States comes the observation that, for all its usefulness, the poverty line has two major economic weaknesses: (1) it relies too heavily on annual money income, which is extremely difficult to obtain accurately from the individual households being surveyed, and (2) the monetary income itself is an inadequate indicator of command over resources.[5]

Nevertheless, all countries undertaking serious poverty research find themselves treading the well-worn path of researchers in India, honing a definition of the poverty line that would permit an examination of trends over time and an informed discussion about the impact of government policies designed to alleviate poverty.[6] But it is important to heed a warning, based on long experience, that a "periodic survey and assessment is good enough; what is important is to *do* something about it" (Rath 1994).

Poverty researchers would all agree that fact-finding is not enough – that beyond the collection of data there must be analysis of causes; and that beyond that there must be strategies for action. Although poverty is a profoundly political issue, perhaps precisely because of this fact, there is a strikingly consistent attempt by researchers to maintain objectivity. Social scientists recognize their obligation to uncover the truth as accurately as possible in an environment where, as Miller points out for the United States,[7] the facts themselves can be highly political. The extent to which poverty data are vulnerable to misuse, whether consciously or subconsciously, is itself a powerful reason for the emphasis that researchers have given to its collection. Moreover, researchers from all around the world, from Israel, Scandinavia, Hungary, the United States, Latin America, and elsewhere, report on the sensitivity of results to the tools of measurement or the concepts chosen. Hence the importance of using different means of measuring poverty and of analysing carefully the meaning of differences in the results. One important step towards strengthening this process of verification, suggested by le Roux (1995), is that all researchers should adopt the convention of automatically lodging in some library, or other accessible safe place, copies of their workings and of any computer program used in the analysis of data, thus enabling others to check for any errors in calculation.

It is against this background that, despite legitimate concern about the overemphasis of research on fact-finding rather than on analysis or policy, one can only welcome the recent drive in Western Europe, South Africa, and elsewhere for more comprehensive data on living standards. Indeed, one would go further to take special note of the crippling impact on society of an environment that either denies the existence of poverty, or refuses to allow publication of statistical and other information about it. Fundamental to any democracy must be the collection and placement in the public domain of comprehensive, accurate, and up-to-date statistical and other information about living standards, poverty, and the wider political economy. The advances that have been made in this connection in many different parts of the world as recently as the past decade are most encouraging and need to be consolidated and expanded.

There is, however, one important caveat to which those writing about Latin America draw special attention. It relates to the important role that international organizations such as the International Labour Organization or the World Bank have played in recent years in pioneering poverty research in many different countries. It is clear that in many places external intervention has been crucial in providing funding and expertise that otherwise would have been lacking to collect adequate information. But, coming from the outside, and working with the host government as they are bound to do, these organizations have a built-in bias to avoid, or at least to play down, matters deemed by their hosts to be unduly controversial or political. This is particularly evident when it comes to analysis of the *causes* of poverty, where class conflict and other clashes of interest may be fundamental in understanding the dynamics of a situation in which the government itself may be part of the problem.

As Golbert and Kessler write[8]: "International organizations are focused on the financial-economic cause to explain the poverty increase in the [19]80s ... they analyse the negative effects of the external debt, the fiscal imbalance, and unequal distribution without mentioning the socio-political factors that generated these circumstances. International agencies do not deny the influence of socio-political variables in poverty's increase, but because their objective is to produce a diagnosis of the situation and to propose lines of action they leave the task of the in depth analysis of the causes of poverty in the hands of local researchers." There is no way of completely eliminating inherent biases of this sort. But it is important to be aware of the hidden constraints, if only to encourage a wider diversity of research workers whose public discussion can help to overcome possible blind spots.

Another major weakness of externally driven, donor-funded research, as experience from South Asia makes clear,[9] is that it can increase dependency by failing either to build up local knowledge of relevant issues or to ensure adequate training and experience of analytical and policy-orientated researchers within the country or region concerned. It is important to ensure that all such research programmes build in a properly thought-through and adequately funded process of local "learning by doing", which increases the capacity of the country concerned to understand, analyse, and prescribe strategies for itself in an atmosphere of accessible information and open, independent, and critical debate. An international network of social scientists such as that gathered under the umbrella of the Comparative Research Programme on Poverty (CROP), could do much to consolidate the enormous gains made in recent years, to prevent a relapse into the secrecy of information and hostility to open debate that tempt bureaucrats, and to widen these zones of openness until they include every country on earth.

So much then for the search for precision in definition and measurement of poverty. It seems to be now generally agreed, as Room (1990) has pointed out has happened for Western Europe, that, instead of focusing only on the disposable income or expenditure of individuals or households at a moment in time, researchers have to make a three-fold shift in perspective to: (1) the many dimensions of poverty; (2) dynamic analysis; and (3) from the isolated individual or household to the local community within which that household lives. In other words, there is a new awareness of an old truth: that poverty can be better understood in a wider, more holistic framework in both space and time.

This shift in perspective does not yet take us much further down the road in analysing the causes of poverty. Indeed, one might feel that with the new arguments (coming from the United States by Murray 1984, and others) to the effect that much poverty is now a result of some of the very policies designed to alleviate it, there is less clarity (certainly less consensus) about the causes of poverty than there was, say, thirty years ago. It is illuminating to read analyses of poverty in different parts of the world, but we are far from having reached a stage where we could postulate a general theory. Indeed, as an early newsletter of the Comparative Research Programme on Poverty warned, "The complexity is such that there is no reason to determine *one* encompassing theoretical framework" (Øyen 1994).

Poverty itself is a highly political issue where power and interest groups have had a significant (some would say overwhelming) influence on patterns of distribution and the existence of poverty. In addition, the historical context from which the particular present of a specific country or region has emerged is often interpreted in different ways. Thus the analysis of the causes of poverty is itself contested territory where all who tread, including social scientists themselves, cannot be completely unaffected or neutral. Hence the need for all of us to be open to critical attacks on our most cherished theories and to recognize the corrective value of a diversity of hypotheses in the search for understanding. Moreover, despite the extent to which poverty can be fully comprehended only in the context of a particular place and time, there are nevertheless some important observations and ideas whose relevance is by no means confined to one specific situation. Reading through the wide collection of papers in this book there are a number of striking parallels that provide stimulating starting points for further thinking. Let us consider some of these, one by one.

First is a general recognition of the fact that the debate on poverty is part of the wider debate on development and underdevelopment. Despite the difficulties of definition noted earlier, the concept of "poverty" is less ambiguous than that of "development", which is what some writers have called a "suitcase" word able to contain any meaning one chooses to pack into it.[10] Nevertheless, the dual process of understanding the causes of poverty and of devising strategies to reduce or even uproot it is the central component of the development debate. Recognition of this reality serves partly to reinforce appreciation of the difficulties of the problem, which is as broad and diverse as the global economy, and partly as a reminder that the search for strategies and understanding of poverty must draw on the wider body of knowledge accumulated in the general field of development. Any attempt at a brief overview cannot expect to do more than scratch the surface here and there in the hope of stimulating deeper thinking about certain aspects of the matter. At the same time, insights from development theory can be useful when considering specific instances of poverty. Thus, in reviewing poverty research in Turkey for example, Petmesidou calls attention to Ozbudun's pessimistic predictions about the possibility of reducing poverty through effective redistributive policy:

> In a third world country trying to speed up development, both the populist model of development and the technocratic model generate their own vicious cycle. In the former [model], growing public expenditure limits economic growth and increases social conflicts as more groups become participant in the political game and attempt to share a stagnant or slowly growing pie; the result is social and political instability. In the latter [model], a high rate of economic growth can be achieved, [but] at the expense of social justice and political participation, and this will increase polarization and social unrest.

Thus, concludes Ozbudun, "the complex relationships among development, participation and equality will provide the key to the future of Turkish politics".[11] Which is not to say that substantial reduction of poverty is impossible, but it does serve as a salutary reminder of the political context and constraints within which particular policies would unfold.

Against this "development" background let us turn more specifically to note some of the various theories of poverty that have been used in different parts of the world. In South Asia, Silva and Athukorala[12] identify four theoretical frameworks: (i) the neoclassical approach, with market-led development; (ii) the political economy approach, focusing on history and on the creation of poverty through conflict of interests; (iii) the culture of poverty approach, which tends to blame the victim and to reinforce the status quo; (iv) the participatory approach, whereby the energies of the poor themselves are harnessed to alleviate their plight. These four frameworks are not entirely mutually exclusive nor do they cover exactly the same ground. Some analyse the past and others focus on future strategies, but the categorization helps to identify different emphases in the search for understanding.

These four frameworks are by no means absent from Europe, but Jürgen Kohl looks at the matter somewhat differently, drawing on two research traditions.[13] One (Anglo-Saxon) is concerned primarily with distributional issues and the lack of resources at the disposal of the household or individual. The other (continental, intellectual) looks at relational issues, including such matters as inadequate social participation and the problem of integrating the poor into the larger society. The nub here is "poverty as social exclusion". This focus on exclusion is reinforced in the Nordic countries where, of the four classes of explanation (namely marginalization, underclass, feminization, and subculture), it is theories of marginalization and of underclass that are most widely used.

In the United States of America, Miller points to a four-part classification of causes: (i) demographic; (ii) neighbourhood effects; (iii) cultural, and (iv) a large bag of labour market causes, including different pockets or aspects such as human capital, mechanization, and other economic changes; macro/Keynesian explanations; immigration ebbs and flows; and (for some such as Charles Murray) welfare disincentives. The high degree of politicization of poverty in the United States implies not only a vigorous, indeed rancorous, debate about causes and strategies but also sometimes bias in the selection of data to prove preconceived conclusions, and misuse of facts to bolster arguments with statements that appear factual but that in reality lack empirical support. Despite such froth which bubbles in the political cauldron it is possible in North America to distinguish, as Mishra has done, between two approaches to the study of poverty, namely social engineering, which focuses on policy and administration, versus social structural, which focuses more on the institutions and processes through which poverty is produced, reproduced, and sustained. Mishra argues that there is need to move beyond these "conservative" and "liberal" approaches to a third, structural, approach that takes due account of power and of conflict.

It is worth noting that the demographic model to which Miller draws attention in the United States is implicit in an important analysis of the causes of continuing poverty, if not impoverishment, in South Asia where Silva and Athukorala pinpoint the impact of steady population growth in rural areas where agrarian reform has failed and land concentration remains high. With little or no extension of cultivated land, more and more people become landless. It is this steady decline in the asset base of the vulnerable rural population that seems to be one of the primary fators leading to increases in the numbers in poverty. This analysis is also true in South Africa for people living in those rural areas that, until recently, were delineated as apartheid's Bantustans. The persistence of poverty in rural India despite growth in agricultural labour productivity leads Dutta to point to the need for better wage data so as to be able to trace what impact such increases in productivity may have on the real incomes of agricultural labourers.

In Anglophone West Africa, Akeredolu-Ale laments the widespread anti-intellectualism and the non-theoretical orientation of such studies as exist, but suggests that the most appropriate theoretical framework in that context might be one that, while rooted in historical anlysis, combines insights from social stratification and from marginalization theories of poverty.

What is one to make of this welter of theory? Social scientists long for the simplicty of $E = mc^2$ or a Grand Unified Theory, but must settle instead for that other vital lesson of twentieth-century natural science: namely that, with limited understanding, two ways of looking at a problem may be contradictory yet both true. Physicists have learnt to live, if not happily at least creatively, with the duality of light conceived of both as a particle and as a wave. Human beings and their social structures are far more complicated than light, so social scientists have to learn to live, no less creatively than the physicists, with the inclusive diversity and tension of apparently contradictory truths.

From analysis and the search for more powerful theoretical understanding I turn now to consider briefly some of the comparative evidence that certain policies have actually worked more effectively than others in achieving their goal of reducing poverty. In South Asia, anti-poverty programmes have been divided into two main types: (i) those that stimulate production and income-generating processes amongst the poor, and (ii) those that guide the flow of income or consumption through such devices as food stamp programmes or employment guarantee schemes. Silva and Athukorala conclude that the first set of policies, which aim to stimulate income generation (and which are further subdivided into policies focused on land redistribution and tenancy reforms; on increasing the asset base and productivity of the rural poor; and on specific areas), are more effective than the second set. Thus, for example, the Grameen Bank in Bangladesh and the Janasaviya programme in Sri Lanka are widely believed to have been remarkably successful. But this conclusion is not without its critics. Raymond Apthorpe (1994), for one, questions whether either Grameen or the Amul Dairy in India have in fact achieved all that is claimed.

One of the most successful of more recent strategies against poverty has been in Malaysia, where comprehensive affirmative action programmes in a context of rapid economic growth led to a reduction of the proportion of households in poverty from 60 per cent in 1957 to 12 per cent in 1993. Similarly in Korea, rapid economic growth combined with other policies led to a rapid reduction in relative and absolute poverty in the seven years from 1979 to 1986, although the extent of urban poverty is still a matter for considerable dispute. Malaysia and Korea are two of a number of countries in Asia (including Singapore, Thailand, and Indonesia) that demonstrate that significant advances in poverty reduction are possible where growth-promoting policies are pursued along with targeted programmes for the poor. These are the ones that have attempted to make the maximum possible use of the poor's only known asset – their labour power.[14]

Growth alone is not enough. In South Asia as a whole average GNP growth of 3.1 per cent during the 1980s failed to trickle down,[15] and there are many countries in Asia (including Bangladesh, India, China, Pakistan, Mayanamar, the Philippines, and Vietnam) where significant poverty reduction has not really taken place. In Latin America during the thirty years 1950–80 the average annual growth of employment in formal sector activities reached 3.7 per cent. But this was not enough to absorb all those seeking work, and poverty, together with inequality, remained acute. Much the same can be said about South Africa over the four decades of almost unchecked growth that began with the rise in the price of gold as a result of Roosevelt's devaluation of the dollar in 1934, and continued through the industrial expansion of the Second World War. The subsequent growth was not decisively halted until the Soweto uprising of 1976. Similarly in the United States it is argued that growth needs rethinking, for two reasons: first, because growth of GNP does not necessarily imply a concomitant increase in jobs—the phenomenon of jobless growth is becoming increasingly apparent; second, because of greater awareness of the environmental consequences of growth.[16]

Policies do indeed make a difference. The evidence from North America is that social insurance type programmes have done far more to lift people out of poverty than means-tested programmes. The paradox, argues Mishra, is that targeted programmes (in the USA and Australia) do much less to lift people out of poverty than those that emphasize universal and comprehensive programmes (such as in the Nordic countries). In the United States, reduction of poverty among the elderly has been the great success story of social programmes there.[17] In Australia, by contrast, the worst problem of poverty is to be found amongst those over the age of 64. Differences between Sweden on the one hand, where poverty is mainly a problem for young people, and Australia, on the other, are primarily due to differences in old-age pension schemes.[18] Similarly, urban poverty studies in Greece emphasize the absence of substantial social benefits compared, for example, with Israel, where maintenance of a stable pattern of income distribution and relative poverty requires large investments and well-planned social policy.

It is obvious yet relevant to point out that the socio-political environment within which poverty occurs will itself be a major factor in determining whether steps will be taken to try and deal with the problem. Contrast, for example, increasing political pressure in the United States to reduce government expenditure on social welfare programmes with the situation in Israel, where evidence that the proportion of the population in poverty was increasing led to a huge public outcry and immediate passage of a law for "the reduction of the extent of poverty and income disparity", which provides for increased universal transfer payments (for children, maternity, unemployment, old age, etc.) plus selective (means-tested) guaranteed income maintenance.[19] Social scientists (who have their own political biases) are still a long way from consensus on how best to tread the fine line between using a safety net to help those who have fallen on hard times and seeing this safety net as a factor encouraging indolence, along the lines of the argument that giving money to beggars simply increases the demand for beggars. However, one of the most exciting products of the new network of poverty studies is the possibility of comparing and contrasting the very different practices pursued at both the macro and the micro level in so many countries around the world and learning from them. There is still a vast amount of basic research work to be done in this area.

Although it is obviously worthwhile, as well as encouraging, to focus on those policies and programmes that have succeeded, one should also examine those policies that fail, because it is often possible to learn as much, if not more, from well-documented failure than from many success stories. In this context it is salutary to note that, in Asia, particular attention has been drawn to the failure, or perhaps the limitations, of state-sponsored poverty alleviation programmes. It is worth quoting Samad's careful conclusion at some length.

> The restructurings in the concepts of poverty alleviation programmes and the mechanisms of their implementation thus would centre around a) restructurings of the designs, b) the delivery system and c) the antenna of the recipients. This would be possible only in a mileu of genuine democracy and decentralised administrative arrangements. Too much centralisation in the past did not allow otherwise

viable ... [poverty alleviation programmes delivery systems] to deliver. This is the lesson of the past. We have to remember that the more remote a decision-making entity from the subjects of those decisions, the lower the probability of those decisions having their intended impacts. People must participate in as close a proximity as possible in decisions that affect their lives, living, workplace and interactions with the exterior world. Any worthwhile programme restructurings at the conceptual and implementation levels must acknowledge this simple but often ignored truth. (Samad 1994)

Another salutary warning, this time from the United States, is Miller's caveat:

Be suspicious of the siren call of education and training as the preferred remedy for poverty. Certainly they are good things of themselves, especially when they aim to do more than slot people into narrow work situations and also provide some civic education. ... [but] a crucial, often-neglected question is whether the jobs will be there when the poor complete their training. Many poor people are shifted from one training programme to another – they are being trained to be trained. ... Training does not solve basic problems of low employment growth, especially for low-trained persons. (Miller 1994)

Where they have not already done so, other countries may yet have to learn these lessons. It is to be hoped that the growth of comparative studies in this field will enable them to glean wisdom from the experience of those who have had to learn the hard way. Thus South Africa, for example, which has embarked, with high hopes, on a highly centralized Reconstruction and Development Programme may find that the Asian experience is not without relevance in order to achieve the goals to which the government of national unity is committed.

One final point emerging from the essays in this volume remains to be commented upon. It relates to the surprising lack of attention paid to the impact of the political boundaries of the modern nation state in so many situations of poverty. Mishra draws attention to the fact that most studies work, as they were commissioned to do, within the boundaries of the nation state. As he points out: "Relatively little has been done by way of cross-national poverty research ... [yet] it is a particularly promising area of research. ... It should help to put the national problems and issues in a broader international perspective, bringing a fresh, new look at domestic issues."[20] All this is true, and more. We would want to go even a step further to argue that the assumptions implicit in many national studies make it possible to miss, or simply to ignore, important forces that should be considered in any analysis of causes or of strategies of alleviation.

The experience of southern Africa has been particularly helpful in this regard because it is here, perhaps more than anywhere else, that the economic consequences of political boundaries that have acted as a one-way filter or membrane affecting flows of labour, of investment, or of tax revenue have been most visible. Lesotho, for example, or Mozambique have contributed, by way of migrant labour supplies, as much as any other area in the region (including rural South Africa) to the development of the mining industry during the past century. But little of the wealth accumulated during that process trickled through in the form either of income or of capital investment (whether private or public) to these "peripheral" areas. Indeed, it seems likely that, for many of these reasons the consequence of being organically part of the "development" of South or southern Africa was to reduce rather than to increase per capita income. The geography of distribution, whether within countries, as in China with its impoverished mountain areas,[21] or between countries, as in southern Africa and elsewhere, is a matter requiring further work.

To conclude, I return to where I began: to reiterate that this overview can do no more than reflect upon some of the insights and contradictions that emerge from reading the chapters that make up the core of this book. If this essay has done no more than whet the appetite of readers to work through the fascinating detail of the individual case studies it will have done its job. They are offered to readers in the hope that they will provide a good starting point for a deepening understanding of, and effective action against, the scandal of mass poverty that permeates the world as it enters the twenty-first century.

NOTES

1. This chapter draws directly and heavily on the other chapters in this book. In an attempt to keep notes to a minimum, specific facts and ideas from these different chapters are not always directly acknowledged.
2. S. A. Samad, "Regional State-of-the-Art Reviews on Poverty Research/Asian Chapter", Crop conference paper, Paris, December 1994, p. 35.
3. Valencia, Chapter 8.
4. Halleröd et al., Chapter 16.
5. Miller, Chapter 25.
6. Dutta, Chapter 7.
7. Miller, Chapter 25.
8. L. Golbert and G. Kessler, "Regional State-of-the-Art Reviews on Poverty Research/Latin America", Crop conference paper, Paris, December 1994, p. 19.

32 PART I: POVERTY AND POVERTY RESEARCH

9. Evidence from South Asia about the danger of externally funded research increasing dependency by not ensuring adequate training.
10. I am indebted to Marie-Dominique Perrot for an introduction to the important Francophone debate on development, which includes reflection on "*le mot valise*".
11. M. Petmesidou, "Review of Poverty Research in Greece, Turkey and Cyprus", Crop conference paper, Paris, December 1994, p. 20.
12. Silva and Athukorala, Chapter 5.
13. Kohl, Chapter 14.
14. Samad, op. cit., p. 63.
15. Silva and Athukorala, Chapter 5.
16. Miller, Chapter 25.
17. Mishra, Chapter 21.
18. Halleröd et al., Chapter 16.
19. Bar-Yosef, Chapter 20.
20. Mishra, Chapter 21.
21. Ruizhen and Wang, Chapter 9.

REFERENCES

Apthorpe, Raymond (1994) Personal communication at the UNESCO/ CROP Scientific Symposium on The Regional State-of-the-Art Review on Poverty Research, Paris, December.

Eden, Sir Frederick Morton, Bart. (1797) *The State of the Poor, or a History of the Labouring Classes in England from the Conquest to the Present Period. In which are particularly considered Their Domestic Economy with respect to Diet, Dress, Fuel and Habitation; and the various Plans, which from time to time have been proposed and adopted for the relief of the Poor*. London.

Le Roux, Pieter (1995) "Pensions and poverty in South Africa". Cape Town, preliminary draft, May.

Miller, S. M. (1994) Conference paper presented at the UNESCO/ CROP Scientific Symposium on the Regional State-of-the-Art Review on Poverty Research, Paris, December.

Murray, Charles (1984) *Losing Ground: American Social Policy, 1950–1980*. New York: Basic Books.

Øyen, Else (1994) Editorial *CROP Newsletter*. 1(2).

Rath, Nilakantha (1994) Verbal communication at the UNESCO/ CROP Scientific Symposium on The Regional State-of-the-Art Review on Poverty Research, Paris, December.

Room, Graham (1990) *"New Poverty" in the European Union*. London: Macmillan.

Samad. S. A. (1994) Conference paper presented at the UNESCO/ CROP Scientific Symposium on The Regional State-of-the-Art Review on Poverty Research, Paris, December.

Wilson, F. and M. Ramphele (1989) *Uprooting Poverty: The South African Challenge*. New York: Norton.

Chapter 3
The Present Situation in Poverty Research
Syed Abdus Samad

There is an enormous variety of perceptions and opinions on poverty research at the present time, as can be gauged from some of the papers presented in this volume. Depending on the doctrinal/ideological leanings or background of the respective observers, poverty research is diversely viewed as a public good with incredible externalities, a private good with some utility for academics, researchers, and decision makers in the public domain, and an instrument for linking theories to policy. There seems to be some agreement, globally, on the need for a deeper understanding of the concepts, hypotheses, theories, and explanations of poverty. In the absence of such an understanding, it would be futile to search for any sustainable solution to the problem of poverty.

In this chapter, I review the present situation in the realm of poverty research, largely drawing from the existing literature and ongoing CROP work. I will first make some general observations, which will be followed by comments on the different regions of the world as reflected, mainly, in the CROP literature.

General remarks

The basic configuration of poverty and its global distribution are fairly well known and documented. Its causes and consequences, however, continue to generate heated debates, leading occasionally to polarized positions. Some feel that in current research poverty is viewed mostly and primarily as an economic problem – that economists seem to have dominated the research arena, to the exclusion of social scientists from other disciplines. Most of the research has been based on secondary data and grey literature, with very little interdisciplinary and qualitative analysis.

Research in many cases has been carried out in isolation, leading to parallel and overlapping efforts and the resultant waste of critical resources. Many therefore feel the crucial need of sharing research outputs through better multinational networking and other means of information dissemination.

On the conceptual issues, there is no uniform definition of poverty or agreement on its most precise form of measurement. More theoretical and empirical clarification of published research is needed. Data on poverty are derived from broader, general purpose household income–expenditure and national accounts surveys. The concept of a poverty line based on such data can have but limited validity. Specific-purpose data must be generated for further poverty research. The relationship between the individual and poverty and the relationship between a class of poor people and society are not the same thing. Poverty results from some limitations, maladjustments, and shortcomings at the individual as well as at class levels. A free and perfectly functioning market will pick the natural winners (those with the initiative, enterprise, imagination, and power of observation to discern an opportunity). Current poverty research does not seem to highlight the underlying factors behind the winners and the losers, who belong to the set of the poor. The concept of a poverty line seems to have elements of arbitrariness and, even though for obvious reasons it cannot be the same for all countries and regions and/or for all times, still research should be able to throw up some common basis for its conceptual grounding and operational validity.

Poverty, it is now perceived, is neither an economic nor a purely social problem, but is multi-faceted, with economic, social, political, cultural, and demographic dimensions. It is a *condition* as well as a *process* (Valencia 1994), a *cause* and an *effect*. It should be viewed as an involuntary rather than a voluntary affliction. Its macro, rather than micro, analysis requires to be focused. Many feel that the differentiation between absolute and relative poverty is often arbitrary. The limitations of using income alone in determining poverty status (relative/absolute) are well known. For example, it does not take into account the degree or extent of the monetization of the economy, the scale of the parallel/informal/underground economy, or the prevailing disequilibria in the different markets, as well as in-kind transfer payments. But still researchers seem to continue to favour the concept of a threshold income (McAuley 1994). Poor data on income distribution, food security, the shares of different income classes in the economy, etc. make the estimation of the incidence of poverty a lot more difficult than is usually believed (Choo et al. 1994). Poverty research up till now has contributed little by way of new or original ideas and theories.

Approaches and methodologies

Most poverty research comprises studies in comparative statics. This limits their intertemporal relevance. Many use the neoclassical economist's approach with reliance on the power of the market to cure the poverty problem in the long run, and on the responsibility of the individual to upgrade his/her marketable skills, etc. At the other end of the spectrum, the radical approach (centre–periphery) is rather critically limited in its operational dimensions. Research often leaves it unclear as to how the major anti-poverty programmes would be operationalized. Some research works use highly suspect methodologies, developed by the central planning agencies and other functional ministries of the government concerned (Dutta 1994). Some works tend to focus on the effects of growth in alleviating poverty, to the exclusion of distribution. Choice and uncertainty are often ignored. Poverty may appear as an ambiguous concept unless the methodology of its analysis is clearly and precisely described. Some approaches and research methodologies ignore the risks of reducing very complex socioeconomic and cultural phenomena to single numbers (Wilson 1994).

The globalization of research approaches and methodologies has resulted in certain dominant values and opinions prevailing over their indigenous counterparts. This calls for a new survey method, exclusively for generating data on poverty. Conventional household income–expenditure and other stereotyped general-purpose surveys do not fulfil the requirements of focused poverty research (Akeredolu-Ale 1994). Some approaches to poverty research have failed to incorporate the major shifts in development paradigms and their consequences for poverty research, while a large number of works on poverty lack a sound and generally acceptable conceptual framework.

Research coverage

Concepts and measurements (in particular head counts) currently dominate research coverage. In contrast, the causes, consequences and explanations relating to poverty have not been adequately addressed. For example, the labour market, capital market, and wages and incomes policies of different political regimes have not been studied in the context of poverty. Other under-researched areas according to present perceptions are the following:

- the power structure and its implications for poverty;
- non-economic factors responsible for causing poverty;
- inequality of access and opportunities;
- structural adjustment measures and their impact;
- the control and manipulation of statistics and the structural framework of primary research;
- the relationship between poverty and internal as well as international labour migration.

Research is also rather ambiguous in its treatment of benefit payments. Whether they alleviate or sustain poverty would be an interesting research question. The heterogeneity and diversity of poverty certainly do not lend themselves to plausible explanation by any one theory. This message comes across quite clearly from all existing research.

Hypotheses and theories

There seems to be near-consensus that current theories, being partial and inadequate, lack the necessary rigour and scientificity to explain the phenomenon of poverty. Many of the hypotheses are ambiguous at best and cannot be tested on the ground. Some of the theories are aimed at explaining inequality, while others attempt to examine the relationship between development and inequality. The anti-intellectual mind-set of those who are in charge of allocating research and development resources in many developing countries in particular has definitely impaired more focused and higher-quality research on theories of poverty. Much of the research work on theories tends to deal with national and domestic poverty issues and relatively little work of any consequence has been done by way of cross-national research in developing testable hypotheses and theories.

Some general issues and gaps

Many research works focused on poverty alleviation programmes have observed the following gaps, which are responsible for programme failures:

- poor programme design and delivery systems;
- a lack of commitment from sponsors and staff;
- inadequate resource allocation;

- an incomplete understanding of the complex issues that impinge on poverty and the socio-political contexts in which the poor live.

Some hold the opinion that anti-poverty programmes should not degenerate into some kind of cultural imperialism in which the poor are treated as meek objects. The spatial dimension of poverty is seldom incorporated in research. The entire process of politicization and ideologization of poverty considerably narrows the focus of research debates. Structural analyses of poverty are not necessarily radical; some can be quite conservative. A few research initiatives fail to capture the fundamental characteristics of the control groups. Some research can be frustrating inasmuch as it leads to nothing.

On a more positive note, however, not all research works have been in vain. It is now recognized that poverty is as much a problem of "underdevelopment" as of "development" of particular genre. The direct results of poverty research include an increasing emphasis on better governance, participation, ethics in decision-making, empowerment of the disadvantaged and other vulnerable groups, the demystification of poverty, and an improvement in our understanding of poverty and the poor.

Poverty research in the different continents

I now proceed to discuss the present situation in poverty research in Africa, Asia, Europe, Latin America, and North America. This discussion is almost entirely based on the materials presented in this volume.

Africa

Poverty research has been viewed as somewhat frustrating because no use seems to be made of its outputs. African researchers view poverty primarily as a problem of development. In African research it is widely acknowledged that it would be folly to globalize the concept of poverty because it cannot mean the same thing to every country or region, let alone the world itself. Poverty in Africa is *shared*, and social scientists and other poverty watchers therefore prefer to speak in terms of *group poverty*, rather than the poverty of the individual or even the household or family. Research is full of the articulation of the failures of government programmes and the negative impacts (as viewed by African scholars) of structural adjustment measures (in East Africa in particular). The need for better data, specifically generated for poverty research, is repeatedly highlighted in nearly all major works of recent years (Akeredolu-Ale 1994). Africans also increasingly question the extent to which poverty policies relate to theories. Much African research work advocates that the poor should have a say in the decisions affecting their lives, without however spelling out how best this can be achieved in the existing circumstances.

Wilson (1994) points out that the uncertainty factor is often ignored in the definition of poverty. Akeredolu-Ale (1994) claims that the globalization of poverty research has resulted in the dominant values overwhelming local values, and that persistent poverty in Africa symbolizes a failure of the state.

In African research there is little debate on whether the individual or the society is responsible for poverty. The urbanization of poverty gets an occasional mention, as does NGO-led research and its contextualization.

Asia

Poverty research in Asia is rich in country-specific studies which include the incidence of poverty, some hypothesis formulation, policies and poverty alleviation programmes, with the last accounting for a disproportionate share in the later period of research (the 1980s and 1990s). I would like to make the following general comments on the coverage and quality of these research initiatives.

- Most research works have been funded or sponsored by aid donors or designed with a heavy concentration on concern for the donor poverty agenda and focus only tangentially on the agenda of indigenous government policy makers.
- The statistical systems and theoretical frameworks borrowed from industrial countries are not particularly well suited to the kind of poverty analyses that would be relevant to Asian realities and concerns. Although this is not to say that they are not useful (Chenery et al. 1974).
- A large number of studies lack a sound conceptual foundation. Most describe or report events or data, rather than offer coherent analyses. Quite a few thus have low *a priori* analytic content.
- Most studies tend to focus on the incidence (head counts), definitions, and measurement of poverty. Few offer scientific explanations of poverty.

- Most of the hypotheses are implicit and not rigorously formulated.
- Very few theories of poverty have been created by research.
- Most of the studies are partial analyses and do not have a general equilibrium perspective. Poverty seems to have been studied in isolation.
- Governance, dysfunctional bureaucracy, and poverty programmes and their shortcomings represent the most extensively researched areas in Asia.
- There is considerable ambiguity, vagueness, and uncertainty in defining poverty. Some authors tend to assume that it is known, which is a most unrealistic assumption.
- Many treat poverty and inequality in the distribution of income as coterminous.
- The definitions and descriptions of the data or units used are not standard or uniform.
- A related limitation is the researchers' inability to utilize the incredibly rich sources of data that are now available in the region, most preferring to use their own bases (Bhatnagar, 1994).
- The effects of alternative household sizes and structures on poverty and the risks associated with it at a given level of income distribution have been very little researched in Asia (Lipton 1988).
- The non-availability of adequate data and information on the intra-household distribution of consumption, income, and assets compels many authors to use highly aggregative data, which might understate both inequality as well as poverty.
- Regional and ethnic dimensions of poverty have been little researched in many plural societies of Asia. This could be due to the great political sensitivity of the issue.
- Another often mentioned weakness is that research on poverty is "soft", intuitive, and value laden, with the result that there is an excess of low-quality and overlapping research output.

The lack of indigenous research funding and the customary reluctance of governments to support poverty studies continue to remain major lacunae. Because the outcome of research is seldom obvious to policy makers in a Third World setting, it is necessary that the missing bridge between research and policy-making should be built soon. The difficulties inherent in quantitative methods of attempting generalizations about relationships between poverty and growth are extremely well known, well researched, and well documented. This relationship is associational and represents certain stylized facts that are observable but do not automatically lead to theory formulation (Ahluwalia 1976). What, however, is missed by social scientists or public officials is the direct link between misdirected and lopsided development and poverty.

Poverty research in Asia – when all is said and done – comprehensively reflects the poverty scenarios of the continent at the present time.

Europe

The European Community portrays diverse images of poverty. To the European researcher, however, both conceptualization as well as operationalization of the various research issues are important. There is an ongoing debate on the structuralist versus individual explanations of poverty, the former having led to a few policy interventions. The relationship between welfare and poverty occupies a key area of poverty research.

Methodological issues are considered fairly important in appropriately defining poverty within the context of large welfare systems and elaborate institutional arrangements for transfer payments (Kohl 1994). Relative deprivation features prominently in contemporary European empirical poverty research. Likewise, social exclusion, income poverty, and the failure of public assistance programmes have been widely researched (Kohl 1994).

The European Community has played a key role in initiating poverty research. It sponsored three community action programmes (CAPs), between 1975 and 1994, to combat poverty. These generated several national reports on poverty incidence, which now constitute an important source of data for poverty research. These stocktaking materials have generated new policy debates in the countries concerned (Kohl 1994). The resulting improvements in statistical infrastructures have helped comparability in the measurement of aggregate poverty and of different social classes. The involvement of Eurostat, the EC statistical office, meant the setting up of working groups on poverty indicators in 1986. The use of household budget surveys and the need for better-quality data have been articulated ever since. Earlier, the Luxembourg Income Study (LIS 1983) had undertaken a complete representative household income survey in the OECD countries, to standardize them for comparative cross-national analysis (for common concepts, explanations, etc.). The survey outputs represent the most comprehensive and reliable database available for analysis of the processes of income distribution (and hence relative poverty). LIS is also a model for a comparative interactive research network and has produced large sets of disaggregated data, working papers, and poverty profiles. We may, however, note some of the limitations of LIS:

- The analysis is limited to income poverty and therefore no indicators of relative deprivation in natural living conditions can be derived from it.
- It is not possible to study the subjective consequences of objective poverty.

European Research on Poverty and Social Inequality (EURO-PASS) represents another major work on substantive poverty research issues, the adequacy of social security systems, and subjective as well as objective standards of poverty measurements. The Social Assistance Dynamics Panel Study, involving eight OECD countries, enquires into the dynamic aspects and causal processes leading into and then out of poverty, whether for sustained or transitory periods.

European research is particularly rich in methodological and analytic descriptions. There is a discernible attempt on the part of researchers to provide a detailed description of the particular research methodology used; the unit of analysis is the individual, household, or group; and there is some analysis of the intensity of poverty by using different poverty lines (40, 50, or 60 per cent of the mean income, for example), duration of poverty spells, etc. At least one opinion (Kohl 1994) views the head-count measure as rather limiting because it neutralizes poverty intensity – all poor become equal, irrespective of their relative poverty levels. There is a recommendation to use the concept of an aggregate poverty gap instead, which specifies the total amount of resources that will be needed to raise the incomes of all poor households to the level of the poverty line.

The paucity of research coverage can be observed in the areas of poverty risk, relative poverty risk, composition of the poor, etc. European research recognizes the importance of regular social reporting on poverty in order to inform all concerned.

Latin America

Poverty research in Latin America has usually been carried out within the broad framework of the political economy of poverty with, at times, strong ideological or doctrinal biases. Latin American research views of poverty, briefly speaking, are as follows (Golbert et al. 1994):

- Poverty is a byproduct of distributional and unbalanced conditions that sustained economic prosperity would alleviate. But, for this, more integrated public policies are needed. Social policies must fundamentally improve the pernicious and other undesirable effects of economic policies.
- Poverty and citizenship, poverty and unemployment, poverty and social structure, poverty and family, and new poverty are some of the under-researched areas and should be taken up for serious investigative research.
- Poverty research in Latin America is primarily oriented to the assessment of public policies, and the debate usually centres around the strategies of state interventions.

Most research tries to articulate some form of a poverty line and is concerned with the quantitative assessment of the intensity of poverty. It usually does not assess the growing vulnerability and exclusion of the hardcore poor. Research on these dimensions of poverty should be promoted to obtain a wider and fuller perspective on poverty. In the process, the linkage between poverty and other socio-political variables needs to be carefully analysed. The Latin American poverty research domain is currently constrained by:

- inadequate funding;
- insufficient academic and intellectual interchange among researchers (this to a certain extent has been overcome by the international development network database, which services the social science and development research community of the region from the Latin American Social Science Council based in Argentina);
- the need to review national assessment tools;
- the phenomenal public debt of many Latin American countries, which have slackened efforts at poverty research because of its high opportunity costs in the context;
- the fact that poverty research is by and large led by NGOs and at present there is no attempt to develop a linear econometric model of poverty that might throw up some interesting survival strategies for the poor.

North America

In the USA some believe that poverty is an artefact generated by Washington based liberals; it is not a real problem any more. The problem is dependency on welfare and handouts as well as state transfer payments. In other words, poverty is the result of the perverse effects of liberal social policy (Mishra 1994). Welfare liberalization has further aggravated its intensity. The current research debate in the USA centres on the liberal–conservative divide in its interpretations. Poverty research thus has been anchored in the ideological leanings of the researcher–analyst. There is extensive research on welfare and what it does to the underclass which continues to grow, causing concern for the conservatives in particular. This has narrowed the horizon of poverty research in the USA. The emergence of a new identity group – white males who claim to have lost out to the blacks and women – has further complicated the research agenda. However, an official poverty line was eventually adopted to serve as a benchmark for poverty measurement. According to some researchers, this is an unrealistic abstraction from reality and the debate centres around poverty in terms of net earning capacity (i.e. the potential of a household for income/wealth generation) and the level of living notion of material well being. American researchers largely view poverty as a situation of relative deprivation of material things, other than merely income, because they feel that the standard of living and income are poorly correlated.

The following are some of the more visible aspects of the current situation in poverty research in the USA:

- There are two views on theory: according to one, poverty has been overtheorized, while the other maintains that it is undertheorized.
- There are too many casual explanations, few of which are stated with the necessary precision and rigour; they are broad frameworks, rather than bounded hypotheses (Miller 1994).
- There is research galore on public assistance systems, but the specific obstacles encountered by poor households, which prevent them from coming out of the poverty trap, have not been adequately addressed in any major research.
- The characteristics of the poor are incorrectly deployed as the causes of poverty rather than its consequences. The low human capital of the poor is likewise a symptom rather than a cause of their poverty.
- The phenomenon of social exclusion is not adequately researched, nor is the relationship between politics and poverty, e.g. the role of power in determining poverty conditions.
- Poverty has been researched within the context of the political economy of social policy, which means that it has been of residual rather than prime concern.

- Dominant ideological paradigms and currents have influenced the research content and goals. Social research, including poverty research, is seen as part of the political debate about the social scenario of the times and how it might be shaped in accordance with particular values, beliefs, and interests.
- The disregard of transfers-in-kind and the under-reporting of income make the income approach to poverty research inadequate (Mishra 1994).

Researchers seem to be obsessed with the definition and measurement of poverty (head counts in particular), the poverty line, and public assistance programmes. Because poverty can perhaps be treated as normative, and hence a contentious subject, there are not many objective definitions around. In the USA, research on poverty is mainly concerned with applied issues rather than with the philosophy of poverty analysis. A major finding of American poverty research is that social insurance type programmes fare better in poverty alleviation than means-tested ones. Targeted programmes seem to do much less to lift people above the poverty line than the non-targeted ones (just the reverse of the Asian experience). There is agreement among poverty researchers in the USA that more work is needed on the aged, children, and one-parent families who constitute a large set of vulnerable people.

Economists have played a leading role in the realm of poverty research so far. The War on Poverty was launched in 1964, under President Lyndon B. Johnson, on the assumption that poverty could be eradicated through human capital formation (Mishra 1994). Historians, political scientists, sociologists, and philosophers often take a more critical and social-structural approach compared with the abstract-technical approach of the economists.

In Canada, unlike in the USA, there is no formal poverty line, albeit some quasi-formal hybrid varieties are available for researchers and policy makers. Canadian official research agencies update the statistics on absolute poverty on a regular basis. In Canadian research, if someone spends more than 55 per cent of their earnings on food, clothing, and shelter, they will be classified as poor. Poverty is neither politicized nor ideologized in Canada. Most of the poverty research there is carried out in the unofficial realm, rather than in the universities and parastatal think tanks (Mishra 1994). Links between crime and poverty or the role of NGOs in poverty alleviation has not been adequately researched in Canada, where poverty is treated more like a residual problem than a problem of prime concern.

Poverty research in North America is mainly grounded in domestic issues, within broad national frameworks. There is very little cross-national study. However, from existing literature, it is obvious that academics and researchers in North America feel that poverty research can have a vital role in the debate on the issues of equity, distributive justice, and overall human welfare. There is also a felt need for the codification of the major findings and generalizations on poverty research in North America.

Conclusions

Although current research does provide a great deal of systematic and refined data and information as well as analyses of the concept, definitions, measurements, and theories of poverty, the possibilities for investigating the causes and consequences of poverty are still rather limited. This is clear from the foregoing review. Even though there remain as yet many unexplored and unexplained areas of quality research, the efforts so far made globally in understanding poverty do tend to capture some critical issues on the subject. A variety of theoretical and conceptual perspectives has, however, not led to a gradual build-up of any systematic knowledge on the key relevant issues of better explanation of poverty.

I nonetheless want to conclude this review on a positive note and therefore enumerate the following affirmative elements as constituting an important part of current poverty research:

- Research has led to a better understanding of the concepts and how they get operationalized in policy terms.
- Some positive affirmative actions and interventions have created a large pool of all kinds of critique and research data and information that can be useful in the analysis of poverty-related social issues.
- The participatory/democratic approach to decision-making and interdisciplinary/thematic, rather than segmented/sectoral, research have been promoted under the umbrella of poverty research.
- A growing awareness of the critical need for a sound conceptual framework for action and results has been created.
- There is a rich and growing literature on different facets of poverty .
- National anti-poverty interventionist strategies have evolved from specific programmes such as the Grameen Bank (Bangladesh), the New Economic Policy (Malaysia), the Agha Khan Rural Support Programme (Pakistan), Philippines

Business for Social Progress (Philippines), Janasawiya (Sri Lanka).
- There is a better perception of the role of cultures, caste, ethnicity, and religion in the creation of poverty and of poverty as an aspect of social discrimination.
- The inadequancy of social indicators in measuring poverty is recognized.
- Surveys exclusively for poverty research have not been mounted so far anywhere in the world, even though the data requirements for refined and targeted poverty analysis are better understood now and hence the need for poverty data surveys (for example, the need for consumer price indices for the poor).

Because scientific research relies heavily on data, primary data on poverty need to be collected, refined, collated, and analysed extremely carefully. For example, data and information on poverty as a situational syndrome, the reproduction of social relations and transfers, etc. are not easy to generate and interpret. The political economy approach to poverty would, in addition, call for data on public support, popular consent, the social legitimacy of budget supported programmes, etc. So far these aspects seem to have gone unresearched. Political perspectives on socioeconomic development and how these could impact on poverty research remain as yet a largely unexplored area. One nonetheless has to acknowledge that poverty research has led to new questions being asked on development itself – its processes, priorities, models, strategies, and policies. It has shaken many dominant paradigms in development thinking and encouraged the search for new ideas on many development-related issues. Rome was not built in a day.

References

Ahluwalia, Montek S. (1976) "Inequality, poverty and development". *Journal of Development Economics*, 3.
Akeredolu-Ale, Dayo (1994) "Poverty without research". CROP.
Bhatnagar, S. C. (1994) *A Network of Institutions in Information Technology: Proposal for a Resource Centre @ IIM, Ahmedabad.* Information Technology.
Chenery, Hollis et al. (1974) *Redistribution with Growth*, Brighton, Sussex: World Bank and Institute of Development Studies.
Lipton, Michal (1988) *The Poor and the Poorest.* World Bank.

The other authors mentioned in this chapter are all found in the present volume.

Chapter 4
Concepts of Poverty
Mojca Novak

Introduction

The social security of citizens, as well as their poverty, have passed, in the past century, through various stages of scientific interest. The original Rowntree poverty research has developed into a number of approaches that depend principally on the ideas of subsistence, basic needs, and relative deprivation (Townsend 1993). Any classification, however, is inherently biased by the author's contextual preferences and the limitations of his or her knowledge. Regardless of how detailed, analytically far-reaching, and imaginative it may be, any such effort shows only a tentative organizing of a specific field of human knowledge. Another classification, which is at present more frequently in use, makes a clear distinction between absolute and relative poverty, silently incorporating the notion of (in)equality into the debate.

Heated debate about the conceptual problems of poverty and its measurement among such scientists as Townsend, Piachaud, and Sen (Townsend 1993) shows that this social science field is far from being without conflict. It was Piachaud (1987) who particularly stressed the question of whether the poor have an "opportunity to choose" at all, but the problem of which concept is more productive in explaining the incidence of poverty and its rate left this question merely "untouched". Apart from a lack of material resources, the poor also suffer a lack of opportunity to choose their lifestyle. They have no opportunity to choose whether to eat meat or vegetables, being forced to consume them in insufficient quantity and quality. Hence, dilemmas such as whether to be a vegetarian or have five o'clock tea are locally "coloured" and also reveal cultural preferences. What counts substantially is living involuntarily in conditions that are below what is commonly considered to be a decent standard of living. It appears that the poor are forced to live a life of lack of various resources. Therefore, what should be observed in poverty investigation is primarily the way of life of the poor in terms of social characteristics such as gender, age, education, race, etc., and secondarily the lifestyle and feeling of deprivation. In accordance with expectations, the incidence and rate of poverty and the risk of impoverishment in terms of the lack of various resources dominate most observations. Unfortunately the measurement of resources is also frequently reduced to disposable income. These questions of conceptualization and measurement were transcended to a certain extent by Nordic social scientists who established "the third stage in measuring poverty", applying Titmuss's idea of "command over resources" (Erikson and Åberg 1987).

Regardless of how productive these conceptualization debates are, they focus on poverty as observed by Westerners in the West. A global perspective on poverty research is missing from their (re)consideration. This lacuna can to some extent be remedied in the "state-of-the-art" on poverty research in this book, which extensively documents an enormous variety of approaches employed in non-Western regions. Social scientists from these regions productively apply poverty concepts "produced in the West" to specific local conditions but they employ a unique conceptual framework as well. In this respect, they frequently abandon observation of the incidence of poverty that is strictly limited to the individual level. They also consider this phenomenon at the intermediate level and at the macro level with respect to groupings and stage of development. It has been proved elsewhere (see Ahmad et al. 1991, for example) that the macro perspective contributes a fresh aspect to the stock of poverty knowledge by focusing primarily on poverty seen as the result of the impact of various "macro" processes and structures, such as business cycles, the economic structure, regional development, politics, and international relations. It is not the individual inability to adapt to changes at the macro level alone that should be considered as poverty's "prime cause", but these processes themselves. Interestingly enough, the poverty investigation "boom" in Western regions was initiated by employing social indicators in measuring poverty as both an economic and a social phenomenon. Evidence has shown that this venture was conceptually framed by the basic human needs idea (Doyal and Gough 1991; Drewnowski and Scott 1966), but this was soon "replaced" by the micro level perspective, reducing poverty simply to the individual experience and situation.

In contrast to this broadening of the poverty concept perspective, an opposite direction can also be revealed. The "(mal)nutrition" or lack of food approach to poverty is applied particularly in Asia and Africa. Despite the widespread reduction in the subsistence approach to food, it domonstrates that the incidence of poverty in these regions differs significantly from that observed in the West. Hunger and poor shelter and clothing, frequently accompanied by ill health, illiteracy, overcrowded housing, and totalitarian political regimes, are features that would move any social reformist, active either a hundred years ago or today.

Given the different contributions to the global stock of poverty knowledge, it makes sense to diversify the concept review in this chapter. The guiding principle in this is to consider the dominant "Western" concepts, on the one hand, and those poverty concepts that are coloured by specific features in other regions on the other hand. In this respect the reviewed concepts can be classified into two major categories. The concepts employed in Western Europe and North America make up the first category and, although revealing many local characteristics, they are considered to be poverty concept classics. The second category consists of concepts employed in poverty investigations in other regions.

All the findings and conclusions arrived at here relate only to the reports on the "state-of-the-art" of regional poverty research compiled in this handbook. Therefore they ought to be evaluated in the light of this fact. Apart from this, it could be concluded that a worldwide "communication" of poverty concepts is needed. Poverty conceptualizations in the West could be fruitfully and productively improved by the judicious introduction of contributions from the non-Western regions. Then poverty conceptualizations would "sound" more global. Moreover, certain other fields of social science fields have already experienced a similar undertaking. For example, dependency theory has to date usually been employed in framing modernization in the Third World. Over the past decade, the modernization theory and dependency theory have been linked together to enable better explanation of underdeveloped Western regions and sectors. It would seem that if lacunae fail to be conceptualized by the tools in use, the intervention of fresh tools is needed. Therefore the implicit intention of this chapter is to draw attention to such potential for future directions in this field.

Poverty concept classics

Various social scientists employ different principles in classifying applied poverty concepts and if a common dividing line is applied, a dichotomized picture appears. The classic poverty concepts can be grouped around two pillars. The first one deals with poverty "causes", focusing on (the lack of) resources, and the second one deals with poverty "outcomes", observing them by means of a poor way of life, poor living conditions, and customs and attitudes towards poverty. The concepts making up the first category are labelled "Anglo-Saxon", "indirect", or "subsistence". However, they are far from dealing with the prime causes of poverty, although from the individual's position and everyday life situation they might appear to do so. Concepts labelled "continental", "direct", or "basic needs" and "relative deprivation" make up the second category. It is hard to say whether this distinction is the only possibility, but it represents an attempt to bring together the variety of poverty concept classifications as presented in Figure 4.1. Different labels frequently mislead the reader to conclusions about dissimilarities among reviewed conceptualizations; therefore looking at similarities is an important aspect of this venture.

Frequent debates on the explanatory capacities of the poverty concepts, e.g. between Townsend, Piachaud, and Sen (Townsend 1993), undoubtedly showed that the subsistence idea applied in the poverty "causes" concepts offers a more transparent and less ambiguous picture of poverty. On the other hand, it was proved to be weak in sketching the broad range of incidence of poverty and demonstrated a considerable lack of in-depth analysis. In contrast, the poverty "outcome" concepts cope with wide variations in poor living conditions. They provide a clear distinction between opportunity and choice, but remain vague as regards the distinction between way of life and lifestyle.

Poverty "causes" concepts	Poverty "outcomes" concepts
Main labels Anglo-Saxon Indirect Subsistence	Continental Direct Basic needs Relative deprivation

Major topics
Lack of resources such as:
  Money
  Material assets
  Capital (physical, human)
  Time
	Poor situation as regards:
	  Living conditions
	  Way of life
	  Customs
	  Attitudes towards poverty

Figure 4.1 The double pillar classification of poverty concepts

The Western poverty concept tradition, taking into account the (lack of) resources aspect, can be reviewed in terms of various classifications as discussed in detail in subsequent chapters of this book. The "Anglo-Saxon" conceptualization focuses on distributional issues: the lack of resources at the disposal of an individual or a household is of principal interest. The lack of disposable income and opportunities can be seen as an indirect conceptualization of poverty, as stressed by Ringen (1987). In the USA, the subsistence concept of poverty is employed either in absolute terms (e.g. the "Orchansky index") or in relative terms (e.g. the median).

Among the fresh contributions from these countries, Douthitt (1994) conceptualizes poverty as "time-adjusted", focusing on families with young children that need time as well as money to provide child care, to prepare meals, and to perform other housekeeping functions. This "time approach" can be interpreted as one form of social capital that might be considered in conceptualizing poverty. It is not only the deprivation of the adult who is unable to spend time with the children that is considered, but, more importantly, the deprivation of the child. The child does not get the cultural and intellectual stimulus that interaction with adults can provide.

The "net earnings capacity" concept is an interesting innovation (Haveman and Burton 1993) that concentrates on the potential to generate income that households with working-age adults would have if they were able to use their human and physical capital to full capacity. Capital assets are taken into account, as well as personal characteristics such as age, gender, education and race.

The direct conceptualization of poverty concentrates on the "outcome" aspect of the poverty situation. It deals primarily with living conditions, stressing either a poor way of life or poor consumption standards or attitudes towards living in poverty. Furthermore, as employed in the "continental" conceptualization of poverty, relational issues (inadequate social participation and integration of the poor into the broader society) are the focus of consideration. This approach relates to Townsend's conceptualization of poverty as relative deprivation, in which participation in the customary lifestyle of a particular local community is the central issue.

The Nordic approach to living conditions represents a special contribution to the relevant stock of knowledge. Two major points of departure – first, poverty must be visible, and, second, poverty is not how people feel but how people live – shape this attempt to analyse the issue of poverty. It is seen as an accumulation of social deprivation and represents a "third stage in measuring poverty" (Ringen 1985). This approach combines the ideas of income-related measurement and living conditions research. In Ringen's terms (1988), observation of income offers only indirect evidence of poverty. The additional criterion is the actual inability to reach the minimum standard of living owing to a lack of material resources. Data are consequently needed on income, assets, and other material means and on actual well-being in terms of housing, health, education, work involvement, etc. This kind of reasoning comes close to Townsend's idea of a deprivation index. In Swedish poverty research, a "consensual poverty approach" is added, which specifically investigates people's attitudes towards material consumption and the actual patterns of consumption. One purpose is to replicate the pioneering study of Mack and Lansley (1985), who define poverty as "an enforced lack of socially perceived necessities". A similar orientation was adopted by Douthitt et al. (1992), who applied Duesenberry's "emulation hypothesis" to prove that people consume not just relative to their income. On the contrary, they basically follow the consumption pattern of the reference group. Furthermore, as Duesenberry claims, the higher the income, the less the reference group consumption pattern is followed. In the USA, Mayer and Jenks (1993) have found that the distribution of basic necessities is less unequal than the distribution of household income. Moreover, the distribution of household expenditure is less unequal than the distribution of household income. Therefore, they argue in favour of developing a way of measuring the material well-being of households similar to the measurement of income, expenditure, and consumption patterns, which brings them close to the Nordic approach where poverty measurement is confined to the measurement of outcomes.

The regional reports in this book mention few qualitatively orientated poverty studies, and the poverty culture approach is almost absent. It seems that the American tradition presented particularly in Oscar Lewis's works and Herbert Gans' (1992) works attracts few followers. Anthropological methods and devotion to particular research topics such as the marginalization of the poor, the underclass, the feminization of poverty, and the subculture of the poor attract less research interest than the topics already mentioned. As stated in the Nordic report (Chapter 16), this "outcome" aspect of poverty concepts has attracted interest to any great extent only in Nordic poverty research. Apart from this, "the social history of the poor", particularly in terms of life history analysis, is not a perspective that appears in the presentations in this volume. Consequently, the Americans, at least, await their Dickens in vain. As Harrington (1981) stated, the poor need (an American) Dickens who would describe their language, their psychology, and their conception of life. To be poor means to have less access to those resources that are viewed as common in a local community. To be poor means to be an alien in one's native country and in its culture. If this perspective is abandoned, poverty as a pattern of socialization in which children adopt values and psychological characteristics from their poor parents (Corcoran et al. 1985) remains unrevealed.

Social features such as gender, race, age, and education (Haveman and Burton 1993), by which the most vulnerable and truly disadvantaged social groups (Miller 1994) are brought into focus, attract limited analytical attention. In contrast to scarce employment, the introduction of social variables into poverty research means a return to the "original" sociological perspective on poverty that was abandoned a decade ago.

Despite the variations, the subsistence idea of poverty, which dominates the poverty "causes" concept, attracts the vast majority of investigators. The poverty "outcome" concept arouses substantially less interest, regardless, perhaps, of its most productive development, e.g. Mack and Lansley's (1985) approach and the Nordic approach. What is most striking is that the basic human needs conceptualization has been virtually abandoned. Decades ago it represented a fresh view of poverty, considering it in terms of both individual experience and local community conditions (Drewnowski and Scott 1966). Nevertheless, it has recently gained a certain renewed analytical interest (Doyal and Gough 1991).

Regional variations on poverty concept classics

Regardless of the classification principle employed, the classic poverty concepts show a common feature: they consider poverty simply as an individual and, less frequently, a group experience. Moreover, it is believed (e.g. Piachaud 1987), that extreme poverty as described by Charles Dickens has been eradicated. In contrast, empirical evidence, particularly from Asia and Africa, fails to prove the same for these continents. The lack of food for many groups of people affects poverty investigation in these regions to a considerable degree. Furthermore, the significant impact of the stage of national development on the incidence of poverty, specifically in Asia, is the second feature distinguishing poverty conceptualization in this area from the concepts in operation in the West. Any consideration of poverty focused on either a national or an international perspective should include these factors.

Empirical evidence on poverty investigation in Asia undoubtedly proves that the concept of poverty is far from being constant and that it has temporal, contextual, and spatial attributes. In certain cases, poverty can be conceptualized as a "disequilibrium phenomenon" and, hence, ephemeral and transient. Apart from being a significant economic problem, poverty also has fundamental social and political implications. The major perspectives employed in poverty investigations focus on access to sufficient food on the one hand and on the stage of development on the other. In terms of the differentiation between poverty "causes" concepts and poverty "outcomes" concepts, both perspectives can be considered as dealing with the poverty "causes" aspect. Furthermore, both perspectives deal with (the lack of) resources as the core issue (although at different levels), and therefore this "level" innovation should be explored more carefully. The poverty "outcome" concepts fail to attract the same conceptual interest.

At the micro level, the poverty concepts applied focus primarily on individual experience. The lack of sufficient food marks the consideration of poverty in India in particular. It can be focused either on cereal consumption or on adequate food or command over commodities; limited particularly to food intake and the consumption basket, the "(mal)nutrition" approach prevails. Reviewing the poverty concept either in South Asia specifically or in Asia in general, poverty is conceptualized either as extreme poverty, in terms of calorie intake per day, or as material poverty, defined as a lack of the means to satisfy purely material needs such as food, clothing, and shelter. Specifically in India, some criticism has been addressed to the overworked "diet" approach, with the proposal that it should be replaced by the level-of-living approach. In contrast to these poverty conceptualizations, investigators in Korea observe poverty primarily in terms of a lack of money, stressing either household expenditure or distribution of income. Furthermore, they also explore the subjective perception of living conditions, which brings them close to the "outcome" aspect of poverty concept classification.

The poverty situation of various groups of people dominates consideration at the intermediate level. It is observed as mass poverty related to minority poverty, particularly exploring whether it encompasses a large majority of the population or certain minority groups. The "cumulative long term" concept, focusing on particular groups such as children and pregnant or breastfeeding women, is also employed.

Because poverty is far from being just an "individual" matter, although it is frequently considered as such, observation at the macro level adds a productive contribution to a better understanding where overwhelming impoverishment of societies and particular regions is the core research subject. The "regionalization" concept considers poverty separately as a rural phenomenon and as an urban phenomenon in India, Korea, and China.

Poverty as a side-effect of economic development is viewed as resulting in unemployment, a high infant mortality rate, the prevalence of malnutrition, and low literacy rates such as in the Philippines. It is also seen as "seasonal poverty" in rural areas, or as "cyclical" poverty in Sri Lanka, where the extent of poverty significantly depends on electoral cycles, which can be another factor determining the living conditions of the poor. The fact is, governments tend to lower the cost of living and to create additional employment opportunities in preparation for an election. "External poverty" is observed with respect to the non-poor, which brings this approach close to understanding poverty as a function of wealth (Gans 1992). Like "natural poverty", it can be a result of malfunctioning of the socioeconomic system and underdevelopment.

China's poverty investigations in particular reveal a strong "macro level" orientation. Poverty is conceptualized with respect to different "economic development" theories. The most influential initiatives come either from Rostow's theory of economic growth, stressing different stages of economic development or from theories distinguishing between the (active) centre and the (inactive and disadvantaged) periphery. Theories of a dualistic economic structure and its potential for transformation frame poverty research where it is observed in relation to different growth capacities in various sectors.

A twentieth-century Dickens could be left without words but without work too, if we compare modern England with the England of a hundred years ago. Shifting his interest to Asia, he could be deeply frustrated by observing the range and rate of destitution and misery. Asia's poverty investigators attempt to transcend this embarrassing situation by introducing novelties to the stock of poverty conceptualization in particular, and poverty knowledge in general. They do observe the phenomenon in terms of locally adjusted classic concepts by focusing on malnutrition and respecting the subsistence idea of poverty. Apart from this, it ought to be stressed again that they broaden the poverty conceptualization by contributing the fresh idea of its investigation at the macro level as well. According to this innovation, poverty may be considered as an individual situation but it must be observed primarily as resulting from "macro-level" processes in the economy, in politics, and in society. Western poverty investigators apparently abandoned this perspective long ago. The social exclusion concept, by which the incidence of poverty is related to civil rights on the one hand and "macro" processes on the other, should overcome this deficiency. Moreover, in this respect Townsend (1993) advocates introducing the perspective of "social structure" and global economic relations. Hence, the "non-Western" poverty conceptualizations undoubtedly show that the West could learn some lessons from this part of the world, too.

The predominance of subsistence concepts focusing on the lack of resources also shadows poverty investigation in Africa, although they mutate into a number of varying approaches that reflect local features. Though poor living conditions are far from ignored, the prime focus is on food and malnutrition. Similarly to Asia, particular vulnerable groups, such as women and displaced persons in East Africa, are recognized; on the other hand, the significant difference between rural and urban poverty is taken into consideration as well. Interestingly enough, in Anglophone West Africa (Nigeria and Ghana) an absolute and a relative approach serve as an "umbrella concept" for developing a concept in terms of social inequality and a poverty culture. This concept has been developed in response to criticism of the original concepts. More specifically, it has been argued that the poverty concepts employed should transcend the limitation to the micro level, which focuses primarily on personal income and expenditure. Poverty should be seen in the context of access to all forms of resources and facilities provided by or within a nation, and therefore socioeconomic factors ought to be taken into consideration as well. The macro-level perspective of poverty conceptualization may not yet have matured. As a criticism, however, it may accelerate productive development in this respect, at least.

To a limited extent, South Africa's poverty conceptualization has undergone a similar development. Research started with a very simple approach that focused primarily on white people, and poverty was defined very subjectively. A major step forward was made by an explicit examination of the nutritional basis of poverty and by analysing the distribution of the whole population – blacks and whites. Surveys that followed dealt with varying standards of living, employing a similar concept but viewing poverty predominantly as a relative condition. The second Carnegie Inquiry broadened poverty concepts further. It was suggested that researchers should go out into the country to listen to the poor people in order to be able to understand poverty. Unfortunately, tensions between in-depth case study scientists and the advocates of representative data led to constant switching between the two concepts. Nevertheless, the above suggestion initiated the quiet but valuable inclusion of the in-depth "anthropological" approach to poverty studies. The question "Where is your next meal coming from?" neatly sums up this evolution in poverty research and clearly reveals the shift from focusing on the "statistical" individual to the concrete individual and groups who are truly disadvantaged, as Wilson (1990) provocatively remarks.

Poverty conceptualization in the Western area that is excluded from "producing territories", e.g. New Zealand, the Mediterranean basin (Israel, Greece, Cyprus, and Turkey), and Central and Eastern Europe (the former Yugoslavia, Hungary, the former Czechoslovakia, Poland, and the former Soviet Union), reveals, on the one hand, the widespread strict adoption of classic concepts and, on the other, a lack of local adjustment in employing them. The range of specific local contributions to poverty knowledge varies, but investigators in other regions, e.g. in Asia and Africa, have shown more imagination in applying the classic poverty concepts in their analysis.

Regardless of the variation in poverty research approaches, lack of resources is the major subject investigated and poverty "causes" concepts provide the most frequently used framework. The subsistence idea of poverty applied in terms either of low income or household expenditure or of economic hardship is the leading concept. Poverty "outcome" concepts frame poverty observation less frequently, and if applied they relate to living conditions (Poland, the former Yugoslavia) and relative deprivation (Hungary). Additionally, social scientists from Hungary and the former Czechoslovakia seem to be concerned with studying the historical roots of poverty as well, focusing on official or scientific poverty considerations.

However, in Central and Eastern Europe it is frequently overlooked that both welfare strategies and their consideration should incorporate the basic assumption of an unstable society that is different from that in the West. Apart from this, poverty trends in these countries should be considered in terms of the welfare state concept as well. Full employment and the high employment of women had a greater impact on social welfare than the welfare state concept and the social policy model implemented. Moreover, the following question arises: What is the desirable type of society in these countries? What really counts? A new philosophy of change that apparently fails to restore impoverishment but provides greater access to various welfare and different income resources? Rising above the poverty line in terms of the poor "taking off" would represent the desired qualitative change.

In contrast to the above view, recent poverty research in Israel takes a multidimensional view, using income, housing density, and number of dependent children as parameters and stressing the degree of deprivation caused by factors such as social unrest and protests. A second type of research deals mostly with the social mobility of lower-income categories, stressing their disadvantaged position. This analytical orientation substantially connects both types of investigation to the sociological survey classics, i.e. social stratification and mobility research. Moreover, poverty is grasped conceptually and analysed indirectly by a combination of the social stratification and mobility approaches and a living standards approach. Analysts are primarily concerned with social inequality and particularly with "vulnerable" categories – groups at risk of poverty such as the unemployed, immigrants, and ethnic minority groups. This represents a fresh contribution to the stock of knowledge about poverty from the Western territories considered.

Poverty research conceptualization in Latin America has its own locally adjusted framework, too. The poverty issue is frequently framed in terms of permanent income insufficiency, resulting in a critical lack of basic necessities. This reveals the poverty "causes" concept to be the most "attractive" source employed for building the conceptual background. Apart from this, investigations of minimum living standards and other, locally produced concepts regard poverty from the "outcome" aspect, viewing it as a situational syndrome in which a combination of underconsumption, malnutrition, precarious housing conditions, and low education is stressed. Or it can also be considered in terms affecting future events and processes in potential, which is particularly important for public policy makers. The concept of a situational syndrome has a contextual relationship with the Nordic standard of living approach, stressing the multidimensional and complex nature of the phenomenon and viewing it as a "vicious circle", which brings it close to the classic poverty concepts.

Conclusion

Of the classic concepts, the subsistence idea of poverty in terms of a lack of resources has proved to be the most popular worldwide, but it shows very clear local variations that differ in both range and extent. Local innovations and fresh contributions to the global stock of poverty knowledge, particularly with respect to the perspectives of stage of development, social stratification, and mobility, should also be stressed. However, the findings and conclusions arrived at enable us to consider a tentative poverty conceptualization. It is far from being merely a combined macro and micro level of poverty assessment, which is once again preferred as an analytical perspective. The need to transcend the view of poverty as an individual condition at the micro level primarily stimulates the search for a framework that would include the social inequality perspective as well as the social system perspective.

Claims that the poor, either as individuals or as groups, should be observed as a function of the rich (Wilson 1992), and that poverty should therefore be (re)considered as a function of wealth, prove that the vast majority of concepts currently employed are inadequate. Regional poverty conceptualizations reveal an "escapism" in cases where attempts are made to apply the available poverty concepts to specific local circumstances. Again, it could be assumed that the further the country is from the West, the greater the need for a genuine mutation of the classical concepts. On the other hand, poverty in the West also needs to be reconsidered from a macro/micro perspective and should include a social inequality perspective.

Regarding the above suggestions, which come from different parts of the world, it might be concluded that a holistic approach to the issue of poverty would present a way out from the "hyper-individualization" of the poor, since it is individual living conditions that are the subject of the main analytical efforts with regard to poor local communities. Such a "holistic" and "structural" view of poverty can also serve as a guide to the "highways and byways" of the specifically local incidence of poverty.

Using this approach, poverty could be observed as a three-level phenomenon. At the micro level, two approaches could frame poverty investigation. In terms of an "anthropological" perspective, the meaning of poverty – its smell, colour, and sound, its cry and its whisper – would be the core subject. Social indicators can also serve as measures for investigating living standards and social inequality. At the intermediate level, various vulnerable and disadvantaged groups could be observed, taking into account a similar framework. At the macro level, a "development" approach could be applied, analysing poverty in terms of economic and political processes in the national and international perspective.

To be fair, the above contextual suggestion is rather utopian, but its main aim is to stress that poverty as a phenomenon that should be considered from a much broader perspective than occurs in the vast majority of investigations, where strict individualization in terms of both the incidence of poverty and its eradication has been the leading context and strategy. A maturing of poverty investigation could be achieved by the global interweaving of different concepts. The pictures of poverty thus produced would, perhaps, "sound" richer. This handbook proves it is possible.

REFERENCES

Ahmad, E., J. Dreze, J. Hills, and A. Sen (1991) *Social Security in Developing Countries.* Oxford: Clarendon Press.

Corcoran, M., G. J. Duncan, G. Gurin and P. Gurin (1985) "Myth and reality: The causes and persistence of poverty." *Journal of Policy Analysis and Management* 4: 316–36.

Douthitt, R. A. (1994) "Time to do the chores? Factoring home-production needs into measures of poverty." Discussion Paper no. 1030–94. Madison: University of Wisconsin, Institute for Research on Poverty.

Douthitt, R. A., M. Macdonald and R. Mullis (1992) "The relationship between measure of subjective and economic well-being: A new look." *Social Indicators Research* 26: 407–422.

Doyal, L. and I. Gough (1991) *A Theory of Human Need.* London: Macmillan.

Drewnowski, J. and W. Scott (1966) *The Level of Living Index.* Genevea: UN Research Institute for Social Development, Report No. 4.

Erikson, R. and R. Åberg (1987) *Welfare in Transition; A Survey of Living Conditions in Sweden 1968–1981.* Oxford: Clarendon Press.

Gans, J. H. (1992) "Über die Positiven Funktionen der Unwurdigen Armen – Zur Bedeutung der 'Underclass' in den USA". in S. Leibfried and W. Voges (eds), *Armut im modernen Wohlfahrtsstaat, Kölner Zeitschrift für Soziologie und Sozialpsychologie* 32, pp. 48–62.

Harrington, M. (1981) *The Other America: Poverty in the United States.* Harmondsworth, Middx: Penguin.

Haveman, R. and L. Burton (1993) "Who are the truly poor? Patterns of official and net earnings capacity poverty, 1978–1988", in D. B.

Papadimitriou and E. N. Wolff (eds), *Poverty and Prosperity in the USA in the Twentieth Century*. New York: St. Martins Press.

Mack, J. and S. Lansley (1985) *Poor Britain*. London: Allen & Unwin.

Mayer, S. E. and C. Jenks (1993) "Recent trends in economic inequality in the United States: Income versus expenditures versus material well-being", in D.B. Papadimitriou and E.N. Wolff (eds), *Poverty and Prosperity in the USA in the Twentieth Century*. New York: St. Martins Press.

Miller, S. M. (1994) "Poverty and respect". Paper presented at the World Congress of Sociology, Bielefeld.

Piachaud, D. (1987) "Problems in the definition and measurement of poverty", *Journal of Social Policy* 16: 147–164.

Ringen, S. (1985) "Toward a third stage in the measurement of poverty." *Acta Sociologica*, 28: 99–113.

―――― (1987) *The Possibility of Politics. A Study in the Political Economy of the Welfare State*. Oxford: Clarendon Press.

―――― (1988) "Direct and indirect measures of poverty." *Journal of Social Policy*, 17: 351–365.

Townsend, P. (1993) *The International Analysis of Poverty*. London: Harvester Wheatsheaf.

Wilson, W. J. (1990) *The Truly Disadvantaged. The Inner City, the Underclass, and Public Policy*. Chicago: University of Chicago Press.

―――― (1992) "Ghettoisierte Armut und Rasse; Zur öffentliche Meinungsbildung in den USA", in S. Leibfried and W. Voges (eds), *Armut im modernen Wohlfahrtsstaat. Kölner Zeitschrift für Soziologie und Sozialpsychologie* 32, pp. 221–236.

Part II
The Asian Region

Poverty research in Asia is considerable, in terms of coverage and its thematic as well as intertemporal distribution. Most of the research in the 1960s investigated the equity aspects of growth, the trickle-down thesis and its validity, the relevance of the "bootstraps" strategy, redistribution of income through fiscal and other policy instruments, absolute and relative poverty, a fixed vis-à-vis a variable or moving poverty line, using a mix of positive as well as normative concepts and instruments of poverty measurement. In the 1970s and 1980s, however, the focus of research shifted more toward an understanding of the political economy of poverty, its structure, and how it generated differential incidences of poverty and inequality. The six chapters in Part II review some of these approaches, with particular focus on poverty lines and their refinements, regional dimensions of poverty, and ethno-religious explanations with regard to the causative factors.

The chapters cover only a fraction of the vast region that Asia-Pacific represents. But, in a wider sense, they do depict the basic configuration of poverty and its intensity. Its causes and consequences, however, continue to generate heated debates, leading at times to polar positions. According to one estimate of the World Bank there were 633 million poor people in the world in 1990, more than two-thirds of whom (425 million) were in Asia, a continent that represents enormous diversity in terms of stages of development, ethnicity, culture, religion, language, and human development. Quite understandably, research on poverty in this vast and heterogeneous region has not followed any uniform pattern. An analysis of the Human Development Index country ratings by the United Nations Development Programme in 1993 shows there is no obvious link between income and human development, and secular economic growth does not automatically lead to an improvement in the quality of life. Independent analytic research carried out by individual academics or donor agencies has often arrived at similar conclusions.

All the papers call for more focused research, more refined and specific-purpose poverty data, and the need for comparative research. Given the diversity of Asia, it is somewhat reassuring from the point of view of comparative research that researchers doing independent investigations have been able to reach a certain broad consensus on the needs for higher-quality poverty research in Asia.

Chapter 5
South Asia: An Overview
K. Tudor Silva and K. Athukorala

Introduction

This chapter reviews selected research on poverty in South Asia published between 1980 and 1994. South Asia includes India, Bangladesh, Pakistan, Nepal, and Bhutan, comprising the Indian subcontinent and the island nation of Sri Lanka. The volume of literature on poverty in this region is very extensive indeed, even when limited to a period of fourteen years. Therefore, this review only deals with selected poverty research in the region in the period covered, bearing in mind the broader project objective of comparative poverty research. In selecting material for this review the best access has been to the relevant literature on Sri Lanka, Bangladesh, and India, in that order of coverage. This limitation must be borne in mind in assessing the review.

The significance of South Asia in poverty research

In 1991 South Asia had a population of 1.1 billion or roughly about 20 percent of the entire world population (SAARC 1992: 1). According to World Bank estimates for 1990, one half of the entire poor population in the world lived in South Asia (World Bank 1992). Thus, as a region, South Asia has by far the largest concentration of poor people in the world. A report published in November 1992 by the Independent South Asian Commission on Poverty Alleviation appointed by the South Asian Association for Regional Cooperation (SAARC) estimated that 30–40 per cent of the population in the region is below the poverty lines set in the respective countries (SAARC 1992: 1). South Asia is also one of the most densely populated regions of the world, with an average population density of 242 km² in 1992 (ibid.: 143). Thus the twin problems of widespread poverty and high population pressure characterize this region as a whole.

Given the above situation it is natural that poverty is a key social problem and a target of social policy and interventions, as well as a principle focus of research in the region. In one way or another poverty influences almost all aspects of society and culture, including politics, social instability, broad social and economic processes, literature, and entertainment. Accounts of poverty in South Asia vary from journalistic accounts and reports by various agencies to serious academic writing. This raises the question of how to classify and evaluate poverty research in the region.

Towards a classification of South Asian poverty research

South Asian poverty research can be classified on the basis of disciplinary focus (e.g. economics, sociology, geography, political economy, theology, etc.), academic versus applied research, who funds or carries out research (e.g. international donor agencies, government agencies, non-governmental organisations (NGOs), universities or individual researchers), or the nature and content of the reporting of research results. Considering the nature, content, and authorship of the publications, poverty research in the region may be broadly classified as follows.

- Publications by international agencies such as the International Labour Organization (ILO), especially under its Asian Employment Programme (ARTEP), the World Bank, the Asian Development Bank, the Economic and Social Commission for Asia and the Pacific (ESCAP), and SAARC. The aims of these reports are varied, but they often monitor trends in poverty in countries in the region (for example, Islam 1985; Khan and Lee 1983; SAARC 1992; World Bank 1992). Often these reports use secondary data obtained from national sources.
- National survey reports containing primary data. Examples are consumer finances surveys conducted from time to time by the Central Bank of Sri Lanka, Labour force and socio-economic surveys conducted on a similar basis by the Department of Census and Statistics of Sri Lanka, household expenditure surveys periodically conducted by the Bangladesh Bureau of Statistics, and periodic household surveys

conducted by the National Sample Survey Organization affiliated to the National Planning Commission in India.
- Evaluations of specific interventions against poverty in the respective countries, such as the Grameen Bank in Bangladesh (e.g. Osmani 1989; Quasem 1991), the Janasaviya Programme in Sri Lanka (e.g. Hettige 1994; Mendis 1992; Ministry of Policy Planning, Sri Lanka 1990; Ratnayake 1994), Integrated Rural Development Programmes in India (see Bandyopadhyay 1985), and the Small Farmers' Development Programme in Nepal (e.g. Banskota 1985).
- Analytical studies dealing with poverty trends, their causes, and their consequences in a limited geographical region. These studies in turn may range from those proceeding from a specific theoretical perspective (see Chambers 1983; Griffin 1985; Moore 1990) to those simply reviewing certain empirical observations relating to poverty or income inequality (see Glewwe 1988; Gunatilleke et al. 1991; Minhas et al. 1991). Because these studies seek to understand the hard realities of poverty, they often take the form of academic rather than applied research.
- Ethnographic research. These studies involve first-hand experience of living in selected rural or urban communities on the part of the researchers themselves. Ethnographic research in urban low income communities (e.g. Silva and Athukorala 1991; Sinha 1985) or selected village communities (see Ratnapala 1989) typically presents a qualitative description of the life of the poor and their feelings and perceptions about their condition. Although these studies may be of limited relevance for understanding macro issues such as the changing wage structure in agriculture or how the poor adjust to changing global processes, such studies best bring out the subjective aspects as well as the social and cultural dimensions of chronic poverty.

The above categories are not necessarily mutually exclusive because the same research may sometimes be classified under more than one category.

Concepts of poverty used in South Asia

Poverty researchers in South Asia conceptualize poverty in different ways depending on their objectives, the theoretical perspectives from which they approach poverty and the nature of the data available. The definitions of poverty in turn may rest on income criteria, ownership of assets, physical quality of life, occupation, quality of housing, or subjective views of the populations. The main distinction is between *absolute* and *relative* poverty. Whereas researchers dealing with absolute poverty have a notion of minimum living standards, those dealing with relative poverty stress inequities within the social and economic systems with a focus on the bottom layers of society. Most poverty research and interventions in South Asia use a notion of absolute poverty, which typically involves an estimate of the level of income needed to ensure a minimum diet estimated in calorie terms.

Theoretical perspectives on poverty in South Asia

Poverty research in South Asia over the period 1980–1994 varies in regard to the level of theoretical sophistication with which it approaches the problem of poverty. The basic question why there have been such high levels of poverty in this region throughout the past several decades has not received the attention it deserves, in spite of the large volume of literature on poverty in South Asia. Hence one researcher noted "a poverty of poverty research" in the region (Griffin 1985: 32).

To the extent that poverty in South Asia has been approached theoretically, there are four broad perspectives from which the issue of poverty has been addressed:

- the neoclassical theory of market-led development;
- the political economy of poverty;
- the culture of poverty;
- a participatory approach to poverty alleviation.

These theories employ varied explanations of poverty and lead to varied policy recommendations for the alleviation of poverty.

The neoclassical approach

This approach argues that market-led development is the only sure way to reduce poverty and improve living standards in the long run. It does not argue against "safety nets for the poor" insofar as such protective measures do not inhibit the operation of market forces. Under the influence of the structural adjustment policies advocated by the World Bank, this approach has increasingly acquired a hegemonic position in development thinking worldwide. A variant of this approach is found in World

Bank funded studies on Sri Lanka by Bhalla and Glewwe (1986, 1988). In comparing the social indicators for Sri Lanka for the pre-liberalization era and the post-liberalization era, with 1977 as the point of transition, Bhalla and Glewwe concluded that "the evidence examined in this paper . . . suggests that the post-1977 policies have not been detrimental to the equity objectives and may offer more promise than those which they replaced" (1986: 62). As one commentator noted, this approach assumes "that all development activities implicitly embodied objectives of poverty reduction, and that positive progress would be achieved through the process of 'trickle down'" (Easter 1980: 1). There are, however, wide-ranging criticisms against the market-led policies as they relate to poverty in South Asia. Using Sri Lankan data, Lakshman (1994) argued that market-led policies have had adverse repercussions on the poor.

In other examples of the application of the neoclassical approach in South Asia, some authors have highlighted the positive economic and social benefits of the green revolution in Pakistan and parts of India. Commenting on the green revolution in Panjab, the SAARC report on poverty alleviation noted, "The green revolution transformed the rural-traditional economy, created work with good wages even for the landless, stimulated a different type of industrial growth which evolved spontaneously out of the input and demand linkages produced by agricultural production and incomes" (1992: 17). Others are more cautious in interpreting the social outcomes of the green revolution. Mundle, writing about the recent changes in agriculture in rural Panjab, reported:

> The principal factor accounting for the decline in rural poverty in Panjab would appear to be the improving production performance of agriculture, measured here as the level of per capita food grain production. The positive income effect of agricultural performance has been reinforced by the positive income effect of rising food grain prices . . . However, the latter effect is quite weak. This is because the rising food grain prices have a positive income effect on the class of net-selling cultivators, but this positive income effect is offset to some extent by the negative income effect of rising grain prices on agricultural labourers who may have to buy at least a part of the family's grain requirements from the market.
> (Mundle 1984: 104).

Another group of ILO and ARTEP funded studies concluded "that broad-based programmes of the productivity-raising type have benefitted the rural poor to some extent but their benefits to the rural rich have been disproportionately high" (Mukhopadhyay 1985: 29).

The political economy approach

The political economy approach contends that poverty is a product of certain economic and social processes that are intrinsic to given social systems. It assumes that there is a conflict of interest between the rich and the poor in society, and that the poor remain poor not because of any individual or personal qualities, but because society denies them the legitimate share of benefits that should accrue to them. The notion of class is central to the political economy approach to poverty. Griffin and Khan reported:

> Our empirical work has demonstrated that poverty is associated with particular classes or groups in the community, e.g., landless agricultural labourers, village artisans, plantation workers, etc. Yet most theories and models are couched in terms of *atomistic households* in a *classless* society. This neo-classical assumption is closely associated with the assumption of the universal *harmony of interests*.
>
> We do not believe it is possible to get very far in understanding the problems of the Third World until it is more widely accepted that there are *classes* in society and that the interests of the various classes often are in *conflict*. (Griffin and Khan 1978: 302; emphasis added)

This approach pays considerable attention to the historical context within which poverty evolved in South Asia. According to this approach, the roots of the current crisis in South Asia go back to the colonial period.

> Rural poverty cannot be studied in isolation. It has an historical origin and setting which simultaneously connect the present to the past and establish boundaries to what is possible in future. The history of rural poverty is of course part of the history of underdevelopment. ... Europe did not "discover" the underdeveloped countries; on the contrary she created them.
> (Griffin 1985: 29–30).

Using this same historical perspective, the significance of the development of a plantation economy in generating poverty and inequity in South Asia has been highlighted by other authors. De Silva (1982), for instance, argues that the super-exploitation of labour and the transfer of surplus from the periphery to the centre were the twin principles around which plantation economies were developed throughout the underdeveloped world.

In this approach, rural poverty is typically seen as a product of extreme inequalities in land ownership and control. Writing about Bangladesh, Rahman, Mahmud, and Haque noted: "Given the importance of agriculture in Bangladesh and of land as the primary agricultural factor of production, landlessness is perhaps the most crucial element explaining the level and the growth of poverty" (1988: 49). According to another commentator on poverty in Bangladesh, "Given the significance of land in the production process in a largely unmodernized agriculture and its rather unequal distribution over rural households, it is no wonder that a more egalitarian land distribution would be considered essential for ensuring a better living of the most disadvantaged" (Rahman 1986: 24). Commenting on the agrarian structure in rural Panjab, Mundle wrote:

> The extreme inequality of the pattern of land ownership can now be seen clearly. At the bottom of the scale, roughly half the total number of households, in size class of one acre or less, own barely 1 percent of the total area and operate even less. At the other end, less than 5 percent of all households own as well as operate about 30 percent of the total area or roughly 20 to 25 percent of all households own or operate around 80 percent of the total area.
> (Mundle 1984: 92)

The contrast between the neoclassical and the political economy approaches comes into sharp focus when their analyses of the effect of the green revolution are compared. Whereas neoclassical approach highlights the positive effect of the green revolution for all income categories, including the poor, the political economy approach, as exemplified by critics of the green revolution such as Satya (1990) and Harris (1992) sees growing class differentiation as a negative outcome of the green revolution.

One of the weaknesses of the political economy approach, however, is that it leaves us with only a limited range of options for alleviating poverty.

The culture of poverty approach

Following the work of Oscar Lewis in the 1950s, the culture of poverty approach became important in the study of urban poverty, especially in North America. This theory holds that poverty is not merely a lack of adequate income, but rather a way of life handed down from generation to generation. In contrast to the theory of political economy, which looks for the root causes of poverty in the larger structures of society, the culture of poverty attributes poverty to the subjective views of the urban poor themselves.

Only one study employed the theory of culture of poverty in the South Asian context. In their study of the urban poor in Sri Lanka, Silva and Athukorala (1991) discovered that films and football played an important role in shaping thinking and attitudes towards life. These authors, however, questioned the validity of the culture of poverty thesis as a universal explanation of the behaviour and attitudes of the urban poor. Other studies too examined cultural beliefs as a factor in perpetuating poverty in parts of South Asia, but typically they did not consider them through the culture of poverty thesis. One of the main criticisms against this theory is that it justifies the status quo and blames the victims themselves (namely the poor) for their condition. Because cultures are hard to change through intervention, it is of limited practical use.

The participatory approach to poverty alleviation

Many past efforts to deal with poverty involved interventions from outside, whereby the poor themselves were seen as targets rather than decision makers cum actors capable of improving their own condition, given the right incentives and skills. The participatory approach argues that the only way the poor can overcome their difficulties is by directly participating in the formulation of social policy, the development of programmes, implementation at ground level, and sharing the benefits of such programmes. The participatory approach has the dual goal of promoting growth and equity while also ensuring the development of democratic processes at the grass roots. During the 1980s this approach became a dominant model for analysis and intervention in South Asia (see SAARC 1992; Wignaraja 1990a). Both governments and NGOs have increasingly turned to this approach in their anti-poverty programmes.

> In the past ten to fifteen years, a sufficient body of experience has emerged which demonstrates that where the poor participate as subjects and not as objects of the development process, it is possible to generate growth, human development and equity. An indepth analysis made of the participatory process at the micro terrain such as the Women's Development Programme in India, the Aga Khan Rural Support Programme in Pakistan . . . reflect the kind of social mobilization taking place where the poor have contributed to growth and human development simultaneously under varying socio-political circumstances. They also demonstrate that at relatively lower levels of income it is possible to achieve a high level of human development. The participatory process itself ensures that the poor assert their right to resources and a fair share of the surplus.
> (SAARC 1992: 50)

Lack of influence over decision-making has been identified as an important feature of poverty in South Asia. In a study of poverty in rural Sri Lanka, the authors concluded: "An important dimension of poverty is lack of access to extra village resources, a result of lack of information, of useful social and political contacts and, very importantly, the ability to extract services from agencies of government". (Moore and Wickramasinghe 1980: 64).

The *empowerment* of traditionally disadvantaged segments of the population such as women, scheduled castes and tribes, and ethnic minorities is seen as an important means of promoting growth and equity. Describing the condition of poor women in South Asia, Wignaraja (1990a: 19) stated that they suffer from "a double burden" in being women and poor at the same time. "It is now well established that poor women have the least access to basic needs, such as food, health and education, both within the family and without" (ibid.). Although achieving a level of success in promoting community participation, the ability of this model to alter fundamental structures in society and to promote growth and equity simultaneously is yet to be demonstrated in South Asia. In contrast to the political economy model, the participatory approach advocates a gradual and a bottom-up process of social change where the poor and the underprivileged gradually become full participants in development and decision-making processes.

Data sources on poverty in South Asia

Two categories of data sources that may be used in a comparative study of poverty can be identified:

- regional databases covering the whole or parts of South Asia;
- national databases in each South Asian country.

South Asian regional databases

SAARC

Of the regional databases, perhaps the most up to date is the Report of the Independent South Asian Commission on Poverty Alleviation appointed by the SAARC (SAARC 1992). This report covers the SAARC countries of India, Pakistan, Bangladesh, Sri Lanka, Bhutan, Nepal, and the Maldives. The Commission consisted of fifteen representatives from the above countries. It represented both government agencies and the NGOs in the region. Its chairman was Mr K. P. Bhattarai, a former prime minister of Nepal, and its deputy chairman was Dr P. Wignaraja, a Sri Lankan national and a leading poverty researcher in the region. The main tasks of this Commission were to evaluate the past attempts at poverty alleviation, draw positive lessons from them, and recommend a future strategy of poverty alleviation for the member countries.

Based on available published and unpublished data in the member countries, the Commission reported the incidence and trends in poverty in the different countries and in the region as a whole for the previous two to three decades. In addition, based mainly on UN data, its report presents the latest social indicators for the member countries. Finally, the report lists some of the innovative approaches to poverty alleviation in the region. For the first time this report gives an authoritative account of poverty and selected anti-poverty programmes in the whole region. The report identifies gaps in available data and the need for continuous surveillance of poverty in the whole region. Its analysis of ongoing anti-poverty programmes tends to be somewhat dogmatic and rather uncritical. The database developed by this Commission is located in the SAARC Secretariat in Kathmandu.

ILO-ARTEP

Under the Asian Employment Programme of the ILO, the Asian Regional Team for Employment Promotion (ARTEP) currently operating from Bangkok has implemented a series of research, workshops, and publications on poverty and employment in selected countries in South and South-East Asia since 1981. In 1983, ARTEP completed a series of research studies on poverty in India, Bangladesh, Pakistan, Nepal, Sri Lanka, Indonesia, and Thailand. The results are published in Islam (1985). Most of these studies evaluated the results of selected anti-poverty programmes, usually from a microeconomic perspective.

In an earlier study conducted in the same countries, a team of ARTEP-supported researchers examined trends in rural poverty from 1960 to 1979 using available secondary data. The results of these studies are published in Khan and Lee (1983).

Based on field research in selected rural communities, ARTEP also published a series of monographs on the theme of local resource mobilization for employment generation. The study conducted under this project covered two villages in Sri Lanka and examined labour and employment patterns, land use, crop production, non-crop activities, income distribution, and poverty (Wickramasekara 1983). ARTEP has developed one of the most extensive databases for understanding rural poverty in parts of Asia.

Other regional databases

ESCAP, based in Bangkok, the Asian and Pacific Development Centre (APDC) in Kuala Lumpur, the Asian Development Bank in Manila, and the World Bank have important databases on poverty and related issues in South Asia. The United Nations University South Asian Perspective Project has generated a database on the theme of participatory development, democracy, and women's status in South Asia (Wignaraja 1990b).

National databases on poverty

Owing to a lack of information, this description covers only Sri Lanka. In Sri Lanka the two primary sources for data on poverty are the labour force and socio-economic survey (LFSS) conducted periodically by the Department of Census and Statistics, and the consumer finance survey (CFS) conducted periodically by the Central Bank. The last two LFSSs were conducted in 1980/81 and 1985/86 and the last two CFSs were conducted in 1980/81 and 1986/87. Both LFSS and CFS are based on stratified random samples covering the whole nation. Whereas the LFSS concentrates on unemployment, the CFS focuses on income distribution and household expenditure. The results of these surveys are widely used in planning and evaluation as well as in research.

The Ministry of Plan Implementation in Sri Lanka has developed its own computerized database for monitoring and evaluation purposes. This database primarily covers information about Janasaviya and food stamp recipients. This database is not accessible to researchers from outside the ministry.

The Agrarian Research and Training Institute (ARTI), which is under the Ministry of Agricultural Development and Research, has conducted a series of studies on land tenure, landlessness, farm wages, rural labour, indebtedness, and rural marketing. Similarly, the Slum and Shanty Division of the National Housing Development Authority has the only database on urban poverty in Sri Lanka.

A large number of NGOs operating in Sri Lanka have developed their own databases for monitoring and evaluation purposes. But typically they are not accessible to researchers from outside these organizations. The Marga Institute, an independent research organization specializing on development issues, has conducted a wide variety of research on rural and urban poverty (e.g. Marga Institute 1981). The results of these studies have been published in a variety of formats.

Poverty incidence and trends in South Asia

The Report of the Independent South Asian Commission on Poverty Alleviation estimated that, in 1991, 30–40 per cent of the total population in South Asia was below the poverty line as determined in the respective countries. According to these estimates, of the 440 million poor in the region in 1991, 360 million, or 82 per cent, lived in rural areas, whereas the remaining 18 per cent comprised the urban poor. The report concluded "that the magnitude and complexity of the problem of poverty in South Asia is staggering. When confronted with the multifaceted crisis currently facing South Asian countries, the problem is becoming unmanageable, not only putting democracy at risk, but also posing a threat to the fabric of South Asian societies" (SAARC 1992: iii).

Considering the lack of uniformity in the procedures adopted to determine the poverty lines, it is necessary to be cautious in comparing poverty levels across countries and between different estimates in the same country. According to the latest estimates available (see Table 5.1), the highest levels of poverty are reported in Nepal, Bangladesh, and India, followed by Sri Lanka and Pakistan. Of the different countries in the region, Pakistan recorded a substantial decrease in poverty from 1962 to 1984, Bangladesh and India recorded a marginal decrease in poverty over the past one to two decades, and Sri Lanka and possibly Nepal have recorded a notable increase in poverty in recent years. The recorded increase in poverty in Sri Lanka has been associated with corresponding increases in malnutrition, indicating that the reported increase in poverty is not merely an artefact of the survey procedures used. The SAARC Report concluded that, "given the present trends in population and economic growth and in the absence of a concerted effort at poverty alleviation, the number of poor in the Region is likely to increase substantially" (SAARC 1992: 1).

Factors affecting recent trends in poverty in South Asia

One of the key areas of poverty research in recent and ongoing studies in South Asia is the issue of the effect of structural

Table 5.1 The incidence of poverty in selected countries in South Asia (latest available estimates)

Country	Rural (R) urban (U) total (T)	Estimated by[a]	Year	Poor as a % of population
Bangladesh	R	BBS	1985–6	51.0
	R	Rahman	1985–6	47.1
	R	Hossain	1985–6	49.9
	R	BBS	1988–9	48.0
India	T	NPC	1972–3	51.5
	T	NPC	1977–8	48.3
	T	NPC	1983–4	37.4
	T	NPC	1987–8	29.9
	T	Minhas	1970–1	56.3
	T	Minhas	1983	48.1
	T	Minhas	1987–8	45.9
Nepal	T	NPC	1976–7	40.3
	T	NPC	1988–9	40.0
	T	WB	1988–9	71.0
Pakistan	T	WDR	1962	54.0
	T	WDR	1979	21.0
	T	WDR	1984	20.0
Sri Lanka	T	MPI	1978–9	19.0
	T	MPI	1986–7	27.0
	T	Korale	1985–6	39.5

Source: SAARC (1992: 5).
Note:
[a] BBS= Bangladesh Bureau of Statistics; NPC = National Planning Commission; WB = World Bank; WDR = World Development Report; MPI = Ministry of Plan Implementation.

adjustment policies (SAP) on poverty levels in South Asia. In this regard the SAARC report argues: "The Structural Adjustment Policies, which accompany the open-economy industrialization strategy currently being adopted by most SAARC countries, are likely, in the shorter term, to put further strains on the poor" (1992: iii). A poverty researcher in Sri Lanka argued that "SAPs do not have any in-built mechanisms integrated into the package for a fair distribution of the benefits" (Lakshman 1994: 3). In contrast some World Bank researchers found that under the SAPS Sri Lanka managed to consolidate its achievements in social development started in the previous period.

A key factor in the prevailing high levels of poverty in South Asia has been the failure of agrarian reforms in most of the subcontinent. Reviewing various "land to the tiller" programmes in South Asia, Herring (1983) concluded that, given the existing hierarchical social organization, agrarian reform is highly unlikely to succeed unless it is accompanied by firm political commitment and social mobilization of the poor. Islam and Lee noted:

> The literature on poverty is replete with the suggestion that growing impoverishment in Asia can be explained largely by an agrarian structure characterized by high degree of land concentration, steady population growth and little or no extension of cultivated land – all leading to rising landlessness and dependence on wage labour. In such analyses, increasing poverty is associated with a steady decline in the asset base of the vulnerable group of rural population. (Islam and Lee 1985: 7)

The progress of anti-poverty policies and programmes

As noted earlier, the anti-poverty policies and programmes in South Asia have increasingly moved towards the participatory model over the past two decades. This in turn resulted from the failure of agrarian reform programmes implemented since the 1950s, the participatory policies promoted by the UN agencies and other foreign donors, and lessons from certain innovative interventions within the South Asian region itself.

Islam and Lee (1985) developed the following classification of anti-poverty policies in rural Asia.

A. Policies designed to stimulate production and income-generating processes.

(i) Land policies: tenancy reforms and land redistribution.
(ii) Policies for increasing the asset-base and productivity of the rural poor. The Integrated Rural Development Programmes (IRDP) in India and other countries, the Small Farmers' Development Programme (SFDP) in Nepal, the Grameen Bank in Bangladesh, and the Janasaviya Programme in Sri Lanka are examples of this kind of policies.
(iii) Area-based programmes such as the Drought Prone Area Programme in India and the Remote Area Development Programme of Nepal.

B. Policies designed to guide the flow of income or consumption so as to benefit needy groups.
  (i) Employment creation schemes such as the rural works programmes in different countries, the Food for Works Programme and Infrastructure Development Projects in Bangladesh, the People's Work Programme in Pakistan, and the National Rural Employment Programme in India.
  (ii) Other target group oriented programmes such as the Food Stamp Scheme in Sri Lanka.

Of recent anti-poverty programmes in South Asia, the Grameen Bank (GB) Programme in Bangladesh has received the widest attention as a model of participatory development. The main positive lesson to be learnt from the GB is that the rural poor, including women, could be brought into the nexus of rural banking provided that they are organized into effective small groups that are bankable. In an independent evaluation of this programme, Hossain (1988) found that the project villages had consistently higher income levels, less unemployment, and higher asset levels relative to a control group of villages. The households in GB villages also reported higher average expenditure on education, health, and housing compared with those in control villages. These researchers concluded that the GB made a positive contribution to the alleviation of poverty in the areas of its operation.

On the negative side, the researchers found that the GB covered only a small fraction of the rural poor in Bangladesh. In an article entitled "Limits to the alleviation of poverty through non-farm credit" another researcher (Osmani 1989) argued that rapid expansion of self-employment through the GB may influence market prices in ways that are unfavourable to the rural producers unless there is a simultaneous increase in the income levels of the whole population pushing the demand for goods and services. His recommendation was to integrate the GB scheme with national and regional development plans so as to create a macro-level total atmosphere conducive to this programme.

Towards an evaluation of poverty research in South Asia

Poverty research in South Asia has made considerable progress over the past three decades. Largely through the support of international agencies such as the ILO, ARTEP, ESCAP, SAARC, APDC, and UNICEF, a large volume of research on the subject has been conducted, an array of government and non-government research organizations addressing poverty as a key research issue has been developed, networks among researchers in the region have been created, and arrangements for dissemination of research results have been made. However, given the magnitude of poverty in the region it is necessary that the problem of poverty be given a higher priority in research and intervention.

Some of the main achievements in poverty research in South Asia over the past decades are as follows:

1. Increased clarification of the concept of absolute poverty for research and intervention purposes. As an outcome, most of the countries in the region have adopted a poverty line for intervention purposes. This has facilitated the quantitative measurement of poverty and its monitoring. However, as noted earlier owing to variations in the definition of poverty lines the comparison of poverty levels in different South Asian countries has proved to be difficult.
2. Even though it is difficult to say that poverty research in the region provides a lead for the formulation of social policy and interventions, the Grameen Bank in Bangladesh is a good example of a national programme evolved from an action research project. The experiences of such positive interventions, in turn, have been widely disseminated throughout the region.
3. Largely as an outcome of poverty research, widespread poverty is increasingly seen as a major social problem requiring urgent attention on the part of government agencies, NGOs, and the public at large. The poor themselves have become increasingly aware of their condition, rights, and capabilities. This indicates further possibilities for using *participatory research* as a means of empowering the poor and the underprivileged.
4. A wide range of databases covering poverty, unemployment, income disparities, malnutrition, gender relations and, consumption patterns has been developed or is being developed in all South Asian countries. These databases are being used with varying degrees of success for monitoring poverty levels, assessing the correlates of poverty, and evaluating social policies and interventions.

Despite these achievements, poverty research in the region tends to be externally funded and donor driven rather than generated from within the region in response to perceived local needs. Most poverty research has taken the form of crude empirical investigations and evaluation of specific projects and interventions. Even though a variety of theoretical perspectives has guided some of the research and interventions, as noted earlier, it has not led to a gradual build-up of knowledge regarding the relevant issues. The participatory approach currently in vogue in South Asia tends to be ideologically stimulated rather than research oriented.

In our opinion the following gaps exist in current knowledge about poverty in South Asia:

1. Urban poverty in South Asia remains relatively under-explored and under-researched. Even though the magnitude of urban poverty in South Asia is much smaller relative to rural poverty, there are signs that urban poverty is growing at a faster rate following the market liberalization policies currently being pursued in these countries. We do not agree with the claim that "urban poverty is, to a considerable extent, a spillover of rural poverty" (SAARC 1992: 1). It is necessary that urban poverty is examined in its own right considering its special character in terms of lifestyle, employment, and living conditions.
2. The role played by some aspects of South Asian culture in perpetuating poverty in the region has not been explored satisfactorily. One of the issues is the roles of caste, ethnicity, and gender divisions in perpetuating discrimination against the so-called "low castes" – ethnic minorities including tribal populations and women in parts of South Asia.
3. Many of the current studies use measurable economic criteria to the neglect of issues of powerlessness, discrimination, and prejudice as factors affecting the life chances of the poor. On the whole, this points to the need to examine poverty as an aspect of social stratification in society. One of the important issues that needs further research is the rate and determinants of social mobility in different circumstances.
4. Participatory research, where the poor participate in the research process not merely as subjects of research but also as collaborators and potential users of information, offers good prospects for improving the positive impact of poverty research. Even though some efforts have been

made to initiate participatory research as part of some intervention programmes in South Asia, this line of research is yet to be developed as a key strategy in poverty research.

5. The effect of international labour migration on poverty levels in South Asia needs to be examined. A large number of unskilled and semi-skilled workers from impoverished backgrounds in several South Asian countries have found work in the Gulf region and in some newly industrializing economies in East and South-East Asia. For instances, remittances by these workers have become a major source of income in some of the South Asian countries. This aspect of the emerging world economy may or may not be an important avenue for relieving poverty in parts of South Asia but it requires further research.

REFERENCES

Bandyopadhyay, D. (1985) "An evaluation of policies and programmes for alleviation of rural poverty in India" in R. Islam (ed.), *Strategies for Alleviating Rural Poverty in Asia*. Bangkok: ARTEP, pp. 99–152.

Banskota, M. (1985) "Anti-poverty policies in rural Nepal", in R. Islam (ed.), *Strategies for Alleviating Rural Poverty in Asia*. Bangkok: ARTEP, pp. 153–174.

Bhalla, S.S. & Glewwe, P. (1986) "Growth and equity in developing countries: A reinterpretation of the Sri Lankan experience". *World Bank Economic Review* 1(1): 35–63.

—— (1988) "Is Sri Lanka an exception? A comparative study of living standards", in T. N. Srinivasan and P. K. Bardhan (eds), *Rural poverty in South Asia*. New Delhi: Oxford University Press.

Central Bank of Sri Lanka (1988) *Consumer Finances Survey 1986–87*. Colombo: Central Bank.

Chambers, R., R. Longhurst and A. Pacey (eds) (1981) *Seasonal Dimensions to Rural Poverty*. London: Frances Pinter.

Chambers, R. (1983) *Rural Development: Putting the Last First*. London: Longman.

Chandrasiri, J. K. M. D. (1993) "Poverty and land". *Sri Lanka Journal of Agrarian Studies*. 8(1&2): 45–62.

Department of Census & Statistics, Sri Lanka.

—— (1986) *Labour Force and Socio-Economic Survey of Sri Lanka, 1985–86*. Colombo: The Department of Census & Statistics.

De Silva, S. B. D. (1982) *The Political Economy of Underdevelopment*. London: Routledge & Kegan Paul.

Easter, C. (1980) "What can be done about poverty in developing countries?" in C. Easter (ed.), *Strategies for Poverty Reduction*. London: Commonwealth Secretariat, pp. 1–15.

Glewwe, P. (1988) "Economic liberalization and income inequality: further evidence from Sri Lankan experience". *Journal of Development Economics*, 28(2).

Griffin, K. (1985) "Rural poverty in Asia: Analysis and policy alternatives", in R. Islam (ed.), *Strategies for Alleviating Rural Poverty in Asia*. Bangkok: ARTEP, pp. 29–66.

Griffin, K. and Khan, A. R. (1978) "Poverty in the third world: Ugly facts and fancy models". *World Development*, 6(3): 295–303.

Gunatilleke, G. et al. (1992) "Income distribution and poverty in Sri Lanka: Priority issues and policy measures". *Asian Development Review*, 10(1).

Harris, J. (ed.) (1992) *Rural Development, Peasant Economy and Agrarian Change*. London: Hutchinson University Library.

Herring, R. J. (1983) *Land to the Tiller: The Political Economy of Agrarian Reform in South Asia*. New Haven, Conn: Yale University Press.

Hettige, S. (1993) "Alcoholism, poverty and health in rural Sri Lanka". *Sri Lanka Journal of Agrarian Studies*, 8(1&2): 27–44.

────── (1994) "Health and rural poverty in Sri Lanka: Some policy implications". Paper presented at the Asia Pacific Second Social Science and Medicine Conference, Quezon City, Philippines, 23–27 May.

Hossain, M. (1988) *Credit for Alleviation of Rural Poverty: the Grameen Bank in Bangladesh*. Washington DC: International Food Policy Research Institute, Research Report No. 65.

Islam, R. (ed.) (1985) *Strategies for Alleviating Poverty in Rural Asia*. Bangkok: ARTEP.

Islam, R. and E. Lee (1985) "Strategies for alleviating poverty in rural Asia: Introduction", in R. Islam (ed.), *Strategies for Alleviating Poverty in Rural Asia*. Bangkok: ARTEP, pp. 1–27.

Khan, A. R. and E. Lee (eds) (1983) *Poverty in Rural Asia*. Bangkok: ARTEP.

Lakshman, W. D. (1994) "Market-oriented policies and poverty in Sri Lanka". Paper presented at the National Seminar on poverty, NARESA, Colombo, June.

Marga Institute (1981) *An Analytical Description of Poverty in Sri Lanka*. Colombo: Marga Institute.

Mellor, J. W. and G. M. Desai (eds) (1985) *Agricultural Change and Rural Poverty: Variations on a Theme by Dharm Narain*. Baltimore, MA: Johns Hopkins University Press.

Mendis, P. (1992) "The economics of poverty alleviation: The Janasaviya programme in Sri Lanka". *South Asia Journal* 5(3): 289–298.

Minhas, B. S., L. R. Jain, and S. D. Tendulkar (1991) "Declining incidence of poverty in the 1980s: evidence versus artifacts". *Economic and Political Weekly*, 6–8 July.

Ministry of Policy Planning, Sri Lanka (1990) *Employment and Poverty Alleviation Project: Draft Report*. Colombo: The Ministry.

Momin, M. A (1993) "Strategies for poverty alleviation in Bangladesh". *Sri Lanka Journal of Agrarian Studies* 8(1&2): 9–26.

Moore, M. P. (1990) *Economic Liberalization, Growth and Poverty: Sri Lanka in Long Run Perspective*. Brighton: University of Sussex, IDS Discussion Paper No. 274.

Moore, M. P. and G. Wickramasinghe (1980) *Agriculture and Society in the Low Country–Sri Lanka*. Colombo: ARTI.

Mukhopadhyay, S. (ed.) (1985) *The Poor in Asia: Productivity-Raising Programmes and Strategies*. Kuala Lumpur: Asian and Development Centre.

Mundle, S. (1984) "Land, labour and the level of living in rural Punjab". in A. R. Khan, and E. Lee (eds), *Poverty in rural Asia*. Bangkok: ARTEP, pp. 81–106.

Osmani, S. R. (1989) "Limits to the alleviation of poverty through non-farm credit". *Bangladesh Development Studies*, 17(4): 1–18.

Quasem, M. A. (1991) "Limits to the alleviation of poverty through non-farm credit: a comment". *Bangladesh Development Studies* 19(3): 129–33.

Rahman, A. (1986) *The Socio-economic Disadvantages and Development Perspectives of the Poor in Bangladesh Agriculture*. Dhaka: Bangladesh Institute of Development Studies, Research Report No. 52.

Rahman, A., S. Mahmud and T. Haque (1988) *A Critical Review of the Poverty Situation in Bangladesh in the Eighties, vol. 1*. Dhaka: Bangladesh Institute of Development Studies, Research Report No. 66.

Ratnapala, Nandasena (1989) *Rural Poverty in Sri Lanka*. Colombo: Deepani Press.

Ratnayake, R. M. K. (1994) "Alleviation and reduction of poverty". Paper presented at the National Seminar in preparation for the World Summit for Social Development organized by the Ministry of Policy Planning, Colombo, June.

SAARC (1992) *Meeting the Challenge: Report of the Independent South Asian Commission on Poverty Alleviation*. Kathmandu: SAARC Secretariat.

Satya, P. (1990) "Green revolution and poverty among farm families in Haryana, 1969/70 and 1982/83". *Economic and Political Weekly*, 25(39): 105–110.

Silva, K. T. and K. Athukorala (1991) *The Watta-Dwellers: a Sociological Study of Selected Urban Low-income Communities in Sri Lanka*. Lanham, Md.: University Press of America.

Sinha, S. (1985) *Slum Eradication and Urban Renewal*. New Delhi: Inter-India Publications.

Wanigaratne, R. D. (1993) "The concept of poverty". *Sri Lanka Journal of Agrarian Studies*, 8(1&2): 63–70.

Wickramasekara, P. (1983) *Expansion of Employment and Income through Local Resource Mobilization: A Study of Two Sri Lankan Villages*. Bangkok: ARTEP.

Wignaraja, P. (1990a) *Women, Poverty and Resources*. New Delhi: Sage.
────── (1990b) "The theory and practice of poverty alleviation in South Asia". *Economic Review*, 16(5): 3–7, 33.
World Bank (1992) *World Development Report 1992*. New York: Oxford University Press.

Chapter 6

Korea: Poverty in a Tiger Country

Hakchung Choo, Soon-Il Bark, and Suk Bum Yoon

Introduction

Studies on poverty in Korea are relatively scarce, as is the case in many developing countries. The reasons for the lack of poverty studies are even more pronounced in Korea for a number of historical reasons. A three-year internal war from 1950 to 1953 drove the majority of the Korean population into extreme hardship and poverty. After the Armistice in 1953, the remaining years of the 1950s were mainly devoted to reconstruction and rehabilitation, while poverty was too widespread and rampant to attract any serious attention for independent study. The Korean people were forced to persevere through economic difficulties and were urged by the drive to better their living standards. During the early years of rapid economic growth from the early 1960s, Korean researchers perceived only the initial phase of the Hirschmanite tunnel effect (Hirschman 1973), where even growing disparity is welcomed in the anticipation of the trickle down effect. It was not until the late 1970s that a growing concern emerged among Korean researchers with regard to distributive equity and the issues of poverty (see Choo and Kim 1978; Choo et al. 1979; Choo 1982).

Despite the growing concern about absolute and relative poverty issues among the Korean scholars, the theoretical and empirical problems inherent in poverty studies inhibited such research endeavours. Although poverty may be defined in several ways – such as "a situation in which needs are not sufficiently satisfied" (Hagenaars 1986: 1), "a matter of deprivation" (Sen 1981: 2), or the "inability to attain a minimal standard of living"(World Bank 1990: 26), – these definitions are too general to be workably applied to a society. Even after intensive worldwide research efforts devoted to basic needs and social indicators in the 1970s, there is not even a consensus on a workable concept of primary health care among the researchers, let alone one of absolute or relative poverty.

If poverty studies are to be relevant and meaningful, they must contain empirical analyses. However, useful statistics and data on poverty are much more scarce than any other types of statistical data. For instance, household income and expenditure surveys are carried out in most developing countries. These surveys are designed primarily to derive the weights for the consumer price index, rather than to be used in the estimation of the distribution of income or in the analysis of the poor. Among the price statistics available from developing countries, one can seldom find an index designed specifically for the poor, even though all researchers recognize that there is a wide difference between the consumption basket of the poor and that of an average household.

To conduct a meaningful study on poverty, each poor household needs to be surveyed carefully in terms of all of its unique demographic and socioeconomic characteristics. Such an extensive and detailed sample survey on poverty is in excess of the priorities of policy-makers and the statistical authorities. As a consequence, analysts are forced to use a number of proxies and average figures in a sensitive empirical analysis of poverty. Social scientists in general tend to take least care with data problems in empirical studies placing place greater emphasis on the interpretation of their empirical results. One can hardly expect social scientists to make the effort to crosscheck their empirical findings against relevant and peripheral statistical evidence.

This chapter begins with a summary of the major findings from poverty studies of the past two decades, especially those marking the cut-off poverty line and the incidence of absolute and relative poverty by various measures. A wide variation in the estimated measures considered here is attributed to both the theoretical definitions of estimating poverty and problems in using statistical data. We will attempt to deal with these problems separately, although they are often interrelated, and then end with some concluding remarks.

Major findings of existing studies

Although prevailing poverty issues attracted scholastic attention from the early 1960s, it was in the late 1970s when any significant contributions to poverty studies were made in Korea. Most of the earlier studies confined themselves to a part of the poor section in a city or at most to poor sections of a whole city, and were carried out by social scientists (in economics, public administration, sociology and social services, including public health) (Kwon et al. 1967; Noh, C. S. 1967; Noh, J. H. 1971; Sociology Department, Kyungbuk University 1963). As a consequence, the earlier studies on poverty focused on surveying the income and expenditure patterns of the loosely defined "poor" and analysed their demographic and socioeconomic characteristics as the causes and consequences of poverty. The findings of these studies did, of course, shed some light on the poor, but these studies were far from being comprehensive and representative, for obvious reasons such as the sample sizes, coverage, and survey methods used.

One of the most comprehensive studies on Korean poverty for the years 1965, 1970, and 1976 was carried out by Sang Mok Suh and others at the Korea Development Institute in 1979 (Suh 1979). This study was then extended to 1980 and 1984 by Sang Mok Suh and Ha Chung Yeon (Suh and Yeon 1986). This pioneering study resulted in the estimate of various poverty measures for Korea, as shown in Table 6.1. All the estimated measures of both absolute and relative poverty for the selected years demonstrate trends of rapid reduction consistent with the analysis of the World Bank, except the head-count ratios of relative poverty for 1976 and 1980, which were due to the relative worsening of the distribution of income for these years. For the two benchmark years of 1980 and 1984, the only available measures of poverty are the head-count ratios of absolute and relative poverty, both of which also reveal rapid reductions.

In interpreting the findings of Suh's 1979 study and Suh and Yeon's 1986 study, it must be noted that the cut-off line estimated in the two studies was applied to two different sets of estimated size distribution of income. For the earlier years of 1965, 1970, and 1976, Suh relied on Choo's estimates whereas Sug and Yeon used the results of the social statistics surveys for 1980 and 1984 conducted by the National Bureau of Statistics (1986). For this reason, there may be some discrepancies, although the overall trends may be consistent. The 1979 study by Suh had further been matched and supplemented by the 1980 study by Yoon (Yoon 1994; Yoon and Park 1985), which basically adopted the Leyden method in estimating a poverty line in Korea.

In addition to the studies cited above, there have been two noteworthy studies on urban and rural poverty, respectively, in recent years (Bark 1994; Chung and Oh 1990). Table 6.2 shows the recent estimation of absolute poverty in urban Korea by Soon-Il Bark compared with the estimates of Suh and the

Table 6.1 Estimates of various poverty measures in Korea, 1965–1984

	1965	1970	1976	1980	1984
Head-count ratio (%)					
Absolute poverty[a]	40.9	23.4	14.8	9.8	4.5
Urban	54.9	16.2	18.1	10.4	4.6
Rural	35.8	27.9	11.7	9.0	4.4
Relative poverty[b]	12.1	4.8	12.4	13.4	7.7
Urban	17.9	7.0	16.0	15.1	7.8
Rural	10.0	3.4	9.2	11.2	7.5
Poverty gap (billion won in current prices)					
Total	79.1	60.8	221.0		
Urban	39.7	21.3	139.6		
Rural	39.4	39.5	81.4		
Poverty gap as % of gross national product (%)					
Total	9.8	2.3	1.8		
Urban	4.9	0.8	1.1		
Rural	4.9	1.5	0.7		
Sen's Poverty Index					
Total	0.1489	0.0623	0.0595		
Urban	0.2490	0.0443	0.0728		
Rural	0.1085	0.0733	0.0472		

Sources: Suh (1979); Suh and Yeon (1986).
Notes:
[a] The absolute poverty line is defined as 121,000 won per month in 1981 for a five-member family.
[b] The relative poverty line is defined as one-third of the average household income in a given year.

Table 6.2 Comparison of available estimates of the absolute poverty rate for urban Korea, 1965–90 (%)

Source	1965	1970	1980	1984	1990
Suh	40.9	23.4	9.8	4.5	N/A
Bark	N/A	68.5	48.3	44.4	11.6
MOHSA[a]	10.2	N/A	6.2	N/A	7.7

Sources: Suh (1979); Bark (1994: 74–5).
Note:
[a] The ratio of recipients of public assistance to the total population provided by the Ministry of Health and Social Affairs.

Ministry of Health and Social Affairs. The estimates of the urban poverty rates by Bark are considerably higher than two others, although both of the series show a rapid reduction in the prevalence of poverty. Such wide differences in the poverty rate

Table 6.3 Comparison of two estimates of the absolute and relative poverty rate for the rural Korea, 1967–1988

	Source	1967	1970	1988
Absolute poverty rate	Suh and Suh and Yeon	35.8	27.9	4.4[a]
	Chung and Oh	33.7	23.5	6.5
Relative poverty rate	Suh and Suh and Yeon	10.0	3.4	7.5
	Chung and Oh	31.6	36.1	17.4

Sources: Chung and Oh (1992); Suh (1979); Suh and Yeon (1986).
Note:
[a] 1984.

for the same target population frustrate all serious analysts when they review existing studies.

The comparison of two poverty estimates for rural Korea (Table 6.3) looks much better than that for urban Korea. The Suh and Yeon estimate of absolute poverty for 1970 is somewhat higher than that of Chung and Oh, while the estimate for 1988 is the reverse. However, the two estimated rates of relative poverty reveal pronounced differences, particularly for 1970. Although the difference narrows for 1988, it is still significant at about 10 percentage points. These differences are primarily due to definitional differences: Suh and Yeon took one-third of the average income as the cut-off line, whereas Chung and Oh defined it to be one-half (Chung and Oh 1992; 26). Furthermore, for the same reason, the absolute poverty incidence for 1967 (both Suh and Chung) and 1970 (Suh only) was higher than the incidence of the relative poverty in the same years.

These wide variations in the findings of existing studies on poverty deserve further scrutiny, otherwise these findings may confuse the issue, be abused by diverse interest groups and distort reality. Although some difference may be allowed, the extent should be within the level of tolerance, certainly not as great as in the comparison of Suh and Bark's estimates of urban absolute poverty in 1976 and 1980 (as shown in Table 6.2).

The problem of different findings by different researchers is compounded by the theoretical methods and statistical data used. As is widely known, there exist a number of methods for establishing the minimum cost of living as a cut-off line of poverty, and this results in a wide range of figures (see, for example, Table 6.4 below). In addition, there is a tendency among social science researchers to conserve their efforts in order to make better use, with care, of existing data with their well-known inherent limitations.

What is even more dangerous is the common practice of social scientists of extending a point-of-time estimate into a time series estimate. In relation to poverty studies, the consumer price index is used as the deflator or inflator, not the consumer price index of the poor. In addition, the size of family is often not adjusted, by measuring adult-equivalent scales for different family compositions. The next two sections will attempt to examine these problems further in the Korean context.

Estimation methods

The available poverty studies in Korea applied a number of different methods in establishing the poverty threshold or cut-off lines, ranging from Engel's coefficient method to the poll or perception method. Table 6.4 summarizes representative studies in Korea during the past two decades and the resulting estimates of the minimum cost of living (MCL) per person per month in 1993 constant Korean prices. All of these methods have their respective merits and demerits, which do not need further elaboration here. However, because each of these methods is

Table 6.4 Estimated minimum costs of living per person per month in Korea, 1973–90

Source	Reference year	Method	Estimated MCL (1993 constant Won 1000)
MOHSA	1973	Engel	32
Suh	1973	Engel	35
Yoon	1980	Leyden	63
Chang	1984	Rowntree	66
Lee	1985	Leyden	66
MOHSA(1)	1978	Engel	83
MOHSA(2)	1978	Leyden	110
Bae et al.	1987	Rowntree	181
Lim et al.	1989	Leyden	109
Ahn et al.(1)	1989	Expenditure	99
Ahn et al.(2)	1990	Expenditure	105
Bark et al.(1)	1990	Perception	114
Bark et al.(2)	1990	Perception	127

Source: Bark (1994).

Table 6.5 Comparison of the Engel's coefficient of the poor households and the average urban household, 1962–90 (%)

Source	Reference year	Poor households	Urban households
Kyungbuk University team	1962	77.9	44.4
Kwon et al.	1966	80.0	47.0
MOHSA	1973	52.3	41.1
Ahn et al.	1979	50.2	35.2
Kim	1982	32.0	38.3
Hong et al.	1985	55.3	34.4
Bark et al.	1990	31.8	27.4

Source: Bark (1994: 102).

applied to Korea, the result is a wide range of MCL estimates. The lowest estimate is from the Ministry of Health and Social Affairs, while the highest one (almost six times higher) is reported in the study by Bae et al. The substantial changes in MCL over time may be attributed to changes in the commodity baskets and the ever-increasing aspirations of the poor, along with increasing average per capita income.

Generally speaking, at least in the case of Korean studies, the Engel method tends to yield a low estimate, followed by the Leyden and the Rowntree methods (with the exception of the study by Bae et al.). The expenditure method and the poll (perception) method produce results on the high side, with some variations depending on the assumptions employed in each study. However, the differences between the MCL estimates are so significantly large that the adopted method may not be the whole explanation.

The estimates of MCL in Table 6.4 reveal a tendency to be higher, the more recent the reference year is. Because of the rapid economic growth in Korea during these years, the composition and especially the prices of basic goods and services necessary to maintain a minimum standard of living have changed significantly over the years. It is like finding a difference in the MCL in an international comparison between high- and low-income countries. As partial evidence to support this point, Table 6.5 provides the estimates of the Engel's coefficient for poor households compared with the average urban household over the years. The declining trend in the coefficient for the poor is as apparent as it is for urban households. This explains why the estimates of MCL for recent years are larger: each estimate is multiplied by the inverse of the Engel's coefficient when the Engel method is applied.

As shown in Table 6.6, the differences in the sample of a survey also cause the resultant estimates to differ, for at least three reasons. First, most of the sample surveys were conducted in the poor areas of the metropolitan city of Seoul, Daegu, or, at most, six major cities of Korea. The results from these surveys were inevitably significantly higher than those from a sample survey covering the entire country and including small and medium-sized cities and rural villages.

Second, depending on the survey, the sample households were selected from the absolute poor, poor families assisted under the Livelihood Protection Law, low-income households, residents within poor areas, or households earning below the average income (as shown in Table 6.6). Therefore, the selection criteria of the sample caused the estimated MCL from each survey to vary significantly.

Third, the sample size also differs widely from one survey to another, ranging from a few hundred households to a few thousand. Certainly, a sample of several thousand in a survey of one city (Kwon et al.'s 1966 study of Seoul) may be redundant, whereas Bark's 1993 sample for a national study may be considered to be rather small. These variations in the sample sizes of different studies would inevitably result in varying degrees of possible sampling errors.

The resulting estimates of MCL in 1993 constant prices, as shown in Table 6.4, tend to be somewhat biased, either way, owing to the index number problem implicit in the use of the consumer price index (CPI) as the inflator. Because the CPI is compiled by adjusting the weights of commodities and services every five years in Korea, it would be hazardous to use it to generate an appropriate time-series in order to derive an MCL series in constant terms.

It is safe to say that the application of any method for determining the poverty threshold yields an estimate with some variation, in the case of Korean studies as in any other country. The differences in the estimated poverty line may be to a certain extent attributable to the method of determining MCL, the coverage, the sample size of the survey, and the reference year. In particular, the difference between reference years during the period of rapid economic growth and transformation in a country such as Korea makes the comparison of MCL estimates extremely difficult.

What is evident from the preceding examination is that the existing poverty studies in Korea can provide only a range for the

Table 6.6 Differences in the samples surveyed

Coverage	Name of investigators	Year sampled	Type of households surveyed	Sample size	Area covered
National	Ministry of Social Affairs	1973	Low income households with an income below 24,000 Won per month	1,162	
	Kim	1981	All households assisted under the Livelihood Protection Law	1,292	
	Bark et al.	1990	All low-income households	2,500	
	Bark et al.	1993	All low-income households	830	
Local	Sociology Dept, Kyungbuk University	1962	All low-income households within the area	120	Shinamdong, Daegu
	Noh	1964	"	723	
	Kwon et al.	1966	"	4,222	Dongbu, Ichon-dong, Seoul
	Choi	1968	"	347	16 poor areas of Seoul
	Noh	1970	Low-income households with less than the per capita income of 7,000 Won	2,652	2 poor areas of Seoul
	Yoo	1971	The poor assisted under the Livelihood Protection Law	1,162	
	The city of Seoul	1979	Low-income households	1,292	Poor areas in Seoul
	Suh et al.	1981	Poor households assisted under the Livelihood Protection Law	2,500	
	Yoo et al.	1982	All low-income households	830	40 poor areas of Seoul
	Kim	1982	"	120	Bong-cheon dong
	Hong et al.	1985	The absolute poor	723	2 poor areas of Seoul
	Lim et al.	1989	Low-income households with income below than 765,000 Won per household	4,222	6 cities
	Chun et al.	1989	All low-income households	347	Seoul

Source: Bark (1994: 99–100).

poverty line, not its specific value within a tolerable level of accuracy. Therefore, it is not surprising to find wide variations in the incidence of poverty in Korea.

The adequacy of the data used

Any serious empirical analyst, whether from a developed or a developing country, frequently runs into difficulty with the availability and reliability of necessary data. However, the degree of difficulty varies from one country to another. Analysts tend to be rather eloquent about the theoretical hypothesis to be tested, its mathematical specification, and the interpretation of quantitative results, but they seldom explain the problems of the necessary data to be used in estimating the critical parameters of analytical equations. In order to be economical in academic works, analysts rely almost entirely on the published data of statistical agencies and estimates by a handful of data specialists. The only justification given by the users of these statistics is the citation of the sources, but they seldom assess the data.

Although Korea is considered to be one of the developing countries that is relatively better endowed with adequate statistics, the data required in poverty studies are comparatively scarce and those that are available are far from adequate. For example, the central statistical agency in Korea did not use a large enough sample in its urban household income and expenditure survey for it to be possible to abstract statistical data to represent the urban poor.[1] However, poverty researchers, instead of attempting to survey a large enough sample of the poor directly, often derive a sub-sample of the poor from this survey. Moreover, it is practically impossible to derive any meaningful price series for a particular target population such as the poor from existing price indices.

Even when there is a high-quality sample survey on the poor and the poverty line is scientifically established, the head-count method simply cannot be applied to the size distribution of income for Korea. One of the few serious studies that attempted to measure poverty in Korea was conducted by Suh (1979), who took Choo's income distribution estimates in order to derive a head-count ratio. Suh's study applied a five-step procedure, which estimated the poverty line and borrowed adjustment factors from Statistics Canada (1973) for an adult-equivalent scale. It is still unclear how household-specific information was applied by Suh to the distribution pattern estimated by Choo. In short, it is practically impossible to pool survey results with income distribution data, as they exist in Korea, unless strong assumptions are introduced about the distribution pattern and household characteristics within the lower deciles.

Furthermore, the household income and expenditure survey results used in estimating the size distribution of income for Korea involve a number of problems that deserve a mention. The city household income and expenditure survey (CHIES) conducted in Korea contains elements of both upward and downward bias (Choo 1982: Appendix II). On the one hand the CHIES results are considered to be upwardly biased because the survey excludes all non-farm households in non-city areas, where incomes are basically lower than those in cities. On the other hand, the results are downwardly biased because the survey applied an upper income ceiling until 1976 and thus excluded the highest-income households. Therefore, if an analyst uses the CHIES data to estimate the poverty line, the resultant cut-off line and poverty incidence rate tend to be upwardly biased. However, the most serious defect of the CHIES is the fact that, ever since the survey was first conducted in 1963, it has never released the surveyed incomes, but consumption expenditures of the self-employed and wage income households.

If the farm household income and expenditure survey (FHIES) is utilized for the purpose of a poverty study, its results are likely to be downwardly biased in terms of a head-count, because the survey excludes those farm households cultivating less than 1 danbo (equivalent to 0.235 acres) and landless rural households, which are assumed to be more likely to be poor than property holders. This exclusion had a significant defect until the late 1980s in Korea, when all farm workers were paid at subsistence level. In recent years, however, the shortage of manual workers in Korea has become so serious that a male farm worker is paid more than US$ 50 per day, on average, including fringe benefits of all kinds.

Owing to these deficiencies in the CHIES and FHIES, a number of researchers bravely attempted to carry out sample surveys themselves, which, as mentioned in the previous section, is technically very difficult, to say the least. Moreover, such surveys are useful only for limited purposes in a cross-section study because of seasonality, limited coverage of sampled areas, arbitrary sample selections, and the inexperience of the field workers, among others. Even when the results of an independent cross-section survey prove to be relatively accurate, it is difficult to maintain consistency over time among the surveys and the results would not serve the purpose of time-series analysis, unless an analyst assumed them to be comparable with other results. Any attempt to gather primary data on poverty must be made with extreme care and researchers need to make a concerted effort to solve data problems.

Another spectrum of data and associated problems lies in establishing the poverty line. Despite worldwide efforts throughout the 1970s to make quantum specifications of basic needs, there is no consensus among researchers yet on what constitutes primary health care, let alone basic needs. Without theoretical specifications, one cannot, of course, expect such statistical data to be compiled by the statistical agencies.

Summary and concluding remarks

Numerous empirical studies of poverty have been attempted in Korea, as reviewed in this paper. Owing to differences in analytical methods, reference years, and the coverage of surveys, the findings from one study inevitably differ from those of others. These findings can provide us only with a range of existing benchmarks, which need to be used with careful qualification, both implicit and explicit, in a study. Therefore, further research effort is required in order to gain conclusive evidence on both urban and rural poverty in Korea.

As in other parts of the world, all the available estimation methods have been applied in the Korean poverty studies over the years. A new method has the merit of compensating for the weakness of another method, at least theoretically. However, when there is no conclusive study, the application of different methods complicates the matter by making the clarification of differences in the findings of each study more difficult. It is hard to know whether to attribute the differences to the method itself or to a weakness of the study, such as the data pooled and/or surveyed. Instead of applying all available methods, it might be better to use a few selected or tested ones until conclusive evidence on different aspects of poverty emerges.

As in all countries, the major bottleneck in poverty studies in Korea lies in what we call data problems. These time-consuming problems are too frequently and conveniently overlooked by researchers. Because the relevant statistics compiled by the Korean statistical agencies are not readily applicable to poverty studies, almost all such studies rely on data from sample surveys designed by the researchers. However, conducting a sample survey is not a simple task, especially one on poverty. Therefore, social scientists in all countries should support their statistical agencies in securing adequate staff and budgets to conduct poverty and related surveys regularly.

Although there have been numerous studies on poverty in Korea in the past, these studies are far from conclusive. At their best, they reveal only partial truths, and they are also sometimes misleading. Rapid economic growth during the past thirty years in Korea has alleviated poverty to a great extent. Yet there remain, and will remain, many pockets of absolute and relative poverty in Korea, for which comprehensive policy measures need to be adopted. In the absence of persuasive studies on poverty and policy recommendations to redress it, the sufferings of the poor are bound to remain unnoticed and ignored. Such neglect represents a research and academic failure as much as the administrative and managerial failure of poverty alleviation efforts.

NOTE

1. Until 1977, the sample size did not exceed 2,000 households for the 32 cities surveyed in Korea.

REFERENCES

Bark, S. I., (1992) *A Study of the Social Welfare System in Korea*. Seoul: Korea Institute of Health and Social Affairs (in Korean).
—— (1994) *The Reality of Poverty and Social Security in Korea*. Seoul: Ilshin-sa (in Korean).
Chang, Soo-Man, (1991) "Republic of Korea", in *The Urban Poor and Basic Infrastructure Services in Asia and the Pacific*, vol. 2. Manila: Asian Development Bank.
Choo, H. (1979) *Income Distribution and Its Determinants in Korea*, vol. I. Seoul: Korea Development Institute (in Korean).
—— (1982) *Income Distribution and Its Determinants in Korea*, vol. II. Seoul: Korea Development Institute (in Korean).
Choo, H., and D. Kim, (1978) *Probable Size Distribution of Income in Korea: Over Time and by Sector*. Seoul: Korea Development Institute (in Korean).
Chung, Ki Whan and Nae-Won Oh (1992) "Rural poverty in the Republic of Korea: Trends and policy issues". *Asian Development Review*, 10(1).
ESCAP (1993) "National poverty concepts and national approaches to the measurement of poverty". An Expert Meeting Paper, September.
Hagenaars, A. M. M., (1986) *The Perception of Poverty*. Amsterdam: Elsevier Science Publishers.
Hirschman, A. O. (1973) "Changing tolerance for inequality in development". *Quarterly Journal of Economics*. November.
Kakawani, N. C. (1980) *Income Inequality and Poverty – Method of Estimation and Policy Applications*. Oxford: Oxford University Press.

Kim, Jong-Gie (1993) *Characteristics of Urban Poverty and Policy Measures*. Seoul: Korea Development Institute.
Kwon, I-Hyuk, et al. (1967) "A Study on the Urban Poor". Medical School, Seoul National University (in Korean).
Lim, Chang Ho (1989) *Research on Policy Measures for the Urban Poor*. Korea Research Institute for Human Settlements (in Korean).
National Bureau of Statistics (1986) *Social Indicators for Korea* (in Korean).
Noh, Chang Sup (1967) "Socio-economic characteristics of urban slum areas", in *Collected Essays of Ehwa Women's University* (in Korean). Seoul: Ewha Women's University Press.
Noh, Jeong Hyon (1971). "Study on the poor in Seoul". Yonsei University (in Korean).
Øyen, Else (1992) "Some basic issues in comparative poverty research". *International Social Science Journal*, 34. November.
Sen, A. (1981) *Poverty and Faminies*. Oxford: Clarenden Press.
Sociology Department, Kyungbuk University (1963). *The Survey Report on Low Income Households* (in Korean).
Statistics Canada (1973) "Revision of low income cut-offs". December, unpublished.
Suh, Sang Mok (1979) *The Patterns of Poverty in Korea*. Seoul: Korea Development Institute, Working paper No. 7903.
Suh, Sang Mok and H.C. Yeon (1986) *Social Welfare During the Structural Adjustment Period in Korea*. Seoul: Korea Development Institute, Working Paper No. 8604.
Van Praag, B. M. S., J. S. Spit, and H. Van De Stadt (1982). "A comparison between the food ratio poverty line and Leyden poverty line". *Review of Economics and Statistics*, 64.
World Bank (1990) *World Development Report*. Washington DC: World Bank.
Yoo, J. and H. Choo (1987) "A cross-sectional analysis of the household equivalence scale in Korea". *Korea Development Review* (Seoul: Korea Development Institute), pp. 71–85 (in Korean).
Yoon, Suk Bum (1994) *Poverty in Korea*, Seoul: Sekyung-Sa, (in Korean).
Yoon, Suk Bum and Tae Kyu Park (1985a) "Strategies and programmes for raising the productivity of the poor and the eradication of poverty in Korea", in Swapna Mukhopadhyay (ed.), *The Poor in Asia: Productivity-raising Programmes and Strategies*. Kuala Lumpur: Asian Pacific Development Centre, Chapter 6.
Yoon, Suk Bum and Tae Kyu Park (1985b) "An in-depth follow-up study of the poor rural village of Jukchon", in Swapna Mukhopadhyay (ed.), *Case Studies on Poverty Programmes in Asia*. Kuala Lumpur: Asian Pacific Development Centre.

Chapter 7

India: Tradition for Poverty Research

Bhaskar Dutta

Introduction

During the 1970s, there was increasing awareness all over the world that the development strategies of previous decades would not eliminate or even reduce poverty to any significant extent. Economists and policy makers in India were also aware that the rate of economic growth was too slow to lift the living standards of the bottom half of the population to acceptable levels. Given a relatively rich database on the distribution of consumption expenditures, this awareness generated a lively debate on the trends and causes of poverty in India, as well as the appropriateness of various strategies to alleviate poverty. The purpose of this chapter is to review the main strands of this debate. I start with a discussion of the informational basis for poverty studies in India. I then discuss some methodological issues connected with the measurement of poverty. A crucial step in the measurement of poverty is the specification of the cut-off point in (typically) the level of either consumption or income below which individuals are deemed to be poor. The rationale underlying alternative specifications of the cut-off point in India is discussed in some detail. The trends in the incidence of poverty in India are discussed in the next section. There is now a database to measure the extent of poverty for almost all years between 1956/57 and 1988/89. However, the trend in poverty prior to 1973/74 has been a controversial topic, and this controversy is reviewed in this section in some detail. Another issue that has received a great deal of attention in the Indian literature on poverty has been the efficacy of the trickle-down mechanism. This discussion has focused on whether accelerated growth can reduce the extent of poverty in the rural sector. In particular, the issue has been narrowed down to the role of agricultural growth in reducing rural poverty. Various hypotheses regarding the determinants of rural poverty are summarized.

However, even the most ardent advocate of the trickle-down mechanism will admit that the rate of economic growth in India has been too slow to make any significant dent in the poverty problem. This perception has been widespread, and has resulted in an expansion in the scale of intervention oriented to a target-group by the government. The effects of such interventions and other relevant issues are discussed in the final section.

The database for poverty studies

The only reliable source of time-series data on the distribution of either consumer expenditure or income is the National Sample Survey (NSS) Organization, which has been conducting sample surveys of household consumer expenditure practically every year since 1951. After 1972/73, a decision was taken to start quinquennial surveys with a considerably larger sample size, though the usual annual survey was also conducted in 1973/74 with a relatively small sample. As emphasized in subsequent sections, almost all the studies on poverty in India are based on NSS consumer expenditure data. The sampling scheme of the NSS consumer expenditure surveys is based on a stratified two-stage sampling design. The first-stage units consist of rural villages or urban blocks selected according to a probability that is proportional to population. These are also selected in the form of two independent sub-samples. The second-stage units consist of sample households from the complete listing of households in the first stage units. The sampling errors of the NSS estimates of private consumption may be taken to be very small because the sample sizes are quite large. Indeed, there are about 13,000 first-stage units and 121,000–158,000 second-stage units. The NSS collects detailed itemwise consumption data for the thirty days preceding the date of enquiry from the sample households by interviewing members of the household. The survey period of a round, which is normally of a year's duration, is divided into four sub-rounds. The two independent sub-sample households are equally distributed over the four sub-rounds, and the canvassing is staggered throughout the survey period so as to make the estimates free of seasonal variation.

Doubts have sometimes been expressed about the reliability of NSS data on private consumption expenditure. In particular, it has been pointed out that the NSS estimates are significantly below the total private consumer expenditure estimated from the

National Accounts Statistics (NAS). The NAS estimates of private consumption expenditure are derived as a residual after deducting estimates of government consumption, fixed investment inventories, and exports (net of imports) from estimates of output flows. These adjustments are all subject to errors, and so the NAS estimates of private consumption expenditure need not necessarily be taken as a benchmark. (See Minhas 1989, who discusses several reasons for the divergence between the two estimates of private consumption.)

Another crucial ingredient in the measurement of poverty is the state-specific and all-India consumer price indices, because these are needed to adjust poverty lines for spatial and intertemporal variations in the cost-of-living. Unfortunately, no representative official cost-of-living indices are available. Official cost of living consumer price indices relate to narrow groups such as the consumer price index for agricultural labourers (CPIAL), for industrial workers (CPIIW), and for urban non-manual employees (CPINM). The CPIAL has been widely used in studies measuring the incidence of rural poverty in India. This index, prepared by the Labour Bureau of the Government of India, is constructed on the basis of monthly retail prices of 62 items, the price quotations being collected from a fixed set of 422 villages spread throughout the country. The weighting diagram is based on the consumption pattern of rural agricultural labour households observed in 1956/57. As far as the CPIIW and CPINM are concerned, weekly price data are collected for a large number of consumer items from industrial and urban centres spread all over the country. The weighting diagrams for the construction of the CPIIW and CPINM are obtained from the expenditure pattern available from the family living surveys carried out in 1958/59.

Since agricultural labour households constitute only 30 per cent of the rural population, and only 70 per cent of agricultural labour households are amongst the rural poor, less than half of the rural poor are agricultural labour households. This has raised doubts whether the CPIAL can really serve as a representative cost-of-living index for the entire class of rural poor. However, Bardhan (1973) argues that the weighting diagram used in the CPIAL does conform quite well to the consumption pattern of the rural poor. Dutta (1978, 1980) and Vaidyanathan (1974) also discuss this issue. Similar objections can be levelled against the use of CPIIW and CPINM as a cost-of-living index for the urban poor.

This prompted Minhas et al. (1990, 1992) to construct appropriate consumer price indices for the total rural and urban population of each state, as well as for the "middle-range population" between the 20th and 60th fractile, since the poverty line invariably falls in this fractile group. These price indices were constructed using the same price data going into the CPIAL, CPINM, and CPIIW and weighting diagrams based on NSS consumer expenditure distributions. These price indices have been used in later studies on the incidence of poverty in both the rural and urban sectors, and some of these estimates will be discussed in the section on poverty trends.

Measurement issues

Poverty exists in a given society when a group of its members fail to attain a level of well-being considered to be a reasonable minimum by the standards of that society. Insofar as the extent of poverty is concerned, its measurement must involve two distinct stages. First, the minimum living standard, the so-called poverty line, has to be specified so that the set of "poor" persons can be identified. Second, the actual levels of well-being of the poor below the poverty line have to be aggregated into an overall measure of poverty. Any comprehensive definition of well-being must encompass all factors that affect an individual's standard of living. Apart from command over commodities (measured by either income or consumption expenditure), the list must include at least health and education (see Sen 1985). Unfortunately, because relevant time-series data are seldom available, the usual practice has been to adopt a very narrow concept of well-being, with income or current consumption being identified as the indicator of living standards. Moreover, because the incomes of the poor exhibit greater variability than current consumption, the latter is normally judged to be a more reliable indicator of the current standard of living.

Indeed, the dominant tradition in the specification of a poverty line is to identify some basic consumption needs. Obviously, the most important consumption need is the attainment of some recommended food-energy intake. Since there are many food combinations that can achieve any specified food-energy intake, this specification does not directly yield a well-defined poverty line. An attempt to calculate the minimum cost of attaining the required food-energy intake is likely to be irrelevant because the minimum-cost food bundle may be very unpalatable. One option is to follow Panda (1989), who performs the minimum-cost exercise subject to suitable constraints introduced so as to avoid "corner" solutions. These constraints ensure that the optimum solution is a reasonably balanced meal. In practice, the poverty line is specified by finding the consumption expenditure at which a person typically attains the required food-energy intake. Notice that this procedure also makes an allowance for expenditure on non-food consumption.

The first attempt to specify poverty lines was in 1962, when a Working Group set up by the Government of India recommended a per capita total consumption expenditure (PCTE) of Rs 20 per month in 1960/61 prices. This figure excluded expenditure on health and education, which were expected to be provided by the state. However, it is not clear whether this figure corresponded to any specific consumption basket or food-energy intake because there are no records to reveal the assumptions or calculations implicit in this figure. Nevertheless, this figure came to acquire some legitimacy, with the Draft Fifth Five Year Plan noting that "In the Fourth Plan document, private consumption of Rs 20 per capita per month at 1960–61 prices was deemed a minimum desirable consumption standard".

Subsequent specifications of the poverty line have been more explicit about the assumptions underlying the poverty line estimates, with the poverty lines corresponding to the monthly PCTE at which households can afford either a specified level of nutrients or a specified consumption basket. Of course, the specification of the level of nutrients or the food basket cannot avoid the element of arbitrariness that is inherent in all such exercises. For instance, Dandekar and Rath (1971) used an average calorie norm of 2,250 calories per capita per day for both rural and urban areas as the required food energy intake. NSS consumption data revealed that rural households with monthly per capita consumption expenditure of Rs 14.20 at 1960/61 prices consumed on an average food whose caloric content was 2,250 calories per day. The corresponding PCTE for urban areas was Rs 22.60 at 1960/61 prices. Amongst other early attempts at constructing poverty lines are those of Bardhan (1973) and Rudra (1974). Most of the subsequent studies on the incidence of poverty in the rural sector carried out in the 1970s have used a per capita consumption expenditure of Rs 15 per month as the rural poverty line. There is no agreement about the urban poverty line, except that it has to be higher than the rural cut-off point because of higher prices. However, some results that use monthly PCTE of Rs 20 at 1960/61 prices will be reported here.

Official estimates of poverty in India carried out by the Planning Commission define the poverty line as the per capita expenditure level at which the average per capita daily intake is 2,400 calories in rural areas and 2,100 calories for urban areas.

This is based on the age–sex–activity-specific calorie allowances recommended by a group of nutrition experts, who estimated the average daily per capita requirements for rural and urban areas using the age–sex–occupational structure of their population. Based on the observed consumer behaviour as revealed by NSS data for 1973/74, it was estimated that total consumption expenditure of Rs 49.09 per capita per month in rural areas and of Rs 56.64 per capita per month in urban areas were the appropriate poverty lines. These have come to be the accepted norms in studies carried out in the past 15 years.

The poverty line has to be adjusted for changes in the cost of living across time as well as for spatial variability in prices. As mentioned in the previous section, the CPIAL has been widely used to adjust the rural poverty line. Dutta (1980) has also used the CPIIW to measure the incidence of urban poverty during the period 1960/61 to 1973/74. The next section discusses inter-state movements in the incidence of poverty during 1970/71 to 1987/88. These results use the official (Planning Commission) estimate of the poverty line of Rs 49.09 for rural India and Rs 56.64 for urban India at 1973/74 prices, and adjusted by the price indices for the middle range of the population obtained by Minhas et al. The simplest measure of poverty is given by the head-count ratio, which essentially measures the percentage of people below the poverty line. The head-count ratio is obviously a very crude measure because it ignores both the shortfall of consumption from the poverty line, as well as the distribution of consumption amongst the poor. However, its simplicity is its most appealing feature, and perhaps this has resulted in its widespread use. Also, it turns out that the trends in the incidence of poverty are not very sensitive to the particular index used to measure poverty. In this chapter, all estimates of poverty use the head-count ratio.

Trends in poverty: 1956/57 to 1988/89

This section describes the trends in the incidence of poverty in both rural and urban India during the past four decades. The period is divided into two overlapping sub-intervals, the first being the period 1956/57 to 1973/74, while the second is the period 1970/71 to 1988/89. Note that the two sets of estimates are not strictly comparable because the poverty lines as well as the price indices used to adjust them across time have been different.

Before discussing estimates of the incidence of poverty at the all-India level, it is worth pointing out that two estimation procedures have been followed in the literature. The first is to perform the poverty computations directly on the all-India consumption expenditure distributions, which are published by the NSS separately for the rural and urban sectors. These aggregate distributions are obtained as the population-weighted averages of the state distributions. An obvious defect of this procedure is that it ignores inter-state variations in prices. Since the state expenditure distributions in current prices are not corrected for differences in prices across states, this procedure is equivalent to using a uniform poverty line across all states. The second procedure is indirect, because it first computes the incidence of poverty at the state level, then the incidence of poverty at the all-India level is derived as the population-weighted average of the state-wise poverty levels. The latter would be a theoretically sounder procedure if the poverty levels of all states (and union territories) were aggregated to arrive at the all-India figures. However, since state-wise price indices are not available for all states and union territories, this has not been done so far. For instance, Kakwani and Subba Rao's (1992) all-India rural estimates were based on poverty levels in sixteen major states, whereas Minhas et al.(1991) aggregated poverty levels in twenty states to derive their all-India estimates. Because the indirect method excludes a section of the population, it cannot be called truly representative. Also, the two procedures usually give different estimates, as is borne out by results of Ahluwalia (1978) and Minhas et al. (1991).

The incidence of poverty during 1956/57 to 1973/74

In an early and provocative paper, Minhas (1970) used the NSS percentage distribution of consumption expenditure to allocate the aggregate private consumption figure derived from the NAS amongst different groups of the population. Using two alternative poverty lines of Rs 240 per capita per year and Rs 200 per capita per year at 1960/61 prices, Minhas concluded that between 1956/57 and 1967/68, "there has been a steady decline in the proportion of people below the poverty line".

Two features of his estimation procedure have come in for sharp criticism. First, there does not seem to be any justification for combining the distribution of NSS consumption expenditure along with the estimate of aggregate private consumption expenditure from NAS. As discussed in the section on the database, there is no reason to question the reliability of NSS data simply because of a divergence from the estimates derived from the NAS. Moreover, if the NSS data are considered unreliable, then the use of the NSS percentage distribution of consumption expenditure is bizarre. Second, Minhas used the national income deflator to adjust for price changes across time. As Bardhan (1973) pointed out, national income includes investment as well as consumption goods, and so it is not clear why consumption should be deflated by the national income deflator. Since the weight of manufactured goods in the consumption basket of the rural poor is much smaller than the national average, the national income deflator is singularly inappropriate as a consumer price index for the rural poor.

Bardhan (1973) also estimated the incidence of rural poverty in the 1960s. Unlike Minhas (1970), Bardhan relied solely on NSS consumer expenditure data. As with most studies in this period, Bardhan defined the poverty line to be a monthly PCTE of Rs 15 at 1960/61 prices, and used the CPIAL to measure price rises for the rural poor. Bardhan found that the proportion of people below the poverty line rose from 38 per cent in 1960/61 to 45 per cent in 1964/65, 53 per cent in 1967/68, and to 54 per cent in 1968/69. These figures suggested a secular increase in poverty in rural India during the 1960s, and there were also suggestions that the pattern of development was biased against the poor (see also Bardhan 1970; Rajaraman 1975; and Lal 1976). Ahluwalia (1978) was amongst the first to point out that any firm statements about secular changes can only be made on the basis of a time-series of observations. Otherwise, conclusions can be vitiated by the choice of end points. Ahluwalia (1978) showed that there was no statistically significant time trend in the incidence of poverty (as measured by the head-count ratio) in the rural sector during 1956/57 to 1973/74. Dutta (1980) also established the same result for the period 1960/61 to 1973/74 and for both the rural and urban sectors. There have been fluctuations in the proportion of the population below the poverty line, with a marked tendency for poverty to increase in years of bad harvests and associated high food prices. Indeed, the poverty estimates in both sectors reached their peak in 1967/68, the year in which price rises were highest.

Unlike the incidence of poverty, there has been a statistically significant trend increase in the number of people below the poverty line in both sectors of the economy. On average, there was an annual increase of 5.38 million in the number of the rural poor, while the corresponding increase in the urban sector was 1.3 million. The trend growth rate in the size of the poor population was higher for the urban sector.

The experience between 1970/71 and 1987/88

Many of the studies on the incidence of poverty in India in the recent past adopted the Planning Commission's specification of Rs 49.09 and Rs 56.64 per month PCTE at all-India 1973/74 prices as the poverty lines for the rural and urban sectors, respectively. Kakwani and Subba Rao (1992) also specified a cut-off point for the ultra-poor. This was taken to be 80 per cent of the poverty line, which they took to be Rs 50.00 per month PCTE for the rural sector. Hence, the "poverty line" for the ultra-poor is Rs 40, which is quite close to the earlier poverty line of Rs 15 at all-India 1960/61 prices adjusted by CPIAL.

Both the CPIAL and the new consumer price indices for the middle-range rural and urban populations derived by Minhas et al. have been used to adjust the poverty lines across time and across states. This section relies heavily upon the poverty estimates of Tendulkar et al. (1993), who used the Minhas et al. price indices.

As remarked earlier, the specification of the poverty line is subjective and to some extent arbitrary. Moreover, as with all price index numbers, the consumer price indices used to adjust the poverty line across time are all "approximations" of the true cost-of-living index of the poor population. It is, therefore, reassuring to find that the pattern of the incidence of poverty during 1970/71 to 1988/89 is remarkably robust to alternative specifications of the poverty line, the consumer price indices, as well as the estimation procedure (direct versus indirect methods).

Thus, in the rural sectors, there was a monotonic decline in the incidence of poverty from 1972/73 to 1988/89. The pattern in the urban sector is similar. The head-count ratio declined from 57.33 per cent in 1970/71 to 42.23 per cent between 1970/71 and 1988/89 in the rural sector, while the corresponding figures for the urban sector were 45.89 per cent and 35.07 per cent. Moreover, as in the earlier period, the incidence of poverty in the urban sector was appreciably lower than in the rural sector throughout this period. It is also worth emphasizing the decline in the head-count ratio between 1983 and 1987/88 because the latter was a particularly severe "drought" year, and in previous drought years the head-count ratio had tended to rise. This welcome break from the past must be at least partially due to large-scale government intervention in the form of special wage-employment programmes as well as a huge release of food-grains through the public distribution system to control the price of food-grains.

Notice, however, that the appreciable decline in the head-count ratio was not accompanied by any reduction in the number of people below the poverty line. Indeed, there was a clear increase in the number of poor people between 1970/71 and 1983 according to all the estimates. The further decline in the head-count ratio between 1983 and 1987/88 makes the comparison of the numbers of people below the povery line between 1970/71 and 1987/88 more difficult. The size of the poor population during this period decreased if the poverty line is taken to be a monthly PCTE of Rs 15 at 1960/61 prices, but it increased if the poverty line is taken to be the Planning Commission specification. As far as the urban sector is concerned, there was a noticeable increase in the number of people below the poverty line. However, part of this increase was due to the greater degree of urbanization during this period.

Kakwani and Subba Rao (1992), Jain and Tendulkar (1990), and Tendulkar and Jain (1992) also conducted the exercise of decomposing the changes in the incidence of poverty into changes in average PCTE (growth effect) and changes in distribution (distribution effect). Although the decomposition exercises use somewhat different procedures and different time-periods, the basic principle is identical. This is to identify (i) the growth effect (GE) as the change in the incidence of poverty attributable to change in real average PCTE while keeping the Lorenz curve (of the distribution of consumption expenditure) unchanged, and (ii) the distribution effect (DE), which is the change in poverty attributable to the change in the Lorenz curve between two time points while keeping real average PCTE constant. The sets of results differ because of differences in end points and procedures. For example, Kakwani and Subba Rao (1992) found that between 1973/74 and 1977/78 and between 1983 and 1986/87, the DE actually retarded poverty reduction. On the other hand, Tendulkar and Jain (1992) found that between 1972/73 and 1977/78, the DE was favourable but small, whereas between 1983 and 1987/88 the DE was favourable and large.

In this connection, Tendulkar, Sundaram et al. (1993) observed that, when the end points are similar (local peak to local peak such as 1977/78 to 1983, or drought to drought such as 1972/73 to 1987/88), the GE has an overwhelmingly large influence. Moreover, the DE in urban areas is virtually negligible in the absence of urban anti-poverty programmes. However, the DE in both rural and urban sectors becomes important when one of the time points is a drought year whereas the other is a peak year.

Tendulkar et al.'s explanation for the observed pattern of decomposition is also interesting. If the end points are dissimilar, then the scale of the government's anti-poverty interventions will also be different. For instance, in the drought year 1987/88, massive employment generation under public works programmes must have had favourable distributional effects for the rural population, whereas, in a local peak year such as 1983, the poverty alleviation programmes were on a much smaller scale. This can be expected to lead to a large DE if the period of comparison is between 1983 and 1987/88. On the other hand, the absence of urban anti-poverty programmes leaves the urban poor particularly vulnerable in drought years. This implies that the DE in urban areas will be large and negative (or unfavourable) when the comparison is between peak and drought years. Finally, note that, because many of the anti-poverty programmes such as the public works programmes are targeted at the poorest segments, the distributional effects will be larger when the incidence of poverty is measured by distributionally sensitive measures such as the Sen index. This is also borne out by the results of Tendulkar and Jain (1992).

Determinants of poverty levels

The first systematic attempt to explore a possible determinant of the extent of rural poverty was Ahluwalia (1978), whose main purpose was to examine the relationship between the level of per capita agricultural incomes and the incidence of rural poverty. If there is any "trickle down" mechanism at work in the rural economy, then increases in rural incomes should translate into lower levels of poverty in the rural sector. Since agriculture is the dominant source of incomes in the rural sector, it is natural to test the "trickle-down" hypothesis with some proxy for agricultural income as the independent variable. Ahluwalia used the net domestic product per head of rural population at constant (1960/61) prices (NDPARP), which is a measure of per capita value added, as the proxy for per capita rural income. Ahluwalia found "that improved agricultural performance is definitely associated with reductions in the incidence of poverty". The basis for this assertion is a set of different regression equations in which the dependent variable is the head-count ratio in the rural sector. The coefficient of NDPARP turned out to be negative and significant in these equations.

Ahluwalia also found that there is no significant time trend in any of the equations after controlling for the influence of NDPARP. This indicates that there are no factors correlated with time that are important determinants of the extent of poverty in the rural sector.

The basic hypothesis was also tested at the level of individual states, though Ahluwalia noted that the state-level exercise has to cope with two problems. First, unless the performance of the agricultural sector is uniform across all states, there may be temporary migration from a state in which the harvest has been bad to a neighbouring state with a better harvest. The possibility of inter-state migration implies that the trickle-down mechanism may not be very effective at the level of individual states. Second, in the absence of time-series data on state-wise NDP in agriculture, Ahluwalia was forced to use a two-year average of an index of agricultural production per head of the rural population (IAPPH) as the independent variable. Since this is a "gross output" measure, this would tend to overstate rates of growth if there was any increased intensity of input usage. Ahluwalia's results were ambiguous at the state level. In seven out of fourteen states, the coefficient of IAPPH was negative and significant. Moreover, in many states, the coefficient on time was significant, indicating that there may have been other factors at work that have tended to increase rural poverty.

What can be concluded about the efficiency of the "trickle-down" mechanism from these regression results? Can agricultural growth without major institutional reforms reduce poverty? Some authors have contended that the period of Ahluwalia's analysis, namely 1956/57 to 1973/74, is inappropriate because the new agricultural strategy was adopted only in the early 1960s. Thus, Griffin and Ghose (1979) and Saith (1981) contended that the years prior to the early 1960s should be excluded. Saith also argued for the exclusion of the year 1973/74 because the price index with base weights of 1956/57 understates the importance of commodities whose relative prices rose rapidly from 1970/71 to 1973/74. On a truncated time-series of observations, Saith's regression exercise revealed a statistically significant positive trend in poverty after controlling for CPIAL and variations in agricultural production.

These arguments for the exclusion of some observations are not particularly convincing. However, the question remains whether Ahluwalia's regression results at the all-India level throw much light on the trickle-down hypothesis. In particular, it is important to take note of the fact that there has been no trend increase in NDPARP. Ahluwalia (1986) pointed out that, between 1956/57 and 1977/78, the NDP in agriculture grew at an annual average rate of 2 per cent, which is only slightly faster than the growth in rural population. Hence, even if the trickle-down mechanism is potentially useful in reducing poverty, it could not have actually effected any significant reduction in the extent of rural poverty simply because "there was very little to trickle down at the All-India level" (see Srinivasan 1986). It is also worth pointing out that the state-wise regression results reveal that many states have had statistically significant trend increases in IAPPH, although there have not been any accompanying trend declines in poverty. Indeed, in West Bengal, there have been statistically significant trend increases in both IAPPH and poverty. Clearly, unless IAPPH is a particularly bad indicator of agricultural growth, the trickle-down hypothesis has failed in West Bengal. Indeed, Bardhan (1986) used NSS cross-sectional data on individual households in 550 sample villages of West Bengal for 1977/78 to conduct a logit analysis of the probability that an agricultural labour household falls below the poverty line. The logit analysis revealed that, other things remaining the same, the probability of an agricultural labour household sliding below the poverty line increases if it is in a district where agricultural production has grown at a faster rate! Both Dharm Narain (see Desai 1986) and Saith (1981) also noted a correlation between the consumer price index for the rural poor and the incidence of rural poverty. Narain expanded Ahluwalia's specification by including the CPIAL as an explanatory variable. Narain observed that the nominal price level appropriate for the rural poor is a statistically significant explanatory variable.

The inclusion of the price variable as an explanatory variable has generated a lot of discussion (see, for instance, Ahluwalia 1986; Bliss 1986; Sen 1986 and Srinivasan 1986). A change in the nominal price level can affect the incidence of poverty only through an effect on the distribution of income (and hence consumption). For instance, if money wages and earnings do not rise as fast as the price level, then the real incomes of agricultural labourers and other non-cultivator households will go down. This could then translate into a reduction in per capita consumption expenditure. Recent work by Ravallion and Datt (1994) supports this explanation. A variation of Narain's hypothesis is provided by Bhattacharya et al. (1991), who contended that it is the relative price of cereals, that is, the price of cereals relative to manufactures, that is a major determinant of the extent of rural poverty. Bhattacharya et al. started with the observation that the incidence of poverty in rural India is highly correlated with the per capita consumption of cereals. They advanced two reasons for this observed correlation. First, cereals account for at least 50 per cent of the consumption basket of the rural poor, and the observed pattern of per capita cereal consumption has a very close fit with the pattern of per capita total consumption. Second, their regression results showed that about 88 per cent of the intertemporal variation in the level of poverty is explained by variation in PCTE.

Hence, they sought to explain changes in the incidence of poverty through an examination of factors affecting the per capita consumption of cereals. They postulated an inverse relationship between the extent of poverty and per capita consumption of cereals, and constructed a model to identify factors explaining the latter. Assuming that cereal production (and hence supply) is exogenous, demand functions were specified for the rural and urban sectors. The model was "closed" by specifying that supply must equal demand. Their model predicted that the lagged price of cereals is a determinant of the per capita consumption of cereals, and their regresssion results confirmed this.

Notice that the Bhattacharya et al. results can be used to provide an explanation for Narain's regression equation. This is because the lagged price of cereals is correlated with the current level of CPIAL. Hence, one plausible explanation for the observed dependence of poverty on the CPIAL is that this is actually the combined effect of the dependence of poverty on the lagged relative price of cereals and the latter's correlation with CPIAL.

Public policy for poverty alleviation

Explicit poverty alleviation programmes were formulated and implemented with the initiation of target-group-oriented special programmes towards the end of the 1960s. Thus, the Small Farmers' Development Agency (SFDA) and the Marginal Farmers' and Agricultural Labourers' Development Agency (MFALDA) were set up during the Fourth Five Year Plan (1969–74) to increase the incomes of the currently non-viable small and marginal farmers as well as of agricultural labourers. However, these schemes did not assist more than 15 per cent of the rural households who were eligible for assistance. The Integrated Rural Development Programme (IRDP), initiated during the Sixth Five Year Plan (1980–85), was considerably larger in scale.

The Integrated Rural Development Programme

The IRDP was an ambitious scheme designed to assist 15 million rural households (roughly one-seventh of the total number of rural households) during the course of five years. The beneficiaries were supposed to be selected from amongst the "poorest of the poor". Two-thirds of the beneficiaries were to be covered by projects broadly classified under the heading of "agriculture and allied activities", while the rest were to be provided with self-employment opportunities in village and cottage industries and in the service sectors. Each project was to be chosen so that it would generate a net income flow sufficient to take the beneficiary across the poverty line.

The entire programme was to be financed through a combination of budgetary subsidy and institutional credit. The stipulated rates of subsidy varied according to the type of beneficiary household, the rate being 25 per cent for small farmers, 37 per cent for marginal farmers and agricultural labourers, and going up to 50 per cent for tribals. The ceiling on subsidies was Rs 3,000 per small and marginal farmer and agricultural labourer. A plan allocation of Rs 15,000 million was made for the plan period, and institutional credit of Rs 30,000 million was also to be provided. Assuming a capital–output ratio of 1.5, this investment was estimated to generate additional income of Rs 30,000 million. Even without any detailed consideration of the actual operation of the IRDP, it is apparent that the target of assisting 15 million households from amongst "the poorest of the poor" to cross the poverty line could never be fulfilled. First, as Bandyopadhyay (1989) pointed out, at least 20 per cent of the plan outlay of Rs 15,000 million was required to meet the administrative costs of running the programme. Assuming away about 15 per cent of total investment by way of leakages leaves a total investment outlay of Rs 35,700 million during the course of the five years. Even assuming that the grossly underestimated capital–output ratio of 1.5 is correct, this outlay could generate an income flow of Rs 23,800 million. This works out at less than Rs 1,600 per individual household if 15 million households were to be assisted.

The IRDP also assumed a poverty line of Rs 3,500 per household per annum. This is absurdly low. Taking the average household size to be five, and assuming the Planning Commission's specification of monthly PCTE of Rs 49.09 at 1973/74 prices, the threshold annual consumption level for households in 1983 turns out to be Rs 5,590 when the poverty line is adjusted by the Minhas et al. price indices for the middle range of rural population. This implies that none of the assisted households could have crossed this poverty line.

Of course, the figure of Rs 1,600 as the additional income flow per beneficiary household is a generous overestimate. There are at least two reasons for this. First, the actual capital–output ratio varied from project to project and was also location specific. The Institute for Financial Management and Research (IFMR), which conducted a major country-wide evaluation study of the IRDP, found that capital–output ratios between 2.5 to 3 for IRDP schemes were more realistic than the official estimate. Second, what is really important is the net income flow after adjusting for loan repayments. Obviously, if the debt servicing is taken into account, the additional income flows generated by the IRDP will be significantly lower. However, the main problem with the IRDP is not simply that the total investment outlay was inadequate to provide sufficient assistance to all the 15 million households. As many authors have pointed out, the entire programme was implemented in such a myopic manner that it essentially turned into a subsidized credit scheme for the rural poor. No attempt was made to mesh the individual projects into an integrated development plan for the rural economy. This implied that the sectoral allocation of credit was unbalanced. For instance, in the initial years, animal husbandry programmes, in particular purchase of dairy animals, dominated the programme. There was no match between disbursement targets and the local potential for increased livestock ownership. The new owners faced shortages of both inputs and infrastructural services. Particularly hard hit were the landless labourers who even had to purchase fodder.

Not surprisingly, yields from milch cows were often quite low, forcing owners to resell the cows. In contrast, subsidiary occupation schemes such as fishery and agriculture were very successful, and as many as 50 per cent of households in the "very, very poor" category operating these schemes managed to cross the cut-off mark of Rs 3,500 per annum. Tertiary sector schemes such as petty services also proved to have large income-generation capabilities. The wide discrepancy in returns from the various schemes is symptomatic of large-scale misallocation of resources.

Another aspect of the implementation of the IRDP that has been roundly criticized in almost all studies is the substantial leakage due to improper selection of beneficiaries ("death of animals" and outright sale of assets were other common sources of leakage). The original stipulation was that the poorest households were to be identified with the help of the village council or Gaon Sabha. However, this practice has not been followed uniformly in all states, and there have been reports of the village headman manipulating the selection process. Different macrostudies suggest that 15–36 per cent of borrowers were estimated to be above the official poverty line, while less than a quarter of beneficiaries were from the "very, very poor" category. Micro studies are usually more critical. For instance, Dreze (1990) concluded from his village study on Palanpur that there had been no overall discrimination in favour of the poor in the allocation of loans. Affluent households have been liberally included amongst the beneficiaries, and the head-count measure of poverty amongst the IRDP beneficiaries was 43 per cent whereas the overall measure was 40 per cent.

Despite these defects, the sheer magnitude of the overall programme obviously had some impact on the living standards of the rural households. The various evaluation studies report that between 37 and 49 per cent of eligible borrowers moved above the official poverty line of annual household income of Rs 3,500. Unfortunately, these figures do not account for either inflation or loan repayment. More encouraging is the IFMR study that reported that 84 per cent felt subjectively "happy" or "very happy" with the IRDP, while the Programme Evaluation Organization (1985) estimated that almost 90 per cent of beneficiaries received incremental income.

However, there are several problems in interpreting these figures. Indeed, even the conceptual task of formulating criteria for judging the degree of success of such programmes is not particularly straightforward. As far as the findings of the evaluation studies are concerned, Copestake (1992) pointed out that these are based on relatively small sample sizes. (Dreze 1990 also pointed out the wide divergence between the results of macro- and micro-studies.) Moreover, there are serious problems in the income estimates. First, the income estimates are derived from single-visit interviews, resulting in possible omission and recall errors. Second, the entire change in income levels of beneficiaries is attributed to the IRDP, whereas other determinants of income levels could also have changed during the duration of the IRDP project. Third, a single comparison between income estimates at two points of time says very little about the pattern of income flows because of possible gestation lags or because other exogenous parameters may have changed.

A related point is the argument advanced by Dreze (1990) that an important criterion for judging the success of the programme must be the ability of the project to yield adequate and stable income flows. In the absence of perfect capital markets, consumption smoothing opportunities for the rural poor are limited. This makes long-term average incomes or "permanent" income poor indicators of the living standards of the rural poor. This issue is particularly relevant because the IRDP has often been accused of promoting risky ventures.

It is also misleading to place undue emphasis on a household crossing the poverty line, whatever may be the specification of the line. Given the size of investment outlays and the additional incomes generated, it is not surprising that only a fortunate few amongst the poorest category of households crossed the official threshold of Rs 3,500. This must also have contributed to the pattern of selection of beneficiary households, with zealous officials selecting households from just below the poverty line so as to record magnified success.

Many other issues have been discussed in the extensive literature on the IRDP. A small sample is Bagchee (1987), Bandyopadhyay (1985, 1989), Copestake (1992), Dreze (1990), Sundaram and Tendulkar (1985). Dreze contains additional references.

Special wage-employment programmes

The sheer size of the rural population in poverty meant that complete reliance on self-employment programmes to alleviate poverty was out of the question. The rural economy simply could not have absorbed the required number of small-scale projects. Thus, a multi-pronged strategy was essential, with the creation of massive wage-employment opportunities complementing the self-employment programmes. Special wage-employment schemes such as the Rural Manpower Programme have been in operation since 1960/61. However, until the mid-1970s, these programmes were essentially designed to provide supplementary employment in the lean season to landless labourers. The scale of operations was limited, and they were not really designed to be general anti-poverty programmes. The first major wage-employment scheme was actually the Employment Guarantee Scheme (EGS), which was run by the state government of Maharashtra before similar schemes started at the national level. The scheme offers to provide manual work to all unskilled persons willing to work, and at the statutorily fixed minimum wage rate. The public works were to be organized within fifteen days of demand by fifty or more persons and preferably within 5 kilometers from the village. The first national counterpart of the EGS was the Food for Work Programme launched in 1977, and later merged into a much bigger programme called the National Rural Employment Programme (NREP) at the start of the Sixth Plan.

One advantage of the special employment programmes is supposed to be that a suitable specification of the level of wages and type of work can ensure that only the really poor will take up work in these programmes. For example, self-selection devices were built into the EGS by fixing the wage at the statutory minimum wage rate, which was less than the prevailing agricultural wage rate, and also by offering only unskilled work. However, an official evaluation still reported that small and medium farmers also reported for work under the EGS and NREP. This was one motivation for starting the Rural Landless Employment Guarantee Programme (RLEGP) in 1983. A specific objective of the RLEGP was to guarantee up to 100 days of employment to at least one member of each landless household in the country. The NREP and the RLEGP were brought under a single umbrella called the Jawahar Rozgar Yojana (JRY) in 1989/90.

Whereas the benefits or impacts of the self-employment programmes are hard to measure, the amount of employment created in the special wage-employment programmes is much easier to quantify. The average daily employment generated during the Sixth Plan by the NREP was 1.16 million man days, which was only slightly over 7 per cent of the total daily status of rural unemployment in 1980. The combined "output" of the NREP and the RLEGP during the Seventh Plan period was less than 10 per cent of total unemployment during this period. Indeed, as Dandekar and Sathe (1980) pointed out, the EGS in Maharashtra seems to have had a greater impact.

These programmes also have indirect effects. For instance, availability of employment in the public works programmes has an upward tendency on the general level of wages in the rural sector. Moreover, even this relatively small proportionate increase in employment generation had a significant impact in so far as the incidence of rural poverty is concerned. Recall that the extent of poverty in 1987/88 was lower than that in 1983. This is in spite of the fact that 1983 was a local peak as far as agricultural production was concerned, whereas 1987/88 witnessed one of the worst droughts. This represented a sharp departure from previous trends, when the incidence of poverty would shoot up during drought years. An obvious explanation for this phenomenon is the cushioning effect provided by these special employment and drought relief programmes (see Tendulkar et al. 1993 for a detailed discussion of this point).

The scale of the special employment programmes was dramatically increased in the Eighth Plan period, and the employment generated under the JRY during 1989/90 to 1993/94 was

3,300 million person-days. However, the huge influx of funds has not been without its attendant problems. Perhaps the most serious problem is that, because the primary objective of the programmes is creation of employment, wage costs form a very high fraction of the total investment outlay. This severely constrains the type of construction activity that can be undertaken. Minor irrigation works and roads form the bulk of the works, with the result that the principal beneficiaries are the medium and large farmers. A second problem is that in many districts there is an acute shortage of complementary inputs, particularly technical manpower, because junior engineers have to execute and supervise the public works.

These problems cast doubts on the long-term viability and desirability of such programmes. Public works programmes are obviously important as drought-relief measures or as supplementary sources of income during the lean season. However, should public works on a massive scale be continued on a permanent basis? Notice that, if the scale of these programmes is large enough, then the overall investment pattern in the economy may get distorted from the optimal pattern. The familiar trade-offs between efficiency and distribution, the short run and the long run, come to the fore. The optimum size of public works programmes (and the self-employment schemes) will then depend crucially on the objective circumstances in each region, because these will determine the nature of the trade-offs.

REFERENCES

Ahluwalia, M. S. (1978) "Rural poverty and agricultural performance in India", *Journal of Development Studies*, 14.
―――― (1986) "Rural poverty, agricultural production, and Prices: An examination", in J. W. Mellor and G. M. Desai (eds), *Agricultural Change and Rural Poverty in India: Variations on a Theme by Dharm Narain*. New Delhi: Oxford University Press.
Bagchee, S. (1987) "Poverty alleviation programmes in the Seventh Plan: An evaluation". *Economic and Political Weekly*, 22.
Bandyopadhyay, D. (1985) "An evaluation of policies and programmes for the alleviation of rural poverty in India", in R. Islam (ed.), *Strategies for Alleviating Poverty in Rural Asia*. Dhaka: BIDS; Bangkok: ILO-ARTEP.
Bandyopadhyay, D. (1989) "Poverty alleviation through special employment programmes in rural India", in M. Muqtada (ed.), *The Elusive Target*. Geneva: ILO-ARTEP.
Bardhan, P. K. (1970) "The green revolution and agricultural labourers", *Economic and Political Weekly*, 5.
―――― (1973) "On the incidence of poverty in rural India", *Economic and Political Weekly*, 8 (reprinted in P. K. Bardhan and T. N.

Srinivasan, *Poverty and Income Distribution in India*. Calcutta: Statistical Publishing Society, 1974.

—— (1984) *Land, Labour and Rural Poverty: Essays in Development Economics*. New Delhi: Oxford University Press.

—— (1986) "Poverty and "Trickle-Down" in rural India: A quantitative analysis", in J. W. Mellor and G. M. Desai (eds), *Agricultural Change and Rural Poverty in India: Variations on a Theme by Dharm Narain*. New Delhi: Oxford University Press.

Bhattacharya, N., D. Coondoo, P. Maiti, and R. Mukherjee (1991) *Poverty, Inequality and Prices in Rural India*. New Delhi: Sage Publications.

Bliss, C. (1986) "A note on the price variable", in J. W. Mellor and G. M. Desai (eds), *Agricultural Change and Rural Poverty in India: Variations on a Theme by Dharm Narain*. New Delhi: Oxford University Press.

Copestake, J. G. (1992) "The Integrated Rural Development Programme: Performance during the Sixth Plan, policy responses and proposals for reform", in B. Harris, R. Guhan, and R. H. Cassen (eds), *Poverty in India. Research and Policy*. New Delhi: Oxford University Press.

Dandekar, V. M. and N. Rath (1971) *Poverty in India*. Bombay: Indian School of Political Economy.

Dandekar, K. and M. Sathe (1980) "Employment Guarantee Scheme and Food for Work Programme", *Economic and Political Weekly*, 15.

Desai, G. M. (1986) "Trends in rural poverty in India: An interpretation of Dharm Narain", in J. W. Mellor and G. M. Desai (eds), *Agricultural Change and Rural Poverty in India: Variations on a Theme by Dharm Narain*. New Delhi: Oxford University Press.

Dreze, J. (1990) "Poverty in India and the IRDP delusion", *Economic and Political Weekly*, 25.

Dutta, B. (1978) "On the measurement of poverty in rural India", *Indian Economic Review*, 13.

Dutta, B. (1980) "Intersectoral disparities and income distribution in India: 1960–61 to 1973–74", *Indian Economic Review*, 15.

Griffin, K. and A. K. Ghose (1979) "Growth and impoverishment in the rural areas of Asia", *World Development*, 7.

Jain, L. R. and S. D. Tendulkar (1990) "The role of growth and distribution in the observed change in head count ratio measure of poverty: A decomposition exercise for India", *Indian Economic Review*, 25.

Kakwani, N. C. and K. Subba Rao (1992) "Rural poverty in India; 1973–1986", in G. K. Kadekodi and G. V. S. N. Murty (eds), *Poverty in India: Data Base Issues*. New Delhi: Vikas Publishing House.

Lal, D. (1976) "Agricultural growth, real wages and the rural poor in India", *Economic and Political Weekly*, 11.

Minhas, B. (1970) "Rural poverty, land redistribution and development strategy", *Indian Economic Review*, 5 (reprinted in P. K. Bardhan and T. N. Srinivasan, *Poverty and Income Distribution in India*. Calcutta: Statistical Publishing Society, 1974.

Minhas, B. (1989) "Validation of large scale sample survey database of NSS estimates of household consumption expenditure". *Sankhya*, Series B, 50.

Minhas, B. S., L. R. Jain, S. M. Kansal, and M. R. Saluja (1990) "Cost of living in rural India: 1970–71 to 1983, statewise and all-India", *Indian Economic Review*, 25.

Minhas, B. S., L. R. Jain, and S. D. Tendulkar (1991) "Declining incidence of poverty in 1980s: Evidence versus artefacts", *Economic and Political Weekly*, 26.

Minhas, B. S., S. M. Kansal, and L. R. Jain (1992) "Incidence of urban poverty in different states; 1970–71 to 1983", in B. Harris, S. Guhan, and R. H. Cassen (eds), *Poverty in India*. Bombay: Oxford University Press.

Panda, M. K. (1989) "Planning for basic needs in India". PhD thesis, Indian Statistical Institute, New Delhi.

Perspective Planning Division (1962), *Perspective of Development 1961–1976; Implications of Planning for a Minimum Level of Living* (reprinted in P. K. Bardhan and T. N. Srinivasan (eds) *Poverty and Income Distribution in India*. Calcutta: Statistical Publishing Society, 1974).

Programme Evaluation Organisation (1985) *Evaluation Report on Integrated Rural Development Programme*. Planning Commission, Government of India.

Rajaraman, I. (1975) "Poverty, inequality and economic growth: Rural Punjab, 1960–61 to 1970–71", *Journal of Development Studies*, 11.

Ravallion, M. and G. Datt (1994) "Growth and poverty in rural India". Policy Research Department, The World Bank, mimeo.

Rudra, A. (1974) "Minimum level of living – A statistical examination", in P. K. Bardhan and T. N. Srinivasan (eds), *Poverty and Income Distribution in India*. Calcutta: Statistical Publishing Society.

Saith, A. (1981) "Production, prices and poverty in rural India", *Journal of Development Studies*, 17.

Sen, A. K. (1985) *The Standard of Living*. Cambridge: Cambridge University Press.

────── (1986) "Dharm Narain on poverty: Concepts and broader issues", in J. W. Mellor and G. M. Desai (eds), *Agricultural Change and Rural Poverty in India: Variations on a Theme by Dharm Narain*. New Delhi: Oxford University Press.

Srinivasan, T. N. (1986) "Agricultural production, relative prices, entitlements, and poverty", in J. W. Mellor and G. M. Desai (eds), *Agricultural Change and Rural Poverty in India: Variations on a Theme by Dharm Narain*. New Delhi: Oxford University Press.

Sundaram, K. and S. D. Tendulkar (1985) "Anti-poverty programmes in India. An assessment", in S. Mukhopadhyay (ed.), *The Poor in Asia: Productivity-raising Programmes and Strategies*. Kuala Lumpur: Asia and Pacific Development Centre.

Sundaram, K. and S. D. Tendulkar (1988) "Toward an explanation of interregional variations in poverty and unemployment in India", in P. K. Bardhan and T. N. Srinivasan (eds), *Poverty in South Asia*. Delhi: Oxford University Press.

Tendulkar, S. D. and L. R. Jain (1992) *Rural and Urban Poverty in India: A Decomposition Exercise*. New Delhi: Indian Statistical Institute, Technical Report No. 9206.

Tendulkar, S. D., K. Sundaram and L. R. Jain (1993) *Poverty in India, 1970–71 to 1988–89*. New Delhi: ILO-ARTEP.

Vaidyanathan, A. (1974) "Some aspects of the disparities in levels of living in rural India", in P. K. Bardhan and T. N. Srinivasan (eds), *Poverty and Income Distribution in India*. Calcutta: Statistical Publishing Society.

Chapter 8

South-East Asia: Beyond the Economic Approach

Luzviminda B. Valencia

Poverty research in the Philippines

Most social scientists in developing countries have had their research training in the West. Filipinos usually trained in the United States, whereas Malaysians and Singaporeans mostly trained in England. This is why research on poverty in the Philippines is often conceptualized in the same ways as research published in North America. For example, local researchers tend to study who the poor are, and, characteristically, the pattern is to use income data similar to the 1990 US data, which showed that over 31 million Americans live in households with incomes below the official poverty level (US Bureau of Census 1991). The American poverty level is defined as the minimum income needed to feed, house and clothe household members (Hess et al. 1993: 188–9). Like their American counterparts, Filipino researchers are enamoured of finding the formula for establishing a poverty level, using surveys similar to those of the US Department of Agriculture that showed that families spend about one-third of their income on food. The Department of Agriculture in the USA determines the cost of a minimally nourishing basket of food and multiplies it by three, thereby coming up with a number that is usually adjusted yearly for changes in the cost of the food basket, but without considering that the cost of housing has been rising at a faster rate than the cost of most food items (Hess et al. 1993: 189). This poverty level has become the take-off point for discussion in the Philippines too.

The other recent popular concept or theme in the West is the feminization of poverty. This is a North American concept that is slowly being picked up in the Asian literature. In the USA, most of the poor are females with low incomes, e.g. teenage mothers, single mothers, divorced women of any age, and elderly widows. Increasingly, poverty in the USA has become feminized, with single mothers with young children and old women being among the poorest in the nation. There are still no available and comparable data in the Philippines or in South-East Asia, but soon local researchers will do something about this. The problems of poverty and the aged, which have been addressed by studies in the North American setting, are still to be addressed locally. Given the pronounced American influence on local researchers, it is not far fetched to expect a similar study in the near future.

Concepts of poverty

The literature indicates that researchers conceptualize poverty on many levels, but the predominant orientation of Filipino researchers on poverty is economic. Very few adopt a sociological point of view. Castillo's (1994) article on poverty research noted this lack of sociological direction. Based on the literature, there are certain identifiable poverty sectors (Abad et al. 1986; Andales and David 1985). Four such sectors are present in the Philippines: artisan or small-scale fishermen, upland swiddeners, scavengers, and sugarcane workers. Abad et al. (1986) provide a regional dimension to poverty; their study links development projects and technological changes. A more recent study, Adem (1992), focuses on still another poverty sector in the urban areas – railway squatters, who are mostly migrants to the city and who live along the railroad tracks. Balisacan (1991a,b,c, 1992a,b,c,d) and Abad et al. (1986) also see the farmers from the rural areas as belonging to the poor sector. Among the rural poor are the landless tenant workers, farm workers, farmers owning 5 hectares or less, marginal farmers, sugarcane workers, small-scale producers, and indigenous people/tribal groups. The city poor are railway squatters, scavengers, and migrants.

Poverty is viewed as both a condition and a process (Abad et al. 1986). As a condition, poverty is a "way of life", as displayed by persons lacking cash, capital, and other resources to meet economic demands. Abad et al. characterize the poor as those receiving low pay (if employed), mostly hungry and malnourished, and powerless and assetless. Powerlessness is a result of their being without education (human capital); consequently, they are without employment skills. They live in communities that are often deprived because neither the local nor the national governments have provided such basic goods and services as food, shelter, health, and educational services.

Arboleda et al. (1988) define poverty through certain objective criteria such as unemployment, the infant mortality rate, the prevalence of malnutrition, and a low literacy rate. These measures of poverty are easily calculable for decision makers to base their policies on.

Associated with the general concept of poverty is a concept of "mass poverty", articulated by Lichauco (1986) and Villegas (1986). It means a state of poverty that has been brought about by the colonial powers, with dire consequences for the people of the Philippines. According to Lichauco (1986), the Philippines is poor because of the existing economic structure, which generates profits only for the owners of industries. The profits earned do not filter down to the larger sector of the population. Industrialization is held back by the absence of "economic democratization". Although Villegas (1986) denies that his concept of poverty is coloured by ideological reasoning, he too sees economic development as a correct response to poverty alleviation issues.

Another concept associated with poverty is "absolute poverty" (David 1989). Like Villegas and Lichauco, David (1989) subscribes to the idea that poverty is mainly a function of economic development and of the existing reproduction of gross economic and social inequality at all levels. David uses the quantitative definition of the poverty threshold of the Philippines' National Economic and Development Authority (NEDA): the "monthly income required to satisfy almost 100% of the nutritional requirements and basic needs of a family of 6 persons". According to this definition, the incidence of poverty in the Philippines in 1989 was estimated at 5.67 million, or 59.3 per cent of the total population. When President C. Aquino became President, she wanted to reduce it to 45.4 per cent by 1992. David's ideas were basically echoes of earlier writers, such as Tendero et al. (1984), Andales and David (1985) and Abad et al. (1986). The common theme underlying their studies, which were published over three consecutive years, was the important notion that poverty is a function of the lack of infrastructure, job opportunities, services, and facilities that "ought" to be provided by the government. Likewise, poverty is also the consequence of the overriding and persistent inequalities of land tenure and of an "institutionalized form of oppression" of the disadvantaged and vulnerable sections in Philippine society.

Hypotheses

Andales and David (1985) hypothesize that small-scale fishermen are poor because they lack the necessary capital to buy gasoline and modern fishing gear, and they lack credit facilities and/or storage and processing facilities. Balisacan (1991a–c, 1992a–d), on the other hand, points to the relationship between uneven income distribution and poverty. He also identifies a set of characteristics that describe the rural poor, and shows that household size and household composition are critical variables related to household production and household consumption. In a separate paper, Balisacan (1992a–d) argues that limited poverty alleviation took place in the 1980s as a result of the intrasectoral and general improvement in the distribution of living standards.

Constantino (1989) focuses on the relationship between poverty and the incidence of diseases, while David (1989) points out that low wages or low income have contributed to the emergence of new poverty in the Philippines, and adds that the inability of the government to intervene aggravates the continuing intensity of poverty. Like Mangahas (1984a,b), Veneracion (1985) examines the relationship between the landlessness of agricultural workers or land transfer and poverty incidence; she also raises the question of whether or not nutritional status or access to food is the best measure of poverty. If it is, then she argues that higher priority must be provided to food-related policies. Ortigas (1989) suggests that poor nutrition tends to contribute to poor intellectual development and is a factor in the rise in poverty among Filipinos.

Ellevera-Lamberte (1983) looks at the actual delivery of services and access to services in upland areas in relation to the incidence of poverty. Garcia and Militante (1986), other hand, believe that poverty in itself is one of several social problems of society. They include excessive population growth as an important factor in the persistence of poverty.

The early work of Ganapin (1987) examines the connection of forest depletion with poverty. He predicted that unchecked resource depletion would eventually have a corresponding negative impact, leading to worse cases of poverty among Filipino people.

Pineda's (1991) hypothesis points to how the national debt crisis directly influences the lives of the poor, bringing more hardship and consequently contributing to making more people poor. Santos and Lee (1989), unlike other authors, categorically state that women are the bearers of the burden of poverty; this approximates the "feminization of poverty" theme found in North American literature. However, Pineda (1991) holds the view that the marginalization of women is a function of the ballooning national debt. Thus, both Pineda and Santos and Lee argue that, as the national debt reaches crisis proportions, women assume the greater burden of poverty.

The dominant thinking is that poverty is related to five factors – socioeconomic, health, political, environmental, and agricultural. The socioeconomic factors are: the lack of resources (e.g. the necessary capital to buy essential inputs); income distribution and low wages; the national debt crisis; delivery of and access to services; and excessive population growth. The health factors are the incidence of disease and access to food. The political factor is the inability of the government to intervene meaningfully. The environmental factor is the depletion of the forest and other resources. Lastly, the agricultural factors are the large number of landless agricultural workers and the issue of land transfer.

Other studies portray poverty not merely as a dysfunctional consequence but also as a necessary product of other social forces, such as the colonialism that took place in the past and the persisting inequalities in land tenure and gender. The majority of the writers and researchers frame their hypotheses in a fashion that states the obvious, i.e. poverty is caused by factors arising from the physical, sociocultural, economic, and political environment. According to Fernandez and de la Torre (n.d.), for example, these factors determine the intensity and structure of poverty in a community. These generalizations are inherent sources of weaknesses in past and current poverty research at the local level, because they present a merely unilinear view of poverty, leading to oversimplification and stereotyping.

One of the more interesting hypotheses generated from the literature is the association of poverty with "learned helplessness" (Licuanan, 1981). To understand the psychological dynamics of poverty, the following measures were designed to observe the psychological experiences of the poor as compared with the non-poor: feelings of self-worth (assertiveness, appreciation of criticism, self-confidence), orientation towards others (attitude towards authority, attitude towards peers, openness to innovation), orientation towards collective action (preference for collective action, belief in group's capability to influence), social responsibility (community participation, cooperation). However, it seems that what Licuanan (1981) presented as original studies were similar to the studies previously presented by the Singaporean researcher Kuo (1976), in his work *Families under Economic Stress* (1975). Kuo studied the relationship between poverty status and certain variables similar to those used by the Filipino researcher.

Data sources

In the Philippines, the family income and expenditure survey (FIES) is the most commonly used database for determining who is poor (Balisacan 1991a–c). Other important data sources are UN reports, such as those from UNICEF and the International Labour Organization. The National Census and Statistics Office and the Nutrition Research Institute are also popular sources of data for researchers.

For example, David (1989) used World Bank and NEDA figures for his concept of absolute poverty. Other poverty studies usually refer to income levels based on the 1980 Census. Figures for birth rate, unemployment rate, average income (which in 1989 was P 3,000 a month – c. US$150), and family income come from NEDA. Pineda (1991) used the 1988 World Bank *World Development Report*. This report indicated the percentage share of Philippine household income: the bottom 20 per cent pegged at 5.2 per cent in 1985, while the highest 10 per cent of households accounted for a hefty 36.4 per cent share. Pineda (1991) is a favourite source of data. One of its reports states that low-income families are characterized by a lack of productive assets or of control over such assets, limited use of modern technology in their production activities, limited access to basic economic and social services, and limited human capital (Pineda 1991).

Now there is a growing trend among researchers to do their own fieldwork. One example is the research of Veneracion (1985), who interviewed landless agricultural workers in three provinces of Central Luzon. Another result of field research is Andales and David's (1985) poverty profile of fishermen in Iloilo province Some of their findings show that most fishermen have a mean number of five years of schooling; their income ranges from P40.00 to – P80.00 a month; and the majority do not have contacts with or knowledge of government and political agencies or service organizations in the area. A third example of a study based on field research is that of Cadeliña (1986), who studied the lowland migrant swiddeners in the Balinsasayao Forest, Negros Oriental. The swiddeners had very little education, they engaged in farming purely for subsistence, and, on average, the family household head earned P90 a week. There were no appliances in the house and the diet was basically carbohydrate with minimal protein. The data sources, then, cover the range from use of secondary data to collection of primary and empirical field studies data.

Evaluation

The review brings out the different and varying approaches used by researchers on poverty, which would explain why comparative studies on the topic could be difficult. One reason is that the research and essay materials reviewed a mixture of definitions of poverty, some relating to causes and some to effects of poverty. This implies that there is a need to address such basic problems in poverty research as definition and measurement issues. The review also indicates that the Philippines is divided into separate spheres of rural and urban poor, which calls for a new conceptualization and makes it advisable in future poverty research to focus on the rural–urban differentials. In fact, Balisacan (1994) pays attention to this very dimension. It is also necessary to focus on the role of the national government and its inability or unwillingness to respond to the people's demand for basic social services, and its responsibility for the promotion of poverty in the region.

Valencia (1994) lists the basic concepts utilized by poverty researchers in the Philippines as: rural poverty, urban poverty, mass poverty, absolute poverty, poverty as a process and as a condition, and poverty as an "institutionalized form of oppression". Valencia examined the published materials on poverty prior to 1985 and found that as early as 1978 Alburo had already examined a range of poverty definitions provided by poverty researchers. Alburo concluded that the definitions, even at that time, were already suffering from serious theoretical weaknesses, prompting him to say that the definitions were inadequate, and thus insufficient to provide a basis for policy options for government to direct resources towards poverty alleviation. The following year, Alburo and Roberto (1979) reiterated the arguments, saying that alternative poverty measures related to energy use, source of drinking water, toilet facilities, size of households, type of tenancy, and occupation would strengthen a methodological approach that could provide a better definition of poverty among certain groups. Alburo's analysis was reproduced by Aldaba-Lim (1986), who argued for the utilization of the same type of data on the plight of women and children all over Asia as a measure of poverty and development in the region. In 1976, a survey team led by Almario studied the poverty profile of rural Philippines (Almario et al. 1976). They observed that most of the research on poverty that they reviewed lacked any coherent theoretical perspective. To arrive at a better understanding of poverty in rural areas, Almario and his team proposed a three-pronged theoretical approach: historical, structural–functional, and cognitive.

This criticism regarding the inadequacy of theoretical frameworks on poverty is just as valid among researchers today. One reason for the lack of a clear theoretical perspective may be the oversimplification of the causal links between poverty and other variables. Another reason is the excessive use of economic approaches to the study of poverty, which is in fact a multiple affliction caused by a plurality of forces. The shortage of other social science approaches to the phenomenon of poverty may be traced to the minor and peripheral interest expressed by social scientists (other than economists) in embarking on field studies on poverty. Most of the time, discussion about poverty among social scientists is merely a serendipitous occurrence.

Poverty research in South-East Asia

Because of a dearth of materials, only a modicum of analysis is possible here. Because there are too few materials to enable the selection of basic concepts, hypotheses, and data sources, the presentation of this section of the paper will be different from that of the first section. Valencia (1994) provides a profile of four countries (Indonesia, Philippines, Malaysia, and Singapore) and highlights some of the common indicators of comparisons to assess poverty.

Table 8.1 shows some basic indicators for the period 1965–87. Among the four countries, Indonesia had the highest population and the largest area. On the other hand, Singapore had the highest GNP per capita, average annual growth rate, and life expectancy. Malaysia and Singapore had the lowest average annual inflation rate from 1965 to 1980. Malaysia had the lowest average annual inflation rate from 1980 to 1987.

The growth of production was different in the four countries. In terms of GDP, Singapore had the highest growth rate from 1965 to 1987. In agriculture, the Philippines had the highest growth rate from 1965 to 1980, and Malaysia had the highest growth rate from 1980 to 1987. In industry, Indonesia and Singapore had the highest growth rate from 1965 to 1980, and Malaysia had the highest growth rate from 1980 to 1987. In manufacturing, Singapore had the highest growth rate from 1965 to 1980, and Indonesia had the highest growth rate from 1980 to 1987. In services, Singapore had the highest growth rate from 1965 to 1987.

Table 8.1 South-East Asia: Basic indicators

Country	Population (millions)	Area ('000 km^2)	GNP per capita Value (US$) 1987	GNP per capita Ave. annual growth rate (%) 1965–80	Average annual rate of inflation 1965–80	Average annual rate of inflation 1980–87	Life expectancy at birth (years) 1987
Indonesia	171.4	1,905	450	4.5	34.2	8.5	60
Philippines	58.4	300	590	1.7	11.7	16.7	63
Malaysia	16.5	330	1,810	4.1	4.9	1.1	70
Singapore	2.6	1	7,940	7.2	4.9	1.3	73

Source: World Bank (1989: 164–5).

Table 8.2 indicates central government expenditures. Singapore had the highest percentage of total expenditure earmarked for defence in both 1972 and 1987. Malaysia had the highest percentage of total expenditure going to education in 1972, whereas Singapore had the highest percentage in 1987. Singapore also had the highest percentage of total expenditure used for health in 1972; whereas in 1987 the Philippines had the highest percentage. Malaysia had the highest percentage of expenditure on housing amenities in 1972, while Singapore had the highest percentage in 1982. In 1972, Indonesia had the highest percentage of total expenditure going to economic services, while in 1987 the Philippines had the highest percentage.

As for the total external debt for the four countries, in 1987 Singapore had the lowest and Indonesia had the highest public and publicly guaranteed long-term debt. In the same year, the Philippines had the lowest and Indonesia had the highest private non-guaranteed long-term debt. In addition, Indonesia had the highest and Singapore had the lowest short-term debt. All in all, Indonesia had the largest total external debt, while Singapore had the lowest total external debt.

Table 8.3 indicates the population growth and projections for the four countries. In terms of average annual growth of population, the Philippines had the highest rate from 1965 to 1980; Malaysia had the highest from 1980 to 1987 and will still be the highest up to the year 2000. In terms of population size, Indonesia had the largest population in 1987 and will still have the biggest in the years 2000 and 2025.

Table 8.4 indicates the demography and fertility of the four countries. In 1987, Malaysia had the highest crude birth rate per thousand population, while Singapore and Malaysia had the lowest crude death rate per thousand and Singapore had the highest percentage of women of childbearing age. The Philippines had the highest total fertility rate, but Malaysia was projected to have the highest rate in the year 2000. In 1985, Singapore had the highest percentage of married women of childbearing age using contraception, while the Philippines had the lowest percentage.

As regards health and nutrition indicators (Table 8.5), in 1984 Indonesia had the highest population per physician, and the Philippines had the highest population per nurse. Singapore had the highest daily calorie supply per capita. In 1985, the Philippines had the highest percentage of babies with low birth weights, while Singapore had the lowest percentage.

Table 8.6 shows the education indicators of the four countries. In 1986, Indonesia had the highest percentage enrolled in

Table 8.2 South-East Asia: Central government expenditure

As a percentage of total expenditure

Country	Defence 1972	Defence 1987	Education 1972	Education 1987	Health 1972	Health 1987	Housing amenities; social security 1972	Housing amenities; social security 1987	Economic services 1972	Economic services 1987	Others 1972	Others 1987	Total expenditure % of GNP 1972	Total expenditure % of GNP 1987	Overall 1972	Overall 1987
Indonesia	18.6	8.6	7.4	8.8	1.4	1.5	0.9	1.7	30.5	23.5	41.3	55.9	15.1	24.0	−2.5	−0.9
Philippines[a]	10.9	9.2	16.3	18.0	3.2	5.5	4.3	3.8	17.6	50.5	47.7	12.9	13.4	13.5	−2.0	−5.0
Malaysia	18.5	–	23.4	–	6.8	–	4.4	–	14.2	–	32.7	–	26.5	31.9	−9.4	−8.2
Singapore	35.3	19.0	15.7	18.2	7.8	4.1	3.9	15.9	9.9	19.9	27.3	23.0	16.7	28.9	1.3	1.4

Source: World Bank (1989: 184–5).
Note:
[a] Refers to budgetary data.

Table 8.3 South-East Asia: Population growth and projections

Country	Average annual growth of population (%) 1965–80	1980–87	1987–2000	Population (millions) 1987	2000	2025	Hypothetical size of stationary population (millions)	Assumed year of reaching next reproduction Rate of 1	Population momentum 1990
Indonesia	2.4	2.1	1.7	171	214	279	345	2005	1.7
Philippines	2.9	2.5	1.9	58	74	101	127	2010	1.8
Malaysia	2.5	2.7	2.2	17	22	30	37	2010	1.7
Singapore	1.6	1.1	0.8	3	3	3	3	2030	1.2

Source: World Bank (1989: 214–15).

Table 8.4 South-East Asia: Demography and fertility

Country	Crude birth rate per thousand population 1965	Crude birth rate per thousand population 1987	Crude death rate per thousand population 1965	Crude death rate per thousand population 1987	Percentage of women of child-bearing age 1965	Percentage of women of child-bearing age 1987	Total fertility rate 1965	Total fertility rate 1987	Total fertility rate 2000	Percentage of married women of child-bearing age using contraception[a] 1970	Percentage of married women of child-bearing age using contraception[a] 1985
Indonesia	43	29	20	9	47	50	5.5	3.5	2.5	–	48
Philippines	42	30	12	8	44	49	6.8	3.9	2.7	2	44
Malaysia	41	31	12	6	43	51	6.3	3.8	2.8	7	51
Singapore	31	17	6	6	45	60	4.7	1.7	1.7	45	74

Source: World Bank (1989: 216–17).
Note:
[a]Figures include women whose husbands practise contraception.

Table 8.5 South-East Asia: Health and nutrition indicators

Country	Population per Physician 1965	Population per Physician 1984	Nurse 1965	Nurse 1984	Daily calorie supply per capita 1965	Daily calorie supply per capita 1984	Babies with low birth weights (%) 1985
Indonesia	31,700	9,490[a]	9,490	1,260[a]	1,800	2,579	14
Philippines	–	6,700	1,130	2,740	1,924	2,372	18
Malaysia	6,200	1,030	1,320	1,010	2,247	2,730	9
Singapore	1,900	1,310[a]	600	–	2,297	2,840	7

Source: World Bank (1989: 218–19).
Note:
[a] Figures for years other than those specified.

Table 8.6 South-East Asia: Education indicators

Percentage of age group enrolled in education

Country	Primary						Secondary						Tertiary	
	Total		Male		Female		Total		Male		Female		Total	
	1965	1986	1965	1986	1965	1986	1965	1986	1965	1986	1965	1986	1965	1986
Indonesia	72	118	79	121	65	116	12	41	18	45[a]	7	34[a]	1	7
Philippines	113	106	115	107	111	106	41	68	42	66	40	69	19	38
Malaysia	90	101	96	100[a]	84	99[a]	28	54	34	54	22	54	2	6[a]
Singapore	105	115[a]	110	118[a]	100	113[a]	45	71[a]	49	70[a]	41	73[a]	10	–

Source: World Bank (1989: 220–1).
Note:
[a] Figures for years other than those specified.

primary education, while Singapore had the highest percentage enrolled in secondary education, and the Philippines had the highest percentage enrolled in tertiary education.

One of the few studies that discusses poverty in three of the countries is Mehmet (1979). Another study is the one by James (1981) on regional inequalities. Both articles represent the usual economic approach to poverty, using some of the above indicators, and the two authors agree that the incidence of poverty in South-east Asia is significantly greater than in other regions of the world.

More in-depth material is provided by Kuo (1976) who, unlike Mehmet and James, defines a sociological study of poverty as one that involves more variables than the income level and the expenditure pattern of households. Although the economic situation, including material deprivation, is crucial, a study should explore both the possible causes and the likely consequences of economic stress. Education and occupation, for example, are brought in as important elements in explaining the poverty status of the individual. For instance, Kuo (1976) states that, in an urban industrial society, education determines to a great extent the type of occupation one is likely to get in the labour market. A person with a low level of education gets less pay, less stability, and lower social prestige, and is more likely to face temporary or constant economic difficulties.

Kuo also explored the relationship between poverty status and various variables related to the following major areas of interest: income, expenditure, and possession of household items; feelings and responses to inflation; perceived well-being and relative deprivation; education and occupation; and marital relationships, including marital disorganization, interactional patterns, division of labour, and decision-making. Since most of the other studies reviewed are economic in context and approaches, many of the relationships posited by Kuo need to be explored.

Poverty is expressed in different conceptual terms in Singapore, Indonesia, and Malaysia. In Singapore, one index of poverty indicates a strong correlation between slum living conditions and a high incidence of gastroenteritis. Another index measures poverty in terms of certain minimum standards of nutrition, clothing, household expenditure, transport expenses, and rent (Kuo 1976). A third measure of poverty is the "disposable income ratio", which determines the extent to which disposable income (net of rent and transport expenses already incurred) is sufficient to provide for a minimum standard of living, excluding the costs of supporting outside dependants, medical expenses, and luxuries such as entertainment and cigarettes.

"Living in poverty" then refers to households whose disposable income ratio is less than 100, or whose income was less than that required to support a strictly defined minimum standard of living. The "poverty line" is set in the range of S$2,040–2,280 per year for a family of six (including a working man, a working wife, one child aged below 7, one child aged between 7 and 11, and two children aged 12 or over – i.e. five equivalent adults).

In Indonesia, the poverty gap index is the average of the gap between poor households' standards of living and the poverty line, as a ratio of the poverty line. Related concepts are depth of poverty, severity of poverty, direction of poverty change, and aggregate poverty. Such concepts are usually missing in the literature from the Philippines, owing to the lack of exposure to problems of measurements, noted specially among those researchers trained in the "soft" social sciences. The coping strategies studied among the poor, such as increasing hours of work, taking a second job, drawing on savings, or obtaining assistance from a network of friends and relatives (community safety-nets), as discussed by Ravallion and Huppi (1991), may be used as a take-off for interregional comparisons of the poor in Indonesia, Malaysia, Singapore, and the Philippines. The associated concept of informal social insurance arrangements in the region could be studied to understand poverty as it exists in these countries.

In Malaysia, "shared poverty" as discussed by Mehmet (1979) is a concept earlier espoused by Clifford Geertz to represent a social response to agricultural "involution" (*sic*). It also implies that there is apparent harmony and harmonious accommodation of the poor in a society. The term "poverty" implies not only a state of material deprivation, but also a way of life, and a complex nurturing set of social, economic, cultural, and political relationships and institutions evolved to find security within an insecure situation (Buchanan 1972: 225). Buchanan also says that one can define and measure poverty statistically as a state of existence, and one can analyse it (but not quantify it) as a kind of culture, or subculture, within the wider society. Thus, the term "poverty" essentially means economic deprivation to a level below adequate subsistence.

Regarding data sources, in Singapore, Buchanan (1972) used the 1966 Sample Household Survey, which provides limited data on the income level of household heads; official health statistics record notifiable diseases such as cholera, diphtheria, and smallpox. In 1950–3 there was a Social Survey of Singapore. The data obtained from this survey estimated that in nearly 90 per cent of all urban households no income-earner earned more than S$400 a month. Singapore regularly conducts sample surveys amongst people in squatter slum areas and low-cost housing estates. In addition, Singapore also conducts so-called general surveys. For instance, general surveys were made of some 500 households living in slum conditions in the Kallang-Tanjong Rha Area in order to determine the pattern of employment and household composition. Data from the Research and Statistics Department of the Ministry of Education are also used by researchers. Mehmet (1979) used budget data from 1957 and household savings in 1970 to estimate the average monthly income of households.

In Indonesia, Ravallion and Huppi (1991) decry the difficulty of analysing the effects of policy changes on the poor because of lack of data on poverty. The authors maintain that a useful indicator of a household's economic well-being must be readily quantifiable, and must reflect the range of different sectors, regions, and periods. This quantification of an economic well-being indicator is lacking in social science approaches. Another measure of poverty is a head-count ratio which measures poverty simply as the proportion of the population whose standard of living lies below a given poverty line.

Ravallion and Huppi (1991) used household survey data for 1980, 1984, 1987 to determine indicators of economic well-being and poverty lines, and to make some assumptions about the poor. The Indonesian Central Bureau of Statistics is consulted by writers on poverty as often as they consult World Bank data. Indonesia's national socio-economic surveys were consulted to produce data on consumption from both market expenditures and production for 50,000 randomly sampled households comprising 250,000 persons.

In Malaysia, Hainsworth's (1982) article is the only one that touches on absolute poverty as it exists in Indonesia, Malaysia, and the Philippines. Citing a World Bank report, he said that there were 17 million poor in the Philippines in 1975. Hainsworth tried to trace the roots of poverty in the three countries in an effort to understand how the phenomenon became part of the larger scenario. He used data from the Asian Development Bank (1971–5) and the UN Protein-Calorie Advisory Group.

In Indonesia, a new poverty measure was generated based on income, food expenditure share, and calorie intake as indicators of level of living. Actual household consumption levels can be expected to correspond to a given food share and will generally vary according to relative prices, demographic factors, and tastes. The poverty measure is based on the distribution of household consumption per person, adjusting for inflation by using the consumer price index and modifying the underlying expenditure weights to correspond more closely with the spending patterns of the poor. Not surprisingly, poverty and undernutrition are directly related, and a correlation is demonstrated between the incidence of poverty and ownership of land.

From Singapore's available materials, there is a clear correlation between low per capita income, low occupational status, and low levels of living. The poorer 50 per cent tend to be those whose breadwinners have irregular or casual employment and low occupational status, and those with below minimum daily food expenditure, high living densities, and disposable income ratios of well below 100.

So, summing up, it can be said that researchers from Indonesia, Malaysia, and Singapore tend to explore approaches besides the economic one in their studies of poverty. Because poverty is a multi-faceted and complex human condition, it cannot be understood by a simple and myopic research tool. Only by adopting a multidisciplinary approach and imaginative perceptions can research cut deep into the heart and soul of poverty.

REFERENCES

Abad, Ricardo G., Rowe V. Cadelina and Violeta Lopez Gonzaga (eds) (1986) *Faces of Philippine Poverty*. Metro Manila: Twin A Printing.

Adem, Elisea S. (1992) *Urban Poverty: The Case of the Railway Squatters*. Manila: Social Science Research Center, University of Sto. Tomas.

Alburo, Florian A. (1978) "Towards a re-definition of poverty". Discussion Paper 78–16, School of Economics, University of the Philippines, Diliman, Quezon City.

Alburo, Florian A. and Eduardo L. Roberto (1979) "An analysis and synthesis of poverty research in the Philippines". Philippine Institute for Development Studies.

Aldaba-Lim, Estemania (1986) *Plight and Rights of Women and Children in the Context of Poverty and Development*. Quezon City: University of the Philippines Center for Integrative and Development Studies.

Almario, Emelina, et al. (1976) *National Profile of Poverty in the Rural Philippines. Preliminary Report*. Quezon City: Institute of Philippine Culture, Ateneo de Manila University.

Andales, Venancio B. and Fely P. David. (1985) "Poverty among small-scale fishermen in Iloilo". *Philippine Sociological Review*, 33 (1–2).

Arboleda, Heidi et al. (1988) "A monograph for the estimator of the 1985 poverty and subsistence thresholds and incidences". The Technical Working Group on Poverty.

Balisacan, Arsenio M. (1991a). "Agricultural growth, employment growth and rural poverty." *Philippine Economic Journal*, No. 70, 30, (1&2): 113–142.

――― (1991b) *Agricultural Growth, Landlessness, Off-farm Employment and Rural Poverty in the Philippines*. Research and Training Program on Agricultural Policy.

――― 1991c. "Aggregate poverty measures, poverty targetting and the determinants of household welfare: The Philippines, 1985 and 1988". Paper presented at the Consultative Workshop on the FIES, Poverty and Income Distribution, Communication Foundation for Asia, Manila.

――― (1992a) "Equivalence scale and poverty assessment in a poor country." *Journal of Philippine Development*, No. 34, 19 (1): 81–95.

――― (1992b) *The Poor During a Period of Macroeconomic Adjustment: The Philippine Case*. University of the Philippines, School of Economics.

――― (1992c). "Parameter estimates of consumer demand systems in the Philippines". Paper presented atthe Technical Change in Agriculture, Income Distribution and Economic Policy in the Philippines. Project reported by the Australian Centre for International Agricultural Research.

――― (1992d) "Rural poverty in the Philippines: Determinants and policies". *Asian Development Review*, 125–63.

――― (1994) *Poverty, Urbanization and Development Policy: A Philippine Perspective*. Diliman, Quezon City: University of the Philippines Press.

Balisacan, Arsenio M., R. E. Evenson, T. N. Srinivasan, M. C. Bantilan, G. T. Castillo, C. A. Florencio, P. S. Intal, Jr, M. Mangahas, A. Quisumbing (1993) *Perspective on Philippine Poverty*. Quezon City: Center for Integrative and Development Studies.

Buchanan, Iain B. A. (1972) *Singapore in Southeast Asia: An Economic and Political Appraisal*. London: G. Bell.

Cadeliña, Rowe V. (1986) *Poverty in the Upland: Lowland Migrant Swiddeners in the Balinsasayao Forest, Negros Oriental*. Philippine Social Science Council, Silliman University.

Constantino, Letizia. (1989) "Health (what makes Filipinos sick)". *Issues Without Tears*, 8: 16–30.

David, Randolf S. (1989) "Poverty in the Philippines: Its social roots". *Kasarinlan*, 2nd quarter: 9–24.

David, Randolf S. (1977) "The sociology of poverty or the poverty of sociology? A brief note on urban poverty research." *Philippine Sociological Review*, 25 (3&4).

Ellevera-Lamberte, Exaltacion. (1983a) "Macro-level Indicators of upland poverty: The case of the delivery of and access to services in upland areas." *Philippine Sociological Review*, 31 (1–2).

――― (1983) "Indicators of upland poverty: A macro review." *Dimensions of Upland Poverty: A Macro-view and a Micro-view*. Manila: Research Center, De La Salle University.

Fernandez, Joseph and Amalia de la Torre. (n.d.) *Scavengers in Cebu City: A Case Study of Urban Poverty.* University of San Carlos.
Ganapin, Delfin J., Jr (1987). "Our forest resources and timber trade." *Solidarity* 115: 53–64.
Garcia, Manuel and Leorigildo Militante (1986) *Social Problems.* Manila: National Bookstore.
Hainsworth, Geoffrey B. (ed.) (1982) "Village-level modernization in Southeast Asia: the political economy of rice and water." Vancouver: University of British Columbia Press, p. 41.
Hess, Beth B., Elizabeth W. Markson, and Peter J. Stein. (1993) *Sociology*, 4th edn. New York: Macmillan.
James, William (1981) "By-passed areas, regional inequalities and development policies in selected Southeast Asian countries". Paper prepared for ADC/NIRA/JCIE Symposium, Okinawa, Japan, 15–19.
Kuo, Eddie C. Y. (1976) *Families under Economic Stress: The Singapore Experience.* Singapore: Institute of Southeast Asian Studies.
Lichauco, Alejandro. (1986) *Towards a New Economic Order and the Conquest of Mass Poverty.* Quezon City: A. Lichauco.
Licuanan, Patricia B. (1981) "A psychological look at development". Paper presented at the 16th Annual Convention of the Psychological Association of the Philippines, Quezon City.
Mangahas, Mahar. (1980) *Poverty Analysis: Some Fundamentals in Training of Trainers on Social Welfare Policy Formulations.* Expert Group Meeting and Workshop, UN Social Welfare and Development Centre for Asia and the Pacific, Manila.
—— (1984a) "The relevance of poverty measurement to food security policy". *Journal of Philippine Development*, No. 20, 11 (2): 191–201.
—— (1984b) *Rural Poverty and Operation Land Transfer.* Research for Development Department, Development Academy of the Philippines.
—— (1985) "Rural poverty and operation land transfer in the Philippines". in R. Islam (ed.), *Strategies for Alleviating Poverty in Rural Asia.* Dhaka and Bangkok: Bangladesh Institute for Development Studies and ILO/Asia Employment Programme.
Mehmet, Ozay (1979) *Poverty and Social Change in Southeast Asia.* Ottawa: University of Ottawa Press.
Ortigas, Carmela D. (1989) "The culture and psychology of poverty: Dynamics of improvement". *Pantas*, 24–31.
Øyen, Else (1992) "Some basic issues in comparative poverty research". *International Social Science Journal*, 134: 615–26.
Pineda, Rosalinda Ofreneo (1991) *The Philippines: Debt and Poverty.* Oxford: OXFAM.
Ravallion, M. and M. Huppi (1991) "Measuring changes in poverty: A methodological case study of Indonesia during an adjustment period". *World Bank Economic Review*, 5: 57–82.

Santos, Aida Fulleros and Lyn F. Lee (1989) *The Debt Crisis: A Treadmill of Poverty for Filipino Women*. Manila: Kalayaan Publications Collective.

Tendero, Avelino P., Dolores A. Reyes, and Ma. Socorro F. Manas (1984) *Philippine Development Issues: An Inquiry*. Manila: National Bookstore.

US Bureau of Census (1991) Censuses of population and housing. Census tracts. Final report PHC. Washington DC. US Govt Printing Office. vol. 18.

Veneracion, Corazon (1985) "Coping with crisis: Landless agricultural workers in central Luzon". *Philippine Sociological Review*, 31 (1–2).

Villegas, Bernardo (1986) "Corporate strategies against mass poverty". *Economics and Society*, vol. 12, pp. 13–18.

World Bank (1989) *World Development Report 1989*. Washington, DC: Oxford University Press.

Chapter 9

China: Poverty in a Socialist Market Economy

Ruizhen Yan and Wang Yuan

A history of poverty research in China

Poverty research in China was initiated in the 1980s. Before that time it had been generally thought that, although China was a developing country, there was not much difference in people's incomes and living standards, owing to the system of publicly owned means of production and equally distributed means of subsistence. Poverty was found only in certain individual families and these were treated as individual cases, which were supposed to be remedied from the public welfare fund established by the people's communes and the relief provided by civil affairs institutions.

When the mechanism of the market economy was introduced into China as a result of China's economic reforms starting in 1978, a big difference in economic growth resulted between the developed region of East China and the underdeveloped region of West China. The sharp contrast in growth attracted nationwide attention in China, especially as a greater part of the impoverished areas was densely populated by ethnic groups and used to be the old revolutionary bases that supported the Chinese communist revolutions during the era of China's revolutionary wars. Therefore, a political dimension was added to the poverty research that had just begun.

The emphasis on poverty research, apart from its political components, was also determined by great economic interests: the potential to escape from China's past low economic growth lies in the impoverished areas, which are of economically strategic importance. China's impoverished regions are concentrated in mountain areas where the land, accounting for 70 per cent of China's territorial area, is rich in natural and economic resources, which are not fully exploited. At present, resources in the plains area are running out, and a shift in development from the plains area to the mountain area has become a strategic need for China's current economic growth. The eco-environment and its balance in the East China plains area, including the protection of water resources, soil conservation, the supply of clean air, the prevention and control of natural disasters such as floods, droughts, and wind and sand storms, depend on the protection and improvement of the eco-environment in the West China mountain area, which acts as an ecological protective screen for the plains area. The underdeveloped mountain area and the developed plains area are complementary parts of the national economy, and their mutual dependence and promotion could give great impetus to the continued development of the national economy.

China's poverty research has so far been confined to the rural areas. This can be explained by the following two points: (1) for a long time a strict household registration system was used, which restricted the influx of rural population into urban areas; (2) the cities had a comparatively perfect system of employment and social security. Therefore, China's urban poverty had not become as serious as its rural poverty. In recent years there have been some changes. The market economy is beginning to break the barrier between the rural and urban areas, and this has led to a flow of some 70 million rural surplus labourers into the cities in search of employment. The introduction of an enterprise management system where bankruptcy is now possible and the abolition of the former system of lifetime employment in urban state-run industries have attracted greater attention to urban employment. An increasing gap between the rich and the poor in the urban population is inevitable when the old social security system is in decline and a new one is not yet established, due to the implementaion of enterprise management. Research into China's urban poverty is, therefore, beginning to appear. The conclusion that follows from the above discussion is that the history of China's poverty research is rather short.

Concepts of poverty

The classification of poverty

Poverty may be classified as absolute poverty or relative poverty. Absolute poverty refers to a situation in which the labourer is engaged in a shrinking reproduction, and their ill-fed and ill-clad condition results from this limited production. Relative poverty is characterized by the income differences between people, and generally refers to the living conditions of low-income people, who account for about 20 per cent of the total population (Ministry of Agriculture 1989). This is the mainstream classification in China. Others tend to regard poverty as a state in which, under certain conditions (political, economic, social, cultural, natural), people are unable to make or earn sufficient income to maintain, in the long run, a basic standard of living that is physiologically, socially, and culturally acceptable. In this connection three points are especially emphasized:

1. Poverty is a non-self-eliminating phenomenon over a comparatively long period of time. Therefore, poverty alleviation targets should be worked out on the basis of a long-term and stable goal.
2. The connotation of poverty in essence consists of production and consumption.
3. The definition of poverty requires the examination of physiological as well as social and cultural standards.
   (a) *Physiological* needs include an intake of calories necessary for survival, the level of nourishment required to maintainf human productive activities, and the necessary clothing and shelter in relation to the weather, as well as the needs of one's spouse and family.
   (b) *Safety* needs include safe drinking water, the prevention and cure of disease, old age care, job security, and a reliable and stable income.
   (c) *Educational* needs include being able to receive a regular education up to at least secondary level.
   (d) *Consumption* needs stemming from social exchange and traditional customs include social exchange etiquette, traditional customs with regard to marriages, funerals, and birthdays, and religious conventions.

The study of poverty on the basis of absolute and relative poverty

Most Chinese poverty scholars tend to study absolute poverty using the definition of an absolute poverty line and poverty alleviation practices. Relative poverty, on the other hand, concerns social equality. It exists in any country and at any stage of economic development. Unbalanced growth, as an objective law of the material world, stimulates competition within reasonable limits (Ministry of Agriculture 1989). At present there are some seven viewpoints on how a standard of poverty should be formulated (Zhao Dongyuan and Lan Xumin 1994).

The Engel's coefficient

The generally adopted poverty standard worked out by the Food and Agriculture Organization (FAO) defines five categories according to the percentage of average income used for food:

- absolute poverty – over 59 per cent
- minimum subsistence – 50–59 per cent;
- well-offness – 40–50 per cent;
- affluence – 30–40 per cent; and
- most affluence – below 30 per cent.

In China, however, the adoption of this method is generally opposed for the following two reasons: (a) under low-income conditions an increase in income is first used to improve food intakes, thereby causing a counter-reaction shown by a rise in the Engel's coefficient; (b) in countries where subsistence necessities are subsidized by the state, the proportion of expenditure used for basic needs (other than food) accounts for only a low proportion of income, and incremental income mainly goes on food consumption, so that the Engel's coefficient often stays at a rather high level. This makes it difficult to use this coefficient as a standard measure for evaluating poverty and its intensity.

Per capita net income

The advantage of the per capita net income standard is its simplicity and ease of use. However, because of its great fluctuations, it is difficult to use it as the basis for an objective absolute poverty line. Moreover, because per capita net income varies with changes in the price index, what exactly reflects absolute poverty in one period may not do so in another. All this will result in measurement difficulties.

Daily necessities consumption expenditure

For an ill-fed and ill-clad peasant, basic physiological needs are of utmost importance. Then other needs will follow, e.g. safety needs such as a job, security, health insurance, savings in case of emergency, etc. Daily necessities consumption expenditure is composed of two parts: the minimum requirements of food for survival, and other needs for minimum daily necessities (including services). On this basis, the poverty line for Chinese rural areas in 1985 was calculated as Y200. However, this poverty line is not considered to be static. It should be adjusted according to changes in the structure of food consumption and the price index, as well as in family size, and taking account of regional differences (Tong Xing and Lin Mingang 1994). This is in accordance with the view held by most Chinese scholars' on how to formulate a standard poverty line (Yan Ruizhen and Wang Yuan 1992; Yao Quanzhuo and Yang Daojie 1994).

The World Bank's target system for evaluating impoverished countries

This system suggests a standard for absolute poverty according to the minimum level of nourishment per person (a daily intake of less than 2,250 kcal) and the proportion of total income spent on food (about 75 per cent).

The comprehensive target system

This is a poverty-evaluation system comprising the three components of a subsistence environment, subsistence quality, and a subsistence effect using fifteen targets. The targets include: per capita GNP and its rate of increase; the proportion of non-agricultural output value in GNP; the "four basic facilities" ratio (referring to the proportion of villages having access to electricity, telephone, public bus service, and running water); the index of natural defects (inverse); per capita net annual income and its rate of increase; per capita expenditure on clothing; per capita daily intake of three main elements of nourishment; the proportion of the expenditure on cultural activities; the proportion of expenditure on food; per capita meat consumption; per capita savings balance; the proportion of per capita family property; the ratio of natural population growth (inverse); average life expectancy; and the number of years of regular education per labourer. Each of the targets is presented a quantity ratio value. This is a comprehensive and systematic way of evaluating poverty, ranging from static targets to dynamic ones. However, a comprehensive evaluation has not yet been worked out and its actual operation is difficult (Zhao Dongyuan and Lan Xumin 1994).

The multi-level poverty line

This standard uses the extreme poverty line (the survival line), the food and clothing satisfaction line (the poverty line), and the growth line (the poverty alleviation line) instead of the current single poverty line (a poverty alleviation line). The three different lines were drawn as follows.

The extreme poverty line refers to the World Bank method. The minimum daily intake of calories required for survival was taken from a country-wide investigation of peasants. The per capita of annual food consumption by rural residents was worked out for different groups. This figure was multiplied by the mixed average price of the food consumed that year, and the result was the minimum per capita annual income of rural residents required for survival. The final result was Y250.

For the food and clothing satisfaction line a formula was used to get the final result: the cost of minimum food consumption was divided by the Engel's coefficient of impoverished households in the poverty-stricken region. According to statistical data analysis the coefficient was 63.6 per cent and so the result (i.e. the poverty line) was Y350.

The growth line was created on the basis of a country-wide investigation of peasants, where peasant households were divided into groups according to the per capita net income of each household, and the relationship between household net income and the value of savings was defined. The marginal value of savings was then introduced so as to find the per capita net income group with the greatest propensity to save. Thereafter the savings ratio of each of the groups was worked out on the basis of the classification according to per capita net income, so as to decide which one was linked to the most obvious change in the savings ratio. Then, by comparing the per capita net income of the peasants of the whole country that year (as a publicly recognized average living standard) with the above-mentioned figure, the growth (poverty alleviation) line was calculated as Y600 (Tong Xing and Lin Mingang 1994).

China's official poverty standard

The following counties are considered to be poor, and therefore entitled to financial aid from the state: counties in rural areas where per capita annual net income was below Y150 in 1985; counties in the old revolutionary base areas and the minority autonomous counties where per capita annual net inome in rural areas was below Y200 in 1985; pastoral counties in rural areas where per capita net income was below Y300 between 1984 and 1986; and semi-pastoral counties in rural areas where per capita net income was below Y200 between 1984 and 1986 (State Council 1989).

Hypotheses

Poverty is a comprehensive social and economic phenomenon, and different scholars make different assumptions when studying it. In China, most studies are based on regionalism.

Poverty in the peripheral areas

The so-called peripheral areas are regions located away from the economic growth centres (central areas). The economy develops slowly and contributes only little to the economic growth of the country. Judging from the distribution of the 667 poverty-stricken counties designated by the Chinese government, all of them are located in the peripheral areas of the national economic growth centres.

Poverty in the mountain area

In "The Development of China's Impoverished Mountain Areas", the co-authors Yan Ruizhen and Wang Yuan express the view that in the impoverished counties the population is mainly concentrated in the mountain areas. Some 80 per cent of the poverty-stricken regions in China are located in the mountains. Out of a total of 679 impoverished counties, 514 (accounting for 75.7 per cent) are located in the mountain areas, and most of them are located in West and Central China. In the peripheral and impoverished mountain areas the following conflictual elements are present:

- In poverty-stricken counties with low per capita income the birth rate is higher, leading to a vicious circle of increasing impoverishment and an uncontrollable population explosion.
- Because of a scarcity of cultivated land and the inability to be self-sufficient in food, hilly fields have to be reclaimed. This causes severe soil erosion and ecological imbalance, and grain yields get increasingly smaller. The more impoverished the people become, the more land is reclaimed; and the more land is reclaimed, the greater the impoverishment. Poverty and environmental degradation thus reinforce each other.
- The comprehensive use of resources and control of the environment demand a big effort and take time, but there is a scarcity of the necessary funds, materials, technology, and infrastructure (including communications, energy resources, water supply, level of urbanization, etc.)
- The isolation of the natural economy prevents the possible stimulus generated by a market economy outside the poverty-stricken counties from having an impact. As a result, poverty stays year in and year out, generation after generation (Yan Ruizhen and Wang Yuan 1992; Zhanf Shaobin 1991).

Poverty caused by policy miscarriage

Because a basically self-sufficient natural economy has been prevalent in the remote impoverished mountain areas, and the planned economy, in contrast to a commodity economy, has greatly encouraged the trend towards a natural economy, a superior structure for harnessing and allocating resources has been prevented from being established. In addition, policies aimed at helping the poor have misfired because the practice of relying on relief without promoting economic growth. It is like giving a blood transfusion without fostering the function of blood formation. Year in and year out this results in nothing but sustained poverty. The implementation of policy is also deficient in the following aspects:

- more emphasis is put on economic than on ecological effects in the exploitation of resources;
- more attention is paid to taking than to giving, as shown by the resource plundering mentality and management;
- more importance is attached to food production than to forestry and animal husbandry;
- there are frequent changes in property ownership, with subsequent destruction of resources;
- the population policy has been wrong (Yan Ruizhen 1990).

Short-run and long-run goals

What should be the goals in order for the impoverished mountain areas to achieve economic growth? In general there are two stages: the short run and the long run. Short run goals involve reversing the present fall in production and changing the resulting malnutrition and poor living conditions. The long run goals call for a policy that will provide areas with a flourishing economy, a good ecological cycle, a healthy environment, prosperity, and a sophisticated culture so that the differences between the mountain areas and the plains areas gradually disappear. This should be the future goal of economic growth efforts in the mountain areas (Du Keqin 1988; Lu Dongsheng 1991).

Theoretical systems

Generally speaking, poverty is normally studied under the guidance and within the framework of the theories of development economics, a theoretical system formed by different doctrines.

The growth pole/centre theory

There are two routes to the development of a growth pole: automatic formation, i.e. the concentration of industries and trades in the developed regions of certain towns, through the spontaneous regulation of the market mechanism, and deliberate formation by the government through economic plans and major investment. Ever since the 1980s, in the pursuit of different models of regional growth theories, most Chinese scholars have been in favour of the growth pole theory as an effective of policy tool.

The theory of stages of economic growth (Shen Hong et al. 1992)

The Western economist Walt Whitman Rostow's theory of economic growth stages has been applied to the study of China's poverty and poverty alleviation strategy (Zheng Dahao 1990) – i.e. the stages of traditional society, preconditions for take-off, take-off, the drive to maturity, and the final stage of mass consumption.

The theory of the dualistic economic structure

The economic growth and development theories of "equilibrium vs. disequilibrium" and "balance vs. imbalance" have been perfected and revised by the Chinese scholars, who have applied them to the study of the issue of economic growth in the impoverished regions in China (Liu Jiagui and Cha Hongwang, 1993; Ye Xingqing 1990).

The theory of the transformation of the economic structure

The mountain area needs to make use of both internal and external factors to change its economy from a natural economy to a socialist market economy, that is, to make the transformation from the middle stage of a simple commodity economy to the final stage of a specialized socialist commodity economy. This change requires two conditions: (1) surplus products or key elements of surplus production after self-sufficient consumption has been satisfied are a prerequisite for the exchange of commodities; and (2) comparative economic advantage of key elements of commodities, that are immune to competition from outside must be established. At present, only by satisfying these requirements will China be able to make full use of the internal and external elements critical to the development of a commodity economy in China's impoverished mountain areas (Li Yunzhu 1993; Yan Ruizhen and Wang Yuan, 1992).

The theory of the differential land rent

Compared with the suburbs and the plains areas, the peripheral areas and the impoverished mountain regions have a disadvantage as regards the differential land rent. In these regions, low-quality land brings fewer profits from the same investment; long-distance transportation results in a higher purchase price for industrial products and a lower sale price for agricultural products. A big investment is also demanded of the regions to protect the ecology of the plains. Peasants have to suffer the economic loss resulting from the price scissors; and, as peasants in poverty-stricken regions, they have to suffer a further loss brought about by the differential land rent. This is the theoretical basis on which the government is expected to apply special preferential policies for these regions (Yan Ruizhen and Wang Yuan 1992).

Conclusions

Establishing a socialist market economy and developing a mountain-area economy

Yan Ruizhen (1992) has suggested the establishment of a socialist market economy and the vitalization of the mountain area economy by using the data collected from an investigation of typical examples to analyse the impoverished mountain areas in detail. According to him, the following elements should be taken into consideration as regards the development in this region: the ecological environment and its control; the exploitation of the natural resources; the problem of meeting nutritionl requirements and a way of addressing it; economic growth and the introduction of technology and education; the lack of funds and finding a solution; the construction of infrastructure; and special economic policies (Tong Xing and Lin Mingang 1994). All these elements are necessary for a dynamic strategy of systematic development in the impoverished mountain areas (Sun Yingzhou 1989; Yan Ruizhen and Wang Yuan, 1992).

Establishing a regional economic growth pole and developing the economy of the impoverished counties

In view of the destitute situation of Midu County in Yùnnan Province, Liu Jiagui and Cha Hongwang (1993), using the theory of the growth/centre pole and the investigative method of typical examples, have suggested the establishment of an economic growth pole as a way of solving the problems of the impoverished regions.

Establishing the centre–periphery system and developing the economy in the peripheral areas

Ye Xingqing (1990) advances a doctrine of the centre–periphery system in which the periphery is defined as being similar to the impoverished region and the central area as being similar to non-impoverished regions. Three relationships are closely connected with the system: the export of capital from the central and provincial governments to the peripheral area is larger than that from the peripheral area to the centre and the provinces; the influx of high-quality labour into the peripheral area from the central region is greater than the outflow; the influx of average labour into the peripheral area from the central region is smaller than the outflow; and there are more technical exports from the central region to the peripheral area than from the periphery to the centre. This conclusion demonstrates the rule governing the circulation of key productive elements between the poverty-stricken area and the developed area (Ye Xingqing 1990).

Developing a system of new technology imports and achieving growth for small-scale peasants

Shen Hong et al. (1992) studied the process of achieving the satisfaction of food and clothing needs and alleviating poverty in an effort to break the chain of poverty (including periodic poverty). There seem to be two prerequisites for the completion of the process:

- A change in the external economic environment. Macro-economic development is considered to be an induced condition for economic growth in the peripheral area, and the induced function should be powerful enough to overcome

local traditions and the yoke of traditional circumstances governing the economic behaviour of small-scale peasants.
• An effective transmission mechanism between the poverty-stricken area and the external economic environment.

Therefore, the following should be taken into account as part of a poverty eradication task: the transmission of technology as the crucial link in the poverty alleviation chain; the principles for choosing new technology, such as the comparative advantage of technology and the low threshold entrance; and the policies corresponding to these principles.

Another important conclusion drawn by Shen Hong et al. is a doctrine of growth centred on small-scale peasants. The subject for growth can only be the poor themselves, so we must do away with the old concept that regards traditional small-scale peasants as passive objects needing comfort and relief. However, they will not be able to break their poverty chain without help, support, and encouragement from outside. The government should take responsibility for initiating the "first promotion". Therefore, the poverty alleviation process should be seen as a two-way interaction between the small-scale peasants and the government, demanding an equal and active "conversation" between the two sides (Shen Hong et al. 1992).

Suggestions for the future

First, we call on social scientists to attach greater importance to the study of poverty. Poverty will continue to remain a major problem in the world for a long time to come. Even in Asia, which is experiencing rapid economic growth, the gap between the rich and the poor keeps widening. This can be considered to be a source of instability.

Second, a worldwide system and an international institute for the study of poverty should be established. Financial support for relevant studies could possibly be obtained by raising funds from international donor institutions and by forming a special poverty study foundation.

Third, an international symposium on world poverty should be held every three years in Asia, Africa, or Latin America, in turn, to discuss the urgent and critical current issues on poverty and its analysis and research.

Fourth, it is a good idea to undertake comparative studies on poverty, and possible fields of study are as follows:

• concepts of poverty;
• definition of a standard measurement of poverty;

- evaluation of the current situation, and forecasts for the future;
- the causes and effects of poverty;
- the position and significance of the economies of impoverished regions in the whole process of economic growth;
- poverty alleviation strategies;
- the exploitation of resources in poverty-stricken regions and their optimum use;
- ecological/environmental parameters in the regions;
- population and birth control;
- food strategy;
- the relationship between eradication of poverty and economic growth, and the correct way to handle it;
- the industrial structure in the impoverished areas;
- the introduction of technology;
- raising funds and reasonable investment;
- cooperation between the developed zones and the impoverished zones;
- the functioning of cooperative economic organizations;
- the way to mobilize a multitude of people and institutions against poverty;
- aid for the poor from the government;
- preferential policies for the impoverished areas;
- theories of poverty; and
- the methodology for the study of poverty.

Fifth, data banks for the study of poverty should be formed and abstracts from the literature of poverty study should be made available from a central database, such as the Comparative Research Programme on Poverty.

REFERENCES

Ai Yunhang (1993) "In accordance with the new market economy situation further strengthening the development focusing on aiding the poor", *China's Rural Economy*, 11: 50–52.

Chen Houji and Zhang Tong (1990) *The Agricultural Development in the World's Underdeveloped District*. Beijing: China Science and Technology Press, pp. 32–46.

China Editing Committee for the Anti-Poverty Cases (1991) *The Choice for Subsistence and Growth*. Beijing: China Development Press, pp. 1–12.

Du Keqin, (1988) *China Mountain-Area Economics*. Hunan People's Publishing House, pp. 50–84.

Jiang Changyun, (1992) "An analysis of the economic behavior of the town and township enterprises in the poverty-stricken region". *China's Rural Economy* (Beijing), 1: 39–43.

Li Yunzhu (1993) *The Deeper Utilization of Mountain-Area Resources & Science Technology*. Beijing: China Agriculture Science and Technology Press, pp. 1–13.

Liu Jiagui and Cha Hongwang (1993) *The Choice out of Poverty*. Beijing: Economic Science Press.

Lu Dongsheng (1991) *China Mountain-Area Economic Strategy"*. Yunnan People's Publishing House, pp. 19–56.

Ministry of Agriculture, Department of Policy, Law and Regulation, (1989) *Poverty and Growth*. Taiyuan: Shanxi People's Publishing House, pp. 3–5, 295–305.

Research Group Studying Resources Circulation and Poverty (1993) "How to use the funds for aiding the poor and the economic growth in the poverty stricken area". *China's Rural Economy*, 2, 49–54.

Shen Hong, Zhou Lian and Chen Shengli (1992) *The Small-Scale Peasants in the Peripheral Areas*. Beijing: People's Publishing House, pp. 161–177.

Song Shuqing (1991) "A tentative comment on the risk-securing mechanism for the establishment of pillar industries in the impoverished region". *China's Rural Economy*, 5: 53–57.

State Council, Leading Group Office for the Economic Development of the Poverty-Stricken Areas (1989) *A Summary of the Economic Development in China's Poverty-stricken Areas*. Agriculture Press, pp. 10–11.

Sun Yingzhou (1989) *An Introduction to the Scientific and Technological Economy in the Mountain Area"*. Beijing: Cultural World Press, Beijing, pp. 164–190, 220–285.

Tong Xing and Lin Mingang (1994) "A study of China's standard poverty line in the rural areas". *China's Social Sciences*, 3: 86–89.

Wang Sangui (1994) "Anti-poverty and governmental intervention". *Rural Economy Affairs*, 3: 44–49.

Wang Yining (1993) "The key strategy points for anti-poverty beyond the century". *Market Economy Research* (Beijing), 4: 26 pp.

Xiao Kefei (1988) *China Mountain-Area Economics*. Beijing: Earth Press, pp. 137–367.

Yan Fenfen (1992) "The economic development and investment in the impoverished region". *Rural Economy Affairs*, 7: 53–55.

Yan Ruizhen (1990a) *A Study of the Development of China's Impoverished Mountain Areas—A Collection of the Papers Presented at the Academic Symposium on the Development of China's Impoverished Mountain Areas*. Beijing: People's University of China Press, pp. 136–147.

Yan Ruizhen (1990b) "The economic development of China's impoverished mountain areas". *Rural Economy Affairs*, 8: 22–3.

Yan Ruizhen and Wang Yuan (1992) *Poverty and Development*. Beijing: New World Press, pp. 17–23, 67–81.

Yang Zhong (1991) "Strengthening the study of the impoverished mountain-Area development". *China's Rural Economy*, 7: 5 pp.

Yao Quanzhuo and Yang Daojie (1994) "A study of the evaluation of the poverty line for China city and town residents". *Financial and Trade Research* (Beijing), 1: 44–48.

Ye Xingqing (1990) *The Economic Growth of China's Peripheral Areas*. Beijing: People's Publishing House, pp. 162–173.

Zhang Shaobin (1991) "A comment on the population loss in the poverty-stricken area". *China's Rural Economy* (Beijing), 1: 57–58.

Zhao Dongyuan and Lan Xumin (1994) "A study of China's poverty-evaluation target system and its quantity ratio". *China's Rural Economy*, 3: 45–49, 59.

Zheng Dahao (1990) *A Study of the Exploitation of Agricultural Resources in the Mountain Areas in Terms of Technology and Economy"*. Beijing: Beijing Agriculture University Press.

Zhou Binbin (1991a) "A few questions worth studying with regard to the Chinese policies for aiding the poor". *Rural Economy Affairs* (Beijing), 10: 46 pp.

Zhou Binbin (1991b) *Challenge to Poverty*. Beijing: People's Publishing House, pp. 11–46.

Chapter 10

New Zealand: A Search for a National Poverty Line

Charles Waldegrave and Paul Frater

Poverty in Aotearoa, New Zealand, is a concept many have found difficult to accept. Not only is New Zealand rich in natural resources, it is also a country that has, at various times, been internationally regarded as a significant social policy innovator, a country of social and economic equality.

However, poverty has emerged as a topic of public discussion in recent times, and the history of research on the subject goes back a number of decades before that. As New Zealand's economic fortune has plummeted, the country has found it increasingly hard to continue to perpetuate the myth of equality. The complacent postwar reliance on the guaranteed market of a colonial economy, has been replaced by market insecurity, large-scale unemployment and the significant removal of state social provisions.

The development of the Welfare State, modern constraints, industrial and employment changes, and official definitions of poverty

New Zealand's political and social development has been atypical when compared with the majority of modern democratic states. By 1900, New Zealand was very advanced in terms of social policy, with voting rights for women, legislation that prevented sweated labour in factories, guaranteed minimum wages, instituted compulsory arbitration, and a pension scheme for elderly people in need.

In the 1930s, New Zealand further distinguished itself with the passing of the Social Security Act 1938. It was one of the most comprehensive pieces of social protection legislation in its time. Poverty was defined in terms of an absolute level of minimum needs, and a social welfare system was devised to remove it.

> An Act to provide for the payment of superannuation benefits and of other benefits designed to safeguard the people of New Zealand from disabilities arising from age, sickness, widowhood, orphanhood, unemployment, or other exceptional conditions; to provide a system whereby medical and hospital treatment will be made available to persons requiring such treatment; and, further, to provide such other benefits as may be necessary to maintain and promote the health and general welfare of the community.

From the 1950s on, however, New Zealand began to lag behind developments in most other welfare states. Bertram (1988) noted "that compared to the United Kingdom, the New Zealand Welfare State has been relatively limited both in scope and in the scale of post 1945 expansion and has been less committed to universalist systems of delivery".

Castles (1985) identifies the working-class quest for wage and employment security as the fundamental influence on the shape of New Zealand's social policy. Industrial protection, wage regulation, and restricted immigration were means of preventing poverty and ensuring full employment. Flat-rate and means-tested benefits, financed from general tax revenue, typified a social regime that – "built on a scarcity of labour, consequent full employment and minimum wages, and guaranteed by compulsory conciliation and arbitration – required only a welfare safety-net for those outside the labour market".

In 1949, New Zealand was one of the world's leading spenders on social security, but during the 1950s it started falling behind other Western democracies (Castles 1985). At a time when other countries were expanding welfare provision, New Zealand did not. Bertram noted Castles' notion that employment, not citizenship (as in Europe), has been the basis of the New Zealand welfare state. He suggested that there is a fundamental ambivalence between these two principles in the design and provision of welfare. Hence the lower spending and more minimalist tendencies alongside certain universal provisions, such as health care. Shirley (1990) identified the comparatively weaker labour movement in New Zealand, because of its small size and dispersed nature, as the reason for a less comprehensive welfare state.

Most analysts agree that New Zealand's social policy regime has had a peculiar Australasian mixture of a northern European rights-based model alongside a minimalist needs-based one (Boston 1992; Castles 1985; Esping-Andersen 1990; Shirley

1990). O'Brien and Wilkes (1993) summarized the development of social policy in the period between 1950 and 1984.

Ostensibly universal social policies were commonly hedged about with qualifications, both moral and practical, and any assessment that New Zealand had reached a "pure" form of universalist welfare state aimed at solving poverty as an entirely practical matter is clearly misguided.

A notable policy exception to this trend was the creation, in 1972, of the Accident Rehabilitation and Compensation Insurance Corporation (ACC). It prevented poverty for those who were disabled through an accident. Compensation came in the form of a lump sum and weekly payments of up to 80 per cent of the victim's former income. Like the social insurance provision of welfare in northern Europe, this enabled them to maintain a similar standard of living, in marked contrast to the benefit system. The scheme was financed by employers, the self-employed, and motor vehicle owners, supplemented by government.

In the 1970s, in the face of growing international concern about poverty, Henderson et al.'s (1970) research into poverty in Australia, and the beginnings of the country's changing economic fortune, New Zealand took an in-depth look at its social security system with the appointment of a Royal Commission.

The 1972 Commission stated that "need and the degree of need, should be the primary test and criterion of help to be given". It suggested that need should be defined relative to the accepted standards in the New Zealand community at the time, and that the social security system should ensure "that everyone is able to enjoy a standard of living much like that of the rest of the community, and thus is able to feel a sense of participation in and belonging to the community".

The Commission radically redefined the official concepts of social welfare and poverty in terms of a standard of living comparable with the rest of the community. This relative definition went beyond earlier official definitions in terms of meeting immediate physical needs, to a concept of the right to an active and involved place in New Zealand society.

The fiscal crisis of the 1970s and 1980s impacted heavily on the New Zealand economy. Debt levels, inflation, and unemployment escalated, as economic growth plummetted. By the early 1980s there was increasing pressure to change economic direction. For some, particularly those associated with "new right" ideology, the opportunity enabled the possibility of fundamental changes to the New Zealand welfare state as well. From 1984 on, successive Labour and National governments obliged, and as a result the country's welfare regime has become increasingly targeted and residualist (Boston 1992; Shirley 1990; Stephens 1992; Waldegrave 1991).

The overdue economic reforms were introduced very quickly by the Labour government. However, it introduced social reforms more gradually in the areas of health, education, and fundamental changes to the progressive tax system. Personal tax for those on the highest incomes was halved. A regressive goods and services tax and a guaranteed minimum family income were created.

The National government in 1990 and 1991 followed Labour's lead, but dramatically lifted the pace and extremity of change. The net result has included major cuts in the nominal value of most social welfare benefits, stricter eligibility criteria, benefits ceasing to be indexed to inflation, longer stand down (unpaid waiting period) for the unemployment benefit, the introduction of a raft of new part charges for health care and education along with tighter targeting, the removal of lump-sum payments for accident victims and the introduction of employee contributions to the scheme, targeted cash subsidies for accommodation, and a move to market rentals (replacing income-related rents) for state-provided housing.

With official unemployment running at 10 per cent in the early 1990s, many households were adversely affected by these moves. On top of this, industrial deregulation, particularly the Employment Contracts Act, significantly eroded the take-home pay for those on low incomes. A recent study (Rose 1993) has shown that the average household income from wages and salaries fell 5.1 per cent for those on lowest earnings (quintile 1, bottom 20 per cent), whereas they actually increased (though minimally for middle-income earners) for all other groups.

The combination of high unemployment, the reduction and targeting of state social provision, and industrial legislative changes has created greater hardship in New Zealand. The 1990s have been characterized by constant media reminders from community agencies of the widespread nature of poverty. The creation, by them, of a chain of nationwide voluntary run foodbanks is but one of many examples of the public concern about poverty in their communities.

It is not surprising, given the changes over the past decade, that the New Zealand government has found it difficult to live with the official definition of poverty, set out in relative and participatory terms by the 1972 Royal Commission on Social Security and reaffirmed by the 1988 Royal Commission on Social

Policy. In 1990, a study of income adequacy (Brashares and Aynsley) was commissioned by the New Zealand Treasury. Among its recommendations was the suggestion of an absolute poverty measure based on minimal food costs. Though not adopted officially, the Cabinet had this study before them when they made the decision significantly to reduce benefits and other welfare provision in 1991 (Campbell 1991). By implication, it could be argued that a return to an "absolute" rather than a "relative" official definition of poverty has taken place.

The debate, discussion, and measures of poverty have gone full circle in New Zealand, always influenced by its economic fortunes. Discussion and research are very active at this time. Recent work owes much to earlier pioneers in the modern field of research. Early income distribution studies (Rosenberg 1968, 1971; Seers 1946), historical economic studies (Oliver 1988; Sutch 1969), the work of the 1972 Royal Commission on Social Security, the Department of Social Welfare deprivation study (1975), and the poverty measurement studies of the early 1970s (Bedggood 1973; Cuttance 1974, 1980; Easton 1976) are among those that stand out.

The following review of recent poverty research in New Zealand is set in the above context. As in most countries, the approaches to such research vary greatly. Particular emphasis will be given to the differing methodologies used. For the purposes of this chapter, and in line with the CROP guidelines for the various regional overviews, only studies carried out from 1980 to the present will be examined. They will be reviewed under three headings: descriptive and self-report approaches; income distribution and equality approaches; and poverty line approaches.

I take the view that all these approaches contribute significantly to our understanding of poverty. No one approach gives us all the information; rather this requires the collection of the different approaches in both qualitative and quantitative forms. Not every study will fit neatly into the assigned categories, but the categories offer a helpful basis for comparison.

Descriptive and self-report approaches

Numbers of local studies have been carried out around New Zealand with a view to investigating the experiences of low-income families. Their primary concern has been to identify the economic pressures on those families, how they dealt with those pressures, and some description by the families of their own situation.

One such study was commissioned by the Low Incomes Working Party in Christchurch (Crean 1982). Survey data were collected by structured interviews, using a questionnaire. The questionnaire was constructed in association with experienced academic researchers, and consisted of seventy-two main questions. A careful definition of low income was used: Grade 2 of the very low-paying Clerical Workers Award Wage. A sample of fifty-three families with children were interviewed.

The results indicated that the families' total budgets were absorbed in maintaining basic survival necessities, such as food, shelter, health expenses, etc. Constant anxieties were reported about balancing household budgets, with 70 per cent of families claiming that their weekly budgets ranged over the year from NZ$30 surplus to NZ$30 deficit. The families reported their daily living to be "full of constraints and limited choices".

Similar local, small-scale studies have been carried out in Auckland (Auckland District Council of Social Services 1982), Palmerston North (Brosnahan et al. 1983), and Lower Hutt (Trego and Leader 1988). A somewhat larger study was commissioned by the Manukau City Local Authority (Crothers 1993) to survey economic hardship. The sample consisted of 370 randomly selected Manukau households. The study found that 40 per cent considered themselves financially worse off than they were a year before; 20 per cent were better off. Respondents reported problems in the following areas: health costs 22 per cent; housing costs 21 per cent; children's costs 15 per cent; food costs 15 per cent; and transport costs 9 per cent. 48 per cent put off visits to the dentist and 43 per cent visits to the doctor. Despite this 59 per cent reported that they were satisfied with their standard of living, with 16 per cent dissatisfied. In summary, however, the report stated, "it is clear that many of the households surveyed were suffering considerable financial difficulties".

An early Christchurch study (Fergusson et al. 1981) took another approach by attempting to measure material well-being rather than economic well-being, as exemplified in income-, expenditure- or budget-based methods. Material well-being was analysed along two correlated dimensions: the level of family ownership, and the economizing behaviour the family was required to undertake. The project was developed as an adjunct to the longitudinal Christchurch Child Development Study. For the study, 1,169 mothers who gave birth to children in the Christchurch urban region a year earlier than the study were administered forty-nine questions in precoded checklist form. The responses were factor analysed. The item endorsements for

the ownership and the economizing scales were set out in household income deciles.
9 Ownership was very low over the first five deciles (lower-income groups) and rose rapidly over the last five. The profile of the economizing dimension was more skewed, but nevertheless showed considerable decline for the higher-decile groups. Both dimensions demonstrated moderate to good reliability and showed systematic correlations with the predictive measures.

A number of national descriptive and self-report studies have also been undertaken. Like the local research, these projects have also demonstrated considerable hardship for households on low incomes. The Department of Social Welfare (Rochford 1987) carried out a survey of living standards of 1,114 randomly chosen beneficiaries, which was added on to the routine quality-control interviews with domestic purposes (DPB) and unemployment beneficiaries (UB). This study attempted to replicate, for different groups, an earlier survey on the aged (Department of Statistics 1975). The questions largely focused on affordability criteria such as accommodation costs, visits to the doctor, and clothing and food costs.

The results indicated "*a high overall level of financial difficulties*". About half reported postponing visits to doctors or dentists and repairing old clothes because of lack of money, over a quarter acknowledged difficulties with accommodation costs and about a third went without meat or fish because of a lack of money. Despite this, more than half the sample were satisfied with their standard of living.

A comparative examination of particular sub-groups was also carried out. DPB single parents with more than one child, UB long-term single, singles aged 18–19, and two-parent families all experienced greater financial difficulties than other beneficiary types.

In 1984, Television New Zealand commissioned a commercial research company (Heylen Research Centre 1984) to carry out a national wealth and poverty survey, in which 826 randomly chosen household decision makers were interviewed in their houses. The results exposed increasing distinctions between the rich and the poor. While 19,000 New Zealanders missed a meal because they couldn't afford it, 88,000 families reported dining at a licensed or B.Y.O. restaurant at least once a week. 90,000 families postponed doctors visits because of lack of money, while 103,000 put up with feeling cold to keep down heating costs. Ten percent of households couldn't afford even 3 days away from home in a year while 77,000 families could holiday regularly overseas each year. The survey claimed that the main group of dispossessed were children, a quarter of a million were living in relative poverty.

Poor New Zealand (Waldegrave and Coventry 1987) is one of the very few books written specifically on the subject of poverty. The authors drew together many studies and the stories of New Zealanders on six dimensions: housing; income; race; employment; health; and gender. The book described poverty in personal, micro, and macro ways using a mixture of personal accounts, local studies, and national statistical data.

Written as "An Open Letter on Poverty", the authors did not attempt to identify a poverty line, but rather indicated the growing body of poverty evidence under each of the six dimensions noted above. Unlike most other studies, they viewed the growth of poverty from each of the six perspectives, tracing New Zealand's history and performance in each. The wide range of studies used, though not establishing a single measure, allowed a multidimensional picture of the complexities of understanding poverty more than one-dimensional measures do. In contrast to the other studies noted thus far, *Poor New Zealand* identified the disproportional way in which Maori and Pacific Island people and women (particularly single-parent women) shoulder the burden of poverty on almost every measure.

The last national study in this section adopted a quite different methodological approach. *Neither Freedom nor Choice* (Craig et al. 1992) was a major qualitative investigation into the experienced impacts on low-income households of the benefit cuts and other social policy changes. A novel method to gather data was chosen. A People's Select Committee, composed of four prominent New Zealanders (a bishop, a Maori elder and academic, a women's studies academic, and the national coordinator of the Unemployed and Beneficiaries Movement), was established to conduct the enquiry.

The People's Select Committee found that there were major social and economic consequences arising from the benefit cuts and other social policy reforms. They noted the "pervasive and overwhelming effect on all aspects of people's lives ... the creation of greater poverty, greater inequality and greater social division", and the use of charity foodbanks to supplement inadequate benefit payments.

They identified the particular groups most exposed to poverty. These included many women, many families, many children, people with disabilities, the elderly, the unemployed, low-paid workers, people with health problems, Maori, and Pacific Island people. The report recorded pages of verbatim statements under various categories. There was one major recommendation from the report: the establishment of an adequate minimum income as of right, to enable all to belong and participate. It is noteworthy that the recommendation echoes a relative definition of poverty along the lines of the 1972 Royal Commission on Social Security.

A variety of self-report and descriptive studies have been undertaken in New Zealand, both locally and nationally. These studies helped highlight the changing New Zealand circumstances.

The Report of the People's Select Committee and some aspects of the self-report research have contributed important qualitative data to our understanding of poverty that are not available in other approaches. The comprehensive focus on the poverty bias to cultural and gender groupings in *Poor New Zealand*, and the emphasis in the People's Select Committee Report, help identify the structural make-up of those in hardship. There is, however, a lack of recent work on material well-being as opposed to the more focused economic approaches.

Income distribution and equality approaches

Because income is the necessary resource for food, shelter, and other necessities in modern capitalist economies, the study of income, particularly income distribution and equality, has made a major contribution to the analysis of poverty. The following studies illustrate the range of interesting research being carried out in New Zealand on income distribution and equality measures. They can be divided into those that simply focus on income distribution and those that seek a more complex measure of equality as well. Those that focus simply on income distribution will be addressed first.

The Department of Statistics (1991) examined income trends in New Zealand between 1981/82 and 1989/90. It analysed personal and household income using national data collected by the Department. These included its Wage and Salary Earner Statistics, its Household Expenditure and Income Survey (HEIS), and A Simulation System for Evaluating Taxation (ASSET) model.

It reported that the purchasing power of the top income quintile increased by 10 per cent, compared with a decline of 4–6 per cent in the bottom three quintile groups over the nine years. It noted that benefit income and taxation did redistribute some income, but did not remove the marked disparities between quintile groups. They "probably did more to improve the positions of those on higher incomes than those on lower incomes". Gender was a key determinant of income, with 30 per cent of females and 10 per cent of males in the bottom quintile. The Department noted that paid work was the most important determinant of individual income level: "It protects the earner from poverty."

These findings probably reflect the tax changes of the Labour government in the mid-1980s, referred to in the first section of this paper. They also help to emphasize the significance of employment over citizenship to stay out of poverty in the New Zealand welfare state. Further evidence of the unequal redistributive impacts of tax and benefit changes was also revealed in a further study.

O'Brien and Wilkes (1993) analysed income distribution changes over a similar period – 1984–90. They used the Department of Statistics' survey data, such as the Household Expenditure and Income Survey, the consumer price index, and the real disposable incomes index. They found that the benefit increases were 18 per cent less than the rate of inflation increase for the period.

Real disposable income for wage and salary earners had dropped for low- and middle-income earners in quintiles 1 and 3, whereas top earners in quintile 5 experienced an increase. We should note that there is some concern about how well the Real Disposable Income Index tracks market incomes, and how sensitive it is to variations within industries. Though still being published by the Department, it may be withdrawn. Nevertheless, average tax rate changes for the same groups revealed a 9 per cent increase for low earners in quintile 1, a 3 per cent decrease for middle-income earners, and a 10.5 per cent decrease for top earners. When indirect tax was also taken into account deciles 1 and 10 were both taxed at around 48 per cent. The authors noted, "all the Tables point in the same direction, namely that the most significant increases and improvements in economic position have been at the higher end of the income scale".

These two studies analysed data from the period prior to the fundamental social policy changes of the National government in 1990 and 1991. Waldegrave and Frater (1991), however, led a research team that measured the cost of those announced policy changes in household disposable income for different family types, in household income quintiles. All data were sourced from HEIS, and the ASSET model allowed both tax calculations and categorization by family type. The Real Disposable Incomes Index was not used.

The results indicated that beneficiaries in the lowest quintile lost around NZ$2,500 per annum, which was 20 per cent of their disposable income. For the middle quintile, the loss was around NZ$900 or 4 per cent of their disposable income, and for quintile 5 it was around NZ$1,100 or 2 per cent of disposable income. The results also revealed that households with children lost considerably more, in every quintile, than households without children. The measure that caused the greatest loss of income in the bottom two quintiles was the change in housing assistance.

Whereas these studies have focused almost solely on income distribution, others have also tried to measure equality by separately analysing redistribution through social welfare cash payments, other public social services, and taxation. One such project is an Australian and New Zealand study of income equality and redistribution (Saunders et al. 1988). The researchers reproduced, for Australia and New Zealand, the original comparative analysis for six countries in the Luxembourg Income Study (LIS). The New Zealand analysis utilized the HEIS 1981-2 and the ASSET model, noted above. Calculations were sought for the four basic LIS cash income concepts of factor income, market income, gross income, and net income.

New Zealand demonstrated the highest redistributive impact of direct taxes on unadjusted income of the two countries, and of the original six: Canada, Germany, Norway, Sweden, the United Kingdom, and the United States. When adjustments were made for family size through the use of an equivalence scale, however, New Zealand fell considerably to rank with Canada, below the Scandinavian countries and the UK. The authors stated that, overall, "neither [New Zealand nor Australia] can be accurately described as relatively egalitarian" when compared with the other six countries.

Snively (1987a, 1987b, 1988, 1993) has carried out an extensive analysis of the distributive effects of governments' budgets. Utilizing the Department of Statistics' HEIS, the ASSET Model, and SEBIRD (Study of the Effect of the Budget on Income Redistribution and Distribution), she measured the budgets' redistributive impacts (1981/82, 1985/86, and 1986/87). The results demonstrated that the impact of the budgets was redistributive for all three years, when analysed by household market income deciles.

Analysis by household type revealed distributive differences. Two adult national superannuitant households had the greatest net gains. Households with two or more adults (non-superannuitant) and no children had a smaller share of market income adjusted for the budget (MIAB) than market income. However, the results concerning households of adults and children were the most disturbing. All such households, with the exception of single-parent households, ended up with an MIAB slightly below their share of market income. Although single-parent households gained through budget redistribution, their share of market income was very low, and their share of MIAB was well below their share of the population, suggesting very low incomes and gender bias.

These themes of increasing relief for those on higher incomes and increasing burdens for those on lower incomes, particularly households with children, persist through the poverty research of the past decade. Because women are much more involved than men in child-rearing and have less access to market income, they are disadvantaged more than men. The themes reappear in two published reports of the New Zealand Planning Council entitled *For Richer and Poorer* (Income Distribution Group 1988) and *Who Gets What?* (Income Distribution Group 1990).The reports drew on Snively's work, and went on to analyse Maori incomes, gender differences in incomes and personal wealth distribution.

They found that real incomes fell during the 1980s, and income became less equally distributed among households after 1985. The main reasons suggested for this, as we have noted before, were the changes to taxation and the increase in joblessness. The reports noted the persistent gap between male and female average incomes, caused by lower participation in paid work, child-care responsibilities, and occupational segregation. Despite the increasing participation rate of women in wage and salary positions, the average full-time earnings of women were 72.6 per cent of those of men in 1986/87. This was a small change from 72.2 per cent seven years before in 1981/82. The reports noted that personal marketable wealth was more unequally distributed than income.

These reports confirmed that Maori were economically disadvantaged, with a larger proportion of Maori households in the lower income brackets. As with other low-income groups, their position deteriorated during the 1980s. The relative income position of Maori households fell from an average position in relation to all other households in 1981/82 to 21 per cent below the all household average in 1987/88.

The cultural and gender focuses of these studies are important, because there is little numerical research on special groups in New Zealand. The HEIS data, which are most often used in income distribution studies, do not carry large enough samples of sub-groups of the population for statistical reliability. It is possible to calculate the overall poverty incidence for Maori, but the data are much less reliable for family-type sub-groups. They are not sufficiently reliable to calculate the overall poverty incidence for the Pacific Island population. This presents a problem for New Zealand researchers, because identifying the sub-grouping make-up of poverty incidence is important for understanding its structure and devising effective ways of eliminating it.

Income inequality statistics for Maori and Pacific Island people are often gleaned from the Department of Statistics Census and Household Labour Force Survey. The 1991 census noted that the median income for full-time employed men was NZ$27,279, whereas for Maori men it was NZ$22,750, and for Pacific Island Polynesian men NZ$19,846. For all women it was NZ$21,461, for Maori women NZ$18,572 and for Pacific Island Polynesian women NZ$17,438. These figures clearly indicate gender and cultural bias. The cultural bias is even greater if the disproportionate number of Maori and Pacific Island people, who currently live off benefits because of unemployment, is taken into account. The official unemployment rate for all New Zealanders in the workforce is 9.1 per cent, whereas for Maori it is 22.9 per cent and Pacific Island people 22.1 per cent (Household Labour Force Survey, for March 1994).

Mention should be made of two other fiscal incidence studies that followed directly from the Planning Council Reports. The Department of Statistics' Fiscal Impact on Income Distribution study (1990) recalculated the earlier report in terms of equivalent income. Stocks et al. (1991) simulated the benefit reductions of 1991, alongside the earlier report results, using the Gini coefficient. The results showed increasing inequality in disposable income.

The final piece of research in this section, a project of the Massey University Social Policy Research Centre (Chatterjee and Srivastav 1992), is significant in that it has established a longitudinal database for the study of income distribution and inequality in New Zealand. *The Statistics of Incomes and Income Taxes*, published by the Inland Revenue Department in 1983–4, were the subject of analysis in this first study of inequality estimates. Subsequent reports will expand on the time-frame.

The measurement of income inequality adopted positive (without reference to any notion of social welfare) and normative measures (start from a social welfare function). The Gini coefficient was used to extract positive measures. An additional positive measure along the lines of the Nelson Inequality Index, using the ratio of the income of the highest 5 per cent and the lowest 20 per cent of the given distributions, was also employed.

The Atkinson Index was chosen as the normative measure to assess the social welfare implications resulting from income inequality changes. The Gini coefficients were then decomposed to assess inequality changes between the genders and between income components.

The findings indicated that the female population recorded a significant overall measure of inequality, both positive and normative. The income distribution was also more unequal for them than for either the male population or the total population. Two factor incomes, those of wages and salaries and business income, were found to be inequality enhancing, while all non-factor incomes were inequality reducing. The authors noted that "results based on the normative measure, demonstrate dramatically the potential gain in the welfare of society that could result from a more equal distribution of existing incomes".

The income distribution and equality studies, although recognizing significant redistributive elements in the New Zealand welfare state, consistently demonstrate basic inequalities. Furthermore, the inequalities have been growing with the tax and benefit changes. Only a small number of studies in this section, however, address data since the major social policy reforms in 1991. Those that do, indicate that the trend has continued.

Where cultural and gender sub-groups are analysed, bias against women, Maori, and Pacific Island people is revealed. Unfortunately, the New Zealand databases are not adequate to analyse many sub-groups reliably. The longitudinal database being developed at Massey University can be expected to make a major contribution to research on income distribution and equality in the future. Finally, it is noteworthy that recent equality research in New Zealand has not adopted more complex measures of material well-being alongside those of economic well-being, as is characteristic of some other countries. This reduces the breadth of New Zealand research in this area.

Poverty line approaches

The use of equivalence scales is fundamental to most poverty line research, as it is to much of the income distribution and equality approaches. An equivalence scale is a means of adjusting incomes so that differing sizes and types of households can be compared.

By the early 1970s (Cuttance 1974) equivalence scales had been developed in New Zealand. The better-known ones, however, were developed by Easton (1976) and Jensen (1978). Easton took a budgetary approach, by using the New York Family Budget quantity weights (Community Council of Greater New York 1970), with New Zealand prices. Jensen derived his scale from a blend of McClements' (1977, 1978) method, a sophisticated food expenditure approach, and Rainwater's Boston study (1974) attitudinal approach.

Easton's basic parameters of the scale were: single adult 0.64; couple 1.00; couple and four children 1.83. Jensen's parameters were 0.6, 1.00, and 2.00, respectively, for the same household types. Easton (1979) later presented another equivalence scale formula based on the Household Expenditure Survey, and Jensen (1988) subsequently revised his scale.

Today Jensen's scales are the most commonly accepted in New Zealand (Rochford and Pudney 1984; Rutherford et al. 1990). They are criticized (Brashares and Aynsley 1990; Easton 1979), though, as being somewhat arbitrary. Easton (1979) has argued that there is still a lot of work to be done in this area and that we cannot continue to depend on foreign studies. The Department of Statistics (Smith 1989) is currently working to see if an empirically derived scale can be developed for New Zealand.

Easton has a long history of poverty research in New Zealand. His work in the 1970s drew the earlier contributions and thinking (including the relative definition of poverty outlined in the 1972 Royal Commission on Social Security) into a coherent paradigm and research programme. Benefits had been rising towards this level during the previous decade. The Commission's definition, in terms of "participation" and "belonging", Cuttance's (1974) study of large families in Hamilton, the Department of Social Welfare's (1975) survey of the elderly, and Easton's (1976) national estimates of poverty in New Zealand were all marks of poverty research development in New Zealand that could stand alongside any in the world.

Though carried out before the period of this overview of poverty research, Easton's study deserves to be mentioned. He used what he refers to as the Pensioner Datum Level (PDL), set at the married rate of the age benefit in force at the time, as his standard of relative poverty. As a result of changes to the benefit system, his later writings (Easton 1980, 1986) refer to the Benefit Datum Line (BDL), which was set at the same standard but was in fact the social security benefit rate for a married couple. He considered the PDL/BDL to be socially defined. The level had been recommended by the Royal Commission on Social Security (1972) as a relative standard, and benefits were set at that level and adjusted for inflation up to the time of his study.

Easton took his income data from the newly instituted Household Expenditure and Income Survey (1973/74 figures), and used his original equivalence scales to gain different household measures of a standard of living equal to that of the married rate of the aged benefit. He then calculated the number of households whose income did not attain the standard. The results suggested that 18 per cent of the population or 550,000 persons lived below the poverty line; 20 per cent of persons over 60, 25 per cent of children, 20 per cent of their parents, and 5 per cent of other adults fell below the Pensioner Datum Line.

This study marked a turning point in the history of poverty research in New Zealand. Given the official definition of that time, Easton's research programme provided a coherent, national estimate of those below the standard. It also provided a method for future studies. Unfortunately, the initiative was not taken up and funded by government. Nevertheless, in a later study (Easton 1986), he commented that there were more working families with children below the BDL than all other households, and that their standard of living had tended to slip behind that of social security beneficiaries.

Since Easton's major work in the 1970s, two poverty line initiatives have been taken by New Zealand government departments. The research programmes, however, were very different. Rochford and Pudney (1984), in a Department of Social Welfare study, applied three equivalence scales to a New Zealand household income distribution taken from the Department of Statistics' 1981 Social Indicators Survey. The scales used were Jensen (1978), those implicit in the benefit system, and a theoretical scale based on the assumption that all members of a household require the same amount of income.

The results found that the choice of scale had a marked effect on the number of households below a poverty line. They chose an equivalent income level between the married sickness benefit rate and the married national superannuation rate as a poverty line. Their study revealed that 8.1 per cent of households and 10.2 per cent of individuals fell below the line. The results supported Easton's contention that many New Zealanders lived in poverty, but the estimate in this study was around half his number.

The second initiative came from Treasury, the Ministry of Finance in New Zealand. It commissioned Brashares and Aynsley (1990, Brashares 1993) to carry out a study on income adequacy standards. This was a quite different research programme, which provided relative and absolute measures of poverty. The reintroduction of absolute poverty line standards is indicative of a shift in official thinking about poverty that has already been alluded to in this paper.

The researchers used a variety of income adequacy standards based on different methodologies, with the standards ranging from subsistence- and absolute-based measures to more generous relative ones. Three food-cost multipliers were used to generate three possible absolute income standards. The Otago food plan, calculated by FOCAS Information Service at Otago University, was employed for estimates of food costs. The relative income standards involved 50 per cent of median household income for two different family types, and two relative earnings standards. These were the award rate for a builder's labourer and 65 per cent of the average wage.

They quantified numbers in poverty, the poverty gap, and a severity index. The HEIS was used as the basis of their analysis, and government housing assistance, using Housing Corporation data, was added to income. The Jensen equivalence scales (1988) were employed.

The results ranged from measures of 2.7 per cent of the New Zealand population below the standard (the most stringent multiplier, the food plan × 3) to 13.3 per cent (65 per cent of the average wage). The authors noted that, if the two extremes were disregarded, the other measures clustered within a range of about NZ$3,000, identifying 4.4–7.8 per cent of the population below the remaining standards. The incidence of poverty was reduced after housing assistance was taken into account.

This study has been heavily criticized (Campbell 1991; Easton 1991, 1994; Sinclair 1992; Stephens 1992). Criticisms have included the use of a low-cost rather than a normal food plan, the inaccuracy of the food prices, major differences in regional housing prices, the addition of housing subsidies to the income of state house tenants and not adding net imputed rents to the income of owner-occupiers, the arbitrary use of multipliers, disregard for other New Zealand studies, and non-value-free assumptions. Easton (1991) and Stephens (1992) argued that Brashares and Aynsley's preferred standard, the low-cost food plan times four, was the basis for setting the significantly reduced level of the unemployment benefit in April 1991.

It is little wonder that controversy has surrounded the move away from a relative and participatory measure of poverty. It is also not surprising, given the extraordinary changes in social policy in New Zealand outlined in this paper over the past decade, that a definition based on minimal needs would again emerge.

The final piece of research to be outlined in this overview is a major study in progress that is adopting a quite different methodology. The Foundation for Research, Science and Technology is funding the New Zealand Poverty Measurement Project, which is carrying out a multidisciplinary and multi-agency study (Stephens, Waldegrave and Frater 1995). The agencies involved are a business economic research unit, a university public policy department, and a community-based social policy research unit.

The study is attempting a combination of a "top–down" macro analysis with a "bottom–up" micro analysis. The measurements reflect the results of the two parallel studies, with a poverty level based on focus group results. The macro study has been investigating the data of the Department of Statistics Household Expenditure and Income Survey (HEIS). These data are then run through the ASSET model, and the Jensen (1988) equivalence scales (set for two adults and one child) are used. Both income and expenditure data are extracted.

In order to make the results internationally comparable, calculations at both 50 per cent and 60 per cent of the median equivalent household disposable income and expenditure lines are extracted, after the application of the equivalence scales. This enables the flexibility of four measures to relate to other studies, and in particular the emerging data from the micro study. The Luxembourg Income Study (LIS), for example, uses an income measure, whereas the European Union (Eurostat) employs an expenditure measure.

The use of a percentage of a median is, of course, arbitrary. It may or may not reflect poverty in New Zealand. Its main advantage lies in the ability to relate to other established studies and commonly used measures of poverty. The micro-study component of this research, on the other hand, anchors the analysis in the experience of those who live on low and/or inadequate incomes.

The micro study has employed a focus group methodology. The initial focus group work for this project was carried out by Cody and Robinson (see Stephens, Waldegrave and Frater 1995). It involves a series of meetings with low-income families, during which they estimate "minimum adequate household expenditure" for different family types.

The focus groups have been designed to encourage the low-income households to share their experience and knowledge with their peers. A consensus is not required, but a common mind is sought. In reality, those who live on low incomes provide an expert consultation of the day-to-day practical and necessary expenditures, which the facilitator receives and conveys to the project. As the project has developed, another estimate has been sought, that of "minimum expenditure that is fair for households to participate adequately in their community". This enables a relative and participatory estimate from the low-income householders.

The macro and micro studies have developed separately, but already the micro data are having an impact on the macro findings. The results from the various focus groups have been remarkably consistent, despite the fact that they were carried out quite separately, with different communities (cultural and household types), and without contact between the groups. Early results indicate estimates for minimum adequate household expenditure clustering around 60 per cent of the median equivalent household disposable income for two-parent households. The estimates for single-parent households were consistently higher, suggesting the Jensen equivalence scales may not be appropriate, especially for this group. Cody and Robinson, in the earlier work, considered the scales underestimated the costs for teenage dependants.

The focus group findings have indicated that the line should be drawn at 60 per cent of median equivalent household income or expenditure (around NZ$500 or less per annum between them throughout the 1990s – Department of Statistics), rather than 50 per cent. This is comparable with the LIS which uses 50 per cent and 60 per cent of median equivalent household disposable income. We should note that New Zealand's decline in living standards in the past decade is such that 50 per cent of median equivalent household disposable income in 1984 is much the same as a 60 per cent measure in 1993 (Department of Statistics). The 60 per cent measure is also comparable with the Eurostat (1991) measure, which is 50 per cent of *mean* equivalent household expenditure. In 1990, 50 per cent of the *mean* equivalent household expenditure in New Zealand was virtually the same as 60 per cent of *median* equivalent household expenditure (Mowbray 1993).

To date, the macro data have been extracted for the 1983/84–1992/93 years. Using the preferred 60 per cent income and expenditure measures for the 1992/93 year, Table 10.1 indicates that 10.8 per cent of households and 13.4 per cent of persons, and 21.1 per cent of households and 20.4 per cent of persons, respectively, were poor. A second estimate was also taken after housing costs, lifting the preferred measure to 18.5 per cent of households and 20.5 per cent of persons on the income standard, and 24.1 per cent of households and 23.2 per cent of persons on the expenditure standard.

In Table 10.1, the results have omitted households with

Table 10.1 Incidence and severity of poverty, in New Zealand 1992/93

Poverty measure	Poverty incidence		Per cent reduction transfers		Poverty gap Mean % poverty line equivalent $	Mean total equivalent $	$m
	Households	People	Households	People			
Before housing costs							
50% expenditure	12.9	12.3	–	–	24.9	3,624	502.2
50% income	4.3	5.5	88.2	82.4	13.6	1,905	87.26
60% expenditure	21.1	20.4	–	–	26.0	4,530	1,026
60% income	10.8	13.4	73.2	68.4	15.8	2,656	308.5
After housing costs							
50% expenditure	16.6	16.0	–	–	31.6	3,808	676.1
50% income	11.5	13.3	71.1	61.3	31.6	3,699	454.2
60% expenditure	24.1	23.2	–	–	32.2	4,656	1204.4
60% income	18.5	20.5	58.1	51.3	29.7	4,169	826.5

Source: Frater, Stephens and Waldegrave (1994). Derived from Department of Statistics.

self-employed losses and those reporting expenditure three times or more greater than their income. The removal of these "outliers", which are not omitted in the LIS, decreases the number of households and persons in poverty.

The column "percent reduction transfers" indicates the extent to which the payment of social security benefits reduces the incidence of poverty. For the 60 per cent income standard, social security payments reduce poverty incidence in households by 73.2 per cent. The poverty gap, that is the severity of poverty, was also estimated by calculating the extent to which households fall below the poverty line. For the 60 per cent level, using income, the mean poverty gap was NZ$2,656 per household, or 15.8 per cent of the poverty line, which would cost NZ$309 million to remove. For the 60 per cent expenditure level, the mean poverty gap was NZ$4,530 per household, or 26.0 per cent of the poverty line, which would cost NZ$1,025.95 million to remove.

The calculations indicate a significant increase of poverty incidence, at every measure, after housing costs have been taken into account. This points to the major part housing plays in the occurrence of poverty in New Zealand. The measures are so marked that the project team consider that a poverty line in New Zealand should be calculated after housing costs have been taken into account.

The research team has agreed to the setting for a poverty standard. In the light of the focus group results and the greater accuracy of income as opposed to expenditure figures, 60 per cent of median equivalent household disposable income after housing costs has been chosen as the poverty standard.

The 60 per cent measure before housing costs are taken into account indicates the amount of income people need to be free of poverty, not including variations in housing costs. Because housing costs are so variable and major changes in both lending and renting policies have occurred in New Zealand as a result of the social policy changes, housing expenditures have a disproportionate impact on low and modest incomes. By using the 60 per cent standard after housing costs are taken into account, a more realistic costing of poverty elimination can take place. This latter measure will include the significant rental increases for those in state houses and young families on modest incomes whose mortgage payments push them below the poverty standard.

Using the currently preferred standard, i.e. 60 per cent of median equivalent household disposable income after housing costs, the cost of bringing all New Zealanders above that line for the 1992/93 year would have been NZ$308.51 million in terms of income adequacy and NZ$826.45 million in terms of income adequacy and housing expenditure, as Table 10.1 shows.

It is interesting to note that the cost of bringing all New Zealanders above the poverty line in the 1990/91 year, immediately prior to the social policy reforms that cut benefits and moved state rentals to market rates, would have been NZ$157 million less, using this standard.

The study is developing a database that enables the poverty measures to be calculated for household types, household numbers, the elderly, children, tenure of dwelling, and owner of dwelling. The focus group work is being carried out in different regions. Note is being taken of differing transport costs, housing costs, and cultural budget items. The Maori and Samoan focus groups in this study, for example, both replaced a budget category, common to all the other groups, with an extended family commitment category. The second estimate concerning participation in the community is also being sought.

Another early result has raised a problem with the use of a relative poverty line rather than an absolute one. Between 1983 and 1993, living standards in New Zealand reduced greatly, largely because of high unemployment and the social policy changes, such that the median equivalent household disposable income has fell 17 percentage points. As a result, there was a fall in the real poverty line. Despite this, the poverty rate has remained essentially constant. Had we used the 50 per cent income measure in 1983/84 as an absolute standard, for example, the household incidence, before housing costs were taken into account would have been 4.3 per cent, and would have grown to 11.3 per cent by 1992/93.

This sort of consistent decline does not appear to have occurred in other similar countries. It raises problems for comparative research when using this sort of relative measure, but it may help explain the consistency of the focus group results. Furthermore, it underlies the importance of the micro aspect of the study in terms of determining the poverty line as a percentage of the median at any one time. The focus group results indicate the adequacy of income at a given period. As a percentage of household income, the figure will vary from year to year according to the adequacy of the income available to low-income families. Significant changes to the poverty standard, as a percentage of median equivalent household disposable income, could be expected, for example, as a result of major social policy changes or changes in the macro economy.

This latest project is interesting because of the range of

measures it produces, and the consequent ability it gives for comparisons with a variety of studies in New Zealand and internationally. Because there is an arbitrary element to any poverty standard, the range of measures give a fuller picture. The micro work anchors the standard in the experience of those who have to live on low incomes. In a real sense, the poor have their say and share their practical expertise in the measure. The project is new, of course, and there is a need for a wider range of focus group work to test the current results, and this is being undertaken.

The use of HEIS data enables an historical series of results that can be consistently maintained in the future, which is very important in developing a credible standard to quantify the increases and decreases in poverty. The project has endeavoured to draw a broad group of researchers together to reflect and advise at each stage of the research. To this end a Statistical Working Party, consisting of independent academic, community, and economic researchers alongside Department of Statistics and Social Welfare researchers, has been instituted to advise the project team.

The various approaches to national poverty line research in New Zealand have all been quite different. As yet, neither an official poverty line nor methodology has been agreed to. Because fundamental economic and social reforms have taken place in the past decade, there has been no official standard to quantify the increases/decreases in poverty. It can only be hoped that developments in this field will lead to an agreed measure.

Acknowledgements

We wish to acknowledge the valuable assistance of Grace Garnham in the literature search. We also wish to thank, Ian Shirley, Suzanne Snively, Dennis Rose, Mike O'Brien, Brian Easton, and Srikanta Chatterjee for their various insightful comments and contributions to earlier drafts of this paper. While deeply appreciative of the help received, the views in this paper reflect those of the leaders of the New Zealand Poverty Measurement Project – Paul Frater (Business and Economic Research Limited, BERL), Bob Stephens (Public Policy Department, Victoria University, Wellington), and Charles Waldegrave (The Family Centre).

We wish to acknowledge the ongoing support, knowledge, and broad range of experience at all levels of poverty research of both the Family Centre staff and the New Zealand Poverty Measurement Project.

This paper is a part of the New Zealand Poverty Measurement Project, which is funded by the New Zealand Foundation for Research Science and Technology. The Project leaders acknowledge that, without its support, the project could not have been attempted.

REFERENCES

Auckland District Council of Social Services (1982) *Poverty in Auckland or It Costs More to be Poor*.
Bedggood, L. R. (1973) "The political economy of the welfare state in New Zealand". Paper presented at the Conference of the New Zealand Sociology Association, Wellington.
Bertram, A. (1988) "Middle class capture: A brief survey", in *Future Directions: Report of the Royal Commission on Social Policy*, vol. III, part 2, April, pp. 109–68.
Boston, J. (1992) "The future of the welfare state social assistance for all or just for the poor", in J. Boston and P. Dalziel (eds), *The Decent Society*. Aukland: Oxford University Press.
Brashares, E. (1993) "Income adequacy standards for New Zealand". *N.Z. Economic Papers*, 27 (2), December.
Brashares, E. and M. Aynsley (1990) *Income Adequacy Standards for New Zealand*. Wellington: The Treasury.
Brosnahan, N., J. Chilcolt, D. Henderson, T. Holdaway, D. Miller, and M. O'Brien (1983) *Surviving on the Breadline*. Palmerston North, Massey University.
Campbell, A. (1991) "Building the poverty prison". *Listener and TV Times*, 25 March.
Castles, F. (1985) *The Working Class and Welfare: Reflections on the Political Development of the Welfare State in Australia and New Zealand 1890–1980*. Wellington: Allen & Unwin.
Chatterjee, Srikanta and Nirankar Srivastav (1992). *Inequalities in New Zealand's Personal Income Distribution 1983–1984: Measurements and Patterns*. Social Policy Research Centre, Massey University, Income Distributions Series No. 1.
Community Council of Greater New York (1970) *Family Budget Standard*. New York.
Craig, A., C. Briar, N. Brosnahan, and M. O'Brien (1992) *Neither Freedom nor Choice*. Report of the People's Select Committee, Easter. People's Select Committee, Box 295, Palmerston North.
Crean, P. (1982) *Survey of Low Income Families*. Low Incomes Working Party, Christchurch, December.
Crothers, C. (1993) "Manukau Quality of Life Survey: Overview Report". Manukau the Healthy City, Manukau City.
Cuttance, P. F. (1974) "Income poverty among large families in Hamilton". MSS thesis, University of Waikato.
——— (1980) "Income poverty among large families in New Zealand: A case study". *New Zealand Economic Papers*, 14: 75–92.

Department of Social Welfare (1975) *Survey of Persons Aged 65 Years and Over*. Wellington: Government Printing Office.

Department of Statistics (1990) *Fiscal Impact on Income Distribution*. Wellington: Department of Statistics.

—— (1991) *New Zealand Social Trends: Incomes*. Wellington: Department of Statistics.

Easton, B. (1976) "Poverty in New Zealand: Estimates and reflections". *Political Science*, 28 (2) December.

—— (1979) "Three New Zealand household equivalence scales". Paper presented at the New Zealand Statistical Association Conference, June.

—— (1980) *Social Policy and the Welfare State in New Zealand*. Allen & Unwin Australia.

—— (1986) *Wages and the Poor*. Allen & Unwin Zealand Limited.

—— (1991) "Calculating the benefit level". *Dominion*, 25 May.

—— (1994) "Properly assessing income adequacy". Economic and Social Trust on New Zealand, 18 Talavera Tce, Wellington.

Esping-Anderson, G. (1990) *The Three Worlds of Welfare Capitalism*. Polity Press.

Fergusson, D. M., L. J. Horwood, and A. L. Beautrais (1981) "The measurement of family material wellbeing". *Journal of Marriage and the Family*, August.

Henderson, R. F., A. Harcourt, and R. J. Harper (1970) *People in Poverty, A Melbourne Survey*. Melbourne: Cheshire.

Heylen Research Centre (1984) *Wealth and Poverty in New Zealand*. Television New Zealand Heylen Poll, The Heylen Research Centre, PO Box 3470, Auckland.

Income Distribution Group (1988) *For Richer or Poorer: Income and Wealth in New Zealand*. Wellington: New Zealand Planning Council.

—— (1990) *Who Gets What? The Distribution of Income and Wealth in New Zealand*. Wellington: New Zealand Planning Council.

Jensen, J. (1978) "Minimum income levels and income equivalence scales". Wellington: Department of Social Welfare, mimeo.

—— (1988) *Income Equivalences and the Estimation of Family Expenditures on Children*. Wellington: Department of Social Welfare, January.

McClements, L. D. (1977) "Equivalence scales for children". *Journal of Public Economics*, 8.

—— (1978) *The Economics of Social Security*. New York: Heinemann.

Mowbray, M. (1993) *Incomes Monitoring Report 1981–1991*. Wellington: Social Policy Agency.

O'Brien, M. and Chris Wilkes (1993) *The Tragedy of the Market. A Social Experiment in New Zealand*. Palmerston North: Dunmore Press.

Oliver, W. (1988) *Social Policy in New Zealand: A Historical Overview*. Royal Commission on Social Policy, *The April Report*, vol. 1. Wellington: Royal Commission on Social Policy.

Rainwater, L. (1974) *What Money Buys: Inequality and the Social Meaning of Income*. New York: Basic Books.
Rochford, M. (1987) *Survey of Living Standards of Beneficiaries*. Department of Social Welfare Research Report Series No. 8. Wellington: Research Section Department of Social Welfare.
Rochford, M. and K. Pudney (1984) *An Exploratory Application of Income Equivalences to Examination of Household Living Levels*. Department of Social Welfare Research Section Working Paper, September.
Rose, D. (1993) *Redistribution, Employment and Growth*. A briefing paper for New Zealand Council of Christian Social Services.
Rosenberg, W. (1968) *A Guidebook to New Zealand's Future*. Christchurch: The Caxton Press.
—— (1971) "A note on the relationship of family size and income in New Zealand". *Economic Record*, 47: 399–409.
Royal Commission on Social Security (1972). Wellington: Government Printer.
Royal Commission on Social Policy (1988). Wellington: Government Printer.
Rutherford, S., A. Khan, M. Rochford, and G. Hall (1990) *Equivalent Income: A comparison of 5 equivalent scales applied to the distribution of income in New Zealand*. Department of Social Welfare Research Report No. 11.
Saunders, P., G. Hobbes, and H. Stott (1988) *Income Inequality in Australia and New Zealand. International Comparisons and Recent Trends*. Social Policy Research Centre Discussion Paper.
Seers, D. (1946) *The Challenge to New Zealand Labour*. Christchurch: The Christchurch Cooperative Book Society, November.
Shirley, I. (1990) "Social policy", in P. Spoonley, D. Pearson, and I. Shirley (eds), *New Zealand Society*. Palmerston North: Dunmore Press.
Sinclair, J. (1992) "Poverty definition and measurement". Research Section Department of Social Welfare. Discussion Paper, mimeo.
Smith, H. (1989) *Working Paper 5*. Department of Statistics. Wellington.
Snively, S. (1987a) "Evaluating the government budget's distributive influence on household incomes". Discussion paper delivered to New Zealand Association of Economists, February.
—— (1987b) *The 1981/82 Budget and Household Income Distribution*. Wellington: New Zealand Planning Council.
—— (1988) "The government budget and social policy". A paper prepared for the Royal Commission on Social Policy, Department of Social Welfare, April.
—— (1993) *Survey of New Zealand Income Distribution Studies*. Wellington: Coopers & Lybrand.
Stephens, R. J. (1992) "Budgeting the benefit cuts" in J. Boston and P. Dalziel (eds), *The Decent Society*. Aukland: Oxford University Press.
Stephens, R., C. Waldegrave and P. Frater (1995) "Measuring poverty

in New Zealand", *Social Policy Journal of New Zealand, Te Puna Whakaaro*, Issue 5, December.

Stocks, P., D. O'Dea, and R. Stephens (1991) "Who gets what now?" Paper delivered at the New Zealand Association of Economists' Conference, Lincoln University, August.

Sutch, W. B. (1969) *Poverty and Progress in New Zealand: A Reassessment*. Wellington: A. H. & A. W. Reed.

Trego, E. and S. Leader (1988) *Hard Times: The Breadline Study: A Physical, Mental and Emotional Spiritual Well-being of Lower Hutt Valley Residents*. Lower Hutt District Council of Social Services.

Waldegrave, C. (1991) "Full employment, equity, participation and a viable New Zealand economy", in R. Pelly (ed.) *Towards a Just Economy: Employment Economics and Social Justice in Aotearoa New Zealand in the 1990's*. The Combined Chaplaincies, Victoria University of Wellington.

Waldegrave, C. and R. Coventry (1987) *Poor New Zealand: An Open Letter on Poverty*. Wellington: Platform Publishing.

Waldegrave, C. and P. Frater (eds) (1991) *The National Government Budgets of the First Year in Office: A Social Assessment*. A Report to Sunday Forum. The Family Centre and Business and Economic Research Ltd.

Part III
The African Region

The three chapters in this part present a picture of some of the important variations of the region. Africa, in particular south of the Sahara, is the poorest continent, and predictions from the World Bank, UN agencies, and other economic reports hold no promises of improvement for the next generation.

There seems to be a direct relationship between poverty in a country and the occurrence of poverty research. The poorer the country, the less is the institutionalized and systematic knowledge about poverty. One explanation is, of course, that poverty research is a luxury commodity that a poor country cannot afford. Another explanation is the immature development of the social sciences in general in many of the African countries. A third explanation, which comes across strongly in the chapter on South Africa, is the fear of the political impact of poverty research. During early apartheid, official research was done only on poor whites, while research on poor blacks, i.e. the majority of the South African population, was made invisible by defining it as a non-issue. Throughout the papers it is shown that shifts in the political climate are marked by the acceptance or rejection of poverty research as a legitimate activity.

The gap in poverty research has been filled by outside agencies, such as the World Bank and non-governmental agencies, which have carried out studies on different aspects of poverty. The major definition of poverty has been economic, thereby imposing an international understanding of poverty rather than a definition of poverty tailored to national perceptions of poverty. Water, for example, stands out as a central element in an African poverty definition. Poor people have less access to clean water. Fewer of the poor have tap water in the house, they have to go a greater distance to fetch water, and the physical effort expended on carrying water requires the energy of an ordinary labourer. On top of all this, the poor are likely to pay more per litre for clean water than the non-poor. But water is not part of the regional poverty definitions.

All three chapters call for new, reliable, and longitudinal data as a first step towards more systematic knowledge on poverty. The data should be collected on a national basis, that is, they should cover the entire country. But they should also be comparable in order to benefit from data and research in other African countries, as well as in countries outside Africa.

Chapter 11

Egypt: Comparing Poverty Measures

Karima Korayem

Concepts of poverty

In poverty studies on Egypt, three definitions have been used of the poverty line: the basic needs approach, the relative income definition, and the sociological definition. The subjective definition of poverty has also been applied, but on a very small scale.

Basic needs

The basic needs approach was used in defining the income poverty line in the studies of Adams (1985), Radwan and Lee (1986),[1] Korayem (1987a, 1994a), and the World Bank (1990b). Although the basic needs approach provides a relatively more comprehensive basis for the measurement of poverty compared with other definitions, it certainly has its limitations and shortcomings. This is reflected mainly in the arbitrariness implied in defining a household's basic needs of food and non-food items, and in the prices used to measure a household's expenditures on those basic needs items, because prices are dependent on incomes, on location, and on social status (Kyereme and Thorbecke 1987; Van Praag and Baye 1990). Arbitrariness is also reflected in estimating the minimum food requirements for individuals in terms of calories level and protein, because individual calorie requirements depend on several factors, such as sex, age, size (i.e. weight and height), and the type of work performed (Kyereme and Thorbecke 1987). The calorie intake needed for the average individual is also disputable, and has been falling in recent years (Lipton 1983). To overcome, or at least to mitigate, the arbitrariness of calorie intake, some studies used more than one recommended daily allowance (RDA) to estimate the poverty line; for example Paul (1989) used three RDAs in estimating the poverty line.

Relative income

The relative income approach was used by El-Laithy and Kheir-El-Din (1994) and the Institute of National Planning (INP 1994) to define the poverty line in Egypt. According to this approach, the poverty line is defined relative to income per capita; it is set at one-half or two-thirds, etc. of income per capita. The shortcoming of this approach is that it lacks the criteria that guarantee that the relative income chosen as the poverty line satisfies the basic needs of the individual. It overlooks the fact that poverty signifies a certain state of being in which the individual does not have enough income to meet his or her basic needs of food, shelter, etc., no matter whether the income is one-half or two-thirds etc. of the per capita income. Also, the studies that define the poverty line according to the relative income approach do not state why a certain relative income has been chosen as the poverty line; e.g. why poverty is defined as one-half (and not as two-thirds for example) of per capita income.

Sociological definition

In a study on structural adjustment in the social welfare sector in Egypt, the sociological definition of poverty was applied (Shawky 1989/90). Shawky defined the poor as those who receive social assistance from the Ministry of Social Affairs (MSA). The sociological definition of poverty is open to serious criticisms. Among those criticisms is that it fails to define poverty objectively, because it implies that people are not poor unless they are recognized by a society as being poor by giving them social assistance. This is difficult to accept. Poverty signifies economic and social conditions in which the individual does not have enough income to meet the basic minimum needs of physical existence of food, clothing, and shelter. In these conditions, the individual must be defined as poor, no matter whether society recognize their poverty or not. Furthermore, a society may give different forms of assistance to people without considering them as poor, e.g. tax exemptions and grants (Jones 1990). Thus, dependence only on social assistance as a measure of poverty is deceiving; social assistance is a sufficient, but not a necessary, condition for poverty.

Subjective definition

The subjective definition of poverty has also been applied in Egypt, but on a very small scale. Radwan and Lee (1986), in their study of agrarian change in Egypt, acquired data on people's perceptions of their basic needs requirements through a one day interview with the inhabitants of a small village (fifteen houses), which was part of the 1977 International Labour Organization (ILO) sample survey. People's perception of the level of income they required to meet their basic needs was £E5 per capita per month in 1977, which comes very close to the poverty line estimate in the study, which is £E67 per capita annually (Radwan and Lee 1986: Appendix). This indicates the modest aspirations of rural people, which runs counter to what is expected from such a definition. One serious shortcoming of this subjective definition of poverty is that people's perceptions of their basic needs requirements are likely to give an overestimated income poverty line (Paul 1989).

Studies of poverty in Egypt

Basic needs approach

Adams (1985), Radwan and Lee (1986), the World Bank (1990b), and Korayem (1987a and 1994a) all estimated an income poverty line following the conventional basic needs approach, which entails first estimating the minimum food requirements needed for the individual and/or household (based on sufficient minimum intakes of calories and protein), and then estimating basic consumption expenditures on non-food items.

Differences exist between the income poverty lines estimated in the five studies. First, Adams and Radwan and Lee estimated the income poverty line in the rural sector only, while the World Bank[2] and Korayem estimated it for both rural and urban sectors. Second, Adams and Radwan and Lee used survey data (different surveys though[3]) in estimating the rural income poverty line in 1982 and in 1977, whereas Korayem used household budget survey (HBS) data for 1981/82 and the household income and expenditure survey (HIES) of 1990/91 in estimating the income poverty line. However, Adams used the HBS data for the rural poverty line estimate in 1958/59, 1964/65, and 1974/75. The poverty line estimates of urban and rural households in 1981/82 that are adopted by the World Bank are just an updating of the estimates for 1974/75 in Ibrahim's study (1982), using the official consumer price index. However, the urban poverty line estimate for 1974/75, and consequently for 1981/82, is subject to serious criticisms.[4] Third, the poverty line estimated by Adams and Radwan and Lee is actually an *expenditure* poverty line, because they did not account for any savings in their poverty line estimates. Korayem, in contrast, estimated the *income* poverty line – she accounted for the savings factor.[5] Fourth, Radwan and Lee and Korayem considered the age and sex structure of the average household in their estimation of the poverty line, whereas Adams ignored this factor. Fifth, because of the above differences, as well as the differences in the methods and prices used to estimate food costs, the studies came up with different estimates for the income poverty line and for the poverty level (see below).

The basic needs approach adopted by Adams, Radwan and Lee, the World Bank, and Korayem makes their estimates of the income poverty line subject to the shortcomings and limitations of this approach, as explained above. Moreover, estimating household expenditure at the poverty line by assuming that the size and age structure of the households follow the average national pattern, which is the case in Korayem's studies, is quite arbitrary because poor households are likely to be larger and to have a higher dependency ratio compared with the average household on the national level. By using survey data, Adams and Radwan and Lee minimized the arbitrariness of this factor in their poverty line estimates, because they derived household size from the sample data.

Relative income approach

El-Laithy and Kheir-El-Din (1994) and the Institute of National Planning Report (INP 1994) applied the relative income approach in estimating the poverty line in urban and rural sectors in Egypt in 1990/91, using HIES data.[6] El-Laithy and Kheir-El-Din defined the expenditure poverty line in urban and rural sectors at two-thirds of per capita expenditure in each sector as estimated from the HIES, while the INP defined the income poverty line in urban and rural sectors at 40 per cent and 30 per cent, respectively, of national per capita income. Both estimates are subject to the shortcomings of the relative income approach as cited above.

The sociological approach

As said before, Shawky (1989/90) applied the sociological definition of poverty, which defines as poor people those who are recognized by society as poor. Thus, the poor in Egypt were defined as those who receive social assistance from the MSA.

According to the MSA definition of poverty, the household income poverty line ranges from zero to £E100 a month.

Comparing the results of poverty estimates

The relative level of poverty

Comparing the relative level of poverty in Egypt – or the headcount index – as estimated by the above studies in the years 1974/75, 1981/82, and 1990/91, where comparable estimates exist, one finds the following.

In 1974/75, the percentage of rural households below the poverty line was estimated as 60.7 per cent by Adams (1985) and 50.9 per cent by Korayem (1987a). Radwan and Lee (1986) estimated the percentage of poor rural households in 1977 (which is close to 1974/75) as only 35 per cent according to their broader definition of poverty (i.e. excluding the "marginal" poor), while this percentage increased to 56 per cent according to the income poverty line definition.

For the 1981/82 estimates, the lowest estimated level of poverty is 10.3 per cent of the population, which represents the MSA beneficiaries (Shawky 1989/90),[7] and the highest estimates are those of Korayem, ranging between 29.7 and 43.0 per cent of rural households in scenarios A and B respectively, and between 30.4 and 44.4 per cent of urban households in the two scenarios.[8] In between fall the estimates of Adams (1985) and the World Bank (1990b). Adams estimated 17.8 per cent of rural households to be poor, while the World Bank estimates 24.2 per cent of rural households and 22.5 per cent of urban households for 1981/82.

For 1990/91, the poverty level in the urban sector is estimated at 29.2 per cent (El-Laithy and Kheir-El-Din 1993), 35.9 per cent according to Korayem's HED estimate (1994a),[9] and 39.7 per cent by the INP (1994) estimates. In the rural sector, the poverty level is estimated at 20.8 per cent by El-Laithy and Kheir-El-Din (1993), 31.6 per cent by the INP (1994), and 54.5 per cent (HED estimate) by Korayem.

Extreme poverty

Four studies have addressed the issue of extreme poverty in Egypt (El-Laithy and Kheir-El-Din 1994; INP 1994; Korayem

1994a; World Bank 1990b). The relative income approach is widely used in the literature to estimate extreme poverty. This conventional method has been applied by three out of the four studies: the World Bank, El-Laithy and Kheir-El-Din, and the INP.

The World Bank adopted Lipton's method of estimating the extremely poor as those whose expenditure on food is 80 per cent of the expenditure on food that is estimated to be required to meet the minimum individual calorie requirements (Lipton 1983). According to this definition, and using the HBS, the extremely poor were estimated as approximately 12.8 per cent of rural households and 10.8 per cent of urban households in 1981/82 (World Bank, 1990b: 9 and Annex K). These World Bank estimates of the extremely poor, especially the estimate of the urban extremely poor, are quite close to the estimate of poverty provided in Shawky (1989/90).[10] El-Laithy and Kheir-El-Din estimated the extreme poverty expenditure line in urban and rural sectors in 1990/91 as one-third of per capita expenditure in each sector as derived from the HIES. The INP (1994) estimated an extreme poverty income line for Egypt for 1990/91[11] as 25 per cent of the national per capita income for urban and rural sectors.

The fourth study (Korayem 1994a) applied a different methodology in estimating extreme poverty in Egypt. Here it was argued that the estimated extreme poverty income line has to fulfil two constraints: to be at the lowest possible level below the income poverty line, and at the same time to be above the starvation level of income. Since there is no guarantee that the arbitrarily defined level of relative income is high enough to meet the second constraint, the relative income approach is rejected. The extreme poverty income line is estimated on the basis of the least-cost diet planned in the study of urban and rural households.[12] Because of the impossibility of eating one diet all year, estimating the extreme poverty income line on the basis of the cost of one diet only implies that, for most days of the year, the destitute eat poor diets in terms of calories and protein intake. In this way it is guaranteed that the estimated extreme poverty income line will be above the starvation level and at the same time at the lowest level possible below the poverty line.

The extremely poor in 1990/91 were estimated by El-Laithy and Kheir-El-Din (1994) at 4.7 per cent of urban households and 5.0 per cent of rural households, by the INP (1994) at 6.5 per cent and 8.7 per cent of urban and rural households, respectively, and by Korayem (1994a) as 0.5 per cent of urban households and 22.2 per cent of rural households (HED estimate).[13] The three studies that have estimated poverty and extreme poverty at the level of the governorates, using the HIES of 1990/91, came to the conclusion that Upper Egypt has the highest poverty and extreme poverty levels compared with Lower Egypt and the urban governorates.

Other dimensions of poverty

Apart from the selection of the poverty line itself, few indices have been developed in the literature that reflect three other dimensions of poverty: the incidence of poverty (measured by the head-count ratio), the intensity of poverty (measured by the poverty gap), and the degree of inequality among the poor (Foster et al. 1984; Grootaert and Kanbur 1990; Haagenaars 1987; Sen 1976; World Bank 1990a). Sen's index was estimated by Adams (1985) and Radwan and Lee (1986) using detailed survey data, while Foster's index was estimated by El-Laithy and Kheir-El-Din (1994) using the preliminary data of the HIES for 1990/91. The Sen index estimates by Adams, and by Radwan and Lee for 1974/75 and 1977, which are the two closest years that could be used for comparison, differ considerably. Sen's index of poverty in rural Egypt as estimated by Adams in 1974/75 was 0.212, whereas the estimated index by Radwan and Lee in 1977 was 0.113, which is almost half Adams' estimates. This shows how sensitive the value of those indices is to the data used.

The poverty gap was estimated for the rural sector by Adams (1985) and by Radwan and Lee (1986), and for both urban and rural sectors by Korayem (1990b, 1994a). Significant differences are found in the average poverty gap estimates. Comparing the estimates in the two closest years, 1974/75 and 1977, it is found that Adams' estimate of the average poverty gap per adult unit equivalent (AUE) per year was £E30.5 in 1974/75, whereas Radwan and Lee's estimate for 1977 was £E19.4. To assess the impact of alternative policy packages on poverty, Korayem (1990b) estimated the poverty gap in 1983/84 using a general equilibrium model for Egypt (GEMET);[14] the estimated poverty gap was £E979.8 million in the rural sector and £E1467.2 million in the urban sector. The poverty gap and the income gap ratio[15] have also been estimated for 1990/91 by Korayem (1994a) using the conventional method. The poverty gap was £E1827.8 million in the urban sector and £E1991.7 million in the rural sector, while the income gap ratio was 75.8 per cent in the urban sector and 85.3 per cent in the rural sector. Both indices show that poverty was more acute in the rural sector compared with the urban sector in 1990/91.

The main features of poverty and how the poor adapt

In reviewing the literature on poverty in Egypt, one may point to three issues that describe the main features of the Egyptian poor. The characteristics of the poor; sources of income for the poor; and how the poor are adapting to the state of poverty.

The characteristics of the poor

Some of the literature on poverty in Egypt has discussed the characteristics of the poor as a group (El-Laithy and Kheir-El-Din 1994; World Bank 1990b; Radwan and Lee 1986), while other studies deal with the characteristics separately, depending on the subject under discussion (Korayem 1987a).

One of the common characteristics of the poor is malnutrition. It is not equally distributed with respect to sex and age, being more common among mothers and children.

Another characteristic of the poor is the relatively large household size compared with the non-poor. For example, in the 1977 ILO survey in the rural sector, it was found that the average size of poor households was 6.4 members compared with 5.3 members for the non-poor (Radwan and Lee 1986). This fact is also confirmed by other studies (Aazer et al. 1991; El-Laithy and Kheir-El-Din 1994; Oldham et al. 1987). The large size of poor households is accompanied by a high dependency ratio, indicating a bias in the household structure towards lower age groups (Radwan and Lee 1986).

Regarding the male/female structure of the poor households compared with non-poor households, Radwan and Lee (1986) found a slightly higher female/male ratio for poor households, while the World Bank (1990b) found no such difference. In other countries, it has been found that the female/male ratio is higher in poor households as a result of the fact that female-headed households have, in general, lower incomes than male-headed households (World Bank).

Another characteristic of the poor in Egypt, as in other countries, is the lack of assets, whether material assets (land, property, etc.) or human capital (e.g. education, skills). Data on the distribution of assets in the rural sector in Egypt can be derived from the 1977 ILO survey. This shows that the "definitely" poor group, who represented 35.3 per cent of rural households, owned 19.7 per cent of cultivated land, whereas the non-poor, who represented 44 per cent of households, owned

67.5 per cent of agricultural land. Besides, 25 per cent of the poor households who work in agriculture are landless. The distribution of non-agricultural assets (houses, the establishments, non-agricultural land, etc.) is also unequal (Radwan and Lee 1986).

There is a strong correlation between the incidence of poverty and the level of education. The World Bank study (1990b) shows that, generally speaking, the governorates in Egypt with a higher incidence of rural poverty have higher levels of illiteracy. Using the 1981/82 HBS data, it has been found that the highest poverty level is in households with an illiterate head; the incidence of poverty in this category is 41.4 per cent for urban households and 51.2 per cent for rural households (El-Laithy and Kheir-El-Din 1994). The 1977 ILO survey showed that whereas 95.4 per cent of the rural poor had not completed primary education, and could therefore be regarded as illiterate or semi-illiterate, this ratio fell to 87.6 per cent for the rural non-poor (Radwan and Lee 1986). This is also the case in the urban sector. In a study of eighteen squatter markets in Cairo, it was found that the illiteracy rate among the market vendors was substantially higher than the rate for the Cairo population as a whole – 52 per cent as against about 35 per cent (Tadros et al. 1990). Illiteracy and low education levels mean that the poor will be engaged in low-paid jobs, receiving low income and, hence, having less chance to educate their children. In this way, social mobility decreases and poverty is inherited generation after generation.

Finally, one of the characteristics of poor rural households that recent studies have revealed is the changing image of women's work. Women's work, which used to be common and acceptable in the rural Egyptian society, is not so anymore; it is taken as a sign of poverty (Abaza 1987).

Income sources for the poor

One may distinguish two approaches to income sources in the literature on poverty in Egypt, depending mainly on whether the study is sociological or economic. The sociological approach tends to focus on a group of people who share a common low-income activity (vendors, landless labourers, etc.) or on poor residential districts; in either case it studies the socioeconomic factors of the people involved (Aazer and Esshak 1987; Oldham et al. 1987; Tadros et al. 1990). The economic approach focuses only on the economic activities that generate income equal to, or less than, a defined income poverty line (El-Laithy and Kheir-El-Din 1994; Korayem 1991; Radwan and Lee 1986).

Reviewing both types of literature, one may point out four well-defined types of low-income activity: the informal sector (e.g. vendors), the public sector (employees at second grade level and below), agricultural landless labour, and small agricultural land holders (less than 3 feddans). This list is by no means comprehensive. For example, another low-income source that is not covered in the literature, because of a lack of data, is old-property owners.

Other sources of income for the poor are the social assistance schemes administered by the Ministry of Social Affairs (MSA) and non-governmental organizations (NGOs). However, the social assistance given by the MSA to the poor is extremely low.[16] This is due to the relatively small budget assigned to the MSA, in spite of the large number of beneficiaries. The effectiveness of the NGOs is limited because of their relatively small budget; on the one hand, the subsidy that the NGOs receive from the MSA is small, and, on the other hand, they are subject to legal constraints regarding fund-raising to finance their activities (World Bank 1990b).

Remittances are another source of income for the poor. However, some studies show that the impact of remittances on poverty is small (Adams 1991; Radwan and Lee 1986), whereas others imply that they may represent an important source of income for the poor (Korayem 1986).

How the poor are adapting to poverty

Adaptation mechanisms

Five adaptation mechanisms have been identified (Korayem 1994b): clustering of the poor in certain residential districts; raising household revenue through earned incomes and other means; minimizing household expenditure; exercising solidarity; and the woman's role in managing the household's life.

The clustering of the poor in certain districts helps them to survive financial hardship (such as events that call for additional expenses), whether this is caused by a mishap (such as death) or a happy event (such as marriage) or even an unexpected social event (such as an unexpected guest at meal time).

Because of the widespread illiteracy and the low educational level of the poor in general, many of them are engaged in low-paid and temporary jobs. The poor adapt to this situation by several means. On the one hand, they try to increase their earned income (e.g. by working longer hours or having more than one job). On the other hand, they try to get additional intermittent revenue by ways other than work (selling some of their belongings, borrowing, etc.).

Household expenditure can be minimized by several means, e.g. sharing a house with other household(s); buying defective low-priced items (e.g. perishable vegetables and fruit, defective textiles, used clothes); decreasing expenditure on health by reducing the dosage of a medicine below what is prescribed by the doctor to make the medicine last longer, and so on.

Different forms of solidarity exist among the poor and enable them to cope with the hardships of poverty: solidarity between household members, between relatives, within the community, and within the society as a whole.

One of the important means of coping with poverty is the vital role that the woman plays, as a wife and mother, in the survival of her family. For example, it is the woman who makes the small income cover the household's needs; and she is the one who takes reponsibility for finding ways to get an income to feed her children (by working, or selling some of her belongings, or borrowing) when the father is unemployed or just walks away from his family responsibilities.

Adjusting to a fall in real income

When real income falls, substitution takes place between food and non-food expenditures, between food items, and between non-food items. Given the already low expenditure on non-food items by the poor, how do they adjust if their incomes fall and/or prices rise? The question is answered by estimating the expenditure and price elasticities of seven main non-food items for the poor: housing and utilities, clothing, transportation, health, education, cigarettes (and tobacco) and beverages, and furniture and household appliances. Expenditure on these seven items represents more than 75 per cent of total expenditure on non-food items of households on the poverty line and below in both urban and rural sectors.

Estimating the expenditure elasticity for those items, it has been found that, when the income of the urban poor falls, the relatively largest cut in spending will be on education and the relatively smallest reduction will be on housing and utilities, and then on health. For the rural poor, the relatively larger cut in spending will be on furniture and household appliances and on education, while the relatively smallest cut will be in expenditure on housing and utilities, then in expenditure on cigarettes (and tobacco) and beverages, and thirdly in expenditure on health.

The price elasticities of the non-food items were estimated assuming that the substitution effect is zero. The values were considerably low (Korayem 1994b).

The effects of poverty

The effects of poverty are addressed explicitly by one study, but only with respect to the impact on children and health (Korayem 1987a). The consequences of poverty for children are manifold. The poor housing and sanitary conditions in which poor children grow up expose them to health hazards that make them vulnerable to diseases and increase child mortality. For example, the child mortality risk is nearly three times as great in the lowest social class compared with the highest class (Shorter 1989).

Child labour is another important effect of poverty. All the literature based on field surveys that has discussed this phenomenon in Egypt points to poverty as the main cause (Abdellatif and Mohamed 1990; Besheer 1991), or one of the main causes (Aazer et al. 1991; UNICEF 1990) of child labour. Many of the children work in industrial jobs without protective measures,[17] which exposes them to injury and ill-health. An important negative aspect of child labour is the spread of illiteracy among children: over 50 per cent of the working children in the samples were illiterate (Abdellatif and Mohamed 1990; Besheer 1991). Illiteracy will probably be carried with them into their adulthood in most cases.

Infant and child mortality is the most common indicator of the strong direct link between health and poverty. Several studies demonstrated a positive relationship between a high rate of infant and child mortality and poor living conditions, a low educational level (especially of mothers), and the rural–urban population distribution (Korayem 1987a; Sayed et al. 1989; Shorter 1989; World Bank 1990b). The strong correlation between poverty and poor health is also indicated by the extent of stunting of poor children compared with well-fed children. Stunting, which is measured by height-for-age, is associated with poor overall economic conditions and is ten times the level expected in a well-fed population (Sayed et al. 1989)

The unfavourable health conditions of poor children applies also to poor adults in Egypt. The poorest section in the population is usually exposed to high morbidity and to chronic infections and parasitic diseases (World Bank 1990b). Unsafe water supplies in the rural areas and in poor urban districts increase the risk of exposure to serious diseases such as typhoid, paratyphoid, and infectious hepatitis.

Structural adjustment and the poor

The effects of structural adjustment and stabilization policies on the poor

The main components of the structural adjustment and stabilization policies in Egypt are: currency devaluation, liberalization of international trade, raising the price of utilities, reducing subsidies, and applying tight monetary and fiscal policies.

One may distinguish two approaches in the literature on the effects of structural adjustment and the stabilization package on the poor in Egypt. The first approach divides society into groups and analyses the impact of the stabilization package on each of those groups; the impact on the poor is dealt with as a side issue (World Bank 1990b). The second approach examines the effects on the poor as one group (Korayem 1987a, 1990b, 1994b). In spite of the different approaches adopted, all agree that the poor will suffer and that something should be done to minimize the social cost involved.

As postulated by the World Bank (1990b), adjustment measures can affect the population via three means: incomes, consumption, and public services received. Accordingly, the study divided society into three groups – producers, consumers, and the beneficiaries of government social services – and assessed the impact of stabilization on them. When assessing the impact of the policy package on consumers, the study discusses the impact on the poor. It anticipated that the reduction in food subsidies would have a negative effect on the bulk of the population, especially the poor, who spend a large share of their budget on food. The study also argued that the planned increase in the prices of water, electricity, fuel products, and transportation would have diverse effects on the poor depending on the goods and services under consideration. For example, the increase in the prices of utilities would hurt the urban poor, but would not affect the rural poor because most rural households have no access to piped water and electricity. The study also anticipated that the cuts in government expenditure under the stabilization measures would entail a further decrease in the per capita expenditure of the Ministries of Social Affairs, Education, and Health, which would hurt the bulk of the population, especially the poor. However, the study emphasized that the social costs would have been higher if structural adjustment had not been implemented.

Korayem (1987a) examined the effects of the stabilization measures on the economy in general, with special focus on the impact on the poor. Currency devaluation, the elimination of subsidies, and cuts in government expenditures on investment and wages hurt the poor the most. This is because the poor spend a large portion of their budget on subsidized food commodities; in addition, a large share of those commodities is imported and hence their prices would be raised by devaluation. Also, the cuts in government expenditures on wages and investment would decrease job creation in the public sector at a time when job creation was not increasing in the private sector, owing to the contractionary policy applied. These measures have a larger negative impact on the employment of the poor, who are disadvantaged because of their low educational level and poor social contacts.

In another study, Korayem (1990b) compared the impact of the IMF stabilization package on poverty with alternative policy packages, using a simple general equilibrium model for Egypt (GEMET). Six policy scenarios, including the IMF policy package, were applied with different combinations of tight and moderate measures of fiscal, external, and monetary policies. It was found that the two strongly contractionary policy scenarios (the IMF package is one of them) gave the relatively worst impact on poverty, measured by the level of absolute poverty and the size of the poverty gap.

Korayem (1994b) assessed the impact on the poor of the economic reform and stabilization package (ERSAP) applied in Egypt since 1991/92. She pointed out three types of policy in ERSAP, and examined the impact of each on the poor. These are: (i) the macroeconomic policies, which affect the poor and the population in general through their impact on prices, employment creation, and income distribution; (ii) policies designed specifically to support the poor (the Social Safety Net and the Social Fund); and (iii) policies affecting the provision of subsidized social services by the government (specifically education and health services).

Poverty alleviation measures during adjustment

Two studies have proposed measures to alleviate poverty during structural adjustment (World Bank 1990b; Korayem 1994b), while another study offered an alternative adjustment package, instead of the IMF package, which aimed to minimize the negative impact on the poor (Korayem 1987a).

The elements of the poverty alleviation strategy proposed by the World Bank (1990b) are:

- measures to increase the income-earning opportunities of the poor by increasing their access to employment and assets;
- measures to improve the effectiveness of public expenditures in health and education in order to increase the poor's opportunities for human capital formation;
- measures to achieve effective targeting of all secondary income transfers (consumer and producer subsidies, and direct welfare transfers);
- the creation of an Emergency Social Fund to foster the above efforts and to protect the low-income population from the negative impact of adjustment measures.

Korayem (1994b) suggested different measures to reduce poverty within the three approaches proposed by the World Bank: the economic approach, the human capital approach, and the welfare approach. The economic approach deals with measures that increase the access of the poor to productive employment and assets; the human capital approach includes measures that increase investment in human capital to promote the productive potential of the poor (such as investment in education, training, and health); and the welfare approach depends on measures that cope with poverty through transfer payments and subsidies.

Korayem (1987a) offered an alternative adjustment programme that was anticipated to reduce the negative impact on the poor as compared with the IMF package. It was argued that the IMF adjustment programme is directed mainly to reducing aggregate demand and restoring balance between the demand and supply sides of the economy at a lower level of national income. The proposed alternative package operated mainly on the supply side by increasing the productive capacity of the economy.

Gaps in poverty research in Egypt

None of the available studies explores the dynamics of poverty in Egypt. The main reason for this is the non-availabilty of data. To analyse the dynamics of poverty in Egypt, detailed information would need to be collected on a sample of households over an extended period of time. Longitudinal surveys, which interview the same people over a number of years, are the best source of information on the dynamics of poverty (Klein and Rones 1989).

A second best to the longitudinal surveys, which will save on cost and time, is to design a cross-generational sample survey, i.e. a sample survey that includes three generations. Applying the longitudinal surveys or the suggested cross-generational surveys in order to estimate the dynamics of poverty in Egypt will reveal how much of poverty is transitory and how much is permanent. This may show that the currently available single-year estimates of absolute and relative poverty overestimate the state of poverty in Egypt, because part of it may be just transitory. It has been found in other studies that the static estimate of poverty is usually greater by about one-third than the dynamic estimate of poverty (Klein and Rones 1989; Smith 1989; World Bank 1990c). The estimation and analysis of the dynamics of poverty in Egypt are important areas of research that are still unexplored.

NOTES

1. Radwan and Lee (1986) used a second criterion in addition to the income poverty line to differentiate between the poor and the non-poor according to a broader definition of poverty. This criterion is nutritional deficiency, which means the shortfall (or surplus) between calorie intake and calorie requirements. Depending on the two criteria, they differentiated between two groups among the rural households whose income falls below the estimated income poverty line: (i) the "definitely" poor, who suffer from nutritional deficiency as well as income deficiency, and (ii) the "marginal" poor, who satisfy their nutritional requirements but suffer from income deficiency.
2. In this study, the poverty line estimates of Ghattas, which were made in an earlier unpublished World Bank study (1989), were adopted.
3. Adams used the data of the 1982 consumer budget survey undertaken by the International Food Policy Research Institute (IFPRI), while Radwan and Lee used the data of the 1977 ILO survey; both surveys are carried out in rural areas.
4. The urban poverty line in 1974/75 is estimated by just increasing the rural poverty line by 30 per cent! For an assessment of the poverty line estimates adopted by the World Bank, see Korayem (1993).
5. On the poverty line, some savings may take place to provide funds for future needs (such as getting married), or to meet extra expenses for unexpected events (such as becoming sick), or to make "GAMIAH", which is an organized form of collective savings to get a total sum of money to meet a household's needs (such as buying a durable consumption good, or paying key money for a place to live in, etc.). Thus, saving at the income poverty line exists, but should

be considered as "postponed" consumption and not as a source of investment.
6. The two studies used different sets of data, though. El-Laithy and Kheir-El-Din used preliminary estimates for HIES data, while the INP used a semi-final set of HIES data.
7. The estimate in Shawky refers to the financial year 1982/83.
8. Korayem provided two estimates (scenarios A and B) for the income poverty line, and hence for the level of poverty, in urban and rural Egypt in 1981/82. In scenario A, official prices were used in calculating food costs at the poverty line, while in scenario B food costs were calculated at prices 20 per cent higher than the official prices because, it was argued, official prices are unrealistically low.
9. Korayem provided one estimate for the income poverty line in each of the urban and rural sectors, and two estimates for each sector for the head-count index (or relative poverty): the HED estimate and the HID estimate. The HED estimate refers to relative poverty when the households' expenditure brackets are used, while the HID estimate refers to relative poverty when the households' income brackets are used; both sets of data are taken from the HIES 1990/91. For comparison with other estimates, we are using the HED estimate because it seems more reliable. This is because, generally speaking, expenditure data are expected to be more reliable compared with income data, and also because of the exclusion of remittances in the income questionnaire, whereas the expenditure data implicitly include the part of remittances that is spent on consumption.
10. Shawky argues that "the MSA in Egypt concentrates on the poorest of the poor and not the poor" (Shawky 1989/90: 18).
11. Although the estimates in the INP report are put under the year 1990, they belong to the financial year 1990/91, because the report is using the HIES data of 1990/91, as mentioned in the text.
12. The estimate of the poverty line was based on the average cost of six planned diets that meet the safe level of calories and protein intake for urban and rural households.
13. The HID estimate for the extremely poor is 6.6 per cent of urban households and 7.3 per cent of rural households (Korayem 1994a).
14. The poverty gap for Egypt has been estimated using actual data for 1983/84, which form the base scenario; then other estimates for the poverty gap have been provided by GEMET using different policy scenarios and compared with the actual gap in the base scenario to find out which policy scenario(s) gives the lowest poverty gap.
15. The income gap ratio = average income of the poor/income poverty line.
16. For example, the total average payment for the individual in 1988/89 was £E57 annually, which is approximately half the statutory pension, which amounts to £E10 monthly (World Bank 1990b).
17. For example, 91 per cent of the working children surveyed did not use any protective clothing or equipment (UNICEF 1990).

Bibliography

Aazer, A. and T. Esshak (1987). *The Marginalised*. Cairo: National Center for Social and Criminological Research (in Arabic).

Aazer, A., N. Ramzi, A. Korayem, and O. Mostafa (1991). *Child Labour Phenomenon*. Cairo: National Center for Social and Criminological Research, and UNICEF (in Arabic).

Abaza, M. (1987). The changing image of women in rural Egypt. *Cairo Papers in Social Science*. Vol. 10, Monograph 3, Autumn.

Abdel-Khalek, G. (1987). *Stabilization and Adjustment Policies and Programmes: Country Study, Egypt*. Finland: World Institute for Development Economics Research of the United Nations University (WIDER).

Abdellatif, S. O. and A. E. Mohamed (1990). *The Arab Family, Reality and Requirements*. Cairo: High Institute for Social Work (in Arabic).

Adams, Jr, R. H. (1985). "Development and structural change in rural Egypt, 1952 to 1982". *World Development*, 13(6). (1991). *The Effects of International Remittances on Poverty, Inequality, and Development in Rural Egypt*. Washington DC: International Food Policy Research Institute.

Behrman, J. R. and A. B. Deolalikar (1991). "The poor and the social sectors during a period of macroeconomic adjustment: Empirical evidence for Jamaica". *World Bank Economic Review*, 5(2).

Besheer, A. Y. M. (1991). "Towards planning indicators to meet child labour phenomenon in the Egyptian society." *The Egyptian Child and the Challenge of the Twenty First Century*. Proceedings of the Fourth Annual Conference on the Egyptian Child, vol. 3, 27–30, April. Cairo (in Arabic).

Boateng, E. O. et al. (1990). *A Poverty Profile for Ghana, 1987–88*. Washington DC: World Bank SDA Working Paper

Center for Economic and Financial Reseach and Studies (Cairo University) (n.d.) *An Assessment of the Economics of Income-Generating Activities Undertaken by Rural Women in Egypt*. Egypt: A Report Presented to the United Nations Children's Fund (UNICEF).

Edmundson, I. C. and P. V. Sukhatme (1990). "Food and work: Poverty and hunger?" *Economic Development and Cultural Change*, 38(2)

El-Aassar, K. (1991). *Agricultural Labor Market in Egypt During the Seventies*. Cairo (in Arabic).

El-Laithy, H. and H. Kheir-El-Din (1994). "Assessment of poverty in Egypt using household data". in G. Abdel-Khalek and H. Kheir-El-Din (eds), *Economic Reform and its Distributive Impact*. Proceedings of the Economics Department's Conference, Faculty of Economics and Political Science. Cairo University, 21–22 November 1992.

Foster, J., J. Green, and E. Thorbecke (1984). "A class of decomposable poverty measures". *Econometrica*, 52.

Gittinger, J. P. et al. (1990). *Household Food Security and the Role of Women*. Washington, DC: World Bank Discussion Papers.

Glewwe, P. and J. Van Der Gaag (1990). "Identifying the poor in developing countries: Do different definitions matter?" *World Development*, 18(6).

Grootaert, C. and R. Kanbur (1990). *Policy-Oriented Analysis of Poverty and the Social Dimensions of Structural Adjustment*. Washington, DC: World Bank, SDA Working Paper

Grootaert, C. et al. (1991). *The Social Dimensions of Adjustment Priority Survey: An Instrument for the Rapid Identification and Monitoring of Policy Target Groups*. Washington, DC: World Bank SDA Working Paper

Hagenaars, A. (1987). "A class of poverty indices". *International Economic Review*, 28 (October).

Hagenaars, A. and K. de Vos (1988). "The definition and measurement of poverty". *Journal of Human Resources*, 23(2).

Hansen, B. and S. Radwan (1982). *Employment Opportunities and Equity in a Changing Economy: Egypt in the 1980s, A Labour Market Approach*. Geneva: International Labour Office.

Ibrahim, S. E. (1982). "Social mobility and income distribution in Egypt, 1952–1977". in G. Abdel-Khalek and R. Tignor (eds), *The Political Economy of Income Distribution in Egypt*. New York: Holmes and Meier Publishers

(INP) Institute of National Planning (1994). *Egypt: Human Development Report 1994*. Cairo: Institute of National Planning.

International Environment Quality Office (n.d.) *Income Generating Program for Women Headed Families (Mansheat Nasser-Cairo)*. Cairo (in Arabic).

Jones, J. D. (1990). *Poverty and the Human Condition: A Philosophical Inquiry*. UK: The Edwin Meller Press.

Kanbur, R. (1990). *Poverty and the Social Dimensions of Structural Adjustment in Cote d'Ivoire*. Washington, DC: World Bank SDA Working Paper

Klein, B. W. and P. Rones (1989). "A profile of the working poor". *Monthly Labour Review*. 112 (October).

Korayem, K. (1986). "The economic impact of labour migration on rural Egypt". *L'Egypte Contemporaine*. 77 (April) (in Arabic).

——— (1987a) *The Impact of Economic Adjustment Policies on the Vulnerable Families and Children in Egypt*. Cairo: The Third World Forum (Middle East Office) and the United Nations Children's Fund (UNICEF).

——— (1987b) "Fiscal policy and income distribution in urban Egypt". *L'Egypte Contemporaine*, 78 (July and October) (in Arabic).

——— (1990a) "Adjustment and equitable growth: the case of Egypt". A study prepared for the Organization for Economic Cooperation and Development (OECD), January, unpublished.

——— (1990b). "The impact of adjustment measures on income and on poverty in Egypt: A Model Specification". *Statistics and Computer Modelling in Human Sciences*. Proceedings of the Second Annual Conference of the Center for Information and Computer Systems

(CICS), Faculty of Economics and Political Science, Cairo University.

——— (1991) *The Eyptian Economy and the Poor in the Eighties (Main Features and the Identification of the Poor)*. Cairo: Institute of National Planning, Memo No. 1542.

——— (1993) *Poverty in Egypt (Literature Review; 1985–1991)*. Center for Economic and Financial Research and Studies, Faculty of Economics and Political Science, Cairo University.

——— (1994a) *Poverty and Income Distribution in Egypt*. Cairo: Third World Forum (Middle East Office).

——— (1994b) The impact of structural adjustment and stabilization policies on the poor in Egypt, and how do they adapt. *Cairo Papers in Social Science*, The American University in Cairo (AUC), forthcoming publication.

Kyereme, S. and E. Thorbecke (1987) "Food poverty and decomposition applied to Ghana". *World Development*. 15(9).

Lipton, M. (1983) *Poverty, Undernutrition, and Hunger*. Washington, DC: World Bank Staff Working Papers No. 597.

Loza, S. F. (1987) "An exploratory study on the child's value in a rural society". *Population Studies*. 13 (March) (in Arabic).

Mahmoud, N. Y. K. (1991) "Preschool education for the children of poor families". *The Egyptian Child and the Challenge of the Twenty First Century*. Proceedings of the Fourth Annual Conference on the Egyptian Child, vol. 3, 27–30 April, Cairo (in Arabic).

National Center for Social and Criminological Research, and the United Nations Children's Fund (UNICEF) (1989) *Report of the Interministerial Committee on Child Labour in Egypt*. October.

Newman, J. et al. (1991) "How did workers benefit from Bolivia's Emergency Social Fund". *World Bank Economic Review*, 5(2).

Oldman, L., N. El-Hadidi, and H. Tamaa (1987) "Informal communities in Cairo: The basis of a typology". *Cairo Papers in Social Science*, vol. 10, Monograph 4, Winter.

Paul, S. (1989) "A model of constructing the poverty line". *Journal of Development Economics* 30 (January).

Radwan, S. (1977) *Agrarian Reform and Rural Poverty: Egypt, 1952–1975*. Geneva: International Labour Office.

Radwan, S. and E. Lee (1986) *Agrarian Change in Egypt: An Anatomy of Rural Poverty*. London: Croom Helm.

Ramzy, N. and A. Aazer (1990) "Child Labour". *National Journal of Sociology*, 27 (September) National Center for Social and Criminological Research, Cairo.

Sahn, D. E. and A. Sarris (1991) "Structural adjustment and the welfare of rural smallholders: A comparative analysis from sub-Saharan Africa". *World Bank Economic Review*, 5(2).

Sayed, H. A., M. I. Osman, F. El-Zanaty, and A. A. Way (1989) *Egypt Demographic Survey*. Cairo: National Population Council, and Maryland, USA: Institute for Resource Development Macro Systems.

Sen, A. (1976) "Poverty: An ordinal approach to measurement". *Econometrica*, 44(2).
Shawky, A. M. (1986) "The Childcare in the Poor Families in Egypt". Cairo: Third World Forum, unpublished.
(1989/90) "Structural adjustment in social welfare sector". A study prepared for the Third World Forum and the United Nations Children's Fund (UNICEF), unpublished.
Shorter, F. (1989) "Cairo's leap forward: People, households, and dwelling space". *Cairo Papers in Social Science*, vol. 12, Monograph 1, Spring.
Shoukry, A. A. (1993) "Poverty and adaptation mechanism: A sociological perspective of the studies on Egypt in the eighties". A study prepared for the Third World Forum and UNICEF, November, unpublished. (in Arabic).
Smith, J. P. (1989) "Children among the poor". *Demography*, 26 (May).
Soliman, A. A. (1987) *An Analytical Study for the Health Services in the Governorates of the Arab Republic of Egypt*. Cairo: Institute of National Planning, Memo No. 1432 (in Arabic).
Squire, L. (1991) "Introduction: Poverty and adjustment in the 1980's". *World Bank Economic Review*, 5(2).
Tadros, E. R., M. Feteeha, and A. Hibbard (1990) "Squatter markets in Cairo". *Cairo Papers in Social Science*, vol. 13, Monograph 1, Spring.
UNICEF (United Nations Children's Fund) (1988) *Veterinary Report on Income-Generating Activities of the Rural Women Project*. Cairo, July.
——— (1990) *Child Labour in Cairo*. Cairo, May.
United Nations, Economic and Social Commission for West Asia (n.d.) *Exploratory Study on the Characteristics and Problems of Women in the Informal Sector in a Poor District in Cairo City*. Studies on Arab Women in Development No. 15 (in Arabic).
Van Praag, B. M. S. and M. R. Baye (1990) "The poverty concept when prices are income-dependent". *Journal of Econometrics*, 43(1–2).
World Bank (1989) "Arab Republic of Egypt: A study on poverty and the distribution of income". A Draft Report of the Country Operations Division, CD111, EMENA, 5, January unpublished.
——— (1990a) *Making Adjustment Work for the Poor. A Framework for Policy Reform in Africa*.
——— (1990b) *Poverty Alleviation and Adjustment in Egypt*. 6 June.
——— (1990c) *Poverty. World Development Report 1990*.

Chapter 12

Anglophone West Africa: Poverty Without Research

Dayo Akeredolu-Ale

The coverage of this review

Only two countries of Anglophone West Africa, namely Nigeria and Ghana, are covered in some depth. Incidentally, these two countries together account for over 94 per cent of the total estimated population of Anglophone West Africa. However, certain indicators (notably, life expectancy at birth, infant mortality rate, under 5 years mortality rate, and percentage of adult population literate) seem to suggest that the poverty pattern in the three countries not covered in depth (Sierra Leone, Liberia and The Gambia) may be significantly different from that in either or both of Nigeria and Ghana.

Profiles of poverty research in Anglophone West Africa

Introduction

For this sub-region, 1983 represents a rough but meaningful demarcation for assessing poverty research. Whatever poverty or poverty-related research was done before that year reflected above all the perceptions, development strategies, and priorities of the governments of the countries concerned and the intellectual perspectives of their research communities. Research after 1983 reflects, very largely, the effects and exigencies of economic reform programmes imposed from outside in the context of economic and political globalization.

The demarcation is particularly meaningful because globalization here represents a definite move to establish and institutionalize in the countries concerned the core values of economic and political liberalism, as well as the orientations and institutional tendencies that go with them. Thus, concepts of poverty, theories of poverty, attitudes and approaches to poverty reduction, as well as the orientations and trajectory of poverty research itself – all these are now crystallizing in these countries as integral parts of the agenda of global economic and political liberalization.

Nigeria

Scope of poverty research and data situation

The 1975 Annual Conference of the Nigerian Economic Society (NES), reported in the book, *Poverty in Nigeria* (NES 1975), represents a watershed in the history of poverty research in Nigeria because it raised many important questions regarding the poverty situation in the country and indicated an agenda for future work on the subject. Also, in the context of mainstream public administration, the Federal Office of Statistics (FOS) had been involved in the conduct of household surveys since the early 1950s and had formally launched the National Integrated Survey of Households (NISH) in June 1980 under the National Household Surveys Capability Programme (NHSCP) sponsored by the United Nations.

Thus, to some extent, poverty had been indicated for the research agenda of the academic community by 1975. By 1980, the FOS had firmly embarked upon a special programme to generate data that could be used for poverty research. However, the truth is that very few, if any, further empirical studies of poverty have been done in Nigeria since the 1975 NES conference, though there has been some further academic research on the related subjects of income distribution and social service distribution. The FOS has also pressed on with the NISH and generated a vast amount of data, for example, on household structure, household economic–production activities, household income and expenditure, employment, health/nutrition, and housing conditions.

NISH, as the details provided in Table 12.1 show, is designed to be a comprehensive system of national economic, social, and demographic statistics. As such, an effective NISH programme will constitute a very rich source of systematic data for the study and analysis of poverty patterns.

From the information available from each module, the data generated by the following could be very relevant in poverty research:

Table 12.1 NISH modules and their implementation, 1980/81–1992/93

Survey Module	
1. General Household Survey (GHS)	x x x x x x x x x x x x x
2. National Consumer Survey (NCS)	x x x x x x x x x[a]
3. Rural Agricultural Sample Survey (RASS)	x x x x x x x x x x x x x
4. Health and Nutritional Status Survey (HANSS)	x
5. Survey of Housing Status (SHS)	x
6. Labour Force Survey (LFS)	x x x x x x x x x x
7. National Agricultural Sample Census (NASC)	
8. Survey of Internal Migration	x
9. Survey of Household Enterprises (SHE)	x
10. National Demographic and Health Survey (NDHS)	x
11. Consumer Shuttle Survey	x
12. Family Planning Survey	x

Source: Compiled from Federal Republic of Nigeria (1992: Tables on pp. 2 and 10).
Notes:
x = Module implemented.
[a] This survey, which ought to have come up in 1990/91, was postponed. Fieldwork began in 1992.

- GHS, which generates basic data on demographic characteristics, education, employment, health, housing, household enterprise, income, etc. from each individual member of sampled households.
- NCS, which generates basic data on consumption patterns.
- NDHS, which generates basic data on a wide range of relevant variables, including housing characteristics, household durable goods, infant and child mortality, prevalence of certain

diseases, access to certain health services, household population structure, household composition, current/total fertility rate, school enrolment, and so on.
- SHE, which generates basic data on types of household enterprises as well as purchases, receipts, and number of persons engaged by such enterprises.

These particular modules seem to have done fairly well in terms of the regularity with which the surveys relating to them have been conducted. The GHS has been conducted every year since 1980/81. The NCS was conducted every year from 1980/81 to 1985/86. Now it is planned to be done on a five-yearly basis; the 1990/91 survey was postponed to 1992/93 and the next survey is scheduled for 1997/98. The NDHS was conducted for the first time in 1990 and the repeat, which is planned for 1995/96, is expected to cover the general health status of the population even more fully than was done in the 1990 survey. The SHE was run as a component of the National Census of Industries and Businesses (NCIB) in 1988/89, but the NISH 1993–98 work programme envisaged a strong SHE component of GHS in 1994/95 in what FOS expected to be "a major contribution to the study of the informal sector".

There are, however, certain important operational problems that must have implications for the suitability of FOS-based NISH as a possible major source of data for poverty research. Among such problems are the recent reductions in the sample size, principally to reduce the cost of data collection, the pile-up of field data awaiting analysis, and the resulting delay of publications.

Concepts, theoretical orientations, and major findings

Poverty as such did not feature prominently or consistently in Nigeria before 1975, either as an important issue of public policy or as a subject of serious academic research. In fact, the 1975 NES conference remains the only forum to date at which poverty in Nigeria has been discussed seriously as a distinct subject of academic enquiry and as a distinct issue of public policy.

The conference examined the questions of the definition and identification of poverty, and the availability and quality of data required for testing whatever hypotheses there are regarding causation, as well as for assessing the impact of poverty-reduction policies and measures.

With respect to the definition of poverty, the conference noted that poverty is a complex phenomenon, often not amenable to objective definition or assessment. It noted also the need to examine critically the validity and relevance of existing methods by which the incidence of poverty is commonly determined. Even more specifically, it was argued that the concept of poverty is largely independent of and stretches well beyond that of personal income and expenditure; that "a full and proper appreciation of poverty within a society must be seen in the context of access to all forms of resources and facilities provided by or within a nation" (Aboyade 1975: 31). It was also argued that the appropriate research procedure would be a statistical survey that had as little perception of a "poverty line" as possible, but included as many as possible of the socioeconomic variables that are likely to be important for analytical and policy controls.

Furthermore, the conference identified a possible alternative to the poverty-line approach, similar to Galbraith's "island" and "case" types (Aboyade 1975: 34); it stressed the need to recognize a distinct urban and spatio-cultural dimension to the concept of poverty (Mabogunje 1975: 71); it considered an outline of a possible theoretical framework for the systematic study of poverty; and it identified many probable causes of poverty in Nigeria, such as the slow rate of economic growth, the exclusion of large segments of the population from the processes and benefits of growth, market imperfections that discriminate systematically against low-income groups (Edozien 1975: 38–41), and a high degree of income/wealth inequalities that the power structure has tended to sustain and exacerbate (Akeredolu-Ale 1975: esp. 55–8; Onimode 1975: 335–48; and Abubakar 1975: 177–90). In all this, social stratification seems to be of critical importance. The established structures of inequality (economic, political, and social) reproduce and determine the life chances of particular groups and individuals.

At least four main factors have been reported repeatedly as explanations of widespread poverty (mass poverty) and of its persistence in Nigeria: the poor growth performance of the national economy; non-participation of the poor in the limited economic growth processes available; inadequate public policies; and national economic disabilities associated with dependency. And, of course, many other lower-order factors have been reported as explanations of each of these main causes of mass poverty.

However, given the characteristics of the studies and data on which these findings are based, the findings themselves can only be regarded as tentative and only as a possible basis for hypotheses to be tested more rigorously in future studies. There has been no specific anti-poverty focus in public policy, and this has adversely affected the growth and quality of poverty research. Consequently, the findings on poverty summarized above have been drawn for the most part from limited case studies and from the analysis of secondary and partial data, rather than from hard primary data derived from empirical studies of the country as a whole.

In fact, since 1980 there have been no empirical studies of poverty as such covering the whole country. The very few poverty studies identified have, typically, been case studies dealing with some particular aspect, none of them being recent. The studies available on income distribution are hardly better. For instance, the 1975 NES conference papers on income distribution were based on research already completed during 1975 or earlier, the Bienen and Diejomaoh papers (1981) were based on research already completed by 1979, and, even though the FOS had conducted the NISH/GHS every year since 1980/81 (as already indicated), the results of all GHSs since 1986/87 are yet to be processed or published, except for the Preliminary Report of the 1991/92 survey, which was published in December 1992.

On the whole, six particular research themes have received some attention: general poverty (or mass poverty); urban poverty; rural poverty; interpersonal income distribution; inter-household income distribution; and possible remedies to poverty. However, given the limitations of the data on which the relevant studies and findings have been based, both poverty and income-distribution research in Nigeria remain largely exploratory and tentative.

Ghana

Scope of poverty research and data situation

The study of poverty as a distinct phenomenon has featured more clearly and more prominently in Ghana than in any other country covered by this review. There has been a more deliberate focus on the poverty situation in the country in the context of both academic and policy research. Thus, unlike in Nigeria, it is possible to identify a number of empirical studies in Ghana that have focused on poverty and that have raised and addressed some of the methodological issues of poverty research, including concepts, theoretical approaches, data, and policy implications. The particular studies on which the review presented in this section are based are the earlier set of studies (namely, Boateng et al. 1989; Brown 1979, 1984; Dei 1992; Ghana Statistical Service 1994: ISSER 1983).

The focus of most of the earlier studies was on the regional dimension of poverty, especially rural–urban and interregional differences. Indeed, some of these studies were, strictly speaking, not poverty studies as such. They were studies of the situation of uneven development in Ghana, a situation that was presumed to correspond to differences in the incidence of poverty. For example, Ewusi's 1976 report on "Disparities in levels of regional development in Ghana" belongs in this category. So does Brown's 1984 study, entitled, rather tantalisingly, *Social Structure and Poverty in Selected Rural Communities in Ghana*, its title and conclusions on the poverty situation notwithstanding.

Brown's 1979 study, based mainly on the analysis of secondary data (census, school enrolment figures, public expenditure, etc.), examined the phenomenon of marginalization, especially the exclusion of rural areas from natural resources and the decision making processes of the country. The "five basic elements of social consumption, namely, education, health care, housing, water and electricity", were all said to be "social services that take the lion's share of government expenditure in the social sector" and "the main areas of social consumption in which the poor feel most deprived". Also identified and examined in the study were processes that tended to reinforce urban privileges, such as the regressive tax system, which was also confiscatory in effect as far as cocoa producers were concerned, and the pricing of food, which kept the terms of trade more or less permanently in favour of the urban areas.

In his 1984 paper, Ewusi analysed the income data of the 1974 National Household Budget Survey and, based on this, attempted to estimate the patterns of poverty in Ghana, defining the "poverty line" as per capita household income of less than US$100. Also examined were the wider economic context and government policies and programmes, especially in the area of rural development, as a basis for explaining the rural poverty patterns observed.

During 1979/80 the Institute of Statistical, Social and Economic Research (ISSER) of the University of Ghana launched what was meant to be a five-year project, entitled, "Poverty in Ghana: Its Scope, Extent and Impact on Development". Conceived as an interdisciplinary, comprehensive, and long-term research programme, the survey was expected to analyse the scope, extent, cause, and policy implications of poverty in Ghana, as part of the search for "alternative models of development" (ISSER, 1983: 4). Unfortunately, the project ran aground halfway and, in a sense, became significant more for what it could not do than for what it did. By the date of the Mid-Project Report (May 1983), the analysis of most of the phase I data had not even begun. And, from all indications, the project ended there.

Apparently, the project stalled as a result of problems such as a cumbersome organization, poor funding (especially after the initial funds had been exhausted), inauspicious timing (it was interrupted at the onset of the December 1981 revolution and subsequently collided with the Economic Reform Programme, which had a very low priority for social policy issues), adverse interpersonal relations within the coordinating organization, stiff opposition to the project *ab initio* by some senior members of ISSER, and the sheer scope of the project itself. But perhaps the most significant feature of the project, methodologically, was its lack of conceptual rigour and theoretical focus. Perhaps this was also its most fundamental problem.

In Boateng et al. (1989), which came under the World Bank initiated/assisted poverty profile assessment project, in the context of the Social Dimensions of Adjustment (SDA) in the Sub-Saharan Africa Programme co-sponsored by the UNDP Regional Bureau for Africa, the World Bank, and the African Development Bank (ADB), an attempt was made to create a baseline and a structure for poverty research. Its target was policy-oriented analysis of poverty in Ghana, based on data from the Ghana Living Standards Survey (GLSS) being conducted by the Ghana Statistical Service.

The survey adopted what was called a "poverty focus" rather than an "inequality focus" (because it concerned itself only with the lower end of income distribution, not with distribution as a whole). Here, a baseline poverty profile for Ghana was suggested based on the first-year results of the GLSS and it was also recommended that "for operational purposes, real household expenditure (or income) per capita be used as the measure of individual welfare" (Boateng et al. 1989).

In Dei (1992), the author analysed "hardships and survival", especially the effects of the Economic Reform Programme (ERP) on the poor and the disadvantaged in society. The case study of a Ghanaian Community, Ayirebi, was based on data from two main sources:

- participant and non-participant observations of everyday life in the Ayirebi community;.
- household surveys by means of interviews and questionnaires on demographic, ecological, and socio-demographic parameters, first in 1982 and again in 1989. In 1982/83, 412 households representing one-quarter of the community's

households were covered, the total population of the research sample being 1,543 persons. Of the 412 households in the initial survey, 407 were among the 405 households in the 1989 follow-up survey, which had a sample of 1,722 persons.

Dei's study is methodologically significant in many ways: it is longitudinal in concept (though this may not have been so *ab initio*); it attempts a holistic approach not normally feasible under statistical surveys; and it suggests the need for community-based monitoring research, especially for assessing the impact of the policy process or of particular policies or measures addressed to the poverty situation.

Finally, the Ghana Statistical Service (through the Government Statistician) addressed the University of Ghana (Research and Conferences Committee's) Seminar on "Poverty Profile from the GLSS". Again (as in Boateng et al. 1989) it was based on the results of the 1987–88 survey, since the data from the other two surveys already conducted are yet to be processed.

Concerning the data situation, it is true that practically all past studies of poverty in Ghana, except Boateng et al. (1989), Ghana Statistical Service (1994), and the empirical community-based survey by Brown, were based on incomplete and out-of-date data. For example, even the UNICEF estimate of the Physical Quality of Life Index for the various regions of Ghana, produced in 1984, had to use 1970 data! But the situation seems to have started to improve.

For example, under the GLSS, Ghana has commenced a five-year survey programme under the Ghana Statistical Service (GSS), with the active support and advice of the United Nations Household Survey Capability Programme (NHSCP), the UN Economic Commission for Africa (ECA), and the SDA project of the World Bank/UNDP/ADB. The GLSS started in September 1987 and, as the GSS informed the "Poverty in Ghana" seminar at Legon in 1994, three rounds of the survey have been conducted since take-off: 1987/88, 1988/89, and 1990/91.

Ghana's GLSS collects information at the level of the community, the household and the individual and on a wide range of variables, e.g. health, migration, income, expenditure, savings, remittances, anthropometric measurements for both children and adults, etc. It is also generating data that will make it possible to analyse sources of income and consumption patterns by poverty groups as well as basic needs achievement by poverty groups, especially in the domains of health and education.

The GLSS sample consists of 3,200 households across approximately 200 Enumeration Areas (EAs) stratified by urban/rural and ecological zones; a household being defined as a "group of individuals who live and eat together for a period of at least nine months of the year preceding the interview", a standard World Bank definition.

Admittedly, the GLSS is primarily a policy-oriented data system. Its purpose is to monitor the experiences of all sectors of the population during the process of economic reform, and to develop a tool for policy and intervention to alleviate the hardships of the vulnerable groups. However, given its national coverage, its rigorous sampling procedures, and the wide range of relevant economic, demographic, social, and living conditions data that it collects, the GLSS also provides a potentially rich source of good-quality data for systematic poverty research. In this regard, it promises to be a significant improvement over the older National Household Budget Survey of the Central Bureau of Statistics.

Concepts, theoretical orientations, and major findings

None of the pre-1989 Ghanaian surveys reviewed here can be said to have addressed the problem of the definition of "poverty" critically or in a rigorous manner. Neither has any of them made explicit a theoretical framework or even seemed to have worked consciously under any particular theoretical framework. Rather, the "poverty line/absolute poverty" concept seems to have been adopted by the surveys, at least implicitly, though they did differ in their specific operationalization of the concept. However, in Brown (1979) "poverty" was defined, again implicitly, in terms of relative exclusion from the so-called "five basic elements of social consumption" and from the exercise of political power, rather than in terms of any monetary measure or poverty line.

Boateng et al. (1989) and the Ghana Statistical Service (1994) both addressed the issue of definition. The former recommends that, "for operational purposes", real household expenditure (or income) per capita be used as the measure of individual welfare. As to where a poverty line should be drawn, it takes the basic position that "the nature and meaning of poverty are country and culture specific" (Boateng et al. 1989: 5) and, where a poverty line does not already exist in a given country, it suggests the following "two conceivable operational procedures":

> (i) Given a distribution of individuals by real household expenditure per capita, choose a poverty line which cuts off a certain fraction, say the bottom 30 per cent of individuals. In addition, choose a "hard core" poverty line which cuts off a smaller fraction, say the bottom 10 per cent, of individuals in some base period. These become the

poverty lines with which to evaluate changes in poverty over time and differences across regions at a point in time.
(ii) ... use a given fraction of mean expenditure per capita as the poverty line.

The Ghana Statistical Service's operationalization of the poverty line differs in some detail from that of Boateng et al. Instead of using the mean expenditure per capita as its basis, it uses the Mean Welfare Index, a measure that incorporates not only expenditure but also actual self-provision; i.e. the portion of household production consumed by the household. Thus, the Mean Welfare Index for 1987/88 was estimated at 296,400 Cedis and for 1990/91 at 309,200 Cedis. Also, although regarding two-thirds of the mean as the cut-off point for defining secondary/ relative poverty, as in the Boateng et al. analysis, it takes 50 per cent (and not 33 per cent) of the mean as the cut-off point for defining primary or "hard core" poverty.

Brown's presentation (1979) is perhaps the closest in this review to any clear theoretical orientation, i.e. the author's structural perspective on the causation of poverty in Ghana – a perspective that sees poverty as a manifestation of "social marginalisation and as a necessary consequence (and concomitant) of the stratification and polarisation of the Ghanaian society". Thus, a reversal of the trend is seen to lie only in a radical reorientation of national development policy and strategy, entailing, among others, "a change in the distribution of public services to the poorest sectors of the society", institutional reforms (e.g. land reform and public ownership of major industries), and "a basic restructuring of the political, economic and social balance of power within the country", as a condition for ensuring "far-reaching changes in the pattern of distribution of benefits".

Perhaps the most general finding of the studies reviewed is that, in Ghana (as elsewhere), poverty is a complex phenomenon in terms of both its nature and probable causation. But, of course, there were more specific findings reported regarding the incidence and pattern of poverty, especially of absolute poverty in the country. For example, the earlier studies all found that poverty was concentrated in rural areas, whether poverty was defined in monetary terms or in terms of access to basic amenities. Also reported by such studies was a north–south difference, with greater poverty in the north, as a reflection of uneven development.

The finding that poverty in Ghana is predominantly a rural phenomenon has also been confirmed by more recent surveys, including Boateng et al. (1989) and Ghana Statistical Service (1994).

Six basic factors have been identified to explain the worse position of rural areas: a slow rate of economic growth, high rates of rural population growth; the exclusion of the rural poor from the processes and/or benefits of economic growth; an inequitable distribution of income, especially along the rural–urban dimension; the inability of the rural poor to influence the course of public policy, and external factors that precipitate and/or exacerbate Ghana's economic crisis.

Other countries

As stated above, the other countries in Anglophone West Africa (representing only about 6 per cent of the population of the subregion) could not be covered in depth. But it is also true that each of them presents a somewhat difficult research environment in terms of the political situation prevailing right now. Yet, from the scanty evidence available, poverty is probably a very serious problem in each of them, particularly for The Gambia and for Sierra Leone.

Even though all five countries concerned fall into the "Low Human Development" category in terms of the UNDP Human Development Index (HDI) as at 1992, the rankings for Liberia, The Gambia, and Sierra Leone are 131, 154, and 159, respectively, which makes the Gambia the seventh least developed nation in the world.

The only available study, an ILO survey (ILO 1982a), assessed the incidence of poverty in Sierra Leone. Using a poverty line based on the costing of a basic needs food basket, topped up to take account of non-food needs (especially housing, fuel, furniture, and transport), the survey found the pattern summarized in Table 12.2.

The Population and Housing Census conducted by the Central Statistics Department of the Ministry of Economic Planning and Industrial Development of The Gambia in 1983 devotes its volume II (Republic of The Gambia 1989) to housing and household characteristics. A copy of that particular volume was not available to us but it probably contains information with which some poverty research on The Gambia could start off.

In view of the fact that the problem of poverty is probably serious in these countries and that the patterns of poverty and inequality prevailing in them may prove unique in some ways, there is an urgent need for systematic poverty research in each of them.

Table 12.2 Sierra Leone: Comparative data showing the proportion of urban and rural populations falling below poverty line

	Urban	Rural
Poverty line[a] (Le/month)	64.0	39.0
% population falling below	50	45
Food poverty line[a] (Le/month)	42.0	27.0
% population falling below	20	20
Target groups	Hawkers, casual labourers, unskilled workers	Subsistance upland rice farmers

Sources: ILO (1982a: Table 7).
Note:
[a] It is significant that the poverty line in each case was set higher for the urban than for the rural areas, which may tend to exaggerate urban poverty relative to rural poverty. The basic idea makes sense, because the cost of living tends to be higher in urban areas, especially if the difference in the poverty lines adopted exactly reflects the urban–rural differences in the cost of living.

Summary evaluation of poverty research in Anglophone West Africa

The three criteria in terms of which this evaluation is conducted are the quality of data used, theoretical orientation and policy relevance.

Most of the studies reviewed in this presentation were based on fragmentary and out-of-date secondary data. Official data sources, even when they were able to generate, analyse, and publish data of satisfactory quality, were often hamstrung by serious resource constraints. Furthermore, the inflexible emphasis on economic statistics has persisted in these countries, which means that demographic and social statistics have not received enough attention. Even in research institutes with social policy or development units, such units were invariably rated low when it came to funding. Even though the 1970s are sometimes referred to as the active period for the development of demographic and social statistics in Africa (for example in ECA's *A Strategy for the Implementation of the Addis Ababa Plan of Action for Statistical Development in Africa in the 1990s*, March 1992, esp. paras 62–70), there is little to show for the period in terms of data relevant to social policy analysis in general or poverty research in particular.

Worsening the data gap was the dearth of empirical social science and social policy studies, even in the universities and research institutes, especially in studies not directly linked to income generation and economic growth. This situation arose not just because of weak financial support for social science generally, but also because of a distinct lack of financial support for social policy research in particular, both by governments and by the major international development agencies.

The 1980s saw the intensification of the process of economic globalization and, in most cases, drastic cutbacks in public expenditure. In that context, no attention could, understandably, be spared for such concerns as poverty research or poverty alleviation; at least not until even the promoters of unconditional liberalization began to see the immense social costs of their strategy. For example, the UNDP 1986 Roundtable on "Development: The Human Dimension" noted that "the human costs of the current process are unacceptable from a humanitarian perspective" and that they could not be accepted even "from an economic perspective" (UNDP 1986).

It is to be hoped that the various initiatives aimed at strengthening the survey capabilities of the countries, initiatives to which reference has already been made above, derive from a new appreciation of the importance of social statistics and of social policy analysis broadly conceived, even in the context of economic liberalism. It is also to be hoped that such initiatives will, in the medium term, ensure a much-improved data situation for social policy and poverty research in the sub-subregion.

With respect to theoretical orientation and contribution, as was noted concerning the studies in Ghana, poverty research in this sub-subregion has not been informed by any strong theoretical orientation as such, and there does not seem to have been any particular interest in developing or advancing the theory of poverty or in contributing to the comparative knowledge of poverty. Rather, the studies were, typically, policy oriented and, even though some of them were rigorous in their conceptualization and analysis, the implications of the surveys were directed towards policy and development action, not towards theoretical issues. This does not mean that policy-oriented research is inherently incapable of making important contributions to theory development; only that such potential can best be realized if policy-oriented research is consciously formulated and executed with theory development as part of the objective in view.

As for the policy relevance of these studies, there are two important dimensions, namely, their suitability for use in the policy process, and the extent to which they have actually been used.

In terms of these considerations, the bureaucracy has generally tended to find these studies not as suitable as it would have wished. In particular, the studies have often been dismissed by the bureaucracy as invariably selective, largely subjective, and not reflective of national priorities. Of course, although this assessment may, to some extent, reflect the true worth of these studies (use of partial and out-of-date data, generalization beyond analysis and data, conclusion and recommendations not necessarily implied in or supported by data/analysis, and so on), there is no doubt that it also reflects the prevailing anti-intellectualism of the policy class in particular and the ruling class in general.

The 1980s have, for the most part, seen social research at its lowest ebb in all the countries covered by this review. Some recent initiatives dating back to the UNDP 1986 Roundtable on Development, and now involving all the major international development institutions, especially UNDP, World Bank, ECA, and ADB, seem to have set in motion a process that could, in the medium term, lead to significant improvement in the data situation in these countries.

However, even a major improvement in the data situation or even in the survey capabilities of the countries concerned will not lead automatically or necessarily to a corresponding improvement in the level or quality of social research activity. More specifically, it will not lead to any improvement in the level or quality of poverty research activity, whether by government agencies or by researchers based in the universities and national research institutions. There are still difficult problems of funding, of accessibility of data for researchers, and of delays in the processing and publication of data. There is also the problem of how to sustain the improvements now being promoted.

The fundamental obstacles seem to be the low priority still accorded social policy, social statistics, and social research in these countries at the level of resource allocation; the prevailing anti-intellectualism among the policy class; and the low ranking that human social welfare concerns and issues have in the context of the current economic liberalization campaign.

REFERENCES

Delaine, G. et al. (1992) *The Social Dimensions of Adjustment Integrated Survey. A Survey to Measure Poverty and Understand the Effects of Policy Change on Households* Washington, DC: World Bank SDA Working Paper No. 14.

Morales-Gomez, D. A. (1993) "The social challenge in development: From economic to social policies", in M. Torres (ed.), *Research on Social Policy. Proposal for a Future Agenda*.
International Development Research Centre. Torres, Mario (ed.) (1993) *Research on Social Policy: Proposal for a Future Agenda*. International Development Research Centre, July.
UNDP (1986) *Adjustment and Growth with Human Development*. New York: United Nations Development Programme.
World Bank (1991) *Making Adjustment Work for the Poor: A Framework for Reform in Africa*. Washington, DC: World Bank.

Nigeria

Aboyade, O. (1975) "On the need for an operational specification of poverty in the Nigerian economy", in NES, *Poverty in Nigeria*. Ibadan: Nigerian Economic Society, pp. 25–34.
Abubakar, Iya (1975) "Poverty in Nigeria: Remedies in NES *Poverty in Nigeria*. Ibadan: Nigerian Economic Society, pp. 371–6.
Akeredolu-Ale, E. O. (1975) "Poverty as a social issue: A theoretical note", in NES, *Poverty in Nigeria*. Ibadan: Nigerian Economic Society, pp. 43–62.
Bienneg, H. and V. P. Diejomaoh (eds) (1981) *The Political Economy of Income Distribution in Nigeria*. New York: Holmes & Meier.
Edozien, E. C. (1975) "Poverty: Some issues in concept and theory", in NES, *Poverty in Nigeria*. Ibadan: Nigerian Economic Society, pp. 35–42.
Federal Republic of Nigeria (1992) *National Integrated Survey of Households (NISH): Fourth Status Report*. Lagos: Federal Office of Statistics, April.
Mabogunje Akin L. (1975) "Prolegomenon to urban poverty in Nigeria", in NES, *Poverty in Nigeria*. Ibadan: Nigerian Economic Society, pp. 69–92.
NES (Nigerian Economic Society) (1975) *Poverty in Nigeria*. Proceedings of the 1975 Annual Conference of the Nigerian Economic Society, Ibadan (edited by O. Teriba, A. O. Phillips, and E. O. Akeredolu-Ale).
Onimode, B. (1975) "The dialectics of exploitation: Poverty and power in Nigeria", in NES, *Poverty in Nigeria*. Ibadan: Nigerian Economic Society, pp. 335–48.

Ghana

Boateng, E. Oti et al. (1989) *A Poverty Profile for Ghana 1987–88*. Washington, DC: World Bank, Social Dimensions of Adjustment in Sub-Saharan Africa Working Paper No. 5.
Brown C. K. (1979) "Rural poverty and socio-economic marginalism in Ghana". Paper presented at the 10th European Congress for Rural Sociology, Cordoba, Spain, 5–10 April.
—— (1984) *Social Structure and Poverty in Selected Rural Communities in Ghana*. Legon, Accra: Institute of Statistical, Social and

Economic Research (ISSER) Technical Publication No. 54 University of Ghana, Legon.
Dei, George, J. Safa (1992) *Hardship and Survival in Rural West Africa: A Case Study of a Ghanaian Community*. Dakar: CODESRIA Monograph Series No. 3/92.
Ewusi, K. (1976) "Disparities in levels of regional development in Ghana", *Social Indicators*, 3(1).
—— (1984) *The Political Economy of Ghana in the Post-Independence Period: Description and Analysis of the Decadence of the Political Economy, etc*. ISSER Discussion Paper No. 14, November.
Hutchful, E. (1990) *The IMF and Ghana: The Confidential Record*. London: Zed Books.
ISSER (Institute of Statistical, Social and Economic Research) (1989) *A Research Proposal on Poverty, Its Scope, Extent and Impact on Development*. Legon, Accra: ISSER, October (revised April 1980).
—— (1983) *Mid Project Report on the ISSER Poverty Study* (prepared by N. O. Addo) Legon, Accra: ISSER, May.
Ghana Statistical Service (1994) "Poverty profile from the Ghana Living Standards Survey (GLSS)". Position paper presented at the Seminar on Poverty in Ghana, convened by the University of Ghana Research and Conferences Committee, University of Ghana 29–30 September.

Other Anglophone West Africa

Ahmed, Iqbal et al. (1991) *Poverty in The Gambia. Preliminary Findings of a Study Initiated and Sponsored by UNDP, JCGP, FAO and WHO*. Geneva: ILO.
ILO (1981) *Ensuring Equitable Growth: A Strategy of Increasing Employment, Equity and Basic Needs Satisfaction in Sierra-Leone*. Addis Ababa: ILO/JASPA.
—— (1982a) *Rural–Urban Gap and Income Distribution: The Case of Sierra Leone*. Addis Ababa: ILO/JASPA.
ILO (1982b) *Rural–Urban Gap and Income Distribution: The Case of Liberia*. Addis Ababa: ILO/JASPA.
Republic of The Gambia (1983–1990) *Population and Housing Census 1983*. Banjul: Central Statistics Department, Ministry of Economic Planning and Industrial Development.
—— Vol. I: *Administrative and Analytical Procedure*, October 1987.
—— Vol. II: *Housing and Household Characteristics*, May 1989.
—— Vol. III: *Economic Characteristics*, October 1983.
—— Vol. IV: *Statistics on Settlement*, May 1990.
United Nations (1990) *UN Conference on Least Developed Countries Country Presentation by the Government of Sierra Leone*. New York: United Nations.
—— (1990) *UN Conference on Least Developed Countries Country Presentation by the Government of The Gambia*. New York: United Nations.
World Bank (1981) *The Gambia: Basic Needs in the Gambia*. Washington, DC: World Bank.

Chapter 13

South Africa: Poverty Under Duress

Francis Wilson

Poverty is not knowing where your next meal is going to come from, and always wondering when the council is going to put your furniture out and always praying that your husband must not lose his job. To me that is poverty.

(Mrs. Witbooi,
Philipstown, Karoo)[1]

Introduction

The biggest change in the poverty research that has taken place in South Africa over the past decade relates to the context within which it has occurred. Before 1990 few people even dreamed that the old pattern of political power, with whites in control of the legislature, the army, and the budget, would change in the forseeable future.[2] But since February 1990 and the unbanning of the African Congress organizations, together with the release of political leaders, all research into poverty has occurred with the knowledge that any issues uncovered, or policy proposals made, would engage the immediate interest of the government of the country. In 1984 the Prime Minister (P. W. Botha) virulently attacked a major scientific conference on poverty in South Africa. (*Debates of Parliament*, 27 April 1984).[3] Ten years later, President Nelson Mandela is leading a government of national unity whose primary commitment, expressed through the Reconstruction and Development Programme (RDP), is to eliminate poverty (see *White Paper on the Reconstruction and Development Programme*, 1994).

In the context of South Africa it is clear to most people that poverty is a profoundly political issue. For this reason research workers there are aware of the degree to which the prevailing power structure shapes the whole research agenda in this field.

Thus, it is important to begin an assessment of poverty research in South Africa with explicit recognition of the political environment in which that research was or is being done. For the first three-quarters of the twentieth century South Africa was dominated both politically and economically by the white minority. Successive challenges to the ideology and practices of white racism were put down, often with brute force. Trade Unions were banned and, after 1960, the major African political organizations were banned and the leadership banned, imprisoned, or exiled.

However, looking back from the vantage point of 1995, it is possible to see that a sea-change began to take place in the balance of power between black and white during the 1970s. The re-emergence and rapid growth of the black trade unions, the rise of black consciousness, the Soweto uprising of 1976, were all both manifestations and causes of profound changes taking place within the society. Certainly by 1980, despite the harsh crackdown of the state, the certainties and seeming permanence of the Verwoerdian apartheid era were giving way to a recognition that South Africa had a future beyond apartheid. People were beginning to talk and think about a post-apartheid society. Those undertaking research in poverty during the 1980s were explicitly conscious that they were part of that broader historical process (Wilson and Ramphele 1989: ix).

Against this background it is perhaps helpful to recognize that poverty research in South Africa can be divided into four time zones: before 1980; the decade when the shift taking place in the balance of power became manifest, though few people expected the transfer of power; the extraordinary period between President De Klerk's speech in 1990, announcing the beginning of fundamental political change, and the inauguration of President Mandela in the wake of South Africa's first democratic elections in 1994; and the period of democratic government since then.

Turning briefly to the period before 1980, we recognize that research into poverty is not a new phenomenon in South Africa. An annotated bibliography by Wilfred Wentzel (1982) provides a useful guide to the literature. As early as 1906 a government commission was appointed in what was then the colony of the Transvaal to look into the matter of "indigency". The Report of the Transvaal Indigency Commission 1906–1908 was fatally flawed in that its terms of reference limited it to consider only the indigency of whites, with very little explicit attention on black poverty, except insofar as it affected whites. Nevertheless it is a fascinating document, not only for the definition of indigency (para. 7) and detailed factual information, but also for its insistence on the importance of a methodology that deals with general, social and economic causes, and aims at preventing the growth of indigency" (T.G. 13/08 para. 9, cited by Wentzel 1982: 20).

For the next two generations the most conspicuous poverty research undertaken in the country focused primarily on whites. Thus, for example, the famous Carnegie Commission into the Poor White Problem (*Arm Blanke Vraagstuk*) was set up in 1928 by a team of university and church people with help from a non-profit American philanthropic trust. The Commission published five major volumes in 1932/33 (Carnegie Commission 1932[4]), which, whilst breaking new ground in poverty research methodology, also set the scene for the development of a range of political strategies focusing exclusively on white poverty. It was precisely some of these strategies that were introduced or strengthened (or, as some would say, hijacked and misused[5]) by the National Party after it came to power in 1948. Thus one strand of South Africa's research history provides an immediate warning about the possible ambiguities inherent in action-orientated research that has too narrow a focus. For, with hindsight, it is possible to interpret the apartheid policies of the National Party as an anti-poverty programme – *for whites only*. It is this sorry history that should make all research workers duly humble and cause us to be vigilant against anti-poverty programmes that incorporate strategies that will benefit some poor people at the expense of others even poorer and more vulnerable.

But there is a second, more inclusive, strand of poverty research in South Africa. W. M. Macmillan published an important and influential book in 1930 which analysed both black and white poverty within the single South African political economy. This book, together with the Native Economic Commission (1932) plus the work of the South African Institute of Race Relations (see, for example, Jones and Hoernlé 1942), ensured that the issue of poverty as it affected black as well as white South Africans during the decades before apartheid remained in the national consciousness if not at the top of the political agenda. Details of further research into poverty during the three decades of high apartheid, after 1948, are contained in Wentzel's bibliography. A number of individual studies, often by those trained in anthropology or sociology rather than economics, provided important insights into living conditions, including poverty datum lines, in particular urban areas or job categories (e.g.

domestic workers). However, despite periodic calls for another Carnegie Inquiry to look at the full ramifications of poverty in South Africa, it was not until fifty years after the first one that this idea took root.

In January 1980, a feasibility study was commissioned. Thus began more than two years of preparatory work. This period included time spent assessing other research around the world. The rash of poverty studies during the 1970s in Britain, Ireland, the European Community, Australia, and the United States were compared and contrasted with numerous studies, often sponsored by the World Bank or the International Labour Organization, in Kenya, Sri Lanka, Brazil, India, and elsewhere.[6]

During the preliminary phase, when soundings were being taken, three important aspects of the inquiry became abundantly clear. First, any study of poverty could be truly meaningful only if there was real inside understanding and participation of those communities that had to endure poverty. In the South African context, where the vast majority of those who are poor are black, this meant that, as far as possible, the centre of gravity of the inquiry had to be black rather than white. Second, it became clear that the inquiry should be designed as an open-ended, ongoing process rather than as a once-off affair. Third, while the study gradually took shape in discussions around the country, a striking contrast in views became apparent. White South Africans were generally enthusiastic about the need for research to gather facts on poverty. Black South Africans were unimpressed by data-gathering. "Why spend money finding out what we already know?", they asked. "What we need is action against poverty." This view was crucial in guiding the subsequent work of the second Carnegie Inquiry during the ten years leading up to the publication and dissemination of its main report in 1989 (Wilson and Ramphele 1989).[7]

The next major thrust in poverty research came in 1992 with the Project for Statistics on Living Standards and Development (PSLSD). This involved a comprehensive survey of 9,000 households drawn from a carefully selected sample throughout the length and breadth of the country. The principal purpose of the survey was to collect hard statistical information about the conditions under which South Africans live in order to provide policy makers with the data required for planning strategies to implement such goals as those outlined in the Government of National Unity's Reconstruction and Development Programme. The idea for such a survey was first mooted by a delegation of

South Africans from the African National Congress and the Congress of South African Trade Unions when they met officials of the World Bank in Washington in April 1992. A South African research unit was asked to coordinate and manage the collection of data required, which was done in a fruitful interaction between South Africans responsible for the survey and staff and consultants of the Bank. From the beginning it was agreed that the data, once collected and cleaned, would be in the public domain and would not belong to any particular university, or government department, or to the World Bank. In this way, those involved in the survey hoped to encourage and consolidate an attitude in South Africa that sees public accessibility to all such data, from whatever source, as a fundamental attitude of a democratic society. It is in this spirit that computer disks and code books containing the data are also available to anybody who wishes to use them.[8] Before embarking on the actual survey, a comprehensive search of the available literature was undertaken in order to collate all information about living standards and development in South Africa in the decade since the main empirical work of the Carnegie Inquiry had been done. Altogether, thirteen such papers, each containing a relevant bibliography, were published in 1993 and 1994. Nine of the papers focus on different regions of the country, and four focus on cross-cutting themes of water, energy, nutrition, and housing.[9]

Building on this work there are two further research initiatives to be noted, both begun in the period since the Mandela Government of National Unity took office – one driven by the government's Central Statistical Service (CSS), the other led by the independent Data Research Africa (DRA) working in collaboration with the World Bank. The CSS, in October 1994, undertook a household survey throughout the country (including the TBVC areas[10]) and was able to release the first set of informative tables in March 1995 (CSS 1985). The DRA programme is aimed at clothing the bare bones of the statistics collected in recent years with a more qualitative assessment of the nature of poverty. Drawing also on some of the Carnegie studies in the early 1980s it aims to gain some insight into the way in which poverty may have changed, qualitatively, over the past decade. Lessons from these various research initiatives have and are being fed into the drafting of the questionnaire for the 1996 census, whose results it is hoped will take our knowledge of the South African political economy to a new level of comprehensiveness and accuracy.

Concepts of poverty

The earliest definitions of poverty in the South African context focused, as explained above, on whites and they were highly subjective. At the time of the first Carnegie Commission in the early 1930s the definition was essentially based upon individual personal estimates of what constituted "a decent standard of living for white men [sic]" against varying traditional standards in different parts of South Africa (Carnegie Commission 1932: vii). But throughout the inter-war years, from 1918 on, regular government commission reports on the cost of living focused attention on the relationship between incomes and the costs of basic needs, including housing. In 1938 the South African Institute of Race Relations published a paper examining wages and the cost of living for black South Africans (Ballinger and Ballinger 1938). A major step forward in poverty studies was taken during the Second World War by the Professor of Sociology at the University of Cape Town, who published a number of papers calculating a local Poverty Datum Line, with explicit examination of its nutritional basis, and analysing the distribution of poverty among "Coloured" and "European" households in Cape Town. Following Batson's pioneering work, the Poverty Datum Line, variously evolving into a Minimum Living Level and a Supplementary Living Level (University of South Africa), a Household Subsistence Level, and a Household Effective Level (University of Port Elizabeth), was refined and modified during the 1970s as black trade unions re-emerged as a force for change and guidelines were needed in the ongoing debate with management about minimum wages (Wilson and Ramphele 1989: 16–17).

The second Carnegie Inquiry made use of these definitions in the course of its work during the 1980s to calculate the proportion of households falling into poverty. However, its work began with a much broader concept of poverty being like illness – manifesting itself in different ways in different circumstances. Research workers were not provided with a nice clean definition of poverty that they could measure but were told instead to go out into the highways and byways of the country to meet people who endured poverty and those who lived or worked with them and to *listen* to what those people, from their own experience, understood poverty to mean. And then to describe and try to measure that. This, as the Carnegie report noted, "is an untidy process and was scathingly condemned by an economist of the

World Bank, at a seminar in Washington on the Inquiry, as one that produced mere 'anecdotal evidence'. . . . We do not wish to be misunderstood: statistical analysis is essential, and the effort to toughen up the soft social sciences by improving the quality of statistics is one of the most significant intellectual advances of our time. But precisely because the numbers are so important it is vital to pause at the beginning to consider what we are measuring and, perhaps even more significant, what we are not measuring" (Wilson and Ramphete, p. 15).

The process of delving deeper was marked, in the Carnegie Inquiry, by a constant interaction between empirical and theoretical insights. Thus the first six (out of more than 300) (see Wilson and Ramphele 1989: appendix 1 for details) conference papers reported not only on "major problems as perceived by the community" or on the perspectives of life as seen by migrant workers ("men without children"), but also on systematic consideration of the different dimensions, or levels, of poverty as well as problems of measurement in rich and poor countries. The next three papers focused on basic needs and on the link between income distribution and poverty in some of the poorest rural areas of the country. Thus the inquiry emerged with a concept of poverty that had many different characteristics or faces.

These "many faces of poverty" were isolated and then described with the aid of the specific detail emerging from the mass of empirical studies. Where possible, statistical estimates of the prevalence of these faces on the national level were calculated. They included hunger and sickness, malnutrition and tuberculosis; the absence of such basic needs as the ready availability of fuel for cooking and lighting, clean water for drinking, adequate shelter for households, sewerage facilities, jobs for those who wanted and needed them, reasonable and safe working conditions for those who had them, access to land for rural households without alternative sources of income. Other less tangible characteristics of poverty were also uncovered and considered, including the fundamental sense of uncertainty about "where your next meal is going to come from"; the humiliation felt by those without adequate housing at not being able to offer hospitality; the shame felt by fathers unable to feed their families because they could not find work; the sense of desperate inadequacy felt by mothers whose children were hungry; the vulnerability of those "on the edge of survival", for whom a sudden shift in circumstances such as drought, a rise in food prices, or loss of job can plunge them into destitution. (See Wilson and Ramphele 1989: Chapter 9).[11]

Hypotheses

The first hypothesis, or perhaps it is really the first assumption, in South African poverty research relates to the value of the research work itself. How do those undertaking such research respond to the question posed by those enduring (or close to those enduring) poverty: "Why spend money to find out what we already know?". The answer is that, it is necessary for two reasons. First, facts are themselves politically powerful. The particularity of what it means to be poor, combined with accurate information about the extent of that poverty, raises consciousness in society in such a manner as can generate or strengthen action to try and deal with the problem. The second reason arises from the fact that the planning of any strategy against poverty is facilitated by the existence of a detailed map of the terrain. To know that 50 per cent of households are living below the current minimum living level is interesting and important, but not very helpful as a guideline for developing appropriate action. But to find out that, in a country whose capacity to generate electricity is greater than the amount currently being consumed, the proportions of black and white households without access to such energy are 63 per cent and 0.2 per cent, respectively, confronts one with a reality about which one can begin to think very creatively. Thus in South Africa the concept of poverty research has been expanded into a three-stage process: facts; causes; strategies. It is no longer acceptable (if it ever was) to conceive of poverty research as being confined to collecting data, or even analysing causes. Research is all focused on finding ways of preventing and curing the syndrome. But, in order to do this, the facts of the matter and the analysis of causes are vital.

The second hypothesis is that history is important. Nowhere is this more true than in South Africa, where the burden of history weighs heavily upon the present. To put it another way, the removal of racist laws and practices from the body politic is no more likely to change the distribution of wealth in the country than is the removal of scaffolding likely to change the shape of a building constructed with its help. Thus abolition of the Land Act, which in effect prevented black farmers from owning and farming all except a small fraction of the country, will not, by itself, ensure a more equitable distribution of land between black and white in the country. To understand the differences in entitlements between white and black, rich and poor, old and young, men and women, urban and rural in South Africa today, it helps a great deal to understand something of the dynamics of the history, particularly with regard to the consequences of conquest, of the migrant labour system developed in the diamond and gold mines, of the differential state expenditure on black and white education over the past century, and of the ever more stringent anti-black urbanization policies of the apartheid government, to name only four hugely powerful influences.[12]

The third hypothesis, closely associated with the previous one, relates to the relevance of political power in any economic analysis of the phenomenon. Poverty is a profoundly political issue. This can be seen most clearly perhaps in a close-up analysis of the conditions that gave rise to the establishment, over a hundred years ago, of the single-sex compounds that are the basis of the notorious migrant labour system and that still, in 1995, housed over 95 per cent of the black workers in the gold mines.[13] The then existing pattern of distribution of political power in the society is central to understanding the shape of the labour system that emerged in the aftermath of the mineral discoveries (see, for example, Turrell 1987).

Another hypothesis that underpinned poverty research during the 1980s lay in the tension between macro and micro perspectives. Implicit rather than explicit, this hypothesis was based on the premise that, to understand the *nature* of poverty and its impact on human beings, to describe it best, one needs micro analysis. But, to understand the *causes* of poverty the emphasis must shift to both a deeper historical as well as a wider macroeconomic perspective.

Finally, in terms of hypotheses, the report of the second Carnegie Inquiry concluded that, just as it was inadequate to reduce so complex a phenomenon as poverty to a single number or characteristic, so was it hopelessly oversimplifying to focus on a single cause of whatever kind, even so pervasive a one as "apartheid". Rather it was necessary to tease out the significance of various strands in a network of interacting causes. This led, in the three-stage process of facts, causes, and strategies, to explicit recognition that any plan of action against poverty must itself include a whole array of strategies at different levels.

Theoretical framework

The theoretical framework that emerged from these hypotheses during the 1980s laid far less emphasis on the personal characteristics of causation compared, for example, with the first Carnegie Commission fifty years previously. There a whole volume of the report was devoted to answering the question, "To what extent have psychological factors played a causal part" in creating the poor white problem? In the second Carnegie Inquiry, researchers were far more concerned to identify structural and other causes beyond the control of individuals enduring poverty than in any form of victim blaming. Although there was explicit recognition of the relevance of the rate of population growth in any consideration of the causes of poverty, as well as the impact of despair and failure to believe in themselves and in crippling the initiative and energy of those enduring poverty, nevertheless the emphasis lay primarily on structural (i.e. historical–political) and on economic (e.g. lack of investment, inadequate growth) causes.

It is perhaps a little too early to pinpoint exactly the change in emphasis of the theoretical framework used in writing about poverty as South Africa moved from the 1980s to the 1990s. However, if one contrasts the Carnegie report (1989), written by South Africans, with the World Bank discussion papers (1994), written largely by well-informed outside observers (see, particularly, Fallon and Perreira da Silva (1994)). There is a clear shift from historical and institutional causes to current economic causes. This change should not be overemphasized. The World Bank writers are mindful of historical causes such as those highlighted in the Carnegie Inquiry, but they build on this to consider many more economic aspects (such as tariff policy or investment strategies) than were looked at in detail, or even considered at all, in the 1980s. But neither in the 1980s nor in the 1990s are those writing about poverty focusing much on individual psychological considerations that, at other times and in other places, have occupied so much attention.

Data sources

Like the curate's egg, South African statistics are good in parts – but extremely patchy. Censuses in 1904, 1911, 1921, 1936, 1946, 1951, 1970, 1980, 1985, and 1991 combined with a whole set of industrial, agricultural, and other censuses, together with careful statistical records from individual sectors such as the mining industry, enable the researcher to uncover many aspects of the South African political economy over an unusually long-time period.[14] However, the data are also full of holes, which make sustained analysis difficult. For example, the declaration by South Africa's apartheid government of political independence for the Transkei in 1976 was accompanied by the removal of any reference to people living in Transkei from the national statistics. Similarly for Bophutatswana, Venda, and Ciskei. The fact that in economic and demographic terms these areas were impoverished rural reserves where the vast majority of the people were unskilled, had little education, and were black meant that their exclusion from the national data sets biased the results in such a way as to understate, to a considerable extent, such characteristics as the degree of poverty, the level of unemployment, or the prevalence of illness such as tuberculosis. By 1993, for example, the total population of the TBVC areas was estimated to be 7.6 million, i.e. 19 per cent of the total of 40.1 million.

The second Carnegie Inquiry, which published a good deal of information about poverty during the 1980s, did not confine itself in this manner. Indeed, a number of papers attempted to examine issues of poverty within these four TBVC areas as well as in the rest of South Africa.[15] But the weakness of the Carnegie Inquiry was that it did not itself generate any new overall statistical data. What it did was to initiate a whole set of individual micro studies in both urban and rural areas as well as to stimulate a number of statistical studies that were themselves based on existing official data and thus subject to the limitations inherent in those data.

It was in an attempt to overcome the weaknesses in the national data sets as collected by the apartheid government that the Project for Statistics on Living Standards and Development was conceived in 1992 (see above, page 230). Most of the fieldwork was carried out and the data collected in the last five months of 1993. The first selection of tables was published in August 1994 (PSLSD 1994).

Major results

Perhaps the best way to convey the results of the latest statistical research is to lay out, as succinctly as possible, some of the salient facts emerging from the Project for Statistics on Living Standards and Development, confirmed where relevant by findings from the CSS October 1994 Household Survey, and backed up by some of the insights from the earlier Carnegie Inquiry. The corrections, connections, and conclusions flowing from analysis of the new wave of statistical information have yet to be published. But it is likely that a number of articles, drawing from this material, will be published soon after this volume appears.[16]

If inequality is not taken into account it is possible to classify South Africa, in terms of average GNP per capita, as an upper-middle-income country, where it is so placed in the tables of the annual *World Development Report*. However, according to a survey based on fifty-seven countries for which data were available in 1978, South Africa then had the highest measured Gini coefficient (= 0.66) in the world (see Wilson and Ramphele 1989: 18, for details). Calculation of the coefficient, based on the 1991 census data (thus excluding the TBVC areas), produced a similar result, with a Gini of 0.68 (McGrath and Whiteford 1994). Later work by the World Bank[17] on the SALSS data, as finally cleaned by 1995, suggests a 1993 Gini coefficient for the country as a whole of 0.61. Further confirmation of the size of the gap between rich and poor can be seen in the fact that in 1993 the richest 10 per cent of households had an average monthly income one hundred times greater than the average monthly income of the poorest 10 per cent of households: R9,938 v R97 (PSLSD 1994: Table 13.6). Using an exchange rate of R3.5 to the dollar, the average household income of the poorest 10 per cent is approximately $1 per day. The vast majority of those who are this poor are African, and their average household size is 4.8 persons; thus the average income of those who are in the poorest 10 per cent of households works out at approximately 19 cents per person per day. Hardly what one would expect in a country that, in average terms, falls into the upper-middle-income range on the world scale.

Another way of measuring the depth of the inequality is simply to note that the poorest 40 per cent of individuals (where individuals are assumed to earn the household per capita income) earn 6 per cent of total income, whereas the richest 10 per cent earn almost half (47 per cent) and the richest 20 per cent earn more than two-thirds (69 per cent) of total income (Whiteford and McGrath 19940).

South Africa, as we have seen above, has long been part of the international attempt to construct poverty datum lines. Whiteford and McGrath (1994) construct seven different poverty lines for African households only. The World Bank, pending the emergence of further consensus, uses a relative poverty line of the poorest 40% of households, equivalent to approximately 53% of the total population, as measured by the 1993 South Africa Living Standards Survey.[18]

For the rural poor in South Africa, as in other parts of the world, access to arable land and landlessness are critical. What is peculiar about South Africa is: the extent to which the distribution of land is racially based; the speed with which population has been growing in precisely the areas that can least afford greater density on the land; the fact that this growth is quite different from the pattern on large-scale commercial farms where population has been decreasing and farms getting bigger.

Analysis of the 1993 data has not yet been done, but from the Carnegie Inquiry we know that the population density in the rural parts of the reserves is almost ten times the density on the largely white-owned commercial farms – 57 and 6 persons, respectively, per km².

In 1954 a government commission (Tomlinson) calculated that the reserves could support approximately 60 per cent of the population counted there in the 1951 census if small-scale agriculture were to be properly developed there. But the remaining 40 per cent would have to move off the land. Instead of this decrease, we find that between 1960 and 1980 the population of the reserves rose from 4.5 million to 11 million. In 1951, approximately one-third of the black population lived in the reserves, one-third on the white-owned commercial farms; and one-third in towns. But, over the next thirty years, whilst people were pushed off commercial farms by mechanization and other changing techniques of production, combined with pressures of apartheid policy, they were prevented by the pass laws of that same policy from going to town. The only place to go was to the overcrowded reserves, where population rose astronomically. In the Ciskei during the twelve years (1970–1982) before "independence", the population doubled. This represented a population growth rate of 5.9 per cent compared with the then natural rate of 3.3 per cent. Similarly in Qwa Qwa, a remote area without an urban economic base, population grew by at least 21 per cent per annum, and possibly even two or three times as fast as that. The consequences of these astronomical increases in rural population throughout the reserves are (a) to reduce the amount of land of those who have, and (b) to increase the number of those who have not. Thus in the Chata Valley, near Keiskammahoek in the Ciskei, between 1946 and 1981 the average size of land holding fell by 75 per cent from 1.72 ha to 0.43 ha, and the proportion of households without land increased from 10 per cent to 43 per cent.

It is not only land, however, that is in short supply for the poor. Also inadequate is access to basic needs such as energy, water, and shelter. The Project for Statistics on Living Standards and Development has collected a mass of data that provide a much clearer picture than previously of availability by geographic area and race, thus facilitating better targeting by policy makers.[19] With regard to electricity, for example, we find that, whereas 100 per cent of white and Indian and 86 per cent of coloured households have access to electricity, only one-third (37 per cent) of African households enjoy the same amenity. The geographic dimension of poverty in the country can be seen by considering the availability of electricity to African households in two provinces: the largely urban PWV and the predominantly rural Eastern Cape. In the former, 71 per cent of households can get electricity from the national grid, whereas in the latter the figure is only 9 per cent. Again considering African families only, we find that the main sources of energy for cooking are: wood 35 per cent, paraffin 29 per cent, and electricity 26 per cent. But for whites, no fewer than 97 per cent use electricity for cooking. For lighting in African homes, candles are the primary source, used by 40 per cent, followed by electricity (34 per cent) and paraffin lamps (25 per cent). With regard to the time taken to collect wood, of those African families that have to collect wood, although 14 per cent take less than 30 minutes, 37 per cent take up to 2 hours, 33 per cent take 2–4 hours, and 16 per cent (one in six) take 4 hours or more. (PSLSD 1994: Table 4.9 ff.)

With regard to clean drinking water, a similar picture of racial and geographic differentials applies. Piped water into the house is enjoyed by virtually all white and Indian households and by 79 per cent of coloured. But for Africans only 18 per cent of households (less than one in five) households have internal water on tap. If we expand our definition of water availability to include households with taps in their yards then virtually all coloured households also have water, whereas African households with water remain in a minority at 44 per cent. Urban–rural differences are no less striking, with inside taps available to less than one in ten (8 per cent) of rural African households compared with two in five (40 per cent) in metropolitan areas.

These statistics confirm and consolidate the insights gleaned ten years previously from the micro studies of the Carnegie Inquiry, where time and again research workers reported something of the daily burden borne by individuals, mainly women in rural areas, in collecting water for their families. One study reported women in three different villages spending an average of 187 minutes per household every day collecting water. Another study of nineteen villages measured the physical energy expended and concluded that carrying the heavy (21 kg) plastic containers to the homestead required the energy equivalent of that needed by a miner wielding a pick. A third described in some detail the problems facing a community, many of whose members were afflicted by a strange, painful type of progressive arthritis (Mseleni joint disease), who had to travel for more than an hour to collect water from the largest freshwater lake in South Africa, which could easily have been connected to the village by some relatively inexpensive plastic pipes. Another study reported an average of one water tap available for every 760 people. Perhaps the most striking statistic of all was that for many poor people, in different rural parts of the country, the actual cash payment per litre of water was up to sixty-seven times greater than it was for urban middle-class households to run water out of their kitchen taps. Poverty, concluded the Carnegie Inquiry in more than one context, can be expensive (Wilson and Ramphele 1989: 48–51).

This focus on water helps to illuminate the value of having both the representative statistical sample as well as the detail of the in-depth case study, as discussed above (page 233). In the case of water, the work that has been done from the universities and other research centres has been incorporated into one of the first of the new South African government's White Papers, which sets out a strategic plan to provide clean drinking water for all (Department of Water Affairs and Forestry 1994).

Listening to those who themselves endure poverty it is clear that one of the most painful aspects is unemployment. "Now I am not working," cried one man, "it is just like these hands of mine have been cut off and I am useless" (Thabane and Guy 1984). In story after story during the course of the Carnegie Inquiry, women and men talked of the pain of being unable to find work. Table 13.1, drawn from the 1993 survey, provides the bare bones of the picture.

From this table one can see something of the profile of poverty in South Africa. Differences in the levels of unemployment are marked between racial categories, between men and women, between urban and rural areas, and between different age groups.

Table 13.1 Unemployment in South Africa

	All	Male	Female	Rural	Urban	Metro-politan	Age 16–24	Age 55–64
African	39	34	44	42	35	34	65	20
Coloured	21	17	25	10	26	19	41	9
Indian	11	8	17	–	10	12	24	5
White	5	4	6	4	4	5	11	2
Total	30	26	35	40	26	22	53	15
CSS[a]	33	26	41	40	28			

Source: PSLSD (1994: 141 ff)
[a] For comparative purposes we include the CSS data for unemployment, similarly defined but including also 15 year olds wanting work, almost exactly one year later in October 1994.
Note: These figures include those who want work but who were too discouraged to continue looking for it.

Current research and lacunae

A good deal of analytical research, using the 1991 census, the October 1994 Household Survey, and the data collected by the Project for Statistics on Living Standards and Development, is currently being done (see note 16), but there are five or six areas where a good deal of empirical work needs to be undertaken.

First, although the PSLSD survey covered a national sample from all over the country, the fact is that, for a number of reasons including difficulty of access, the situation on white-owned farms was not properly investigated. This is not surprising because these areas have been notoriously difficult to get into. There is a good deal more information available now than previously but, despite agricultural censuses, it remains true that a fully comprehensive sample survey of living standards (including production by black households living on these farms) remains to be done. Our information on conditions in rural areas outside the old homelands or reserves is still not good enough.

Second, agricultural output in the reserves is known to be relatively insignificant, as was confirmed by the 1993 survey. But for those exploring strategies of wealth creation by poor people living in and near this small-scale agriculture, there is still not enough detailed information available. It would be useful to know not only the actual but also the desired levels of production by households, especially in the rural areas.[20]

Third, sampling for the 1993 survey was done before the boundaries of the nine new provinces were done. Thus, the results of the situation in each province are not always as significant as they should be. The October 1994 Household Survey has gone a long way to remedying this deficiency at the provincial level, but there is still a need for surveys down at the magisterial and even more localized levels in order to pinpoint more accurately those communities most in need of infrastructural and other investment.

Fourth, proper and more comprehensive monitoring of current development projects, such as the Small Enterprise Foundation in Tzaneen, Northern Transvaal, is needed in order to learn from experience what works in terms of achieving its goals, and what does not, and why. There is not even a readily available list of the wide range of current initiatives, much less adequate ongoing analysis of their work, year by year.

Fifth, research is also required to explore the impact of changes at the macro level on the lives of those enduring poverty down at the grass roots. South Africa has so far done almost none of the sort of research, pioneered by UNICEF amongst others, that examines the impact of various forms of structural adjustment on the nutritional status of children. In South Africa, for example, there has been little investigation of the impact on children in poor households of such macroeconomic measures as the removal in recent years of the subsidy on bread or of cuts in social spending. But this, like other gaps mentioned above, requires more refined and more regular statistical surveys to make possible longitudinal monitoring of the impact of different policy changes on poverty.

There is one final gap that needs to be considered. This relates to poverty that has long been linked to South Africa but that is endured by people living outside its political boundaries, in the limitrophe countries. Analysis during the course of the second Carnegie Inquiry showed that any study of poverty should be made with a clear recognition of the wider regional context in which it occurs.

> Southern Africa is a region in which a century of industrial revolution centred on the gold-mining industry and based on a system of oscillating labour migration has forged a single economy whose boundaries are far wider than those of the political nation-state in which the gold mines are located.
>
> In the light of the region's economic history, it is clear that any attempt to localise poverty by focussing on one small area (for example the Ciskei) in isolation from the wider economy would be profoundly misleading. Even more seriously, too narrow a geographic focus could easily result in strategies being developed to reduce poverty in one area (such as the Transkei) but which did so primarily at the expense of poor people somewhere else (such as in Lesotho or Mozambique). (Wilson and Ramphele 1989: 27–28).

A too narrow economic nationalism could develop a set of policies profoundly damaging to poor people living in countries surrounding South Africa. Table 13.2, which provides basic data for the eleven countries of southern Africa, helps to add some perspective to South Africa's position, with roughly one-third of the region's population generating three-quarters of its total wealth.

In terms of GNP per capita, Mozambique in the 1990s is by far the poorest country in the world. Yet for the full century of South Africa's industrial revolution Mozambique has contributed a significant proportion of the labour that has made that industrial transformation possible. More work needs to be done to understand more fully the process by which Mozambique has become poorer while South Africa has grown richer. One fundamental lesson from southern Africa is that it is not sufficient to focus on

Table 13.2 Southern Africa: basic indicators, 1992

Country	Area ('000 km^2)	Population (million)	GNP/capita US$
Angola	1,247	9.7	676–2,695[a]
Botswana	582	1.4	2,790
Lesotho	30	1.9	590
Malawi	118	9.1	210
Mozambique	802	16.5	60
Swaziland	17	0.9	1,090
Tanzania	945	25.9	110
Zambia	753	8.3	–
Zimbabwe	391	10.4	570
Namibia	824	1.5	1,610
South Africa	1,221	39.8	2,670

Source: World Development Report, 1994.
[a] Estimated as lower-middle income.

poverty within the political boundaries of a particular nation state without considering in some detail, and in historic perspective, the nature and impact of economic linkages between that economy and other countries. Although not included in the scope of this paper, a good deal of poverty research has been done in the former frontline states. The most famous of these studies is undoubtedly the 1974/75 Rural Income Distribution Survey in Botswana, undertaken by the Central Statistics Office in consultation with the Ministry of Finance and Development Planning of the government of Botswana. Twenty years later it remains a model of its kind.

NOTES

1. Cited by Morifi (1984).
2. For discussion on this point, as it was understood in 1989, see Wilson and Ramphele (1989: 6–8 & 258–260).
3. See *South African Outlook*, June 1984, for text of the Prime Minister's statement and the University's reply.
4. The five parts are: 1. Economic; 2. Psychological; 3. Educational; 4. Health; 5. Sociological
5. Those actually involved in the work of the Carnegie Commission clearly saw it as important as part of the process of removing political obstacles to black economic advancement (See Butterfield (1929). The problem arose with the uses to which the findings of the report, focusing exclusively on white poverty, were put by Professor Verwoerd and others.
6. This and the subsequent paragraph are drawn from the Preface to Wilson and Ramphele (1989), which contains further details on how the inquiry was organized.

7. Bibliographical details of the papers produced during the course of the second Carnegie Inquiry into Poverty and Development in Southern Africa are contained in Wilson and Ramphele (1989: appendix 1).
8. This material, from what is now known as the South Africa Living Standards Survey (SALSS), may be obtained, for a nominal fee (currently R250), from SALDRU, School of Economics, University of Cape Town, Rondebosch 7700, South Africa. Fax: 021–6504053 or e-mail: adams@socsci.uct.ac.za.
9. Bibliographical details of the thirteen volumes are contained in PSLSD, *South Africans Rich and Poor: Baseline Household Statistics* (1994), p. 344.
10. See the discussion on pp. 236–237 about data sources and the omission of Transkei, Bophutatswana, Venda and Ciskei from government statistics over the eighteen years (for the Transkei) before 1994.
11. The report made use of the distinction made by John Iliffe (1987) between poor and very poor or destitute; between *pauvre* and *indigent*.
12. Two chapters (10 and 11) in Wilson and Ramphele (1989) are aimed at uncovering the roots of the existing pattern of poverty.
13. The Report of the Commission of Inquiry into Safety and Health in the Mining Industry, RP/1995, draws specific attention to the prevalence of the migrant labour system and its harmful consequences. See also Public Information Centre, (1995).
14. For those wishing to go directly to these data, a good place to begin is with Bureau of Census and Statistics, *Union Statistics for Fifty Years, 1910–1960* (1960). Subsequent annual volumes (starting in 1964) from the same source (variously renamed the Department of Census and Statistics and currently Central Statistical Services) maintain the flow.
15. Sets of these Carnegie papers are lodged not only in South African libraries but also in other parts of the world, including the Oxford Institute for Economics and Statistics and the Africa Collection of the Yale University Library.
16. Those wishing to be kept up to date regarding work in progress on the PSLSD data may do so via e-mail to adams@socsci.uct.ac.za. One significant early benefit of the policy to place all data immediately into the public domain has been the discovery, particularly by Pieter le Roux in his preliminary analysis of pensions, of the need for further cleaning of the data, especially with regard to assumptions about the frequency of pension payments and also about the imputed value of housing owned by households.
17. Ministry in the Office of the President: Reconstruction & Development Programme, *Key Indicators of Poverty in South Africa*; An analysis prepared for the office of the RDP by the World Bank, based on the South Africa Living Standards Survey, co-ordinated by the Southern Africa Labour & Development Research Unit at the University of Cape Town (forthcoming, 1995).

18. Ibid.
19. This picture has been further clarified by the October 1994 Household Survey of the Central Statistical Service published as this overview was being revised for publication. Unless otherwise stated, the data in this section are taken from the earlier PSLSD tables.
20. I am indebted to David Sanders for this point, as well as for discussion clarifying what research is needed to monitor aspects of structural adjustment.

REFERENCES

Ballinger, W. H. and M. Ballinger. 1938. *Native Wages and the Cost of Living*. Johannesburg: South African Institute of Race Relations.
Bureau of Census and Statistics (1960) *Union Statistics for Fifty Years 1910–1960*. Pretoria: The Bureau.
Butterfield, K. L. (1929) *Rural Conditions and Sociological Problems in South Africa*. New York.
Carnegie Commission (1932) *The Poor White Problem in South Africa: Report of the Carnegie Commission*. Stellenbosch: The Commission.
Central Statistical Service (1995) *October Household Survey 1994*. Statistical Release PO317. Pretoria: CSS, March.
Central Statistics Office/Ministry of Finance and Development Planning (Botswana) (1976) *1974/75 Rural Income Distribution Survey*. Gaberone: Government Printer.
Debates of Parliament, 27th April 1984. Cape Town: Government Printers.
Department of Water Affairs and Forestry (1994) *Water: An Indivisible National Asset*. White Paper on Water Supply and Sanitation. Cape Town: The Department, March.
Fallon, P. and L. A. Perreira de Silva, (1994). *South Africa: Economic Performance and Policies*. Washington DC: World Bank, Informal Discussion Paper No. 7.
Gould, S. J. (1981) *The Mismeasure of Man*. New York: Norton.
Iliffe, J. (1987) *The African Poor: A History*. Cambridge: Cambridge University Press.
Jones, J. D. R and A. Hoernle. (1942) *The Union's Burden of Poverty*. Johannesburg.
McGrath, M. and A. Whiteford (1994) *Inequality in the Size Distribution of Income in South Africa*. Stellenbosch Economic Project.
Macmillan, W. M. (1930) *Complex South Africa*. London.
Morifi, M.-J. (1984) *Life among the Poor in Philipstown*. Cape Town: SALDRU, Carnegie Conference Paper No. 33.
Native Economic Commission (1932) *Report of the Native Economic Commission 1930–32*. U.G.22. Pretoria: Government Printer.
PSLSD (Project for Statistics on Living Standards and Development) (1994) *South Africans Rich and Poor: Baseline Household Statistics*. Cape Town: SALDRU.
Public Information Centre (1995) *Mines and Migrancy*. March.

Schumpeter, J. A. (1954) *History of Economic Analysis.* New York: Oxford University Press.
South African Agriculture: Structure, Performance and Options for the Future. Washington, DC: World Bank, Informal Discussion Paper No. 6.
Thabane, M. and J. Guy. (1984) *Unemployment and Casual Labour in Maseru: The Impact of Changing Employment Strategies on Migrant Labourers in Lesotho.* Cape Town: SALDRU, Carnegie Conference Paper No. 124.
Turrell, R (1987) *Capital and Labour on the Kimberley Diamond Fields.* Cambridge: Cambridge University Press.
Wentzel, W. (1982) *Poverty and Development in South Africa 1890–1980: A Bibliography.* Cape Town: SALDRU, Working Paper No. 46.
White Paper on the Reconstruction and Development Programme. August 1994.
Whiteford, A. and M. McGrath (1994) "Income distribution, inequality and poverty in South Africa". Paper presented at the SALDRU conference on poverty, Cape Town, December.
Wilson, F and M. Ramphele. (1989) *Uprooting Poverty: The South African Challenge.* Cape Town: David Philip.

Part IV
The Western Region

The West European approach to poverty research is notable for its concern with the conceptualization of poverty. Significant for the long run of poverty research and policy is the development of less economistic measures of poverty. The subjective poverty line, for example, is based on public opinion surveys of what is considered an inadequate income; deprivation indices measure deficiencies in health, housing, education, etc.; while the broader concern for social exclusion focuses on participation of all citizens in the community. In general, poverty researchers in Western Europe regard poverty as linked to inequality, not just to subsistence. The language of social inclusion is becoming important in policy circles.

Poverty research has had a shorter and more restricted role in the authoritarian Europe of the Soviet Union and the former East European nations in the Soviet orbit. Poverty research was banned, discouraged or limited, and certainly under-researched compared with the West. In the post-1989 and post-1991 period, the impact of a narrow conceptualization of poverty is still visible in the minimum-subsistence approach to poverty measurement and alleviation in the East Central and the former Soviet Union nations. They are now late-comers both to poverty research and to high poverty rates.

The Western region is experiencing economic difficulties that affect social policies. In Eastern Europe, the break-up of communist rule has resulted in the uncertainties of the market, inflation, and high unemployment as well as in new economic growth. Enterprise-based social policies – a staple of the previous regimes – have deteriorated and the social policies left over from the past are not coping well with the new situations.

Economic strains are forcing a re-evaluation of some of the social policies of Scandinavia and Canada. The welfare state in these countries has provided a model, perhaps a yardstick, for assessing poverty policy. Universalistic social programmes providing an income floor and extensive social services are the cornerstone of the welfare state model. As in Eastern Europe and the former Soviet Union, social policy was based on a full employment economy and limited inflation, and political consensus made possible high taxes and high public transfers. Now, these conditions for a strong welfare state have changed, and poverty is re-emerging. In Scandinavia and in many of the other high-income countries in the Western region, the *rediscovery* of poverty is the theme. The new economic conditions force the awareness that poverty is a problem again, and that poverty research is needed. Large-scale research programmes on poverty have been launched, as for example on the urban underclass in the United States and on social exclusion in the European Community.

Chapter 14

The European Community: Diverse Images of Poverty

Jürgen Kohl

Introductory note

This chapter gives an overview on trends in poverty research in Western Europe, focused primarily but not exclusively on the member states of the European Union. The concern is with poverty *research* rather than with poverty itself, and, more specifically, with *comparative* poverty research, that is, with studies covering more than one country. This excludes studies of a purely national character as well as studies carried out at a regional or local level within nations – unless they are of some broader theoretical and methodological significance. Since it is virtually impossible to detail results for twelve (as of the beginning of 1995, even fifteen) countries – some of them with a relatively well-developed tradition in poverty research – within the constraints of one report, the chapter emphasizes *types* of research and *"paradigmatic"* approaches rather than attempting to give an exhaustive overview.[1]

First, some major conceptual and methodological issues are discussed. Then some typical approaches and larger comparative studies undertaken during the past decade are characterized with regard to these distinctions. Finally, I attempt to draw some conclusions from these studies and highlight some promising avenues for future comparative poverty research in Western Europe.

Conceptual and methodological issues

The conceptualization of poverty is certainly a politically sensitive issue charged with political and ideological connotations and prejudices. It is necessary, therefore, to make explicit the methodological choices the researcher is faced with and that determine – to a certain extent – the empirical results. This is a prerequisite to ensure validity and reliability and to allow an adequate interpretation of the findings.

Of course, counting the poor and analysing their composition in terms of socio-economic and socio-demographic attributes do not by themselves lead to explanations of why they are poor and to predictions whether they will stay poor in the future or manage to escape poverty. Nor does such an analysis immediately provide us with policy proposals concerning what can be done politically to prevent poverty or to assist the poor to escape poverty. But in order to tackle such more far-reaching questions, it is first necessary to identify the 'target population', namely people in poverty or at the risk of poverty. "Indeed, the definition, the measurement and the explanation of poverty are closely interdependent, as also are the policy implications which the social investigator may draw" (Room 1990: 37).

In this context, questions of conceptualization and operationalization become critically important; for the extent of poverty as well as the social distribution of poverty largely depend on how poverty is defined and measured.[2] It is always possible to identify social sub-groups with high rates of poverty incidence (meaning disproportionate risks of poverty). In turn, this draws our attention to possible causal factors associated with these social attributes. Whether high rates of poverty are found, for example, among the elderly or among families with children at least suggests where causal mechanisms and explanations have to be sought.

Similarly, empirically tested and corroborated explanations can serve as starting-points for designing strategies to combat poverty. For, in order to combat poverty successfully, policies are bound to intervene into the causal mechanisms of how poverty is generated and eventually perpetuated. Structural explanations of poverty lend themselves more easily to policy interventions than, for example, individualist explanations. In this way, issues of conceptualization gain relevance not only for poverty *research*, but also for (anti-)poverty *policy*.

These general methodological considerations are of special importance to cross-national research on poverty. Whatever options are chosen to define and measure poverty in such studies, it is important that they are consistently applied to all countries under study in order to arrive at valid conclusions.

Researchers are, however, seldom in the position of designing and conducting *ex ante* comparative studies on poverty – in which case they would have to agree on certain standards in advance. More often, they are confined to *ex post* comparisons, that is, to taking stock of existing national studies on poverty, which may differ in their methodological approach and definitions: they can try to render them comparable only in a second step. To perform this task, it is most helpful that the pertinent information is provided and the rationale for making these choices is clearly recognizable in the first place.

Direct vs. indirect concepts of poverty

Graham Room (1992), in his report on poverty research in the European Community, distinguishes between two research traditions: a predominantly Anglo-Saxon tradition focusing on *distributional* issues, namely the lack of resources at the disposal of an individual or a household, and a primarily Continental intellectual tradition focusing on *relational* issues, namely inadequate social participation and social integration of the poor in the larger society.[3] In both traditions, however – it should be pointed out – poverty is treated not as a residual social problem separated from the rest of society but as an integral part of a broader analysis, be it of the distribution of resources in society or of social inequality and social integration.

In a similar way, Stein Ringen (1987a: ch. 7, 1987b, 1988) differentiates two main concepts in poverty research. Following the first concept, people are considered poor "if they do not have the necessary resources, capabilities, or rights to achieve what is defined as a minimum standard in their way of life" (1987a: 145). According to the second concept, people are poor "if they have a way of life which is below the defined minimum standard, irrespective of what has determined this way of life" (1987a: 145f.). The first concept is called "indirect" because "poverty is defined indirectly through the determinants of way of life" whereas in the second case it is defined "directly by way of life" (1987a: 146).

Obviously, these two concepts of poverty are rooted in two competing concepts of welfare (see Figure 14.1): one referring to the *resources* at the disposal of individuals or households, the other referring to the *actual living conditions* of individuals and households. Income is usually considered as the "common denominator" of resources, as "the essential individual resource for choice" (Ringen 1987a: 19), but "other individual resources matter in addition to income (for example property, education or knowledge, or other personal capacities, such as health)".[4] In this perspective, resources of various kinds can be regarded as

	Indirect concepts	Direct concepts
Concepts of welfare	Resources, in particular income (= determinants of way of life)	Living conditions, way of life, quality of life
Concepts of poverty	Lack of resources, in particular income	Social exclusion, lack of social integration
Concepts in empirical poverty research	Subsistence minimum concept	Relative deprivation concept
Measuring devices	Poverty line, equivalence scales	Deprivation scale, index of deprivation
Social policy goals	Guaranteeing minimum income	Combating social exclusion

Figure 14.1   Direct and indirect concepts of poverty.

inputs that are to be converted into actual living conditions by the activities of individuals and households themselves.

The *resource approach* has been advocated especially in the Scandinavian tradition of welfare research on the grounds that command over resources enables individuals to control and direct their living conditions. Moreover "resources are the object of social policies" (Erikson and Uusitalo 1987: 189). Social policies (should) aim at influencing the level and distribution of resources available to individuals, whereas the *use* of resources to create one's way of life should be left to individual preferences.

Ringen seeks to combine the virtues of these two approaches in the concept of "standard of living", which covers both resources (as determinants) and way of life (as a result). Accordingly, he defines poverty as a combination of the two – "as a low standard of living, meaning deprivation in way of life because of insufficient resources to avoid such deprivation". But he insists that "both these understandings of poverty reflect an objective condition of welfare" (1987a: 146). This is important because some authors treat 'deprivation' as a subjective feeling – a subjectivist approach bluntly rejected by Ringen: "To be poor depends on how you live, not how you feel" (1987a: 145).

When reviewing the main concepts applied in empirical poverty research, Ringen – as others (see Atkinson 1989) – distinguishes between the *subsistence minimum concept* and *the relative deprivation concept*. The subsistence minimum concept is exemplified by the early poverty studies of Rowntree, but also by the official poverty index used for statistical purposes in the United States nowadays. In principle, it is aimed to establish "the minimum income which an individual, a family or a household would require to obtain the physical necessities of life" (Room 1990: 39).

The relative deprivation concept is most clearly reflected in the pioneering work by Peter Townsend (1979, 1987) who defines poverty as follows:

> Individuals, families and groups in the population can be said to be in poverty when they lack the resources to obtain the types of diet, participate in the activities and have the living conditions and amenities which are customary, or are at least widely encouraged or approved, in the societies to which they belong. Their resources are so seriously below those commanded by the average individual or family that they are, in effect, excluded from ordinary living patterns, customs and activities (Townsend 1979: 31).[5]

In Townsend's definition, it is recognized that "the needs which an individual or a family must satisfy in order to live as a member of his society are socially rather than physically determined" (Room 1990: 39).

The quasi-official definition of poverty that the Council of Ministers of the European Community adopted when it launched the second Community programme to combat poverty also stands, broadly speaking, within the Townsend tradition: "'the poor' shall be taken to mean persons, families and groups of persons whose resources (material, cultural and social) are so limited as to exclude them from the minimum acceptable way of life in the Member State in which they live" (Council of the European Communities 1984: Article 1.2).[6]

Lee Rainwater interprets these two approaches as expressing a more important underlying difference between an economic and a social definition of poverty: "An economic measure of poverty determines an income sufficient to provide a minimum level of consumption of goods and services... A sociological measure of poverty is concerned not with consumption but with social participation" (Rainwater 1992: 5). Although he strongly argues that "poverty is essentially a matter of social standing or social class" and thus in favour of a sociological concept of poverty, this should not be mistaken as implying a subjective or consensual definition of poverty. His argument rather is that "objectively people cannot carry out the roles, participate in the activities, maintain the social relations, that are definitive of mainstream members of society if their resources (over some period of time) fall short of a 'certain minimum'" (1992: 6) and that this objective condition is reflected in the behaviour of the members of society in that "they respond to others in terms of their perceived social standing and reinforce definitions of each other as poor or prosperous, average or just getting along, etc." (1992: 7).

Ringen, however, draws a different distinction. He characterizes the subsistence minimum concept as an *indirect* concept of poverty because it refers to a *lack of income resources* to buy the necessities of food, clothing, and housing as determined by individual needs. In contrast to this, the relative deprivation concept is characterized as a *direct* concept of poverty, referring to *deprivations in way of life*, determined by social requirements in order to be able to participate in normal social activities and to avoid social exclusion: "The meaning of poverty under the relative deprivation concept is to be excluded from the ordinary way of life and activities of one's society" – Ringen 1987a: 149).

Ringen continues to argue that "if there are indirect and direct *concepts* of poverty, there should also be indirect and direct *measures* of poverty. Under the indirect concept we should measure poverty by income or other resource indicators; under the direct concept by consumption or other way of life indicators" (1987a: 146). The conventional measurement of specifying a poverty line – whether absolute or relative – is regarded as an example of an indirect measure, but, in his view, no direct measurement corresponding to the concept of relative deprivation has been developed. Consequently, he criticizes the "lack of correspondence between concept and measurement" (1987a: 157) and argues in favour of a "third stage in the measurement of poverty" (Ringen 1985), epitomized by an index of deprivation or a deprivation scale summarizing various items of deprivation. He admits, however, that Townsend's pioneering work to construct an "index of deprivation based on a series of way of life indicators" is "a step towards direct measurement" (1987a: 157, fn 32).

Poverty as a multi-dimensional phenomenon

There is widespread consensus that poverty is a multidimensional phenomenon. Whether it is conceived indirectly (as a lack of resources) or directly (as deprivations in the way of life), a multitude of aspects have always to be taken into consideration.

"Income is useful only in markets, but what we get out of markets depends not only on our income but also on other resources which influence how we are able to use our income, for example, education, knowledge, and information" (Ringen 1987a: 160). This means that, even if we prefer an indirect concept of poverty, we should aim to include other dimensions than just income.

For the relative deprivation concept, measuring the various components of way of life directly seems to be the only adequate measurement procedure.[7] "Several indicators of various forms of deprivation are needed in order to identify a network of deprivations" (Ringen 1987a: 161). In order to derive a summary measure of deprivation, one could then think of constructing a *scale* or an *index of deprivation*; for only the *cumulation* of a number of deprivation items can be said to constitute severe deprivation.

However, relying on "way of life" or "deprivation" indicators alone is also insufficient to measure poverty because "people may live as if they were poor without being poor" (Ringen 1987a: 162). "A 'different' way of life which is the result of 'different' preferences and free choice is not a result of deprivation and, must, therefore, be excluded from the measurement of poverty" (Ringen 1987a: 162). Only if their state of deprivation is caused by insufficient resources should it be considered as poverty.[8]

Having accepted in principle Ringen's position that the relative deprivation concept of poverty requires direct measurement by indicators of living conditions, this still leaves us with the problem of which aspects of possession of goods, use of services, and participation in certain activities have to be taken into account in a multidimensional set of indicators (e.g. food, clothing, housing, health, education, family relations, cultural activities, etc.).

Although a number of proposals specifying such items of living conditions have been developed by researchers such as Townsend (1979: ch. 6), Mack and Lansley (1985), Whelan (1992), and Muffels et al. (1992), it seems difficult to reach a consensus about the dimensions to be included and about their relative importance. Moreover, in order to arrive at some aggregate measure of deprivation and to distinguish degrees of deprivation, one has to agree on a weighting procedure for the various dimensions as well as on certain minimum (and normal) standards in each dimension – an even more difficult decision.

In cross-national comparisons, the problems are further exacerbated because some aspects of living conditions may seem less relevant in certain countries than in others. This would mean that different weighting schemes and/or minimum standard definitions have to be constructed for each country. This leads to the conclusion that such a research strategy, although desirable for theoretical reasons, poses severe problems to ensure cross-national comparability.

In empirical poverty research, poverty is most often measured in terms of income, by specifying some kind of poverty line and counting the number of people falling below that line. It is obvious that income is a resource indicator and, hence, corresponds to an indirect concept of poverty. The use of income in order to measure poverty is often justified on the grounds that:

(a) it is the *most important resource* at the disposal of individuals (and can, therefore, be used as a *proxy* for other kinds of resources), and
(b) command over income largely *determines individual living conditions* so that it can be used as a *predictor* of poverty, understood as relative deprivation, even if in theory we would prefer a direct concept of poverty.

A number of objections can be raised against such reasoning: Using income as the only indicator of poverty would seem to be adequate only if an individual's life chances depended entirely upon the goods and services he or she could buy for money (in an ideal-typical system of market exchange). Obviously, this limits the usefulness of "money indicators" in less "monetized" economies where the subsistence sector or the shadow economy may be of considerable size.

Even in developed market economies, however, life chances typically do *not* depend solely on cash income and marketable resources. Private property and wealth (acquired in the past), such as owner-occupied housing, can be utilized in the present to derive a "use value" that would otherwise have to be paid for as rents. Furthermore, there is "income in kind", such as the value of home production, unpaid care work, or mutual assistance within kinship or the neighbourhood. And there are public goods and services provided free of charge or at reduced rates (for example, health services, public housing).[9]

For theoretical reasons, it would be desirable, therefore, to incorporate such forms of non-cash income into a comprehensive measure of economic well-being. Because of the limited availability of such data in some countries, on the other hand, such attempts may lead to less comparability in cross-national studies. In order to achieve cross-national comparability of results, it seems to be more important to use *consistent* definitions and operationalizations than to use the ideal ones in some cases but flawed ones in other cases (see Saunders 1991).

The question of linkages between resources and actual living conditions is also at the heart of the controversy about Townsend's *relative deprivation* concept. Townsend (1979; see also Donnison 1988) holds that below a certain level of income an individual's risk of being deprived of enjoying the benefits and participating in the activities customary in society increases dramatically. But other researchers have questioned whether such a sudden increase of risk can be identified (see Piachaud 1987; Ringen 1988).

It is suggested here that such controversies should be treated not as issues of definition but as propositions that need to be further investigated in order to establish empirically the degree of correlation between income and other resource indicators as well as between income and other indicators of living conditions. Studies making use of different types of indicators seem to be especially suited, therefore, to provide valuable insights into these interrelationships.

Absolute vs. relative poverty lines

Whatever the concept of poverty – whether direct or indirect, focusing on resources (as *potential* living conditions) or on actual living conditions – it is necessary to set certain minimum standards below which people are regarded as poor. With regard to the resource concept of poverty, this is usually done by establishing a *poverty line*. In principle, there are two possibilities:

- an *absolute* poverty line characterized by the amount of resources deemed necessary and sufficient for survival in a given society, or
- a *relative* poverty line defined in relation to some average resources available in that society.[10]

It has rightly been pointed out by various authors (see Ringen 1987b; Veit-Wilson 1987) that even an absolute poverty line represents more than just a (scientifically determined) physical minimum of subsistence; it can be derived only with reference to the level of development of a society, the availability of goods, etc. and, hence, cannot remain unchangeable over time. "What kinds of living situations are described as poverty, depends on the social and economic circumstances and the level of prosperity of a society at a certain moment" (Deleeck et al. 1992: 2).

Nonetheless, the underlying idea is that it represents the monetary value of a "basket of basic goods and services" in a given society and a given time-period. In comparing different countries, comparability would require the use of the same basket of goods for each country, only calculated in the respective national currencies.[11] However, using the same basket of goods may not be adequate for each country, because of differences in consumption patterns and relative price levels. An alternative procedure would be to determine different baskets of goods adequate for each country. It is, however, difficult to define criteria for the inter-country adequacy or 'equivalence' of such baskets of goods.

A methodologically interesting proposal to tackle this problem is based on the observation – generally known as *"Engel's law"* – that the share of food expenditures in total expenditures decreases as income increases. On this basis, it has been suggested that equal food budget shares (of, say, 30, 35, or 40 per cent of total consumption expenditures) be regarded as roughly equivalent absolute poverty lines in cross-national comparisons (see Teekens and Zaidi 1990). This procedure avoids the problem of specifying the composition of a basket of basic necessities as well as that of converting national currencies into a common currency.

Even if it is admitted that any definition of poverty is always "relative", in the sense that it relates to the circumstances prevailing in the country and time-period under study, a methodological distinction can and should be maintained between a poverty line designed to represent a basket of basic goods and services (however those may be defined or selected), and a poverty line expressed as a share of (some measure of) average resources in society.

While the monetary value of the former has to be adjusted to account for price changes in order to keep the 'real value' of the basket of goods and services constant, the latter automatically varies in line with changes in economic performance, as reflected in the fluctuations of average income, for instance.

It is in this technical sense that the terms *absolute* and *relative* poverty lines are used in this report. Of course, this does *not* imply – as is often erroneously assumed – that "an absolute definition will result in far fewer persons officially in poverty than will a relative definition" (Villemez 1992: 1526). The basket of goods and services, for example, may be generously defined as including many items beyond the necessities of physical subsistence (e.g. telephone, TV, car), whereas a relative poverty line may be set at a level so stringent (e.g. 40 per cent or less of average income) as not to allow the purchasing and operation of such amenities.

The major advantage of using a relative poverty line in comparative studies is that the same method of definition can be applied to each country in a consistent manner, for example by setting the poverty line as a percentage of the national mean (or median) disposable income. Such a definition avoids the problems of defining "equivalent" baskets of goods and services for different countries (as with an absolute poverty line) as well as the even more tremendous difficulties of defining "equivalent" living conditions in various countries (as would be required in a multidimensional living conditions approach).

In the case of an absolute poverty line, the underlying assumption is that it is not affected by changes in real income in the society as a whole (income elasticity = 0), whereas in the case of a relative poverty line, a parallel trend is assumed (income elasticity = 1). This poses the question of which of these assumptions is socially more realistic and reflects more accurately the opinions held by the public about the amounts of income necessary "to get along" or to just escape poverty. In a secondary analysis of American opinion polls over a period of four decades, Rainwater has convincingly demonstrated that "the average amount given by the respondents increases exactly proportionately to the increases in average incomes" (1992: 10) and that a poverty line so conceived would have amounted to between 45 and 50 per cent of mean household income. This empirical evidence lends strong support to the sociological adequacy of a *relative* conceptualization of poverty, and also to the adequacy of the *level* of the poverty line often used in conventional poverty research.

Of course, defining a relative poverty line as a percentage of average income always involves a certain arbitrariness.[12] But this unavoidable arbitrariness can be controlled and to a certain extent remedied by using multiple poverty lines at different levels of income (e.g. 40 per cent, 50 per cent, 60 per cent). It is thus possible to take account of the gradual character of poverty by distinguishing different levels of stringency of poverty, for example "severe poverty", "insecurity of subsistence", and "low income". By comparing poverty rates obtained by using multiple poverty lines, one can further infer how sensitive the measurement of relative poverty is to variations in the poverty line.

Defining a relative poverty line in this way links the measurement of poverty necessarily to the shape of the income distribution curve. The more unequal the distribution is, the higher are *ceteris paribus* the resulting poverty rates. On the other hand, the measurement of poverty is independent of the general *level* of income of a country. Sometimes it is argued, therefore, that by applying a relative poverty line it is inequality that is measured and not poverty (see Hansen 1989). In my view, however, this is not a valid argument.

Poverty as a social problem cannot be adequately understood and analysed without reference to the more general issue of social inequality. This is quite in accordance with the conceptualization of poverty as a particular aspect of the broader issue of the distribution of resources in society – mentioned at the beginning. Poverty has, therefore, to be measured by taking as a frame of reference the distribution of resources, here the income distribution in the larger society, with a special emphasis on the lower part of that distribution.[13]

This is not to say, however, that poverty is the same as inequality (of resources or income). The two problems can and should be analytically distinguished although they are interrelated empirically. It is, for instance, quite conceivable to abolish relative poverty (in the sense defined above) without completely equalizing the distribution of income. What is required is only that the *range of variations below the average income* is effectively limited; but variations in the larger part of the distribution are still allowed (see O'Higgins and Jenkins 1990: 207). It is, therefore, a matter of empirical research (not of definition!) to determine how the extent of poverty and the degree of inequality in a given society are related to each other.

Equivalence scales

The second methodological problem in the measurement of income poverty, closely related to the definition of a poverty line, is the choice of an appropriate equivalence scale. This is required in order to account for "economies of scale" when comparing incomes between families or households of different size and composition. By means of equivalence scales, household income is "deflated" into adult equivalent income units that can be interpreted as indicating the real living standard or economic well-being of a household (and of all the individual members belonging to it). In cross-national comparisons, equivalence scales also serve the purpose of accounting for differences in the socio-demographic structure between countries.

Here again there is no single best solution; but it should be evident that a realistic choice has to be located somewhere between the extremes of unweighted household income (elasticity coefficient = 0) and the per capita income (elasticity coefficient = 1). Whiteford (1985), Buhmann et al. (1988) and Hagenaars et al. (1992) have scrutinized a wide range of equivalence scales used in different contexts, discussed the underlying methodologies, and demonstrated their empirical consequences.

The choice of any equivalence scale for the measurement of poverty implies a normative statement about how the "marginal need" of an additional person in the household should be assessed. It has, therefore, a direct impact on household-specific poverty lines and an indirect impact (via the socio-demographic structure) on the mean equivalent income in society at large. The empirical consequences for household-specific poverty rates and, hence, for the social composition of the poor population may be tremendous. "The composition of the population of the poor may drastically change with the choice of another scale" (Hagenaars et al. 1994: 24). Again, as in the case of relative poverty lines at different levels, it is suggested that different equivalence scales be applied in order to control for these effects.

The equivalence scales most commonly used in poverty research in Western Europe are:

- the scale recommended in the OECD "List of Social Indicators" (1982), which equals 1 for the first adult in the household, 0.7 for each additional adult, and 0.5 for each child (under 14 years),
- the modified OECD scale, which gives less weight to additional persons in the household and equals 1 for the first adult, 0.5 for each additional adult, and 0.3 for each child.[14]

A difficult question in cross-national comparisons is whether the same equivalence scale should be used for all countries (see Hagenaars et al. 1994: 15). Because social attitudes and institutions differ from country to country, an alternative option may be to derive equivalence scales *by the same methods* for each country, even if they may differ in the quantitative values.

This ambiguity gives rise to the question of who ought to decide about the appropriateness of a poverty line or an equivalence scale. In the preceding discussion, it has implicitly been assumed that the social researcher (or some social policy expert) should take the decision (perhaps based on some empirical information). There is, however, another approach to this problem, which has become known as *the consensual (or subjective) approach* to determine poverty lines as well as equivalence scales.[15]

Consensual poverty lines and equivalence scales

The rationale of this approach is that citizens themselves should take these decisions about appropriateness because they are supposed to know best what *they* consider as "poor" or as the minimum income necessary to keep or get people out of poverty. There are various methods to determine such subjective poverty lines and equivalence scales empirically (see Bradbury 1989; Hagenaars 1986; Hagenaars et al. 1994: 19ff.; Van Praag et al. 1982; Walker 1987). Following this approach, the role of social researchers is reduced to finding out correctly people's views, without making their own value judgements. In a certain sense, this can be considered as a genuinely sociological approach that reflects the "subjective reality" in people's minds and, by doing so, is socially more realistic than an expert's or researcher's judgement, which may differ from social reality. On the other hand, people's perceptions of equivalent income levels may be distorted – depending on the methods used to identify them – by such factors as lack of information about the *needs* of different household types or depressed *aspiration levels* among larger households.

In general, the subjective method using survey questions about the income required "to make ends meet" tends to result in much lower elasticities with regard to household size, that is, to give less weight to the needs of additional persons in the household than, for instance, the OECD scale or the scales implied by national social assistance schemes. Although accurately reflecting social perceptions, it can be argued that this method does not really measure the same level of welfare and should not be accepted as a normative standard for social policy measures.

Moreover, when applied in cross-national comparisons of poverty, the empirical research needed to establish poverty lines for each household type in each country separately is enormous. Even more important, this approach is likely to yield national poverty lines and equivalence scales that reflect differences in generosity and aspiration levels across countries rather than differences in the "real" extent of poverty. In addition, they are unstable over time (for empirical illustrations, see Deleeck et al. 1992: 43ff.). This situation severely limits cross-national and intertemporal comparability of empirical findings based on the subjective approach.

A pragmatic half-way solution could be to take available empirical evidence from such surveys as estimates for a realistic range of equivalence scales, but then to apply the same equivalence scale consistently to all countries concerned.

Major projects of comparative poverty research

Most poverty research(ers) are driven by the desire to investigate the causes as well as the consequences of poverty and to help develop policy strategies to combat or at least alleviate poverty. These multiple goals are well reflected in many of the empirical studies undertaken in recent years. Definition and measurement of poverty are then needed – as was argued at the beginning – in order to identify the target population of anti-poverty measures. But they are certainly not the ultimate goal of poverty research, and definitions should not be confused with explanations.

Hypotheses about causes and consequences of poverty that have been prominent in recent research can be systematized as shown in Figure 14.2 (for a similar, yet more elaborate heuristic scheme, see Øyen 1992: 617).

Explanations of cross-national differences of poverty certainly need to take into account the socio-economic and demographic conditions prevailing in each country. For example, because (relative) poverty is a function of the inequality of the income distribution, even the distribution of market income and the structure of earnings are likely to have an impact on the rates and structure of poverty. On the other hand, the redistribution of income by means of taxes and transfers, i.e. the *size* of the welfare state, is a major intervening variable because the alleviation of poverty is among the most widely shared goals of the welfare state and a number of transfer programmes are geared towards low-income groups. It can further be hypothesized that the *type* of welfare state regime, its underlying principles and the structure and functioning of its institutions, will make a difference.

If the number of people who are typically found in low-income situations and in need of social transfers, such as the elderly, is growing over time for demographic reasons, this is a structural factor increasing the risk of poverty in society. The same is true if certain socio-economic risks, such as unemployment, hit larger parts of the labour force. In both cases, however, the respective social security schemes, their eligibility conditions, as well as the level and structure of the benefits they provide are at least equally important factors mediating the impact of socio-economic risk conditions. The characteristics of social assistance schemes as programmes purposefully designed to prevent or at least alleviate poverty are of particular relevance. For this reason, it should be a major concern of poverty research to monitor the effectiveness and adequacy of social security schemes and of anti-poverty programmes.

Concerning the consequences of poverty, these can be studied on the individual level as well as on the level of collective behaviour. Leaving aside multiple forms of deprivation in living conditions that are better understood as manifestations than as

Distribution of welfare

	Resources (income)	Living conditions
Input	*Measuring devices:* poverty line, equivalence scales *Indicators:* – no. of poor – poverty gap – distribution among the poor – duration of poverty	deprivation scales – no. of deprived – cumulation of deprivations – duration of deprivation

Causes

Socio-economic, e.g.
– distribution of (primary) income
– unemployment

Politico-administrative, e.g.
– social security schemes
– social assistance

Consequences

Individual, e.g.
– subjective well-being
– deviant behaviour

Social, e.g.
– marginalization
– discrimination

Figure 14.2 Topics of poverty research

effects of poverty, individual consequences of poverty can be observed, for example, in subjective (dis)satisfaction with economic well-being, in the self-images of the poor, and in various forms of deviant behaviour.

Social consequences of poverty can best be studied in the relations and interactions between the poor and the non-poor parts of the population, for example as they manifest themselves in various forms of discrimination, stigmatization, and marginalization of those groups labelled "poor". In addition, the discussion about "functions" of poverty can also largely be understood as generating hypotheses about macroscopic consequences of poverty for the larger community or society.

An important research question that follows from the above analytical distinction is "what is the empirical relationship between consequences on the individual level and the social level?" (Øyen 1992: 622). Indeed, the approaches that are most rewarding and promising attempt to link the research questions outlined above in a methodologically consistent way within the framework of a comprehensive research design.

Research sponsored by the European Community[16]

As part of its attempts to place the "social dimension" of the Single Market on the political agenda and to increase public awareness of the issues of poverty and social exclusion, the Commission of the European Communities has played a major role in sponsoring poverty research since the mid-1970s. It initiated three Community Action Programmes to Combat Poverty, with somewhat different emphases and goals.

In the first programme (1975–80), national reports on poverty and anti-poverty policy were commissioned in the (then nine) member countries, on the basis of which a summary report was prepared. These national reports served the purpose of stocktaking of existing knowledge about the extent and the ramifications of poverty at the national level and helped to identify information gaps and to specify needs for further research. In several countries, the publication of these reports spurred a renewed policy debate because it directed attention to an issue that was rather neglected in the "affluent welfare societies" of Western Europe.

The second programme (1986–89) called for action to combat poverty rather than for research. Nonetheless, several studies of national policies were undertaken as part of the evaluation of "model projects" carried out at the local level, which were mostly of limited scope. In addition, efforts were undertaken to strengthen the statistical infrastructure and, thereby, improve comparability in the measurement of aggregate poverty and the poverty of social groups (see Teekens and Van Praag 1990). For example, the first coordinated estimates of the extent of poverty in the European Community (EC), based on a common methodology, were produced (see O'Higgins and Jenkins 1990).[19] Eurostat, the Statistical Office of the European Communities, became involved in these efforts; a Working Group on Indicators of Poverty was established in 1986, and plans were discussed for the use of household budget surveys as a better database for the study of low income groups. (Results of the re-analysis of existing household budget surveys are published in Eurostat 1990).

In 1987 a research group with consultants for each country of the EC was commissioned to keep track of the social and economic changes of the late 1970s and the 1980s and their impact on emerging new forms of poverty. Their synthesis report focused on how labour market development, increasing unemployment, changes in family structure and the life cycle affected the manifestations of poverty, and reviewed governmental policies in response to these problems (Room 1990; Room et al. 1989).

Moreover, a multinational research consortium with participation from seven member countries was set up, partly funded by the Commission, partly by national governments. The so-called EUROPASS project had both methodological and substantive goals: it aimed at developing poverty indicators for cross-national comparison and testing the utility and feasibility of various approaches to defining poverty lines, as well as at stimulating poverty research in some countries not well researched before. The design and main results of this project are discussed below.

In the course of the third programme (1990–4), these initiatives were further developed and some new instruments were added.[18] First, Eurostat was funded to conduct, in collaboration with national statistical offices, a European Community Household Panel. This would provide an improved and more reliable database for cross-national comparisons, especially for monitoring income dynamics (see Eurostat 1993). The plan is to repeat such a panel on income and living conditions annually with a sample size of at least 1,000 households per country and an overall sample size of 20,000 households in the EC.

Second, so-called "observatories" were set up to monitor policy trends in areas of social concern, such as employment policy, family policy, policies for the elderly, and – most relevant in the present context – policies to combat social exclusion. The last interest is especially concerned with the extent to which different groups in society enjoy access to basic public services (education, health, social services, etc.) or suffer disadvantages from reduced levels of social participation. Although, for the most part, these observatories lack the resources to generate new research data of their own, they offer "comparative reporting which covers all twelve countries at a time when up-to-date materials on some of these countries . . . is very scarce" (Room 1992: 20).

Finally, a procedure was set in motion for establishing a research programme that goes beyond the mere measurement of poverty and addresses certain key issues presumed to be causally related to poverty, such as detachment from the labour market, migration, or the perverse effects of public policies. In each of these areas, preliminary feasibility studies were carried out to identify topics of high priority for further research. These should be followed by larger cross-national studies, again co-funded by the EC and by national sources. This procedure, it is hoped, will help to establish multinational research networks and at the same time "promote areas of convergence in the research agendas of different national research councils" (Room 1992: 11).

The Luxembourg Income Study project

The Luxembourg Income Study (LIS) project, directed by Timothy Smeeding and Lee Rainwater and hosted at the Center for Population, Poverty and Policy Studies (CEPS) in Walferdange, Luxembourg, is not linked to or sponsored by the European Community. It was started in 1983 and has since grown into a major cooperative research project with many innovative features. The basic idea is to compile representative household income surveys from advanced Western countries ("the OECD world") in a large data bank, to standardize them, and thereby to make them available for comparative cross-national analyses. In order to achieve this goal, cross-national comparability of the original data sets has to be improved by applying common concepts and definitions and by developing new methods and techniques of statistical analysis.

In the meantime, the LIS data bank includes data sets for most West European countries (Austria, Belgium, Denmark,

Finland, France, Germany, Ireland, Italy, Luxembourg, the Netherlands, Norway, Spain, Sweden, Switzerland, the United Kingdom) as well as some major overseas countries (the United States, Canada, Australia). The list of countries is currently being extended to include some formerly socialist countries of East Central Europe as well (the Czech Republic, Hungary, and Poland). For a number of countries, data sets are meanwhile available for several years, which allows analyses of changes over time.[19]

Despite certain remaining shortcomings in data comparability, the LIS project certainly represents the most comprehensive and most reliable database currently available for the analysis of processes of income distribution and redistribution. Moreover, it provides a model for a cooperative network of researchers at institutions in several countries to utilize the same data resources for secondary analyses of their own. It thereby opens up new prospects for comparative social policy research (see O'Higgins et al. 1990).

The data sets provide detailed information on the income composition of households by sources, including taxes and transfers, as well as on socio-demographic and socio-economic background variables (composition of households, labour force participation of spouses, etc.). With these characteristics, the LIS project is of particular relevance for the comparative study of poverty issues (see Smeeding 1990). The availability of large disaggregated microdata files allows researchers to apply their own conceptualizations of the income distribution process, to define their own poverty lines and equivalence scales, and to focus on particular sub-groups of the population, such as the elderly, the unemployed, or single-parent families.

The LIS project has so far produced a large number of working papers illustrating the vast range of topics that can be fruitfully explored by this new approach. Among those specifically concerned with issues of poverty research, there are studies by Kohl (1988, 1983) on "Inequality and poverty in old age", by Rainwater (1988) on "Inequalities in the economic well-being of children and adults", by Smeeding, Torrey, and Rein (1988) on "The economic status of children and the elderly", by Smeeding et al. (1990b) on "Income poverty in seven countries", by Hedström and Ringen (1990) on "Age and income", by Smeeding and Rainwater (1991) on "Income poverty and dependency of young adults", and by Gustafsson and Lindblom (1990, 1993) on "Poverty as inefficiency of the welfare state". Major methodological advances in exploring the implications of the choices between various poverty lines and equivalence scales have been made by Buhmann et al. (1988), Rainwater (1990), and Förster (1993, 1994).

Some of the more interesting substantive findings are the following:

Defining a relative poverty line at 50 per cent of median income and using the OECD equivalence scale (see above), the incidence of poverty was found to vary between 5 per cent and 10 per cent in the European countries (Germany, the Netherlands, Norway, Sweden, Switzerland, the United Kingdom), while the overall poverty rates were consistently above 10 per cent in overseas English-speaking countries (the United States, Canada, Australia). Using equivalence scales with lower elasticities (such as subjective scales) tended to yield higher poverty rates in general, but did not significantly change the pattern of cross-national variations: the European countries were still characterized by a lower incidence of poverty (see Buhmann et al. 1988). Because the relative poverty line is a function of the shape of the income distribution curve, these findings also point to lower degrees of inequality in the distribution of income in European countries in general.

Relating "age" and "income", the life-cycle pattern of poverty can be confirmed. Young families (with a head of household below 25 years of age) and older families (with a head of household 65 years and over) suffered from disproportionately high rates of poverty. Cross-national differences were more pronounced in the upper age brackets, which points to the strategic importance of public pension schemes in shaping the poverty risks of the elderly (see Hedström and Ringen 1990).

In an attempt to identify vulnerable groups on an individual instead of a household basis, it was also found that, on the average, the elderly's risk of falling below the poverty line was about 50 per cent higher than the risk in the general population. In Germany and in the United Kingdom, for instance, the poverty rates of the elderly were double and three times, respectively, the general poverty rate. In some countries (Sweden, Norway, the Netherlands), however, the poverty risk of the elderly was even lower than in the population at large. These differences testify to the potential effectiveness of public pension schemes in limiting poverty (see Kohl 1988, Smeeding et al. 1990b).

The relative risk of children was found to be only slightly higher, and sometimes even lower, than in the population at large, at least in the European countries in the USA, Canada, and Australia, however, children suffered a markedly increased risk of poverty. The poverty risk of children is especially high in incomplete (single-parent) families, whereas in two-parent families it is generally below average (although increasing with the number of children per family). The overall risk of children falling into poverty is, therefore, largely dependent on the incidence of "broken families" in society, which seems to be much higher in the overseas English-speaking countries (see Smeeding 1990).

As a consequence, the profile of poverty (i.e. the socio-demographic composition of the poor) shows characteristic variations: in the countries with high overall poverty rates, more than two-thirds of the poor live in families with children. In some European countries (Germany, the United Kingdom), one-third of the poor live in elderly households, and another third in families with at least two children. In those European countries with low overall poverty rates (Sweden, Norway), a larger part of the poor come from such atypical groups as single persons below 60 years old or married couples without children.

If there is a common pattern behind the bewildering variety of rates and risks of poverty in the advanced Western countries, it is perhaps this: Differences in the extent and the relative risks of poverty reflect the differing capabilities and/or willingness of welfare states to cope with social risks and problems by means of social policy programmes. Neither demographic nor economic factors (such as share of the aged or unemployment rates) nor the prevalence of social problems (such as broken families) determine the extent and structure of poverty as such. In each case, cross-national comparisons provide examples that adequate social programmes can contain the poverty risks of vulnerable groups and, thereby, the extent of poverty in society in general (see Kohl 1992).

Certain limitations of LIS-based analyses are also apparent: mostly owing to limitations of the original national databases, analysis is restricted to *income* poverty, and almost no indicators of relative deprivation in "natural" living conditions can be derived. In a separate project, efforts have been undertaken to include certain non-cash items in the analysis of income distribution (see Saunders 1991; Smeeding, Saunders et al. 1992). Notably, it has been attempted to evaluate the distributional impact of health and education expenditures. Although these in-kind benefits tend to level differences in economic well-being during the life cycle and to diminish somewhat the poverty risks of the most vulnerable social groups, "overall, the results ... do not give rise to a pattern of national differences in poverty rates markedly different from that to emerge from previous LIS research based on cash income" (Saunders 1991: 28).

No subjective measures of poverty or other non-monetary aspects of poverty (such as social exclusion or lack of social activities) are included in the surveys. This makes it virtually impossible to study the subjective consequences of "objective" poverty and material deprivation. This point can be generalized: although LIS analyses provide a wealth of systematic and sophisticated descriptive information concerning the measurement of poverty, the possibilities for investigating the causes and consequences of poverty are rather restricted.

Policy aspects such as the effectiveness of social policy programmes in alleviating poverty can be studied only at an aggregate level. For example: post-tax and transfer poverty rates are compared with pre-tax and transfer rates, and the percentage reduction of the poverty rates is then taken as a proxy for the relative effectiveness of the redistribution. Measured in this way, the tax and transfer systems in the European countries seem to be much more effective in alleviating poverty (by about 70–90 per cent) than those, for instance, in the USA (about 40 per cent) and Canada (about 50 per cent) (see Smeeding et al. 1990b). But not much attention is paid to the organizational forms, the rules and principles of the respective social programmes that have these effects.

The European Research on Poverty and Social Security (EUROPASS) project

The EUROPASS project covered seven European countries: Belgium, France, Greece, Ireland, Luxembourg, the Netherlands, and Spain.[20] The research consortium, directed by Herman Deleeck of the Centre for Social Policy at Antwerp, consisted of national research teams in these countries that collected the respective data, using the same methods and the same analytical framework.

The project pursued substantive as well as methodological goals. Substantive research issues were first to measure the incidence of poverty, and to identify social groups at high risk of poverty and the social composition of the people living in poverty. The second major concern was to analyse the impact and effectiveness of social security transfers in alleviating poverty and thereby to evaluate the adequacy of the social security system as a whole and of its most important constituent parts (pensions, unemployment benefits, family allowances). This latter goal was achieved by comparing poverty rates before and after social transfers and by measuring the reduction of the "poverty gap" (defined as the distance between the income of the poor and the poverty line).

Methodologically, four different methods to derive poverty lines and equivalence scales were applied to the same data sets and evaluated with regard to their characteristics:

- two 'objective' poverty lines:
  - the EC poverty line mentioned above (50 per cent of mean disposable income in each country, adjusted for household size by means of the OECD equivalence scale),
  - the "legal" poverty line (and the respective equivalence scales), as defined and applied in the context of the various national social security regulations, e.g. as the guaranteed minimum income level;
- and two subjective standards:
  - the CSP poverty line, introduced by the Centre for Social Policy at Antwerp,
  - the Subjective Poverty Line (SPL), developed by a Dutch group at the universities of Leyden and Tilburg (see Van Praag et al. 1980; Van Praag et al. 1982).

The difference between the two subjective standards lies in the way that the minimum amount of income needed "to live decently" or "to make ends meet" is estimated. In the case of the CSP poverty line, only the answers of people saying they could get by "with some difficulty" are taken into consideration for establishing the minimum income necessary to make ends meet. In the case of the Dutch SPL, the minimum income is estimated by a regression equation from the answers given by all respondents (for details see Deleeck et al. 1992: Appendix D). Both subjective poverty lines are estimated for different household types separately so that equivalence scales are implied in this procedure.

The procedure of applying these different standards in measuring the incidence of poverty or poverty risks of social groups allows the assessment of the empirical consequences and relevance of the methodological choice of one or the other standard. For instance, the subjective poverty lines turned out to be at a much higher level than the EC line, while the "legal" standards applied in the context of national social policy mostly fell below the EC standard. Consequently, they also yielded different poverty rates and resulted in a different composition of the poor population (for details see Deleeck et al. 1992: ch. 4 and Appendix A).

In addition, some attention has also been given to measuring living standards and deprivation directly by an index of certain lifestyle indicators (mostly possession of consumer durables) and to exploring the subjective dimension of the insecurity of subsistence and its relationship with objective measures of poverty and insecurity of subsistence.

A second methodological concern has been using the panel method in an attempt to measure change across time and to distinguish between temporary and long-term poverty. However, only two waves of surveys were carried out in only five of the seven countries studied. The preliminary conclusions suggested that "income mobility across the poverty line occurs frequently in almost all social categories" and that "the general risk of 'longer-term' poverty is much smaller than that of poverty at one moment" (Deleeck et al. 1992: 110).

In addition to and in preparation of the comparative publications (Deleeck and Van den Bosch 1992, Deleeck et al. 1992; Van den Bosch et al. 1993), the project triggered a number of studies by the national research teams exploring in great detail and with sophisticated methods particular aspects of poverty in the individual countries (see Callan et al. 1989; Dirven and Berghman 1991, Muffels et al. 1992; Nolan and Callan 1989, 1994). This project, therefore, represents a good example of how the collaboration of a multinational network of research teams can produce results that are relevant in the national policy context and at the same time contribute to a better understanding of cross-national variations in the degree and the manifestations of poverty.

The "Social Assistance Dynamics" study

This project, which has not yet been completed, consists of a series of coordinated studies undertaken in eight countries (the USA, Canada, France, Germany, Ireland, the Netherlands, Sweden, and the United Kingdom). The major goal of the project is to investigate the dynamic aspects and causal processes leading into and out of poverty. These cannot be adequately captured in conventional cross-sectional analyses, but call for a longitudinal perspective (see Duncan, Voges, Hauser et al. 1992; Walker 1994).

Although there are certain differences in the design and the database of the national studies forming part of the project, the major research questions and methodological advantages can be explained by reference to the German study carried out at the Centre for Social Policy at the University of Bremen (for first analyses, see Duncan and Voges 1993; Leisering and Voges 1993; Voges and Rohwer 1992). In this case, the database consists of a fairly large number of social assistance files, supplemented by retrospective interviews of recipients. This allows the reconstruction of the "social assistance career" of recipients in a life history perspective, that is, the singling out of individual characteristics and significant life events that disrupt "normal" lifestyles and social relations and ultimately lead to claims on social assistance. In this way, it seems possible to distinguish typical sequences of events and the cumulative impact of such events that result in repeated poverty spells or permanent dependence.

An important finding is that, hidden behind the "net figures" of recipients at a certain time-point as revealed in cross-section analyses, there are many more people experiencing shorter periods of poverty. On the other hand, administrative statistics that count "cases" of poverty rather than persons tend to overestimate the extent of poverty because of persons frequently moving into and out of poverty within a year. Distinguishing between persistent and transitory poverty (by the number and length of poverty spells) should lead to policy-relevant conclusions for the better targeting of poverty alleviation measures.

Another aim that can be better pursued by an event history design is to study how the social administration treats the claimants and recipients of social assistance. For example, how does information about eligibility conditions and the stigma eventually attached to means-tested programmes affect the actual take-up of benefits (see Van Oorschot 1991)? Or do social security institutions create their own clients (see Leisering and Voges 1993)? Such studies should provide insights into improving the administrative procedures dealing with poverty and deprivation. In sum, this type of research seems to be well suited to identify crucial factors and sequences leading to poverty and escaping from poverty and, thereby, to provide more adequate information for social policy strategies of intervening into these causal mechanisms.

The limitations of this approach stem from the fact that it is bound to rely on national administrative definitions of poverty, as laid down in the respective social assistance schemes. These definitions, of course, reflect different approaches and traditions of poverty policy. They usually lack a common and coherent understanding of poverty; they may be more or less restrictive, which, in turn, may adversely affect the cross-national comparability of resulting poverty estimates. Such a procedure may still provide valuable empirical evidence to assess the adequacy of administrative procedures in implementing these policies – according to their own criteria. Obviously, it does not allow evaluation of the adequacy of a given level of benefits according to some independent judgement. This approach, therefore, needs to be supplemented by a comparative institutional analysis of existing social assistance arrangements that assesses their degree of generosity or rigidity by common standards.

Some conclusions and recommendations

The basic methodological alternatives outlined above have been discussed for a rather long time, and reasonable arguments have been put forward for each of them. Pro's and con's can be offered for almost every approach, especially when the differing purposes of the enquiry are taken into account. There is a growing consensus that no single definition of poverty is capable of serving all purposes, and that different approaches may complement each other in capturing various aspects of the same complex phenomenon.

Because, on the other hand, it is often difficult to judge whether differences in results obtained in a number of studies reflect

- *real* differences between countries or *real* changes between one time-point and another, or
- just differences or changes in definition, or
- differences in the (quality of) the database,

two pragmatic conclusions may be drawn. First, specific methodological details should be given in every study and possibly every table in order to allow adequate interpretation. Even if definitions and operationalizations are not identical, it may, nonetheless, be possible to arrive at valid conclusions by careful *ex post* analysis. Second, there is a merit in applying various definitions and operationalizations to the same database. Such a procedure can serve as a sensitivity test and allow us to gauge the significance of variations in definition.[21]

Fortunately, for the purposes of cross-national comparisons, the range of alternative options in poverty research can be narrowed down to some extent. Partly as a result of theoretical considerations, partly as conclusions drawn from empirical studies, the following recommendations have been proposed:

- "Because of problems of measurement ... a comparable poverty definition should be a resource-type definition mainly based on income and not a definition of the living-conditions-type" (Hauser 1984: 349). An additional reason is that "the

reliability, replicability and comparability of deprivation standards have not been tested to the degree that they can provide information to guide social policy" (Deleeck et al. 1992: 135).
- "Poverty should be defined with respect to the available resources of the family, and not only of the individual" (Hauser 1984: 349). Even when we are ultimately interested in individual well-being, it is necessary to take account of the situation of the household or family as the income-receiving, resource-pooling unit that shapes the opportunities of the individuals participating in it.
- "Disposable income" is the most appropriate income concept to measure economic well-being and – if equivalenced (see below) – can be used as a proxy for measuring "standard of living". Disposable income comprises all earned income and income from capital assets, as well as public and private transfers received. (Direct) taxes and social security contributions should be deducted. If possible, non-cash income (for example, the value of owner-occupied housing and of transfers in kind) should also be included.
- "The available resources of the 'inner family' should be calculated on a per adult equivalent unit basis", that is, disposable household income has to be attributed to individual members by means of equivalence scales. These define the amounts of income necessary for different household types to ensure similar standards of living. "For each country the necessary equivalence scales should be derived by the same method" (Hauser 1984: 350).
- "Relative poverty lines should be used for comparative studies of developed countries" (Hauser 1984: 351). Poverty lines should be set at various levels (for example, 40 per cent, 50 per cent and 60 per cent of the average disposable income per adult equivalent unit) as a sensitivity test to improve the reliability of measurement.
- So-called statistical methods to define a poverty line should be preferred in international comparisons over both subjective methods and legal-administrative definitions because "they are easy to construct, they are exact and they produce plausible results across countries as well as across time" (Deleeck et al. 1992: 134).

Even when, for pragmatic reasons, attention is focused on *income poverty*, there arises further the question of adequate statistical measures to capture various dimensions of income poverty. Traditionally, and in political contexts, attention is mostly limited to counting the number of the poor. In recent debates, however (see Atkinson 1987; Foster et al. 1984, Sen 1976, 1983), it has been pointed out that such an approach is insufficient because it counts all poor equally no matter how poor they are. It thereby neglects the distribution of resources among the poor.

It has been suggested, therefore, that the traditional *"head counts"* (the number of poor persons or households) should be supplemented by measures of:

- the *"average poverty gap"* (the relative distance between the income of the poor and the poverty line);
- the *"aggregate poverty gap"* (the total amount needed, theoretically, to raise the incomes of all poor households to the level of the poverty line);
- the *"duration of poverty spells"* in order to distinguish between short-term and long-term poverty.

To describe the social distribution of poverty, the following indicators have been suggested (see Deleeck et al. 1992: 5f.):

- the *"poverty risk"*: the percentage of all households within a certain social category that are poor,
- the *"relative poverty risk"*: the poverty risk in a certain social category relative to the poverty risk in the whole sample; and
- the *"composition of the poor"*: the share of a certain social category within the total number of the poor.

These measures should form part of a standardized system of social indicators that can serve as a framework for describing and analysing the various dimensions of the poverty issue in a cross-nationally comparable way (see the example given in Deleeck et al. 1992: 11). Regular social reporting on poverty would certainly help to raise the awareness of the general public, which seems to be a precondition for focusing the attention of policymakers on the issue and for mobilizing public support for more forceful action to combat poverty in practice.

NOTES

1. Because some countries of the (now enlarged) European Union are also dealt with in other reports in this volume (Scandinavia and Greece), the reader is referred to these chapters for further country-specific references.
2. "How much poverty you find depends almost completely on how you define poverty and the tools you use to measure it" (Ringen 1987a: 154). "The number of poor depends on the definition used and the method of measurement applied" (Deleeck et al. 1992: 3).

3. In contrast to Ringen (see below), however, he views Townsend's work as an example of the traditional British resource approach, although a sophisticated one aiming to incorporate relational elements.
4. It seems, however, debatable whether health should be considered a "resource" or an "actual living condition".
5. The careful reader may note, however, that even Townsend, in this quotation, refers to (a lack of) resources as a determinant of the inability to participate in normal social activities. This sheds some doubt on whether Ringen is right in classifying Townsend's approach under "direct concepts of poverty" (see below).
6. It should be noted that this definition also suggests a link between (lack of) *resources* and (exclusion from a) *way of life*.
7. This follows from the multidimensional concept of welfare, which suggests breaking down "level of living" or "way of life" into a set of components each of which is then measured by indicators (cf. Erikson and Uusitalo 1987).
8. Following this logic, Mack and Lansley (1985) have defined deprivation as involuntarily not possessing goods and services that the majority of the population regards as necessary.
9. Of course, public goods and services also have to be paid for collectively, by means of taxation, but not individually (and are, hence, not taken into account by individual disposable income).
10. A similar distinction can be drawn with regard to the living conditions concept: in the first case, *absolute* minima have to be determined (perhaps in only some dimensions of living conditions deemed necesssary for survival), whereas in the second one, *relative* minimum standards have to be defined in relation to "normal living conditions" prevailing in society.
11. When taking the national poverty line of a certain country as the baseline, it should be converted into other currencies by using purchasing power parities, not the official exchange rates. But even this does not avoid the problem that the consumption patterns of the "model country" are taken as a kind of normative standard that is imposed on the other countries.
12. "Each possible level of a poverty line represents a more or less arbitrary choice, as to where, in the gradual continuum from getting along easily to a state of dire need, one wants to draw the line" (Deleeck et al. 1992: 3).
13. "The very meaning of the relative theory is to define poverty in relation to the general standard of the population and not in relation to those at the top" (Ringen 1987b: 126).
14. In the early LIS analyses (see below), a simplified scale was applied, the so-called LIS scale, which equals 1 for the head of household and attributes a weight of 0.5 to each additional member of the household.

15. The consensual approach is here discussed only with reference to an *indirect* concept of poverty, namely lack of income, in order to establish poverty lines. It should be noted, however, that the same reasoning can be applied to *direct* concepts of poverty, based on actual living conditions. In that case, the research task would be to find out *empirically*, which items are defined as "necessities" by public opinion and, on this basis, to develop a deprivation index in order to identify the people who cannot afford these items.
16. This section draws heavily upon the report by Graham Room (1992) and a 1994 update to this report which I gratefully acknowledge.
17. In this study, 50 per cent of mean disposable income in the respective countries (not in the EC as a whole), adjusted by use of the OECD equivalence scale, was used as the common definition of the poverty line.
18. Ramprakash (1994) gives a synthesis report of the statistical research completed and in progress under the Commission's third Poverty Action Programme. His article also presents comparative research results illustating the significance of different methodological options.
19. For technical and methodological details, see Smeeding and Schmaus (1990), for an updated list of available data sets, see De Tombeur and Ladewig (1994), *LIS Information Guide*.
20. In the case of France and Spain, the actual surveys were confined to a particular region: Lorraine and Catalonia, respectively.
21. As mentioned earlier, it can further serve to highlight the empirical interrelationships, for example, between resource and living conditions indicators, or between objective and subjective measures of poverty.

REFERENCES

Atkinson, Anthony B (1987) "On the measurement of poverty". *Econometrica*, 55: 749–64.
——— (1989). *Poverty and Social Security*. Hemel Hempstead: Harvester Wheatsheaf.
Buhmann, Brigitte, Lee Rainwater, Günther Schmaus, and Timothy M. Smeeding (1988) "Equivalence scales, well-being, inequality, and poverty: Sensitivity estimates across ten countries using the Luxembourg Income Study (LIS) database". *Review of Income and Wealth*, 34: 115–42.
Callan, Tim, Brian Nolan, Brendan J. Whelan, Damian F. Hannan, and Sean Creighton (1989) *Poverty, Income and Welfare in Ireland*. Dublin: Economic and Social Research Institute.
Council of the European Communities (1984) *Council Decision on Specific Community Action to Combat Poverty* (85/8/EEC).

Deleeck, Hermann and Karel Van den Bosch (1992) "Poverty and adequacy of social security in Europe: A comparative analysis". *Journal of European Social Policy*, 2(2): 107–120.

Deleeck, Herman, Karel Van den Bosch, and Lieve De Lathouwer (1992) *Poverty and the Adequacy of Social Security in the EC*. Aldershot: Avebury.

De Tombeur, Caroline and Nicole Ladewig (eds) (1994) LIS Information Guide. Luxembourg: LIS-CEPS Working Paper No. 7.

Dirven, Henk-Jan and Jos Berghman (1991) *Poverty, Insecurity of Subsistence and Relative Deprivation in the Netherlands. Report 1991*. Tilburg:

Donnison, David (1988) "Defining and measuring poverty. A reply to Stein Ringen". *Journal of Social Policy*, 17(3): 367–374.

Duncan, Greg J. and Wolfgang Voges (1993) *Do Generous Social Assistance Programs Lead to Dependence? A Comparative Study of Lone-Parent Families in Germany and the United States*. Bremen: ZeS-Arbeitspapier Nr. 11/93. Centre for Social Policy (Working Paper).

Duncan, Greg J., Wolfgang Voges, Richard Hauser, et al. (1992) *Armuts- und Sozialhilfedynamiken in Europa und Nordamerika*. Bremen: ZeS-Arbeitspapier Nr. 12/92. Centre for Social Policy (Working Paper).

Erikson, Robert and Hannu Uusitalo (1987) The Scandinavian approach to welfare research", in R. Erikson, E. J. Hansen, S. Ringen and H. Uusitalo (eds), *The Scandinavian Model. Welfare States and Welfare Research*. Armonk, NY: M. E. Sharpe, pp. 177–193.

Eurostat (1990) *Poverty in Figures. Europe in the Early 1980s*. Luxembourg: Eurostat.

—— (1993) *European Community Household Panel: Strategy and Policy*, Luxembourg: Eurostat.

Förster, Michael F (1993) *Comparing Poverty in 13 OECD Countries: Traditional and Synthetic Approaches* Luxembourg: LIS-CEPS Working Paper No. 100.

—— (1994) *Measurement of Low Incomes and Poverty in a Perspective of International Comparisons*. Paris: OECD Labour Market and Social Policy Occasional Papers No. 14.

Foster, James E., Joel Greer, and Erik Thorbecke (1984) "A class of decomposable poverty measures". *Econometrica*, 52(3): 761–766.

Gustafsson, Björn and Mats Lindblom (1990) *Poverty as Inefficiency of the Welfare State. A Cross Country Comparison*. Luxembourg: LIS-CEPS Working Paper No. 61.

—— (1993) "Poverty lines and poverty in seven European countries, Australia, Canada and the USA". *Journal of European Social Policy*, 3(1): 21–38.

Hagenaars, Aldi J. M. (1986) *The Perception of Poverty*, Amsterdam: North Holland.

Hagenaars, Aldi J. M., Klaas de Vos, and S. R. Wunderink (1992) "Family equivalence scales". Discussion Paper, Department of

Economic Sociology and Psychology, Erasmus University, Rotterdam.
Hagenaars, Aldi J. M., Klaas de Vos, and M. Asghar Zaidi (1994) *Poverty Statistics in the Late 1980s: Research Based on Micro-data.* Luxembourg: Eurostat Series 3.C.
Hansen, Erik Jørgen (1989) *The Concept and Measurement of Poverty. A Danish Point of View.* Copenhagen: Danish Institute of Social Research.
Hauser, Richard (1984) "Some problems in defining a poverty line for comparative studies", in: G. Sarpellon (ed.), *Understanding Poverty.* Milan: Angeli.
Hedström, Peter and Stein Ringen (1990) "Age and income in contemporary society", in: T. Smeeding, M. O'Higgins and L. Rainwater (eds), *Poverty, Inequality and the Distribution of Income.* Hemel Hempstead: Harvester Wheatsheaf, pp. 77–104.
Kohl, Jürgen (1988) *Inequality and Poverty in Old Age. A Comparison between West Germany, the United Kingdom, Sweden and Switzerland.* Luxembourg: LIS-CEPS Working Paper No. 11.
—— (1992) "Armut im internationalen Vergleich. Methodische Probleme und empirische Ergebnisse", in S. Leibfried and W. Voges (eds), *Armut im modernen Wohlfahrtsstaat.* Opladen: Westdeutscher Verlag, pp. 272–99.
—— (1993) "Minimum standards in old age security and the problem of poverty in old age", in A. B. Atkinson and M. Rein (eds), London: Macmillan, pp. 224–252.
Leisering, Lutz and Wolfgang Voges (1993) *Secondary Poverty in the Welfare State. Do Social Security Institutions Create Their Own Clients? An Application of Longitudinal Analysis.* Bremen: ZeS-Arbeitspapier Nr. 10/93. Centre for Social Policy (Working Paper).
Mack, Joanna and Stewart Lansley (1985) *Poor Britain.* London: Allen & Unwin.
Muffels, Ruud, Jos Berghman, and Henk-Jan Dirven (1992) "A multimethod approach to monitor the evolution of poverty". *Journal of European Social Policy*, 2(3): 193–213.
Nolan, Brian and Tim Callan (1989) "Measuring poverty over time: Some robust results for Ireland 1980–87". *Economic and Social Review*, 20(4): 309–28.
Nolan, Brian and Tim Callan (eds) (1994) *Poverty and Policy in Ireland.* Dublin: Gill and Macmillan.
O'Higgins, Michael and Stephen P. Jenkins (1990) "Poverty in the EC: Estimates for 1975, 1980, 1985", in R. Teekens and B. M. S. Van Praag (eds), *Analysing Poverty in the European Community. Policy Issues, Research Options and Data Sources.* Luxembourg: Eurostat News, special edition 1-1990, pp. 187–209.
O'Higgins, Michael, Lee Rainwater, and Timothy M. Smeeding (1990) "The significance of LIS for comparative social policy research", in T. Smeeding, M. O'Higgins, and L. Rainwater (eds), *Poverty, Inequality and the Distribution of Income.* Hemel Hempstead: Harvester Wheatsheaf, pp. 158–71.

Øyen, Else (1992) "Some basic issues in comparative poverty research". *International Social Science Journal*, 134: 615–26.

Piachaud, David (1987) "Problems in the definition and measurement of poverty". *Journal of Social Policy*, 16(2): 147–64.

Rainwater, Lee (1988) *Inequalities in the Economic Well-Being of Children and Adults in Ten Nations*. Luxembourg: LIS-CEPS Working Paper No. 19.

―――― (1990) *Poverty and Equivalence as Social Constructions*. Luxembourg: LIS-CEPS Working Paper No. 55.

―――― (1992) *Poverty in American Eyes*. Luxembourg: LIS-CEPS Working Paper No. 80.

Ramprakash, Deo (1994) "Poverty in the countries of the European Union: A synthesis of Eurostat's statistical research on poverty". *Journal of European Social Policy*, 4(2): 117–28.

Ringen, Stein 1985 "Toward a third stage in the measurement of poverty", *Acta Sociologica*, 28(2): 99–113.

―――― (1987a) *The Possibility of Politics. A Study in the Political Economy of the Welfare State*. Oxford: Clarendon.

―――― (1987b) "Poverty in the welfare state?", in R. Erikson, E. J. Hansen, S. Ringen, and H. Uusitalo (eds), *The Scandinavian Model. Welfare States and Welfare Research*. Armonk, NY: M. E. Sharpe, pp. 122–38.

―――― (1988) "Direct and indirect measures of poverty". *Journal of Social Policy*, 17(3): 351–65.

Room, Graham (1990) *"New Poverty" in the European Community*. London: Macmillan.

―――― (1992) *Poverty and Social Exclusion: ESRC Research Review*. Bath: Centre for Research in European Social and Employment Policy.

Room, Graham, Roger Lawson, and Frank Laczko (1989) "'New poverty' in the European Community". *Policy and Politics*, 17(2): 165–76.

Saunders, Peter (1991) "Noncash income and relative poverty in comparative perspective: Evidence from the Luxembourg Income Study". Paper presented at the Conference on Comparative Studies of Welfare State Development, Helsinki.

Sen, Amartya (1976) "Poverty: An ordinal approach to measurement". *Econometrica*, 44: 219–31.

―――― (1983) "Poor relatively speaking. *Oxford Economic Papers*, 35: 153–69.

Smeeding, Timothy M. (1990) "Use of LIS Data for Poverty Analysis: An Overview of Lessons Learned and Still Being Learned", in: R. Teekens and B. M. S. Van Praag (eds), *Analysing Poverty in the European Community. Policy Issues, Research Options and Data Sources*. Luxembourg: Eurostat News, special edition 1–1990, pp. 431–48.

Smeeding, Timothy and Günther Schmaus (1990) "The LIS database: technical and methodological aspects", in T. Smeeding, M. O'Higgins, and L. Rainwater (eds), *Poverty, Inequality and the Distribution of Income*. Hemel Hempstead: Harvester Wheatsheaf, pp. 1–19.

Smeeding, Timothy M. and Lee Rainwater (1991) *Cross-National Trends in Income Poverty and Dependency: The Evidence for Young Adults in the Eighties*. Luxembourg: LIS-CEPS Working Paper No. 67.

Smeeding, Timothy, Barbara Boyle Torrey, and Martin Rein (1988) "Patterns of income and poverty: the economic status of children and the elderly in eight countries", in J. L. Palmer, T. Smeeding, and B. Boyle Torrey (eds), *The Vulnerable*. Washington, DC: Urban Institute Press, pp. 89–119.

Smeeding, Timothy, Michael O'Higgins, and Lee Rainwater (eds) (1990a) *Poverty, Inequality and the Distribution of Income*. Hemel Hempstead: Harvester Wheatsheaf.

Smeeding, Timothy M., Lee Rainwater, Martin Rein, Richard Hauser, and Gaston Schaber (1990b) "Income poverty in seven countries: Initial estimates from the LIS database", in T. Smeeding, M. O'Higgins, and L. Rainwater (eds), *Poverty, Inequality and the Distribution of Income*. Hemel Hempstead: Harvester Wheatsheaf, pp. 57–76.

Smeeding, Timothy M., Peter Saunders, et al. (1992) "Noncash income, living standards, and inequality: Evidence from the Luxembourg Income Study". Paper presented at the 10th World Congress of the International Economic Association, Moscow.

Teekens, Rudolf and Bernard M. S. Van Praag (eds) (1990) *Analysing Poverty in the European Community. Policy Issues, Research Options and Data Sources*. Luxembourg: Eurostat News, special edition 1–1990.

Teekens, Rudolf and M. Asghar Zaidi (1990) "Relative and absolute poverty in the European Community" in: R. Teekens and B. M. S. Van Praag (eds), *Analysing Poverty in the European Community. Policy Issues, Research Options and Data Sources*. Luxembourg: Eurostat News, special edition 1–1990.

Townsend, Peter (1979) *Poverty in the United Kingdom*, Harmondsworth, Middx: Penguin.

—— (1987) "Deprivation". *Journal of Social Policy*, 16(2): 125–46.

Van den Bosch, Karel, Tim Callan, Jordi Estivill, Pierre Hausman, Bruno Jeandidier, Ruud Muffels, and John Yfantopoulos (1993) "A comparison of poverty in seven European countries and regions using subjective and relative measures". *Journal of Population Economics*, 6(3), 235–59.

Van Oorschot, Wim (1991) "Non-take-up of social security benefits in Europe". *Journal of European Social Policy*, 1(1): 15–30.

Van Praag, Bernard M. S., Theo Goedhart, and Arie Kapteyn (1980) "The poverty line – A pilot survey in Europe", *Review of Economics and Statistics*, 62: 461–65.

Van Praag, Bernard M. S., Aldi J. M. Hagenaars, and J. Van Weeren (1982) "Poverty in Europe". *Review of Income and Wealth*, 28: 345–59.

Veit-Wilson, John H (1987) "Consensual approaches to poverty lines and social security". *Journal of Social Policy*, 16(2): 183–211.

Villemez, Wayne J (1992) "Poverty", in E. F. Borgatta and M. L. Borgatta (eds), *Encyclopedia of Sociology*, vol. 3. New York: Macmillan, pp. 1525–31.

Voges, Wolfgang and Götz Rohwer (1992). "Receiving social assistance in Germany: Risk and duration". *Journal of European Social Policy*, 2(3): 175–91.

Walker, Robert (1987) "Consensual approaches to the definition of poverty: Towards an alternative methodology", *Journal of Social Policy*, 16(2): 213–26.

Walker, Robert (ed.) (1994) *Poverty Dynamics: Issues and Examples*. Aldershot: Avebury.

Whelan, Brendan J (1992) *A Study of Non-Monetary Indicators of Poverty in the European Community*. Dublin: Economic and Social Research Institute.

Whiteford, Peter (1985) *A Family's Needs: Equivalence Scales, Poverty and Social Security*. Canberra: Department of Social Security, Development Division, Research Paper no. 27.

Chapter 15

Greece, Turkey, and Cyprus: Poverty Research in a Policy Vacuum

Maria Petmesidou

Introduction

Greece and Turkey are both late industrializing countries whose historical trajectories have been influenced, though to a varying degree, by Eastern socio-political and cultural traditions. This characteristic distinguishes them from the rest of the South European countries. Yet there are also significant differences between the two countries in terms of level and strategy of socioeconomic development, and in this respect Turkey is closer to some other Asian Third World countries, whereas Greece is closer to other countries of the European Union periphery (i.e. Portugal, Spain, Italy, and Ireland). The population of Turkey is more than five times the population of Greece, but GDP per capita in Turkey is much lower than in Greece (US$1,128 and US$3,988, respectively, in 1986). On the other hand, Turkey exhibited a comparatively high rate of economic growth in the 1980s; for the period 1982–7 the average annual rate of growth of GDP was 6.0 per cent in Turkey and 2.1 per cent in Greece.

Cyprus differs in many respects from the other two countries examined here. It has a very small population – a little over half a million inhabitants – and experienced very fast economic growth from the early 1960s, which transformed it from an underdeveloped to a rapidly developing country. Also, its colonial past accounts for some significant socio-institutional influences of a North European origin (i.e. as regards state and administrative structures and the state–economy relationship). From 1960 – the year of its independence – until 1974 the Cypriot economy grew at a high speed, the average annual rate of GDP reaching 7 per cent (Mavros 1989). The Turkish invasion slowed down economic growth in the late 1970s; yet in the early 1980s the economy succeeded in resuming its upward trend. In 1990, GDP per capita reached US$8,434, an indicator ranking Cyprus among the twenty-five richest countries of the world (Papandropoulos 1991: 30).[1]

A common characteristic of Greece and Turkey is the large proportion of the labour force employed in agriculture – amounting to about 50 per cent of the economically active population in Turkey and 30 per cent in Greece. Turkey is still predominantly an agricultural country, and urbanization has not proceeded as fast as it did in Greece. In the early 1980s the urban population in Turkey reached 47 per cent of the total population, while the corresponding percentage for Greece was 62 per cent. Furthermore, employment in the tertiary sector (mainly trade, tourism, and personal services) has always been comparatively high in Greece and in Turkey – though to a lesser extent – because employment in industry has remained low. Other common characteristics are the large size of the black economy, high self-employment, and widespread practices of multiple employment by economic actors crossing the line between the formal and informal sectors.

The sectoral structure of the Cypriot economy exhibits many similarities with those of the other two countries, with agriculture and services being the most important sectors. Yet the very good economic performance of Cyprus during the 1980s in relationship to comparatively high welfare indicators, the achievement of almost full employment, and the absence of acute problems of social marginalization, distinguish it sharply from Greece and Turkey.

In Turkey, the 1960s and 1970s were a period of economic recovery through import-substituting industrialization, comprehensive planning, and labour market liberalization, which, however, ended in a deep crisis in the late 1970s. In the early 1980s the stabilization strategy adopted by the military regime facilitated the transition to a pattern of export-oriented growth, which suppressed internal demand and increased socioeconomic inequalities. Greece turned to an export-oriented strategy of economic development quite early – in 1961 – when the agreement for joining the European Communities was signed. In the 1960s significant changes are observed in the structure of production favouring industrialization and technological change; per capita income was rising fast and GDP was growing at an accelerating rate. However, these trends weakened in the 1970s and 1980s, and Greece entered a period of persistent economic stagnation, rising inflation, and increasing unemployment. Further, political changes in the early 1980s favoured policies of redistribution and expansion of internal demand. Yet these policies were soon replaced by stabilization programmes as the public deficit and external debt reached very high levels.

A historical tradition of paternalistic/statist structures and clientelistic forms of social and political integration, which characterizes the Mediterranean area, had a stronger influence on South-eastern Europe. This characteristic is closely related to the "weakness of civil society" in these countries; and, as argued elsewhere, among the Mediterranean countries "Greece and Turkey constitute examples of very weak civil societies, extensively depending on the state" (Petmesidou and Tsoulouvis 1994: 507). This feature accounts to a large extent for the political instability experienced by both countries in the postwar period.

As is stressed below, in both countries social exclusion and poverty are higher in rural areas; moreover, welfare institutions and research on socioeconomic inequalities are little developed. For a long period fast economic growth was a top priority in both countries. Poverty alleviation was not considered a primary issue of public policy, but rather it was thought that the welfare of the population would increase as a result of economic growth. Furthermore, in both societies, on the one hand the legacy of paternalistic/statist patterns supports state intervention in the creation and distribution of wealth, income, and jobs, as well as an ideology about the "father state". On the other hand, the weakness of civil society and the pattern of social conflicts hinder any consensus among social strata about the development of consistent and systematic social policies. It is interesting to note here that, in the case of Greece, "access to the state constitutes the main aim of social conflicts, and those groups which are the winners in the struggle to power can use the state mechanism as a means for appropriating resources" (Petmesidou and Tsoulouvis 1994: 508; see also Petmesidou 1987 and Tsoulouvis 1987). Closely related to this is the extensive involvement of economic actors in informal economic activities and clientelistic forms of social and political integration, "which undermine the capacity of society to make explicit a number of processes through which value is created and distributed and such a capacity is, indeed, a precondition for the development of any consistent social planning processes and welfare state institutions" (ibid.).

Poverty research in Greece

In Greece, during the whole postwar period, policies for redressing socioeconomic inequalities remained rudimentary. This accounts for the lack of data on distributional issues and the limited research on the extent and intensity of poverty. During the 1960s and 1970s the Greek economy achieved high rates of economic growth, and it was thought that the general improvement in the standard of living would in itself be sufficient to alleviate poverty. Since the late 1970s the deterioration in Greece's economic performance has shaken this over-optimistic attitude. In addition, rising unemployment in the cities has increased urban poverty, while immigration flows from other Balkan countries and the former USSR (e.g. the Greek Pontians) to Greece in the 1990s have created new pockets of poverty in both urban and rural areas.[2]

Still, poverty issues are not in the forefront of public debate, and no official poverty line exists below which the individual or the household would be entitled to public support. To the extent that a limited debate on the degree of poverty and its causes is developing in Greece, this has been induced mainly by the European Community (EC) initiatives to gather information on poverty and social exclusion across the member countries; to finance pilot studies on policy experimentation at the local level; and to promote the exchange of "best practices" to combat social exclusion among national and supranational social policy agencies (e.g. the First, Second, and Third Poverty Programmes of the EC).

A few studies on income inequalities conducted during the 1960s and 1970s drew upon the national accounts and income declarations to the tax office and focused mainly on the "functional" distribution of income, that is on the distribution of total income to the basic factors of production (Athanasiou 1984; Germidis and Negreponti-Delivani 1975; Karagiorgas 1973; Lianos and Prodromidis 1974). On the basis of the data concerning the incomes earned by the three factors of production in the period 1959–71, Lianos and Prodromidis found that the Gini coefficients varied between 0.41 and 0.46. Germidis and Negreponti-Delivani pointed out that indirect taxes contribute significantly to income inequality, while Karagiorgas's study focused on the unequal distribution of the tax burden in Greece. A study by Babanasis offers a historical description of the living conditions of workers' households in Greece from 1900 to 1981, with an emphasis on wage trends, nutritional habits, housing conditions, and other aspects of consumption. Babanasis locates five groups with a high risk of falling into poverty: the homeless, the low-income/low-wage earners, the non-economically active without any resources, migrants and illiterates. He estimated that at the end of the 1970s 20 per cent of the population belonged to these groups and lived in poverty in Greece, whereas the EC average of poor population was 10 per cent (Babanasis 1981 and 1983). These early studies faced severe limitations in terms of the availability of data and most of them were criticized for their limited focus on inequalities between the shares of the factors of production and their neglect of within-shares inequalities (Kanellopoulos 1986: 24).

Poverty in the 1970s

Beckerman's study (1979) constitutes the first systematic attempt to examine the extent of poverty in Greece. It was carried out in the context of the World Employment Programme, coordinated by the International Labour Office, and based upon the grouped data of the 1974 household expenditure survey (HES) conducted by the National Statistical Service of Greece (ESYE). Consumption expenditure was defined so as to include, apart from purchases, consumption of own production, consumption of incomes in kind, as well as imputed rents for owner-occupied accommodation evaluated at market prices. Beckerman defined the poverty line for a two-member household as the average per capita expenditure calculated on the basis of the 1974 national accounts data. The equivalence scales used by the author for households with one, two, three, four, five, and six members were 0.625, 1.00, 1.203, 1.404, 1.611, and 1.866 respectively. By applying this poverty line on the 1974 household expenditure data he arrived at the conclusion that 28.2 per cent of all households and 25.7 per cent of the total population of Greece were living in poverty at that time. These findings indicate that poverty was higher among small rather than large households, though this is contradicted by other studies.[3] There is agreement on two of the conclusions: first, that poverty was highest in rural areas (45 per cent of households), and lowest in the Greater Athens Area (11.7 per cent of households); and, second, that the relationship between household size and degree of poverty is U-shaped, because poverty strikes households with one, two, and six members more often, and households with three, four, and five members less often.

Karantinos's study (1985) also drew upon the grouped data of the 1974 HES by ESYE. In contrast to Beckerman, his definition of consumption expenditure excluded consumption of own production, consumption of incomes in kind, and imputed rents for owner-occupied accommodation evaluated at market prices. The poverty line was defined as an income or expenditure limit that is assumed to reflect the minimum socially accepted standard of living: 5,000 drachmas monthly expenditure per household, or 1,645 drachmas per capita monthly expenditure, at average 1974 prices. On the basis of this definition, which comes closer to a definition of absolute rather than relative poverty, Karantinos calculated that, in 1974, 30.85 per cent of all households and 24.6 per cent of the total population were poor. In agreement with Beckerman, small households were found to be in poverty more often than large ones (Karantinos 1985: 187; see also Karantinos 1981).

Karantinos examined the distribution of poor households by geographical area; the number of economically active members of the household; the socio-professional category to which the household head belongs; and the age group of the household head. On the basis of this analysis, the following high-risk categories were identified – that is, categories in which more than 45 per cent of households are in poverty – and classified in descending order of risk: (1) households with a head in the age group of 75 years and over; (2) households with no economically active member (the head has retired); (3) households with a head in the 65–74 age group; (4) households living in communities with less than 1,000 inhabitants; (5) households in which the head is a farmer or a fisherman; (6) households in which the head is not working or is seeking work; and (7) households living in communities of 1,000–2,000 inhabitants. Other categories at risk are the households with one economically active member only and those with a self-employed head.

The poverty gap varied from 2 per cent in the Greater Athens Area (GAA) to 17 per cent in the rural areas, while at the national level it was 6.6 per cent. Moreover, though 30.82 per cent of the population lived in the rural areas, the share of these areas in aggregate poverty amounted to 57 per cent. The Sen indices and the Gini coefficients calculated for the four types of geographical areas examined – rural, semi-urban, urban, GAA – also showed that the intensity of poverty was highest in the rural areas. Karantinos concluded that a model of economic development that promotes growth but increases inequalities cannot be successful in the long run.[4] Consequently, in order to combat poverty, "marginal changes in the already existing policies and mechanisms of redistribution are not enough". Instead, drastic changes are required and the first step in this direction is to define an official poverty line and find out which groups of the population are below this line (Karantinos 1985: 192).

Another study, by Kanellopoulos (1986), examined poverty on the basis of the income data provided by the 1974 HES. This was the first study to use the primary data of this survey – mainly the primary data on the income of the household head, and only secondarily the primary data on household consumption – as well as the first study to experiment with different poverty lines.

The 1974 HES recorded the monthly net income of the household head; this excluded income taxes and social security as well as income in kind, but included incomes from rents, dividends, or other owned sources of material wealth (Kanellopoulos 1986: 29). The author remarked that the income data of the 1974 HES were very underestimated because they amounted to 71 per cent of the personal disposable income of the national accounts; and the underestimation was highest for the incomes of employers and self-employed, incomes accruing from owned assets and business activities, as well as agricultural incomes (ibid.: 36–8). Kanellopoulos used the equivalence scales of 1.0 for the household head and 0.7 for the rest of the members, and by drawing upon the EC's First Poverty Programme he defined the poverty line as 50 per cent of the average per capita income per equivalent adult. On the basis of this definition it was found that, in 1974, 26.4 per cent of households and of the total population lived in poverty. The size of the poor households did not differ significantly from that of the non-poor ones.

The poverty gap, as a percentage of the total personal income of the sample, amounted to 10.27 per cent, being much higher than the poverty gap calculated by the two previous studies. This happened mainly because the author did not take into account incomes in kind, and he was criticized for this (Tsakloglou 1993a: 378). Also, Kanellopoulos was criticized because he took the household and not the individual as his point of reference, thereby assigning equal weight to small-size and large-size households.

The characteristics of the poor can be summarized as follows (Kanellopoulos 1986: 66–73):

- poverty strikes mostly the rural areas where one in two households live in poverty; in urban areas only 15 per cent of the households are poor;
- poor households are located mainly in the border regions of Epirus, Thessaly, Eastern Macedonia, and Thrace;
- among households with a head employed in agriculture, cattle breading, and fishing, 40.2 per cent are poor; whereas as regards all other sectors of the economy the percentage is below the national average;
- a strong negative relationship is found between the level of education of the household head and the degree of poverty

(92.1 per cent of poor households are headed by a person with education up to primary school level);
- old age is positively related to poverty; elderly couples and old persons (especially old women) living alone constitute an extremely high-risk group;
- the incidence of poverty in respect to family size is U-shaped; also, the more children under 14 there are in the household, the higher is the incidence of poverty;
- only 2 in 10 households are headed by a female breadwinner, and the incidence of poverty is higher than in those headed by a male breadwinner;
- all households with no economically active members are poor, and poverty decreases as the number of household members earning an income increases.

Kanellopoulos concluded that, for the purposes of developing an efficient policy targeted to the groups in the greatest hardship, more research was needed for locating small and homogeneous poverty groups (ibid.: 71). Kanellopoulos also stressed that, in view of increasing unemployment in urban areas and the improvement of the terms of trade for agriculture since the late 1970s, a convergence in the incidence of poverty between rural and urban areas should be expected in the future (ibid.: 75).

Poverty in the 1980s

The study by Karagiorgas and his associates (1990) constitutes more comprehensive research into poverty issues in Greek society, including both the income and non-income aspects of poverty. Owing to the lack of reliable data on income distribution, the study was based on the consumption expenditure data of the 1981/82 HES of ESYE. Also, the data of the previous HESs were taken into account for examining changes in the incidence and intensity of poverty in the postwar period. By adopting the same equivalence scales as Kanellopoulos, the authors defined the poverty line as 55 per cent of total consumption expenditure, because expenditure is less equally distributed than income (Karagiorgas et al. 1990: 77). On the basis of this assumption, in 1982, 20.6 per cent of households (641,000) and 22.4 per cent of the population (about 2 million people) were living in poverty (ibid.: 73) – almost double the EC average of 11.4 per cent. Moreover, the poverty gap amounted to 3.22 per cent of total consumption expenditure per equivalent adult. On the basis of the same method, it was found that, in 1974, 25 per cent of households and 27 per cent of the population were living in poverty, while the poverty gap was 4.54 per cent of total consumption expenditure per equivalent adult. The authors remarked that in 1974 Greece appeared to have the largest percentage of poor households within the European Community (ibid.: 146).

Through an analysis of poverty with respect to household size, stage in the family life cycle, geographical area, age, and employment of the household head, Karagiorgas et al. arrived at similar conclusions about the profile of poor households to those of the above-mentioned studies. Poverty increases progressively in relationship to the following factors:

- large household size (three, four, or more children);
- employment of the household head in the primary sector and household residence in one of the border regions (Epirus, Eastern Macedonia and Thrace, Aegean Islands);
- old age of the household head (65 or over);
- low educational level of the household head; and
- insufficient social security coverage.

Karagiorgas et al. also examined the extent of absolute poverty in Greece from the early 1950s to the early 1980s. They defined the absolute poverty line as 10,000 drachmas (average monthly consumption) for urban areas in 1981/82 and 8,000 and 9,000 drachmas for the rural and semi-urban areas, respectively. Then the equivalents at 1957/58, 1963/64, and 1974 average prices were calculated. On the basis of this definition, it was found that, in 1957/58, 100 per cent of the population of the urban areas were poor, whereas in 1981/82 only 6.84 per cent were below the absolute poverty line. Also, in 1963/64 100 per cent of the population in semi-urban and rural areas were poor, whereas in 1981/82 the poor decreased to 47.35 per cent and 27.95 per cent of the rural and semi-urban population, respectively (ibid.: 131). The authors concluded that in the early 1980s absolute poverty was greatly reduced in Greece. This was due mainly to the high rate of economic growth in the two previous decades, which improved the standard of living of the population, and only marginally to social policies.[5]

Relative poverty increased in the urban centres between 1957/58 and 1974, but decreased between 1974 and 1982 because of the considerable improvement of the economic position of the lower income groups since the middle of the 1970s. Yet, given the fact that in rural areas relative poverty steadily decreased in the period under study, the contribution to aggregate poverty by the urban areas – and particularly by small households – was expected to increase significantly. Karagiorgas et al. also observed a convergence of patterns of consumption between urban and rural areas in the early 1980s.

As regards educational inequalities, the analysis showed that the members of poor households aged 13 years and over reached only 55 per cent of the level of education of the corresponding category of members of better-off households, while the level of education of the heads of poor households was less than 50 per cent of that of heads of better-off households. To the extent that the children of poor households experienced intergenerational upward mobility, this was considered to be of a structural rather than an exchange type, because it was accounted for mainly by changes in the employment structure. On the other hand, among the children of better-off households exchange mobility occurred more often; and this showed that the better-off children were able to realize their ambitions to acquire a higher educational capital, often independently of the requirements of the labour market (ibid.: 464). For poor children, education was unable to break the cycle of cumulative social deprivation intergenerationally.

Although housing conditions for the poor had improved in the period under study, there were still considerable inequalities in the early 1980s. In 1981/82, the number of poor households living in overcrowded conditions (more than one person per room) was 1.5 times higher than for the better-off. This ratio stayed constant during the whole postwar period, although the percentages of poor and better-off households living under conditions of overcrowding decreased. House ownership was found to be higher among poor than among better-off households. Moreover, a convergence was observed in terms of amenities such as running water, kitchen, toilet, and electric refrigerator; while great differences still existed as regards central heating and washing machine and car ownership.

Tsakloglou's study (1990 and 1993b) also focused on changes in the extent and degree of poverty in Greece between 1974 and 1982 by using the same data sources as the above study. The definition of consumption expenditure by Tsakloglou included, apart from purchases, consumption of own production, consumption of income in kind, and imputed rent for owner-occupied accommodation evaluated at market prices.[6] Following an OECD definition of the poverty line, Tsakloglou set this line at two-thirds of median consumption expenditure per equivalent adult in the relevant year. On the basis of this definition, 24.3 per cent of the 1974 HES sample were classified as poor, while in 1982 the corresponding percentage was slightly lower (22.7 per cent).[7] In 1982, the aggregate poverty gap was equal to 3.41 per cent of total consumption expenditure and its elimination would have required the transfer of 3.77 per cent of the consumption expenditure of the better-off to the poor.

By examining poverty with respect to geographical area, the occupational and demographic characteristics of households, and the level of education of household heads, Tsakloglou concluded that:

- poverty is more acute in rural areas and when household heads engage in primary production (rural poverty contributed between two-thirds and three-quarters of aggregate poverty in both surveys);
- poverty is high in households headed by retired persons; moreover, 63.7 per cent of this group were living in the countryside, that is, poverty is high in households headed by retired farmers;
- poverty is relatively high among households belonging to the heterogeneous group "other" (households headed by housewives, students, unemployed, unpaid family workers, etc.).

Furthermore, with the rapidly declining number of farmers and the increasing number of retired persons, Tsakloglou expected "that in the near future the latter may be the single most important group in poverty". Since about 30 per cent of aggregate poverty was accounted for by two groups where the household head was not an employed person ("retired" and "other"), it might be reasonable to expect that in Greece – as in many other European countries – poverty is associated with a lack of economically active persons in the household (Tsakloglou 1990: 392).

Tsakloglou maintained that any variations in the extent and degree of poverty can be only marginally attributed to demographic and occupational changes that occurred in the period 1974–82. His analysis showed that, when the population is grouped according to various criteria (demographic, occupational, etc.), over 84 per cent of the recorded decline in relative poverty was attributable to changes in poverty within groups. The picture was completely different when the population was grouped according to the educational level of the household head: the poverty indices calculated by Tsakloglou[8] showed that about two-thirds of the decrease in poverty was due to changes in population shares. Thus the improvement in the educational level of household heads had a strong positive effect on poverty alleviation (ibid.: 398).

In 1982, when the HES to which Tsakloglou referred was completed, the PASOK party came to power and implemented a programme of redistribution that substantially increased minimum salaries, wages, and pensions, and extended social security coverage to groups that were not previously covered. Tsakloglou maintained that "these policies had a positive impact on poverty alleviation" by redistributing money from the better-off to the poor. However, the effects of these policies on economic growth were considered detrimental by the author, given that between 1981 and 1985 the average annual growth rate of GDP per capita was only 1.0 per cent and the central government deficit as a proportion of GDP rose from 6.5 per cent to 9.8 per cent. In 1985, a stabilization programme was put into effect that most probably increased aggregate poverty in the middle of the 1980s (ibid.: 401).

Urban poverty

There are very few studies on urban poverty. Bouzas (1990) used the grouped data of annual net income (excluding direct taxes and social security contributions) for the year 1984, collected in the context of a study of income distribution in the Greater Athens Area (GAA) conducted by Karagiorgas, Kasimati, and Pantazidis (1988), in order to examine poverty in Athens. The poverty line and equivalence scales were defined in the same way as in Karagiorgas et al. (1990). In 1984, 19 per cent of households and 22.5 per cent of the population in the GAA were living in poverty. The incidence of poverty increased with the size of the household: households with six members exhibited the highest deviation from the poverty line. The aggregate poverty gap amounted to 3.1 per cent of the total net income. Bouzas rejected the approaches that locate the causes of poverty in the characteristics of the poor (e.g. the poverty culture) and emphasized factors such as economic and social policy and especially the absence of substantial social benefits related to the constitution and size of the household.

In the context of the EC's Third Poverty Programme, in 1991 a survey of income distribution was conducted by Kanellopoulos (1993) in the municipality of Perama (on the periphery of the GAA) on the basis of a sample consisting of 10 per cent of the households of this municipality.[9] The Gini and Theil coefficients for Perama – 0.408 and 0.275 respectively – were found to be higher than those for the GAA (0.345 and 0.221 respectively).[10] Thus income inequalities in the Perama community were higher than aggregate inequalities in the GAA.

Relative poverty in Perama and its extent and intensity were examined on the basis of alternative definitions of the poverty line (i.e. the first quintile, 50 per cent of the median income per equivalent adult, and subjective methods). By setting the poverty line at 50 per cent of the median income per equivalent adult (with equivalence coefficients defined as 1.0 for the household per head, 0.70 for every other adult member, and 0.50 for each child under 15 years of age), Kanellopoulos found that 135 households in the sample (19.6 per cent) were living in poverty. These were mostly large households with more than six members (35.8 per cent of households in this category were living in poverty, whereas only 7.3 per cent of one-member households were found to be poor). However, the highest contribution to poverty was exhibited by four-member households, even though this category did not exhibit the highest percentage of poverty. Also the income of this category of households was 42 per cent below the poverty line, thus exhibiting the highest poverty gap. On the basis of these findings the author concluded that, if we want to design an efficient and effective policy to combat poverty, its primary target should be four-member households with the highest intensity of poverty, and not the six-member households with the highest incidence of poverty.

In order to alleviate poverty in the community under study, 1.16 per cent of aggregate income would have had to be redistributed from the better-off to the poor, on the basis of the above definition of the poverty line. On the basis of the method of the first quintile, 5.28 per cent of aggregate income would have had to be redistributed, and this would have been even more if poverty had been defined by subjective criteria (1993: 143). Kanellopoulos also used a number of poverty indices, belonging to the group of Sen indices, that showed a positive relationship between household size and the poverty gap.

A striking characteristic is that one in every two poor households was headed by a person who was employed. Unemployed persons and housewives as household heads constituted a very small percentage of the sample. Also, the incidence of poverty for the households headed by a retired person was equal to the average (19.6 per cent). Household heads with technical education qualifications exhibited a lower incidence of poverty than household heads with general education qualifications. Equally striking is that the incidence of poverty was higher among the self-employed (29.6 per cent) than among the salaried and wage-earners (15.3 per cent) – a finding that can be accounted for by the underrating of the incomes of the self-employed persons of the sample. As regards the occupation of the household head, a higher incidence of poverty was exhibited by tradesmen and sales personnel and by persons employed in transport and restaurants, and partly by "a natural attitude of self-protection in view of the absence of state intervention and state institutions for social protection" (1992: 14). Given this tradition, Chtouris argued that social policy in Greece would be more efficient if based on decentralized institutions, at a community level, that could activate citizens, rather than on "classical methods" of social policy implementation through the development of public institutions for social protection controlled by the central state. Also, he questioned "the likelihood of functional success of institutions of protection based purely on private economic criteria, such as firms offering social services, since they do not incorporate in any special way the existing forms of protection provided by social institutions and particularly the family" (ibid.). However, Chtouris seems to ignore the fact that, in the field of social protection, Greece lacks any tradition of strong voluntary organizations and processes of self-help at the local level on which his policy recommendations could draw; and, as has been stressed by other studies, this is mainly due to the weakness of civil society in Greece (Petmesidou 1987, 1992).[11]

It was estimated that 8.5 per cent of the households in Argyroupolis were living in relative poverty, which is defined as "the inability of a person to reach 50 per cent of the average per capita income" (Chtouris 1992: 114). Yet, on the basis of an alternative definition of poverty, taking as a point of reference the minimum wage as defined through collective bargaining, 21 per cent of the households were considered poor. This was also supported by subjective opinions about poverty in this community. Chtouris's remarks about the relationship between local economic conditions and the existence of less privileged groups living in poverty are rather contradictory. At one point he assigned the causes of poverty to local economic problems, yet at another point he stressed that most of the economically active population of the community were employed or seeking jobs in other parts of Athens and Piraeus (ibid.: 57 and 39). The complex interrelationships between local conditions and broader socioeconomic processes in the Greater Athens Area were not touched upon by the author.

Social policy in Greece

Petmesidou's work on social inequalities and social policy in Greece (1991 and 1992; see also Petmesidou and Tsoulouvis 1990) raises the central question: why in Greek society has a wide consensus about the necessity of developing extensive welfare policies as well as about the aims of such policies scarcely been achieved?

In Greek society the amount of resources appropriated by economic actors through direct or indirect state intervention is quite substantial. This is manifested by the high ratio of public expenditure to GDP (about 50 per cent in the 1980s), and by the high share of the salaries of public employees in the total of salaries and wages: in 1985 it reached 33.5 per cent, and, if we include the rest of the public sector (public utility corporations, banks, and nationalized industries), the ratio comes close to 50 per cent. Yet, despite the high level of public expenditure, state intervention has always been very ambivalent and has rarely, until now, led to any consistent and systematic planning processes; urban and regional planning policies have been rudimentary and state welfare institutions little developed. Moreover, Petmesidou underlines the absence of compromises among conflicting social groups about the goals of social and economic planning. During the whole postwar period, the only context in which it was possible for a social and political consensus to be achieved in Greek society concerned the use of the state machinery for the appropriation of the social surplus by the winners in the struggle for power.

On the basis of the grouped data of the HESs by ESYE (1957/58, 1967/68, 1974, and 1982) Petmesidou showed that in the period in which Greece experienced comparatively high growth rates – from the early 1960s to the middle of the 1970s – the standard of living of low-income groups deteriorated. In parallel, public spending on social welfare services remained stagnant at a very low ratio to GDP (around 3 per cent). Inequalities in consumption expenditure among socio-professional groups decreased significantly only from the late 1970s; while a rapid expansion in social expenditure was observed in the early 1980s – that is, in a period of economic stagnation. These findings sharply contrast Greece to North-west European countries.

By examining the trends in the social budget, Petmesidou stressed that transfer payments constitute the most important component of social expenditure (consisting mainly of pension expenditure), absorbing a comparatively large share of GDP over the whole postwar period. Yet, for fifteen years after 1960, transfer payments expenditure increased very slowly in absolute figures. In the second half of the 1970s, a substantial increase was discerned; but a steep upward trend occurred after 1982. The rapid increase in government expenditure and in the social budget by the successive PASOK (Panhellenic Socialist Movement) governments in the 1980s, and a rhetoric about and a lower incidence by workers in industry (e.g. workers in heavy industry). The sex of the household head did not seem to be a decisive factor in poverty.

Kanellopoulos stressed that poverty is a multidimensional phenomenon that cannot be restricted to income factors. For instance, when we observe a density of more than one person per room, as happened in 15 per cent of the households of the sample, we should consider it an aspect of poverty as well. On the other hand, house ownership is not decisive for distinguishing the better-off from the poor, because 82.4 per cent of households were living in owned accommodation.

On the basis of a subjective poverty line, poverty in Perama was very extensive: 55.4 per cent of households considered themselves to be poor, and poverty was extremely high among one-member households (95.1 per cent of these households), as well as among large households (53.4 per cent of six-member households), and lower among medium-size households (47.1 per cent of the four-member households). Moreover, one in every two households considered the unemployed to be poorer than the disabled, though unemployment was not very high in this community. Only 6.1 per cent and 1.0 per cent of households considered idleness and illiteracy, respectively, to be the main causes of poverty. On the other hand, 44.4 per cent stressed that poverty is accounted for by macroeconomic conditions such as unemployment and inflation or by overall governmental policy (30.3 per cent); and 1.3 per cent blamed poverty on a deficient social security policy. The author concluded that subjective definitions refer to economic difficulties in a wider sense rather than to poverty in the strict sense of the term.

Finally, Kanellopoulos stressed that a large percentage of the households in Perama (mostly the poor households) had very scanty information about the social services offered at the local level. Their information was restricted to the services addressed to the disabled and to families with many children. This raises the issue of the deficiency of the local information system as regards citizens' rights and the kinds of social services offered by various agencies.

A study by Chtouris (1992; also Chtouris et al. 1993), undertaken in the context of the EC's Third Poverty Programme, focused upon the least privileged groups and the role of the family in social protection in the municipality of Argyroupolis (part of the GAA too). Chtouris considered the family to be "the most important institution for social protection in Greece today". According to him, this was accounted for partly by the until recently dominant agricultural tradition in Greek society, institutional reforms "hardly led to the development of a welfare state of Keynesian type (and variations of it) or socialist type" (Petmesidou 1991: 32). This was owing not so much to the recession as to the particular characteristics of statism in Greek society in relation to the rise to political power of the middle classes. The expanding influence of the middle-class strata on the state machinery considerably limited the possibilities of any consensus about the goals of social and economic planning. On the one hand, it discouraged any dynamic involvement of the state in the economy (i.e. construction of big infrastructure works, public investment in manufacturing). On the other hand, middle-class demands continuously pressed for ever-increasing state intervention in the functioning of the market (i.e. increasing demands for the provision of social services and various kinds of benefits and subsidies). Since the late 1970s, an intensified competition for access to political power and the state among the middle classes has increasingly dominated the processes of distribution of social benefits. This has brought to the fore a number of social and economic deadlocks and made even more distant the goal of a systematic social policy in Greek society.

Poverty research in Turkey

There are very few studies on income distribution and poverty in Turkey.[12] The essays in the volume edited by Özbudun and Ulusan (1980a) examine Turkey's income distribution experience from the early 1950s to the mid-1970s. Hansen's comparative study (1991) of socioeconomic development in Egypt and Turkey includes an analysis of income distribution and poverty in Turkey from 1923 to 1985. In addition, a few articles focusing on issues such as illegal housing, land development, and indicators of life satisfaction in Turkey provide valuable information about socioeconomic inequalities in the country.

Existing data are of poor quality. According to Özbudun and Ulusan, "there are few observations, definitions shift through time in the same 'series', sources are not fully documented, and the comparability of concepts and methods is weak across official sources, let alone across the various ad hoc scholarly studies on which one must partially rely" (Özbudun and Ulusan 1980b: 7).

Neither of the above studies produced its own extensive survey research data, but relied largely on available data sources, such as national accounts, population censuses, and industrial surveys and censuses, as well as the published and unpublished results of a set of three nation-wide household surveys (1963, 1968, and 1973). The data prior to the 1973 household survey do not allow a detailed decomposition of income distribution, apart from a two-sector distinction (agricultural and non-agricultural sector). Moreover the 1968 survey is considered to be flawed in many respects: income is found to be underreported by about 38 per cent, while 17 per cent of households were excluded from the survey on the basis of a "shocking choice" to exclude households with a male head whose wife was over 45 years old (Hansen 1991: 278). A more detailed analysis of income distribution is possible only on the basis of the 1973 survey data derived from the fertility and population survey conducted by Hacettepe University (Dervis and Robinson 1980: 85). Yet this survey is also strongly criticized. Among other things, Hansen stresses that "income in non-agricultural activities was underreported by 19.5 per cent and in agriculture (after corrections) by 6.6 per cent; agricultural population was underestimated; and the results for agriculture, which were deemed to be unreliable, were replaced by indirect estimates" (Hansen 1991: 278).[13]

Modernization and changing socioeconomic inequalities

The essays in the volume edited by Özbudun and Ulusan covered a period in which Turkey exhibited dynamic growth that made possible "the emergence of a considerable ferment of populist, redistributive change" (1980b: 3). The essays focused on "the distribution of material benefits – in an income or flow sense"; although this does not mean that the authors did not recognize the importance of the distributions of non-traded, non-monetized material benefits and the way these are linked to income distribution. There was no agreement on a preferred definition of a poverty line, but, instead, several definitions used by official sources were adopted by the authors (ibid.: 6). On the other hand, the authors agreed that the net effects of public policy efforts to reduce inequality were rather weak in the period under consideration. Inequalities increased considerably and the structure of inequalities changed as the gap between the agricultural and non-agricultural sector narrowed.

Özbudun advanced the hypothesis that income distribution becomes a political issue when a society is extensively modernized. In addition, Özbudun and Ulusan adopted the view that "societies in the middle phases of socioeconomic development" tend to exhibit more inequalities than "societies that are less or much developed" (1980b: 14). Özbudun describes the dominant traditional cleavage in Turkish society as a centre–periphery cleavage. This is a politico-cultural distinction, in which the centre denotes the state apparatus and the social strata that have access to it, while the periphery consists of the social strata excluded from such an access. This cleavage originated in the social and political culture of the Ottoman Empire and gave rise to social conflicts and a class consciousness very different from those we find in Western countries. For a long time in Turkish society the main social conflict was between the ruling bureaucratic class (or "the political ins") on the one hand, and the outsiders ("the political outs") on the other. What is more important, in contrast to Western societies where such a political cleavage reflected other social cleavages and conflicts (e.g. between rural and urban interests, the bourgeoisie and the working class), in the Ottoman Empire – and in Turkish society until the early 1960s – it acquired a salience that made it the basis of all social conflicts. The social strata in the centre were mainly the state bureaucracy, the military, and big landowners, while the periphery consisted of the commercial and industrial middle classes and commercialized farmers – although some social groups, for instance landowners, are sometimes seen as located in the centre and sometimes in the periphery.

Closely related to this characteristic is a legacy of a highly centralized governmental authority and a pervasive culture and ideology accepting "the paramountcy of 'father-state' – a sovereign and autonomous entity, almost independent from society" (Özbudun and Ulusun 1980b: 3). The legacy of statism and paternalism in relationship to the homogeneous character of Turkish society – owing to the absence of ethnic and religious conflicts that might be cumulative with class conflicts – apparently favours the pursuit of redistribution policies. Yet, as long as the traditional centre–periphery cleavage dominated Turkish society, equity issues hardly came to the forefront of political debates on redistribution. Such issues acquired political significance with the emergence of "a new functional or class cleavage" with growing industrialization and urbanization. The 1960 Revolution – as the military coup of 1960 is called – and the new Constitution of 1961 are considered to be a turning point in the socioeconomic and political development of Turkey.

As regards economic development, at the end of the 1950s the possibilities of agricultural development and raw material exports were exhausted and a change of policy towards planning and investment for industrialization is observed. The decades of the 1960s and 1970s constituted a period of import substitution and expansion of the home market (Özbudun 1980: 67–75; see also Ayata 1990; Hansen 1991: ch. 6; and Keyder 1987). During these decades significant changes took place aiming to strengthen the legal position of various institutions of civil society (i.e. voluntary associations, chambers representing occupational groups, pressure groups, and trade unions). With the 1961 Constitution, the right to combine, form unions, undertake collective bargaining, and go on strike was firmly established on the legal plane. In parallel, the scope of basic human rights was extended formally through the provision of institutional safeguards against the violation of individual freedom of thought and action, and "social rights" were recognized as the Constitution assigned an active role to the state to redress socioeconomic inequalities and maintain the welfare of its citizens. Some other major decisions taken by the military government in the early 1960s were: "the establishment of the State Planning Organization (SPO), the introduction of the declaration of wealth which would make tax evasion more difficult, the expropriation and distribution of the lands of 55 large landowners in eastern Turkey, and the preliminary studies made of land and tax reforms" (Özbudun 1980: 62).

These conditions "provided a first genuine forum for a discussion of social and economic inequalities in the country", while for the first time "the term social state was adopted as one of the principal characteristics of the republic" (ibid.). The two main parties that successively ruled the country from the 1960s to the 1980s – with some short intervals of military rule during the early 1960s and early 1970s – both accepted the minimum requirements of the social state: the Republican People's Party (RPP) was committed to a populist model of development supporting an interventionist economic policy, political participation, and the expansion of government expenditure; while the Justice Party (JP) adopted a technocratic model stressing economic growth and minimum welfare provisions to those below the poverty line. A concern about equity issues was introduced from above through the 1961 Constitution. But such issues attracted the attention of a large part of the electorate later – in the mid 1970s – when most of the urban low-income groups shifted their electoral support from the conservative party (the Democratic Party transformed into the Justice Party) to the social democratic RPP.

Özbudun concluded that these developments made Turkey a good example of the association between level of socioeconomic development and the relative importance of issues of distribution in a society. Yet, his predictions about the possibility of an effective redistributive policy were rather gloomy. In a Third World country trying to speed up development, both the populist model of development and the technocratic model generate their own vicious cycle. In the former model, growing public expenditure limits economic growth and increases social conflicts as more groups become participant in the political game and attempt to share a stagnant or slowly growing pie; the result is social and political instability. In the latter model, a high rate of economic growth can be achieved, but at the expense of social justice and political participation and this will increase polarization and social unrest.

The patterns of inequality in Turkey were examined by Dervis and Robinson (1980) with reference to the degree of "dualism" in this society. According to them the gap between output per man in agriculture and in the rest of the Turkish economy (called, after Kuznets, the "K ratio") constitutes a main indicator of the extent of inequality in a developing country. It was found that in 1968 the K ratio was 5.09, considered to be one of the highest values, which made Turkey an extreme case by international standards. A combination of factors, such as "rapid migration, a sharp movement in the terms of trade in favour of agriculture, and quite rapid technological change and mechanization" in the 1970s had as an effect a small reduction in the K ratio, which fell to 4.26 in 1973. From disparities in productivity they calculated per capita and per household income disparities, which were found to be quite high and confirmed inter-sectoral inequality as a major source of overall inequality in Turkey in the middle of the 1970s. In 1973, per capita non-agricultural income was 3.74 times per capita agricultural income; per household non-agricultural income was 3.12 times per household agricultural income; and per household disposable non-agricultural income (net of direct taxes) was 2.28 times per household disposable agricultural income (Dervis and Robinson 1980: 98).

Among other things, a progressive improvement in the terms of trade in favour of agriculture was expected by Dervis and Robinson to narrow the gap between agriculture and the rest of the economy in the future; and this would change the pattern of inequalities significantly. The divide between industrializing urban centres and the rural poor would cease to be a major break in society as intra-urban inequalities increased and the expanding urban–industrial sector came to dominate the distribution debate (ibid.: 98–9).

Within the urban sector, the authors distinguished four major socioeconomic groups:

- The capitalist urban elite together with the socioeconomic group of professionals constituted the wealthiest group, com-

posed of exporters, importers, contractors, industrialists, traders, doctors, lawyers, engineers, and top-level managers; it comprised 1.6 per cent of the population (with an average household size of 4.7 persons).
- Government employees constituted a very large socio-economic group in Turkish society (9.8 per cent of the population; average household size 4.9 persons). Their mean income was only one-fifth of the professional mean income and was very close to the overall mean, yet the within-group variance was quite high, with significant proportions of the wealthy and the very poor. These two groups together, with the small groups of white-collar workers and rentiers, constituted the educated, urban middle class.
- The urban working class comprised 21 per cent of the total population (average household size 5.3 persons). The mean income of skilled workers was slightly below but very close to the national average, whereas that of unskilled workers was very much below the overall average.
- The urban traditional sector comprised mainly artisans and small traders (15.4 per cent of the population; average household size 5.6 persons). It is interesting to note that the traditional sector had a mean income higher than the mean income of urban labour and its within-group variance was also very high.

In order to measure the extent of poverty in Turkish society, Dervis and Robinson took an annual household income in 1973 of TL12,000 (approximately US$840, constituting 50 per cent of average annual household income) as the extreme poverty line "below which people are unlikely to be able to adequately feed themselves and unable to enjoy even the minimum standards of a dignified human life" (1980: 110). On the basis of the 1973 Hacettepe–SPO population survey, which included data by socioeconomic group, Dervis and Robinson found that 30 per cent of households were in this condition: 55.6 per cent of the very poor were farmers, 16.6 per cent unskilled labourers, 13.2 per cent artisans, and 5.5 per cent government employees. The next cut-off point was defined at TL 24,000, and households below that income were considered by the authors "as definitely poor". This income group included 40 per cent of the Turkish population: 14.5 per cent were government officials, 15.2 per cent labourers, 14.3 per cent unskilled labourers, 18.4 per cent artisans, and 36 per cent farmers and rural labourers. Households earning between TL24,000 and TL72,000 constituted 25 per cent of the Turkish population, while the very rich households earning more than TL72,000 amounted to only 5 per cent (of them 26 per cent were capitalists and professionals, 8 per cent government officials, 10 per cent artisans, and 49 per cent farmers).

An important characteristic is the spread of agricultural households in all income ranges, accounting for the high within-group variance. The mean income of the top decile was 54 times the mean income of the bottom decile for agricultural household, while the corresponding ratio for non-agricultural households was 29. The proportion of agricultural households in poverty was much greater (49 per cent) compared with non-agricultural households (29 per cent);[14] while the mean income of the bottom decile of non-agricultural households was 2.69 times that of the agricultural bottom decile (ibid.: 111–12).

The highly unequal ownership of land accounted for the high within-group variance in the agricultural sector. According to an SPO study of land distribution in 1973, 22 per cent of rural households in Turkey were landless and 20 per cent owned less than 1 hectare. However, the land owned by these 42 per cent amounted to only 3 per cent of total privately owned land. Conversely, households with 100 or more hectares of land constituted only 0.12 per cent of rural households (and owned 5.27 per cent of the land). Land distribution was particularly unequal in eastern and south-eastern regions (Ulusan 1980).

Interregional inequalities were also very high and, as Danielson and Keles argued, the overall effects of urbanization have been "the perpetuation of serious disparities between rural and urban areas, between eastern and western Turkey, and among different kinds of cities" (Danielson and Keles 1980: 301). In terms of regional incomes, Dervis and Robinson argued that "there is not so much a clear-cut dualism as a more gradual progression from the relatively rich big cities to the poorest eastern region [eastern Anatolia], with the other non-big-city regions forming an intermediate group" (Dervis and Robinson 1980: 118). In the three largest cities (Instabul, Ankara, and Izmir) mean income was more than twice as high as that in the poorest eastern region of eastern Anatolia. Moreover, more developed regions displayed less within-region inequality. For instance, in the three big cities 14 per cent of the households were very poor and 9 per cent extremely wealthy, compared to 38 per cent and 5 per cent, correspondingly, for the country as a whole. On the other hand, in eastern Anatolia 54 per cent of the population were very poor and only 2 per cent very wealthy (ibid.: 118).

The extent of squatter housing constitutes an indicator of intra-urban inequalities. In the middle of the 1970s 27 per cent of the urban population lived in squatter housing (*gecekondu*) and more than two-thirds of them were in the three big cities (70 per cent in the early 1990s), accounting for about 50 per cent of urban space. Also 60 per cent of squatter housing was owner-occupied and the rest was rented to migrants. Although squatter housing in Turkey tends to be a good deal more substantial than the flimsy shanties found in many Asian and Latin American cities, it has many deficiencies such as severe overcrowding and lack of sewerage, running water, and electricity (Ergun 1991). The *gecekondu* play a significant role "in easing the assimilation of migrants", and because public resources are inadequate to meet the housing problems of the migrants, the Turkish state came to view *gecekondu* as an essential aspect of urbanization and modernization (Danielson and Keles 1980: 298).

A field in which public policy has succeeded in bringing about some equalizing effects is education. As Aral (1980) observed, provincial inequalities in enrolment rates and in teacher/student ratios decreased significantly between 1950 and 1970 at all three levels of education (primary, middle, and lycée). In this respect, a majority of provinces moved closer to the national norm in the period under study. Nevertheless, the way in which the Turkish educational system operates has the effect of increasing, rather than decreasing, inequalities in income.

The main conclusion of the studies in Özbudun and Ulusan (1980a) was that various trends in Turkish society would, sooner or later, increase pressures for redistribution. These trends were: increasing inequalities in the agricultural sector owing to growing landlessness and the differential effect of public support policies to agriculture, which tended to make big landowners even better off (Ulusan 1980; Ergünder 1980); the emergence of class-based politics with increasing modernization (Özbudun 1980); limited opportunities for external migration and the poor economic performance of the Turkish economy at the end of the 1970s, which led to rising urban unemployment and a growing radicalization of the poor. Moreover, given the still large size of the agricultural sector and the high degree of inequality within it, any policy of redistribution, in order to be effective in reducing overall inequalities, should first succeed in reducing inequality within this sector.

Estimates of poverty in the 1970s and 1980s

As stressed above, Hansen was very critical of the available information on income and wealth distribution in Turkey, which he considered to be "of poor quality, in terms of both size and functional distribution" (1991: 275). On the basis of the available information he calculated some indicators of income distribution for the period 1952–83. Yet he stressed that they could not provide any basis for firm conclusions about trends in income distribution: "The national Gini coefficient points to a slight decline in inequality but the lowest quintile share points, if anything, in the opposite direction while the highest quintile share tends to support the national Gini coefficients" (ibid.: 275).

Equally difficult was to draw a firm conclusion about trends in the distribution of income by region on the basis of the 1968 and 1973 surveys: "The differences between 1968 and 1973 for the big cities are too large to be credible" (for instance, the average household income in Izmir, as a percentage of the country average, was found to be 355.9 in 1968 and 159.9 in 1973). Furthermore, "the ratio between the weighted average of house-hold income for the metropolitan regions and the predominantly rural regions is 3.3 in 1968 against only 2.3 in 1973, a decline that does not seem credible in view of the fact that agricultural income was relatively low in the latter year" (ibid.: 280).

Estimates of poverty based on the 1973 survey of income distribution were considered to be flawed because of the weaknesses of that survey, mentioned above. Most importantly, "because the poverty line [TL12,000] is kept constant over time and the same for agricultural and non-agricultural families, one should already for that reason expect poverty to be more pronounced in than outside agriculture". Extrapolations for 1978 and 1983 based on the data of the 1973 survey were considered to be dubious and there was no evidence against which the results could be tested (ibid.: 288). On the basis of the adjusted data for 1973 by Celasun, Hansen calculated that 32 per cent of households in Turkey were below the poverty line in that year; the estimates for 1978 and 1983 exhibited a significant decrease in the percentage of households living in poverty at the end of the 1970s (25 per cent), but an increase in the early 1980s (30 per cent). This shows, that after the reforms and change in development strategy in 1980, poverty increased, though it was less pronounced than a decade earlier. In agriculture, in 1973 50 per cent of households were below the poverty line; and though there was an improvement at the end of the 1970s (42 per cent of households were found to be below the poverty line in 1978), the situation deteriorated again in the early 1980s, when, it was estimated, 51 per cent of households were living in poverty (ibid.: 288, table 6.15).

Some other indicators of "human wealth" calculated by Hansen concern nutritional status, life expectancy, enrolment ratios, rates of illiteracy, and years of completed formal education. During the two decades of state planning – the 1960s and 1970s – intakes of calories, protein, and fat increased substantially. In the early 1980s (a period of stabilization, recession, and reform) this trend slowed down. Hansen stressed that before the Second World War Turkey was at the same level as China and India in 1985 in terms of caloric intake, and in 1985 it reached the level of the upper-middle-income countries (but was well below that of industrial market economies; ibid.: 281).[15] Life expectancy increased from 51 years in 1965 to 61 years in 1980, while illiteracy rates for the population over 15 years old fell from 71.5 per cent in 1945 to 25.8 per cent in 1984.

Poverty research in Cyprus

Two studies on income distribution and expenditure patterns in Cyprus conducted in the late 1980s and early 1990s show that inequalities are rather moderate in this society: they are much lower than in other developing or less developed countries, but a little higher than in some developed countries (e.g. Germany, Norway, Japan).

The first in-depth study of income inequalities in Cyprus took place in the late 1980s (House 1988) on the basis of the household income and expenditure survey data collected by the Department of Statistics and Research (Ministry of Finance) in 1985. Poverty was only marginally examined by this study. The emphasis was on absolute deprivation and a poverty line was defined in accordance with a study conducted by the Department of Welfare Services (Ministry of Labour) on the basic needs and minimum income requirements that a household would be expected to meet under the prevailing social and economic conditions of the country. Although there is no officially declared poverty line in Cyprus, below which all households would be entitled to welfare benefits, the Department of Welfare Services' study set some minimum expenditure standards for nutrition, rent, and basic social needs as criteria of eligibility to financial support offered on a means-tested basis to some of those unable to meet the minimum expenditure requirements. On the basis of the minimum expenditure standards for a two-person household, House estimated the poverty line at C£808 per person per year (in 1987 average prices), and this led him to the conclusion that 4.4 per cent of all households fell below the absolute poverty line.[16]

House's definition of an absolute poverty line was found to be defective because it cannot take into account variations in the characteristics of the members of the household and assigns equal weight, in relationship to the head, to all other members, irrespective of whether the second person is a child or an adult; or whether the two-member household consists of two retired people or is a young, childless couple.[17]

House also examined the incidence of poverty among households of differing sizes and with different ages of the household head. Poverty struck mostly single-person households as well as households with six or more members. About 16 per cent of single-person households overall, and one-third in rural areas, had incomes below the absolute poverty line. Two-person households were found to be in a better position with only 5 per cent overall and 9 per cent in rural areas below the poverty line. On the other hand, very few households with three to five members were poor. The incidence of poverty increased dramatically with the old age of the household head: 18% of households overall, and 29 per cent in rural areas, with a head over 75 years old fell below the poverty line. Moreover, 13 per cent of the households with an inactive head were living in poverty; the corresponding percentages for urban and rural areas being 6 per cent and 24 per cent.

In the early 1990s a second study of income distribution and expenditure in Cyprus was carried out on the basis of the Household Income and Expenditure Survey data of 1990/91 collected by the Department of Statistics and Research (Department of Statistics and Research 1993). This was a more detailed study of the incidence and degree of poverty in Cyprus, focusing mainly on relative poverty.

By using a similar definition of absolute deprivation to that suggested by House, an absolute poverty line was also constructed by the authors of this study in order to be able to compare poverty levels in 1991 with those of 1985. Yet some adjustments were made to House's equivalence scales so as to take into account the unequal weight (in correspondence to the head) of other members of the household according to their age.[18] The relative poverty line was defined as equal to 50 per cent of the average national per capita income of all households.

For a single-person household, the absolute poverty line in Cyprus, in 1991, amounted to C£1451 per year and the relative poverty line to C£1542. Because the difference between the two lines was small, the authors assumed that a poor household with respect to relative poverty was likely to be poor with respect to absolute poverty as well. In the early 1990s, 4.39 per cent of all households in Cyprus earned incomes below the relative poverty line (7.9 per cent in rural areas and 2.94 per cent in urban areas).[19]

Households with the highest risk of being poor were those with an elderly head, a female head, or a head with a low educational level or no education at all. Moreover, a high incidence of poverty was found among household of smaller sizes. About 16.5 per cent of single-person households and 10 per cent of two-person households were in poverty in 1991, a great part of these households being headed by an elderly and retired person. Single-member households in rural areas exhibited a higher incidence of relative poverty (28.57 per cent) than those in urban areas (9.68 per cent). An important finding was that poverty among larger households (with two or more members) was almost non-existent, the incidence of poverty for these households ranging from zero to 2 per cent for all Cyprus. Even though there is not much comparability between the two studies reviewed here – the 1991 study used a relative poverty line that was much higher than the 1985 absolute poverty line – the results of the 1991 study point towards a substantial improvement in the standard of living of large households in Cyprus. For instance, in 1985 six-member households exhibited an incidence of poverty around 10 per cent, which decreased to less than 2 per cent in 1991. Households with seven or more members experienced a greater improvement (in 1985, 10 per cent of them were found to be below the absolute poverty line, whereas in 1991 none of these households fell below the relative poverty line).

Another characteristic is the feminization of poverty. Female-headed households had a higher poverty incidence (14.2 per cent) than male-headed ones (2.96 per cent). Also, 21 per cent of single-member households headed by a woman were living in poverty, compared with only 6.6 per cent of single-member households headed by a male person. Poverty was virtually non-existent among households with a head aged under 55. Households with a head aged 65–69 had a poverty incidence rate of 8.7 per cent, while more than one in every four households with a head aged over 75 were poor.

The level of education of the household head was negatively related to the risk of falling into poverty. About 30 per cent of households whose heads had no education at all were found in poverty (the rate being the same for urban and rural areas). The incidence of poverty decreased sharply for households whose head had at least some elementary education, ranging around 3 per cent; and, as the level of education increased, the risk of poverty was eliminated.

The degree of poverty is not very high in Cyprus: 82 per cent of the poor households in all Cyprus earn incomes amounting to over 70 per cent of their respective poverty line, and 28 per cent are only 1–9 per cent away from their respective poverty line. Moreover, the urban poor are in a better position than the rural poor: in the urban areas only 9.5 per cent of the poor households earn incomes below 70 per cent of their respective poverty line, while the corresponding percentage for the rural areas is 24.3 per cent (Pitiris 1993b).

In all Cyprus, three out of four poor single-person households have incomes over 80 per cent of their respective poverty line, and only 11 per cent of them are very poor. The degree of poverty is even less among the few poor households with more than two persons: all of them earn incomes between 71 per cent and 90 per cent of the value of their respective poverty line. Yet, if the degree of poverty is measured on the basis of expenditure instead of income, inequalities tend to be higher. As the Department of Statistics and Research indicated, "14% of the poor households expend less than half the amount suggested by the poverty line compared to less than 1% in the case of income" (1993: 4).

Although the incidence of poverty increases for households with an elderly head, the magnitude of poverty does not increase in parallel. Among poor households, a high degree of poverty is experienced by those with a relatively younger head, as well as by those with a head aged 55–64, the incomes of most of these households ranging below 70 per cent of the poverty line. On the other hand, only a small percentage of poor households with a head aged 70–74 (16 per cent) or over 74 (18 per cent) have incomes of 70 per cent or less of the poverty line. On the basis of these findings, the authors concluded that pension levels in Cyprus are not very low, while a small increase in these pensions would be sufficient for poor households with an elderly head to improve their standard of living and get above the poverty line. Moreover, according to Pitiris's estimates, the total elimination of poverty in Cyprus would require that an amount of C£2,866,000 per year (in 1991 average prices) be distributed to the poor. If this is difficult to achieve, a short-term policy of redistribution of about C£500,000 to the poor in one year could reduce poverty by one quarter (Pitiris 1993b).

Concluding remarks

In the three countries examined here poverty research has been little developed, and available data on economic inequalities are deficient in many respects. In Turkey, even the more recent studies on poverty have as a data source a survey conducted in the early 1970s and estimates of poverty in the next decade derive from these data. In Greece, most of the studies published in the 1990s rely upon the 1981/82 household expenditure survey of ESYE. The data from population censuses and other surveys regularly conducted by ESYE usually become available a number of years after the completion of data collection.

Cyprus differs from the other two countries in terms of the availability of income and expenditure data. The Department of Statistics and Research of the Ministry of Finance has been collecting such data at approximately five-year intervals for some time. The first in-depth study of income distribution took place in the late 1980s, but with a marginal focus on poverty. In the early 1990s, for the first time, poverty issues were addressed in a detailed way. As in the other two countries, an officially defined poverty line below which a household would be entitled to some form of financial support is non-existent. Yet, in contrast to Greece and Turkey, Cyprus is in a much better position with respect to poverty problems because the incidence and magnitude of poverty are comparatively low.

In Greece and Turkey, there are no studies of income distribution and poverty based on reliable personal income data collected on the basis of a nation-wide sample and standardized processes. As a result, there is no comparability in the measurement of socioeconomic inequalities in the two countries. The large size of the black economy and the widespread practices of multiple employment by economic actors in both countries make any attempt at recording personal incomes a very difficult and sometimes even futile task. The absence of policies for defining a poverty line and securing a minimum income for the groups below this line constitutes another side of the phenomenon of the unwillingness of economic actors in both societies to make explicit the processes through which income is created and distributed.

What is more important, poverty research in both countries only marginally touches upon the causes of poverty. Attempts at relating poverty issues to macroeconomic factors (the overall model of development, income policies and their impact on economic growth, etc.) lead to rather vague explanations or express value-judgements rather than empirically grounded hypotheses as, for instance, when it is argued that a development model that benefits a few social groups at the expense of the other social groups cannot be considered successful (Karantinos

1985). Yet how is success measured, what are the causes of social exclusion, and under what conditions can poverty be eliminated?

Another deficiency of poverty research, which partly accounts for the low concern about the causes of poverty, is its primary focus on the income dimensions of poverty. Large-scale empirical studies based on primary data and concerning processes of social change and social mobility in Greek and Turkish societies (as well as in Cypriot society)[20] in the postwar period are absent. Yet such studies are complementary to poverty research, because they provide substantial background information for the intertemporal examination of the causes of poverty and its income and non-income aspects.

In addition, poverty research is little related to policy considerations. This is a main reason why concern about the causes of poverty and strategies for combating it is rather limited. Up to now, poverty research at either the national or the local level, has hardly been integrated into any ongoing social planning processes in which research is linked with various phases of these processes (i.e. defining social exclusion, designing and implementing alternative strategies for combating social exclusion, evaluating the effects and cross-fertilizing experience from various social policy sectors and at various scales of implementation). A few isolated studies of poverty and of the least privileged groups at the local level in Greece have been induced by EC initiatives. These attempts have scarcely been integrated into any local social planning processes and may be discontinued as soon as EC priorities change.

Nevertheless, on the basis of the existing literature, one can identify the profile of the poor. In the 1970s and early 1980s, in Greece and Turkey, the rural/urban divide was still a crucial distinction for defining inequalities. Other factors contributing to poverty were old age and a low level of educational qualifications – with poverty increasing in the case of rural households headed by an elderly and/or illiterate person. In this respect, until the early 1980s, Greece and Turkey were still characterized by a "traditional" type of poverty, in contrast to North-western European societies in which the expansion of the welfare state in the first two decades of the postwar period considerably limited the risk of poverty for the retired and the elderly, whereas social and economic restructuring in the 1970s and 1980s led to the emergence of new high-risk groups, such as the long-term unemployed, the homeless, and single-parent families.[21] The profile of the poor in Cyprus exhibits similarities with the profiles of the poor in Greece and Turkey (especially as regards the higher incidence of poverty in rural areas and in households whose head has a low level of education), but at the same time it differs considerably given the very low degree of poverty among old and retired persons and the virtual non-existence of poverty among large households, in the early 1990s.

Although most of the studies reviewed here stress the fact that modernization processes under way in Greece and Turkey will have significant effects on the incidence of poverty and the profile of the poor, they offer very little insights for understanding social and economic change in Greece and Turkey, in the past decade.

Structural transformation in Southern Europe as a result of European Union integration is expected to have significant disruptive effects on traditional patterns of employment. Changes in the sectoral and geographical distribution of employment may result in making the position of various social groups in the labour market insecure. If, at the same time, traditional forms of family solidarity and paternalistic structures decline – as a result of modernization – without being substituted by alternative forms of social protection, the risk of marginalization of a number of social groups will be high. Considering the increased fragmentation of social interests, the high degree of centralization in economic and social policy issues, and the weak institutional framework for allowing localities to react to situations of hardship in Greek society, it is probable that phenomena of dualism in the labour market and social exclusion will appear. Lavrion (in Attica) and the north-central region of Evia constitute striking examples of severe problems of economic decline and social exclusion: in Lavrion in the early 1990s, almost 70 per cent of the population were unemployed and 45 per cent were living in conditions of absolute poverty; while the recent plant closures in Evia had detrimental effects for the population of more than thirty villages in the region. Moreover, social and economic restructuring in the Balkans and Central-Eastern Europe will have significant repercussions in both Turkey and Greece. Immigration flows from the ex-communist countries of the Balkans southwards have been increasing since the early 1990s. In the case of Greece, legal and illegal migrants from Albania (and to a lesser extent from Bulgaria, ex-Yugoslavia, and Poland) and the increasing number of Greek Pontians coming to Greece from the ex-USSR have led to the emergence of a new underclass in Greek cities, as well as in rural areas.

As a result of the above changes, social exclusion and poverty will continue to be severe problems in Greece and Turkey in the years ahead, though the profile of the socially excluded groups and their geographical distribution at the regional and local level may change considerably. Consequently, the empirical investigation of problems of poverty and marginality and their confrontation through systematic and effective social policy measures should become a top priority for social researchers and social policy agencies in both countries. In the case of Cyprus, on the other hand, the progressive elimination of poverty seems to be an achievable target to which systematic research could contribute significantly.

Notes

1. It should be stressed here that, in the occupied territories, the per capita income of the Turkish-Cypriot population (120,000 persons) amounts to about one-third of that of the Greek-Cypriot population of the Republic of Cyprus.
2. Research on the social exclusion of immigrants is in its infancy; for an analysis of immigration flows and access to labour markets by immigrants and ethnic Greeks returning from Eastern Europe and the former USSR republics, see Karantinos et al. (1992), Kasimati (1993), Katsoridas (1994), Linardos-Rylmon (1993), and Petrinioti (1993).
3. Tsakloglou explains this disagreement as resulting from the different equivalence scales used by each study (1993a, 370–1).
4. See also Livada (1991) for the degree to which middle- and upper-income groups benefited from economic development at the expense of low-income groups in the period 1959–86.
5. On this point, see also Van den Bosch et al. (1993).
6. For the adjustments made to the original data, see Tsakloglou (1990).
7. The author also experimented with several poverty lines set at 50 per cent, 60 per cent, 70 per cent, and 75 per cent of the median consumption per equivalent adult and evaluated the changing number of the poor.
8. The Foster index, F, and an index M, proposed in Tsakloglou (1988).
9. The author admitted that there were problems concerning the reliability of the data gathered, especially because of the significant underrating of the incomes of self-employed persons in the sample (Kanellopoulos 1993: 25).
10. The indices for the Greater Athens Area refer to 1984 and were calculated by Ketsetsopoulou (1990: 148).
11. In a similar vein, Leontidou (1993) considered the family as an important support factor for the unemployed in the two peripheral municipalities she examined, Perama in Athens and Sykies in Thessaloniki. Informal strategies of self-help and activation of extended family networks for the distribution of the unemployed to

new jobs created especially in house-building and renovation substituted for public support policies (i.e. unemployment relief, policies of reintegration of the unemployed in the labour market) which are rather rudimentary in Greek society.

12. It should be noted here that this review includes only the studies on poverty in Turkey that are available in English.
13. In his study, Hansen made use of the adjusted figures for 1973 by Celasun (1986) and the estimates for 1978 and 1983 given by Celasun on the basis of extrapolations from the 1973 survey.
14. On the basis of an official definition of poverty in the Land and Agricultural Reform Act, Ulusan calculated that 70 per cent of agricultural households were are below the subsistence income level (Ulusan 1980).
15. See also the study by Gitmez and Morcöl (1994) on subjective evaluations of the degree of satisfaction of basic needs (nutrition, physical environment, and housing conditions) by a sample of three socioeconomic groups in Ankara. The authors also examined the degree of satisfaction of the respondents with various life domains, such as family, neighbour relations, work, social relations, professional/personal achievement, and voluntary activities.
16. However, in 1987 the Department of Social Services assisted only 0.8 per cent of all households (1,195 households); whereas, according to House's estimates, 6,500 more households should be eligible for financial support.
17. See the methodological criticisms by the research group that conducted the 1991 study on income distribution and poverty in Cyprus (Department of Statistics and Research 1993: 38).
18. In this attempt the researchers relied upon the equivalence scales used by the Supplementary Benefit system of the United Kingdom (Department of Statistics and Research 1993: 38–41).
19. Among urban areas, Larnaca exhibited the highest incidence of poverty (4.49 per cent) and urban Paphos the lowest (2.61 per cent), while, among rural areas, rural Paphos had the highest incidence of poverty (15 per cent) and Famagusta the lowest (4.38 per cent) (Pitiris 1993a).
20. Though in the case of Cyprus the task is much easier owing to the very small size of the country.
21. See Room et al. (1990 and 1992) and Commission of the European Communities (1991).

REFERENCES

Aral, Sevgi (1980) "Social mobility in Turkey", in E. Özbudun and A. Ulusan (eds), *The Political Economy of Income Distribution in Turkey*. New York: Holmes & Meier, pp. 481–99.

Athanasiou, Loukis (1984) *The Distribution of Income in Greece*. Athens: Centre of Planning and Economic Research (in Greek).

Ayata, Sencer (1990) *Social Problems of Technological Innovation in Southern Europe*. Turkish Working Paper. Vienna: International

Social Science Council/European Co-ordination Centre for Research and Documentation in Social Sciences.
Babanasis, Stergios (1981) "Poverty in Greece in the 20th century (1900–1981)". *Greek Review of Social Research*, 41: 110–44 (in Greek).
—— (1983) "The process of disappearance of poverty in Greece". *Review of the European Communities* 4: 303–13 (in Greek).
Beckerman, Wilfred (1979) *Estimates of Poverty in Greece, 1974*. World Employment Programme 2–23, Working Paper No. 80. Geneva: ILO.
Bouzas, Nicos (1990). "Poverty in the Greater Athens Area in 1984". *Greek Review of Social Research*, 73A: 162–81 (in Greek).
Celasun, Merih (1986) "Income distribution and domestic terms of trade in Turkey, 1978–1983". *METU Studies in Development* (Ankara), 13(1–2): 193–216.
Chtouris, Sotiris (1992) *Complex Processes of Social Exclusion and the Role of the Family in Social Protection*. Athens: Praxis.
Chtouris, Sotiris (in collaboration with Giannis Chtouris, Gabriel Amitsis, and Dionysis Gravaris) (1993) *Institutions and Regulations of Social Policy*. Athens: Praxis (in Greek).
Commission of the European Communities (1991) *Poverty 3. Research Problematics*. Lille: Commission of the European Communities, DG V/Animation and Research.
Danielson, Michael N. and Rusen Keles (1980) "Urbanization and income distribution in Turkey", in E. Özbudun and A. Ulusan (eds), *The Political Economy of Income Distribution in Turkey*. New York: Holmes & Meier, pp. 269–309.
Department of Statistics and Research (1993) *Income Distribution and Poverty in Cyprus, 1991*. Nicosia: Department of Statistics and Research, Ministry of Finance, Research Papers and Reports, Series II, Report No. 30.
Dervis, Kemal and Sherman Robinson (1980) "The structure of income inequality in Turkey: 1950–1973", in E. Özbudun and A. Ulusan (eds), *The Political Economy of Income Distribution in Turkey*. New York: Holmes & Meier, pp. 83–122.
Ergüder, Üstün (1980) "Politics of agricultural price policy in Turkey", in E. Özbudun and A. Ulusan (eds), *The Political Economy of Income Distribution in Turkey*. New York: Holmes & Meier, pp. 169–96.
Ergun, Nilgun (1991) "Policies introduced for the integration of squatter areas to the planned metropolitan housing: the case of Instabul Metropolitan City – Turkey". *Proceedings of the 31st RSA European Congress* (Lisbon), pp. 435–48.
Germidis, Demetrios and Maria Negreponti-Delivani (1975) *Industrialization, Employment and Income Distribution in Greece*. Paris: OECD.
Gitmez, Ali S. and Güktug Morcül (1994) "Socio-economic status and life satisfaction in Turkey". *Social Indicators Research*, 31: 77–98.

Hansen, Bent (1991) *Egypt and Turkey. The Political Economy of Poverty, Equity and Growth.* Oxford: Oxford University Press.

House, William J. (1988) *Socio-economic and Demographic Characteristics of Income Distribution in Cyprus.* Nicosia: Department of Statistics and Research, Ministry of Finance.

Kanellopoulos, Constantinos N. (1986) *Incomes and Poverty in Greece: Decisive Factors for Defining Them.* Athens: Centre of Planning and Economic Research (in Greek).

—— (1993) *A Study for Defining Poverty Lines and Deprivation in Perama.* Report in the context of the 3rd programme for the integration of the least privileged groups of Perama (Athens) (in Greek).

Karantinos, Demetrios (1981) "Aspects of income and wealth distribution in Greece". PhD dissertation, Strathclyde University, UK.

—— (1985) "Poverty in Greece". *Greek Review of Social Research*, 56: 186–92 (in Greek).

Karantinos, Demetrios and Jennifer Cavounidis (in collaboration with Cristos Ioannou, Michael Koniordos, and Platon Tinios) (1992) *EC Observatory on National Policies to Combat Social Exclusion. Consolidated Report: Greece.* Lille: Commission of the European Communities, DG V/Animation and Research.

Karagiorgas, Sakis (1973) "The distribution of tax burden by income groups in Greece". *Economic Journal*, 83: 436–48.

Karagiorgas, Sakis, Koula Kasimati, and Nicos Pantazidis (1988) *Research on the Composition and Distribution of Income in Greece. Results for the Greater Athens Area.* Athens: National Centre of Social Research (in Greek).

Karagiorgas, Sakis, Theodoros Georgakopoulos, Demetrios Karantinos, Giannis Loizidis, Nicos Bouzas, Giannis Yfantopoulos, and Manolis Chrysakis (1990) *Dimensions of Poverty in Greece*, vols I & II. Athens: National Centre of Social Research (in Greek).

Kasimati, Koula (in collaboration with Basil Maos, Nicos Glytsos, Vlasis Agtsidis, Maria Vergeti, and Antony Ragousis) (1993) *Pontian Immigrants from the Former USSR. Their Social and Economic Integration.* Athens: Ministry of Foreign Affairs and Panteion University (in Greek).

Katsoridas, Demetrios A. (1994) *Foreign (?) Workers in Greece.* Athens: Iamos (in Greek).

Ketsetsopoulou, Maria (1990) "Economic inequality: An initial approach to its measurement". *Greek Review of Social Research* 73A: 140–61 (in Greek).

Keyder, Caglar (1987) *State and Class in Turkey. A Study in Capitalist Development.* London: Verso.

Leontidou, Lila (1993) "Informal strategies of unemployment relief in Greek cities: The relevance of family, locality and housing". *European Planning Studies*, 1: 43–68.

Lianos, Theodoros P. and K. P. Prodromidis (1974) *Aspects of Income Distribution in Greece.* Athens: Centre of Planning and Economic Research.

Livada, Alexandra (1991) "Income inequality in Greece: A statistical and econometric analysis". *Oxford Bulletin of Economics and Statistics*, 53: 69–82.
Linardos-Rylmon, Petros (1993) *Foreign Workers in the Labour Market of Greece*. Athens: Institute of Labour/General Confederation of Greek Workers (in Greek).
Mavros, Efstathios (1989) "A critical review of economic development in Cyprus: 1960–1974". *The Cyprus Review*, 1: 11–66.
Özbudun, Ergun (1980) "Income distribution as an issue in Turkish politics", in E. Özbudun and A. Ulusan (eds), *The Political Economy of Income Distribution in Turkey*. New York: Holmes & Meier, pp. 55–82.
Özbudun, Ergun and Aydin Ulusan (eds) (1980a) *The Political Economy of Income Distribution in Turkey*. New York: Holmes & Meier.
Özbudun, Ergun and Aydin Ulusan (1980b) "Overview", in E. Özbudun and A. Ulusan (eds), *The Political Economy of Income Distribution in Turkey*. New York: Holmes & Meier, pp. 3–22.
Papandropoulos, Athanasios (1991) "Cyprus among the 25 richest countries of the world". *Economikos Tahydromos*, 32: 30 (in Greek).
Petmesidou, Maria (1987) *Social Classes and Processes of Social Reproduction*. Athens: Exantas (in Greek).
────── (1991) "Statism, social policy and the middle classes in Greece". *Journal of European Social Policy*, 1: 31–48.
────── (1992) *Social Inequalities and Social Policy*. Athens: Exantas (in Greek).
Petmesidou, Maria and Lefteris Tsoulouvis (1990) "Aspects of state policy in Greece: Historical continuity and the impact of the crisis", in *The Functions of the State in the Period of Crisis*. Athens: Karagiorgas Foundation, pp. 288–301 (in Greek).
────── (1994). "Aspects of the changing political economy of Europe: Welfare state, class segmentation and planning in the postmodern era". *Sociology*, 28(2): 499–519.
Petrinioti, Xanthi (1993) *Immigration to Greece*. Athens: Odysseas (in Greek).
Pitiris, Damianos (1993a) "Income distribution and poverty in the eparchies of Cyprus in 1991". *Phileleftheros* 11 July (in Greek).
────── (1993b) "The magnitude of poverty in Cyprus". *Simerini*, 19 September (in Greek).
Room, Graham et al. (1990) *"New poverty" in the European Community*. London: Macmillan.
────── (1992) *Observatory on National Policies to Combat Social Exclusion: Second Annual Report*. Lille: Commission of the European Communities, DG V/Animation and Research.
Tsakloglou, Panos (1988) *A family of Decomposable Poverty Indices*. University of Bristol: Department of Economics Discussion Paper 88/195.
────── (1990) "Aspects of poverty in Greece" *Review of Income and Wealth*, 36(4): 381–402.

────── (1993a) "A critical review of the empirical studies of poverty in Greece", in *Dimensions of Social Policy Today*. Athens: Karagiorgas Foundation, pp. 369–90 (in Greek).

────── (1993b) "Aspects of inequality in Greece. Measurement, decomposition and intertemporal change: 1974, 1982". *Journal of Development Economics*, 40: 53–74.

Tsoulouvis, Lefteris (1987) "Aspects of statism and planning in Greece". *International Journal of Urban and Regional Research*, 11(4): 500–21.

Ulusan, Aydin (1980) "Public policy toward agriculture and its redistributive implications", in E. Özbudun and A. Ulusan (eds), *The Political Economy of Income Distribution in Turkey*. New York: Holmes & Meier, pp. 125–68.

Van den Bosch, Karel, Tim Callan, Jordi Estivill, Pierre Hausman, Bruno Jeandidier, Ruud Muffels, and John Yfantopoulos (1993) "A comparison of poverty in seven European countries and regions using subjective and relative measures". *Journal of Population Economics*, 6(3): 235–59.

Chapter 16

The Nordic Countries: Poverty in a Welfare State

Björn Halleröd, Matti Heikkilä, Mikko Mäntysaari, Veli-Matti Ritakallio, and Charlott Nyman

Introduction

The Nordic countries

Denmark, Finland, Norway, and Sweden[1] are linked together by geography, history, and language. A closer look will, of course, reveal substantial differences among the four countries but these differences are certainly small in an international perspective. The four countries started the postwar era with different experiences of the Second World War. Sweden was not directly involved in the war and had a more or less intact industry and infrastructure. Denmark and Norway had suffered from five years of German occupation and were in the same position as many other European countries when the war ended. Finland had certainly suffered most from the war, with widespread destruction and heavy losses of human life as a result.

All four countries experienced rapid economic growth after the war. Standards of living increased swiftly, unemployment was low, and the prospects for the future were optimistic. The 1950s and 1960s were the period when the so-called Nordic Welfare State model was grounded (Erikson et al. 1987; Esping-Andersen 1990; Kolberg 1993). Sweden, as the forerunner in constructing a welfare state, pursued four lines. First, continuing economic growth and full employment were the cornerstones that would provide the resources on which general welfare was to be built. Second, an income maintenance system would provide income security to the whole population. The goal was not only to provide a minimum income that would keep people above the poverty line but to guarantee everyone earnings that were related to their labour market income. Thus, an extensive public social insurance system covering different forms of pension schemes, sickness insurance, unemployment insurance, paid parental leave, etc. was introduced. Third, important forms of services such as education and health care would be tax financed and provided by the state with no or a very small contribution from recipients. Fourth, an important feature of the Nordic welfare state was that it should be universal. That is, it should cover major portions of the population, include everyone in the same transfer system, and provide the same type of public service to all citizens. This meant that everyone would have something to gain from maintaining the welfare systems. This is an important feature because it contributes significantly to the legitimacy of the welfare state.

The systems, the time of their introduction, and the speed with which the reforms were carried through differed among the Nordic countries. The similarities were, nevertheless, so substantial that it was justifiable to talk about a Nordic Welfare State model (Esping-Andersen 1990). The Nordic countries continued their expansion of their welfare states during the 1970s and 1980s. At the same time, problems began to pile up. The oil shortage shocks of the 1970s put severe fiscal stress on the Nordic countries and the economic downturn made it increasingly harder to maintain full employment.

The crises hit the Nordic countries in different ways. Denmark had the largest problems and followed the rest of the West European countries down the road of mass unemployment. For Norway, the oil shock meant that it could exploit its own oil resources in the North Sea and thereby escape the economic downturn that most other European countries experienced. Finland and Sweden were among the select group of European countries that, without any oil, managed to escape the reintroduction of mass unemployment in Europe during the late 1970s and early 1980s.

The Nordic welfare states seemed to be standing on solid ground during the second part of the 1980s. The economy was booming, Denmark's economy was recovering, and Sweden and Finland continued to expand their welfare states, as did Norway, which was still benefiting heavily from its oil resources. Under the calm surface, problems piled up. The 1990s started with an economic downturn that in Sweden, and even more so in Finland, developed into a depression. Both countries experienced a dramatic increase in unemployment and negative growth. Severe financial problems forced both Sweden and Finland to make substantial cuts in their state budgets, a process that is still going on. Again, Norway was hit less hard by economic problems. Denmark also managed to survive the economic downturn much better than Sweden and Finland. One could say that Sweden and Finland experienced at the beginning of the 1990s in a much more dramatic way what Denmark experienced a decade earlier. The present situation makes the survival of a specific Nordic welfare state more uncertain than ever.

The universal approach, the focusing on income maintenance, and the endeavour to reduce all kinds of inequality moved the spotlight away from the narrow question of poverty and focused it on the distribution of resources and well-being in the total population. Poverty was seen as an aspect of inequality that could be solved without any special measures; poverty, it was believed, would simply disappear as overall inequality decreased. The emphasis on inequality was reflected by the dominant position of level-of-living and living-condition research. Because the goal was to shape equality in the total population, research focused on living standards in the total population. In all four countries, so called level-of-living standard surveys were conducted, with Sweden leading the way in the late 1960s (Johansson 1970). In an international perspective these surveys are unique. They cover a broad range of areas dealing with people's living standard and people's ability to mobilise resources, not only economic resources but also such resources as education, health, political skill and labour market position.

The rediscovery of poverty in the 1980s

Since the early 1980s, especially in Denmark, Finland, and Sweden, a new tradition of poverty research has become apparent, though it is very limited when compared with the totality of social science research. The rediscovery of poverty is propelled in large part by radical change in the societal situation. For example, in all the Nordic countries a means tested income support system is aimed at those who cannot support themselves in any other way. In the 1980s all four countries experienced an increase in the number of households dependent on this social assistance. This growth was clearly troublesome because it indicated increased difficulties in achieving a sufficient labour market income, while at the same time clearly showing that the universal welfare system was unable to cope with this situation.

There is more involved here than the changing situation in the Nordic countries. Behind the rediscovery of poverty lies the redefinition and new understanding of the concept and the nature of poverty in a welfare state. The general belief in the 1960s was that the war against poverty had been won. Then poverty was understood only as an absolute phenomenon – a restriction of physical functioning caused by lack of economic resources. Not until the beginning of 1980s, probably inspired by the work of Peter Townsend (1979), was it also understood in the Nordic countries that economic growth does not automatically alleviate poverty. In fact, it may even produce new kinds of poverty, characterized not only by restricted physical functioning but also by restricted social functioning. This relative poverty, which is defined as a restriction of social function owing to lack of economic resources, was the theme of the new wave of poverty studies in the Nordic countries in the 1980s. It was then that the dynamic nature of poverty was first understood; when conditions change, the criteria of poverty will also change.

In Denmark the poverty discussion was put on the agenda partly because of the fact that Denmark was then the only Nordic country that was a member of the European Union (EU). This fact made it a participant in the poverty programmes conducted by the EU. Denmark was also the Nordic country that was hardest hit by the recession in the late 1970s, experiencing a rapid increase in unemployment. At the beginning of the 1980s journalists and social workers were the first to point out the problem of a rise in poverty (Larsen and Andersen 1989). The new consciousness about poverty was more political than in the other Nordic countries. The Danish Ministry of Social Affairs sponsored a few studies regarding the extent of poverty. The data used were derived from the level-of-living surveys conducted in the mid-1980s (see Hansen 1986).

In Sweden poverty was put on the agenda in the 1980s. This was a period during which Sweden experienced an increase in the number of households dependent on social assistance, a development that occurred despite an economic boom and, particularly during the second half of the decade, an extremely low level of unemployment. It is important to note that social assistance dependency for most households was temporary, not long lasting. This experience raised serious questions about, on the one hand, the ability of the Swedish welfare system to target those sections of the population most in need of help and, on the other hand, the capability of the social assistance system to carry the increasing burden put upon it. These problems emphasized the need for research explicitly concerned with the problem of poverty. Developments in the early 1990s raised an additional and more serious question about the ability of the Swedish welfare state to combat poverty. Financial problems led to major cuts in the universal income maintenance programmes and, more importantly, the unemployment rate increased rapidly from virtually full employment in the late 1980s to about 8.2 per cent unemployment in 1993, the highest level since the 1930s.

The situation in Finland was very similar to that in Sweden. Until the mid-1980s, Finnish poverty research was almost non-existent. Signs of the new wave of poverty research then became discernible. The driving force behind the development was the expansion of social assistance dependence, increasing consciousness about social exclusion and marginalization, and a totally new interest in investigating the variations in the extent and risk of experiencing economic poverty. Socio-political researchers presented in several forums the inexplicable lack of poverty study. The social administration launched a large project dealing with poverty-related issues. It is interesting to note that the rediscovery took place in the mid-1980s, when economic growth and extra investments in welfare policies were still going on (see Ritakallio 1986). Later, it was shown that the 1980s was a period of decreasing poverty in Finland, in the sense of traditional low-income poverty (see Gustafsson and Uusitalo 1990b; Ritakallio 1994a). There are a great many similarities with Sweden as regards the situation in the early 1990s. Unemployment increased in a hitherto unexpected way. In 1994 approximately 20 per cent of the Finnish labour force was unemployed. Because unemployment, and especially long term unemployment, is an important factor in generating poverty the Finnish welfare state is under severe pressure.

Attention to the issue of poverty did not occur in Norway, even though it also experienced a dramatic increase in the social assistance rate. Empirical poverty research has been almost non-existent in Norway since the beginning of the 1980s. It is hard to find an explanation for the lack of poverty study in Norway; the Nordic countries form such a uniform area that one would presume that the same trends would exist in all the Nordic countries at the same time.

Framework of the chapter

The framework of this chapter is based on four schools of thought, three of which use a quantitative approach. The first defines poverty indirectly and focuses on people's access to different kinds of economic resources; the second concerns poverty defined as dependency on social assistance; and the third defines poverty directly and focus on outcomes, that is, on the standard of living people actually enjoy (Ringen 1987: 145;

1988). The fourth deals with qualitative studies of poverty, mainly focusing on specific sub-groups.

The major focus in all four schools of thought has been to describe empirically the extent, depth, profile and risk-groups of poverty. In some studies the task has also been to describe and explain the changing nature of poverty and to make international comparisons. The theoretical discussion has in most case been limited to the concept and measurement of poverty (Halleröd 1991, 1995a; Hansen 1989; Heikkilä 1990; Jäntti 1991; Ritakallio 1994a)

The restriction to statistical descriptions has been especially typical of cross-sectional studies. New perspectives have been opened up by those studies that have dealt with the changing picture of poverty in the longer term (the dynamics of poverty) as well as by studies that have made international comparisons of the capability of different kinds of social security arrangements to alleviate poverty.

Many interesting poverty-related questions require another kind of research methodology. The central task of qualitative poverty research is to question the meaning of poverty from the point of view of the poor. What does poverty mean in everyday life? The problem with this kind of poverty research is that each study concentrates on one sub-group of the poor (single mothers, unemployed youngsters, immigrants, etc.). In some of these cases, the term "poverty" has not even been used.

Quantitative poverty research

Economic poverty

The methodologies used in the area of economic poverty are the traditional ones, based on different poverty lines that measure poverty by the stage of the income formation process (factor income, disposable income, or gross income). This research needs reliable data on people's incomes and assets (income transfers and taxes included). In the Nordic countries, regular household budget surveys and income distribution surveys form a good quantitative base for studies of this type. Generally, the poverty lines are based on income distribution (the relative income method, i.e. 50 per cent of the median). Political or administrative poverty lines are also used. Their fixing points have been the current minimum pension levels or administrative norms for minimum social assistance (income support).

Denmark's membership in the European Union meant that it was a part of the Poverty Programme launched by the EU. A direct result of this was a study by Friis (1981), which contains a thorough discussion of income distribution and income problems in Denmark. Friis, for the first time in the Nordic countries, used the EU's 50 per cent of median income as a poverty line. The results showed that 13 per cent of all families in 1977 fell below this poverty line.

In the mid-1980s Hansen (1986) investigated the extent and nature of poverty in Denmark. Hansen used the Danish living conditions surveys and employed a "two- step" poverty line, classifying as poor those households with a yearly income under DKr 100,000 and where the monthly disposable income (income left for food, clothes, etc. when all fixed expenses such as housing costs were paid) was less than DKr 1,000. This study showed that about 3 per cent of the population were living in poverty. These results were widely debated and criticized for severely underestimating the prevalence of poverty in Denmark. This discussion is an example of the fact that the study of poverty has been much more politicized in Denmark than in the other Nordic countries.

An often debated question within the field of poverty research is the issue of the persistence of poverty. Several studies indicate that most households classified as poor on the basis of cross-sectional data are only temporarily in poverty (Duncan 1984). These results were also confirmed in Denmark by Hansen (1990), who showed that only a minor portion of Danish households could be considered as long-term (four years) low income households.

The study of economic poverty in Denmark differs from research in Finland and Sweden in another way. Danish researchers have to a lesser degree trusted the purely economic measurement of poverty. A certain dissatisfaction with the earlier approaches launched a new research tradition where the pure income measurements (low disposable income left after some basic necessities) were supplemented by certain qualitative interview data to demonstrate the connection between household budgets and social and material needs (Andersen and Larsen 1989). The poverty concept adopted here came from the Norwegian Steinar Stjernö (1985), who introduced the term "poverty as the tyranny of scarcity", which makes an operational distinction between physical and social efficiency. This term was seen to be especially illustrative of the effects of modern poverty.

In Finland the most important contributions concerning the extent of economic poverty have been studies by Heikkilä (1990), Ritakallio (1994a,b), and Uusitalo (1989). Heikkilä used cross-sectional data from the 1986 living conditions survey; the others employed the cross-sectional data of six household budget surveys carried out between 1966 and 1990. The criterion for poverty used in these studies was disposable income, and the equivalent scales (consumption units) were the OECD type. They used several poverty lines side by side. The most common poverty lines were current minimum pension level and 50 per cent of the median equivalent disposable income per consumption unit. Thus, all the studies mentioned analysed relative poverty.

Heikkilä (1990) and Ritakallio (1994a) adapted several operational definitions simultaneously, and Ritakallio also conducted sensitivity analyses within the relative income method. Their results reinforced the view that poverty is such a complex phenomenon that identifying it by means of a single indicator may lead to biased results of the severity of poverty. "Traditional poverty", characterized by continuous subsistence on a low income, seems to have been replaced by new modes of poverty distinguished by unstable labour force position. Furthermore, it has meant that poverty researched indirectly through annual incomes has become more problematic than previously. Given a situation of unstable income, short periods with acceptable income may raise the annual income over the poverty line even though income during the larger part of the year falls below the poverty line.

Uusitalo (1989), Gustafsson and Uusitalo (1990b) and Ritakallio (1994) analysed the shift in the low-income poverty rate over time by using time-series data. They clearly demonstrated the achievements of the welfare state in terms of poverty reduction in Finland. Where the poverty rate decreased steadily from 12.4 per cent in the mid 60s to 2.5 per cent at the end of the 1980s. This was actually the transformation period when the Finnish welfare state developed from marginalism to institutionalism (see Esping-Andersen and Korpi 1987). The decrease in economic poverty in Finland during the whole 1980s was a very different trend compared with several other Western industrial societies. According to Ritakallio (1994c), long term economic poverty almost disappeared until 1990, mainly owing to full employment and effective redistributive policies.

By using Luxembourg Income Study data, Ritakallio (1994c) also made time-series comparisons between six OECD countries in terms of poverty rate and poverty gap. By comparing countries implementing different kinds of social policy he clearly verified the impotence of means-tested social policy in combating poverty. Scandinavian institutional social policy, on the other hand, was proved to be more capable of alleviating poverty equitably among all sections of the population.

In 1984 the Swedish economist Björn Gustafsson published *A Book About Poverty*, in which he discussed a range of topics with relevance for poverty research in a modern welfare state. The empirical part of the book was based on data from the 1979 and 1981 household budget surveys. The incidence and the distribution of poverty in Sweden were estimated, as was the impact of welfare state provision on poverty. Two different poverty lines were used in the study. Both were based on budget calculations but they differed in their generosity. Also shown were the effects of altered assumptions regarding the household's capability of transforming assets into consumption. Another feature of the study is that Gustafsson used both individuals and households as units of analysis. Another study, made in partly similar fashion, was done by Halleröd (1991), using data from the 1986 and 1987 survey of living conditions (ULF). Both Gustafsson's and Halleröd's studies showed that the economic poverty rate in Sweden varied between 5 and 10 per cent of the population. Thus, economic poverty was not a negligible phenomenon in Sweden during the 1980s (see also Gustafsson 1993a). In a more recent study Gustafsson used the 50 per cent of median income poverty line and calculated time-series for the period from the mid-1970s to the beginning of the 1990s. This calculation revealed a continuous increase in relative poverty in Sweden from the beginning of the 1980s and onwards (Gustafsson 1993b).

Two alternative methods of calculating the poverty line have recently been used in Swedish research. The first one was developed by Gustafsson and Lindblom (1993). They defined the poor as those "with a disposable income lower than those for whom the welfare state takes responsibility" (ibid.: 21). The poverty line was set at the mean value for the total range of welfare provision directed to the part of the population that is supposed to work but that does not work for reasons such as disablement or unemployment. Thus, the poverty line is based on norms that in one way or another are related to social policy but are not dependent on one specific budget calculation aimed at a particular purpose. The poverty line is therefore less sensitive to changes in certain social policy programmes at the same time that it allows a broader reflection on the prevailing view of an economic minimum standard in a country. Gustafsson and Lindblom used this poverty line for a comparison of poverty in seven European countries, Australia, Canada, and the USA using data from 1979–82. The results showed, on the one hand, that welfare state provisions in Sweden were relatively generous and, on the other hand, that the poverty rate in Sweden was low compared with most other countries.

The other alternative poverty line recently used in Sweden is the Consensual Poverty Line (CPL) (sometimes referred to as the Subjective Poverty Line) developed in the Netherlands by Goedhart et al. (1977; see also Hagenaars 1986). This approach aims to base the poverty line on people's opinion about a necessary minimum income. The method results in a substantially more generous poverty line compared with the budget calculations used in previous studies and, accordingly, in a higher estimation of the incidence of poverty (Halleröd 1995b). The CPL method has also been used in a comparison of poverty in Sweden and Australia. The results showed that Australia has a higher poverty rate than Sweden and that the distribution of poverty differs between the countries. Poverty in Sweden is mainly a problem for young people. The poverty rate among young people in Australia is also high but the most poverty-stricken part of the population is found among those over the age of 64. The differences in the poverty rate and the distribution of poverty between the two countries can be directly related to differences in welfare state provision and especially in the old age pension schemes (Saunders et al. 1994). The data used to estimate the CPL in Sweden come from a 1992 survey specially designed to study poverty and related problems in Sweden (Halleröd et al. 1993).

Comparative poverty studies

Norway, Sweden and recently Finland, but not Denmark, are members of the Luxembourg Income Study (LIS) (see Smeeding et al. 1990). Comparative studies of poverty based on LIS data emphasize to some degree the distinctiveness of the Nordic countries. Analyses by Mitchell (1993), including Norway and Sweden, and by Ritakallio (1994c), including Finland and Sweden, show that the poverty rate in these countries is comparatively low (see also Jäntti 1993). Another striking feature is that income redistribution in Norway, and even more so in Sweden and Finland, is significantly larger than in other countries. Thus, the poverty-alleviating effect of the welfare state is more radical in these Nordic countries than in most other countries. The basic issues of comparative poverty research have been analysed by several Nordic authors, especially by Øyen (1992).

The social assistance research tradition

Last-resort, means-tested social assistance (income support, supplementary benefit, etc.) forms a strong and widely used criterion for poverty researchers in the Nordic countries. This tradition stems from the conviction that, in a highly developed welfare state, those eligible and actually depending on these benefits are the worst off.

The need for a closer look at welfare clients grew out of administrative and political concerns. Somewhat surprisingly, both the proportion of the population dependent on social assistance and the total costs of social assistance started to increase in the Nordic countries in the mid-1980s. This development caused individual governments to start several studies on the increased dependency risk and also on the more basic social mechanisms behind this shift. Nonetheless, it is important to see that conducting research on social assistance (dependency, client groups, etc.) cannot automatically be equated with poverty research in a strict sense. This distinction has been stressed with differing degrees of emphasis in the different countries included in this review.

In the mid-1980s the Nordic Council of Ministers launched a cross-Nordic research project that started with a pilot study (Tanninen and Julkunen 1988) and then produced a comparative panel study on long-term dependency in the Nordic capitals in the last part of 1980s (Tanninen and Julkunen 1993). The Nordic research team also published an anthology *On Social Assistance in the Nordic Capitals* (Fridberg et al. 1993). The anthology included analyses of national profiles of benefit dependence, work involvement, and persistent poverty, helplessness, and cumulative deprivation.

In studies on social assistance clients, other poverty definitions and lines have also been used. One more or less surprising research finding from Sweden and Finland has been that a great majority of those dependent on income support are not poor according to the traditional income-based poverty lines, e.g. 50 per cent of median income, or by the social assistance norms themselves (see e.g. Halleröd 1991; Heikkilä 1990, and Ritakallio 1994a). On the other hand, their actual material and non-material living conditions are clearly below average. Another surprising finding when several operationalizations are used simultaneously is a tremendous under-use of income support, at least in Finland. A relatively large proportion of the population was eligible for minimum assistance simply by virtue of their low incomes, but, according to the records, they never exercised this right.

There exists a broad consensus among researchers that social assistance is a very special indicator of poverty, because the local authority responsible for supplying the benefits also conducts both needs- and means-testing. Another point of view is that, especially during times of recession and increasing unemployment, the social assistance "rate" is a clear indicator of the functioning of the "first-resort", i.e. earnings-related safety net. In time-series studies the social assistance definition of poverty is problematic because of the major changes caused by organizational reforms.

Finnish studies using social assistance as the indicator of poverty should also be mentioned. Lauronen (1988) collected extensive quantitative material on welfare clients, which showed that the most common reason for dependency was unemployment and the lack or insufficiency of unemployment benefit. This finding later gained support from other studies (e.g. Lehto and Lamminpää 1992; Mäntysaari 1993) done during the economic recession at the beginning of 1990s. Ritakallio (1991), using a rather large amount of survey data, investigated the actual living conditions and welfare hardships of welfare clients in several rural and urban settings. His study focused on the accumulation of welfare deprivation among social assistance recipients. In this way, he aimed to chart the emergence of the process of marginalization among the clientele. One of his findings was that clients differ from each other not only in relation to material resources but also in relation to their abilities to transform the material aid they receive into personal welfare. The Finnish research results also point to two typical population groups that share persistent poverty (meaning long-term income support dependency): single middle-aged marginalized men and single mothers. Within the Nordic comparisons this can be seen as a unique Finnish phenomenon.

In Sweden a rather large body of research deals, in one way or another, with the problem of social assistance. In some of these studies, predominantly the older ones, social assistance is used as an indicator of poverty. Recipients of social assistance have been regarded as poor simply based on the fact that they received social assistance (Inghe 1960; Knutsson and Stridsman 1988; Korpi 1971). The poor in Sweden have therefore often been equated with and defined as those receiving social assistance, with no attempt to derive an independent yardstick. It has been argued, however, that such a definition is tautological and logically incoherent: tautological because the system designed to ameliorate poverty is also used to define poverty; and logically incoherent because it is only those who have received help, and who therefore should not be in poverty, who are defined as poor (Saunders et al. 1994: 4). Scholars in the field of social work have also emphasized a distinction between the poor and the recipients of social assistance (Bergmark 1991: 15; Salonen 1993: 30). There are two main reasons for such a distinction. The first is theoretical. The number of people who receive social assistance is, on the one hand, dependent on political decisions concerning eligibility and generosity in the social policy system and, on the other hand, on people's willingness to apply for social assistance, which, among other things, depends on information and the risk of stigmatization. The incidence and distribution of social assistance recipients are hence not connected with a theoretical understanding of the phenomenon of poverty. The second reason is empirical. There is clearly a connection between social assistance and poverty. People in poverty have, compared with other sections of the population, a higher probability of receiving social assistance. But it is nevertheless the case that most recipients of social assistance are not classified as poor according to more traditional definitions of poverty (Halleröd 1991, 1992).

In Norway it has also been common to distinguish between social assistance and poverty (Stjernö 1985). Terum (1984) described the social assistance rate more narrowly as a measurement of "registered poverty", acknowledging that this definition of poverty has certain limitations. A distinction between social assistance and poverty has also been emphasized in Norway. The recipients of social assistance are not regarded as poor but they are seen as a poverty-threatened group. This view is clearly expressed by Hove (1993), who explored the prevalence of poverty among recipients of social assistance in the capitals of the Nordic countries. According to the measurement of poverty used in this study, 38 per cent of the long-term recipients of social assistance in Helsinki, Oslo, and Stockholm were poor. It was also the case that 59 per cent of the recipients regarded themselves as poor (ibid.: 18).

In the Danish research tradition, the demarcation between social assistance and poverty has been even more strict than in the other Nordic countries. However, it is important to state that much of the research carried out on social assistance recipients has had great relevance for the study of poverty. It is likewise important to be clear that a too narrow focus on social assistance will by definition conceal many aspects of the poverty problem.

Poverty as an accumulation of welfare deprivation

There are two main factors behind the development of the relatively rich Nordic research tradition that tries to combine the ideas of income-related measurement and living conditions research. One is the certain flatness of the picture given by the economic approach; the other is the Nordic tradition of conducting regular level-of-living surveys. To these two we naturally have to add the theoretical development within the field of poverty research. A wide consensus prevails about the inadequacy of income measures: pure incomes do not give a satisfactory picture of poverty and the degree of the satisfaction of material needs achieved by them.

On the other hand, this approach is problematic in trend studies and in international comparisons. The first problem is the lack of comparable data. Another problem is more a question of principle. According to the relative view of poverty, the criteria for poverty are temporally and regionally determined. For example, the criteria for poverty in the Nordic countries were different in the 1960s than they are now. In the same way the criteria for poverty were different, for example, in Sweden and in Portugal in the 1980s. But how do we define the limits of poverty at different times and in different countries even at the same time, if our research material is data on living conditions? There is no universally applicable solution to the problem of the definition of poverty lines in comparative studies when we use the living conditions data as research material. The methodology of social consensus is one attempt to solve this problem. This will be further discussed later when we deal with the Swedish and Norwegian studies in this area.

The basic idea behind the accumulation of welfare deprivation school of thought is that low income forms a necessary but not sufficient precondition for an adequate concept of poverty. Data are consequently needed both from income, assets, and other material means and from actual well-being in terms of housing, health, education, work involvement, etc. This kind of reasoning comes close to the idea of a deprivation index (Townsend 1979). Basically the welfare deprivation school of thought stresses the outcome-based conceptualization of poverty.

A remarkable amount of research has been done in the Nordic countries on the accumulation of deprivation and links between poor living conditions on an individual level. Some general trends in the results can be listed. First, the sociological welfare research based on Nordic data has not demonstrated very strong links between low income and deprivation in other welfare areas (Erikson & Tåhlin 1987; Halleröd 1991; Hansen 1990; Heikkilä 1990; Ringen 1987; Uusitalo 1975). On the other hand, the links between various components of economic well-being (income, housing, labour market position) are relatively strong. Second, the empirical overlap between economic poverty and cumulative deprivation is relatively small (Heikkilä 1990). On the other hand, the accumulation of deprivation as such is relatively strong and is linked to some central structural and background variables (Heikkilä 1990). The accumulation of welfare problems is especially common in some marginal groups. Ritakallio (1991) indicated that separated middle-aged men living alone who were social assistance clients constituted a uniform group that suffered from the worst accumulation of problems (see also Fridberg et al. 1993). The position of men without families as the core group of the worst-off is emphasized by the fact that their risk of becoming social assistance recipients is greater than that of other population groups, and among those who receive income support they continue to form the core group of the excluded.

An elaborated analysis of accumulation of deprivation in Sweden was done by Erikson and Tåhlin (1987). They studied the coexistence of welfare problems in seven different welfare areas: health, housing conditions, social relationships, leisure activities, political resources, working conditions, and economic resources (Erikson and Tåhlin 1987: 259). The study was based on level-of-living standard surveys (LNU) from 1968, 1974, and 1981, which made it possible to analyse the development over time. Erikson and Tåhlin did not define a poverty line; in fact they did not talk about poverty at all, but they identified a group who suffered from accumulated deprivation because they had three or more problems. In 1968, 22 per cent fell into this group, in 1974, 12 per cent, and in 1981, 8 per cent. One conclusion is that conditions have improved over time. However, one has to remember that the indicators of welfare problems were not adjusted in line with the general development of living conditions. Results indicating anything other than a substantial decrease in the prevalence of accumulated deprivation would therefore have been sensational.

Three other findings of Erikson and Tåhlin might be of greater importance. First, financial problems were shown to play a central role and were often connected to other problems. One important conclusion was hence "that economic support would probably alleviate many of the different problems which occur" (1987: 274). Second, the incidence of accumulated deprivation was related to age, class, and gender. Elderly people, women, and members of the working class experienced an increased risk of suffering from accumulated deprivation. This relationship was persistent over time. Third, an individual who suffered from one problem had an increased risk of suffering from problems in other areas as well. Despite the fact that the number of individuals with multiple problems decreased, this pattern was also persistent over time. These results indicated that the mechanism underlying the accumulation of deprivation operated in the same manner in 1981 as in 1968.

Ringen (1985, 1987, 1988) has strongly argued against the use of economic resources as the sole indicator of poverty. Low-income groups "are not homogeneous, either in other resources than income or in way of life" (Ringen 1987b: 164). The actual standard of living will therefore vary considerably among people with low incomes. Poverty should therefore be measured via direct indicators of the living standard that people actually experience. Direct observation of living standards is not enough, however, and low income should still be seen as a necessary precondition for poverty. Ringen therefore suggested a combination of measurement of economic resources and accumulated deprivation. The poor are those who have an income under an economic poverty line and at the same time suffer from accumulated deprivation. "Poverty, in other words, is the result of an accumulation of deprivation in both resources and way of life" (ibid.: 162). Ringen used data from Norway (1985) and Sweden (1987) to show that only a small proportion of the low-income group suffered from accumulated deprivation. His main conclusion was therefore that poverty measured as low income only (or for that matter as accumulated deprivation only) tends to result in a substantial overestimation of the poverty rate.

An unsolved problem in Ringen's approach is that he mixed relative and absolute measures of poverty. He assumed that the economic poverty line should be relative to the income level in the society, but the indicators of living conditions used to measure deprivation were assumed to be absolute and stable over time. It is not clear why we should grant the poor a higher income if the income for the rest of the population is rising but not a higher standard of living if the standard for the rest of the population is rising.

Halleröd (1991; see also Halleröd 1992) discusses different approaches to defining and measuring poverty. Largely following the distinctions made by Ringen (1988), he points out three main strategies used to study poverty. These were measured in the following way:

- an indirect approach based on measurement of money income and a poverty line based on the Swedish Board of Health and Welfare's guiding norm for social assistance;

- a direct definition as an effect of accumulation of deprivation, with those who suffer from at least three problems from a list of nine aspects of living conditions being classified as poor;
- those actually receiving social assistance are classified as poor.

The main object of the study was to investigate to what degree these definitions actually identify the same individuals as poor and if the factors used to explain the prevalence of poverty are the same regardless of definition.

The data set used was the ULF of 1986 and 1987. The overlap of these three definitions was small: 20.6 per cent of the population were poor according to at least one of the definitions, but only 0.5 per cent according to all three definitions. These results were even more striking as a result of the fact that the explanatory factor also differed depending on choice of definition. It was therefore concluded that the concept of poverty does not refer to a single social phenomenon. Poverty is instead a heterogeneous concept and the choice of definition will influence not only the incidence of poverty but also, more fundamentally, the social phenomenon that will be studied.

The latest development in Swedish poverty research is an ongoing project called "Consensual Poverty". The central purpose is to replicate the pioneering study of Mack and Lansley (1985), and poverty is accordingly defined as "an enforced lack of socially perceived necessities" (ibid.: 39). The investigation of people's attitudes towards material consumption and actual patterns of consumption is therefore of central interest. People are regarded as poor if they are deprived to a certain degree of consumption that most other people would regard as "necessary". The first reported results from the project used exactly the same method as Mack and Lansley when identifying the poor; that is, those who lacked three consumption items that a majority of the population regarded as necessities were reckoned as poor (Halleröd et al. 1993).

There are two important reasons that make the direct consensual method preferable compared with earlier attempts to measure poverty in terms of accumulated deprivation. First, the method is designed to measure deprivation in consumption – that is, the part of people's lives that has the closest connection to economic resources. The method is therefore supposed to narrow the gap between economic poverty and accumulated deprivation. Second, we must one way or another decide what is an indicator of deprivation and what is not. In the consensual approach, this decision is to a large degree based on public opinion and therefore is less arbitrary than other measurements of relative poverty. There are nevertheless a number of problems connected with Mack and Lansley's original approach to measuring poverty. An alternative way of using the consensual approach to measure accumulated deprivation has therefore been developed (Halleröd 1994a,b; Halleröd et al. 1995). It is argued that this method is more theoretically appealing, less arbitrary, and more sensitive to people's preferences concerning necessary consumption than Mack and Lansley's approach.

The data used in the "Consensual Poverty" project were collected via face-to-face interviews in 1992 using a specially designed questionnaire and covers a representative sample of the population aged 20–75 (Halleröd et al. 1993). The survey included a broad spectrum of questions that make it possible to relate the topic of poverty to other relevant areas such as work involvement, work conditions, attitudes, housing, etc. It is also possible to study the relationship between the consensual measurement of accumulated deprivation and the consensual measurement of economic poverty referred to above.

Qualitatively oriented poverty research

Although the bulk of poverty research in the Nordic countries has used quantitative methods of research, some qualitatively oriented poverty research has also been going on since the beginning of the 1980s. Qualitatively oriented research very seldom produces any kind of hypotheses about the causes and effects of poverty; instead, it places a strong emphasis on a phenomenological view of the world. To put it very simply, from qualitative research we can learn what poverty is all about when it comes to the daily life of poor people. There are certain limitations connected with this approach. The results of qualitatively oriented research are hardly ever strictly comparable with each other. The logic of qualitative research is simply different from that of quantitative research.

In his useful article on interpretations of modern poverty, Marklund (1990: 136) divided the explanations of poverty into four classes: marginalization, underclass, feminization, and subculture perspectives. Marklund pointed out that, in all Nordic countries, both available data and the interpretations made by social scientists seem to exclude the perspectives of subculture[2] and feminization. Although the problems of ethnic minorities are now more the focus of discussions than previously, the number of minorities is still comparatively small in all the Nordic countries. The relative cultural homogeneity is, of course, a natural explanation for the lack of enthusiasm for a subculture paradigm.

The "level of living" approach that prevailed in the Nordic countries from the 1960s grew out of the assumption that a social continuum descends from the level of living of the rich to the level of living of the poor and that no breaks or lacunas occurred. The subculture paradigm society sees not as a culturally homogeneous entity, but as consisting of many different kinds of cultures that to a limited extent share the same life goals (Andersen et al. 1987: 194). According to this view, modern societies consist of differentiated social organizations and modes of living that differ substantially from each other. Cross-sectional surveys do not take these differences into account, and in fact wipe out fundamental distinctions among different modes of life. Qualitative analysis can serve to put social relations and the organization of everyday life into the centre of the analysis (Henriksen 1987: 388).

An example of such a study is Seija Hautamaa's research on the hidden dimensions of poverty, in a study focusing on tenants of the poorest neighbourhoods of Jyväskylä, a medium-sized Finnish town (Hautamaa 1983; Sipilä 1992, 12). Although Hautamaa was describing poverty and marginalization in an old housing area, her main emphasis was on poverty as the experience of a single person as opposed to the experiences of a group or to a description of a poverty-stricken area.[3] The study was based on data from interviews and participant observations. The poor seemed to live one day at a time, unable to plan their lives weeks or years ahead. On the other hand, it did not seem as though they were suffering from low expectation levels, which sometimes is seen as a central feature of the poor (Lewis 1959). It seems that even the most marginalized people in Finnish society do not form a clear-cut, separate subculture; they still share the same goals and expectations as the non-poor.

Nordic social research has produced many studies on different kinds of social problems. Usually, these studies refer to the fact that the minorities in question are also poor, but there is a lack of research concentrating clearly on the question of poverty. For example, there are many reports done by means of a qualitative paradigm on alcoholics and other substance abusers. Addicts are usually poor, but the focus in these studies is not primarily directed towards the problem of poverty. Instead, the drug or alcohol addiction problem is the focus of attention. There is also, as mentioned above, a large and growing body of social work research on social assistance and its effects (for example, Bergmark 1991; Lilja 1989; Mäntysaari 1991; Rostila 1988; Salomaa

1986; Salonen 1993; Svedberg 1994). These studies are not dealt with here because the subjects focused on are primarily social work clients, not the poor as such.

In recent years some research has been devoted to the hitherto unexpected consequences of poverty in the postwar Nordic countries. According to a recent study conducted by a research group in Finland, even hunger is becoming a problem in parts of the country. Hunger is politically a very sensitive issue in Finland, and for that reason the empirical data were gathered by asking people who had had personal experience of hunger to write a letter to the researchers. The research group received 200 letters during a two-month period in 1994. The conclusion of the research was clear: there are people in Finland who suffer from hunger. Hunger was, however, understood relatively, i.e. respondents operationalized it as a situation in which the refrigerator is empty and one has no money for food. Some of these people are the marginalized poor, who have traditionally suffered from lack of resources. However, there are also unemployed people who come from a middle-class background but who are now without means of livelihood. The third group consists of young people living alone who cannot support themselves (Heikkilä et al. 1994).

The experience of being poor in a welfare state

During the 1980s, the worsening unemployment situation in Denmark together with the cutbacks in welfare state expenditure led to a growing number of people suffering from poverty. Andersen and Larsen's study (1989) dealt directly with the problem of being poor in an otherwise affluent society. They wanted to analyse, on the one hand, the effects of poverty on everyday life and individual actions and, on the other hand, the quality of the social policy efforts aimed at diminishing the effects of poverty.

Andersen and Larsen's theoretical framework was influenced by Marxism. The researchers tried to combine the structural societal level with the individual level. According to the authors, there is always a poverty risk in capitalist societies; poverty can be seen as a form of extreme class inequality (Andersen and Larsen 1989: 54).

Andersen and Larsen were basically following Townsend's theory of poverty (1979) when they developed their own definition of poverty. They say that poverty in Denmark is not a question of being totally without resources, but rather a question of being separated from the way of life that the surrounding society practises and in which they want to participate (Andersen and Larsen 1989: 11). One interesting result of their study was that even the people interviewed defined the concept of poverty in almost the same way as the researchers of the relative poverty school.

As mentioned above, Andersen and Larsen chose to mix a qualitative analysis with quantitative data. The qualitative part of the research was based on interviews with sixteen middle-aged unemployed persons living in the area of Copenhagen. The interviews consisted of questions on the process of marginalization, household budgets, the social consequences of poverty, and the coping strategies of the interviewees. The interviews concerning the life histories of the middle-aged unemployed showed that a typical change had taken place in their lives. In the 1940s and 1950s, life was hard; in the 1960s and at the beginning of the 1970s life was easier and number of opportunities seemed to grow as the expanding labour market and the welfare state provided new opportunities. From the beginning of the 1980s the situation worsened: unemployment increased and social security benefits once again turned out to be insufficient.

Andersen and Larsen also used interviews to gather information about the economic needs of different types of households. These household budget estimations gave a very concrete picture of needs and their costs in a modern society and were widely discussed in the media when the study was published.

In our concluding remarks we will argue that qualitative poverty research seems to be quite underdeveloped in comparison with the quantitative research done in Scandinavia. Studies that explicitly focus on poverty are rare, and the qualitative methods used are not very refined. There are many possible reasons for this. One explanation was suggested by Andersen et al. (1987), who said that Scandinavian welfare researchers find it difficult to accept the central idea of a poverty culture, because this theory sees society as a mixture of contradictory lifestyles and subcultures.

Summary

As has been shown in this review, poverty research has for a long time played a marginal role in the Nordic social research tradition. However, for different reasons, it was put on the agenda during the 1980s. What might then be the concluding, overall assessment of the Nordic state of the art research within the field of poverty studies? We can isolate a few features, positive and negative, and also point out similarities and differences between the countries assessed.

- Until the beginning of the 1980s the question of poverty was not generally dealt with as a central issue in either social research or social policy. One basic reason for this lay in the general objectives of social policy: the basic objective of the Nordic welfare model was to secure overall equality, not just to guarantee a minimum standard. Policies were explicitly, policies were targeted towards inequality reduction and also towards keeping the unemployment level low. Instead of a distinct poverty research tradition such as existed in the USA and the UK, the Nordic countries took the path of welfare research, which has been the dominating discipline since the early 1960s.
- Once poverty was put on the agenda, Nordic research was able to benefit from the relative richness of large quantitative databases provided by level-of-living surveys and social statistics. There is also a long tradition of cooperation between countries both in harmonization of social statistics and also in conducting comparable surveys of living conditions on a frequent basis. The living conditions surveys offer a unique database for ambitious poverty research. This also implies that poverty research has been policy relevant, i.e. its results have formed an evaluation basis for the assessment of social policies.
- Most of the research done so far has not been very ambitious in a theoretical sense. The welfare state itself has usually been used as the central frame for understanding and even explaining the existing forms of poverty. In addition, the marginalization theory and to some degree the underclass theory have been adopted in the Nordic context.
- There are, of course, differences among the Nordic countries, even though they form a relatively uniform group. Denmark was until recently the only country that was a member of the European Union, which partly explains why the rediscovery of poverty took place earlier in Denmark than in the other Nordic countries. Another explanation is, of course, that Denmark was most seriously hit by the economic downturn in the late 1970s. Within the Nordic group, Denmark can also be viewed as more unusual in the sense that the consciousness of poverty was more political in nature. It seems as if Sweden and Finland share the greatest similarities when it comes to the development of poverty research. In both countries the rediscovery of the poverty issue took place at about at the same

time, and mainstream poverty research has been characterized by economic poverty and social assistance studies. In Norway one cannot discern the same kind of rediscovery of poverty as in the other Nordic countries, a fact that almost certainly reflects the strength of the Norwegian economy.

Concerning the major results, we will emphasize the following three. First of all, the research done so far clearly reveals the dynamics of poverty – the changing composition of poverty risk and incidence. Owing to the social policies adopted, the traditional risk factors such as old age, sickness, and also to some degree unemployment have lost their meaning in explaining economic poverty. Typical risk groups in the 1970s and 1980s were students, young people in general, families with a lot of children, and one-parent families, and also, more recently, the long-term unemployed. The uncertain position of the young and families with children reflects to some degree their difficulties in establishing themselves as independent households. Second, the research results provide clear evidence supporting the assumption that social policy does matter. Strong redistributive policies, which have been one central feature of the Scandinavian model, proved their effectiveness in poverty alleviation. The third main result deals more with methodological issues. Much of empirical research teaches us the somewhat controversial lesson that different operationalizations identify different population groups as poor. Analysis has shown that the three main strategies defining the poor – economic poverty, accumulation of deprivation, and social assistance – to a large degree target different sections of the population. The overlap between alternative measurements is surprisingly small. These results clearly demonstrate the complexity of the poverty phenomenon in developed countries.

At the beginning of 1990s changing societal conditions brought the problem of poverty into public debate much more strongly than was the case in the 1980s. This was especially the case in Sweden and Finland. The major change in these countries was the rapid increase in unemployment and particularly the increase in the number of long-term unemployed. At the same time both countries face huge financial problems. A rapid increase in state budget deficits is leading to substantial cuts in welfare provisions. The combination of the increase in unemployment and a decrease in the ability of the welfare state to fund income maintenance makes the prospects for the future rather pessimistic. Thus, it seems likely that poverty research, at least in Finland and Sweden, will be the focus of attention even more in the future.

As a result of the already discussed well-known reasons, Norway is possibly an exception here too.

In Denmark high unemployment rates are no longer a new phenomenon. The unemployment and long-term unemployment rates have stood at nearly 10 per cent and 3 per cent, respectively, during the past decade. In Denmark, then, the poverty caused by high unemployment is no longer "new poverty". Compared with Sweden and Finland, Denmark has produced extensive research results that are relevant for this situation. These studies will be valuable for researchers in Finland and Sweden.

Another significant challenge for the Nordic countries in general but more specifically for poverty research, will be European integration. Denmark has been a member of the EU since the 1970s. Sweden and Finland decided to join the EU in 1994, whereas Norway decided to remain outside. What kind of institutional impact will integration have on poverty and the Nordic welfare model? This will obviously be one focus of future poverty research in the Nordic countries.

At a theoretical level one can discern some new trends and improvements that will affect future poverty research:

- the increased interest in the life-history and longitudinal approach to poverty;
- the social consensus methodology to define poverty;
- comparative studies of public policies directed at poverty alleviation; and
- follow-up studies that make it possible to understand the changing nature of poverty and to explain the dynamics of poverty.

Notes

1. The Nordic area consists of five countries: Denmark, Finland, Iceland, Norway, and Sweden. Iceland is for practical reasons not included in this review.
2. However, the concept of poverty culture has been widely discussed even in the Nordic countries. A very thought-provoking presentation about the discussion can be found in a report by a Danish group of researchers (Anderson et al. 1987: 194).
3. There are also some other poverty studies connected with the question of housing. Jokinen and Juhila undertook an interesting study of an old working-class area in Tampere (Jokinen and Juhila 1987, 1991).

References

Andersen, J. and J. Elm Larsen (1989) *Fattigdom i velfärdsstaten*. Köbenhavns Universitet, Sociologisk Institut, forskningsrapport no. 3.

Andersen, J., J. Henriksen, J. E. Larsen and P. Abrahamson (1987). *Fattigdomens sociologi*. Copenhagen: Sociologisk Institut.

Bergmark, Å. (1991) *Socialbidrag och försörjning*. Rapport i Social arbete nr 55, Stockholms universitet – Socialhögskolan.

Duncan, Greg J. (1984) *Years of Poverty Years of Plenty*. University of Michigan, Institute for Social Research.

Erikson, R. and M. Tåhlin (1987) "Coexistence of welfare problems", in R. Erikson and R. Åberg (eds), *Welfare in Transition. A Survey of Living Conditions in Sweden*. Oxford: Clarendon Press, pp. 258–80.

Erikson, R., E. J. Hansen, S. Ringen, and H. Uusitalo (1987) *The Scandinavian Model. Welfare States and Welfare Research*. Armonk; NY: M. E. Sharpe

Esping-Andersen, Gøsta (1990) *The Three Worlds of Welfare Capitalism*. Oxford: Polity Press.

Esping-Andersen, G. and W. Korpi (1987) "From poor relief to institutional welfare states: The development of Scandinavian social policy", in R. Erikson, et al. (eds), *The Scandinavian Model. Welfare States and Welfare Research*. Armonk, NY: M. E. Sharpe, pp. 39–74.

Fridberg, T., K. Halvorsen, O. Hove, I. Julkunen, S. Marklund, and T. Tanninen (1993) *On Social Assistance in the Nordic Capitals*. Copenhagen: Nordic Council of Ministers.

Friis, H. (1981) *Nederst ved bordet*. Copenhagen: Socialforskningsinstitutet.

Goedhart, T., K. Halberstadt, A. Kapteyn and B. M. S. Van Praag (1977) "The poverty line: concept and measurement". *Journal of Human Resources*, 12(4): 503–20.

Gustafsson, B. (1984) *En bok om fattigdom*. Lund: Studentlitteratur.

—— (1993a) "Poverty in Sweden 1975–85, in E. J. Hansen, S. Ringen, H. Uusitalo, and R. Erikson (eds), *Welfare Trends in the Scandinavian Countries*, Armonk, NY: M. E. Sharpe

—— (1993b) *Ekonomisk fattigdom i Sverige sedan mitten på 1970-talet*. Socialstyrelsens kunskapsunderlag. Department of Social Work, Gothenburg University.

Gustafsson, B. and M. Lindblom (1993) "Poverty lines and poverty in seven European countries, Australia, Canada and the USA". *Journal of European Social Policy*, 3(1): 21–38.

Gustafsson, B. and H. Uusitalo (1990a) "Income distribution and redistribution during two decades: Experiences from Finland and Sweden", in I. Persson (ed.), *Generating Equality in the Welfare State. The Swedish Experience*. Stavanger: Norwegian University Press, pp. 73–95.

—— (1990b). "The welfare state and poverty in Finland and Sweden from the mid-1960s to the mid-1980s". *Review of Income and Wealth* 36(3): 249–66.

Hagenaars, A. J. M. (1986) *The Perceptions of poverty*. Amsterdam: Elsevier Science Publishers.

Halleröd, B. (1991). *Den svenska fattigdomen: en studie av fattigdom och socialbidragstagande*. Lund: Arkiv.

—— (1992) "Fattigdom och socialbidragstagande". *Nordiskt socialt arbete*, No. 4: 17–32.

—— (1994a) *Poverty in Sweden: A New Approach to Direct Measurement of Consensual Poverty*. Umeå: Umeå Studies in Sociology No. 106.

—— (1994b) *A New Approach to Direct Consensual Measurement of Poverty*. University of New South Wales. Social Policy Research Centre, Discussion paper No. 50.

—— (1995a). "The truly poor: Indirect and direct measurment of consensual poverty in Sweden". *Journal of European Social Policy*, Vol. 5 (2): 111–29.

—— (1995b) "Making ends meet: Perception of poverty in Sweden", *Scandinavian Journal of Social Welfare*, 4 (3): 174–89.

Halleröd et al. (1993) *Konsensuell fattigdom: en studie av konsumtion och attityder till konsumtion*. University of Umeå, Umeå Studies in Sociology No. 104.

Halleröd, Björn, Jonathan Bradshaw, and Hilary Holmes (1995) "Adapting the consensual definition of poverty", in Gordon and Pantazis (eds), *Breadline Britain in the 1990's*. A report to the Joseph Rowntree Foundation.

Hansen, E. J. (1986) *Danskernes levekår 1986 sammenholdt med 1976*. Copenhagen: Hans Reitzel.

—— (1989) *The Concept and Measurement of Poverty*. Copenhagen: Danish National Institute of Social Research, Booklet No. 29.

Hansen, F. K. (1990) *Materielle og sociale afsavn i befolkningen*. Copenhagen: Socialforskningsinstituttet, Rapport 90:4.

Hautamaa, S. (1983) *Köyhyydestä ja syrjäytymisestä – tapaustutkimus vanhalta puutaloalueelta*. Jyväskylä: Jyväskylän yliopiston yhteiskuntapolitiikan laitoksen työpapereita nro 33.

Heikkilä, M. (1990) *Köyhyys ja huono-osaisuus hyvinvointivaltiossa. Tutkimus köyhyydestä ja hyvinvoinnin puutteiden kasautumisesta Suomessa*. With English summary: *Poverty and Deprivation in a Welfare State. A Study of Poverty and Accumulation of Welfare Deficits in Finland*. Helsinki: Sosiaalihallituksen julkaisuja 8/1990.

Heikkilä, M., S. Hänninen, J. Karjalainen, O. Kontula, and K. Koskela, (1994) *Nälkä*. STAKES, STM, Raportteja 153. Helsinki.

Henriksen, J. P. (1987) "Some perspectives on Scandinavian welfare research". *Acta Sociologica*, 30 (3–4): 379–92.

Hove, O. (1993) *Relative Deprivation and Subjective Poverty*. Oslo: NKHS-NOTAT Nr. 93:1.

Inghe, G. (1960) *Fattiga i folkhemmet*. Uppsala: Almqvist & Wiksell.

Jäntti, M. (1991) *On the Measurement of Poverty. Conceptual Issues and Estimation Problems*. Abo: Meddelanden från ekonomisk-

statsvetenskapliga fakulteten vid Åbo Akademi, Nationalekonomiska institutionen ser. A: 328.
―――― (1993) *Essays on Income Distribution and Poverty*. Åbo: Åbo. Akademis förlag.
Johansson, S. (1970) *Om levnadsnivåundersökningen*. Stockholm: Allmänna föralget.
Jokinen, A. and K. Juhila. (1987) *Asumisen ankeus ja autuus. Tutkimus puu-Tammelasta ja sen asukkaista*. Tampereen yliopisto, sosiaalipolitiikan laitos. Tampere.
―――― (1991) *Pohjimmaiset asuntomarkkinat. Diskurssianalyysi kuntatason viranomaiskäytännöistä*. Helsinki: Sosiaaliturvan keskusliitto ja asuntohallitus.
Knutsson, G. and K. Stridsman. (1988) *Fattiga i Sverige*. Stockholm: Allmänna förlaget.
Kolberg, Jon Eivind (1992) *The Study of Welfare State Regimes*. London: M. E. Sharpe.
Korpi, W. (1971) *Fattigdom i välfärden*. Stockholm: Tiden förlag.
Lauronen, K. (1988) *Toimeentulotukiasiakkaat ja heidän elämäntilanteensa*. Sosiaalihallituksen julkaisuja 9/1988.
Lehto, J. and K. Lamminpää (1992) *Ruuhkaa ja leikattua perusturvaa toimeentulotukiluukulla*. Helsinki: Sosiaali- ja terveyshallitus, raportteja nro 75.
Lewis, O. (1959) *Five Families*: New York: Basic Books.
Lilja, E. (1989) *Välfärdskapandets dilemma. Om människan och hennes behov i kommunala socialvårdspraktik*. Stockholm: Nordiska institutet för samhällsplanering, Avhandling 7.
Mack, J. and S. Lansley (1985) *Poor Britain*. London: Allen & Unwin
Mäntysaari, M. (1991) *Sosiaalibyrokratia asiakkaiden valvojana*. Tampere: Vastapaino
Mäntysaari, M. (1993) Toimeentulotuki – viimesijainen soujaverkko vai ensisijainen turvajärjestelmä?, in: M. Heikkilä, S. Hänninen, V. Kosunen, M. Mäntysaari, S. Sallila, and H. Uusitalo. *Hyvinvoinnin päätepysäkillä? Aineistoa hyvinvointipolitiikkaa koskevaan keskusteluun*. Jyväskylä: Stakesin raportteja 128.
Marklund, S. (1990) "Structures of modern poverty. *Acta Sociologica* 33(2): 125–40.
Mitchell, Deborah (1993) *Income Transfers in Ten Welfare States*. Newcastle: Ashgate Publishing.
Øyen, E. (1992) "Some basic issues in comparative poverty research". *International Sococial Science Journal*, 134: 615–26.
Ringen, S. (1985) "Toward a third stage in the measurement of poverty". *Acta Sociologica* 28(2): 99–113.
―――― (1987b) *The Possibility of Politics. A Study in the Political Economy of the Welfare State*. Oxford: Clarendon Press.
―――― (1988) "Direct and indirect measures of poverty. Discussion". *Journal of Social Policy*, 17(3): 351–65.
Ritakallio, V.-M. (1986) *Kartoitus suomalaisesta köyhyystutkimuksesta ja arviot tutkimustarpeista. Sosiaalihallituksen toimeentuloprojekti*.

Helsinki: Sosiaalihallituksen julkaisuja 16/1986, Valtion painatuskeskus.

——— (1991) *Köyhyys ei tule yksin. Tutkimus hyvinvointipuutteiden kasautumisesta toimeentulotukiasiakkailla.* With English summary: Poverty Comes not Alone. *A Study of Accumulated Welfare Deprivation among Social Assistance Recipients.* Helsinki: Sosiaali- ja terveyshallitus, tutkimuksia 11/1991. Valtion painatuskeskus.

——— (1994a) *Köyhyys Suomessa 1981–1990. Tutkimus tulonsiirtojen vaikutuksista.* With English summary: *Poverty in Finland 1981–1990. A Study of Effects of Income Transfers.* Jyväskylä: National Research and Development Centre for Welfare and Health, Research Report No. 39.

——— (1994b) "Köyhyyden muuttunut kuva Suomessa 1966–90, in M. Teoksessa Heikkilä and K. Vähätalo (eds), *Huono-osaisuus ja hyvinvointivaltion muutos.* Helsinki: Gaudeamus, 169–90.

——— (1994c) *Finnish Poverty: A Cross-National Comparison.* Luxembourg: LIS Working Paper No 119.

Rostila, I. (1988) *Subjektina sosiaalitoimistossa? Asiakassuhteen analysointia toimeentulotuki-, PAV- ja lastensuojeluasiakkaiden kokemusten avulla.* Helsinki: Sosiaalihallituksen julkaisuja 7/1988.

Salomaa, A. (1986) *Toimeentulotuki asiakkaiden näkökulmasta. Tutkielma toimeentulotuen asiakkaiden elämäntilanteista ja heidän kokemuksistaan toimeentulotuesta.* Tampere: Tampereen yliopisto, sosiaalipolitiikan laitoksen tutkimuksia 80/1986.

Salonen, T. (1993) *Margins of Welfare.* Kristianstad: Hällstad Press.

Saunders, P., B. Halleröd, and G. Matheson (1994) "Making ends meet in Australia and Sweden: A comparative analysis using the subjective poverty line methodology". *Acta Sociologica* 37(1): 3–22.

Sipilä, J. (1992) "Defining, measuring and talking about poverty: the case of Finland". *Scandinavian Journal of Social Welfare.* 1(1): 12–20.

Smeeding, T., M. O'Higgins, and L. Rainwater (eds) (1990) *Poverty, Inequality and Income Distribution in Comparative Perspective.* New York: Harvester Wheatsheaf, The Luxembourg Income Study.

Stjernö, S. (1985) *Den moderne fattigdommen. Om ökonomisk knapphet og ydmykelse i 1980-åra.* Oslo: Universitetforlaget AS.

Svedberg, L. (1994) *On Marginality: A Client Group's Relation to Work.* Edsbruk: Almquist & Wiksell, Stockholm Studies in Social Work, 8.

Tanninen, T. and I. Julkunen (1988) *Utkomststödet i Norden, problem och utvecklingstendenser under 1980-talet.* Copenhagen: Rapport från Nordiska Ministerrådet.

——— (1993) *Elämää säästöliekillä.* Helsinki: STAKES Tutkimuksia.

Terum, L. I. (1984) *Yngre og utan arbeid.* Oslo: INAS Notat 84:11.

Townsend, P. (1979) *Poverty in the United Kingdom. A Survey of Household Resources and Standards of Living.* Harmondsworth, Middx: Penguin Books.

Uusitalo, H. (1975) *Income and Welfare. A Study of Incomes as a Component of Welfare in the Scandinavian Countries in the 1970s.*

Helsinki: University of Helsinki, Research Group for Comparative Sociology No.
—— (1989) *Income Distribution in Finland. The Effects of the Welfare State and the Structural Changes in Society on Income Distribution in Finland in 1966–1985*. Helsinki: Central Statistical Office of Finland, Studies No. 148.

Chapter 17

Russia and the Baltics: Poverty and Poverty Research in a Changing World

Alastair McAuley

Introduction

The growing economic crisis that preceded the collapse of state socialism and the break-up of the USSR was accompanied by a growth in poverty – and a belated recognition on the part of the Soviet government that poverty existed in the USSR. The transition to a market economy has been accompanied by an enormous further increase in poverty in Russia and, indeed, in most of the other successor states of the former Soviet Union (FSU).

The growth in poverty has led to an increase in its political importance and hence to an increase in government concern. This has not, however, resulted in any great increase in the amount of academic research on the subject carried out by domestic specialists. And it has certainly not resulted in any substantial theoretical innovation in the field. But there has been important new research on: the definition of poverty lines; determining the incidence of poverty and its causes; devising social policies to contain and alleviate poverty. Much of the impetus for this work has come from international agencies, primarily the World Bank. Those who collaborate with consultants supplied by the World Bank or other agencies are exposed to recent Western research on poverty, to Western concepts, and to Western measures. The ongoing transmission of ideas is laying the groundwork for future original contributions by specialists from the FSU.

Poverty and socialism

The countries covered by this review are special for three reasons. First, until the collapse of the USSR in December 1991, they did not exist as independent states. Second, as constituent republics of the Soviet Union, they were parts of a socialist state – or at least of a state that proclaimed itself to be socialist. Finally, since achieving independence they have all – or almost all – announced their intention to abandon socialism and central planning and have embarked upon the process of transition to a market economy. These features mean that the new states that have emerged from the FSU share a common – and special – history. They also face problems not experienced by more well-established countries. There is neither room nor time in this paper to explore all the implications of this uniqueness. But it is worth mentioning briefly the following three issues: the legacy of Soviet ideology; the consequences of the relative isolation of the Soviet academic community; and the implications of the Soviet policy heritage.

Ideology

In Soviet eyes, socialism was a progressive ideology. This meant that a socialist state was committed to solving the social problems that disfigured capitalism. Party propagandists liked to claim that, certainly by the 1960s, the USSR had made considerable strides towards the goal of creating a just and equal society. As a result, it was suggested that there could be no poverty. Furthermore, if there was no poverty, there could be no justification for the academic study of the phenomenon.

This claim perhaps oversimplifies the situation in the USSR. During the Khrushchev period, it was recognized that the country had inherited a range of social problems from Stalin; these included poverty. Attempts were made to devise policies to cope with them and some academic specialists were encouraged to study them. (At this time the authorities encouraged the development of sociology.) But it was difficult to "call a spade a spade". It was argued that Soviet social problems were different in nature from those to be found in a capitalist system. One did not talk of "poverty" in the USSR but used a variety of euphemisms instead. Later, under Brezhnev, such camouflage was not enough. Researchers found it more difficult to publish analyses of social problems such as poverty; and this work was discouraged in other ways. On the whole, the Communist Party succeeded in determining the social science agenda. Certainly very little published research on the causes or consequences of poverty in the USSR appeared in the period 1965–85 or 1990. As a result, neither Russia nor any of the other successor states of the FSU possesses a body of experienced poverty analysts. Nor is there a body of literature to which policy makers and others can turn.

The most prominent exception to this assessment is the work of N. M. Rimashevskaia. Starting in the late 1950s she studied problems associated with inequality in earnings and incomes. She has prospered; in the late 1980s she became head of a separate institute, the Institute for the Study of Socio-economic Problems of the Population (ISEPN). This organization and its staff constitute one of the poles of Russian professional work on problems of poverty and social policy. The other source of poverty analysis in the Soviet Union in the 1970s and 1980s was the Research Institute of the State Committee on Labour and Wages. This organization was responsible for the calculation of the so-called *biudzhet minimuma material'noi obespechennosti*, the quasi-official poverty line, in 1965.

Isolation

In the late 1980s, even so-called specialists in the field of poverty research had limited knowledge of the international literature, of recent developments in thinking about policy, of new approaches to the measurement of poverty, and so on. This intellectual isolation was reinforced by two other features of the development of Soviet social science. First, the computer revolution had barely penetrated the USSR. Soviet economists or sociologists did not possess personal computers; many of them even had difficulty gaining access to mainframe machines. Even where they did so, they had few user-friendly software packages to help them analyse their data. Second, the authorities made little attempt to release relevant data regularly or coherently. As a result, Soviet specialists had relatively little experience at hands-on analysis. In this area, the position in republic capitals and most provincial cities was worse than in Moscow and (possibly) Leningrad.

Policy

The FSU nations share a common history in the field of social policy, particularly in anti-poverty policy. Concern about the scale and extent of poverty in the USSR was first expressed in the late 1950s. This was part of Khrushchev's attempt to cope with the legacy of Stalinism. It resulted, among other things, in the adoption of a minimum wage. In the 1960s, it was argued that this policy had failed – there was still substantial poverty. There appears to have been some argument about whether to raise the minimum wage further or to introduce a means-tested benefit. In

1968, the first of these alternatives was adopted – for fear of the impact of benefits on work incentives. Not until 1974 was a limited income supplement programme initiated. (This was payable to families with children under the age of 7 years where per capita income was less than 50 roubles a month. The benefit was set at 12 roubles per child per month.) This approach influenced thinking about anti-poverty policy in many if not all of the successor states.

In the late 1980s, the government introduced other anti-poverty measures – particularly in connection with the attempt to raise consumer goods prices and reduce the burden of subsidies. These programmes led to a bewildering array of ad hoc payments to which families were entitled. Many of them were still being paid by governments in successor states in 1993 or 1994.

Poverty research in transition

The previous neglect of poverty as a topic for academic research has continued into the transition period – certainly in Russia. This situation has several causes. First, it reflects in part the demoralization of the scientific community in the wake of the economic crisis of the early 1990s. The institutes of the Academy of Sciences network have seen their funding fall sharply; this has been translated into substantial reductions in salaries. Newly impoverished scholars have neither the incentive nor the energy to embark upon a new research agenda.

Second, the economic crisis and the collapse of the old Soviet state also resulted in the cessation of much of the routine data-collection activities of the government. Much of the old programme of social monitoring no longer makes a great deal of sense. On the one hand, in the face of very rapid inflation, the old indicators have lost much of their meaning; for example, when nominal wages may increase ten-fold or even a hundred-fold over a twelve-month period, one can learn little from an annual census of wages. On the other, the change in institutions and, in particular, the move to a market economy have undermined the value or even the meaning of traditional data series. Inevitably, this deterioration in accuracy and reliability of statistical information has affected the quality of academic research in Russia – and the ability of scholars to explore new issues.

Two other factors have intensified the data problems facing social scientists in the FSU. The fiscal crisis from which almost all governments have suffered has caused governments to reduce real expenditure on data collection and, possibly more, on its dissemination. And privatization, even when only partial, has led former state enterprises (and private individuals) to be much less willing to cooperate with the statistical authorities.

The FSU has had no tradition of open publication of official statistics; many standard statistical series that were routinely published in other countries were classified or secret in the USSR. If statistics revealed a negative trend or a politically embarrassing development, publication was suspended. (This was what happened to infant mortality rates for example, when they showed an unwelcome increase in the second half of the 1970s.) Old habits die hard. The Russian government has still not established a regular programme of publication of economic and social information. The availability of particular pieces of information may be denied at almost any time. And what is released is often not in a form that is appropriate for analysis using modern statistical methods and information technology.

As a result, little serious scholarly work on poverty – or many other issues in the field of social policy – is being undertaken in Russia's academic institutes or universities. The situation is not, however, completely blank. Policy needs have inspired some work. For example, the Ministry of Labour commissioned a team from ISEPN to develop a new subsistence minimum in collaboration with consultants from the World Bank (Popkin, et al. 1994). A new research institute, headed by the former prime minister Yegor Gaidar, has been exploring regional aspects of inequality and poverty (Surinov and Kolosnitsyn 1994). The Central Council of the Trade Unions has continued to calculate an independent index of the cost of living – and hence its own poverty line. Various institutes in Moscow and in different provincial cities conduct public opinion surveys or other studies that deal, *inter alia*, with the standard of living and poverty. In view of the history of research on poverty in the FSU and considering the problems involving access to data outlined above, it is not surprising that much of this work is of dubious quality.

The position in other parts of the FSU seems essentially the same. In none of the new states has there been a tradition of research on poverty; nowhere is there any substantial body of well-trained and experienced researchers in the field. All or almost all of the new states have experienced difficulties in collecting – and disseminating – reliable data on incomes, expenditures, and prices, which are an essential precondition for successful empirical work on poverty.

In most states, the work that has been done in the field has been inspired by the needs of policy. Often it has been organized in conjunction with consultants hired by international agencies.

(The World Bank and, to a lesser extent, the International Monetary Fund have played an important role here.) But there has also been some autonomous politically inspired work (such as, for example, the monitoring of the cost of living undertaken by the Russian trade union movement). Finally, as in Russia, much of the work on poverty that has been undertaken since independence is of doubtful quality.

In all FSU states the impetus for further research on poverty is policy driven. It is linked to the "social safety-net" programmes that governments have wished to introduce or have been persuaded to adopt and to the burden that these place upon the fragile fiscal balance. Until recently, such research has been partially funded by the IMF, the World Bank or the European Union (EU), through such programmes as TACIS. This state of affairs is likely to persist for at least another year or so. Finally, this research is often undertaken by Western consultants; inevitably, such specialists have little prior knowledge of the FSU nations and their problems.

Concepts of poverty

For all its limitations, the USSR did have a concept of poverty. In certain respects it differed markedly from those developed in market economies in the past fifty years or so. This concept constitutes the intellectual heritage of all the countries of the former Soviet Union. Since the collapse of communism and the break-up of the so-called Soviet empire, individual countries have moved away from this heritage and, under pressure from international agencies such as the World Bank, have developed concepts of poverty that correspond more closely to those familiar to policy makers and scholars in Western Europe. In this section I describe the Soviet poverty concept; I also describe the development of a new concept of poverty that has taken place in Russia since 1991 (or even somewhat earlier). The experience of other member states of the FSU is similar to that of Russia and is discussed somewhat more briefly as well.

A common intellectual heritage: the MMS budget

In the late 1950s and 1960s, a degree of official concern was expressed about the position of particular groups in Soviet society. This led to the development of the so-called *biudzhet minimuma material'noi obespechennosti*, the minimum material security budget (the MMS budget), which functioned as a quasi-official poverty line until 1991. The budget was intended to reflect the minimum levels of consumption needed to "reproduce simple labour power" – that is, to sustain an unskilled worker. A panel of experts determined what quantities of various goods and services such a worker might need to maintain the specified standard of living for himself and for his notional family. In this exercise, nutritionists were consulted over the quantities of food to be included in the consumption basket; other quantities appear to have been chosen fairly arbitrarily – although some attention was paid to what was available on the Soviet consumer goods market and to patterns of expenditure as revealed by the family budget survey.

The basket was then priced at official state prices, making some allowance for the higher prices to be found on kolkhoz markets. This constituted the MMS budget. In the published research report, some allowance was made for regional variations in prices. Also, the calculations revealed some economies of scale in consumption: the cost for a single individual was set at 58 roubles a month; for a notional family of four it was 204 roubles. No more sophisticated attempt at determining equivalence scales was published (McAuley 1979: ch. 1). This calculation formed the basis for the adoption of 50 rubles a month per capita as the quasi-official poverty line in 1968. This figure remained the benchmark until the mid-1980s.

For Soviet scholars and policy makers (and hence, initially, for those in the successor states of the FSU) poverty was a needs-based concept. (The first reference to either a rights-based or a consensual definition of poverty in the Russian language literature appeared in an article that I published in *Sotsialisticheskii trud* in 1991.) Poverty was relative rather than absolute – although policy makers were slow to adjust their poverty line to changes in either the cost or the standard of living. Little attempt was made to reflect the actual consumption patterns of the poor. Little attempt was made to allow for differences in need within the family or for economies of scale in consumption.

The official view appears to have been that poverty was the result of low wages or large families. Hence, the appropriate response to poverty was to raise the minimum wage and to provide child benefits for those with large families. In the 1960s and early 1970s, academic specialists managed to convince policy makers that poverty might also be a consequence of family breakdown or inadequate labour-force attachment. As a result, the Soviet social safety-net was extended and the social insurance system was redirected to cope with current need rather than to provide incentives for long-term labour-force participation.

The view was widespread in the USSR that the "deserving" poor were either old or very young. If those of working age were poor, it was probably because they were unwilling to work – through idleness, alcoholism, or some such other reason. This view persisted right up to the end of the USSR and beyond (it has broken down as a result of the sharp fall in real incomes during the last few years). These attitudes influenced the shape of anti-poverty policy in the Soviet Union and form part of the common heritage of the states of the FSU.

The new Russian concept of poverty: the subsistence minimum

The economic crisis of the 1980s induced a change in official attitudes towards poverty in the USSR. In 1989, for the first time the prime minister admitted in the Supreme Soviet that poverty existed in the Soviet Union. This attitude has carried over into contemporary Russia. Indeed, poverty and the decline in living standards have become something of a national obsession, discussed at all levels of government and in the press.

More formally, the Russian government, in conjunction with the World Bank has developed a new approach to the determination of poverty. It now publishes an estimate of its minimum subsistence level regularly. Furthermore, adjustments in the minimum wage and the minimum pension are linked to this calculation – although neither is explicitly indexed to the so-called official poverty line. The government also publishes estimates of the incidence of poverty.

In addition, the IMF, the World Bank, and UNICEF each continue to study poverty in Russia. For the first two organizations, these studies form part of a general involvement with the country and, informally at least, affect judgements about the conditionality conditions to be attached to support. UNICEF has embarked upon a more formal monitoring of economic and social conditions in both Eastern Europe and parts of the CIS, reflecting its concern about the impact of transition on the position of children in the region.

A lot of space is devoted to poverty and changes in the standard of living in the daily and periodical press. The topic has attracted a lot of attention – and a fair amount of bad analysis – from journalists. It has not yet led to any radical and sustained academic discussion, either about the nature and causes of poverty or about the problems involved in its measurement.

The new official poverty line

At the end of 1989 or the beginning of 1990, the Soviet government agreed to a request by the Group of Seven (G7) that the three major international economic agencies – the IMF, the World Bank, and the Organization for Economic Cooperation and Development (OECD) – should conduct a study and assessment of the Soviet economy with a view to providing multilateral assistance. This study criticized the Soviet approach both to the definition and measurement of poverty and to the provision of a social safety-net. In response, the government agreed to commission research towards the determination of a new subsistence minimum (*prozhitochnyi minimum*), more in line with accepted international practice. In the end it was carried out by Barry Popkin from the University of North Carolina together with Marina Mozhina from ISEPN and Alexander Baturin, a nutritionist from the USSR Academy of Medical Sciences. Russia inherited the results of this study after 1991.

The new subsistence minimum is derived following a procedure similar to that used by Orshansky in determining the US poverty line. It is based on a food basket that guarantees an appropriate number of calories a day and whose composition corresponds to the recommendations of the World Health Organization (WHO) and the Food and Agriculture Organization (FAO). The basket is also supposed to conform to Russian tastes and to the realities of the Russian market. (This has caused some conflict because Russians – and particularly members of the Parliamentary Committee on Social Security – did not agree with the WHO's desire to reduce sharply the proportion of calories to be derived from fats.) This basket was costed at Russian market prices and the total was grossed up to allow for other essential components of subsistence about which fewer scientifically derived requirements exist – clothing, shelter, and so on.

In 1992, it was decided that on average, households could be expected to spend some 68 per cent of their income on foodstuffs (for pensioners the figure was 83 per cent, for children it was 73–74 per cent and for adults of working age 62 per cent (Popkin et al. 1994: 67). This figure for food expenditure is much higher than in other countries that follow a similar approach. But it was chosen with Russia's conditions in mind. First, it was argued that Russia was only just embarking upon the transition to a market economy and, as a result, a substantial part of consumers' expenditure took place at controlled prices; this referred to housing and the cost of most utilities. Second, it was pointed out that, in the last years of Soviet rule, households had engaged in the stockpiling of soft goods and durables; they could be expected to draw down these stocks for a year or so.

The new subsistence minimum specifies a concept of poverty that is based on needs; it is relative in that, in principle, the multiplier factor should be adjusted as the country becomes richer. Furthermore, it provides an answer to policy problems: what part of the population should receive some additional support and, perhaps, how much support should they receive? But it is deficient in a number of ways, and it may need to be extended or modified in the future.

First, and uncontroversially, I believe, as the ambit of price control is changed, the "multiplier factor" must be adjusted. Since the government has gone some way towards the deregulation of rents, this adjustment is urgent. Second, the food basket that lies at the heart of the subsistence minimum pays too little attention to geographical variations in tastes and the availability of foodstuffs. This may need to be modified. Third, Russia is a large country and only partly connected, resulting in significant regional differences in the cost of living and the structure of relative prices. Finally, economies of scale in consumption and differences in need of different categories of people raise the issue of whether an equivalence scale should be adopted.

Comparison between new and old poverty lines

Table 17.1 shows how the new subsistence minimum evolved over the years 1992–4. It also shows how the minimum differs in value from the old MMS budget. In the spring of 1992, the subsistence minimum was set at 1,031 roubles a month per capita; a year later it had risen to 8,069 roubles a month – a 7.8-fold increase. In March 1994, the subsistence minimum was reported to be 60,388; the increase over the same month in the previous year was 7.5-fold. This is a reflection of the very rapid rates of inflation from which Russia has suffered since independence.

In March 1992, the value of the MMS budget was reported as 2,617 roubles a month per capita, some 2.5 times as large as the new subsistence minimum. In June 1993, the MMS budget was valued at almost 37,000 roubles, still more than double the subsistence minimum. Some idea of the problem with the MMS poverty standard can be obtained from the following figures drawn from estimates of the distribution of income in the second half of 1992 (McAuley 1994):

	August 1992	November 1992
Median (roubles)	2,642	4,519
Ninth decile	4,898	8,203
MMS budget	4,883	8,500

These figures show that in 1992 some 90 per cent of the population were living in families with a per capita monthly income below a poverty line derived according to the old Soviet methodology. This may give some indication of the scale of the collapse in living standards. It cannot provide a meaningful guide for policy.

Table 17.1 The evolution of the poverty standard: Russia, 1992–94

	Subsistence minimum (Roubles/month)	Minimum consumption budget (Roubles/month)
1992		
March	1,031	2,617
June	1,639	4,097
September	2,163	5,449
December	4,282	10,694
1993		
March	8,069	20,891
June	16,527	36,984
September	28,183	n.a.
December	42,800	n.a.
1994		
March	60,388	n.a.
June		
September		

Sources: rows 1–6 – McAuley (1994: Table 5.1); rows 7–8 – Surinov and Kolosnitsyn (1994: 4); row 9 – *Sotsial'no-ekonomicheskoe polozhenie Rossii. Yanvar'-Aprel', 1994*, Moscow: Goskom RF po statistikep, 1994: 68.

The concept of poverty in the rest of the FSU

The countries of the FSU inherited the MMS budget as a concept of poverty. Since independence, each has tended to move away from that standard. The impetus for change has usually come from the World Bank or the IMF in the context of a country assessment. And the Bank's pressure has in turn often been connected with a desire to rationalize the social protection programmes provided by the new government – and to relate them more closely to the state's fiscal capacity. The Ukraine will serve to illustrate the changes in the FSU countries.

Until the end of 1991, the Ukraine used the same quasi-official poverty line as the rest of the FSU – the MMS budget. In 1988, this was set at 78 roubles a month per capita. In 1992, the newly independent government commissioned a new poverty study (employing essentially the same methodology), which established the following poverty line, in January 1993 prices (Kakwani 1994: 36):

Food products	9,490 coupons
Non-food goods	2,992
clothes and footwear	1,488
hygiene and medicine	391
household	1,113
Services	1,103
Taxes, etc.	669
Poverty standard	14,345 coupons

In this budget, the total cost of the basket (the poverty line) is some 1.5 times the cost of food. This is higher than the ratio in the new Russian minimum subsistence standard. It is also higher than recommended by the World Bank's consultants. In view of the depth of the crisis being experienced in the Ukraine and taking account of the extensive subsidies being paid in such sectors as housing, health care, education, and public transport, they suggested a multiplier of 1.25 (Kendall et al. 1993, cited in Kakwani 1994: 37). The Kendall multiplier implied a poverty standard (in January 1993 prices) of 11,862 coupons a month per capita.

The MMS budget of 78 roubles a month per capita in 1988, when adjusted for price inflation, yields a poverty line of 11,878 coupons a month. Thus, the old Goskomstat poverty line is almost identical to the Kendall standard.

Data sources

Information about earnings and incomes in the USSR came from one of four sources. For earnings there was a census of enterprises held periodically after 1956 and quinquennially after 1976. This recorded earnings for all employees for the month of March. For incomes, the main source was the family budget survey (FBS). The shortcomings from which this suffered have been described at length: as a result of faulty sampling design the poor were under-represented, average incomes were overstated, and inequality was underestimated (Atkinson and Micklewright 1992: 263–69). There have also been periodical surveys of family composition, income, and housing conditions. The first of these was conducted in 1958; others were conducted in 1967 and 1972. Towards the end of the Soviet period they appear to have been organized every three years. Although the sample used was larger than that for the FBS, it suffered from many of the same weaknesses (McAuley 1979: 54). For all their shortcomings these three sources of data were organized on an All-Union basis. Therefore, they constitute a source of data on the distribution of income, on poverty, and on inequality in each of the successor states of the FSU. They also provide a methodological starting point for whatever income-monitoring programmes the new governments have adopted. The final source of data is the various academic surveys conducted by Soviet economists and sociologists. Although these can provide much interesting information on conditions in particular towns, few provide Union-wide data – or even data that might cast light on the position in more than one republic.

Since the break-up of the USSR the data-gathering activities of the successor states have diverged – not least in the area of earnings, incomes, and poverty. In Russia the FBS continues to operate. But it has been supplemented by a longitudinal monitoring survey designed to a large extent by World Bank consultants. Unfortunately, the government does not publish extensive results from either of these. Nor does the World Bank. Goskomstat also collects information on earnings.

In the Ukraine the government continues to undertake a family budget survey that is essentially the same as the one that operated under the Soviet government. (It is reported, however, that households in the Ukraine, as in Russia, are less willing than previously to cooperate with the statistical authorities and that this has reduced the reliability of the figures derived from this survey.) So far, the Ukrainian FBS has not yet been supplemented by an alternative monitoring survey initiated by the World Bank.

In Kyrghyzstan, however, the World Bank has carried out one wave of a longitudinal monitoring survey. It intends to do the same in Uzbekistan in 1996 or 1997. In principle, the Bank believes that its monitoring surveys should replace the FBS as the source of statistics on income and consumption – and hence on poverty. But this has not yet happened in any of the newly independent states. Many governments have indicated the desire to maintain the FBS.

How widespread was poverty in the USSR in the final pre-crisis decade, 1980–90, and how has it evolved since the collapse of communism?

Measurement

Poverty in the crisis decade, 1980–1990

Table 17.2 introduces three alternative relative poverty lines. The first of these is defined as 60 per cent of average per capita income; this is often used in studies of less developed countries. The second notional poverty line is defined as 50 per cent of average per capita income; this is the level conventionally assumed for advanced industrial societies. Finally, the table proposes the quasi-official poverty line derived from MMS budget studies.

The table shows, first, that in 1980 the 50 per cent poverty line was almost the same as the quasi-official one first set in 1967. This suggests that when it was first established the Soviet MMS budget provided for a relatively generous standard of living. In 1985, the quasi-official poverty line was approximately equal to 60 per cent of average earnings. Again, since the USSR was an industrialized state, this suggests a relatively generous poverty standard. Finally, in 1989, inflation had eroded the generosity built in to the notional poverty standard: the quasi-official MMS budget was again approximately equal to 50 per cent of average per capita income.

Table 17.2 Poverty in the USSR, 1980–9

Year	Poverty line 1 (R/month)	Head count (million)	Poverty line 2 (R/month)	Head count (million)	Poverty line 3 (R/month)	Head count (million)
1980	61.5	42.0	51.3	23.6	50.0	19.3
1985	78.6	57.5	65.5	35.2	75.0	49.6
1989	97.4	66.8	81.4	41.7	81.0	39.5

Source: Cols 1–4 and col. 6 calculated from *Sotsial'noe*, (1991: 117); col. 5 from Rimashevskaia and Rimashevskii (1991: 123).
Notes:
[a] Poverty line 1 is defined as 60 per cent of average monthly per capita total income;
[b] Poverty Line 2 is defined as 50 per cent of average monthly per capita total income;
[c] Poverty Line 3 is the value of the quasi-official *biudzhet minimal'noi material'noi obespechennosti* for the year in question.

The table also shows how the numbers with incomes below the notional MMS budget changed over the decade. In 1980, approximately 20–23 million people fell into this category; this was some 7.5–9 per cent of the population. By the end of the decade, the numbers with incomes below the MMS budget (or 50 per cent of the average) had risen to 40–42 million – 14–14.5 per cent of the population. The numbers with incomes below 60 per cent of the average rose from 42 to 67 million (16 per cent to 23 per cent of the population) over the decade. In these terms at least, the growth in poverty started well before the collapse of the Soviet Union in 1991.

The figures in Table 17.2 relate to the population of the USSR as a whole. It has not proved possible to locate estimates of the level of poverty by republic in 1980. But such figures have been estimated for 1989 and the results are given in Appendix Table 17A.1. The table reports two estimates of the regional distribution of poverty in the USSR. First, poverty is defined relative to 50 per cent of average per capita income for the USSR as a whole. Second, an estimate has been made of 50 per cent of per capita income in each republic. In the table, estimates are given of the distribution of poverty relative to this regionally specific poverty line.

In 1989, relative to the All-Union poverty line, some 14.6 per cent of the population lived in households with a per capita income of less than 81.4 roubles a month. Three-fifths of these were to be found in just three republics: Russia, the Ukraine, and Uzbekistan. Whereas 8 per cent of the population of Russia had incomes below the national poverty line, almost half of Uzbekistan was below this level. In fact, all the Central Asian republics had more than one-third of their population with per capita income below the notional poverty line; so did Azerbaijan. The position in Kazakhstan, Georgia, and Armenia also deserves mention: between one-sixth and one-fifth of the population in each of these republics appeared to have been poor.

The picture changes significantly when we consider poverty relative to republic-specific poverty lines. In terms of this standard, the head count of poverty drops from 42 million to 32 million and its geographical distribution changes too. Not surprisingly, poverty rises in those republics with per capita income above the national average; it falls in the poorer republics of Central Asia and the Transcaucasus.

Table 17.3 attempts to determine poverty changes in the FSU relative to a fixed standard. It is taken from a forthcoming study by Branko Milanovic at the World Bank. It uses a different approach to the definition of a poverty line, starting from the

Table 17.3 The evolution of poverty in the FSU: selected Republics, 1987/88–1992/93

Republic	Percentage 1987/88	Percentage 1992/93	Millions 1987/88	Millions 1992/93	Poverty gap, 1992/93 Percentage of GDP
Russia	2	31	3.0	46.2	2.4
Ukraine	2	12	1.0	6.3	0.7
Belarus	1	41	0.1	4.2	3.9
Kazakhstan	5	–	0.8	–	–
Uzbekistan	24	–	4.8	–	–
Latvia	1	21	0.03	0.5	1.4
Moldova	4	44	0.2	1.9	5.7
Lithuania	1	50	0.04	1.9	4.8
Kyrgyzstan	12	–	0.5	–	–
Turkmenistan	12	14	0.4	–	–
Estonia	1	40	0.02	0.6	3.7

Source: Milanovic forthcoming: Table 5.1.
Poverty line = $ppp120 a month per capita at 1990 prices.

proposition that the poverty line should be set at 4 international dollars per capita a day at 1990 prices. This is then converted into local currency at the purchasing power parity (PPP) exchange rate taken from the UN's international comparison project. Finally, the 1990 local currency poverty standard is inflated or deflated by the cost of living index to obtain the figure for other years. Thus, the table seeks to determine the incidence of poverty relative to a fixed poverty line, one that was intended to ensure a constant command over the volume of consumption goods that could be acquired both in time and in the different parts of the FSU.

Before looking at the available figures on the evolution of poverty in the FSU, it is worth making two points about the level of living implied by this standard. Milanovic observes that "The amount of $PPP4 per capita a day is a relatively high poverty line. It is four times higher than the World Bank line of absolute poverty" (Milanovic forthcoming: ch. 5, p. 11.). This minimum, it should be noted, was substantially less than the quasi-official poverty lines devised by Soviet authorities. As we have seen, in 1987/88 the MMS budget was set at some 78–84 roubles per capita a month; the $PPP4 a day standard was worth only 54 roubles a month. (On the other hand, the Milanovic standard was indexed to the price level and by 1992 or so the two standards had substantially converged).

There are three noteworthy features about the figures given in Table 17.3. First, only some of the successor states are listed, and the entries for some of these are incomplete. This is an indication that the data on which the table is based are incomplete – and unreliable. Nevertheless, the second feature is striking, and well-established: a universal and significant increase in poverty occurred between 1987/88 and 1992/93. Some of the increases have been enormous in percentage terms. In Latvia, the proportion of the population judged to be in poverty according to this standard increased twenty-fold, from 1 per cent to 21 per cent of the population; Belarus had a forty-fold increase! Third, Milanovic claims that, given the scale of poverty, the estimated poverty gap is very small. (That is, the incomes of the poor fall short of the poverty standard by a relatively small amount; the poor are bunched at or near the poverty line.) Since poverty is shallow, one can infer that "unlike in Latin America, the poor do not represent a distinct 'underclass'; their educational achievements seem reasonable and not too different from the rest of the population; their access to social services, ownership of consumer durables and apartments is also close." If output recovers and incomes rise in the reasonably near future, "large numbers of the current poor could be pulled up above the current poverty line" (Milanovic forthcoming: ch. 5, p. 17). For Russia at least, this claim has been disputed (McAuley, 1994: 24).

Poverty in Russia, 1991–1994

Table 17.4 provides estimates of the way in which poverty in Russia has evolved since the collapse of the Soviet Union – when

Table 17.4 The incidence of poverty: Russia, 1991–1994

Date		Poverty line (roubles/month)	Head-count ratio (%)	Poverty gap (% of GDP)
1991		190	11.4	–
1992	March	1,031	23.4	0.59
	June	1,639	23.1	1.13
	September	2,163	18.9	1.23
	December	4,282	15.7	1.85
1993	March	8,069	34.7	1.05
	June	16,527	24.7	1.43
	October	32,400	28.8	3.76
1994	April	66,536	10.7	–

Sources: rows 1–8 – Braithwaite 1994: Table 1); Row 9 *Sotsial'no-ekonomicheskoe polozhenie Rossii (ianvar'-aprel' 1994)* Moscow: Goskom RF po statistike, 1994: 68.

defined in terms of the new subsistence minimum. The table shows that in 1991, just before the collapse of the Soviet Union, the *prozhitochnyi* minimum was set at 190 roubles a month per capita. At this level, some 11.4 per cent of the population was judged to be poor. By March 1992, the head count ratio had more than doubled to 23.4 per cent. A year later, in March 1993, it had increased by a further 50 per cent or so to 34.7 per cent. According to official statistics, in April 1994, the poverty rate had fallen sharply and stood at only 10.7 per cent of the population. This improvement has been challenged. Surinov and Kolosnitsyn (from the Gaidar Institute) claim that in the summer of 1994 an estimated 23 per cent of the population had per capita incomes below the subsistence minimum (Surinov and Kolosnitsyn, 1994: 4). These figures should be compared with those given by Milanovic in Table 17.3. He suggests that, according to the $PPP4 in 1990 prices standard, the poverty rate in Russia in 1993 was 31 per cent; this is of the same order of magnitude as the estimates reported in Table 17.4.

Table 17.4 also reports estimates of the poverty gap. This refers to the extent to which the incomes of the poor fall short of the poverty line, and is an attempt to measure the intensity of poverty. The figures in the table express the aggregate poverty gap as a percentage of GDP. They show, not surprisingly, that the increase in poverty in 1991–2 resulted in an increase in the poverty gap. More interestingly, the gap continued to increase throughout 1992 – even though the head-count ratio fell in the second half of the year. This implies that poverty intensified: the incomes of the poor fell further below the poverty line.

Between the winter of 1992 and the spring of 1993, the headcount ratio more than doubled, but the poverty gap fell markedly. This means that, although a lot more people declined into poverty, the incomes of the poorest members of society were raised. They became less poor, as it were. This improvement was not maintained, however, and by the autumn of 1993, the poverty gap was higher than it had ever been. Data have not been located on what has happened to the intensity of poverty in the last year or so. The figures would probably show something of the same seasonal pattern; they would probably also show an overall decline in the gap, a fall in the head-count ratio, and a slowing in the rate of inflation. This should have allowed government anti-poverty policy measures time to improve the position of the poorest.

If there are significant seasonal variations in the measured poverty gap, this could help to explain the difference between the estimates given in Table 17.3 and Table 17.4. It could be that

Milanovic's estimate relates to a different month in the year. But it is doubtful that the full difference can be explained in this way. Also questionable is the inference that poverty in Russia is shallow. Figures on the share of total income received by different quintiles of the population (see Appendix Table 17A.2) show that the share of total income received by the bottom 20 per cent of the population fell from 11 per cent of the total in 1992 to 7 per cent in 1993; it was still only 8 per cent in 1994. Also, in the third quarter of 1992, some 11 per cent of the population (or almost one-third of the poor) had a per capita income that was less than 50 per cent of the subsistence minimum.

Poverty in Ukraine, 1990–94

The only source of data on the distribution of income in the Ukraine is the family budget survey, and the following information comes from this source. It is important to point out that this survey has been heavily criticized because its sample design under-represents the poor. (Atkinson and Micklewright, 1992; McAuley 1979). Taking the figures at face value, however, Table 17.5 shows that in 1990 some 11 per cent of the population lived in families with incomes below the (somewhat inflated) official poverty line of the new government; in 1991, this had fallen to less than 9 per cent. If we take the poverty line recommended by the World Bank, the incidence of poverty in 1990 was as little as 5.5 per cent; in 1991 this had fallen to 3.2 per cent. The collapse of the USSR resulted in an enormous increase in the level of poverty. According to the World Bank standard, it increased to 17 per cent of the population; according to the official poverty line almost 30 per cent of the population were in poverty. Since

Table 17.5 Poverty in the Ukraine, 1990–1992

	1990	1991	1992
Ukraine standard[a]			
Poverty line in current prices	100	188	2,846
Head count (%)	11.5	8.8	29.75
Poverty gap	2.3	1.3	6.86
World Bank standard[b]			
Poverty line in current prices	83.1	155.7	2,356.4
Head count (%)	5.5	3.2	16.88
Poverty gap	1.0	0.4	3.45

Sources: Kakwani (1994: 37).
Notes:
[a] 14,345 coupons in January 1993 prices.
[b] 11,862 coupons in January 1993 prices.

real wages fell sharply in 1993 and 1994, one must assume that the incidence of poverty has continued to increase.

Table 17.5 also contains estimates of the poverty gap in the Ukraine for the years 1990–92. They suggest that in 1992 this was substantially higher than the figure given by Milanovic. There is, however, some confusion over this: Milanovic is clear that the denominator in his estimate is GDP; Kakwani is not specific – and he may have used personal income. If so, then his estimates should perhaps be halved before being compared with those of Milanovic.

Poverty in Kyrgyzstan

As data in Appendix table 17A.1 show, before 1991 Kyrgyzstan was one of the poorer republics of the FSU. In 1989 over 38 per cent of the population lived in families whose per capita income was less than 50 per cent of the All-Union average. It is claimed that in 1992 some 35 per cent of the population were found to be poor – using the official family budget survey and the officially defined minimum consumption basket of goods (presumably the MMS budget). In May 1993, the proportion of the population in poverty according to this standard had risen to as much as 80 per cent. (Falkingham and Ackland 1994: 2).

As a result of these developments, the Kyrgyz government, together with the World Bank, undertook the development of a new poverty standard. This followed a methodology similar to that adopted by Russia in the calculation of its subsistence minimum. The team that undertook the work, led by same consultant (Barry Popkin), proposed two standards: the low-cost budget amounted to 659 som a year per capita (of which it was assumed that 522 som were spent on food), the high-cost budget was set at 1048 som a year per capita of which 830 som were to be spent on foodstuffs. Both of these budgets are priced in October 1993 prices. In what follows, use is made of the minimum pension as a notional poverty line. In October 1993, this was set at 32 som a month – or 384 som a year.

In addition to developing a new subsistence minimum for Kyrgyzstan, in 1993 the World Bank, in conjunction with the government of Kyrgyzstan carried out an independent household budget survey, which included a representative sample of 1,937 households (9,066 individuals). The following data are taken from this Kyrgyzstan multipurpose poverty survey (KMPS).

The survey showed that mean per capita income in Kygyzstan was 119 som a month. Mean expenditure was somewhat higher –

Table 17.6 Poverty in Kyrgyzstan, 1993

	Households		Individuals	
	Head-count ratio (%)	Poverty gap ratio (%)	Head-count ratio (%)	Poverty gap ratio (%)
Poverty standard:				
Income				
Low-cost	53.9	27.9	62.7	33.8
High-cost	71.5	41.3	77.7	47.6
Expenditure				
Low-cost	25.2	11.6	29.5	14.0
High-cost	39.7	19.5	45.4	22.7
Minimum pension:				
Income				
Per capita	33.7	16.2	41.7	19.9
Equivalent	23.1	10.6	27.5	12.1
Expenditure				
Per capita	13.6	6.4	16.4	7.8
Equivalent	9.5	4.2	11.0	4.9

Source: Falkingham and Ackland (1994: Tables 4, 5, 6a, and 6b).

189 som. When some allowance was made for the size and composition of households – using the OECD equivalence scale – mean income per equivalent adult was 157 som a month and expenditure per equivalent adult was as much as 251 som a month.

As the figures in Appendix Table 17A.3 show, the KMPS showed that both income and expenditure were very unequally distributed in Kyrgyzstan. Gini coefficients in the range 0.5–0.7 are rare, if not unheard of, among the industrialized states of Western Europe. But income was more unequal than expenditure. Further, per capita income and expenditure were more unequally distributed than equivalent income or expenditure.

Falkingham and Ackland draw attention to the low correlation between income and expenditure:

> Using the standard Pearson Correlation Coefficient on ungrouped data for both total household income and expenditure, we find that the association between the two indicators of welfare is surprisingly low, with a correlation coefficient of only 0.2.
>
> (Falkingham and Ackland 1994: 19)

Estimates of both the head-count ratio and the poverty gap using both high-cost and low-cost poverty standards and both income and expenditure are given in Table 17.6. They imply that between one-quarter and almost three-quarters of households in

Kyrgyzstan were poor. Because large families are more likely to be poor than small ones, the estimates of individual poverty are higher than those for households; they suggest that between almost one third and almost four-fifths of the population were poor.

Falkingham and Ackland suggest that expenditure was better observed than income, and that significant amounts of income were omitted, especially among the least well-off. For this reason, they believe that expenditure is a better guide than income to welfare in Kyrgyzstan. They also favour the high-cost subsistence minimum. They conclude, therefore, that some 45.4 per cent of individuals or 39.7 per cent of households were in poverty in October–November 1993.

In October 1993, the minimum pension in Kyrgyzstan was 32 som a month. Using this as a poverty line and comparing it with the distribution of both per capita and equivalent income, Falkingham and Ackland conclude that between one-tenth and one-third of households or one-tenth and two-fifths of individuals were living in poverty in Kyrgyzstan at the end of 1993. Their preferred estimate using this standard is 16.4 per cent.

Table 17.6 also gives estimates of the poverty gap ratio for each of the "head counts". It is not clear how the poverty gap is measured – the estimates are so high that it is unlikely to be GDP. Thus, these figures are not comparable with those given by Milanovic. They indicate that poverty is substantial and not "shallow".

Poverty in the Baltic Republics

Estonia

In 1992 and the first half of 1993, the Estonian government continued to use the MMS budget as the basis for its anti-poverty policy (Kutsar and Trumm 1993: 132). In September 1993, the government passed a decree establishing a poverty line of 280 EEK a month. The government also set out procedures for adjusting the poverty line in accordance with changes in the cost of living. This new Estonian poverty line is based on a physical subsistence minimum, very much along the lines used in Russia and Kyrgyzstan (Viies 1993: 14). Some academic researchers have also made use of a notional poverty line defined as 50 per cent of median income – or expenditure (Kutsar and Trumm 1993: 137).

According to the old MMS budget standard, some 20 per cent of the population was poor in August 1992, whereas in May of the same year the proportion had been as low as 7.5 per cent (Kutsar and Trumm, 1993: 137). A year later, the head-count ratio was still only 20 per cent – but this figure was relative to the government's new (and more stringent) poverty standard (Viies 1994: 19). Viies also reports that poverty was associated with large family size, incomplete families, and unemployment.

The formulation of anti-poverty policy in Estonia has been complicated by ethnic politics. Because Estonians believe that a disproportionate share of the poor are Russian, the government has been unwilling to establish and maintain a universal safety net (Kutsar and Trumm 1993: 132).

Latvia

In 1992 and 1993, the Latvian authorities continued to make use of the system that they had inherited from the USSR for the study of poverty and inequality. Only in November 1993 did the government specify an official poverty line. This was set at 22.3 LVL a month per capita. Families with incomes below this level, however, must satisfy additional criteria before they are entitled to state assistance (Cice 1994: 4). In 1993, some 75 per cent of persons had incomes that fell below the subsistence minimum – that is the old MMS budget corrected for changes in the cost of living (ibid.: 9).

The position of Russians in Latvia is perceived to be different from that in Estonia. Poverty is "spread mainly among Latvians . . . non-citizens who arrived illegally during the Soviet occupation [i.e. Russians] are mainly connected with private structures" (Cice 1994: 10). The groups who have taken advantage of new market opportunities are not poor.

Lithuania

Lithuania was the first Baltic republic to break away from the old Soviet methodology for the study of living standards, poverty, and inequality. The government adopted a new budget survey framework as early as March 1992 (Budreikaite 1994: 1). A year later, in 1993, it introduced a new method of defining the poverty line. This too followed the physical subsistence model favoured by the World Bank and adopted in Estonia, Russia, and Kyrgyzstan (among other successor states). As a result, in August 1993 the minimal living standard (MLS) was set at 54.5 Lits a month per capita (Budreikaite 1994: 11).

At this standard, poverty in Lithuania was less acute than in Estonia. In September 1993, some 14.5 per cent of the population had incomes below the MLS standard. Budrekaite believes that this figure understates the real incidence of poverty in Lithuania.

Explanations of poverty

The risk and incidence of poverty

In Russia in 1992, the incidence of extreme poverty was greatest among children between the ages of 7 and 15 and adults under the age of 30. These two groups accounted for half of all those with per capita incomes less than 50 per cent of the poverty line. On the other hand, the risk of extreme poverty among young adults was only modestly higher than in the population as a whole. On certain plausible assumptions, the probability that a randomly chosen young adult has an income of less than half the subsistence minimum is only 0.13; for a randomly chosen individual the probability is 0.11.

More generally, one can note that both the incidence and the risk of poverty among children are high: almost half of all children live in families with incomes below the subsistence minimum. They make up almost one-third of the poor. They also make up more than one-third of the extremely poor. But these figures need to be treated with caution: no allowance has been made for differences in the needs of persons of different ages – nor for economies of scale in consumption.

Women – of either working or pensionable age – are at no greater risk of being poor than the population as a whole; and they are half as likely to be extremely poor. The incidence of poverty among men of pensionable age is low partly because the risk is low in this social group and partly because men aged 60 and above make up only five per cent of the population (women of pensionable age account for 14 per cent).

One significant feature of the growth in poverty in Russia is the fact that a high proportion of the new poor are actually in employment. For example, the World Bank reported that in 1992 some 63 per cent of the heads of households adjudged to be poor were in employment (Russia 1993: 13). In 1993 the proportion was 66 per cent (Milanovic, 1994: 40). Milanovic shows that substantial numbers of employees descended into poverty because their earnings failed to "keep up with" inflation – and hence with the cost of the subsistence minimum. He shows that, between 1987 and 1990, average earnings were between four and five times the deflated value of the 1990 poverty line; by the beginning of 1993 they had declined to less than three times the poverty line (adjusted for changes in the cost of living). In

1992–3, the average pension was more or less equal to the poverty line. As a result, many families fell into poverty – even when both spouses were in employment. Milanovic shows that a somewhat similar situation developed in the Ukraine: by the beginning of 1993, average earnings were less than twice the poverty line (Milanovic 1994: 41).

Milanovic does not speculate on why earnings have followed the path that they have, but two observations can be made. First, before 1992, wage rates were determined centrally in both the Ukraine and Russia. In Russia, this process has been largely retained for the so-called budget sector. Pay scales here are determined bureaucratically and have been changed relatively infrequently; changes in earnings have tended to lag behind changes in the cost of living. Further, attempts to restore fiscal balance resulted in pressure to keep wages down in the state sector. In the so-called productive sphere, managers have enjoyed more autonomy over the determination of wages since the end of the 1980s. Here too, the financial constraints that have followed from the collapse in output have induced enterprises to restrain wage increases; this policy has been reinforced by the government's tax on excess wage increases. Take-home pay has also been affected by monetary chaos: enterprises have not always been able to pay their workers on time. Wages paid in arrears are not indexed – which can imply a substantial fall in real incomes when inflation is running at up to 20 per cent a month. The decline in real wages has meant that firms have been able to maintain employment at a higher level than would otherwise have been possible.

Inequality and the growth of poverty

This chapter has argued that the transition from the Soviet Union to independent countries has been accompanied by a decline in income and a growth in inequality and that these two processes have resulted in an increase in poverty. This section provides somewhat more detail.

Table 17A.2 reports changes in the distribution of income in Russia between 1992 and 1994. There was a sharp fall in the share of income accruing to the lowest quintile of the population, a significant fall in the share of the second quintile, little change in the shares of the third and fourth quintiles, and a significant increase in the share of the top quintile. In other words, the poor are poorer and the rich much richer. This is reflected in an increase in the Gini coefficient by almost a half – from 0.22 to 0.31.

Table 17.7 The growth in poverty: FSU, 1987–93 (millions)

	Decline in income	Growth in inequality	Demographic change	Total
Baltic states	1.3	0.9	0.0	2.2
Russia	8.5	18.9	0.9	28.3
Rest of FSU[a]	9.3	1.8	0.2	11.3
Total	19.1	21.6	1.1	41.8

Source: Milanovic (1994: 35).
Note:
[a] Excludes Central Asia and the Transcaucasus.

Three "causes" for an increase in poverty are offered in Table 17.7: income decline, inequality increase, and demographic change. The last exists because if population grows or contracts, other things being equal, some of that growth (contraction) will occur among the poor. So far as the parts of the FSU covered by the table are concerned, demographic factors have played only a minor role in the growth of poverty. Had Milanovic been able to extend his calculations to cover Central Asia, the picture might have been somewhat different.

Between 1987 and 1993, the number of persons in poverty in the FSU (excluding Central Asia and the Transcaucasus) increased by about 42 million. Two-thirds of this increase was in Russia. Since there were significant increases in poverty in some Central Asian states, this conclusion possibly overstates the importance of Russia in the growth of FSU poverty. The table also shows that the experience of Russia differs from that of the rest of the FSU. In Russia, more than twice as much of the increase in poverty could be attributed to increases in inequality as to the collapse in income; for the rest of the FSU the position was reversed. In the Baltic states, the decline in output was responsible for almost two-thirds of the increase in poverty; in the rest of the CIS it accounted for more than four-fifths of the total increase. At least for Russia, this analysis suggests that economic growth alone will not reverse this increase in poverty.

The determinants of poverty in Kyrgyzstan

Kyrgyzstan, one of the smaller republics of the FSU, is interesting for two reasons. First, it is the only Central Asian republic for which we have detailed and representative data. Second, it is the only republic for which we have analyses using western concepts and modern statistical techniques. However, the picture it reveals would probably be repeated in the rest of Central Asia and in much of the Transcaucasus.

The Kyrghyz Multipurpose Poverty Survey (KMPS) asked respondents a range of other questions that allow the exploring of the composition of the poor and the examination of hypotheses about the determinants of poverty. First, poverty in Kyrgyzstan is more prevalent in rural areas than in towns. The exact household figures are:

	Headcount	Poverty gap
Urban	28.7	11.5
Rural	48.1	25.5
All Kyrgyzstan	39.7	19.5

(Falkingham and Ackland 1994: 26)

Second, although Kyrgyz and Uzbek households were substantially poorer than Slav households, more than a quarter of the latter had expenditures that put them below the high-cost subsistence budget.

Conclusion

The problem of poverty and anti-poverty policy has become an issue of some political significance in all the successor states of the FSU. The old MMS budget inherited from the USSR, yields levels of poverty so high as to preclude meaningful relief. As a result, all governments have undertaken or commissioned research into the specification of a new, more modest subsistence minimum. Where such work has been completed, it has usually been done in conjunction with consultants provided by or through the World Bank. In Russia at least, there has been some independent locally organized study of poverty; similar work may exist in other successor states. However, much of this is based on dubious statistical sources and employs questionable methodologies.

Second, the economic crisis that has accompanied the transition to a market economy has resulted in a sharp fall in output – and hence in average income – in all republics. In most, this has been accompanied by an increase in inequality as some individuals reap windfall gains or losses and because some people have adapted more quickly to the opportunities afforded by the new economic environment. These two developments have resulted in a substantial increase in poverty in all of the successor states of the FSU.

Third, most of those groups that were at greatest risk of poverty in the Soviet Union remain at great risk in the successor states. These include children, especially those in large families, and women, particularly those who are heads of households. The elderly, if they live alone, are also quite likely to be poor. Since the collapse of the Soviet Union new groups of poor have emerged. There are the unemployed. There are also substantial numbers of employed workers whose wages are now too low to keep them and their families above the poverty line. These include many of those employed directly by the state – teachers, nurses, hospital orderlies, and so on; they also include unskilled and semi-skilled workers in manufacturing, many of whom are women. A more varied poverty population now exists in the FSU.

Appendix

Table 17A.1 The incidence of poverty: USSR and republics, 1989

	All-Union (poverty line = 81.4 roubles/month)			Republics		
	Head count			Republic-specific poverty line[a]	Head count	
Republic	% of republic	Million	% of USSR	(roubles/ month)	Million	% of USSR
Russia	11.5	7.8	27.4	90.7	17.6	54.2
Ukraine	5.0	9.6	11.9	79.1	4.3	13.2
Belarus	0.6	5.9	1.4	87.8	0.9	2.7
Uzbekistan[b]	9.9	49.4	23.6	48.2	[2.6]	–
Kazakhstan	3.3	20.0	7.9	73.1	2.4	7.4
Georgia	0.9	17.2	2.1	76.9	0.8	2.5
Azerbaijan	2.7	38.7	6.4	57.8	1.3	4.0
Lithuania	0.2	4.1	0.5	84.6	0.2	0.6
Moldova	0.7	16.4	1.7	72.8	0.5	1.5
Latvia	0.1	4.3	0.2	100.1	0.3	0.9
Kyrgyzstan	1.7	38.7	4.0	54.5	0.6	1.8
Tadjikistan	2.9	56.7	6.9	39.6	–	–
Armenia	0.6	19.2	1.4	69.7	0.4	1.2
Turkmenistan	1.5	40.8	3.5	54.0	0.5	1.5
Estonia	0.0	3.4	–	107.5	0.2	0.6
USSR	14.6	41.9	100.0	–	32.5	100.0

Source: calculated from Sotsial'noe (1991: 119).
[a] Republic-specific poverty line defined as 50 per cent of average per capita monthly total income, estimated from data on the distribution of income in the source.
[b] For Uzbekistan and Tadjikistan, the poverty line fell into the lowest (open) interval of the distribution; it was not possible to interpolate and estimate the incidence of poverty in these two republics.

Table 17A.2 The distribution of money income by population quintile: Russia, 1992–1994(%)

Money income received by:	1992	April 1993	1994
First (lowest) quintile	10.6	6.8	7.8
Second quintile	15.3	11.6	12.7
Third quintile	19.2	16.4	17.3
Fourth quintile	23.8	23.2	23.4
Fifth (upper) quintile	31.1	42.0	38.8
Total	100.0	100.0	100.0
Gini coefficient	0.217	0.353	0.311
Ratio of average incomes of first and tenth deciles	3.7	9.7	7.5

Source: *Sotsial'no-ekonomicheskoe polozhenie Rossii (ianvar'-aprel' 1994)* (Moscow: Goskom RF po statistike, 1994: 66).

Table 17A.3 The distribution of income and expenditure: Kyrgyzstan, 1993 (%)

	Per capita		Equivalent[a]	
Quintile	Income	Expenditure	Income	Expenditure
First	1.8	2.5	2.0	2.7
Second	4.8	6.9	5.1	7.2
Third	8.3	12.0	8.6	12.7
Fourth	14.4	20.4	14.7	20.8
Fifth	70.7	58.2	69.6	56.6
Total	100.0	100.0	100.0	100.0
Mean (sum per month)	119.1	189.4	157.0	251.2
Gini coefficient	0.678	0.548	0.665	0.531

Source: Falkingham and Ackland (1994: Tables 1 and 2).
Note:
[a] Calculated using the OECD equivalence scale: first adult = 1; additional adults = 0.7; children under 14 years of age = 0.5.

References

Atkinson, A. B. & J. Micklewright (1992) *Economic Transformation in Eastern Europe and the Distribution of Income*. Cambridge: Cambridge University Press.

Braithwaite, Jeanine (1994) "Old and new poor in Russia: Trends in poverty". Washington, DC: IMF, mimeo.

Budreikaite, Danute (1994) Personal income distribution in Lithuania". Vilnius: Institute of Economics, mimeo.

Cice, Ausma-Mare (1994) "Personal income distribution in Latvia". Riga: Institute of Economics, mimeo.

Falkingham, Jane and R. Ackland (1994) "A profile of poverty in Kyrgyzstan, October to November 1993". Paper prepared for the National Seminar on Poverty and Social Protection in the Kyrgyz Republic EDI, World Bank, Washington, DC.

Kakwani, N. (1994) *Income Inequality, Welfare and Poverty in Ukraine*. Washington, DC: World Bank: Research Paper No. 7, Transition Economics Division, Policy Research Division, July.

Kendall, Anne, B. Mills, J. Munoz, and D. Sahn (1993) "Data needs for means testing social benefits in Ukraine". Washington, DC: mimeo, World Bank, August.

Kutsar, D. and A. Trumm (1993) "Poverty among households in Estonia". *Scandinavian Journal of Social Welfare*, No. 2.

McAuley, A. (1979) *Economic Welfare in the Soviet Union: Poverty, Living Standards and Inequality*. Madison: Wisconsin University Press.

McAuley, A. [Makoli, A.] 1991. "Bednost' i ee izmerenie", *Sotsialisticheskii trud*, No. 7.

────── (1994) *Social Welfare in Transition: What Happened in Russia*. Washington DC: World Bank. Research Paper No. 6, Transition Economics Division, Policy Research Division, January 1994.

Milanovic, B. (forthcoming) "Income, inequality and poverty during the transition". Washington, DC: World Bank.

Popkin, B. (1994) "A subsistence income level for Kyrgyzstan". Paper prepared for the National Seminar on Poverty and Social Protection in the Kyrgyz Republic EDI, World Bank, Washington, DC.

Popkin, B., M. Mozhina, and A. Baturin (1994) "Metody obosnovania prozhitochnogo minimuma v Rossiiskoi Federatsii", in *Bednost': vzgliad uchenykh na problemu Demografiia i sotsiologiia vypusk* 10. Moscow: RAN-ISEPN.

Rimashevskaia, N. M. and A. A. Rimashevskii (1991) *Ravenstvo ili spravedlivost'*. Moscow: Finansy i statistika.

Sotsial'noe razvitie SSSR, 1989. Moscow: Finansy i statistika.

Surinov, A. and I. Kolosnitsyn (1994) "Social inequality and poverty in Russia". Moscow: mimeo.

Viies, Mare (1994) "Personal income distribution in Estonia". Tallin, Estonia: Institute of Economics, mimeo.

Chapter 18

Former Czechoslovakia, Hungary, and former Yugoslavia: Poverty in Transitional Economies

Mojca Novak

In past decades the "Iron Curtain" was blamed for dividing Europe into the First and Second World. Both the similarities between Eastern Europe's social policy programmes and those in the West (Atkinson and Micklewright 1992) and assumptions about convergent development (Andorka and Toth 1992; Deacon 1992) have shown this "ideological wall" to be porous. Recently, various initiatives indicate that poverty policy in Eastern Europe needs to be renewed, and the experiences of Western Europe might be seen as models. Any indiscriminate imitation, however, in terms of either poverty-alleviating programmes or methods of adjustment to the poverty standard, would be undesirable. Western poverty approaches may or may not be relevant in Eastern Europe, but the choice of method is in itself a matter of judgement, and the differences must be regarded as an expression of the preferences in these countries.

There may be particular features of pre-reform Eastern Europe that require the use of a scale quite different from that found in the West (Atkinson and Micklewright 1992). This is a very important reason for keeping in mind the fact that Eastern Europe will preserve its "late-comer" features and poor modernizing capacities in this field for the foreseeable future as well. Following the pace of dissemination, the West's standards and programmes will mark related restructuring in the East. The warnings against indiscriminate imitation, frequently experienced in the Second World in the past, should force political authorities and administrators in the East to apply tested models and strategies cautiously, taking into account specific economic circumstances and respecting historical tradition. Hence, the virtual "battlefield" on which the two models, liberal and continental–corporatist, will "fight" for domination will apparently be not in Western Europe but in Eastern Europe (Deacon 1992), which is desperately looking for a new social policy paradigm and trying to attain developed world standards.

Eastern Central Europe in common analytical perspective

According to the World Bank (1990), the countries under consideration in this chapter fit into the category of middle-income countries (GNP per capita of US$ 545–6,000). As regards their indebted situation, they belong either to "severely indebted middle-income" countries (Hungary) or to "highly indebted middle-income" countries (Yugoslavia – at the end of the 1980s); Czechoslovakia has not yet reported the relevant information. The same source reports a slight increase in economic performance in the same period: real GDP growth was 1.4 per cent, and real GDP growth per capita was only 0.8 per cent compared with 4.8 per cent in the period 1965–73. At the end of the 1980s the incidence of poverty for the whole region was approximately 7.8 per cent, and the prospects for the year 2000 were slightly worse – 7.9 per cent.

Decreased economic performance is reflected domestically in an increase in unemployment and an enormous increase in the cost of living owing to price liberalization, which triggered a decline in living standards of approximately 20 per cent (Deacon 1992; 169). The deterioration of the economy and the accompanying deterioration in living standards for the majority of citizens present a specific "challenge" to the social policy sector, which is responding to the emerging problems. The social policy established and implemented by communist regimes was frequently accused of being too comprehensive, promising to care for (privileged categories of) residents "from cradle to grave". Rarely were these promised benefits delivered. Recently, this sector has had to confront dual "social obligations". On the one hand, Eastern Europe must modernize its programmes and strategies, particularly if it wants to achieve Western Europe's standards and become part of the European Union. At the same time, the economic decline and transformation to a market economy are pushing more people onto welfare with the expectation that the state should solve their problems.

Externally, the countries of Eastern Europe present an enormous threat to the West in terms of migration. The turmoil in this region caused huge migration flows into the countries of Western Europe, which lack effective political programmes to meet the emerging problems related to refugees, asylum-seekers, and impoverished immigrants. As usual, the economic migration from East to West is intensified by severe impoverishment owing to the transformation to market economies, ethnic conflicts, and political liberalization (Ronge 1991).

The external impacts of Eastern Europe's current problems attract Western investigators in particular, while the internal problems are responded to by both domestic and foreign social scientists. The latter's findings on poverty measurement and related poverty-alleviation policy will be taken into account next. Comparative studies concerning Hungary, (the former) Czechoslovakia, and (the former) Yugoslavia will be presented. Studies investigating poverty in each individual country will then be considered separately.

Measurement of poverty in temporal perspective

Milanovic's work (1991) and Atkinson and Micklewright's joint effort (1992) made a substantial contribution to income distribution analyses and poverty measurement in an East European comparative perspective. Because the authors highlighted different points in poverty investigation it makes sense to consider their works separately.

Atkinson and Micklewright (1992) used absolute and relative definitions of poverty lines backed up by the subsistence concept of poverty in observing the incidence of poverty in Eastern Europe. Their objective was to prove that the empirically non-verified application of any definition is misleading and professionally incorrect. The absolute is operationalized by the monetary value of a commodity basket, while the relative is operationalized by average income. Taking into account this analytical perspective, the general hypothesis can be summarized as follows: the definition and measurement of poverty in Eastern Europe have distinctive features that differ from those of Western Europe.

The theoretical framework is shaped by analysing the incidence of poverty and related retrospective observation. Several poverty investigators illustrated that poverty was, for many years, a sensitive issue for the communist governments of pre-reform Eastern Europe. This is true even in countries where substantial information was published on inequality and household incomes. In the 1960s poverty surveys were conducted in Hungary (e.g. by Kemeny and Fekete) and Czechoslovakia (e.g. by Hirsl and Kucerak) and poverty rates were estimated, but the results remained confidential. In the 1980s, renewed official interest in poverty line computations and in the estimation of the rate and composition of poverty gave the impetus to new poverty investigations. Apart from this, regularly published data invite comparisons of post-socialist Eastern Europe with the West, and pose the question of which of the concepts and related definitions in use in the West is best for the East.

The major data source used in investigating the subject at hand is empirical evidence on poverty line calculations in comparative retrospective. Atkinson and Micklewright (1992) observed that poverty lines in Eastern Europe (including Poland and the USSR) have a number of similarities: like the US official poverty line, they are quite independent of social security benefits and they are based on a basket of goods; despite the standard of living orientation, the scales are applied to total incomes rather than to total expenditures; the unit of analysis is the household.

Analysis of poverty lines in pre-reform Czechoslovakia indicates that the calculations of subsistence and social minima for different household types were made in the mid-1960s by Hirsl and Kucerak. At that time, 1967 prices were used to determine the minimum standard for a single pensioner. This was based on estimations of subsistence food consumption determined by nutritional experts, in addition to clothing and footwear requirements based on actual expenditure by pensioner households. Also included were other items ascertained directly or taken from observed budgets. The subsistence minimum was set at 75 per cent of the social minima.

The social minimum calculation in Hungary was based on a commodity basket. The first official calculations were made in 1968, and since 1984 the Central Statistical Office has been making regular calculations using the data from the budget survey. The calculation began by establishing a minimum-cost food basket for a number of different types of household; for example, in 1986 the minimum subsistence level for a single pensioner represented 46 per cent of median earnings, and the social minimum was 53 per cent.

In contrast to Hungary, the Czech basket covers all goods, rather than being a multiple of food spending. But in both countries the minimum is arrived at by a more sophisticated version of the food share method used in the USA, which is based on regressions of food spending on income. Apart from this, both countries differ from Western countries in certain other features. The equivalence scales that have been applied in Eastern Europe differ in that they assign higher allowances to active than to inactive workers and they give greater weight to the needs of larger households with children. Since the 1980s the poverty line in Hungary has been indexed to prices, while in Czechoslovakia the indexation is in line with changes in average income. Hungary's price index in the pre-reform period is considered to have been among the best in Eastern Europe – although real wages decreased, the subsistence minimum slightly increased during the 1980s.

Atkinson and Micklewright concluded that the method of adjustment to the poverty standard has particular relevance at a time of economic transition. A poverty line indexed to official prices may overstate the growth in poverty between the pre- and post-reform periods. This may be an argument for indexing by incomes rather than prices. Such a procedure means that any reduction in real incomes during the transition process is transmitted to the poorest section of the population. A government might well want to protect this segment from a general decline in average real incomes. This may point to the need for fresh calculations of the social minima, following the long-established tradition in Eastern Europe.

Like Atkinson and Micklewright, Milanovic (1991) also looks back to the end of the 1970s and points out the significant features of economic performance in Eastern Europe. In observing the rates and composition of poverty in the previous decade he applied a relative definition of the poverty line backed up by the subsistence idea of poverty and welfare as a framing concept. The definition is operationalized by disposable household income. Of the countries concerned, Hungary and Yugoslavia fitted within the developed framework.

Two hypotheses underscore the main analytical scope. First, the slowdown of growth and the reversal in the transfer of resources were so dramatic in East European countries that they were reflected at the household level in an almost uniform decline in real income and an increase in poverty. Second, the low share of capital income and the absence of increased unemployment in socialist economies suggest that the increase in poverty resulting from recession would be less than in a capitalist economy.

The theoretical framework is shaped through hindsight. In the 1980s, the countries in Eastern Europe have experienced declining growth rates, debt problems, reductions in economic productivity, and a widening technological gap compared with the West. Little is known about how the crisis has affected the standard of living or about its impact on poverty. During the 1980s Hungary and Yugoslavia experienced stagnation and crisis, but the recession was not accompanied by increased unemployment. In Hungary, unemployment was actually non-existent, while in Yugoslavia the rate remained unchanged during the entire decade. Salary expenditures were lowered by cuts to all wages, but real per capita income for workers and farmers practically stagnated.

Inter-country comparisons of income inequality and poverty are fraught with difficulties. It can be argued that comparisons are more reasonable when the level of development, the social system, and the macroeconomic performance of the countries are similar. A similar data source, i.e. household surveys, also helps. Hungary and Yugoslavia fit these criteria, though the main results reveal significantly different poverty rates.

In 1978, the Yugoslav poverty rate was 17 per cent and it stabilized at 25 per cent in the mid-1980s. The poverty rate for the non-agricultural sector (workers and pensioners) doubled, but it remained lower than the poverty rate for mixed households and farmers. The average per capita income for non-agricultural households remained higher than that of the other two groups (farmers, mixed). The poverty rate for farmers declined sharply from 42 per cent in 1978 to 27 per cent in 1983, but increased to 45 per cent in 1986 and 1987. Apart from this, the data indicate that urban poverty doubled, from 24 per cent to 47 per cent whereas rural poverty decreased from 76 per cent to 53 per cent.

Hungary did not experience a similar deterioration in the real incomes of households. The poverty rate for workers was 17–18 per cent in the mid-1980s, while the poverty rates for pensioners and farmers decreased from 14 per cent in 1985 to 11 per cent in 1987. At the end of the 1980s, just before the onset of the post-socialist upheavals and turmoil, a crumbling economy and significantly high poverty rates were common features of Hungary and Yugoslavia.

Poverty-related social policy

The observation about an overly lax and comprehensive social policy in Eastern Europe, monopolized by the state, frequently overshadows any debate on its present features and future prospects. The confrontation between civil initiatives and the state monopoly in this area normally receives less attention in related concepts. In this respect Marklund (1993) expresses certain expectations about civil society's initiatives, which should give an impetus to the social welfare reforms. Furthermore, his hypothesis implies the following: learned helplessness or anomie was created by strong state control over all aspects of life and these structures should be replaced by small-scale institutions, the family, and individual responsibility.

In shaping the theoretical framework, it is of substantial help to reconsider social policy in terms of Esping-Andersen's three models of welfare. Formally, the socialist European countries can be classified as institutional redistributive systems. This is based on the fact that the state played a dominant role in all aspects of social policy, which was an integrated part of economic policies at both national and enterprise levels. Apart from findings referred to by various social policy researchers in Eastern Europe, no other specific data source was used in applying the concept to the available information. The analytical results support conclusions that do not contradict the initial assumptions, that is, that in both Czechoslovakia and Hungary the social policy model was developed well before the Second World War and was based on the German corporatist model. After the war, access to welfare benefits was not universal: farmers and the self-employed were excluded. Residual forms of welfare in the sense of private charity and church involvement were weak. As far as social actors are concerned, current dominant social forces are very reluctant to promote cooperation between the state and social movements. The most influential views about civil society are opposed to all forms of social policy reform.

Atkinson and Micklewright's work (1992) again presents a substantial contribution to the unveiling of specific features of poverty-related social policy in a temporal and comparative perspective. The subsistence concept of poverty underlies the investigation, but the definition of the poverty line varies according to country: in Czechoslovakia the relative definition is used, whereas in Hungary the absolute definition is utilized. Furthermore, although both definitions are operationalized by subsistence and a social minimum, this distinction is derived from the indexation. In Czechoslovakia, the minimum was indexed to average income, while in Hungary it was indexed to prices.

Despite these differences, a common hypothesis is advanced: in the process of economic transition existing schemes should be scaled-down with the objective of balancing the state's budget and improving the incentives to work.

The theoretical framework concerns the safety-net features before the beginning of the transition period when, it is commonly held, the state in pre-reform Eastern Europe provided an all-embracing comprehensive system of cash benefits. Empirical evidence on safety-nets in comparative perspective shows that the social security system (all cash transfers) was comparable to those in developed Western countries. Although the state "cradle to grave" policy of support had abolished poverty, the social security system was inadequate in preventing subsistence poverty. In simple terms, pre-reform Eastern Europe can be seen as providing a safety-net through a combination of full employment, generous family benefits, and social insurance linked to employment.

Hungary

The changing structure of prosperity

Professional concern with and investigation of poverty, particularly in the countries of Eastern Europe, usually lack a sociological perspective in that classical topics such as the relation between social and economic change and between social stratification and mobility are not addressed. Owing to Ferge's (1987) early work on poverty and its dynamics, it was not ignored in poverty studies in Hungary. Moreover, although the evolutionary aspect has been dropped, Szanto and Toka (1990) try to comprehend the recent structure of individual well-being using the framework of "classical" conceptualism.

Ferge (1987: 168–169) actually analysed the dynamics of the reproduction of social relations. Of specific concern is the parental generation's transfer of wealth to its children. Multiple deprivation caused by a combination of poor schooling, bad jobs, low incomes, and bad housing is the key concept shaping the analytical background. The central hypothesis concerns the intended or unintended transmission of social advantages and disadvantages, which is a general tendency in all hierarchically structured societies.

The related theoretical framework deals with social change and economic growth after the Second World War, coupled with full employment and a rapidly expanding social policy, which helped to eliminate the massive absolute poverty that had prevailed in prewar Hungary. These events created the belief that constant economic growth and large-scale and multi-step mobility were inevitable concomitants of socialist development, and that all the problems connected with social inequalities, unequal opportunities, poverty, marginality, and the like could be solved. However, social stratification studies showed convincingly that many forms of inequality persisted, although usually on a much reduced scale, and that additional inequalities were constantly being generated by various new mechanisms.

The data used were collected in 1979 by random sampling of 500 families from the micro-census, mostly from the central cohort (born between 1928 and 1934). The major results lead to the conclusion that early poverty made social mobility difficult, though not impossible; its main impact was in hindering multi-step social mobility. Great childhood poverty did not affect shorter upward moves or the opportunities open to the offspring of unskilled workers or farmhands to become skilled or lower white-collar workers. In contrast, the offspring of the prewar, better-off strata, who assessed their childhood as well-to-do, said that they had started their adult life in unsatisfactory circumstances. Only a feeling of relative deprivation can explain these ratios, because it is almost certain that, objectively, unskilled workers or farmhands fared far worse than the majority of the above group, even in that period.

A few decades later, the impact of the introduction of the socialist "equalizing" of Hungarian society was evident. It attracted Szanto and Toka's scientific knowledge in terms of stating the following hypothesis: everybody had an equal share of the goods (Szanto and Toka 1990).

The living standard as a key concept was operationalized by income and assets as central variables. There was no theoretical framework, and the longitudinal data were collected by random sampling of the adult population. The major findings suggest that the role of demographic factors in poverty decreased while that of labour market factors increased. In general, Hungary in the 1980s was closer, in terms of the distribution of material assets, to the type of society characterized by almost equal distribution than to one featuring extreme inequality. The "equalized" income distribution is also revealed by Andorka and Toth (1992) and is supposed to be due to transferred cash benefits. They found the distribution curve to be as flat as income distribution in the observed capitalist countries, for instance Scandinavian countries.

Poverty line calculations

Among researchers of East European poverty, Hungarian social scientists seem to be the most concerned with studying its historical roots. Frequently, they focus on the development of both official and academic attitudes to poverty. Moreover, many studies on the present state of affairs are implicitly backed up by a historical perspective. In this respect, the work of Salamin (1992) and Andorka and Toth (1992) is notable in that it combines dynamics with the calculation of the structure of poverty lines.

The main topic under investigation, i.e. the development of official poverty line calculations, determines the concept to be used. The absolute poverty line operationalized by "minimum of socially accepted needs" underlies the studies of both Salamin (1992) and Andorka and Toth (1992), whose basic conceptual framework is the subsistence view of welfare. The hypotheses put forward do not differ very much and they can be outlined as follows: the social minimum was considered to be an income that adequately meets conventionally accepted basic needs; it was the role of cash benefits to diminish pauperization and decrease inequality.

The major concern of researchers of poverty line calculation was its development during recent decades and it seems this venture consumed their interest, with the result that the theoretical framework lacks comparable consideration. The data come from historiographical evidence on poverty line calculation (Salamin 1992). The historical perspective marks results, which lead to the following conclusions. Calculation of a poverty line began in Hungary in the 1920s. Between 1923 and 1939, trade unions calculated and published weekly poverty reports based upon a worker family of five. In 1955–6 the Central Council of Hungarian Trade Unions estimated poverty using an empirical method based on two types of families (families of three and four). Many people debated the necessity of such calculations under socialist conditions, and the series was subsequently dropped. Other poverty calculations were carried out by the Hungarian Central Statistical Office (CSO) in 1968. During the course of this work, norms were worked out for all products and services. More recently, poverty calculations have been indexed to prices and published regularly, and clearly have an important orientational role in the field of social policy.

Since Eastern Europe's "opening", there has been an explosion of poverty line calculations and poverty rate and composition estimations, which have captured the interest of researchers who refer to the household and/or income survey data (e.g. Andorka and Speder 1993; Szalai 1990, 1992; Toth and Foerster 1994). In these studies, only the subsistence poverty concept is employed, but the poverty line is defined in both absolute and relative terms, and, as usual, operationalized either by socially accepted needs or by disposable household income. The hypotheses are more frequently implicit than explicit; nevertheless, some common assumptions can be outlined as follows:

- poverty in Hungary is a stable and enduring phenomenon;
- in the 1980s there tended to be low levels of poverty among the elderly and high levels of poverty amongst people of working age and in large families;
- the analytical results are influenced by the common use of a per capita concept.

The theoretical framework is frequently lacking, although the subject under investigation is considered in temporal perspective in terms of the development of poverty line calculations (Andorka and Speder 1993; Szalai 1990, 1992) and the data source is the same, i.e. household and/or income surveys, which are conducted regularly by the Central Statistical Office. The major findings lead to the following conclusions. Between 1977 and 1987, the number of people living below the poverty line remained within the same range – between 10 and 17 per cent. The young, families with children, and less educated sectors of society were most vulnerable to poverty. A significant change in the social composition of the poor was also discerned: there was a sharp increase in poverty among urban households with an active earner and in the proportion of children living below the poverty line. This structural distribution of poverty was partly the product of a long-term economic and social crisis and partly the result of a whole set of changes launched in the present time (Szalai 1990).

The main conclusion, therefore, is that income and poverty estimates in Hungary are extremely sensitive to the context chosen (subsistence minimum or economic distance approach) and the method of calculation (per capita or equivalence scale). The sole use of per capita income does not seem to provide sufficiently solid estimates, because it introduces a serious bias into some poverty estimates, for example the overestimation of large households (Toth and Foerster 1994).

Specific poverty aspects

The Hungarian poverty studies differ in many aspects from those from the other countries under consideration. Apart from a frequently implicit temporal perspective, specific features, in particular child poverty, have also attracted considerable research interest (see Szalai 1993). Though not explicit, the poverty concept can be described as the subsistence one using the absolute definition of the poverty line, particularly as the related social policy is considered in the perspective of socialism. An implicit theoretical framework is supported by information on the socioeconomic development of the previous five decades. In contrast to the implied analytical framework, the explicit hypothesis is that child poverty is not transitory in character and is not caused by recent economic factors, but is strongly connected to social origins.

Two data sources are used: statistics from the Statistical Yearbook and the household and income surveys. The major finding of the existence and rapid expansion of child poverty is all the more shocking for Hungarian society, because the prosperous years of the late 1960s and the 1970s inculcated the general belief that poverty would be eradicated. The chronic economic crisis of the 1980s worked to the detriment of the poorer groups, producing stagnation or even a downturn in their standards of living. The infant mortality rate shows that significant improvements were accompanied by sharper inequalities over time. The lower the education of mothers, the higher the infant mortality rate in general, which is assumed to be due exclusively to increasing inequality of access to high-quality services.

Czechoslovakia

As in Hungary, poverty line calculations in Czechoslovakia were initiated in the 1960s, but remained unpublished for reasons of official secrecy. The political authorities declared poverty dead. At the beginning of the 1980s, however, poverty line calculations and poverty-related social policy began to attract the interest of both researchers and government administrators.

Various poverty line calculations

Three studies are particularly significant in providing information about the state of analyses of poverty (Hirsl and Dlouhy 1992; Van Praag et al. 1992; Vecernik 1993). In these studies, the authors apply distinct contextual frameworks that make the results comparable to similar Western approaches.

The concepts of poverty in use explicitly follow recent approaches in Europe by distinguishing between objective and subjective poverty, and between absolute and relative poverty. Both objective and absolute poverty are operationalized by the cost of a commodity basket, simply called the "Orchansky" index. The other two definitions are operationalized, respectively, by the empirical relationship between expenditure on foodstuffs and income (relative poverty), and by individual perceptions (subjective poverty). Despite the contextual variations, apart from subjective approach none of the other definitions exceeds the underlying subsistence view of poverty.

Vecernik's (1993) hypothesis is based on the changes in economic life and material well-being since the "marketization" of the Czechoslovak economy. It can be stated as follows: the threat of poverty emerges as a result of the economics of inequality and security. As a development of Hirsl's relative poverty approach and the earlier "secret" computations of poverty lines, Vecernik built his theoretical framework by reconsidering this "historical" background.

Vecernik follows Hirsl's poverty research legacy by computing family budget survey data and micro-census data for 1958–88, as well as data from the regular sociological survey "Economic Expectations and Attitudes" sociological survey (1990, 1993). Any discussion of the major findings should undoubtedly take as its point of departure the marketization of the Czechoslovak economy and the related liberalization of prices, which enormously increased the cost of living and substantially decreased a "line of social tolerance" (Hirsl and Dlouhy 1992). Surprisingly, a significant increase in personal and household incomes was also recorded. This was thought to be attributable mostly to social benefits (pensions and family allowances).

However, poverty line computations applying different poverty line standards reveal similar results elsewhere: official poverty estimates are slightly lower than the European Community poverty estimates – 2–3 per cent versus 4.2 per cent (Vecernik 1993: 8–9). Unlike those in the official poverty category, the subjectively poor are better economically situated and better educated. They tend to be families with younger and older household heads; with one child or none; and single pensioners.

Van Praag et al.'s (1992) testing of various poverty lines based upon Czechoslovak empirical evidence starts from two assumptions:

- poverty is a feeling of lack of well-being and any statement about it requires at least the possibility of comparing interpersonal utility;
- household income is the yardstick for poverty measurement.

The theoretical framework is shaped by discussing variousy monetary poverty line definitions: the Beckerman line; the Centre of Social Policy poverty line; the subjective poverty line, applying the "minimum income question"; the Leyden poverty line, applying the "income evaluation question"; the official poverty line, etc. The Economic Expectations and Attitudes Survey was used to help determine which definition was most compatible with the empirical evidence. Ten criteria serve as test items: the information value of the poverty line, income distribution (in)stability, population mixing, internal consistency, flexibility, robustness, systematic error, data collection costs, actuality, and intuitive plausibility (Van Praag et al. 1992: 11–13).

Regarding the empirical evidence on poverty available in Czechoslovakia and the outlined conceptual framework, the results suggest that the best choices would be the official poverty line and the Leyden poverty line (based on a subjective definition of poverty). In particular, the subjective poverty line is much more informative, because it is neither wholly relative nor wholly absolute and it is more robust to changes in income distribution and/or compared with other poverty lines. Apart from this, it was discovered that there are no technical difficulties in applying subjective attitude questions regarding income or well-being.

The historical perspective approach to social security programmes in transition

Two authors (Castle-Kanerova 1992; Potucek 1993) have attempted to reassess the future tasks of social security in shielding the residents of Czechoslovakia from the poverty risks experienced in the past. They say that the new authorities and governmental bodies should begin their social security "renovation" activities by revising what has been achieved in the past. Therefore they list arguments to support the "historical" approach in shaping the subject under (re)consideration and establishing (new) programmes to achieve better living standards and quality of life. In this regard, they do not follow any specific concept of poverty or related theoretical framework. Social security is primarily viewed as a sector of the overall social policy system in transition. The data sources mainly concern social policy and social security documents in temporal perspective; and flow-chart analysis is the major method applied.

Hypotheses are put forward implicitly, but the main assumptions are as follows:

- the idea of social justice is an evolutionary product of two liberal periods, the 1920s and the 1960s (Castle-Kanerova 1992);

- political transition is mirrored in the reconstruction of the social security programme (Potucek 1993).

The major results comprise the most significant features of the development of the social security scheme in Czechoslovakia since the First World War. In 1924 the industrial workers' insurance scheme was based on joint contributions, equally divided between employer and employee. It was founded on the principle of an equivalence between wages and expenditure, which did not constitute a firm foundation in times of economic crisis. It was a compromise between the bourgeois and the reformist coalition and it covered the basic risks, such as old age, invalidity, widowhood, orphanage, ill health, and injury (Castle-Kanerova 1992). Moreover, before the Second World War the Czechoslovak social security system was relatively advanced. It was based on the Bismarckian tradition of social insurance (Potucek 1993).

What distinguished the 1970s from the 1960s in social policy was the shift in the income/price relationship. Living standards in the 1950s and 1960s were maintained through a slow growth in wages accompanied by a slow fall in prices. This form of social economic policy was replaced in the 1970s by a model more common to dynamic industrialized societies where fast growth in wages is followed by rapid price increases. This sparked a greater emphasis on social welfare for a wider network of citizens, particularly those with lower earnings. Castle-Kanerova (1992) concluded that the benefit system quite clearly could not cope with the increasing poverty, particularly among the elderly. Social justice and social security emerge as the key concepts of the Czechoslovak social policy at is undergoes important changes. The same concepts were used before by Beveridge, Titmuss and the Czechoslovak social democrats of the 1920s and 1940s, as well as by more ideologically inclined orthodox Marxist–Leninists. In Castle-Kanerova's (1992) view, Eastern Europe in the next decade will remain a test case for the conceptualization of the role of social policy in the broadest sense. But such optimism may be ill founded should certain performance limitations hold sway, such as:

- heavy demands on the state budget owing to increasing unemployment and declines in living standards;
- restrictions on programmes based on insurance principles; and
- inadequately educated and unmotivated staff in social work institutions (Potucek 1993).

Yugoslavia

Apart from Milanovic's poverty studies, almost no other similar analysis has been undertaken of Yugoslav poverty vis-à-vis Eastern Europe. The references below indicate that investigations have most frequently been conducted on the regional level. Moreover, even the "intra-Yugoslav" comparative perspective is lacking.

Reassessment of the methodology of estimating subsistence and social minima in Slovenia

The methodology of estimating the cost of living as proposed by Sumi (1986) has been applied to Slovenia since the beginning of the 1980s. It has undergone a few revisions, but in the late 1980s the commodity basket consisted of 270 items, and subsistence and social minima were computed for categories of individuals depending upon their age and family composition. The monetary value of different commodity baskets is currently adjusted to the prices of goods and services (Novak 1993).

In considering the methodology of estimating the cost of living, both Sumi (1986) and Stanovnik (1991) applied, though more implicitly than explicitly, the subsistence concept of poverty. The absolute poverty line is operationalized by basic needs, which are reflected in the commodity basket items. Apart from Novak (1993), who reconsidered the implications of subsistence and social minima in terms of poverty-alleviating policy in Western Europe, there is no theoretical framework. In contrast to this, a common hypothesis is put forward very clearly, especially by Sumi (1986) and Stanovnik (1991). Both assumed that dietary patterns and the commodity basket underwent a substantial change during the 1980s, and, therefore, that the methodology of estimating the cost of living should reflect this shift. Novak extended this methodology debate further by assuming that any decision on the methodology of estimating the cost of living is purely a political decision. The household survey and related political documents on poverty policy are the major data source for testing the above hypotheses.

The opposing emphases of the researchers affect their conclusions. Sumi (1986) advocated a methodology based on a reassessment of his basic premise, that is, that the subsistence and social minima should reflect the expenditure of the lowest income decile. Stanovnik contended that the established official method of estimating the cost of living was too lax. Moreover, the composition and quantity of items in the commodity basket should reflect actual consumption patterns and different household types. Novak's analytical findings undermine the simplicity and transparency of the methodology debate, revealing that the problem is far from being just a disagreement about methodology. If the poverty-alleviating programmes were to incorporate Stanovnik's suggestion about applying dietary patterns as a basic premise in estimating subsistence and social minima, then transfer entitlements would be considerably reduced. According to Stanovnik's estimation method, which has already been incorporated into new legislation, social benefits should provide only the subsistence minimum, in contrast to the previous benefits, which provided the social minimum.

Surveys of well-being

At the beginning of the 1990s, a very extensive level-of-living survey was conducted by random sampling throughout Yugoslavia, but only a few results are available (Lay 1991 for Croatia, and Novak 1994 for Slovenia). In both studies, a similar conceptual framework was applied. This framework does not include poverty and impoverishment specifically, but uses the concept of low individual well-being as reflected in living conditions. Furthermore, the hypotheses proposed start from a similar assumption: individual well-being and prosperity reflect social class characteristics.

The theoretical frameworks differ for the studies under consideration. Lay's conceptual framework echoes Maslow's basic needs concept, this time operationalized by material needs (to have), social needs (to love), and emotional needs (to be). Furthermore, four clusters related to these basic needs (well-being, security, freedom, and self-fulfilment) were constructed, but only well-being was subjected to statistical analysis. The Scandinavian approach to living conditions, particularly Ringen's suggestion of a "third stage in the measurement of poverty", is evident in Novak's conceptual framework. Moreover, the Scandinavian approach was applied conceptually and methodologically to specific Slovene conditions in the investigation of unequal access to various resources. As stated earlier, both studies lacked a more poverty-oriented theoretical framework, especially as far as monetary measures are concerned.

The differing theoretical frameworks resulted in differing points. However, the conclusions as to lower well-being and prosperity are similar in both Croatia and Slovenia. Lay measured individual well-being by employing a comprehensive indicator and "synthesizing" information on quality of diet, health, housing, work conditions, leisure time, and education. The results indicate that 8.7 per cent of Croatia's residents live in bad conditions. In addition, the findings support the "classical" distribution of well-being: the lower the education and the social class, the lower the access to the resources for well-being (Lay 1991). Novak found similar features of individual well-being and prosperity in Slovenia.

Apart from this, analysis of longitudinal data (1984, 1991) reveals an increase in individual prosperity while at the same time reflecting respondents' fears that the threat to their well-being has become more serious. The available information restricts any reconsideration of outcomes in terms of an interplay between macro factors and their micro reflections, meaning that conditions are to be determined at the individual level. It is perhaps too speculative to ascribe the discrepancy between objective conditions and subjective perceptions to a better commodity supply and higher aspirations, driven by the substantially higher living standard in neighbouring societies (Novak 1994).

Relative poverty estimations

The household survey at either at the federal or regional level is the common feature of the above studies. Regardless of the regional origin – whether Serbian (Posarac 1991) or Slovene (Malacic and Stropnik 1991; Stanovnik 1988, 1990, 1992, 1993) – all studies are based on the subsistence concept of poverty and employ the relative poverty line definition operationalized by household disposable income, and the data source, is the regional household survey. However, there are differences in the hypotheses advocated, the theoretical frameworks, and the major findings.

In their analysis of expenditure on children in Slovenia, Malacic and Stropnik (1991) implicitly assumed that the official standards exceed the accepted standards applied elsewhere in the similar sector. The officially established average expenditure on children is usually 50 per cent or less of household disposable income (as in the USA) – 50 per cent in families with three children or 40–45 per cent in families with two children. The results indicate that the norm – according to official standards – for a one-child family (with two employed parents) in Slovenia is to spend about half of its disposable income on the child. This suggests that a two-child family spends almost 90 per cent of its income on its children.

Stanovnik's name crops up most often when the economic aspect of poverty is raised. In computing different poverty lines or investigating respondents' perceptions of their satisfaction with their disposable income, Stanovnik also applied the relative poverty line definition, framed by the subsistence poverty concept, and uses the same data source, i.e. household survey. The hypotheses reveal small variations in either the relation between poverty concept and poverty estimation method or the relation between declining prosperity and its perception. Apart from this, the theoretical framework is usually supported by two pillars: either the federal administration's ignorance of emerging impoverishment (Stanovnik 1988) or an overly lax methodology for estimating poverty that also lacks the subjective approach (Stanovnik 1990, 1992). The OECD equivalence scale has recently determined the contextual pillars as well (Stanovnik 1993). The different concepts applied and the stagnant data source result in wide variations in the findings.

The analysis of food ratio in the former Yugoslavia reveals that the Yugoslav republics strictly followed Engel's law: the higher the stage of development, the lower the food ratio (Stanovnik 1988). When surveyed as to their perceptions of poverty lines, 10 per cent of residents of urban households in Slovenia reported living below the poverty line and another 25 per cent reported living on its brink. In short, one-third of urban households were subjectively living a sub-standard existence. However, this poverty rate was much higher than the official one, which "assumed" figures three times smaller than those subjectively perceived (Stanovnik 1990, 1992).

Compared with the extensive poverty research in Slovenia, at least as far as the economic aspect is concerned, for Serbia there is only one study (Posarac 1991), and there are no reports from the other regions. Describing the decade of economic regression in Serbia, Posarac implicitly assumed that stagnant growth and increased employment affected the redistribution of the gross domestic product and resulted in a higher poverty rate. Though an explicit theoretical framework is lacking, notions about the enduring economic crisis implicitly support the analysis of the distribution of disposable household incomes. The findings lead to the conclusion that the rate of poverty increased from 15.3 per cent to 21.0 per cent in the period 1978–1989 in Serbia. This was ostensibly due to the stagnant economic growth and persisting economic crisis of the 1980s. At the end of the 1980s, approximately one-fifth of Serbia's residents were living in conditions of relative poverty. In addition, the composition of poverty underwent a considerable transformation – shifting from a rural to an urban setting.

Evaluation

The condition of the poor in Eastern Europe is unusual because of the state's major role in the provision of employment, housing, and other services. Poverty is largely an urban problem associated with low real wages and, increasingly, with unemployment. In several countries, poverty increased during the 1980s. Structural problems accompanied by low growth in productivity and chronic material shortages have caused a drop in real wages for a large segment of the labour force.

This state of affairs is perfectly reflected in the studies considered here. The main results and findings are largely in agreement whether researchers are analysing poverty in a particular country or in the three countries comparatively. It is evident that, regardless of the increase in prosperity of the higher social classes on the one hand, and the increased risk and incidence of poverty of the lower social classes on the other, poverty rates show a considerable increase in all countries, though to differing extents. In those instances where the country was thoroughly investigated (Hungary and the former Yugoslavia), a significant transformation of the composition of poverty is discerned. In both countries it shifted from rural poverty to urban poverty, and from poverty affecting the elderly to poverty afflicting young families with several dependent children.

Apart from the recorded features, poverty-related social policy and administrative measures are similar, and, interestingly enough, are also somewhat similar to certain Western models. A redistributive institutional welfare system and a significant work orientation bring East European safety-nets closer to the corporatist Bismarckian model. However, the future development in terms of "de-etatization" of social policy in general, and of the social security system in particular, is far from being simple and achievable in the short run. As some researchers have remarked, Eastern Europe is confronting two opposing currents of change simultaneously: liberalization (e.g. of prices and economy), which will affect the de-equalization of the distribution of resources (income, wealth, benefits) in the long run, and "de-etatization" of society in general, in which no other social actor can replace the demanded and expected withdrawal of the state. This obvious fact frequently failed to be recognized by the various critiques of the "all-embracing and comprehensive socialist social policy that takes care of privileged categories from cradle to grave". In expressing the options for future social and poverty policy development, some researchers do not clearly distinguish between "wishful-thinking" and the actual capacities of society. This calls to mind the same story about legitimizing socialism in these countries half a century ago.

In this respect, I share Marklund's (1993) observations about the future prospects for East Europe's social policy, which will face many severe restrictions. Perhaps the major obstacle to restructuring will be state intervention in social welfare, which is still influential for a number of reasons. Further limitations will result from economic restrictions and the lack of strong social forces, social movements, or civil institutions that could replace state intervention. Though they are rare, encouraging factors can be observed in the welfare roots of the past, i.e. a strong work ethic and corporate features of social policy, which bring these countries closer to the corporatist model.

The studies from Hungary and Czechoslovakia illustrate a particular approach to the investigation of poverty. Whether explicit or implied, the historical perspective on either poverty alleviation policy or poverty measurement is always the basis of the studies considered. This perspective enables a considerably wider analytical perspective than in other countries. The lack of such an analytical framework is most evident in the Yugoslav studies. Moreover, Yugoslavia was frequently excluded from an overall East European perspective, as if it did not belong.

The majority of studies also lack a sociological (and theoretical) perspective on the results, particularly those that are supposed to take heed of their real professional nature. The reconsideration of poverty either in terms of social (in)equality or in terms of the distribution of the resources necessary for well-being continues to be ignored. The frequently observed inadequacy of the theoretical framework that should be related to the utilized poverty concept, e.g. the subsistence concept, is hypothetically in accordance with the above observation. But, Eastern Europe's poverty researchers are not the only ones to blame for ignoring theoretical considerations. Perhaps, the Western demand for information on Eastern Europe's post-socialist transformation simply does not require such an approach. "Rudimentary" information, not loaded with any additional values, norms of the country it comes from, is desired in order to satisfy Western models on Eastern phenomena. The reported similarity between Western welfare models and Eastern practice is simply unrecognized, owing to a very distinctly one-way exchange of information during the past century.

Prospects on comparative studies

The state of poverty investigation in the countries under consideration is more optimistic than it looks at first glance, although the estimation of poverty rates and composition began much later than in comparable Western countries. Moreover, some efforts in Hungary and Czechoslovakia were brought to a halt by communist regimes and have been revived only recently. What makes this picture more optimistic than it seems is the fact that in all countries the household and income surveys are conducted and published regularly. In addition, the official organizers of these surveys try to follow the related methodologies of the West, particularly those applied by research groups working for the European Union. As one researcher remarked, there is no particular problem in joining this "club", at least not for Czechoslovakia. In this respect, the regions of the former Yugoslavia present a slightly larger problem. The household income survey is still being conducted, at least in Slovenia. However, it is irritating that the comparison of poverty rates and composition in the Yugoslav regions is lacking, at least for the period when the aggregated poverty rates at the federal Yugoslav level were computed.

Acknowledgements

I would have had tremendous difficulty in undertaking the planned analysis had it not been for the help of my colleagues in various countries, who provided articles and papers on the topic under investigation. Therefore, I would like to thank Julia Szalai and Istvan Gyorgy Toth of Budapest, Claire Wallace and Jiri Vecernik of Prague, Nada Stropnik and Tine Stanovnik of Ljubljana, and Bernd Marin of Vienna. However, the responsibility for findings and conclusions lies with me.

REFERENCES

Andorka, R. and I. G. Toth (1992) "Changes in and challenges to the major cash social programmes of the Hungarian welfare-state." Manuscript.

Andorka, R. and Z. Speder (1993) "Poverty in Hungary: Some results of the first two waves of the Hungarian household panel survey in 1992 and 1993". Manuscript.

Atkinson, A. B. and J. Micklewright (1992) *Economic Transformation in Eastern Europe and the Distribution of Income.* Cambridge: Cambridge University Press.

Castle-Kanerova, M. (1992) "Social policy in Czechoslovakia", in B. Deacon et al. (eds), *The New Eastern Europe: Social Policy Past, Present and Future*. London: Sage, pp. 91–117.

Deacon, B. (1992) *Social Policy, Social Justice and Citizenship in Eastern Europe*. Aldershot: Avebury.

Ferge, Z. (1987) "The dynamics of the reproduction of social relations", in Z. Ferge and S. M. Miller (eds), *Dynamics of Deprivation*. Aldershot: Gower, pp. 148–72.

Hirsl, M. and J. Dlouhy (1992) "Minimum standards of living and minimal social benefits in Czechoslovakia", in *Poverty Measurement for Economies in Transition in East European Countries*. Warsaw: Polish Statistical Association & Central Statistical Office, pp. 529–39.

Lay, V. (1991) "Kvaliteta zivota stanovnistva Hrvatske" [The quality of life in Croatia]. Manuscript.

Malacic, J. and N. Stropnik (1991) "Stroski otrok v Sloveniji" [Expenditure on children in Slovenia]. *Slovenska ekonomska revija*, 42: 148–63.

Marklund, S. (1993) "Social policy and poverty in post-totalitarian Europe", *Scandinavian Journal of Social Welfare*, 2: 104–14.

Milanovic, B. (1991) "Poverty in Eastern Europe in the Years of Crisis, 1978–1987: Poland, Hungary, and Yugoslavia". *World Bank Economic Review*, 5: 187–205.

Novak, M. (1993) "Poverty policy in Slovenia in restructuring". Manuscript.

—— (1994) "Decreasing prosperity in the 1980s in Slovenia?" *Revija za sociologiju*, 25: 41–50.

Posarac, A. (1991) "Siromastvo u Srbiji" [Poverty in Serbia]. *Ekonomika*, 27 60–9.

Potucek, M. (1993) "Quo vadis, social policy in Czechoslovakia?" in S. Ringen and C. Wallace (eds), *Societies in Transition: East-Central Europe Today*. Prague: Central European University, pp. 129–36.

Ronge, V. (1991) "Social change in Eastern Europe: Implications for the Western poverty agenda". *Journal of European Social Policy*, 1: 49–56.

Salamin, J. (1992) "Calculation of poverty level (Hungarian experience)", in *Poverty Measurement for Economies in Transition in East European Countries*. Warsaw: Polish Statistical Association & Central Statistical Office, pp. 463–77.

Stanovnik, T. (1988) "Pojmovanje revscine v SR Sloveniji" [Poverty Definitions in Slovenia]. *Informativni bilten – Revija za planiranje*, 12: 39–46.

—— (1990) "Revscina – definicije, analize in implikacije za socialno politiko" [Poverty: Definitions, outcomes of analysis, and implications for social policy]. *Informativni bilten – Revija za planiranje*, 14: 18–28.

—— (1991) "Primernost metodologij za dolocanje minimalnih zivljenjskih stroskov" [Subsistence minimum standard – An assessment of methodology]. Survey Report.

────── (1992) "Perceptions of poverty and income satisfaction". *Journal of Economic Psychology*, 13: 57–69.

Stanovnik, T. (1993) Analiza socialnoekonomskega polozaja slovenskih gospodinjstev v letih 1978, 1983, 1988. (Socio-economic conditions of households in Slovenia in 1978, 1983, 1988). Survey Report.

Sumi, J. (1986) "Metodologija ocenjevanja zivljenjskih stroskov v Sloveniji" [Living expenditure estimating methods in Slovenia]. Survey Report.

Szalai, J. (1990) "Some thoughts on poverty and the concept of subsistence minimum", in R. Andorka et al. (eds), *Social Report*. Budapest: TARKI, pp. 296–304.

────── (1992) "Poverty in Hungary during the period of economic crisis". Manuscript.

────── (1993) "Social policy and child poverty: Hungary since 1945". Manuscript.

Szanto, J. and G. Toka (1990) "The inequalities of material living conditions", in R. Andorka et al. (eds), *Social Report*. Budapest: TARKI, pp. 285–95.

Toth, I. G. and M. F. Foerster (1994) "Income poverty and households' income composition in Hungary". Manuscript.

Van Praag, B. M. S. et al. (1992) "Poverty line concepts; An application to Czechoslovakia". Manuscript.

Vecernik, J. (1993) "Changes in the rate and types of poverty: The Czech and Slovak republics 1990–1993". Manuscript.

World Bank (1990) *World Development Report 1990*. New York: Oxford University Press.

Chapter 19
Poland: Missing Link to Policy
Ludmila Dziewięcka-Bokun, Ewa Toczyska, and Witold Toczyski

Poverty research in Poland has a long and politically determined history. The first surveys were undertaken in the 1920s and focused on various aspects of the living conditions of the Polish population. They concentrated mainly on groups of households threatened with unemployment, insufficient food intake, and poor housing conditions. At that time, models of income distribution were worked out and data from various sources were used. The surveys were conducted by the Central Statistical Office (CSO), by the Institute of Social Economy (ISE), created in 1920 as an autonomous section of the Society of Polish Economists and Statisticians, and also by researchers and scientists from various scientific and research centres.

After the Second World War the term "poverty" was not officially used, nor was it a subject of scientific investigation. However, the Central Statistical Office did start to organize surveys of the living conditions of the population again and step by step developed them in cooperation with other institutions. In 1951 the household budget surveys were stopped and the break lasted until 1957.

In the years 1957-81 household budget surveys (HBS) gradually developed, the methodology improved, the scope was extended, and new research methods were utilized. Experimental household budget surveys attempted to use the methodology of West European countries. In 1960 the surveys of living conditions were started on a larger scale, and they are repeated every few years. These surveys also include poverty-related problems (CSO 1984, 1991; Kordos 1973, 1990).

In the 1970s social scientists and the CSO staff attempted to introduce new sociological and statistical surveys in order to carry out comprehensive analyses of living conditions and the quality of life. For ideological reasons this concept was not implemented in practice, but in the 1980s it became possible to launch large-scale surveys of this type (Kordos 1982; Luszniewicz 1972).

Regardless of the fact that the term "poverty" was not officially used, a number of studies were conducted to determine the "spheres of indigence" (the term used instead of poverty) and social differentiation.

In 1983 Frąckiewicz published a book on the spheres of indigence. Activities in this field were conducted under the supervision of Beskid (1984 and 1989). In 1984 and 1988 conferences were held in Poland on poverty at which a number of interesting papers analysed the surveys and analyses of poverty on the basis of surveys conducted by the Central Statistical Office (CSO 1990b, 1991a; Kordos 1990). Such surveys were also conducted by research institutes (e.g. Budzyński and Lisowski 1991).

In 1982, after the 1980–81 crisis, another attempt was made to establish an integrated system of household surveys. In the same year a continuous method of household budget surveys was replaced with the rotation method. A master sample was designed that made it possible to carry out various social surveys using sub-samples. Uniform concepts, definitions, and classifications were used and training was provided for all the staff involved in the surveys. The quality of training of field personnel was regarded as an important element of this integrated system. In the period 1982–91 some thirty-three surveys of this type were conducted. In 1991 the process of gradual adjustment of the Polish system of surveys extended to all groups of the population, such as employees, workers–farmers, farmers, pensioners, people living exclusively on benefits, those employed in the non-state sector outside agriculture, and the self-employed, who in the past, for various reasons, had not been covered. Attempts were made to undertake surveys as carried out by Eurostat. The surveys of the labour force were carried out on a much larger scale than previously. Preparations were made to conduct surveys on incomes to supplement the existing surveys of living conditions (Kordos 1982).

In 1991 the poverty line was set on the basis of the social minimum for one-person households in which the OECD scale of equivalences was used: first adult in household = 1.0, each addition adult = 0.7, each child = 0.5. The social minimum was calculated on the basis of a specific consumers' basket. The items in the basket were priced at prices quoted by the Central Statistical Office.

The ISE did studies on several aspects of poverty, but the term "poverty" did not appear in any report titles until autumn 1989 when a study entitled "The problems of poverty" appeared. From that time, poverty became the core of the Institute's research activities (Budzyński and Lisowski 1982).

In general, the ISE studies tended to confirm the findings in other countries of similar culture – the people most likely to suffer poverty were: the aged, women, families with many children, single mothers, households with handicapped persons, households with poorly qualified persons, and those affected by illness. General economic progress over the years brought changes in the perception of whether the situation was unsatisfactory. Admittedly this progress was somewhat slower than in democratic countries with different economies. The main feature was that progress was greater in access to knowledge and improvements in education, health, social security, cultural activities and public transport than in individual access to material wealth. Research in the 1980s and subsequently showed that the main factors of poverty were commonly perceived to be: low pensions, a lot of children, isolation, disability, and alcoholism.

Researchers focusing on social dysfunctions in Poland can be divided into two main groups: those who wanted to improve the existing socialist socioeconomic system, and those who felt that a new order would in itself do nothing to rectify these problems and would, indeed, be more affected than the old order because of shortages of the means to correct the dysfunctions. Nonetheless, both groups were obliged to comply with the exigencies of state censorship, which led in turn to self-censorship and avoidance of definitions that conflicted with the official doctrine. It was the practice not to write about a negative situation, but rather to stress the positive steps undertaken by the state to make things better.

The problem of poverty assumed stark reality in research dealing with the satisfaction of societal needs. Investigations by the ISE of problems connected with the non-satisfaction of needs were always conducted with due consideration to the prevailing limitations of social factors – in order of ascending magnitude: the family, the workplace, the nation-wide social security system, the socio-political alignment of the state. The accepted methodology for research into social policies allowed the following conclusion to be reached: needs could be satisfied either by perfecting the existing system, or, if possible, by eliminating the system, if in itself it led to the creation of needs that were impossible to satisfy. In view of this, it was necessary to present research findings in such a way as to link them with poverty in Poland, but to do so in an oblique manner (Lisowski 1985; Budzyński and Lisowski 1992).

Current research on poverty

The Polish "soft" revolution in 1989 allowed the CSO and the ISE to start new investigations into poverty, its social conditions, and its consequences without the need to disguise the topic.

In the ISE the investigations began in late 1989 with attempts to identify areas of concern threatened by encroaching poverty. At first, the ISE staff appraised selected social aid institutions and formulated issues requiring further analysis:

- the establishment of criteria for identifying geographical areas of poverty in Poland;
- the risks in groups affected by non-satisfaction of needs or threatened by the inability to meet basic needs, such as benefit recipients and families affected by unemployment – former ISE research enabled these groups to be identified;
- the risks associated with the socioeconomic changes arising from unemployment and other phenomena;
- the symptoms and causes of poverty in the youngest generation (Lisowski 1986).

Three studies were conducted in 1990 on the following topics: the risks of poverty within employed families with a lot of children (Lisowska 1991); living conditions in female single-parent families (Wolska 1991); and the symptoms of poverty in Warsaw primary schools (Lisowski 1991).

The survey report on employed families with a lot of children contained the following statement: "The current economic changes in Poland and their undesirable effects are affecting (such) families considerably" (Lisowska 1991).

Single mothers and their children are the victims of a whole range of ills, such as difficult housing conditions, low incomes, and heavy parental responsibilities. The single mothers described their material situation as bad or very bad; one-third of them admitted that their families were on the verge of poverty (Wolska 1991).

In April 1990 pupils of Warsaw primary schools were already beginning to betray signs of poverty behaviour stemming from unemployment within their families, even though Warsaw has one of the lowest unemployment rates in the country. Poverty manifests itself in various ways: thefts in school, alcoholism among both parents and pupils, inadequate child care. Although it is usual to attribute these symptoms to the effects of the political and social changes taking place in Poland, the causes were seen to lie in the more traditional areas of social pathology. The extent to which schools can accommodate the needs of underprivileged children is limited by a shortage of resources (Lisowski 1991).

As part of the poverty research programme, the ISE published a special issue of the *ISE Bulletin* containing the abovementioned articles and also:

- a theoretical examination of the possibility of harnessing the results of the CSO household budget surveys to the analysis of poverty (Kordos 1991);
- a report on threats of poverty appearing in the work of social aid centres in Warsaw in late 1989 (Wiśniewska 1991);
- an analysis identifying the causes of poverty in families with small children, based on an ISE investigation in 1983–6 and CSO family budget investigations (Kostrubiec 1991);
- an article dealing with problems of socialization in families with a lot of children threatened with poverty (Rodziewicz 1991);
- an article on the correlation between geographical areas and living conditions in Poland (Rakowski 1991).

In May 1991 social assistance beneficiaries and unemployed persons in five small Polish towns were studied (Kurzynowski 1991). The results revealed that, among the sample populations, families affected by unemployment are relatively young – the median age being 28. Benefit recipients are markedly older, but with a greater age range, which means that there are some very young persons among them (Budzyński and Lisowski 1992). Large differences between the levels of social assistance in different towns indicated a correspondingly large difference in the consequent burden on different local authorities.

A bibliography with over 1,000 items has been prepared on the topic "Requirements for studies of endangered communities during the economic restructuring in Poland", aimed at helping in further investigations of poverty.

A repetition of the territory-based studies of benefit recipients and the unemployed was made in 1991 as part of the series "Restructuring of the Polish economy and changes in living conditions of various groups with particular focus on those threatened with poverty".

Recent and current Central Statistical Office research on poverty and its larger context includes household budget surveys

(CSO 1990a) and surveys on the living conditions of the population (CSO 1984, 1990b, 1991a). During that period the integrated system of household surveys was supplemented with thirty special surveys of various groups in the population (families with a lot of children, one-parent families, elderly people, young people, and women). The surveys covered housing and living conditions, participation in culture, tourism, quality of life, and health status and some of them also covered selected aspects of poverty (Kordos 1985).

According to Kordos, some of the surveys pertained directly to the poverty problem. In 1985, when large-scale surveys of living conditions were conducted, the respondents were asked directly whether they regarded themselves as living below the poverty line, although a definition of poverty was not provided. Only 3.2 per cent of the households stated that they were living in poverty. The question was repeated in 1990, when 7.6 per cent of households admitted that they were living in poverty. If the size of household is taken into account, one-person households constituted the highest percentage (7.7 per cent in 1985 and 12.0 in 1990) and four-person households the lowest percentage (1.9 per cent and 5.4 per cent, respectively). Overall, the highest percentage of households living in poverty were those living exclusively on social benefits (29.6 per cent in 1985 and 42.3 per cent in 1990), while the lowest percentage was of households of self-employed persons (0.5 per cent and 5.4 per cent respectively). Because many people in Poland are unwilling to admit that they live in poverty, the above indices represent not the actual poverty level of the surveyed population, but only the perception of material status in relation to other households. A question about subjective assessment of the material status of the household was asked in 1985, and it turned out that 17.5 per cent of households stated that their material status was bad or very bad; in 1990, that figure increased to 28.8 per cent.

Research work on poverty carried out by research institutes (Beskid 1988, 1989; Budzyński and Lisowski 1991; Frąckiewicz 1993) should also be mentioned here.

Household budget surveys carried out by the rotation method cover about 7,500 households quarterly, which amounts to about 30,000 households covered by the survey within a year. The incomes from work of employees covered by the surveys are verified by employers with full data confidentiality. Every year an annual interview is conducted on selected income and expenditure items in every household that took part in the survey. Annual incomes from work are also verified. In addition, subjective opinions on the material status of the household and household budgeting, as well as on possession of durable goods and on housing conditions, are taken into consideration. The results are published every year in a special publication (e.g. CSO 1990a).

Apart from gathering information on the living conditions of the population, the main objective of large-scale living-conditions surveys is the preparation of a sampling frame for household budget surveys. The sample is replaced every four years (i.e. first-stage units, with only half of the sample being replaced in one year and the other half in the next year), so between 1982 and 1990 two such sample surveys were conducted every four years. The size of the sample in each survey was about 120,000 households (CSO 1984, 1991a). The household budget surveys are potentially a rich source of information on living conditions and on poverty. Before 1988, ideological pressures blocked the full use of these surveys for poverty measurement, although some attempts were made.

Some income data from the Polish household budget surveys (HBS) have been used for poverty measurement. Although such data are a relevant and frequently used indicator of poverty, they suffer from many limitations. An important factor in satisfying the needs of the family are incomes in kind. These are covered by the HBS as goods and services received free of charge. Although the data on incomes derived from HBS are underestimated to some extent, incomes from work, owing to the verification by employers, are quite accurate. Up to the present moment, incomes from property and from self-employment (outside agriculture) have not been covered owing to their negligible relevance (they were specified under "other incomes"). Up to 1990 the surveys covered about 90 per cent of households, excluding the households of policemen, soldiers, the self-employed, and collective households (Kordos 1992).

Expenditure data constitute the core of HBS and are an important source of information on poverty. Sometimes general expenditure data are used instead of income data, but they are treated as less reliable. The composition of expenditures is important for poverty analysis. In poverty analysis one of the relevant components of low-income households is dietary habits. Data on food consumption may be used to calculate caloric and protein intakes and to compare them with nutritional norms. Such comparisons were done in Poland (CSO 1990b) for particular groups of the population, by both age and sex. The nutritional needs of a man over 18 years old was taken as a basic unit and the need of other groups were expressed as a ratio of this. This unit was based only on nutrition norms and, although imprecise, it was applied in household budget surveys till the 1970s.

Data on the socioeconomic characteristics of household members are especially relevant for the classification of households by socioeconomic group and for the analysis of characteristic features of households living in poverty. Parallel to HBS, information on housing conditions and the possession of durable goods is collected. The information makes it possible to work out a multidimensional approach to the concept of poverty.

Large-scale living-conditions surveys allow a focus on different aspects of poverty measurement. Everything points to a strong likelihood that research into poverty will grow in the near future. But then a rapid growth in poverty itself also seems likely.

Main concepts of poverty

Poverty lines and social minima

In Polish statistical practice, examples of subjective evaluations of the material status of households can be found. The problems were dealt with initially by Beskid (1984) and then by the Central Statistical Office, which introduced subjective evaluation surveys as a supplement to HBS and other surveys on the living conditions of the population. Beskid analysed such problems as the income patterns desired by respondents and incomes regarded by them as indispensable. However, no formal method of determining poverty lines was applied in that analysis.

After 1956, the problem of introducing a social minimum in Poland became an issue in several political and social programmes, in the speeches of politicians, and in the mass media. The problem usually caught public attention after each social crisis. The first publication containing the results of calculations of a social minimum was issued in Poland in 1957 (Akoliński 1957). The first book on the social minimum was published in 1973 (Tymowski). An especially large number of articles on the social minimum were published in 1981. In that year also the first official calculations of the social minimum, done by the Institute of Labour and Social Welfare, were published.

The overall concept of the method of calculating a social minimum was worked out in the early 1970s (Deniszczuk 1972; Tymowski 1973), although the issue was dealt with even earlier. In the period 1970–6, the Central Statistical Office calculated the so-called "minimum of cost of living", but these calculations were confidential, meant only for the state authorities. At present, the social minimum is calculated by the Institute of Labour and Social Welfare and is published on a quarterly basis.

In August 1981 the Polish Council of Ministers passed a special resolution on the definition of a social minimum and the research needed. This is the only document in which the social minimum is defined, although the definition was not very precise. It stated that the social minimum is a basic set of goods and services, purchased by particular families and expressed in terms of cash and goods in kind, taking into account actual price levels. Later, when the objectives of relevant research work were described, it was indicated that one of the objectives should be the determination of the "number and structure of families whose incomes are below the social minimum". Another objective should be to determine "changes in the level of the social minimum due to the living conditions and costs of living of the population".

The social minimum is calculated on the basis of a specific consumers' basket (a set of goods and services the consumption of which is regarded as indispensable from the social point of view and corresponds to the economic situation of the country), and on the basis of the actual price level quoted by the CSO. The social minimum is calculated for families of employees (one- and four-person households) and families of pensioners (one- and two-person) (Góralska 1986). The minimum basket includes goods and services such as foodstuffs, clothes, shoes, hygiene and health care, dwelling houses, appliances and furniture, cultural services and recreation, transport and communications. In addition, it is estimated that about 10 per cent of resources should constitute so-called personal funds (to satisfy specific personal needs such as medicines, cigarettes, etc.). The foodstuffs basket was based on nutritional norms in Poland (with foodstuffs bought at moderate prices). The items in the basket are priced at prices quoted by the Central Statistical Office, the prices being those actually paid by consumers (according to household budget surveys). One of the assumptions when setting up the minimum basket was that families live in community blocks of flats fully equipped with facilities, and that the size of a flat is adequate for the size of the family. However, this assumption is far from reality: many families share a flat, and almost one-fifth of the urban population lives in dwellings not equipped with all sanitary facilities.

The social minimum always aroused strong feelings on the part of the general public, government, and trade unions, and in scientific circles. It became an issue in political debates and negotiations. The reliability of its calculation and interpretation was questioned. After the introduction of martial law in Poland in 1981, the calculations of the social minimum ceased to be published, although they were still carried out. Official publication of the results did not start again until 1988, although the category was used in official programmes, declarations, and decisions as well as in political struggles (Kordos 1992).

Many authors point to the limited usefulness of the social minimum for defining the sphere of poverty. Poverty is expressed through several features of the social position of the poor and not just through insufficient income. Further aspects of the social minimum to which they refer include:

- the contents of the basket are not constant, but are adjusted to the economic situation of the country; therefore, there are two minima: basic and critical ones – the minimum for the 1980s was 11 per cent lower than that for the 1970s;
- a fundamental assumption of the basket is that a family lives in a state flat that is adequate for the size of the family and is fully equipped;
- the social minimum relates to the conditions of a market that is relatively stable;
- the basket is intended to fulfil typical needs, with no regard to specific situations such as illness, the characteristics of a particular job, etc.
- the divergence between the level of earnings and actual consumption is not taken into consideration (although it should be remembered that there are previous savings, family help, etc.).
- the standard of living also depends on such factors as the functioning of the social infrastructure, the quality of public goods and services, etc.

The results of the research on the social minimum were not published regularly. It was only in the 1990s that the data were presented regularly in the periodical *Social Policy*.

In 1993 some of the variables were modified. In adddition to "traditional" estimates, comparable with the previous ones, a variant of the social minimum was prepared by using the scale of so-called equivalent earnings. The accepted scale was convergent with the one proposed by the OECD, i.e.:

1.0 for the earnings of the first person of a family household,
0.7 for the earnings of each additional person over 15 years old,
0.5 for the earnings of each member of the family under 15.

By introducing a correction into the estimates of the social minimum, the so called *scale of equivalency* had a crucial significance in the judgement of the extent of the phenomenon of material poverty within households.

As stressed before, the financial situation was not the only criterion for deciding whether a particular family should be considered as "poor". Therefore, for households with low incomes, other living standard factors were also included. These factors were household facilities, density of occupation in one flat, and expenses on cultural and leisure activities. These factors define the stage of "household needs deprivation", and, when combined with the income of a family, may reflect the phenomenon of poverty. The objective of estimating such a social minimum was debated. Most authors claim that the social minimum should not be the determinant of poverty, but rather should be used in social policy (e.g. setting the minimum wage, pension benefits, unemployment benefit, etc.).

Low incomes

Attempts were also made to create measures of poverty based on the criterion of low incomes. In 1981 the Central Statistical Office introduced a category of "low incomes", and prepared a relative method of defining the boundaries of poverty. It stated that an income is low when it corresponds with the lowest fifteenth percentile in the distribution of household incomes. (This approach limits *a priori* the size of the sphere of poverty to 15 per cent of all households.) Later, it was decided that low income should reflect real value, thus it was adjusted in line with the increase in the prices of goods and consumption services.

Rutkowski (1988) argued that low income does not correlate (or correlates only minimally) with the material assets of a given household, and therefore is not a sufficient criterion of poverty. Households with luxury equipment cannot be regarded as poor, even if their recent income is lower than the social minimum. High-quality household equipment suggests that the family has other income sources (work abroad, help from family, or an extra job). Therefore, Rutkowski proposed a joint factor embracing low present incomes and low-quality household equipment.

If we take as a starting point the size of the sphere of financial poverty and add the material equipment in a household, this leads to a reduction in the number of households regarded as poor, mainly among families of non-workers, and to a lesser degree among families of workers, young families, and multi-person families (especially those bringing up one or two children). The joint criterion points to the same social groups as being important in the poverty population as does the criterion of low incomes. However, it gives a different picture of the relative importance of age groups. Older families are more numerous, while fewer young families and middle-aged families are included.

The consequence of using the joint criterion is that it narrows the sphere of economic poverty, while at the same time widening the sphere of social and cultural poverty. To the latter group belong those households that have incomes over the social minimum, but that still have very poor material equipment. Therefore poverty should be considered as two-dimensional, taking into account both current income and material equipment. It is also important to note that the joint criterion leads to changes in the poverty picture.

Other authors also point to the fact that poverty research cannot be limited to the analysis of incomes. A good example of the multidimensional approach is Jarosz and Kozak's work "Experts' report. Spheres of indigency" (1987). As an indicator of poverty they combined a permanent situation of low income (estimated according to the social minimum of the time) with other specific situations. The specific situations that could add to poverty are:

- the family budget (net expenses in relation to net incomes);
- expenditure on food (in all households there is an important correlation between food expenses and the cumulative effect of low incomes and the size of a household);
- the housing situation (owning a flat, its size, density of occupation, having one's own bed);
- basic facilities (cold and hot water, bathroom, shower, WC, gas, etc.);
- permanent household equipment, including luxury goods.

The structure of expenses for typical households is published by the Central Statistical Office. High relative expenditure on food turns out to be a characteristic of poor households.

Jarosz and Kozak concluded that in families suffering from poverty there is an accumulation of negative situational factors in addition to low incomes, such as high density of inhabitants in one flat and a low level of education and culture. Low income is strongly correlated with other poverty indicators.

Gòvalska proposed that instead of examining current incomes, which influence the material situation only to some extent, the level of current consumption should be accepted as a criterion of poverty. Examining actual consumption leads to a consideration of all its sources: current incomes, past savings, future incomes (credits), as well as other sources of consumption, such as natural consumption (e.g. food and home-made clothes) and consumption arising from transfers. Defining the sources of consumption is particularly important because current consumption is often financed with incomes that are not current or with future incomes. In such situations poverty increases.

The subjective boundary of poverty

In recent years other methods of defining the boundaries of poverty have become popular. These methods are based on obtaining opinions from the members of a family on how high their income should be in order to maintain their household at a minimum level.

The Leyden Poverty Line (LPL) was used by Podgórski (1990) in his analysis of the results of living standards research performed by the Chief Census Bureau in 1989 and 1990. Since 1992 this method has also been used in quarterly analyses of research on family budgets, conducted by the monthly rotation method.

Households are asked to state the level of income they would think of as "very good", "good", "merely satisfactory", "unsatisfactory", and "very bad". The subjective boundary of poverty for certain types of households approximately corresponds to the level of incomes stated to be "merely satisfactory". The value of the social minimum income is not high. For one-person and four-person working families, and for two-person pensioners' households, it is possible to equate the subjective boundary of poverty with the social minimum, as calculated by the Institute of Statistics. The analyses make it clear that for small (two-person) households, the subjective boundaries of poverty are slightly higher than the social minimum. In the case of large families (four people) the relation is almost the reverse: the value of the social minimum is higher than the incomes defined as a subjective boundary of poverty.

The application of the LPL method allows the researcher to define both the extent and the intensity of subjective poverty. The subjective boundary of financial poverty is compared with the distribution of real incomes of the respondents. The extent of poverty is then defined on the basis of families earning incomes below the boundary of subjective poverty as a percentage of the total number of households. The intensity of subjective poverty is measured with the indicator of the average poverty gap. The indicator shows how much the average income of a household below the poverty line differs from the level of income subjectively regarded as the poverty line. Both the extent and the size of the income gap are obtained on the basis of comparable incomes of various households.

The concept of "individual income functions of welfare" was introduced in Poland by Podgorski and Dobrowolska (1991). Their research revealed that the boundaries of poverty based on subjective assessment of the income necessary to meet the fundamental needs of the members of a given family do not have the necessity to be higher than the boundaries established objectively. The most interesting conclusion was that "minimum" and "satisfactory" incomes do not differ much according to age, education, or place of residence. This points to a levelling of consumption aspirations in society as a result of the long-term economic crisis. However, there are clear differences in the extent of poverty according to household size, number of employed family members, level of education, and place of residence. The small difference between declared incomes and subjective assessments of poverty undoubtedly reflects the fact that a large part of the social minimum basket goes to meet the most basic needs, which cannot be substituted with other elements of consumption.

Absolute and relative deprivation

"Absolute deprivation, as far as material conditions of living are concerned, assumes that the boundaries of poverty should be defined by the norms that characterize necessary standards of living in certain social and economic conditions" (Beskid et al. 1990). The following elements were used in order to define absolute deprivation:

- per capita income below 50 per cent of the average income;
- the lack of at least two of the following: a washing machine, a refrigerator, a radio, a black-and-white TV-set (in households without a colour TV);
- the lack of at least one of the standard facilities of a flat: i.e. electricity, water supply, WC, bathroom;
- a living space of less than 10 m^2 per person;
- meat consumption below 300 dag a month (the norm in 1982 was lower).

If we analyse the distribution of various levels of particular material elements of living conditions, we observe a low level of cumulation at the 10 per cent extremes of the distribution. However, as the boundary of poverty shifts towards the centre of the distribution, broadly understood deprivation increases.

The range of deprivation can thus be presented as two types of distribution: one according to deciles, and the other as the distribution below or above the average of a given element. The following scale of poverty has been created by combining the elements in these distributions:

1. *Extreme deprivation*: all elements are found in the two lowest deciles.
2. *Moderate deprivation*: two elements lie within the two lowest deciles and the third lies below the average, or one element is within the two lowest deciles yet all three can be found below the average.
3. *Poor living conditions*: three elements lie below the average, but not in the lowest two deciles, or two elements, one of which lies in the lowest two deciles, are below the average and one element is above the average.

Subjective estimation of material living conditions

One of the consequences of the unbalanced distribution of goods is subjective deprivation, in other words, a feeling of being discriminated against in the sphere of living conditions. The following three types of subjective estimation of discrimination can be identified:

- *escalating aspirations*, i.e. when aspirations grow faster than the possibilities of achieving them;
- *diminishing aspirations*, i.e. when there is no chance of achieving aspirations and meeting needs, and earlier opportunities vanish;
- *progressive aspirations*, i.e. when, after a period of feeling deep discrimination, a period of diminishing discrimination emerges.

Measures of the subjective estimation of deprivation require special attention to the correspondence between public opinion and real deprivation. A characteristic feature is that the *per capita* in the family does not seem to influence people's opinions on deprivation. In order to understand the social structure of poverty, it is, however, important to consider the range of subjective feelings of deprivation as presented by the respondents.

Research on the subjective estimations of living standards leads to the following methodological remarks:

1. There exists a logical link between a subjective estimation and the real situation. This is particularly visible when a person's situation is subjectively estimated as low or mediocre.
2. The relationship between subjective and objective estimations is not homogeneous.
3. Correlations between objective and subjective indicators depend on the objective situation. In most cases the middle-range estimations are similar. An objectively low level of material living conditions is often estimated as mediocre in subjective answers, whereas an objectively high level of living conditions is estimated below its actual position. In the case of extreme values the correlation increases again.
4. A feeling of deprivation is not synonymous with objective poverty. In subjective estimations there is a tendency to omit extreme estimations:
   - needs and aspirations are understated, therefore objective poverty is estimated as a mediocre level;
   - among those in a mediocre position, almost 20 per cent think of themselves as poor, and about 30 per cent vary in their opinions (they also include themselves in the group of the poor).
5. Because full correlation between subjective estimations and the objective situation does not exist, it is not possible to substitute one for the other.

The importance of subjective estimations is found in the observed discrepancy between social expectations of material and social needs and the possibilities of fulfilling those needs.

Conclusions

First, research on poverty in Poland has been strongly connected with the state's policy towards poverty itself. Before the upheaval of 1989, neither poverty research nor anti-poverty policy had been attempted on a large or systematic scale. Poverty was considered as temporary and exceptional. Though public discussions on poverty were banned for decades, poverty nevertheless existed and became more evident during the 1980s.

Second, in Poland the predominant influence of the methods of measuring poverty has resulted in a system of state statistics, with particularly well-developed research on family budgets. However, these statistical measurements are directed not towards the nature and structure of poverty, but mainly towards reporting the conditions of living, consumption, and income. Furthermore, poor families, for example alcoholic families, might be insufficiently represented.

Generally, three approaches are used in the statistical measurement of poverty in Poland:

- objective poverty – on the basis of earnings and expenditures;
- subjective poverty – on the basis of household members' opinion on the level of earnings necessary to maintain the household on a proper level;
- non-financial indicators of poverty, such as low level of consumption, living conditions, household facilities, as well as ways of spending spare time, etc.

Third, there is a growing need to develop and improve poverty measurement techniques and the tools for identifying poverty in the current process of political, economic, and social changes. Politically, however, the prevalent tendency is to define poverty in absolute terms.

Recent poverty measurements focus on household budgets using surveys embedded in the official statistics. It is difficult to use these data to make international comparisons. These surveys concentrate on absolute poverty, relative poverty, non-financial poverty factors, and household incomes.

Poverty research in Poland only accidentally focuses on the causes of poverty. As a consequence, limited explanations or subjective value judgements are offered.

Fourth, numerous signs indicate that poverty is still increasing. Some of the main reasons for the growing number of people falling into poverty seems to be the result of political and economic transformation, the financial crisis of the state, high unemployment rates, shrinking of the safety-net and its inefficient administration, the lack of a social welfare infrastructure and inadequate attention to social pathologies, demographic and structural factors, and weak political interest in social policy issues and poverty.

REFERENCES

Akoliński, S. (1957) "Próba ustalenia minimum kosztów utrzymania" [Test to determine the cost of living minimum]. *Przegląd zagadnień socjalnych*, No. 2.

Beskid, L. (1984a) "Wizja społeczna poziomu i proporcji w podziale dochodu [Social vision of level and proportion in income distribution]. *Gospodarka Planowa*, 1988 No. 4.

―――― (1984b) "Społeczna koncepcja sytuacji dochodowej" [(Social conception of income situation], in *Warunki życia i potrzeby społeczeństwa polskiego 1982*, Warsaw.

―――― (1988) "Niedostatek w opiniach społecznych" [Scarcity in public opinion], *Praca i zabezpieczenie społeczne*, No. 9.

―――― (1989) "Subiektywny obraz sytuacji materialnej, potrzeb i aspiracji Polaków w latach 1982–1986" [Subjective picture of the material situation, needs and aspirations of Poles in 1982–1986]), in L. Bestid (ed.), *Potrzeby i aspiracje społeczenstwa polskiego*, Warsaw: Beskid, L. et al. (1990) *Społeczne bariery zagrożenia i skutki realizowanej polityki ekonomicznej*. Ekspertyza zbiorowa [Social barriers, means and consequences of current economic policy. Group's Expertise]. Warsaw:

―――― (1992) "Poczucie zagrożenia bied." *[Feeling of a poverty threatening]*. *Polityka Społeczna*, No. 1.

Budzyński, A. and A. Lisowski (1991) *Aspects of Poverty Measurment in Researches of the Institute of Social Economy in Poland*. Warsaw: Polish Statistical Association and Central Statistical Office. Warsaw.

CSO (1984) "Sytuacja materialna gospodarstw domowych w 1982 r" [Living conditions of households in 1982]. *Opracowania Analityczne* (Warsaw).

―――― (1990a) "Budżety gospodarstw domowycz w 1989 r" [Household budget survey results in 1989]. *Materiały i opracowania Statystyczne* (Warsaw).

―――― (1990b) "Warunki życia ludności 1989 r" [Living conditions of the population in 1989]. *Studia i analizy statystyczne* (Warsaw).

―――― (1991a) "Warunki bytowe gospodarstw domowych w 1985 i 1990" [Living conditions of households in 1985 and 1990]. *Materiały i Opracowania Statystyczne* (Warsaw).

―――― (1991b) "Subiektywne granice ubóstwa a dochody gospdarstw domowych" [Subjective poverty lines and household incomes]. *Studia i Analizy Statystyczne* (Warsaw).

―――― (1991c) "Jakośí życia i warunki bytu" [Quality of life and living conditions]. *Biblioteka Wiadomości Statystycznych*, Vol 40.

Deniszczuk, L. (1972) "Wzorzec konsumpcji społecznie niezbędnej (minimum socjalne)" [A socially necessary consumption standard – a social minimum]. *Studia i Materiały IPiSS* (Warsaw).

Frackiewicz, L. [1983] *Sfery niedostatku* [Spheres of indigence]. Warsaw: IWZZ.

―――― (1988) "Ubóstwo jako kwestia społeczna" [Poverty as a social issue]. *Praca i zabezpieczenie społeczne*, No. 9.

―――― (1988) *Warunki życia i bytu mieszkańców aglomeracji Górnośląskiej* [Living conditions of the Upper Silesia inhabitants]. Katowice: Instytut śląski.

―――― (1991) *Jakośí życia mieszkańców Górnego śląska [Quality of life of the Upper Silesia inhabitants]*. Katowice: Instytut śląski.

―――― (1992) "The syndrome of poverty in the richest region in Poland (Silesia)", in *Poverty Measurement for Economies in Transition in Eastern European Countries*. Warsaw: Polish Statistical Association and Central Statistical Office.

Góralska, H. (1984) "Dochody i konsumpcja ludności żyjącej w niedostatku" [Incomes and consumption of the deprived population]. *Studia i materiały*, Nos 2 and 3, ed. by IPiSS, Warsaw.

―――― (1985) "Sfera ubóstwa przez pryzmat dochodów" [The sphere of poverty through the prism of income]. *Polityka Spoeczna*, No. 4.
―――― (1986) "Minimum socjalne. Metody obliczeń i interpretacja" [The social minimum. Methods of calculation and interpretation]. *Studia i Materiały IPiSS*, z. 4, (Warsaw).
Jarosz, M. and M. Kozak (1987) *Ekspertyza. Sfery niedostatku* [An expertise. Spheres of indigency]. Warsaw.
―――― (1989) "Sfery niedostatku" [Spheres of indigence]. *Studia Socjolgiczne*, No. 2.
Kordos, J. (1973) *Metody analizy i prognozowania rozkładów płac idochodów, ludności* [Methods of analysing and forecasting the distribution of the population]. Warsaw: PWE.
―――― (1982) "Metoda rotacyjna w badaniu budżetów rodzinnych w Polsce" [Rotation method in the family budget survey in Poland]. *Wiadomości statystyczne*, No. 9.
―――― (1985) "Towards an integrated system of household surveys in Poland", in *Proceedings of 45th Session, Bulletin of the International Statistical Institute*, vol. LI. Amsterdam.
―――― (1988) "Niektóre metody określania granic ubóstwa" [Some methods of determining the poverty line]. *Polityka Społeczna*, Nos 11/12.
―――― (1990) "Research on income distribution by size in Poland", in C. Dagun and M. Zenga (eds), *Income and Wealth Distribution, Inequality and Poverty*. Berlin: Springer-Verlag, Studies in Contemporary Economics.
―――― (1991) "Możlowości wykorzystania wyników badań budżetów gospodarstw domowych w analizach ubóstwa" [Possibilities of using the results of the household budgets research in poverty analysis]. *Biuletyn IGS*, No. 1.
―――― (1992) "Poverty measurement in Poland", in *Poverty Measurement for Economies in Transition in Eastern European Countries*. Warsaw: Polish Statistical Association and Central Statistical Office.
Kostrubiec, S. (1991) "Zagrożenie ubóstwem w pracowniczych rodzinach wielodzietnych" [The threat of poverty in employed families with many children]. *Biuletyn IGS*, No. 1.
Lisowska, E. (1991) "Zagrożenie ubóstwem w pracowniczych rodzinach wielodzietnych" [The threat of poverty in employed families with many children]. *Biuletyn IGS*, No. 1.
Lisowski, A. (1989) "Program badań IGS z zakresu problematyki ubóstwa". *Biuletyn IGS*, No. 1.
―――― (1991) "Objawy ubóstwa w podstawowych szkołach Warszawy" [The symptoms of poverty in Warsaw primary schools]. *Biuletyn IGS*, No. 1.
Podgórski, J. and B. Dobrowolska (1991) *Subiektywne granice ubóstwa a dochody gospodarstw domowych* [Subjective boundary of poverty and household incomes]. Warsaw: CSO.
Podgórski, J. (1990) "Subiektywne linie ubóstwa. Zastosowanie metody 'Leyden Poverty Lines' w warunkach Polski" [Subjective poverty

lines. The application of Leyden Poverty Lines in Polish conditions].
Wiadomości statystyczne, No. 11.

———— (1991) "Subjective poverty lines – some results for Poland". Paper at conference on Poverty Measurement for Economies in Transition in Eastern European Countries, Warsaw.

———— (1992) "Subjective poverty lines – some results for Poland", in *Poverty Measurement for Economies in Transition in East European Countries*. Warsaw: Polish Statistical Association and Central Statistical Office.

Rutkowski, J. (1988) "W poszukiwaniu kryterium ubóstwa" [In search of a poverty criterion]. *Polityka Społeczna*, No. 9.

Tymowski, A. (1973) *Minnimum Socjalne. Metodyka i próba określenia* [The social minimum. Method and determination trial]. Warsaw: PWN.

Wiśniewska, H. (1991) "Rozszerzające się sfery ubóstwa" [Widening poverty spheres]. *Biuletyn IGS*, No. 1.

Winiewski, M. (1984) "Zróżnicowanie dochodów w okresie radykalnych zmian warunków bytu – metodologiczne problemy badań epirycznych" [Income differentiation in the period of radical changes in living conditions – Methodical problems of empirical surveys]. *Ekonomia*, 46 (Warsaw).

Wolska, B. (1991) "Wybrane aspekty sytuacji bytowej rodzin matek samotnie wychowujących dzieci w 1990 r" [Some aspects of the material situation of female single-parent families in 1990]. *Biuletyn IGS*, No. 2.

Chapter 20

Israel: Resistance of Poverty to Change

Rivka W. Bar-Yosef

Ideology, concepts, and research since independence

Israel as a state emerged in less than auspicious circumstances: wars with the surrounding, already well-established Arab states, the turbulence of transition from the largely voluntary sectoral organizations to central political, economic, and military institutions, and the influx of large numbers of immigrants from the displaced persons camps of Europe and from the North African and Asian Arab states. Between 1948 and 1952 the population of Israel tripled. The immigrants brought with them the heritage of a variety of cultural backgrounds but no economic resources, and in the majority of cases arrived after severe physical and mental traumas, many of them disease-ridden and members of disrupted families and communities.

In 1949, before the cease-fire agreements with the Arab states, the government appointed a committee to prepare the basic framework for welfare legislation. In 1953 the National Insurance Law was enacted and the National Insurance Institute (NII) was established. Mandatory social insurance for all employed persons was chosen as most suitable both for organizational and for ideological reasons (Doron and Kramer 1991). A system of wage and salary equity, progressive taxation, subsidies on basic consumption items, and social insurance was thought to be sufficiently efficient to eliminate poverty and ensure general well-being.

Although the socialist–collectivist values of the early Israel weakened during nearly five decades of statehood, nonetheless these principles are still sufficiently accepted to incite heated disputes and criticism, to justify continuous monitoring of their implementation, and to serve as legitimation for changes in social policy.

The commitment of various governments – and Labour governments in particular – gave rise to a certain interest in research. The political establishment wanted to document and monitor the success of their policy and present it to the public as documented by independent and reliable research results. Those dissatisfied with the implementation of social policy and who criticized it, whether for ideological, oppositional, or other reasons, were no less eager to use "objective" data.

In the old university and later the new universities a new stratum of social researchers trained in the UK and the USA, who brought with them an appreciation of empirical data, were strongly motivated to work on socially relevant empirical studies. Social research, especially when it is based on large-scale survey data, is expensive and, if the data are produced by several different institutions, their accessibility depends on the interest and the goodwill of the respective organizations.

The researchers, when they were the initiators, were usually motivated by a mixture of theoretical interest, belief in their role of "social monitors", and ideological and professional desire for involvement in the development of Israeli society. In Israel it is impossible to deal with the problem of poverty and the poor according to the rigorous definition of the concept as "deprivation of basic necessities". It is true that until the late 1960s governmental bodies and the media still used the concept of absolute poverty – mainly hunger and lack of shelter – but this was not the trend of research, whether carried out by governmental bodies, public institutions, or academia. The main issues concerned the triple value-complex of welfare, equality, and integration and their opposites of poverty, lack of equality, and lack of integration. Although the issues were in theory separate and often different persons were involved in each field, in many of the empirical studies the concepts overlap or strongly correlate.

Once the level of absolute poverty had been radically diminished in Israel, the question of relative poverty became the main issue and this was nearly inseparable from questions of equality. The database was usually the same and only the focus of interpretation differed according to the interest of the researchers. Immigrants were in most cases the most recent groups of the poor and often the authorities and researchers chose to define poverty and inequality as inevitable but temporary problems of the process of acculturation and absorption of large groups of immigrants. This field of research is one of the most obvious examples of the linkage between research and politics, and the uneasy but inevitable relations between academia and governmental and other public bodies.

Since the 1970s research has grown in volume. In addition to the universities there are research units in various ministries, in the National Insurance Institute, the Central Bureau of Statistics, the Bank of Israel, the General Federation of Labour and several private research institutes. There is an abundance of relevant data. Much of the important data are produced and processed by governmental bodies. Not all of them are published and some are accessible only with the consent of these bodies. In order to use these data, academic researchers need clearance. They also need funding from outside academia, where they are competing with the research departments of various ministries and the independent research institutes. Much of the funding is made contingent on the "usefulness" of the research for what are defined as acute problems.

In this symbiosis between the political power and social research, both sides are treating each other warily. Academic research is often regarded by policy makers with suspicion as too independent, unpredictable, too theoretical, and critical, and hence not very helpful for their immediate needs. Politicians think in fixed time-periods – from election to election – and serious academic research seems to them to take too long to be useful in the between-election period. It is not easy to periodize results of policy nor is it easy to convince politicians that theoretical research is necessary and is able to discover unexpected and new aspects of the issues in question.

The issue of equality

Despite the rhetoric of equality as one of the desired attributes of Israeli society, it was never expected that no differentiation of salaries/wages and of socioeconomic status would occur. The issue is not equality but the level of inequality. As in most democratic countries, a consensual assumption exists that there is a level of inequality that is unacceptable for Israeli society. But neither theoretical nor political discourse has succeeded in defining a level of acceptable inequality. Measuring inequality served not the evaluation of the actual situation in relation to some ideal type of equality, but mostly as a measuring rod of changes in the pattern of inequality and the public reaction toward degrees of inequality.

A schematic analysis of the research studies concerning the issue of equality reveals several recurring themes:

- egalitarianism in Israeli society: ideologies and social policy (Eisenstadt 1967);
- the adequacy of equality-enhancing programmes and their implementation (Doron and Kramer 1991);
- the endeavour to create a theoretically and empirically verifiable map of the crucial variables for the definition of equality: income, housing, consumption, education, labour market participation, prestige, human capital, health, subjective evaluation of inequality (Sharlin et al. 1992);
- the presumed causes of social inequality: discrimination, cultural differences – traditionalism and modernity, demographic attributes, immigration (Hanneman 1991; Smooha 1978);
- the methodology of measurement of the equality variables: indices and causal analyses;
- the socio-demographic composition of groups positioned at the lower levels of inequality scales (Lewin-Epstein and Semyonov 1993; Matras 1975; Smooha 1978);
- regional inequality – geographical peripheries, development towns, and quality of life discrepancies among urban neighborhoods (Ayalon et al. 1993).

The issue of poverty

Poverty as such was a non-issue in the formative years of Israeli social policy. In the first two decades, society was poor, the general standard of living was low, and there was no well-established, visible upper class, so the category of "the poor" was not sufficiently distinct or conspicuous. The main issues of the period were building the state institutions, absorption of immigrants, and economic development that would provide the resources needed for the immediate tasks of survival. The second reason for not relating to the issue of poverty was ideological. The Labour Party and its mainstay, the Histadruth, could not come to terms with the existence of poverty. Admitting its existence in the Israeli state would have been manifest proof of ideological and political failure. In the 1950s, the years of mass immigration, it was easy to explain the scarcity of housing, the obvious lack of basic amenities, and large-scale unemployment as the inevitable temporary pains of the absorption of masses of immigrants (Bar-Yosef 1955). The issue became critical in the 1960s, when social turbulence and the protest of individuals and communities who had lived in Israel for ten or more years could not be explained away as adaptation and absorption difficulties. The issues raised by the protesters were relative poverty, inequality, and discrimination. The protesters were concerned with quality of life variables, especially housing, education, and employment.

Obviously, social policy did not ensure that all groups shared equally the benefits accruing from the rising standard of living. The fact that those left behind had a distinct demographic profile (large families, low level of education, unskilled or semi-skilled father, originally from North Africa) elicited imputations of discrimination. The relative deprivation felt in the 1960s generated stronger feelings of disappointment than did the objectively worse conditions of the early 1950s. A committee of experts appointed by the Minister of Social Assistance in the early 1960s tried to build a "model of family budget which can satisfy the minimum needs within our society and the provision of which to disadvantaged families is within the ability of the government" (Ministry of Social Assistance 1963: 4). Only in the 1970s was relative deprivation recognized as a legitimate basis for the definition of poverty (Rotter and Shamay 1971). In a period when at last the basic needs of food and shelter were satisfied for nearly all the population, policy makers and public opinion had difficulty in making the conceptual transition from absolute to relative poverty.

The object of poverty research was the population at the lower end of the equality scale, who were referred to by distinctive names: they were "the needy", "the indigent", "the underprivileged", or "the weak strata". The questions were similar to those relating to the issue of equality; the main difference was in their focus:

- theoretical discussions about the concept of needs and the definition of poverty (Salzberger 1992);
- the social meaning of various types of measurement (Achdut and Bigman 1987);
- poverty lines (Achdut and Bigman 1987; Achdut et al. 1989, 1993);
- the socio-demographic composition of the poor (Sharlin et al. 1992);
- the effects of a poor lifestyle: mortality and morbidity, school failure, violence, and crime (Adler 1974; Salzberger 1992; Sharlin et al. 1992);
- types of reaction: protest movements, political attitudes (Azmon 1985; Hasson 1983: 157–74);
- the effects of social policy on "pulling people out of poverty" (Rosenfeld 1989; Salzberger 1992; Shamgar-Handelman and Belkin 1986).

It is of some interest to mention the questions that are seldom or never dealt with. Most often, poverty research refers to urban poverty, whether in the larger cities or in the new and/or peripheral townships. Even some of the macro surveys based on large samples did not include the rural areas. One of the reasons was technical, i.e. the difficulty of sampling and gathering data in hundreds of small localities. But it seems that hidden behind the technical explanation was a conception. Israel's rather small rural population (somewhat less than 10 per cent) lives either in cooperative and collective communities or with extended families in traditional villages. In both cases the individual is embedded in a community of mutual help and responsibility in which the individual members seem to be protected from the destructive effects of poverty.

The issue of integration

The concept of integration became linked to the process of immigration, and its subjects were the various groups of immigrants arriving in Israel. Only very recently was its relevance extended to other areas, first and foremost to the non-Jewish minorities of Israel (Bar-Yosef 1993).

Unlike research on inequality and poverty, integration research was in most cases initiated and transacted within university departments. Many studies attached policy recommendations to their theoretical conclusions. In spite of the apparent separation of the issues of integration from those of equality and poverty, there was much overlapping of theory and data. In his now-classic book about the absorption of immigrants, Eisenstadt (1954) defined integration as:

> (a) participation within the social system; and (b) identification with its values and symbols. . . . [T]he main criteria of actual institutionalization [are] . . . The extent of the social field in which the immigrant participates . . . an important question here is how far he takes part in all the main spheres of the social system . . . how far the immigrants' behaviour is patterned according to the accepted institutional norms of the absorbing society. . . . The extent of identification, of active orientation towards the general values of the social system. . . . The extent of the feeling of "belonging" . . . and of belief in the possibility of achieving various positions and changes through individual or concerted action within it.
>
> (1954: 142–43)

In this first major study of the integration of immigrants, Eisenstadt, probably influenced by Parsons (Parsons and Shils 1951), tried to provide a comprehensive perspective on three levels of integration: the institutional, the acculturational, and the psychological. He had two basic assumptions: (a) that these three levels are closely connected, and (b) that at each level there will be a tendency to stable pattern formation. This ambitious research design was not followed by many researchers, who preferred to focus on one or other of these levels. Obviously this approach to integration is equally relevant to all groups in danger of marginality, be they an ethnic or religious minority, women, the poor, the elderly, the handicapped, or the new immigrants.

The main difference between immigrants and the other potentially marginal groups is the time factor. Immigrants are by definition marginals in the new society, so there is a precise date for the beginning of their marginality. In Israeli research it was assumed that integration is an ongoing process from the initial marginality toward full integration. This expectation had an important practical expression. The immigrants were entitled to a package of material assistance and facilitating programmes, such as language and retraining courses. These rights being linked to immigrant status, the question of how long an immigrant is still an immigrant became an administrative problem.

The bureaucratic definition of the duration of integration (three years) was a practical, primarily budgetary decision, but it signified the normative expectation of a short time-period of marginality. Academic research could not provide any formal definition for an "integration line" akin to the "poverty line" by which to distinguish between the integrated and the non-integrated. There was no uniform and universally valid process of integration. Nor were the aspects of integration suggested by Eisenstadt (1954) necessarily correlated. The path toward integration of different groups was not uniform, and large groups of immigrants, especially those coming from Moslem countries, did not succeed in achieving the expected "institutional" dispersion and remained in their partially integrated status as compared with immigrants from Western countries.

The deficiency of theory in specifying probable time limits for the period of integration blurred the differences between the concepts of poverty, inequality, and marginality as a result of immigration. Three theoretical schools tried to explain the disparity: *the power and discrimination model*, which saw the problem as a competition for power positions between the established old-timers who co-opted immigrants with similar backgrounds, but excluded and discriminated against others; *the acculturation model*, according to which immigrants from Moslem countries brought with them traditional cultural values and behavioural norms that hindered their adaptation to a modern industrial society; *the poverty culture theory*, which found an explanation in the vicious circle of a low level of education, poorly functioning family, and inadequate socialization of children, leading to the development of a certain personality structure, which in turn reproduces the poverty chain.

Selected research studies

The first two projects reviewed here are the Income Distribution Committee and the Prime Minister's Committee on Distressed Children and Youth. These two projects have several attributes in common: they were appointed by the government (by the Finance Minister and the Prime Minister, respectively) and the teams were interdisciplinary, with a mixed membership of academics, other professionals, and government officials. The task, set by the government, demanded a combination of reliable research with policy recommendations. It was also assumed that the government and the members of the committee had common values, at least as far as believing in the power of social policy to reduce inequality and poverty. The two projects had a lasting influence both on the pattern of measurement of poverty and inequality and on establishing the standards of social research for social policy.

The Income Distribution Committee dealt mainly with questions of measurement of inequality of incomes and established a template for this type of research. The Prime Minister's Committee on Distressed Children and Youth was asked to come up with policy recommendations. Nearly all of these were accepted and implemented, thus changing the attitude toward poverty and enlarging the scope of social policy for the following decades.

The income distribution committee

The Committee acknowledged the complexity of the issue of inequality and explained its decision to restrict its task to a single facet – income.

> social disparity is the result of many qualitative and quantitative factors. There is no uniform definition of this concept, hence no single accepted way to measure it. ... [Nevertheless] in the absence of reliable and precise non-economic tools of measurement, and with a lack of comprehensive longitudinal research into the development of non-economic variables, the committee was aware that it is unable to deal with the complex question of social disparity and decided to found its conclusions mainly on economic data.
>
> (Ministry of Finance 1971: 6)

The Committee used several measures of inequality of incomes: income distribution tables by deciles of population ranked by size of income, the Lorenz–Gini indices, and income ratios between the lowest and the highest decile of the population. Both gross and disposable net income tables were calculated. The Committee had doubts about the validity of family income data for the measurement of inequality. Obviously the use of family income entails disregarding the effect of differences in the size of households (number of dependants) with equal income. Nor was the Committee satisfied with the use of per capita income, which meant disregarding the economies of size of a large family compared with single people or smaller families. The concept of the standard adult, in use in several countries, adapted to the consumption habits of Israeli families, seemed to be the most satisfactory tool for the task. By according different weights to each person in the household according to the size of the household, the consumption needs of households of different size were equalized. Table 20.1 shows the "standard adult" tables proposed by the Committee and used in Israel since then.

The advantage of a frequency distribution based on incomes calculated per standard adult became evident when the demographic attributes of the lower deciles were examined. When the variable was family income, the lowest decile contained 48 per cent of single people and 40 per cent of two-person households. It contained only 0.4 per cent of households of six persons. This was an obvious misrepresentation of the standard of living of large families, which were by no means better off than small

Table 20.1 Standard adults per family and weights per person

Family size	No. of standard adults	Weight for marginal person	Average weight for one person
1	1.25	1.25	1.25
2	2.00	0.75	1.00
3	2.65	0.65	0.88
4	3.20	0.55	0.80
5	3.75	0.55	0.75
6	4.25	0.50	0.71
7	4.75	0.50	0.68
8	5.20	0.45	0.65
9	5.60	0.40	0.62
Any additional person		0.40	

families. When incomes were calculated per standard adult, 23 per cent of the lowest decile were families with six and more persons, while single people comprised 24 per cent.

Demographic breakdown of each decile has shown that education, age, family size, residential density, the year of immigration, the country of origin, and possession of durable goods are not randomly distributed over the deciles. Both the lowest and the highest deciles had distinctive demographic profiles. The pattern of measurement established by this Committee became the model for the subsequent periodic evaluations of equality.

More elaborate versions of this model for studying inequality were adopted by a considerable number of later studies. All three types of income – family, per capita, and standard adult – are often used in the same study. In later projects, separate income distributions and inequality measures according to age, occupation, family size, education, geographical residence, and gender were calculated. Some of these breakdowns have shown surprising findings. Thus, by calculating separate Gini coefficients for married women and men, it was found that the inequality index of the incomes of married women is considerably higher than the index for standard adult incomes of married men or the joint index of husbands and wives.

> Women in the upper decile of families receive almost 50 percent of all married women's incomes.... more than half the women within the three upper deciles and 70.7% in the upper decile, against only a fraction of women in the lower deciles, are employed in other than household duties. On the other hand, the ratio of incomes earned by women as against those received by their husbands is higher in the lower than in the upper deciles.... Distribution of pension-derived income displays a degree of inequality similar to that of earned income.
>
> (Even-Shoshan and Gabbay 1986: 173)

The Prime Minister's committee on distressed children and youth

This Committee was much larger than the Committee on Income Distribution and the members represented a larger variety of disciplines and practices. From its inception, the Committee adopted a broad social view. It proclaimed that: "[T]he team does not assume that inequality of income distribution is identical with the problem of poverty. It is possible that the number of the poor is increasing while inequality is decreasing" (Prime Minister's Office 1972: 3). It was the basic assumption of the team that, although deprivation is not solely the result of a low income, but the result of a cluster of factors such as housing conditions, level of education, social integration, and other factors, raising the level of income is nevertheless the necessary first step. In this way the Committee defined both its distinctive identity against the Income Distribution Committee while recognizing the importance of income inequality.

The task was ambitious, combining theoretical, empirical, evaluative, and policy application aspects. After lengthy deliberations the Committee decided:

1. to study and to define the dimensions and aspects of deprivation of youth and children;
2. to survey and to evaluate the social services for youth and children;
3. to propose ways of alleviating and preventing the deprivation of Israel's youth and children and programmes for rehabilitation (Prime Minister's Office 1972: 8).

A list of relevant issues was delineated, each to be studied by a separate team: income maintenance; housing and community; preschool and elementary school education; high school, college, and vocational education; informal education and community social work; family personal health and social services; voluntary social services; alienated and marginal youth; the police; the army; and the structure of services and their integration.

The summary of the discussions and the recommendations was printed, published, and brought to the attention of the public shortly after being presented to the government. The recommendations were widely commented upon in the media and the book served as a strong weapon for lobbying and public pressure on policy makers. The recommendations were accepted and implemented by the government, and they are still the backbone of Israeli social policy. The most important among these recommendations were:

- a universal child allowance should be paid to all families with children;
- child allowances should be taxed according to the usual rate;.
- income maintenance allowances should be paid to all families whose income is below a clearly defined poverty line;
- the minimum income and the poverty line should be updated in line with changes in incomes in the population – the Committee accepted the Rotter–Shamay definition of the poverty line (40 per cent of the median income) and

abandoned the concept of a "minimum consumption items package" suggested by an earlier committee with the same chairman;
- child allowances and income maintenance should be paid by the National Insurance Institute and not by the Ministry of Welfare;
- the Committee emphasized the importance of proper housing for the normal development of young people and recommended that housing standards should depend on the size of the family; the Government should subsidize housing for families living in substandard conditions;
- in the field of education, the Committee demanded that special attention should be given to pre-school education.

Two longitudinal studies

Two longitudinal studies (Salzberger 1992, Shamgar-Handelman and Belkin 1986) grappled with some interesting questions about the "career" of poor families over time and the impact of the corrective measures of social policy.

Salzberger studied "the question of how socially deprived child-raising families are affected by a prolonged period of general socio-economic prosperity accompanied by accelerated inputs in social welfare provisions" (1992: 232). The first phase of the project was carried out in 1964–5 at the height of social turbulence and protests. A random sample of 1,000 families with children was interviewed. The families were ranked on a scale of four degrees of deprivation defined by the number of "exigencies", the term used by the authors for any of four indicators of socio-familial deprivation: income – 50 per cent or less of the average per capita monthly family income; housing density – three or more persons per family sharing one room; health – ill health among both parents limiting their functional capacity; children – families raising four or more children under 17. These were the objective quantitative indices. Information was also collected on "predicaments" – the families' self-perceived problems (Matras et al. 1969; Rosenfeld and Salzberger 1973).

The second phase was ten years later (1974–5) during which period "an accelerated overall input of social opportunities and social welfare provisions ... became available ... and were deliberately directed to the weak strata of the population" (Salzberger 1992: 237). For the 1974 study, two groups of the 1964 study were selected: those classified as high and medium deprived (four and three exigencies, respectively) and a 10 per cent random sample for comparative purposes from the mildly and the non-deprived (one exigency or none) – a total of 361 families. Salzberger developed three scales to grade the families according to their level of deprivation: the socio-familial deprivation scale; the socio-familial disadvantage scale; and the family health impairment scale. It was found that

> substantial material improvement . . . occurred . . . over the period of ten years, as reflected in the reduction of income and housing exigencies. In 1965, 98% of the study group suffered from income exigency, compared with 58% in 1974, a 40% reduction, whereas housing exigencies were reduced by a half, from 66% to 32%. The most disturbing change was declining health. In 1965, illness causing functional limitation of one or two parents was the least prevalent exigency (32.8%) . . . In 1974, twice as many families (65.5%) were afflicted by ill health. . . . Nevertheless, the upward mobility of the study families on the four-point socio-familial scale is a most striking finding. In 1965, 45.5% of the families belonged to the "medium" group and 54.4% to the "high" deprived group, having two, three, or four exigencies, respectively. Ten years later, 9% of the families did not suffer from any exigency and another 21% were rated low on deprivation (one exigency). Among the moderately deprived (two exigencies) were 21% of the families, while 49% remained highly deprived. The trend of upward mobility . . . is even more . . . noticeable from the distribution on an 11-point socio-familial disadvantage scale.
>
> (Salzberger 1992: 242–3)

The strongest predictive factor of mobility was the initial status of the family. Of the variables, housing was the most powerful, followed by income. "Among the demographic variables, the most powerful . . . were, in descending order . . .: years of wife's schooling, military service of husband, age of wife and wife working outside home. Country of origin was of negligible magnitude" (1992: 251).

Two more findings are especially interesting. The first is the critical importance of women in the process of mobility. As seen above, women's attributes and behaviour have a strong impact on the chances of mobility. This finding is in accord with one analysis mentioned above (Even-Shoshan and Gabbay 1986) on the importance of wives' income for the lower deciles. At the same time, women were the main sufferers from health deterioration, attributed by them to frequent pregnancies and family and household stresses. The second finding concerns the subjective self-evaluation of the families. The objective improvement in their position did not change the perceived gap between them and the standard of living of average Israeli families. Probably this why the rate of negative feelings about income and housing remained constant. These feelings found their expression in the voting patterns of the families, who showed overwhelming support for the opposition right-wing parties.

Shamgar-Handelman and Belkin (1986) covered a somewhat later period. The first stage was carried out around 1973 and the second between 1982 and 1983. The aim of the study was "the assessment and measurement of the degree of social mobility of a group of families from three lower-class neighborhoods in Jerusalem and that of their married children ten years later. ... All families in stage one had been classified by the welfare and education authorities as disadvantaged. ... they were the target of various governmental and private programs designed to enhance their status vis-a-vis that of the Israeli population in general" (p. 177). The findings show that, measured on the objective indices of socioeconomic status, the second generation (the married children of the original research population) was much better off than the parents were, both in the first and in the second phase of the study. They were better educated, had more prestigious occupations, higher incomes, and significantly better housing, and managed their life opportunities better. They planned their families, married later than their parents, and delayed child-bearing. The wives, even those with young children, entered the labour market. The parents also improved their standard of living and housing conditions. Their job stability and the entitlement to the old-age pension provided at least some economic security. A small minority achieved occupational mobility, while some were worse off at stage two than they had been ten years before.

Shamgar-Handelman and Belkin, like Salzberger (1992), found considerable mobility as measured by income, housing, education, and occupation. Nevertheless "those who failed to rise according to objective criteria, fell behind heavily in both generations. Those who did rise, many among them with great effort and significant achievement ... succeeded only in maintaining their relative position in society ... that is, *no matter how hard they ran, they stayed in the same place*" (Shamgar-Handelman and Belkin 1986: 152). However, unlike the families studied by Salzberger, the second-generation families studied by Shamgar-Handelman and Belkin were more optimistic and self-reliant. They ranked themselves consistently higher on the status scale than their rank would be measured by quantitative socioeconomic variables.

Although the macro-social measurements of inequality and relative poverty display the structural aspect of social disparity, they cannot answer the question about the life-long stability and generational continuity of the low-income groups. These two longitudinal studies arrive basically at similar conclusions: they show the positive impact of massive targeted social policy and at the same time the pertinacity of hard-core poverty.

Income, housing, health, and education

In many studies and in attitude surveys a common map of five major needs was repeatedly found: income, employment, health, housing, and education of the children. There is no clear-cut ranking of the importance of these needs, neither are they seen by the low-income groups, among them new immigrants, as being entirely dependent on income. A large volume of research turned to the study of these areas using different methods – from statistical presentation of levels of inequality, correlational and causal analyses, to anthropological research and case studies. The subjects are varied, such as low-income groups in general, ethnic groups, women, children, or other sub-populations. Comparative data on "real groups" of the population provide a social map of the poor. This is also more meaningful for the public and policy makers alike. People, politicians, academics, media makers, or others do not think in terms of deciles, but think about families, children, the handicapped – people with bodies and faces.

Income

In addition to the recurrent survey and analysis of income distribution and the calculation of equality coefficients, other income-related variables are surveyed such as cash expenditure on consumer items or number and the type of items bought, the value of home and car ownership, service benefits received from employment and from social services, and the possession of durable goods. These data reveal a more visual and more individualized picture of poverty and of the changing lifestyle of the low-income groups than the important but abstract measures of income distribution by deciles. They also highlight the areas where relative deprivation is most visible and felt daily.

Housing

Housing is of special objective and subjective importance. The influx during the past five years of more than half a million immigrants (1989–94) has put heavy pressure on the housing market and there are many who live in housing that is considered substandard in Israel or in crowded circumstances. Some research has been done on the effects of unsatisfactory housing conditions on the school performance of children. Two social experiments intending to improve the overall character of rundown communities or slum neighbourhoods were followed over several years by sociological research.

One study was a case study of a neighbourhood included in a large-scale project initiated by the government under the title "Project Renewal", which is aimed at the physical and social rehabilitation of a relatively large number of metropolitan and other urban neighbourhoods. The project called for the creation in each locality of a steering committee comprising government officers and representatives of the local population, whose task was to ascertain local needs, to propose and approve the renewal plan, and to follow its execution. This qualitative study focused on the organizational problems of this type of joint committee, the power struggles, and the restricted scope of the effective participation of the local representatives (Shelah and Ben-Ari 1989).

The second study was a longitudinal community study of an independent local initiative, the "Settle with Us" project.

> [The] project was aimed at two goals: attracting higher-status groups to an underprivileged community and achieving social integration between these newcomers and the veteran residents ... Prior to the ... project, Mobiltown was socially and ethnically homogenous ..., fairly isolated from the rest of the country. In order to attract new residents of a higher SES and of the dominant Ashkenazi group, Mobiltown's leaders promised them their own neighborhoods....
> The project has created heterogeneity by allowing the establishment of segregative neighborhood groups and, moreover, has produced inequality by being overproportionally beneficial to the stronger and new groups. From the point of view of enhancing the life prospects and self-image of the less privileged group, however, the ultimate goals of social integration have been achieved, at least to some extent. Though the newcomers have benefited most, the veteran residents – at least in relative terms – have benefited too.
>
> (Ayalon et al. 1993: 172)

In the last chapter the authors discuss the advantages of this model as compared with the government-initiated community renewal project and the social cost of the changes induced by it.

Health

In Israel of the 1980s and the 1990s, unlike decades before, hunger and undernourishment are isolated occurrences. The question of the necessary calorie intake is not a central issue. But other aspects of health welfare – infant mortality, life expectancy, and morbidity – are clearly correlated with income and crowdedness, and, for women, with multiple pregnancies (Salzberger 1992; Shamgar-Handelman and Belkin 1986). In spite of universal health insurance, regional differences in the quality of the services between the central and the peripheral regions have not been eliminated (Sharlin et al. 1992). Research on immigrant groups has found that the country of origin, customs, and beliefs are related to health.

Education

As in other modern societies, the number of years of formal education is one of the most valuable items of a person's human capital. Learning is also a traditional value of Jewish culture, equally appreciated in the traditional religious and in the modern secular circles. The ancient self-image as "the people of the Book" is incorporated in the self-image of modern Israeli society. At the same time, education is perceived as the means for mobility, for escape from poverty and low status, but also as an element of self-esteem. A review reveals that, beyond the professional didactic and pedagogic problems, Israeli educational discourse is indivisibly bound into the universe of poverty, equality, and integration (Adler 1974). Integration in the Israeli educational discourse means several problems: integration in the same classroom of children of immigrant parents of such different backgrounds as highly educated professional parents from the former communist East European countries and very traditional parents from the rural areas of Ethiopia; integration of children from poor families or from disadvantaged families and children of the well-to-do ("disadvantaged" being the label for uneducated parents who are not necessarily of low income). Integration also means the endeavour to find a solution for the much analysed and still not satisfactorily explained overrepresentation among underachievers of children with the "disadvantaged profile": large family, low-education parents, originally from Moslem countries (sometimes labelled as Sephardi or Oriental) (Minkovich et al. 1982). Many researchers were or still are actively involved in educational policy, and in the planning and follow-up of the many experiments aimed towards the problems of integration (Nevo 1979). Until recently it seemed that underlying the educational literature was a value consensus on a preference for equality and integration and less for achievement. More recently a dispute about values has become part of the educational discourse – equality versus excellence, and the continuing of forced integration of schools versus free choice.

Monitoring policy

A large volume of studies evaluates and monitors the intended results of policy measures in reducing or at least stabilizing inequality, reducing poverty, and promoting the integration of immigrant groups. The most important monitoring instruments of poverty and inequality are the annual surveys of the National Insurance Institute (NII). Besides routine comparison of income distribution and measures of inequality and poverty over time, the NII publishes data and analyses of special populations such as the unemployed, wage-earners compared with independent business people, new immigrants, families of different sizes and structure, pensioners, ethnic groups, minority groups, and geographic areas (Achdut and Bigman 1987; Achdut and Tzedaka 1989; Achdut et al. 1989, 1993).

In the past decade a new line of research under the general title of social indicators has been carried out and published by the Center for Policy Research.

> [I]n choosing social indicators for inclusion ... [the centre was] guided by the selection criteria used by the OECD. [It] concentrated on output-oriented indicators relating to final social outcomes, rather than on data on inputs and throughputs. [It] preferred indicators relevant to policy, i.e., those describing social conditions amenable to change through public policy ... indicators that would be, as far as possible, independent of particular institutional arrangements, so as to be reasonably comparable over time and between countries.
> (Kop 1988: 2)

The Center focuses on selected problems, among them housing, health, and taxation. It also publishes yearly its version of a social balance sheet for the nation.

From the point of view of social policy, the most important question is the effectiveness of the large-scale policy measures to keep poverty and inequality in check: the financial tools of the tax system, subsidies, the use of the consumer price index and transfer payments, and the provision of services for selected target populations. Since they take up a good slice of the national budget, it is politically vital to prove to voters and to all other interested parties that the theory on which these measures are based is valid and the results are worthwhile.

Subsidies

A policy of subsidies has been used continuously by the government as a relatively easily manageable tool for controlling prices; the target is the reduction of the market prices of basic items of food, transportation, and electricity. The amount of subsidies for various items is changed from time to time. The NII data show that subsidies indeed reduce the inequality of disposable income, but various items have different effects on each decile according to its pattern of consumption. For example, the three lowest deciles obtain 50 per cent share of the total subsidy on bread, whereas the share of the three upper deciles is only 13 per cent. The subsidies on poultry, eggs, and transportation benefit the middle deciles somewhat more, and the upper deciles get more from the subsidy on milk.

The efficiency of subsidies as a tool of social policy is questioned, given the fact that, despite the periodic changes in the subsidized items, a considerable share of the total subsidy aids the upper deciles. In evaluating the relative social and economic cost of the two alternatives, the NII researchers are of the opinion that there are sufficiently good reasons for the use of this kind of universal tool in preference to direct means-test-linked payments to lower-income groups (Achdut and Tzedaka 1989).

The consumer price index

Consumer price index linkage is the most important insurance against the erosion of incomes – earnings or transfer payments – in the inflationary economy of Israel. The crucial importance of the index was especially apparent in the period when the Israeli economy suffered from three-digit inflation. Since then inflation has been more or less stable around 10 per cent. This still means a considerable erosion of the value of incomes without a periodic index-based correction.

Transfer payments

The list of transfer payments has grown over the years and it contains universal (child allowance, maternity, old-age and survivors, unemployment, etc. payments) and selective (means-linked guaranteed income maintenance, housing subsidy), contributory (most of the universal benefits) and non-contributory (most of the selective benefits) rights. The principle of social insurance was expanded to absorb non-insurance-based types of benefits. Social expenditures are the largest item (41 per cent) of the National Budget minus the payment of debts (defence is a near second). The largest expenditure in the social services slice is income maintenance. In the past decade, per capita expenditures on income-maintaining payments have increased, while expenditures on services in kind decreased.

Table 20.2 Selected measures of poverty, 1992

	Extent of poverty (%)		
	Before transfers	After transfers	After transfers and taxes
Families	34.2	15.6	16.4
Individuals	30.8	16.0	17.2
Children	31.9	19.3	21.3
Poverty gap (%)	66.2	27.9	27.1

Source: Achdut et al. (1994).

The monitoring research data are political tools in the dispute about the social necessity of transfer payments and the maintenance of constant relative value by the linkage to the consumer price index. These, as shown by the studies, are irreplaceable tools in the struggle for the alleviation of poverty. The data on the poverty gap prove that a slimmed-down package or its elimination would more than double the poverty gap for many, and it would change the present problem of relative poverty, defined by the changing poverty line, into one of absolute poverty involving deficiency of basic needs.

Table 20.2 shows that transfer payments reduce by half the population under the poverty line (defined now as 50 per cent of the median income of the population). It seems that the effective influence of the tax system is less than expected, probably caused by lack of knowledge about tax deductions, by faulty adjustment of taxes by the authorities, and by the less-than-perfect progressiveness of the tax system. The combination of family allowance and tax exemption for each child was intended to equalize the economic status of large families with that of smaller families. This aim was never realized. The majority of large families are in the lower deciles of the equality scale. They are characterized by the typical poverty syndrome of one earner per family, mostly an unskilled or semi-skilled worker with low education, and consequently low income.

The latest data of the National Insurance Institute have shown that, despite the intended "corrective policy", during 1992 the extent of poverty (the deciles whose income is below the poverty line) increased by 14.2 per cent and in 1993 by another 5.7 per cent. About half of these households are headed by a non-working adult of working age, a quarter are headed by an elderly adult, and another quarter by a non-elderly and employed adult. These facts were headlined by all the written and electronic media. The disappointment with the results of the massive investment in social policy has overshadowed the euphoria caused by the peace process and the distress caused by the difficulties of its realization. The precarious majority of the Labour government is seriously endangered by the vehement public reaction and the acrimonious attacks of the opposition. The immediate response of the government in the form of the law for the "reduction of the extent of poverty and income disparity" was passed with a remarkable speed by the Knesset. The law provides increased transfer payments, promising that these will push 20–25 per cent of the low-income population over the poverty line (Achdut et al. 1994).

This is one of the infrequent instances when research findings had a political impact. A deeper analysis of the timing of publication of the data reveals the roles played by the media, the political constellation, public sensitivity to the problem, and the struggle of the responsible ministers to defend their much attacked status in creating a situation in which the numbers, although often not properly understood by the parties involved, were nevertheless taken up and used.

Concluding remarks

The most disappointing conclusion is the resistance of poverty to substantial change. Even the maintenance of a more or less stable pattern of income distribution and relative poverty requires large investments and a well-planned social policy. It should be made clear that the strategy for raising groups of people above the poverty line is different from a strategy of changing the income dispersion pattern. Comparison of the pattern at different points in time does not reveal the turnover among the poor. We have to know more about movement in and out of poverty. The effort to push groups of people above the poverty line, however worthy, is also dangerous. Resources above the poverty line as measured for political purposes do not ensure a decent standard of living or quality of life. It is very seldom asked how much above the poverty line makes possible a truly non-poor style of life, a stable position, and better opportunities for the future generation. What is the difference between those whose income is 49 per cent of the median income (who are hence below the poverty line) and those whose income is 51 per cent, who are hence officially out of poverty?

A great number of studies expose the substantial influence of the tools of measurement on the results. Without falsifying or manipulating data or their presentation, the final evaluation can be more or less in line with expectations or with desired ends, depending on the tools and the breakdowns used. Hence, the importance of using several different tools and analysing carefully the meaning of differences in the results achieved by various means of measurement – precise-seeming measurements such as the scale of ranked deciles or the rather simple poverty line are attractive to researchers and policy makers alike. Income data are also relatively easy to come by and amenable to statistical manipulation. A rather instructive example is the history of the poverty line. In its present form it was proposed by two economists (Rotter and Shamay 1971), working in the research department of the National Insurance Institute, as an interim trial criterion for the use of the Prime Ministers' Committee on Distressed Children and Youth (see pages 438–439 above). Without any formal decision or critical discussion the temporary poverty line became permanent, the only change having been to raise it from 40 per cent of the median income to 50 percent.

Poverty, equality, and integration are interconnected, whether from the perspective of policy, of values, or of the subjective well-being of those who are at the lower end of whatever scale is used for their measurement. In Israel the most emotive issues for the low-income groups are housing and education. Housing and educational differences are powerful components of the relative deprivation syndrome and they were triggering elements in several protests.

The research studies discussed in this chapter covered not only income but also health, housing, education, and community status. The more intangible aspects of deprivation – representation, participation, and relative deprivation – lurked in the background. On the other hand, employment and unemployment were not discussed in spite of their central importance because their multifaceted influence on the deprivation syndrome needs fuller treatment (Bar-Yosef 1993). The protest movements too were neglected although they should be seen as a step towards the self-help and self-organization of the deprived.

Better theory and more comparative research are needed for understanding the structure of the deprivation syndrome and the relative importance of the various components in different cultural and material situations. More scrupulous analysis of the measurements used is needed to uncover their hidden biases and the images they may project. It is also desirable to include in the measurement of the deprivation syndrome items that are less suited to precise measurement and sophisticated statistics, but that may in some instances be more relevant in representing and communicating the style of life of the deprived, the changes in that style, the preferences of people, and the need for policy intervention.

References

Achdut, L. and Bigman, D. (1987) *The Measurement of Poverty: Theoretical Approaches and Trends in Israel During 1979–1984.* Israel: National Insurance Institute (in Hebrew).

Achdut, L. and E. Tzedaka (1989a) "Subsidies for basic consumption items and the distribution of incomes", in Y. Kop, (ed.), *Resource Allocation for Social Services, 1988–89*, Jerusalem: Center for Policy Research.

Achdut, L., O. Kristal, and Y. Shaul (1989) "The dimensions of poverty and the inequality of income distribution in Israel: 1987 and 1988", National Insurance Institute, *Annual Survey 1988, 1989*.

Achdut, L., Y. Awad, and N. Israeli, (1993) "The dimensions of poverty and the inequality of the distribution of incomes in Israel: 1992", in L. Achdut (ed.), *Annual Survey 1992–1993*. Jerusalem: National Insurance Institute, Research and Planning Administration.

Achdut, L., Y. Awad, Y. Shaul, and N. Israeli (1994) "The dimensions of poverty and inequality of income distribution in Israel: 1993", in L. Achdut (ed.), *Annual Suevey 1993–1994*. Jerusalem: National Insurance Institute, Research and Planning Administration.

Adler, C. (1974) "Social stratification and education in Israel". *Comparative Education Review*, 18.

Ayalon, H., E. Ben-Rafael, and A. Yogev (1993) *Community in Transition: Mobility, Integration, and Conflict.* Westport, Conn.: Greenwood Press.

Azmon, Y. (1985) "The protest of a disadvantaged population in a welfare state', in S. N. Eisenstadt and O. Ahimeir (eds), *The Welfare State and Its Aftermath*. London: Croom Helm.

Bar-Yosef, R. W. (1955) "The Moroccans: The background to the problem". *Molad*, 17: 247–51 (in Hebrew).

—— (1993) "Melting-pot, multiculturalism and pluralism: The Israeli case" in K. Yaron and F. Poeggeler (eds), *Meeting of Cultures and Clash of Cultures: Adult Education in Multicultural Societies*. Jerusalem: The Magnes Press.

Doron, A. and R. M. Kramer (1991) *The Welfare State in Israel: The Evolution of Social Security Policy and Practice*. Boulder, Colo: Westview Press.

Eisenstadt, S. N. (1954) *The Absorption of Immigrants*. London: Routledge & Kegan Paul.

—— (1967) *Israeli Society*. London: Weidenfeld and Nicholson.

Even-Shoshan, O. and Y. Gabbay (1986) "Distribution of family income and taxes", in Y. Kop (ed.), *Changing Social Policy: Israel 1985–8*. Jerusalem: Center for Policy Research.

Hanneman, R. (1991) "Promises in the Promised Land – Mobility and inequality in Israel". *American Journal of Sociology*, 96(6).

Hasson, S. (1986) "The emergence of an urban social movement in Israeli society – An integrated approach". *International Journal of Urban and Regional Research*, 7(2): 157–174.

Israel (1971) *Report of The Committee on Income Distribution and Social Equality* (in Hebrew).
Israel (1972) *Report of The Prime Minister's Committee on Distressed Children and Youth* (in Hebrew).
Kop, Y. (ed.) (1988) *Israel 1988: Socio-Economic Indicators.* Jerusalem: Center for Policy Research.
Lewin-Epstein, N. and M. Semyonov (1993) *The Arab Minority in Israel's Economy: Patterns of Ethnic Inequality.* Boulder, Colo.: Westview Press.
Matras, Y. (1975) *Social Inequality – Stratification and Mobility.* Englewood Cliffs, NJ: Prentice Hall.
Matras, Y., I. M. Rosenfeld and L. Salzberger (1969) "On the predicaments of Jewish families". *International Journal of Comparative Sociology*, 10 (3–4).
Ministry of Social Assistance (1963) Report of Expert's Committee (Hebrew). Jerusalem, Israel: Government Printing.
Ministry of Finance (1971) Report of the Committee on Income Distribution and Social Equality (Hebrew). Jerusalem, Israel: Government Printing.
Minkovich, A., D. Davis and J. Bashi (1982) *Success and Failure in Israeli Elementary Education: An Evaluation Study with Special Emphasis on Disadvantaged Pupils.* New Brunswick, NJ: Transaction Books.
Nevo, D. (1979) *The Gifted Disadvantaged: A Ten Year Longitudinal Study of Compensatory Education in Israel.* New York: Gordon & Breach.
Parsons, T. and E. Shils (eds) (1951) *Toward a General Theory of Action.* Cambridge, Mass.: Harvard University Press.
Prime Minister's Office (1972). Report of the Prime Minister's Committee on Distressed Children and Youth (Hebrew). Jerusalem, Israel: Government Printing.
Rosenfeld, J. M. (1989) *Emergence from Extreme Poverty.* Paris: Science and Service Fourth World Publications.
Rosenfeld, J. M. and L. Salzberger with Y. Matras (1973) *Family Needs and Welfare Provisions.* Jerusalem: The Hebrew University.
Rotter, R. and N. Shamay (1971) "The patterns of poverty in Israel". *Social Security*, 1 (in Hebrew).
Salzberger, L. (1992) "A longitudinal study of social-familial deprivation : The effect of increased inputs of social opportunities on the mobility of socially deprived families". Unpublished PhD thesis, the Hebrew University, Jerusalem, (in Hebrew).
Shamgar-Handelman, L. and R. Belkin (1986) *Ten Years Later: Parents and Children – Processes of Change and Mobility versus Perpetuation and Stagnation in a Disadvantaged Population an Inter- and Intragenerational Perspective.* Jerusalem: The Hebrew University.
Sharlin, S., R. Katz and Y. Lavie (1992) *Family Policy in Israel.* Haifa: Haifa University.
Shelah, I. and E. Ben-Ari (1989) *Urban Renewal, Interorganizational Linkages and Community.* Jerusalem: The Hebrew University.
Smooha, S. (1978) *Israel: Pluralism and Conflict.* Los Angeles: University of California Press.

Chapter 21

North America: Poverty Amidst Plenty

Ramesh Mishra

This chapter presents an overview of the study of poverty in two North American countries: the USA and Canada. Although similar in many respects, these two countries differ in their approach to poverty and are discussed separately. The chapter is in three sections: the first looks at the USA, the second at Canada, and the third discusses the findings and offers some comments and suggestions.[1]

The United States of America

Ever since President Johnson declared an unconditional war on poverty, it has featured prominently as an issue of public policy and as a topic of research in the United States. But that is not to say that there have not been ups and downs in national concern about poverty and the poor. The 1960s represented the high water mark of interest in poverty. In the 1970s, as other issues such as inflation, unemployment, and recession came to the fore, interest in poverty declined. With the resurgence of neo-conservative values and beliefs under the Reagan presidency, the war on the poor replaced the erstwhile war on poverty. And this new departure in social policy seems to have revived the debate about poverty and the poor, with the difference that, whereas in the 1960s the concern was with poverty, in the 1980s it was more with the poor and their behavioural characteristics. By the end of the 1980s the neo-conservative wave seemed to have rolled past and modest reforms and anti-poverty measures once again appeared on policy agendas. Because poverty research is an applied area of study and tends to be policy orientated, the political economy of American social policy has formed the context within which issues have been studied. Naturally enough, the dominant ideological currents have influenced the nature and scope of poverty research.

Research on poverty has undoubtedly been the forte of the USA. With the beginning of the famous war in 1964, there was an "unprecedented flow of public spending for research on the 'nature and causes of, and the cures, for poverty" (Haveman 1987: 4)'. Between the mid-1960s and the mid-1970s federal expenditure on research and development concerned with poverty grew forty-fold in real terms (ibid.: 38). The Institute for Research on Poverty at the University of Wisconsin-Madison was set up in 1966. By the late 1980s it had published over 40 books and some 800 papers on the subject and it continues to be a focal point for poverty research (Sawhill 1988: 1073). Apparently it is a unique research institution in the West in that it is devoted exclusively to the study of poverty. In 1968 a longitudinal study of the economic fortunes of 5,000 American families – the Panel Study of Income Dynamics – began at the Survey Research Center of the University of Michigan. Its findings were reported annually (Duncan 1984). If research and development were the key to winning the war on poverty, the USA would have won it long ago. Alas, poverty not only persists but it appears that the USA leads the industrialized world in poverty. A cynic might conclude that poverty is directly related to the amount of research conducted on it. But such a conclusion would be unwarranted. For research is but one determinant – and a minor one at that – of social policy. Indeed social research – including poverty research – is best seen as a part of the political and ideological debate about the social world and how it might be shaped in accordance with particular values, beliefs, and interests.

Concepts of poverty

Poverty lines

How to demarcate the poor from the non-poor population has been central to the study of poverty. How and where to draw the poverty line is of crucial importance because the notion of poverty has clear value and policy implications. As an index of deprivation and suffering, and as a statement about the size of the nation's population that lacks the basic necessities of life, it has a strong judgemental aspect. Unlike its close cousin "inequality", poverty is a statement about a condition that demands redress – some form of meliorative action. It is not surprising that where to draw the poverty line and how to count the poor have been the staple of controversy in poverty research.

The declaration of the War on poverty in 1964 led to the adoption of an official poverty line the next year. This showed the nature of the enemy to be vanquished so that progress in the war could be monitored. Despite wide-ranging criticism, this official definition has remained the basis for the count of the poor in the United States. The poverty line is based on the cost of buying a minimal diet and other necessities of life. A survey of 1955 had shown that average households spent one-third of their income on food. Hence the cost of a minimally adequate diet multiplied by three was deemed to be the poverty threshold. The poverty line is adjusted according to the family size and, annually, for changing prices. This threshold has remained virtually unchanged since its inception and forms the touchstone for debates on poverty (Ruggles 1992).

This official poverty line is based on an "absolute" rather than a relative standard, if by absolute we mean a standard considered appropriate for the early 1960s and that has been "frozen" in time. There is no clearly articulated rationale for the poverty line except what has been noted already. As the economy grows and the average income rises, the poverty line falls in value in relation to the average income. Thus, from 46 per cent of the median income at its inception in 1965 it had declined to 32 per cent of the median in 1986 (Sawhill 1988: 1076). Measured by an absolute standard, poverty may decline simply as a result of rising average incomes. At any rate, poverty in the USA declined from 19.0 per cent of the population in 1964 to an all-time low of 11.1 per cent in 1973. It then hovered around 11.5 per cent for the rest of the 1970s before rising sharply in the 1980s. After reaching a high of 15.2 per cent in 1983 it declined, but remains at a level higher than in the 1970s (Danziger et al. 1992–93: 2–3). Explaining the persistence of and the recent rise in poverty has formed a significant part of the research and debate on poverty.

Although the official measure of poverty shows a substantial decline in poverty, relative measures tell a different story. Using 50 per cent of the median income as the poverty standard – a commonly employed measure of poverty in cross-national research – a much higher percentage of Americans turn out to be poor. For example, in 1972, 17.9 per cent were poor by this standard, compared to 11.9 per cent by the official measure. Ten years later the corresponding figures were 18.9 per cent and 15.0 per cent, and in 1988 19.5 per cent and 13.0 per cent (Ruggles 1992: 7). Moreover, since the 1960s relative poverty shows a small rise rather than a decline (ibid.).

Critique of the official poverty line

The many shortcomings of the official definition of poverty loom large in American debate over poverty. Much of the critique seems to fall fairly clearly into two main ideological positions. The basic liberal position seems to be that the poverty line is too low, so that it understates poverty substantially and thus inhibits ameliorative action. The conservative critique too finds the official standard misleading but from the opposite viewpoint, i.e. that it grossly overstates the extent of poverty. Naturally, not all critiques fall into these two categories. It is possible to identify a left position as well as one that may simply be described as "technical". The latter aims at refining techniques of measurement and developing more appropriate and sensitive measures, including alternative conceptions of poverty.

A major criticism of the official measure of poverty – and it is conservatives who have made it their forte – is that it does not take into account in-kind transfers. Since the mid-1960s expenditures on programmes such as Food Stamps, Medicare, Medicaid, housing subsidies, and the like have grown enormously. The in-kind benefits represent a very substantial transfer to the low-income population but are ignored when computing income. The result, according to conservatives, is a gross understatement of the resources available to the low-income population and an inflation of poverty figures. Following these criticisms and the ensuing debate, the US Bureau of Census began collecting data on the in-kind transfers. They are assigned a cash value using a number of alternative methods. In 1987, for example, the official poverty rate was 13.5 per cent. Including the value of food stamps and housing benefits reduced the poverty rate to 12.0 per cent. Including the value of medical care reduced it further to 8.5 per cent. And this was without taking into account many in-kind benefits from both government and non-government sources (Ruggles 1990: 142).

Conservatives also believe there is widespread under-reporting of income. The poor, it is argued, obtain a good deal of income through "moonlighting" and other forms of underground activity that remains unrecorded. Estimating such income with any degree of reliability and accuracy is a difficult task. Nonetheless, guesstimates have been made by official as well as other researchers, and these bring down the poverty rate further. A Congressional Budget Office study estimated that taking in-kind transfers and under-reporting into account would bring the poverty rate for 1976 down from 12.0 per cent to 6.4 per cent. Another estimate put it even lower (Anderson 1978: 22–3).

Taking such factors into account, Martin Anderson (1978), policy adviser to the Reagan government, concluded that the war against poverty had been won and that issues such as welfare dependency and the undermining of work incentives by social assistance now needed far more attention. As we shall see below, this line of argument was developed more fully and systematically by Charles Murray some years later.

The official poverty line is based on gross income and takes no account of taxes and contributions. This was of little consequence in the 1960s when the poor paid little in the way of direct taxes. Between the mid-1960s and the mid-1980s, however, the tax burden on low incomes increased a good deal. In more recent debates the issue of taxation has been raised by liberals. The after-tax income of low-income earners would be lower and this increases the poverty population. It is of course difficult to take into account all forms of taxes. The US Bureau of the Census
publishes estimates of income net of federal income taxes and payroll taxes from time to time. An estimate for 1986 showed that adjusting income for the payment of these taxes increased the poverty rate from 12.2 per cent to 13.1 per cent (Ruggles 1990: 137). Whatever the exact nature of incidence, taking direct taxes into account raises the poverty rate slightly, thus counteracting the effect of adjusting for in-kind transfers. Smeeding (1984: 88) estimated that in 1979, when in-kind transfers (including medical care), under-reporting of income, and incidence of taxation were taken into account, the poverty rate dropped from the official figure of 11.6 per cent to 6.1 per cent. It should be noted that tax reforms of the late 1980s and early 1990s have increased earned income tax credit and in other ways eased the tax burden on low incomes, especially on earned income (Levitan et al. 1993: 8).

Poverty researchers differ a great deal on how to treat in-kind benefits and taxation for the measurement of poverty income. Should non-cash benefits be included at all? And, if so, should all benefits, including medical assistance and benefits from non-governmental sources, be counted? And, finally, what is the best way of computing the value of these benefits? These are all questions that await a clear answer. Patricia Ruggles, a leading authority on the measurement of poverty, suggests that "cash-like" in-kind benefits such as food stamps as well as taxes should be taken into account in computing income. She argues quite convincingly that medical care costs are different in that they do not free up income for spending on other items in the way that food stamps or housing assistance, for example, do. The unreality of assigning the value of medical benefits as income for the purposes of measuring poverty can be seen in the case of the elderly population. This group is a heavy consumer of medical care and adjusting the in-kind benefits including medical care results in the poverty rate in 1987 plunging from 12.2 per cent to a mere 2.1 per cent (Ruggles 1990: 142). Yet it is quite clear that the resources available to these individuals do not change even if their income is boosted by the cash value of the medical benefits. An official inquiry was set in motion in 1992 to look into the existing poverty standard and its measurement and no doubt its report and recommendations would be of much interest (Haveman 1992–3: 24).

Absolute vs. relative measure: revising the poverty line

As mentioned earlier, multiplying the cost of a minimally adequate diet by three has remained the formula for calculating the poverty line since its inception. A major criticism of the official poverty measure is that the multiplier of three harks back to the standards of the 1950s when it was first developed. Critics point out that even by mid-1960s the formula was obsolete because the average American family was spending only about one-quarter of its income on food (Ruggles 1992: 2). By the late 1980s this had dropped to about one-sixth (Ruggles 1990: 50). In short, with higher living standards, changing patterns of consumption, and the rise in the cost of necessities other than food – notably shelter – expenditure on items other than food was absorbing a greater proportion of family income. Yet the poverty line was taking no account of these changes. A multiplier of at least four would be needed, according to some critics, to bring the calculation of income closer to the conditions of life in the 1990s.

The subject of updating the poverty line raises, in some quarters the spectre of relativizing the line. Continually updating the line, it is argued, will make it a "moving target". Surprisingly perhaps, this viewpoint receives some support from liberals (e.g. Wilson 1987: 171), who believe that an officially approved, stringent, and "absolute" standard has the advantage of being widely accepted and of providing a modest, and therefore attainable, target for anti-poverty policy. A further advantage, it is claimed, is that it enables the nation to chart the changes in poverty over time and thus provides a clear benchmark of progress, in a way that a revised poverty standard would not.[2]

Many liberal poverty researchers, however, reject the notion of an absolute or unchanging poverty line. Poverty, they argue, is a relative concept, invoking no less an authority than Adam Smith in support of their view. If poverty means not having the means to acquire those necessities of life that "the custom of the country renders it indecent for creditable people, even of the lowest order, to be without", then poverty cannot be defined without reference to the "custom of the country", i.e. the norms and standards prevalent in the community (Ruggles 1990: xv). In other words, the poverty line must be adjusted to the changing standards of the community to which people belong. In short, the relativists argue that poverty is a social and not a physical norm, and that the official poverty line in the United States is clinging to a physical survival notion of poverty. Thus critics point out that the official poverty line has been falling as a proportion of the average household income and thus increasingly slipping below what most Americans in effect believe to be the poverty standard (ibid.: 44). One result of a declining poverty line is that the "poor" come to represent a narrower subset of the population, one that differs a good deal from the average household. More and more of the poor therefore come to be seen as different, e.g. an underclass that is behaviourally different from mainstream America and responsible for its own plight. Such a perception of the poor may "undermine support for programmes designed to combat poverty" as the poor become more isolated politically (Ruggles 1992: 9). A poverty standard that keeps in line with the changing standards of the community, it is argued, would be less atypical and less exclusive.

Although liberals favour a relative notion of poverty, the idea of defining poverty as a proportion of average income finds little favour. Ruggles, for example, argues as follows. Although a relative measure such as half of median household income has the advantage of simplicity, it is little more than a statement of people's relative levels of consumption or their place in the hierarchy of income distribution. But poverty, unlike inequality, implies a value judgement. Therefore what matters for public policy and normative debate is the *actual* rather than *relative* standard of consumption. A measure of poverty based on relative income distribution is not likely to be useful as an instrument of public policy and income transfers. Ruggles favours a relative definition of poverty based on a market-basket approach to minimum needs. A panel of experts could decide on a basket of goods representing minimum need. Apart from adjusting for price changes it could be revised periodically – say every ten years – to take into account changes in consumption patterns. This method would have the advantage of being backed by the authority of "experts" and, although the method would be no more "scientific" or objective than any other, it would at least have a clear rationale. It would steer clear of the Scylla of an abstract relative measure and the Charybdis of an out-of-date relative poverty line masquerading as an absolute measure of poverty (Ruggles 1992: 2).

One thing that becomes quite clear from the debate on poverty and its measurement is that it is unrealistic to draw a rigid line of demarcation between the "poor" and the "non-poor". A more realistic view of living standards suggests a gradation stretching from the very poor to poor to near-poor. The situation of the elderly in the United States illustrates the point. The aged are rightly seen as the success story of anti-poverty policies: their poverty rate is below the national rate and was falling through the 1970s and the 1980s when the general trend was in the opposite direction. However, what this statistic does not show is that a good part of the elderly population has an income not far above the poverty line (Burton 1992: 17). This means that, if the poverty threshold is raised, a disproportionately high percentage of the elderly find themselves in poverty. They belong to the category of the near-poor. The policy implications of being close to the poverty line are not difficult to see. For example, any switch of resources from the elderly to other groups, e.g. children, risks bringing many of the older Americans back into the poverty fold (Ruggles 1992: 8).

A related issue is that of the poverty gap, which shows the actual income level of the poor, or more precisely the extent to which the income of the poor falls short of the poverty level. It thus measures the depth or severity of poverty. Using a 75 per cent of the poverty line measure as an index of "severe" poverty we find that in 1980 more than half of poor children and 42 per cent of the elderly poor were severely poor (Smolensky et al. 1988: 98). Looking at it from another angle, the average poverty gap (after taxes and transfers) for poor households was 38 per cent for families with children and 29 per cent for the elderly (ibid.: 114). Clearly this is an important additional statistic in the analysis of poverty and in ascertaining the condition of the poor.

Alternative conceptions of poverty

Much of the debate on poverty in the United States has centred around income – the level of poverty line income and how to compute it. Relative vs. absolute definitions of poverty have also centred around income. The shortcomings of an income-based approach have led some social scientists to formulate alternative conceptions of poverty.

Haveman and Burton (1993) suggest an approach based on "net earnings capacity", i.e. the potential of households with working-age adults for generating income if they could use their human and physical capital to full capacity. This calculus of the potential income of a household, which takes into account capital assets as well as personal characteristics such as age, gender, education, and race, yields a picture of poverty very different from that based on actual income. For some groups the net earnings capacity (NEC) poverty rate turns out to be a good deal higher than the official poverty rate, and for other groups much lower. For example, in 1988 a female-headed white family with a child under 18 had an official poverty rate of 37.7 per cent. The NEC poverty rate for the same group was 52.4 per cent, i.e. a much higher proportion of this group had a low potential for generating income. This was even truer of the non-white female-headed family. On the other hand, one-person households, e.g. students, showed an NEC rate about half the official poverty rate (ibid.: 65). Dividing the NEC of the household, i.e. its income-generating potential, by the official poverty line, i.e. its need, gives the "NEC welfare ratio". Those with a low ratio of earnings capacity to need are the truly poor. Haveman and Burton believe that this measure says something important about the population that the official measure does not. These comparisons suggest that "a new definition of national poverty is in order, one which would attend to the longer-term capabilities of individuals and families, rather than to their current cash income." (1993: 71). They find that overall only about 40–50 per cent of the official poor are poor in terms of their ability to be independent and self-sustaining. The policy implication of Haveman and Burton's concept is that those identified as earnings-capacity poor might be made the object of special assistance to realize their potential fully. Such assistance might include education and training, help with child-care costs, counselling, and the like. Their approach also takes care of what might be called differences in family preferences, which are not at present reflected in the poverty statistics. For example, there may be two identical families comprised of husband and wife and child. One family might decide that both parents go to work, the other that the mother stays at home. As a result the latter family may fall below the poverty line, given that the role of two earners has become critical in sustaining living standards. By Haveman and Burton's criteria these two families would be identical in terms of their earnings capacity and presumably be above the poverty line. Undoubtedly the concept of "earnings capacity poverty" is both useful and interesting, albeit the calculation of earnings capacity is far from unproblematic. It is also difficult to see how such an approach could replace the income measure of poverty.

However, as a supplementary approach it seems far more acceptable.

Mayer and Jencks (1993), who share Haveman's dissatisfaction with the income approach to poverty, take a different tack. They too believe that the disregard of in-kind benefits and underreporting of income make the income approach inadequate. Moreover, they argue, poverty is not so much about inequality of income as a condition in which a person is deprived of some of the basic necessities of life, e.g. adequate and nutritious food, satisfactory housing, access to medical care. Mayer and Jencks find that the distribution of basic necessities has only a weak correlation with income. Moreover, consumer expenditure surveys for the period 1960–89 show that the distribution of household *expenditure* is less unequal than the distribution of household *income*. Mayer and Jencks reject the view that these discrepancies are a result of borrowing and credit buying, and they imply that income measures present a misleading picture of the resources available to households (ibid.: 137). They also examine disparities in measures of material well-being, e.g. housing conditions, access to cars and telephones, access to medical and dental care, and find that trends in the distribution of these do not show that "the gap between the rich and poor has widened over time". Mayer and Jencks argue in favour of developing a measure of material well-being of households similar to the measure of income, expenditure, and consumption patterns. They acknowledge the difficulty of developing such a measure because it requires a knowledge of the details of household need, e.g. health status, work-related expenses, and the like, in order to assess well-being. A focus on material well-being also leads to the disaggregation of various forms of inequality; for they find that different kinds of material inequality respond to very different technical, economic, political, and social forces. Overall, for the period 1960–89, material inequality in the USA correlated weakly with trends in income inequality, underlining the inadequacy of income as a predictor of well-being (ibid.: 123).

Theories and hypotheses in poverty research

The War on Poverty and the Great Society programmes were aimed primarily at the poor. They expanded existing means-tested programmes or developed new ones. With the notable exception of Medicare, most of the programmes and developments e.g. higher benefit levels and relaxed eligibility rules for the AFDC (Aid to Families with Dependent Children), Food

Stamps, and Medicaid, involved means-tested benefits that helped only the low-income population. On the other hand, Social Security, the major New Deal programme, on the other hand was a contributory insurance programme catering for the general population. Beneficiaries paid into the programme and in this sense "earned" their benefits. It was also based on labour force attachment. By contrast, the social assistance programmes of the Great Society were non-contributory, i.e. beneficiaries had not in any sense "earned" these benefits. The programmes were seen to be supporting what had appeared as a largely undeserving population. Mainstream America saw these as programmes for which it was paying but from which it was not benefiting. By the early 1970s, then, the American welfare state had developed a two-tier structure: one consisting of comprehensive, nearly universal social insurance programmes that enjoyed a great deal of support, and the other consisting of a set of ostensibly "anti-poverty" programmes that had a much weaker base of support and legitimacy (Weir et al. 1988: 422). In the late 1970s it was the latter that became the chief target of neo-conservative attack on the welfare state. Much of the debate in the United States around the poor and poverty focused on these means-tested programmes meant for the working-age population – above all AFDC or "welfare" – and their consequences.

Unlike in the 1960s, the major concern in the 1980s was not with poverty and its reduction, but with the reduction of social expenditure, with the apparent dysfunctions of the welfare state for the market economy, and more generally with restricting government commitment to social protection. Indeed, the Reagan administration replaced the war on poverty with a war on the poor (Katz 1986: ch. 10). Far from being a cure for poverty, social programmes, and especially welfare, began to be seen as a *cause* of poverty and welfare dependency. Not poverty as such but pauperization, i.e. dysfunctional and deviant behaviour on the part of the poor, was now identified as the main social problem of the 1980s, and the early 1990s reflected this shift in agenda from a concern with poverty to a concern with the poor. It must also be remembered that issues of race, especially in relation to work, family patterns, and crime, loom large in American debate over poverty and welfare. If in the 1960s the issues were racial discrimination and injustice, in the 1980s they were about deviant behaviour – single parenthood for example – centred in the black poverty population. Three overlapping questions have dominated recent debate over poverty:

1. Why, despite a massive increase in social expenditures and programmes targeted on the poor, has progress in reducing poverty been so limited?
2. What, if any, is the relationship between social welfare programmes and systems and such phenomena as the rise in joblessness among young blacks and the sharp rise in black female-headed families?
3. Is there a growing underclass – a subset of the poverty population whose attitudes and behaviour depart substantially from the mainstream – and if so what is behind its growth?

These are by no means the only questions being asked and debated around poverty but there is no doubt that, with the shift from a liberal to a neo-conservative definition of social problems, these questions have tended to dominate the public debate. A variety of theories and hypotheses have clustered around each of these questions and defy neat classification. One way of looking at the debate is in terms of conservative theses and their rebuttal by liberal researchers.

On the first question, namely why poverty persists, conservatives have come up with two different answers. One is that in fact the war against poverty has been won. Here the focus is on the limitations of the official poverty count, which leaves out of account in-kind transfers and unreported income. The official poverty rate is said to bear little relation to reality. From this viewpoint, then, poverty is no longer an issue. The social problems confronting Americans are now those of welfare dependency, out of wedlock births, criminality. and other dysfunctional behaviour on the part of the lower strata of the population (Anderson 1978). In short, urban America is faced with a growing underclass. Here social assistance and social welfare programmes more generally are seen as bearing a major responsibility. The second answer, which overlaps a good deal with the first, emphasizes the failure of the war on poverty. In spite of the massive effort of public policy to èradicate poverty and the massive rise in social spending, poverty rates remain disconcertingly high. The problem lies in the behaviour of the poor themselves, for which public policy bears a heavy responsibility. In short, one viewpoint is that poverty is now little more than a statistical artefact, the other that it persists because of the perverse consequences of a liberal social policy. In the 1970s, the dysfunctions of the American economy (inflation, unemployment, budget deficits, etc.) were blamed on government interference with the market economy and increased state spending.

Government economic policy was to blame for the state of the economy. Likewise, government social policy was now seen as the cause of social ills (Gilder 1981; Murray 1984).

The two conservative theses outlined above have stimulated a great deal of debate and research. We have already reviewed the debate on issues related to the measurement of poverty, e.g. in-kind transfers, under-reporting of income, and taxation. We therefore turn to the second of these theses and to the liberal response it has evoked.

Poverty and social policy: the conservative perspective

The theme of the perversity of social programmes was expounded most systematically and provocatively by Charles Murray (1984) in *Losing Ground*. Murray contends that poverty had been declining since about 1940, a decline that continued into the late 1960s. During the Johnson years – when the War on Poverty began and social programmes and expenditures multiplied – this twenty-year-old trend simply continued. The decline in poverty had nothing to do with the growth in social programmes and expenditures, which occurred in the late 1960s and 1970s. Indeed, the decline in poverty came to an end in the early 1970s and subsequently rose to a level higher than in the late 1960s. So what went wrong?

> In 1968, as Lyndon Johnson left office 13% of Americans were poor, using the official definition. Over the next twelve years our expenditure on social welfare quadrupled. And, in 1980, the percentage of poor Americans was 13%. Can it be that nothing changed?
>
> (Murray 1984: 8)

Murray lays the blame squarely on the perverse effect of Great Society policies on the low-income population. "Basic indicators of well-being took a turn for the worse in the 1960s most consistently and most dramatically for the poor. In some cases earlier progress slowed, in other cases mild deterioration accelerated" (ibid.).

Murray's basic argument is that liberal thinking, which dominated the reform of the 1960s, took the view that it was the system, and not the individual, that was to blame for poverty. In absolving individuals from responsibility for their own economic fate it in effect destroyed the moral and material incentive for poor individuals to be self-supporting and responsible. By liberalizing eligibility for welfare, by raising benefit levels, and by teaching that it was the system's fault that people were poor, liberal social welfare policy undermined work incentives. Females were offered the incentive of becoming a single-parent and going on welfare. Murray marshals a wide array of statistics to show that labour force attachment among black youths weakened substantially and joblessness grew apace. There was a large gap between the participation rates of young whites and blacks. The number and proportion of female-headed families, especially among blacks, grew substantially. Growth of female-headed families alone accounted for one-third of the growth in poverty between 1970 and 1980. Murray sees a fairly direct connection between black joblessness and the rise in crime and violence in inner cities. Increasingly, black youth was deprived of the incentive – moral and material – of making an effort and leading a life of independence, self-respect, and hard work even if the rewards were modest. As the work habits of generations of black youths were destroyed, they turned to crime and the underground economy as a way of survival in inner cities. It should perhaps be noted that Murray, along with most other conservatives, is concerned with working age poverty. For the working-age population, the new rules of social policy made it "profitable for the poor to behave in the short term in ways that were destructive in the long term". Moreover, the new rules masked these long-term losses. "We tried to provide more for the poor and produced more poor instead. We tried to remove the barriers to escape from poverty, and inadvertently built a trap" (ibid.: 9).

Murray's thesis has been subjected to a devastating critique and its standing as a "scientific" work may not be particularly high (Wilson 1987: 17). Its importance lies in its pervasive – systematic and redolent with rhetoric and hyperbole – presentation of the perverse-effect-of-social-policy thesis and in giving voice to a set of attitudes towards welfare that is fairly widespread in middle America. The racial elements in Murray's interpretation of poverty and welfare are also quite explicit. Published in 1984, Murray's work is said to have provided a convenient legitimation for Reaganite social policy in the mid-1980s. For Murray, then, poverty had been declining during the war and the post Second World War years as a result of economic growth and might have gone on doing so but for the liberal social policy – well-intentioned but disastrous in its consequences – of treating the deserving and the undeserving poor alike and legitimizing dependency and welfare.

Lawrence Mead's (1986) work is also concerned with the perverse effects of social policy in the United States, in particular "welfare" or social assistance. He too started with the question why, twenty years after the War on Poverty, poverty still existed in America. He locates the problem not so much in the proliferation of social programmes and expenditures as in the permissiveness of the welfare state. The system distributes benefits without demanding anything in return. Clearly this does not help the poor to improve their functioning; for poverty today "often arises from the functioning problems of the poor themselves", such as difficulties in getting through school, in working, and in keeping their families together (ibid.: ix).

Mead too notes the explosive growth in social programmes and expenditures since the early 1960s and the fact that over the same period "welfare dependency and unemployment have grown, standards have fallen in the schools and rising crime has made some areas of American cities almost uninhabitable" (ibid.: 1). The racial aspects of welfare and dependency feature prominently in Mead's work. He writes: "There is substantial agreement about the nature of the social problem. A class of Americans heavily poor and non-white, exists apart from the social mainstream" (ibid.: 3). Reintegration of this growing underclass into mainstream America is for Mead the real challenge. The social problem is not only the destitution of the functioning citizens and their families but also "widespread dependency, with millions of Americans, including many working-age adults, subsisting on federal benefit programs" (ibid: 19). Murray finds that working-age people on welfare (presumably black women with young children) have absolutely no obligations. This makes them a privileged group compared with average Americans, who are obliged to work for a living and to perform a variety of roles to a high standard. It is this absence of any obligation to work or to do anything in return for state benefits that, for Mead, is the nub of the problem. Although the Great Society programmes did some good, such as improve opportunities for non-whites and reduce poverty, they did little to improve work and family problems among the disadvantaged. Indeed these got worse. Expanded welfare rolls, widespread dependency on state benefits such as food stamps, and the existence of a small underclass responsible for a large part of urban disorders cast serious doubt on social progress. Mead's answer to these problems is work. The state must attach conditions – above all work requirements – to programmes that serve the working-age population. Thus Mead's message is that of "workfare", i.e. the state must demand some form of work, education, and training in return for social benefits. Mead thus joined the rising chorus of voices demanding workfare in the United States in the 1980s. Clearly the policy of workfare has been quite influential – even if largely at a symbolic level – as evidenced for example by the Family Support Act of 1988, which includes employment, education, and training provisions for adults on AFDC.

The Liberal and the left response

According to W. J. Wilson (1987), the work of conservatives such as Murray has "lit a fire" under the liberals, forcing them to respond to the conservative challenge. The thesis that readily available and high levels of welfare benefits, notably AFDC, are mainly responsible for the rise in female-headed families has been subjected to close scrutiny and extensive research (see, for example, Ellwood and Bane 1984). Liberals have pointed out that the real value of AFDC payments and food stamps increased only from 1960 to 1972, after which it declined sharply as states failed to adjust the value of benefits to inflation. Yet this fall in the real value of benefits seems to have had no effect on the growth in female-headed families or male joblessness. In 1975 Congress passed the earned income tax credit, which provided an additional incentive for the poor to work. Later, in the 1980s, the tax credit was expanded further. If Murray's thesis of the disincentives of welfare had any validity, the trend in the growth of female-headed families, out-of-wedlock births, and black joblessness should have slowed down or reversed as a result of these changes. But nothing of the kind happened. All of these kept rising.

Inter-state variations in benefit levels provide another test of the same hypothesis. AFDC benefit levels vary widely across states. If Murray is right, the incidence of dysfunctional behaviour by the poor should be higher in states with higher levels of benefits. But no clear relationship has been found between the variables. For example, Cutright (1973) found no association between out-of-wedlock birth-rates and benefit levels. Other studies on the subject report either a slight association or none. True, the generosity of the welfare system and the number of female-headed families in the jurisdiction were found to be positively correlated, but the nature of the causal relationship is unclear (Sawhill: 1988). One relationship that is quite clear is that between the generosity of welfare benefits and the living arrangements of young single mothers. Single mothers tend to move out of extended family arrangements and set up on their own in states where welfare benefits are generous (ibid.).

Income maintenance experiments have also provided a test for their effect on work disincentives and family formation. Guaranteed income experiments show a slight work disincentive effect, and *prima facie* evidence on family formation shows that guaranteed income made some difference. But more careful analysis of the data showed that the income maintenance element in the experiment had no effect on family composition (Sawhill 1988: 1105). The main reason for the growth of black female-headed families is a rise in out-of-wedlock births. And, as noted already, this shows no clear relationship to the welfare system. Overall, then, research findings do not support the view that welfare is a major cause of the growth of female-headed families or out-of-wedlock births. No perverse effects of welfare are in evidence in these respects at least.

Able-bodied single people do not receive welfare. The connection between the unemployment of young blacks and welfare is therefore indirect. A young man whose common law spouse and child could get more from AFDC than he could make from a job paying the minimum wage has little incentive to work in such a job. He is better off "working" in the underground economy and thus enjoying his freedom at the taxpayer's expense. Conservatives such as Murray see this as the main cause of unemployment among young blacks and a major contributor to black female-headed families. Liberal researchers believe other reasons are more important for both these phenomena. On the thesis of black unemployment there is at least one piece of research that has damaging implications for the conservative thesis (Osterman 1991). In the 1980s Boston enjoyed an economic boom that brought virtual full employment in the city. The poor blacks in Boston took full advantage of the economic opportunity and there was a dramatic decline in both unemployment and poverty. In 1988, when the poverty rate for American central cities was 19 per cent, Boston's rate was only 3.5 per cent. Poverty rates also fell substantially for female-headed families. Clearly, given the opportunity for work blacks responded as "good" Americans. What is more, Massachusetts, the state in which Boston is located, is very generous with its AFDC as well as other welfare benefits such as subsidized housing. If generous welfare benefits act as a disincentive then this was an ideal testing ground for the Murray thesis. Furthermore, jobs in Boston were by no means highly paid. Nearly half of the jobs held by the poor paid less than $5.00 dollars an hour at a time when the federal minimum wage was $3.35 an hour. This research offers evidence that is a clear refutation of the Murray thesis.

Beyond these specific hypotheses, which have been tested and found wanting, the conservative thesis as a whole has come under fire for its gross oversimplification of the relation between poverty and social policy. Essentially, writers such as Murray make a one-to-one equation between social spending and the reduction in poverty, ignoring other variables that enter into the equation. Thus critics have pointed out that unemployment in the 1970s was double the rate it was in the 1960s. Real wages, which had grown steadily through the 1950s and 1960s, had stopped growing in the 1970s. It was a decade of severe economic recessions. Murray simply ignores all this. Thus research shows that, for every 1 percentage point rise in the unemployment rate of prime-age males, poverty goes up by 0.7 per cent, after controlling for average income, transfers, and inflation. Moreover, unemployment affects low-income working families far more than middle- or upper-income families (Sawhill 1988: 1089).

Other factors to which liberal research has drawn attention include the demographic factor. For, although the economy grew through the 1970s, growth was not enough to absorb the numbers entering the labour market (the baby boom generation). The state of the economy, then, had a lot to do with why poverty failed to decline. Indeed, the role of the market economy in creating poverty and that of income support programmes in reducing poverty become quite clear from poverty rates before and after transfers (Sawhill 1988).

The relationship between economic growth and poverty is far more complex than is made out in conservative arguments. This becomes clear from the situation in the 1980s. Research shows that between 1982 and 1990 the United States experienced its second-longest economic expansion since the Second World War, yet poverty rates declined relatively little. Why? In a thorough study of the phenomenon of the "unexpectedly slow decline in poverty" in the 1980s, Blank (1993) seeks to answer the question. During the recession of 1981–2 the poverty rate was over 15 per cent. In 1989, towards the end of the long boom, it still stood at 12.8 per cent, well above the historic low of 11.1 per cent in 1973 and at about the same level as in 1980. Given favourable economic circumstances – economic growth, lower unemployment, and lower inflation – the expected rate of poverty was 9.3 per cent rather than 12.8 per cent in 1989. Blank examines a range of explanations for the sluggishness of poverty but finds them inadequate. These include the measurement of poverty (not counting in-kind transfers), changes in income support policies (Reagan cutbacks and restrictions), the regional distribution of the poor, and changes in the family composition of the poor. She locates the main explanation in the substantial real wage declines among low-wage workers throughout the 1980s. With economic growth, unemployment fell rapidly and working-age people in the bottom quintile of the population increased their work effort more sharply than in the 1960s. Despite high labour participation rates, however, declines in the wage rates of low-wage earners made economic growth "a far less effective tool" for reducing poverty than it was in the economic expansion of the 1960s.

Blank does not examine the reasons for the decline in wages but draws attention to some of the reasons suggested by other researchers. These include a decline in the unionization of labour, polarization of the labour market between "good" jobs and "bad" jobs, and the globalization of the economy and its impact on wages. Be that as it may, Blank concludes that, if the trends of the 1980s were to continue, "trickle down" will be dead. It will have very little relevance to poverty reduction and other options, however difficult politically, such as income redistribution and social transfers will have to be considered.

On the relationship between social expenditure and the reduction of poverty, liberal scholars point out that reduction of poverty among the elderly has been the great success story of American social programmes. It has been achieved mainly through social security – a universal, insurance-based programme rather than one targeted on the poor. In fact the social security programme does far more to lift Americans out of poverty than the targeted programmes (Sawhill 1988: 1099). Thus, even among the non-elderly, social insurance programmes have been two to three times more effective in reducing poverty than means-tested cash transfers (ibid.). It is not difficult to see why. Benefits provided by social insurance programmes tend to be a good deal higher than those provided by means-tested programmes. For example, during 1940–70 social security benefits for a retired couple were typically about 40 per cent higher than AFDC benefits for a three person family (Smolensky et al. 1988: 45). After 1970, AFDC benefits, which are not indexed, fell in real value. Social security benefits, on the other hand, were indexed. By 1980 the typical retired couple received almost twice the benefits received by a three-person family on AFDC with a prime-age head (ibid.). AFDC payments typically fall far short of the poverty line. In 1987 the median state payment standard for a family of four was only 44 per cent of the federal poverty line (Meyer and Moon 1988: 183, Table 5). It is not surprising that, despite a large outlay, the very fact of being an assistance programme meant for the poor prevents it from eradicating poverty. Its main purpose is to *relieve* rather than to prevent or eradicate poverty. The point liberals make is that even the function of relieving poverty is not performed by means-tested benefits. For example, in 1990 only 42 per cent of those below the poverty line received cash assistance and over one-quarter of the poor received no benefits at all. Among the elderly, only half of those eligible for supplemental security income (SSI) actually received it (Burton 1992: 7–8). Clearly this raises the question of the take-up of means-tested benefits – a subject that appears to feature little in debates on poverty.

One answer to the question posed by conservatives, namely why poverty persists despite the effort to eradicate it, begins by desegregating poverty. By comparing the poverty of particular groups of people, for example the elderly and children, it becomes possible to ask why age poverty has been reduced so successfully and why, moreover, it continued to decline through 1970s and 1980s against the general trend in poverty. Conversely, we may ask why child poverty has remained higher all along and has been rising in recent years. A comparison between these two groups brings out the role of public policy as well as the part played by social insurance type programmes in combating poverty. Put simply, age poverty has been substantially reduced because public policy willed it. A social insurance programme with high levels of benefits, and meant for the general rather than the poverty population, the supplemental security income (SSI), whose benefit level has been set nationally, the indexing of social security benefits – these policy decisions represent the generous treatment of the aged, who are not expected to be in the labour force. Children, on the other hand, have been treated very differently. Children are expected to be taken care of by the parents, working-age adults who are expected to be independent. The USA is unique among Western industrialized countries in never having instituted a child allowance or family allowance programme. Typically it tends to be a universal programme that helps all families with the cost of child care. The aged have been provided with a floor of income – through the SSI – that is set nationally and is relatively generous. The income floor for children is set in effect set by AFDC – a standard that varies from state to state – at a level far below the not overly generous official poverty line. When we add to this the fact that wages in the low-paid sector have declined and family incomes have been stagnant or declining since the early 1970s, it is not difficult to see why the poverty rates of these two groups are the way they are and why they have diverged in recent years (Smolensky et al. 1988).

Comparative poverty research in the United States has drawn attention to some of the ways in which the United States differs from other countries. A comparison of eight Western industrial countries in 1979–81 shows American poverty rates to be the highest. The data also indicate that countries with the lowest poverty tend to be those that emphasize universal rather than targeted programmes for income support. Thus Australia, another country that uses targeted programmes quite extensively, also shows poverty rates comparable to that of the United States (Smolensky et al. 1988: 96–7, 112). Cross-national research on poverty and social policy more generally is adding a valuable dimension to nationally based studies.

The debate over the underclass

In the United States, the 1980s were without doubt a neo-conservative decade. Because conservatives locate the cause of poverty – or more precisely dependency – chiefly in the attitudes and behaviour of the poor, these issues have been at the centre of the poverty debate. The term "underclass" has served as a loose conceptual underpinning for this debate. However it is the terminology and context of the debate that are new rather than its substance. For one thing, "underclass" has a clear affinity with the "culture of poverty" tradition in the analysis of poverty – a notion that refers to a subset of values, attitudes, and behaviour patterns among the poor that sets them apart from the rest of society and that impedes their integration with mainstream society. For another, it harks back to an older – and recurring – theme in conservative thought, which sees permissive forms of social welfare (poor relief) as causing a great many ills, for example loss of work incentives, habits of dependency, indiscipline, and demoralization among the poor. The arguments of American conservatives such as Murray (1984) and Mead (1986) are a re-run of old themes and concerns (for instance, the attack on the Speenhamland system of poor relief in England in the 1830s). Indeed, some of the remedies proposed by conservatives – workfare and the retrenchment of welfare assistance – are strongly reminiscent of the poor law reform of 1834 in England, with its principles of less eligibility and the workhouse test. The underclass debate also echoes the concern in England in the late 1800s about the "pauperized population" and the growth of "dangerous and criminal classes" in parts of London and other cities.

Be that as it may, the debate over the underclass in the United States has an element to it that was missing in the earlier debates, namely race. As Wilson (1987: ch. 1) argues, conservatives such as Murray seem to have thrust the issue of race in American poverty to the fore – an issue that liberals have tended to see largely in terms of racism and discrimination by whites. High rates of unemployment, female-headed families, out-of-wedlock births, and crime have been seen almost entirely as a product of systemic discrimination – historical and contemporary. The oppression of the black population and its accommodation to its position in the social hierarchy of American society explain the high incidence of such phenomena in the black population. This has meant turning a blind eye to the pathologies of black family and community life. The debate over the underclass has focused attention on the dynamics of black poverty in inner cities and its relation to the changing economic and social structure of urban America.

The "underclass" is not a concept with any clear reference point in either theory or empirical reality. It refers to a class of "disreputable" poor (in the American context, to the black poor) whose values, attitudes, and above all behaviour seem to set them apart from the rest of society – they literally drop out of the class system – and impede their integration into mainstream society. Is there such an underclass in America and has it been growing in recent years? Conservatives believe that that is the case and, as we have seen, that it is liberal social welfare policies that are to blame. There is now a sizeable literature that addresses the issues arising out of the underclass thesis.

One of the most original and influential works on the underclass is Wilson's (1987) *The Truly Disadvantaged*. Wilson, a black sociologist, accepts the conservative thesis that in American society there exists an underclass and that it might be growing. It consists of a heterogeneous grouping of inner-city families and individuals whose behaviour and characteristics are at variance with those of mainstream America, for example in respect of labour force attachment, female-headed households, out-of-wedlock birth and crime. Chronic joblessness, persistent poverty, and social isolation are some of the main characteristics of the ghetto poor or the underclass. Though Wilson's notion of underclass is nominally colour-blind, his focus is on the black underclass. Wilson's analysis owes something to the culture of poverty view of the underclass but offers a structural explanation for the emergence and persistence of the deviant and pathological behaviour patterns.

Wilson's thesis may be summarized, somewhat baldly, as follows. The changing nature of the economy in the United States has resulted in chronic joblessness in inner cities, where most poor blacks live. Jobless black youths have turned to criminal activity. Joblessness and imprisonment have meant a serious drop in the number of marriageable males. As a result, out-of-wedlock births and female-headed households have been growing. Moreover, ghetto poverty has become more concentrated and the ghetto poor more isolated as middle-class and respectable blacks have left inner-city areas for suburbs or other parts of the cities. The race-specific policies of the 1960s and 1970s – equal opportunity, anti-discrimination – primarily benefited the more able and advantaged blacks, enabling them to be upwardly mobile while leaving a substantial minority of disadvantaged blacks – the underclass – in a hopeless situation. Wilson sees the solution in developing European-style social policies that are universal and comprehensive rather than targeted on particular groups – whether economic or ethnic. These include job creation and full employment, family allowances, a national labour market strategy, and a child-care strategy. For Wilson, the life chances of the ghetto underclass can best be improved "by emphasizing programmes to which more advantaged groups of all races and class backgrounds can positively relate" (1987: 155).

Wilson"s work has spawned a good deal of research and debate. The hypotheses implicit or explicit in his analysis have been subjected to empirical test and close scrutiny (see e.g. Jencks and Peterson 1991). Prominent among these are: the increasing concentration of urban poverty – increasingly the poor are to be found in areas characterized by high rates (40 per cent or more) of poverty; social isolation – increasingly the ghetto poor are cut off from social contacts with the mainstream, i.e. middle-class and working-class black families; increasing polarization of income among blacks; the outmigration of black middle-class families from inner cities; the decline in suitable jobs (requiring minimal education) for poor blacks in inner cities; the lack of suitable marriage partners, leading to a rise in female-headed families.

The verdict is somewhat mixed on the Wilson thesis (Jencks and Peterson 1991; Wilson 1989). The economic argument connecting a lack of suitable jobs in the inner city to black unemployment receives ample confirmation. Moreover, wage rates in low-paying jobs also appear to have declined. The connection between the growth of female-headed families and the dearth of marriageable males, however, appears to be more complex than suggested by Wilson and there is little support for a causal connection. Aspects of black culture and changing notions of family and marriage in the United States seem to be more important in accounting for the rise in female-headed families than economic factors. The thesis of the increasing concentration of poverty receives support in the largest central cities of the rust belt. But even here it is not clear whether this is simply due to an increase in poverty in recent years or to greater segregation of the poor. There is no evidence of increasing black segregation along income and class lines between 1970 and 1980 in metropolitan areas. There is also little evidence that the poor have become more isolated from the mainstream than in the past. Finally, the ghetto poor (living in areas of concentrated poverty) seem to differ little in political attitudes and behaviour from the poor living elsewhere.

The concept of underclass itself has come in for a good deal of criticism. Many social researchers find little conceptual validity in a notion that lumps together disparate groups and individuals who do not necessarily share the characteristics associated with the underclass, namely being poor, or being on welfare, living in the ghetto or inner city, being an unwed mother, being unemployed, or engaging in criminal activities. Taken singly, none of these attributes qualifies a person for membership of the underclass. How then do we define the group? For without being able to operationalize the concept we cannot go far in either proving the existence of the phenomenon or showing that the class is growing.

Ricketts and Sawhill (1988) defined underclass areas as those with an above-average incidence of high school drop out, female-headed families, welfare dependency, and non-attachment to the labour force by prime-age males. Analysing 1979 data they found that the total population living in such areas came to 2.5 million or only 5 per cent of the American population.

Ruggles (1991) used the criterion of persistent poverty to identify the underclass. However, in the literature, persistent poverty has been operationalized in a variety of ways, by some as being poor in five out of six consecutive years, by others as being poor over an eight-year period. Leaving aside the elderly and the disabled, Ruggles estimated the persistent poor in urban areas to be less than 2 per cent of United States' population. Ruggles, however, leaves open the question of whether the persistent poor can be seen as "part of a self-perpetuating culture whose members remain in or near poverty over most or all of their lives" (ibid.: 186).

Jencks (1991) believed that the idea of a growing underclass rests on the "illusion of class homogeneity". So that, for example, if one of the behavioural attributes of the class increases (e.g. crime), then the entire class is seen as growing. It is the same with other attributes; for example, if poverty increases, then it is assumed that the class, with all its deviant behavioural patterns, must be growing (ibid.: 97–8). Jencks' approach was to disaggregate the characteristics subsumed by the term underclass and to examine them separately, charting their changing incidence and causation. Thus he examined long-term poverty, the inheritance of poverty, the proportion of black population on welfare, teenage pregnancy, and joblessness, but he did not find that they are all growing or indeed that they move together. Jencks, in short, did not find the notion of underclass very meaningful or useful. W. J. Wilson too favoured dropping the notion of underclass in favour of something less amorphous, such as "ghetto poor".

Left social scientists reject the notion of underclass partly because it is something of a red herring. It distracts attention from the substantive problems of American society and a serious debate about their causes and their solution. Katz (1993: 21), for example, writes: "As a modern euphemism for the undeserving poor, it reinforces the tradition of blaming the victim." Moreover, in concentrating on the "behaviour of a relatively small number of people clustered in inner cities [it] deflects attention from the problem of poverty". (ibid.: 21–2). For Weir et al. (1988), the notion of underclass, with its "emphasis on the individual characteristics of the poor as the solution to poverty", is a natural outgrowth of the agenda of the War on Poverty (ibid.: 425). This particular perspective has had "an enduring influence" on the thinking about black Americans and their problems. They reject this approach to "poverty", which has resulted in a bifurcated welfare state in America – one for the poor and one for the non-poor, socially divisive rather than solidaristic – and which isolates the problem and its solution from broader issues of socioeconomic policy and political action (ibid.: 425–30).

Canada

Social policy development in the United States and Canada has been contrasted in terms of a "big bang" (USA) vs. a "steady state" (Canada) approach. The Canadian approach to poverty seems to fit the description. Unlike the USA, Canada never declared a "war" on poverty. Somewhat along the lines of European countries Canada has developed an array of policies and programmes seeking to ensure a national minimum standard of life for all Canadians. Poverty has been tackled indirectly and change has often been incremental. Yet in the 1960s Canada too felt the impact of the rising concern over "poverty amid affluence" in the United States and elsewhere. In Canada too, poverty became a focus of interest in the late 1960s (Guest 1980: 170–3).

Concepts of poverty

There is no official measure of poverty in Canada. However, the so-called "low income cut off" (LICO), an income level used by Statistics Canada to identify the low-income population, has acquired the status of an unofficial poverty line (Ross and Shillington 1989: ch. 2). The calculation of the LICO, which dates back to 1968, has some similarity with that of the American poverty line. A survey of family expenditures in 1959 showed that the average Canadian family spent about one-half of its income on the basic necessities of food, clothing, and shelter. Thus families that had to spend a substantially higher percentage of their income on the basic necessities would have little left over for other needs. They could therefore be considered as living in "straitened circumstances". Statistics Canada (StasCan) adopted 70 per cent as the cut-off: families that spent more than 70 per cent of their income on essentials would be considered to be living in straitened circumstances. Applying this standard to 1965 incomes, 25 per cent of Canadians were found to be below this LICO income level, i.e. poor. Since 1971 StatsCan has conducted its income surveys annually. The family expenditure surveys, which show the changing expenditure pattern of average Canadians, are carried out every four years and form the basis for estimating the proportion of income spent by average Canadians on food, clothing, and shelter. StatsCan then marks up this percentage by 20 per cent. The income level of families that spend this amount ($x + 20\%$) on the three basic necessities becomes the LICO. The 70 per cent standard based on a 1959 survey gave way in 1973 to a 62 per cent standard based on a 1969 survey and in 1980 to a 58.5 per cent standard based on a 1978 survey (Ross and Shillington 1989: 7). The survey carried out in 1990 brought it down to 54.7 per cent, because the average spending on the three essentials had dropped to 34.7 per cent (National Council of Welfare 1994: 74, n, i). Thus the Canadian LICO, unlike the American poverty line, is a relative rather than an "absolute" standard. The income level is adjusted according to the size of the household and the type of residential community (e.g. rural, small town, city), and updated to take into account changes in the consumer price index.

Among other definitions of poverty in Canada, two in particular deserve mention. In 1973, the Canadian Council on Social Development (CCSD), a leading voluntary organization, developed a measure of income inequality that used 50 per cent of the average household income as the low income standard. In choosing a cut off of 50 per cent of average income the CCSD

Table 21.1 Canadian low income measures (C$)

Household	LICO	CCSD	SPCMT
One person	12,063	11,828	16,398
Three person	21,291	23,655	21,694
Four person	24,534	27,597	30,204

Sources: Ross and Shillington (1989: Tables 2.1, 2.2, 2.4).

Table 21.2 Population in poverty (%)

	National definition	LIS definition
Canada	14.0	12.1
United States	11.7	16.9

Sources: Ross and Shillington (1989: Table 10.1); Battle (1991: Table A); Sawhill (1988: Table 2).

implied that those with an income of less than half of the national average were falling below the desirable minimum standard. In effect the CCSD income measure has also become a measure of the population with less than adequate income, in short the poverty population (Ross and Shillington 1989: 9).

The Social Planning Council of Metropolitan Toronto (SPCMT) – an unofficial body – uses an approach based on the cost of a basket of goods and services. The SPCMT uses a social rather than a merely physical survival standard. A panel made up of experts as well as lay members decides on the type of goods and services necessary for a socially adequate level of living, which are then costed by professional buyers. However, because the SPCMT is a Toronto-based organization, its budgetary standard refers to that city and would not necessarily apply elsewhere (ibid.: 11).

It is of interest to note that these three poverty lines – all of which are relative – are not so far apart, albeit their method of calculation limits their comparability. Table 21.1 shows the figures for 1989.

The Luxembourg Income Study (LIS) provides a useful database for cross-national comparison of poverty lines. The LIS poverty line is based on half of the median disposable income of households. Table 21.2 shows the figures for Canada (1981) and the United States (1979). Table 21.2 shows that, whereas the

American poverty line based on an absolute standard understates poverty, the Canadian measure based on LICO – a relative standard – seems to go the other way.

In Canada the poverty rate, as measured by the LICO, fell from 29.0 per cent in 1961 to 14.0 per cent in 1981 (Battle 1991: Table A). Canada's worst postwar recession in 1981–2 pushed the rate up to 17.0 per cent in 1983. By 1989 it had declined to 13.6 per cent but the recession of 1990–1 pushed it back up again (National Council of Welfare 1994: Table 2). We saw earlier that measured by a relative standard, for example 50 per cent of the median household income, the poverty rate in the United States shows no improvement at all. Comparable figures for Canada are not available, but insofar as the LICO is a relative measure it would seem that relative poverty in Canada shows a steady decline since 1961. The lowest rate of 13.3 per cent was reached in 1977, after which it rose somewhat, dipping below 14 per cent only in 1989. As in the United States, poverty among the aged has fallen sharply since the the early 1960s and the decline continued through the 1980s. The poverty rate for households headed by over 65s fell from 21.9 per cent in 1979 to 9.5 per cent in 1986 (Ross and Shillington 1989: 44). Although by Canadian measures the overall poverty rate for the elderly remains high, a cross-national study shows that, using the American absolute poverty line, only 4.8 per cent of the aged were poor in 1981 compared with 16.1 per cent in the United States in 1979 (Smolensky et al. 1988: 105). The difference narrows, however, when the 50 per cent median household income standard is used (17.2 per cent compared with 23.9 per cent) (ibid.: 96).

The LICO of StatsCan and the poverty line of the CCSD are both based on pre-tax or gross incomes. Benefits in kind are excluded. There has been very little concern in Canada over in-kind benefits, under-reporting of income, or some of the other issues related to the calculation of poverty income. It has to be remembered that Canada has no equivalent of the food stamp programme in the United States. Medical care is a universal programme and there is no medical assistance for the poor.

In recent years, however, the definition of poverty and the method of counting the poor have come under attack from conservatives. Sarlo's (1992) is perhaps the most comprehensive statement. Sarlo objects to the relative measure of poverty, which he believes should more appropriately be considered a measure of income inequality. As an absolutist he takes a physical survival view of poverty. By this standard, Sarlo believes, poverty in Canada has been "virtually eliminated" (ibid.: 2). According to Sarlo, both StatsCan's LICO and CCSD's poverty line are relative measures and therefore "grossly" exaggerate the extent of poverty. He develops a "basic needs" approach of his own with a poverty line income far below the other two measures. Sarlo's figure for a family of four in 1988 of C$13,140 compares with LICO's C$22,371 and CCSD's C$26,941. (ibid.: 3).

By Sarlo's measure, only 2.5 per cent, compared with 14.8 per cent (LICO) and 15.4 per cent (CCSD) of Canadians turn out to be poor. His poverty line is based on a market basket approach with three main sectors of expenditure: food, shelter, and other items. It works out to a level not far from the social assistance or welfare standard, which differs across the provinces – ranging between one-half to three-quarters of the LICO level. On average, Sarlo believes, welfare brings people above what he considers to be the poverty line (ibid.: 172–3). Sarlo's work, published by the Fraser Institute, a right-wing "think tank", follows in the footsteps of neo-conservatives south of the border.

The liberal critique of the LICO has centred around the question of adopting an unambiguous relative definition. It should be noted that Statistics Canada does not regard the LICO as a poverty line and has sometimes equivocated on the question of using the regularly updated expenditure standard for determining the LICO. Responding to the poverty lobby and others, StatsCan has proposed a new low income measure based on half the median family income. It will be adjusted for family size and composition but, unlike LICO, not for community size. StatsCan intends to try out this measure and invite feedback from users of poverty data. Preliminary estimates show that the change is likely to have very little effect on the overall poverty rate (Ross 1992: 63).

In Canada, unlike in the United States, issues of welfare dependency, the growth of female-headed families, and the emergence of an underclass have not featured prominently in debates on social welfare. True, in Canada too issues of workfare and the reform of social security have been acquiring greater visibility. The unemployment insurance programme has been steadily eroded in terms of eligibility and level of benefits. Workfare, education, and training for working-age people dependent on state benefits are being considered, and universality is being supplanted by targeting of benefits and programmes (Evans 1994).

On the other hand, in Canada, as in the United States, poverty researchers have been documenting the plight of the "new" poor, notably female-headed families, children, and families in general, and lobbying governments for action on these issues.

The poverty gap has received a good deal of attention. Some effort is being made to find out more about the duration of poverty, which has not been examined systematically in Canada so far (Ross and Shillington 1989: 19). It must be remembered, however, that in Canada, unlike in the United States, poverty has not been targeted as a special area of investigation and research. Ideological issues pursued with elan by conservatives in the United States evoke only faint echoes in Canada. The ethnic and racial dimension has been much weaker. Overall, poverty research in Canada has remained somewhat low key. It has been industrious rather than innovative, descriptive rather than analytical – more interested in detailing and monitoring poverty than in developing or testing hypotheses. Much of the study of poverty goes on in and around government departments and non-governmental organizations (such as the CSSD) concerned with social policy issues, rather than in a university academic setting. Comparative poverty research has yet to make its mark.

Poverty research: comments and suggestions

What comes across quite clearly when reviewing North American research is the way the poverty line, the measurement of poverty, and related issues of defining poverty loom large in the literature. This is true of both the United States and Canada, although in Canada measurement issues have not been prominent. The near-obsessive concern with the definition and the count of the poor is clearly driven by the ideology and politics of social welfare. Thus it appears that conservatives – who tend to be "absolutists" – would drag the poverty line as far down as possible, whereas the liberals – "relativists" generally speaking – would like to go the other way. Because poverty is a normative concept there cannot be an "objective" definition of poverty, any more than there could be of "justice" or "liberty". Indeed poverty seems to be a matter of distributive justice in society. Thus poverty is and must remain a contested concept. At any rate, insofar as it involves state action and redistribution, the basic divide seems to be between a "stringent" and a "liberal" concept of poverty. And a great deal of poverty research, focused on definitional issues, seeks to validate normative judgements with reference to empirical data. The need to demarcate the "poor" or "needy" from the non-poor is essentially a bureaucratic and not an intellectual or conceptual need, although the implications for society and the "poor" are substantive. From a social science viewpoint, the logical approach seems to be to see the distribution of income or well-being as a continuum, at the lower end of which one might locate various positions that could be described as "very poor", "poor", "somewhat poor", "near poor", and so on (George and Howards 1991: 10–11). At any rate, North American research on poverty has been concerned less with philosophical arguments and more with "applied" issues. The inadequacy of an income-based approach for the assessment of levels of living and material well-being is a point that has been made quite well. And both the "earnings capacity" and "material well-being" approaches suggest complementary methods of estimating the resources available to an individual or family.

A major finding of American poverty research is that social insurance type programmes have done far more to lift people out of poverty than means-tested programmes have. This is an important point that merits emphasizing because it draws attention to a fundamental issue in the fight against poverty. It is that "prevention is better than cure" is as true of poverty as of other things. The insight of poverty researches in the USA, namely that insurance-type programmes do far more in this respect, also suggests that the wide array of means-tested programmes in the United States cannot really be considered as *anti-poverty* measures. In a sense, of course, all means-tested programmes are aimed at helping the poor, but this does not mean that they aim at *lifting the poor above the poverty line*. For example, a glance at any social assistance programme should be enough to dispel the notion that it is an anti-poverty programme. In fact, most social assistance programmes keep the clients below the poverty line. They are most appropriately considered as programmes for the *relief* of poverty. Hence the "paradox" (poverty studies are teeming with paradoxes of one kind or another) that targeted programmes do much less to lift people above poverty than non-targeted programmes. This is a "paradox" that is worth emphasizing, especially in the context of American anti-poverty policy. Cross-national studies show quite clearly that countries that rely more on means-tested programmes (the residual model of welfare) tend to have higher rates of poverty (for example, the USA and Australia). Conversely, countries with the lowest rates of poverty (e.g. Sweden) are often those that emphasize universal and comprehensive programmes (the institutional model of welfare). Indeed, the United States' own social policy operating through its two-tier welfare state shows that it has developed virtually an institutional welfare system for the aged while retaining a residual welfare system for the working-age population. Not surprisingly, poverty among the aged has continued to decline since the early 1960s, a decline that continued right through the 1970s and 1980s. On the other hand, poverty among families and children stopped declining in the mid-1970s and has been on the rise. Although factors other than social policy are also responsible for this difference, the role of a universal, entitlement-type income transfers policy cannot be underestimated.

However, as Greenstein (1991) among others points out, the distinction between universal and selective programmes is not the whole story. Thus, the US means-tested programme for the aged, viz. the supplemental security income (SSI), differs in a number of ways from the other means-tested programmes meant for the "undeserving". It is national rather than state based, its benefits are far more generous than, for example, those of the AFDC, and it has far stronger support in the community. In short, all selective programmes need not be the same. This is a good point, which is corroborated by Canadian programmes. The guaranteed annual income (GAI) for the aged, the child tax credit and several other tax credits, as well as the American earned income tax credit (EITC) programmes show that targeted programmes may have a useful role to play. Canada has been something of a pioneer in developing *income-tested* programmes, including refundable tax credits, in the context of a more or less institutional welfare state. These Canadian programmes and their potential for reducing poverty may be worth examining in some detail. And here there seems to be a gap in Canadian poverty research that needs filling: little is known about the contribution that the different programmes make in reducing poverty. More generally, studies of the anti-poverty strategies of different nations and their effectiveness in reducing poverty could be very helpful in suggesting the most effective lines of action.

More systematic work also needs to be done – both within and across nations – in comparing different groups of vulnerable population, e.g. the aged, children, one-parent families. For example, one of the most informative and interesting cross-national studies compares the aged and children in a number of countries in respect of relevant social policies, poverty rates, and trends (Smolensky et al. 1988). Among other things it shows how, and suggests why, society has extended adequate social protection to some groups but not to others. More inter-group comparisons of poverty and poverty policies – nationally and cross-nationally – could be a growth point in poverty research, helping us to develop appropriate strategies for dealing with poverty in different groups.

It is possible to distinguish between two different approaches or orientations to the study of poverty: the "social engineering" approach and the "social structural" approach. This is an ideal-typical distinction and a particular study or piece of research may include elements of both (and some, e.g. conceptual studies, may not fit either of these categories). But overall the distinction is a useful one.

The social engineering approach tends to concern itself with research problems closely related to issues of policy and administration. It could also be described as "operational" research. Thus work on the measurement of poverty, calculation of incomes, and the like falls into this category. The social engineering approach tends to abstract the issue of "poverty" from the larger social structure and sees it largely as an administrative problem that can be solved by policy makers by applying "rational" methods. This also leads to a tendency to reify the "poor" – viewing them as a statistical category of needy persons whose problems are amenable to administrative solution rather than as a range of social groups that are a part of the larger society within which the dynamics of poverty take place. A good deal of poverty research has this operational or social engineering character. To say this is not to detract in any way from the necessity and usefulness of this type of research. It is rather to draw attention to the limitations of this type of practice and policy-orientated research. This should become clear when we look at the social structural approach.

In contrast to social engineering, the social structural approach is not policy orientated – at least not in any direct sense. Its policy implications are often indirect. It is more concerned with the societal institutions and processes through which poverty is produced, reproduced, and sustained. Unlike the social engineering approach, the focus of interest here is not on discrete and concrete problems of poverty policy (measurement, drawing the poverty line) but on broader structural issues and their relationship to poverty. These may include, for example, unemployment, macroeconomic policies, income distribution, deunionization, and urban development. Social structural analysis tends to be more sceptical; it does not, for example, take the professed objectives of government policy – as proclaimed through political rhetoric, etc. – at face value. Approaching poverty in this way can offer a very different perspective on initiatives, e.g. the War on Poverty, and on questions such as why in spite of the War on Poverty, poverty persists (Weir et al. 1988; Katz 1989).

Whereas the social engineering approach takes a *consensus* view of social problems and their solution, the social structural approach often takes a *conflict* view. It implies that the reduction of poverty entails a redistribution of income, which in turn raises questions of vested interests, the ideology of state action, and conflict. From a conflict perspective, an explanation for the persistence of poverty in the United States may be sought, for example, in the distribution of power and in the capacity of the propertyless to organize and make use of political institutions and processes. Thus the tendency of poor Americans not to vote (another "paradox": "greatest apathy amidst greatest democracy"?) and the recent decline, if not annihilation, of unions in the United States may be important for understanding the persistence of and increase in poverty. In short, a realistic understanding of poverty requires that the politics of poverty not be left out. Although work of this kind does not focus directly on poverty, its critical edge of understanding is important in demystifying and demythologizing American poverty policy and discourse. Scholars such as Katz (1989) and, in a broader policy framework, Weir et al. (1988) offer examples of research of this genre. My own review has focused mainly on "social engineering" type research, but the importance of the social structural approach needs to be acknowledged fully and work that can forge a link between these two types of research should be encouraged.

But how does this distinction relate to my earlier discussion of poverty in terms of conservative and liberal perspectives? To some extent the type or orientation of research cuts across these ideological divisions. Nonetheless, both conservatives and liberals seem to work within a consensus view of policy-making and change. Neither looks at power and conflict as concepts relevant to the analysis of poverty. And it is here that the third or "structural" approach becomes important in widening the parameters of poverty research and shifting the terrain of the discourse on poverty – largely defined by neo-conservatives in recent years – in a different direction. It is perhaps not surprising that the disciplinary base of the structural approach is often history, politics, or sociology rather than economics.

This brings us to the issue of the various disciplines involved in the study of poverty and their respective contribution. There is little doubt that, in the USA at least, economics has been prominent in poverty research. The War on Poverty itself was based on the belief that poverty could be eradicated through human capital development, labour market participation, and the like. The economics profession was called upon to play a major part in directing and conducting poverty research. In the 1960s sociologists too played a part but later the field was left largely to economists. The Institute of Research on Poverty has, for example, been very largely weighted towards economists. No doubt, from the viewpoint of operational research, economics offers many strengths – modelling, a quantitative approach, methodological sophistication – and these may explain the preponderance of economists. On the other hand, contributions from other disciplinary perspectives, e.g. sociology or politics, have been marginal. These disciplines are more likely to take a social structural approach than is economics – an "abstract" social science. What seems particularly lacking is a synthesis of knowledge derived from different disciplinary sources. This, among other things, is perhaps what makes the work of W. J. Wilson (1987), for example, an outstanding contribution.

What is the place of theory in poverty research? In fact the bulk of poverty research has tended to be atheoretical. Research questions and hypotheses have often been ad hoc, driven by contemporary ideological debates and administrative or political rather than disciplinary interests and theoretical consensus. As Sawhill for example remarks:

> Few researchers have approached the task of analysing the effects of different variables on the poverty rate in the context of a coherent overall model of the process by which income is generated. Although economists are often criticised for devoting too much time to theory at the expense of empirical information ... I believe that where the distribution of income and poverty are concerned just the opposite is the case.
>
> (Sawhill 1988: 1085)

The same may be said of other disciplines as far as most poverty research is concerned. Thus Katz's (1993: 14) judgement that poverty research has "contributed few new ideas and little in the way of theory", though somewhat harsh, is not unfair. This raises the question of whether "poverty research" tends to be abstracted and empiricist, given the applied, policy-orientated nature of the field and given that a good deal of funded research is driven by current policy issues and concerns.

Be that as it may, in the absence of an explicit theoretical orientation on the part of researchers, it is the current dominant ideology that fills the vacuum and shapes the debate and the research agenda. Thus one of the main questions in the recent poverty debate – namely why, despite large social spending, poverty persists – makes little sense outside the ideological framework of neo-conservatism and the brand of liberalism associated with the War on Poverty. The fact is that the vast majority of industrialized nations spend a good deal more on social programmes than the United States. But nowhere, not even in Mrs Thatcher's Britain, has such a question been posed let alone been the subject of so much research and debate. At any rate the research generated as a result of the debate has been useful in pinpointing the weakness of the War on Poverty and Great Society programmes as anti-poverty measures. Indeed, in subjecting conservative theses on poverty and welfare to empirical tests. Liberal social research has made a solid contribution towards an understanding of poverty and policy. What is lacking – and what is badly needed – is a *codification* of the major findings and generalizations of recent poverty research. This could well form the nucleus of a revised liberal perspective on poverty in the 1990s. For what seems clear is that, unlike conservatives, the liberals lack a coherent and well-grounded viewpoint on poverty and allied issues and how to tackle them in the 1990s. Liberals may need to borrow from both the "structuralists" and the "conservatives" in order to develop a credible framework for the understanding of poverty and relevant policies. The basic assumptions of the 1960s can hardly suffice for the 1990s.

Much of North American poverty research – and I suspect this is true of other regions as well, as one might expect – has been concerned with domestic issues within a national framework. Relatively little has been done by way of cross-national poverty research. Although this is a growing field, especially in the USA, it is a particularly promising area of research and would seem to offer considerable growth prospects. It should help to put the national problems and issues in a broader international perspective, bringing a fresh, new look at domestic issues. It should help to develop hypotheses relevant to national issues and to test, against cross-national data, hypotheses generated through national poverty research. For example, the proposition that universalistic income support programmes are more effective against poverty than targeted programmes could be examined more thoroughly in a cross-national perspective than has been done so far. Finally, cross-national research should help to break down the isolation of national researchers and promote mutual understanding of issues and problems related to poverty. In the past, lack of comparable data has hindered cross-national research on poverty. With the development of the Luxembourg Income Study (LIS) database this deficiency is being overcome.

Both the USA and Canada are a part of the LIS data set as are an increasing number of industrialized nations. Although difficulties relating to data may still inhibit work in this area, there is ample scope not only for quantitative analysis of a cluster of nations but also for in-depth study ("social structural") of, say, two or three nations. Thus a comparative analysis of poverty and the anti-poverty policies of, say, Canada and the USA might be quite interesting and instructive. Thus far, most of the cross-national work has been of a "quantitative" kind; more "qualitative" research would help to redress the balance.

If in the euphoric days of the 1960s and the early 1970s it seemed that poverty could be abolished once and for all, we now know – or should know – better. However affluent a society, it does not follow that income and wealth will be distributed evenly. A rising economic tide not only does not lift all boats, it can upturn, destroy, and sink many boats. It is the task of the social welfare system to ensure that through the redistribution of income and other measures the fruits of economic growth are shared more evenly and that the cost of economic change is not allowed to lie where it falls. Indeed, momentous changes have taken place in global economics and politics since the mid-1970s. The conditions that create and sustain poverty have worsened. Gone are the days of full employment; we now have chronic unemployment throughout the OECD area. Gone are the days of unionized workers being able to negotiate good benefits and wages; we now have a much more fragmented labour market with "flexibility" (i.e. low wages and few benefits) the order of the day. Unions are weak and on the defensive; in some countries, notably the United States, they have been virtually eliminated. Globalization of the economy and the demand for international competitiveness is exerting a downward pressure on wages and on social protection everywhere. Inequality of income distribution and regressivity of taxation are on the increase. At the same time, marriage and family patterns are undergoing significant changes, for example the increase in the number of single-parent families. This is a context in which poverty is likely to rise and will probably remain at a higher level compared with the 1960s and early 1970s – the "golden age" of welfare capitalism. It is important therefore to renew the commitment to fight poverty, to chart the changing nature and incidence of poverty, and to look for new and imaginative ways of preventing and reducing poverty. Final solutions to this age-old problem – whether through a War on Poverty or by the simple expedient of defining it out of existence, not to speak of the creation of a socialist utopia – have proved illusory. The dynamics of the social and economic structure of advanced capitalist societies – and not only these societies – require that the struggle against poverty be waged perpetually. Perhaps the time has come to open a "second front" at the international level. At any rate, poverty research – both national and cross-national – will have a vital role to play in these developments.

Notes

1. "Poverty research" has been interpreted here somewhat freely. There is an immense literature, especially in the United States, directly or indirectly related to poverty. It is difficult to convey in this paper the range, versatility, and richness of American poverty research. This paper has focused on the work related to some of the major issues around poverty in the past ten to fifteen years. It is therefore, and necessarily, a highly selective presentation. Little has been said, for example, about evaluation research (effectiveness of programmes), an aspect of poverty research where the United States has been particularly strong.

    As for data sources, the paper does not list specific sources. The two government departments responsible for most of the poverty-related data are the United States Bureau of the Census and Statistics Canada.
2. A justification of sorts for this line of reasoning can be found in the Canadian measure of low income (poverty), which is a relative measure and does create some confusion with its changing baseline. However, such problems can be overcome, e.g. by publishing two parallel series of poverty figures.

References

Anderson, M. (1978) *The Political Economy of Welfare Reform in the United States*. Stanford, Calif.: Hoover Institution Press.
Auletta, K. (1982) *The Underclass* New York: Random House.
Battle, K. (1991) "Poverty myths, misconceptions and half-truths". Mimeo.
Blank, R. (1993) "Why were poverty rates so high in the 1980s?" in D. B. Padadimitriou and E. N. Wolff (eds), *Poverty and Prosperity in the USA in the Late Twentieth Century*. New York: St. Martin's Press.
Burton, C. E. (1992). *The Poverty Debate: Politics and the Poor in America*. Westport, Conn.: Greenwood Press.
Canadian Council on Social Development (1984) *Not Enough: The Meaning and Measurement of Poverty in Canada*. Ottawa: Canadian Council on Social Development.
Corcoran, M. et al. (1985) "Myth and reality: The causes and persistence of poverty". *Journal of Policy Analysis and Management*, 4 (4).

Cutright, P. (1973) "Illegitimacy and Income Supplements", *Studies in Public Welfare*, paper no. 12, pt. 1. Washington, DC: Government Printing Office.

Danziger, S. H. and D. H. Weinberg (eds) (1986) *Fighting Poverty: What Works and What Doesn't*. Cambridge, Mass.: Harvard University Press.

Danziger, S. H. et al. (1992–3) "Excerpts from Editor's Introduction". *Focus*, 14 (3).

Duncan, G. J. (1984) *Years of Poverty, Years of Plenty: The Changing Economic Fortunes of American Workers and Their Families*. Ann Arbor, Mich.: Institute for Social Research, University of Michigan.

Ellwood, D. T. (1988) *Poor Support: Poverty in the American Family*, New York: Basic Books.

Ellwood, D. T. and M. J. Bane (1984) "The impact of AFDC on family structure and living arrangements". Washington, DC: Department of Health and Human Services, Grant 92A-82.

Evans, P. (1994) "Eroding Canadian Social Welfare: The Mulroney Legacy, 1984–1993", *Social Policy and Administration*, 28(2).

George, V. and I. Howards (1991) *Poverty Amidst Affluence*. Aldershot: Edward Elgar.

Gilder, G. (1981) *Wealth and Poverty*. New York: Basic Books.

Greenstein, R. (1991) "Universal and targeted approaches to relieving poverty: An alternative view", in C. Jencks and P. E. Peterson (eds), *The Urban Underclass*. Washington, DC: The Brookings Institution.

Guest, D. (1980) *The Emergence of Social Security in Canada*. Vancouver: University of British Columbia Press.

Harrington, M. (1984) *The New American Poverty*. New York: Holt, Rinehart & Winston.

Haveman, R. (1987) *Poverty Policy and Poverty Research*. Madison, Wis.: University of Wisconsin Press.

—— (1989) *Starting Even: An Equal Opportunity Programme to Combat the Nation's New Poverty*. New York: Simon and Schuster.

—— (1992–93) "Changing the poverty measure: Pitfalls and potential gains". *Focus*, 14 (3).

Haveman, R. and L. Burton (1993) "Who are the truly poor? Patterns of official and net earnings capacity poverty, 1973–88" in D. B. Papadimitriou and E. N. Wolff (eds), *Poverty and Prosperity in the USA in the Late Twentieth Century*. New York: St. Martins Press.

Jencks, C. (1991) "Is the American underclass growing?" in C. Jencks and P. E. Peterson (eds), *The Urban Underclass*. Washington, DC: The Brookings Institution.

Jencks, C. and P. E. Peterson (eds) (1991) *The Urban Underclass*. Washington, DC: The Bookings Institution.

Katz, M. B. (1986) *In the Shadow of the Poorhouse*. New York: Basic Books.

—— (1989) *The Undeserving Poor: From the War on Poverty to the War on Welfare*. New York: Pantheon Books.

—— (ed.) (1993) *The "Underclass" Debate: Views from History*. Princeton, NJ: Princeton University Press.

Korpi, W. (1980) "Approaches to the study of poverty in the United States: critical notes from a European perspective" in V. T. Covello (ed.), *Poverty and Public Policy: An Evaluation of Social Science Research*. Cambridge, Mass.: Schenkman Publishing Co.

Levitan, S. A. et al. (1993) *Working But Poor*. Baltimore, MD.: Johns Hopkins University Press.

Mayer, S. E. and C. Jencks (1993) "Recent trends in economic inequality in the United States: Income versus expenditures versus material well-being", in D. B. Papadimitriou and E. N. Wolff (eds), *Poverty and Prosperity in the USA in the Late Twentieth Century*. New York: St. Matin's Press.

Mead, L. M. (1986) *Beyond Entitlement*. New York: Free Press.

Meyer, J. A. and M. Moon (1988) "Health care spending on children and the elderly" in J. L. Palmer et al. (eds), *The Vulnerable*. Washington, DC: The Urban Institute Press.

Murray, C. (1984) *Losing Ground*. New York: Basic Books.

National Council of Welfare (1994) *Poverty Profile 1992*. Ottawa: Supply and Services Canada.

Osterman, P. (1991) "Gains from Growth? The Impact of Full Employment on Poverty in Boston", in C. Jencko and P. E. Peterson (eds), *The Urban Underclass*. Washington, DC: The Brookings Institution.

Palmer, J. L. et al. (1988) *The Vulnerable*. Washington, DC: The Urban Institute Press.

Patterson, J. T. (1986) *America's Struggle Against Poverty*. Cambridge, Mass.: Harvard University Press.

Perron, P. and F. Vaillancourt (1989) *The Evolution of Poverty in Canada 1970–1985*. Ottawa: Economic Council of Canada, Discussion Paper No. 343.

Peterson, P. E. and M. C. Rom (1990) *Welfare Magnets. A New Case for a National Standard*. Washington, DC: The Brookings Institution.

Piachaud, D. (1987) "Problems in the definition and measurement of poverty" *Journal of Social Policy*, 16(2).

Ricketts, E. R. and I. V. Sawhill (1988) "Defining and measuring the underclass" *Journal of Policy and Analysis and Management*, 7(2).

Ross, D (1992) "Current and proposed measures of poverty, 1992" *Perception*, 15(4)–16(1).

Ross, D. P. and R. Shillington (1989) *The Canadian Fact Book on Poverty 1989*. Ottawa: Canadian Council on Social Development.

Ruggles, P. (1990) *Drawing the Line: Alternative Poverty Measures and their Implications for Public Policy*. Washington, DC: The Urban Institute Press.

────── (1991) "Short and long term poverty in the United States: Measuring the American underclass", in L. Osberg (ed.), *Economic Inequality and Poverty: International Perspectives*. Armonk, NY: M.E. Sharpe, Armonk.

────── (1992) "Measuring Poverty" *Focus*, 14(1).

Sarlo, C. A. (1992) *Poverty in Canada*. Vancouver, BC: The Fraser Institute.

Sawhill, I. (1988) "Poverty in the U.S.: Why is it so persistent?" *Journal of Economic Literature*, 26: 1073–119.
Smeeding. T. M. (1984) "The anti-poverty effect of in-kind transfers: A 'good idea' gone too far?" in R. Goldstein and S. M. Sachs (eds), *Applied Poverty Research*. Totowa, NJ: Rowman & Allanheld.
Smolensky, E. et al. (1988) "The declining significance of age in the United States: Trends in the well-being of children and the elderly since 1939" in J. L. Palmer et al. (eds) *The Vulnerable*. Washington, DC: The Urban Institute Press.
Statistics Canada. Various publications (Ottawa).
US Bureau of the Census. Various publications (Washington, DC).
Weir, M. et al. (1988) *The Politics of Social Policy in the United States*. Princetown, NJ: Princeton University Press.
Wilson, W. J. (1987) *The Truly Disadvantaged: The Inner City, The Underclass and Public Policy*. Chicago and London: University of Chicago Press.
—— (ed.) (1989) *The Annals of the American Academy of Political and Social Science*, 501, *The Ghetto Underclass: Special Science Perspectives*.

Part V
The Latin American Region

Poverty research in Latin America demónstrates the close relationship between politics and academia in the search for useful knowledge. Much of the poverty research is applied, in the sense that studies are geared towards finding solutions to overwhelming poverty problems and providing data that can be used as a base for national social policies. During this process academics are developing a political role that involves them in debates and public consultations on poverty issues, as well as in the making of concrete social policy measures.

The Latin American continent has undergone economic and political turbulence during the past couple of decades, which has had an impact on the incidence of poverty. A succession of adjustment and restructuring policies has run its course in most of the countries, many of which used to have wealthy economies. Macroeconomic policies aimed at poverty alleviation have not been too successful. Poverty seems to have increased both in metropolises and in the rural areas, as have income differences. This development has influenced research on poverty in several ways. Powerful theories on the macro level have appeared, trying to explain the causes and consequences of economic and social changes, directly or indirectly including poverty. Indicators have been developed to capture the manifestations of changing policies and compare them across the different Latin American nations. The cruption of research on poverty lines can likewise be seen as part of this picture.

Here, as elsewhere, a major aim in applied research is to create a poverty line that adequately portrays poverty and at the same time is easy to administer. Politicians and bureaucrats alike are pressing the researchers to come up with an efficient and unambiguous social policy instrument. So researchers and official data collecting institutions are attacking the problems of constructing a fair and unambiguous poverty line as fiercely as if they were attacking the complex problem of poverty itself. Numerous poverty lines are constructed, and poverty lines created elsewhere are tried out in a Latin American context.

The debate on various aspects of poverty is widespread and influenced by structural explanations of poverty. The many economic crises have spurred an overall feeling that poverty is produced in the social and economic system, and the redistribution of resources and a more equitable development are proposed as necessary to curb injustices and poverty.

Chapter 22

Latin America: Poverty as a Challenge for Government and Society

Laura Golbert and Gabriel Kessler

Introduction

Poverty has been a persistent problem throughout the history of most Latin American countries (LACs). The typical problems of developing regions – their economic dependence, their position in international trade as producers of primary products, the behaviour of their dominant classes, the existence of "enclave economies" in many countries, the predominance of large landed estates, and the intensity of the distributional struggle among different groups – explain the widespread presence of poverty, especially in rural areas. However, this general pattern does not apply to every country. For example, Argentina and Uruguay, which experienced the processes of industrialization and urbanization prior to other countries in the region, have performed better in terms of income distribution and access to social services.

By the end of the Second World War, Latin America was one of the fastest-growing areas of the developing world. Between 1950 and 1980, the average annual formal employment growth in urban areas reached levels comparable to those of the industrialized countries. However, this growth was not enough to absorb the marked increase in the urban labour supply caused by high urban demographic growth, rural–urban migration, and the increase in labour force participation. Furthermore, by the mid 1970s, the import-substitution model adopted by most LACs began to show signs of decay.

At the beginning of the 1980s, Latin America underwent a series of shocks as a result of the crisis in the developed world.

These countries' economic recession caused not only a decrease in capital flows into Latin America, but also a massive transfer of resources from this region to the rest of the world as countries settled external debts. The deterioration of the terms of trade and the governments' difficulties in revenue collection further aggravated the financial situation of the Latin American economies.

In this context, by the mid 1980s, most countries decided to apply adjustment policies to reduce expenditures and balance public finances. This strategy resulted in the rapid decline of growth rates, with consequent impacts on salaries and employment. The presence of high inflation further affected the decline in real wages. The loss of family income, the increase in unemployment, and the expansion of the informal sector were not counterbalanced by compensatory social policies owing to the significant reductions in social spending imposed by fiscal adjustment.

By the end of the decade, urban poverty was extensive and had intensified to unprecedented levels in most of the region. Inequality in income distribution was exacerbated. For these reasons, the 1980s were called the "lost decade".

The poverty debate in Latin America

In the 1960s, Latin America had a remarkable role in the development of theories, that in a direct or indirect manner, tried to explain the poverty phenomenon. Some examples are the studies by Raul Prebisch of the Economic Commission for Latin America and the Caribbean (ECLAC), the theory of dependence (Cardoso and Faleto 1970), the theory of modernization (Germani 1973) and theories on marginality (Nun 1969; Quijano 1977).

Paradoxically, thirty years later, in a context of even more drastic circumstances as regards poverty and social exclusion, no similar intellectual response has taken place. The debate has been oriented basically towards poverty measurement or assistance strategies for the poor. Some of the causes of the paradox are the crisis in the world paradigm, local academic deficiencies, and the need for immediate concrete action in view of the declining socioeconomic conditions. The predominant neo-liberal ideology favouring safety-nets for poverty alleviation has further hindered new theoretical developments.

However, this apparent absence of theoretical frameworks does not, in any way, imply a lack of research. In fact, the seriousness of the situation and the need for the implementation of policies to reduce poverty have led to important studies aimed basically at poverty diagnosis and measurement.

In fact, the consequences of the crisis of the 1980s in terms of the magnitude and type of poverty are recognized by academics and experts on the subject. The differences arise when poverty concepts, explanatory hypotheses, and the soundness of the theoretical frameworks are discussed.

While both international agencies and local researchers have been important participants in this debate, the former have been more successful at setting the agenda for debate. In fact, international organizations in Latin America such as the World Bank (WB), the International Labour Organization (ILO), the Economic Commission for Latin America and the Caribbean (ECLAC), and the United Nations' Development Programme (UNDP) have had and continue to have a preponderant role in poverty studies. The guidelines elaborated by these agencies are the ones that dominate the poverty research field for the following reasons: (a) these are the only organizations that systematically produce comparative research on the magnitude and extent of poverty; (b) prestigious professionals provide academic legitimacy to the studies; (c) the mass media consider these sources more reliable than national ones; (d) these organizations not only provide information, they also, in some cases, finance public policies.

These organizations address the issue of poverty in different ways. In this chapter, the questions that have occupied a prominent position in the debate of the past decade will be analysed from these different perspectives. It is necessary to remark that there are some ambiguities in the position of each agency owing to the fact that in many cases the consultant researchers produce documents that do not necessarily reflect the views of their organizations.

In addition, studies carried out by relevant local researchers were taken into account. In this case, topics that are not studied by the international agencies are also considered in order to give as complete a picture as possible of the "state of the art" in the region.

The concept of poverty

Currently, the notion of poverty refers to an essentially permanent situation of income insufficiency resulting in basic needs not being satisfied. Although it is known that such a concept is ambiguous, there is little discussion about it. Thus, the word "poverty" denotes phenomena of non-uniform meaning (Katzman 1989). This theoretical ambiguity leads to problems when operationalizing concepts to assess the phenomenon's magnitude.

The World Bank defines poverty only as not having the possibility of reaching a minimum living standard. Its major concern is to try to obtain an operational definition. To render this definition useful, the World Bank considers three questions that need to be answered: How do we measure living standards? What do we mean by a minimum living standard? Once "the poor" have been identified, how do we express the degree of poverty using only one index or measurement?

The UNDP elaborated a concept of poverty linked to "basic human needs": "Poverty is defined as a situation which prevents the individual or the family from satisfying one or more basic needs and from fully participating in social life" (UNDP 1990: 33). Even though it considers poverty to be essentially an economic phenomenon, it also takes account of its social, political, and cultural dimensions. "The poor find themselves compelled to choose some necessities, sacrificing others that are also basic. This is why poverty is a state of need in which there is no freedom" (ibid.: 33).

The ECLAC researches are based on pioneer studies by Oscar Altimir (1979) carried out at the end of the 1970s. Some years later, Altimir (1993) acknowledged the difficulties of elaborating a poverty theory. He considered poverty to be a "situational syndrome in which the following are combined: underconsumption, malnutrition, precarious housing conditions, low educational levels, poor sanitary conditions, either unstable participation in the production system or restriction to its more primitive strata, attitudes of discouragement and anomie, little participation in the mechanisms of social integration and possible adherence to a particular set of values different to some extent from the rest of society's" (1993: 2).

Ruben Katzman (1989), a well-known regional researcher, made an interesting contribution when he emphasized the necessity of determining the temporal extension of poverty, an important distinction when designing public policies. "If the extension over time is not defined, it can involve situations varying from a circumstantial economic recession up to chronic poverty" (1989: 99).

Numerous studies have had the objective of determining the size of the sectors below the "poverty line". In some cases this approach has been framed in a general income distribution context (Beccaria 1993; Bergsman 1980; Camargo and Giambiagi 1991; Filgueira 1994; León 1994; Lopes 1990; Rocha 1992).

Poverty and the adjustment policies

During the 1980s, the decline of the accumulation model and the devastating effects of the external debt crisis on the socioeconomic system became evident. Thus, most Latin American governments saw the need to reduce public expenditure in order to balance their budgets. Therefore, the poverty debate in the 1980s was framed within the context of (and sometimes displaced by) the discussion on "what to do" with the state and the economy.

There is no consensus between the different international agencies about the consequences of the adjustment policies applied by most Latin American governments during the 1980s. The World Bank (1993) considers that poverty has been a chronic problem in Latin America, and that without adjustments the condition of the poor would undoubtedly have become worse than it did.

The UNDP recognizes the negative effects of the adjustment programmes. However, it believes that without these programmes the situation of the poor today would be worse. The historically unbalanced condition of the regional economies would have had even more unfavourable consequences. Considering the adjustment programmes as emergency programmes, the UNDP believes that it is necessary to create other policies to attack the structural obstacles to development of Latin American societies.

The ILO/PREALC (Regional Employment Programmes for Latin America and the Caribbean) (ILO 1988) criticizes the adjustment strategy, suggesting that it would have been possible to apply alternative economic measures at lower social cost. According to the ILO, the debt was not distributed equally in society. The costs of adjustment fell disproportionately on social groups with low purchasing power, thereby increasing the countries' "social debt".

ECLAC (ECLAC 1992) similarly states that the adjustment programmes have led to a more uneven distribution of income and a higher incidence of poverty in most Latin American societies. The rare exceptions are the result of a deliberate and persistent effort in favour of equity in the design and practice of economic policies.

Outside the realm of international agencies, specialists in these topics agree that adjustment policies have increased poverty and have exacerbated the unequal income distribution. (Beccaria and Orsatti 1989; Lustig 1989; Melgar 1989).

Poverty and the labour market

According to Faria: "From the late '50s until the early '70s, – as the population grew at very high rates, urbanization rates skyrocketed, and deep changes occurred in rural and urban productive structures – Latin American scholars turned their attention to the capacity of the modern urban industrial activities to provide adequate employment to the increasing urban laborforce. A large amount of work revolved around the concept of 'urban marginality'" (Faria 1994: 7).

One of the characteristics that has marked the development of the region is the high incidence of informal labour. The crisis of the 1980s intensified informal relations even more and increased underemployment and open unemployment, together with a fall in real wages. Today, there is widespread agreement among the different agencies (supported by evidence gathered from a variety of sources) on the association between these factors and the growth and intensification of urban poverty.

ECLAC, apart from describing the effects of the economic crisis on the labour market, suggests that, paradoxically, informality has had a positive effect on employment. It argues that, although open unemployment increased, the transfer of labour between sectors has somewhat mitigated its impact. In most countries, employment in manufacturing and the public sector declined, and a percentage of the unemployed moved to less productive areas of the service sector.

Faria adds in this regard:

> during the 1980s, under the intellectual influence of the PREALC, the attention was placed again on the employment generation problem resulting, first, from the economic crisis, then, from the adjustment policies implemented to face the crisis and, finally, from the regional economic restructuring resulting from the new patterns of dynamic integration into the world economy. One of the main contributions of these studies has been the indication of the growing vulnerability of several segments of the labor market (even some modern urban-industrial segments), the increasing precariousness of work, and the progressive dualization of urban labor markets. Another contribution has been the awareness of the need of improving labor-force's skills and qualifications as an essential step to overcome the crisis. Last but not least, this literature strongly

supports the idea that, in the next two decades, the generation of productive jobs will continue to be one of the crucial issues regarding poverty and exclusion in the region. (1994: 7; see also ECLAC 1991a; Galin and Novick 1990; Monza 1993; ILO/PREALC 1988, 1992; Rodgers 1989; Souza 1980)

Poverty and social policies

As mentioned earlier, there is agreement regarding the connection between poverty and employment. However, implementing a strategy for creating employment requires certain economic, social, and political conditions that are difficult to establish in the short term. So, in addition to confronting the problem of unemployment, it is necessary to implement programmes designed to mitigate poverty. This matter is perhaps one of the most controversial in the poverty debate. There are three main points to this debate.

Economic policies plus social policies versus integrated public policies

According to the World Bank, poverty is a product of distortions or unbalanced conditions that would be alleviated by sustained economic growth. It is in this context that it considers poverty to be a problem that may be ameliorated with the application of palliative policies targeted at the poorest groups. Social policies must be destined fundamentally to improve the pernicious and undesired effects of economic policy.

ECLAC, on the other hand, questions the "capsulization" of social policy, that is, its separation from economic policy. As far as ECLAC is concerned, this problem is worsened by the internal segmentation of social policies in problematic sectors. The Commission believes that it is necessary to elaborate an integrated view that would transcend partial approaches. Emphasis must be placed on "the effort to achieve an integrated approach to social policy – together with economic policy – molded in an institutional reform of the State which would increase its capacity for unified action" (ECLAC 1990: 22).

According to the UNDP, social and economic policy constitute a whole, as is expressed in its Social Reform proposal (UNDP 1993). This reform is conceived as a process that contributes to human development through the integration of policies and instruments aimed at incorporating all members of society in an efficient way. The Social Reform proposal argues that the entire population's access to economic opportunities is an essential component of economic reform.

Targeted policies versus universal policies

Various organizations have elaborated views on how to conduct the struggle against poverty. The World Bank is the most important and principal defender of targeted policies. Its primary concern is extreme poverty and it considers social spending targeted at the most needy as the most rational and efficient allocation of social spending.

The UNDP criticizes this view, which emphasizes policies geared toward the needs of the victims of structural adjustment, and argues instead for the integration of excluded sectors. It believes that policies should serve not only to provide an adequate supply of goods and services to satisfy basic human needs, but also to generate a more equal distribution of the surplus and the progressive incorporation of excluded sectors.

The ILO/PREALC has measured the poverty gap and calculated the social debt that Latin American societies owe to the less protected sectors. Its institutional profile is based on employment policies rather than on classical policies.

Academic studies (in the fields of political philosophy, political science, sociology, and related fields) are concerned with absolute poverty as well as with relative poverty.

State versus non-governmental organization action

During the past decade the redefinition of the state's role and the roles of non-governmental organizations (NGOs) in social policies has been debated. NGOs have taken a more active role as a result of state reforms (for example privatization) and reduced public expenditures. The main issues in the debate are the proper roles of each actor, the scope of intervention, the levels of efficiency, and the administration of funds. In general, it is not an issue of NGOs versus the state, but rather how the two might complement one another.

Poverty measurement

When referring to poverty measurement in Latin America, two aspects of the discussion will be taken into account: (a) methods of measurement, and (b) a focus on relative or absolute poverty.

Certain general characteristics are shared by most of the poverty assessments in the region. The first concerns the unit of analysis. The usual unit of analysis is the household. Therefore, what is identified as "poor" or "not poor" is the household and not each of its members. This brings about a series of problems in the measurement of intra-familial differences. Second, all the comparative studies use the same data sources: the periodic surveys of household income produced by national statistics and census offices, institutes, or departments. In many studies, these databases are used to elaborate specific statistical calculations. Third, a great number of the studies warn that the data are not absolutely reliable. This leads to a fundamental problem in the measurement of poverty in the region, which can be solved only once the national governments improve methods of statistical measurement.

In the 1980s, the most studied group was the urban poor. The development of these studies was related to the growth in urban poverty, the availability of data – in comparison with data on rural poverty – and the development of measurement standards and data-collection methods for this population. The severity of the 1980s' crisis inspired numerous studies on poor households (Altimir 1982; ECLAC 1985; Filgueira 1994; León 1994; Lopes 1994; Minujin 1992; Rocha 1992). Thanks to UNICEF's efforts in the region, poverty among children received greater attention (Albanez et al. 1989; Anaya et al. 1984; Galofre 1981).

As regards the methodological approach, in Latin America there is widespread use of the internationally accepted methods: the measurement of "unsatisfied basic needs" (UBN) and the poverty line (PL). At the national level as well as in regional comparisons, both of these methods have advantages and disadvantages. Nevertheless, some international agencies have developed their own indicators while using the same national databases used by other organizations.

As is widely known, the "poverty line" presupposes the specification of a basket of basic needs and services, which must relate to the cultural consumption standards of a society in a particular historical period. This basket is valued by calculating its total cost. This monetary value is "the poverty line". By using this criterion, those households or persons whose incomes are below the poverty line would be identified as poor.

The UBN measurement refers to material evidence of the lack of access to certain type of services such as: housing, drinking water, electricity, education, and health, among others. This method requires the definition of minimum standards that would indicate unsatisfied and satisfied needs considered "basic" at a particular moment of a society's development. Consequently, those households that cannot satisfy some of the needs defined as basic would be identified as "poor".

A great deal of the literature assumes that the two poverty assessment methods, the PL and the UBN, would theoretically evaluate similar situations. However, several studies carried out in Latin America during the 1980s and 1990s (Beccaria and Minujin 1991; Desai 1989; Katzman 1989; Minujin 1991) using the data obtained by household surveys, revealed important differences in poverty measurement depending on the method used. Researchers consider that the results of these two methods reflect two different phenomena:

> "the UBN criterion would be detecting structural poverty – owners of a deficient house or persons with low educational levels, or others – whereas the PL criterion would detect the pauperized households since it characterizes poverty according to the household income"
> (Cortés and Minujin 1988: 12).

It is widely accepted that both methods have limitations, some of which are intrinsic and some of which are particular to the quantitative methodology. Some of the main problems of the UBN method relate to defining the basic wants, their minimum thresholds, the relative importance of each of them, and the operationalization of the variables. In fact, the number of variables is limited and the operationalization of the variables is simplified. In terms of comparative studies, the main problem is that the variables used and the way they are evaluated vary from country to country. As a matter of fact, whereas in some countries, like Argentina, most indicators refer to housing conditions, in others they are related to education or health.

When choosing the variables to define poverty in each country, a theoretical definition is usually combined with an appraisal of the most salient local manifestations of poverty. Consequently, because different variables are used, the definition of poverty in each country depends on what is locally considered to be a basic need. Actually, if we applied the UBN indicators from one country to another, the population in poverty would vary. The absence of regional criteria hampers the establishment of homogeneous criteria; and therefore hampers accurate comparisons.

The problem with the PL method concerns the various alternative definitions of the poverty line and its application to households, as well as the estimation of income. The differences in the PL estimates in the Latin American case arise from variations in methodological approach, such as: (a) how to impute nonresponses, (b) the measurement of goods and services consumed by the household but not acquired in the market, (c) how to adjust for understatement, (d) how to impute rent, and (e) how to measure the value of income according to the age of the household members.

Nowadays, there is general consensus in the region about the problems posed by each of the methods. Consequently, the choice of one or the other is related to the theoretical perspective, the availability of data, and the objectives of each research project. In general, in previous decades there has been a greater tendency towards the UBN method. The most important factors in its choice were that (a) it was a suitable method for measuring structural poverty, which has historically been the prevailing type of poverty in the region, (b) the information needed could be obtained from census data, whereas the income data needed for PL measurements could not be obtained in this way.

Nonetheless, in the 1980s, research based on the PL criterion flourished. This was due to the many problems posed by the UBN method, such as how to treat households whose situation was acceptable regarding some needs but not others. The PL approach seemed more attractive, because it provided a reasonable way to average the importance of different needs. But apart from these methodological problems, the growing interest in the PL method seemed to be greatly enhanced by the increase in poverty. This implied that new population groups had recently experienced declining social mobility, which could be better detected by the PL method.

Theoretical frameworks and the causes of poverty

When comparing the studies carried out in the region during the past two decades with those undertaken in the 1950s and 1960s, the latter exhibit clear cohesion within diverse theoretical frameworks, whereas the most recent studies appear more empirical and lacking theoretical analysis. In fact, in the earlier studies, we find a broad range of theoretical frameworks such as the reproduction of poverty and intergenerational transmission of poverty, offshoots of the culture of poverty perspective or the family survival strategies, studies based on Marxist perspectives of different kinds, and others based on the dependency theory and the centre–periphery theory, among others.

The crisis in modern social theory has had an impact on poverty studies. In fact, many studies admit that such a complex, multidimensional problem as poverty cannot be understood through only one theory. However, it would not be fair to criticize the studies of the 1980s for being theoretically weak. Although strict adherence to theoretical frameworks is not explicitly stated, the paradigms persist.

Taking a general look at the studies of the 1960s and 1970s, one can perceive signs of the core concepts in vogue at the time. Thus, as a hypothesis, we could make several assertions about more recent studies.

First, signs of the dependency theory and – to a lesser extent – the centre–periphery theory are present in studies that associate the increase in poverty in the past decade with: (a) the characteristics of the external debt in the 1980s – the creditors being large transnational banks; (b) the deterioration of the public sector; and (c) the processes of economic concentration. In other words, the structuralist view is still used to explain the historic genesis of regional poverty and its recent increase.

Second, these explanatory hypotheses are linked with those from other theoretical frameworks when policies are proposed to mitigate poverty. In fact, at the end of the 1980s and the beginning of the 1990s, the "safety-net" emerged as the predominant policy measure aimed at alleviating the immediate needs of the poorest sectors. It is noteworthy that diverse researchers and organizations have converged from different perspectives to reach broad consensus on the types of measures needed to mitigate poverty (Bustelo and Isuani 1992; Castañeda 1990; Faria 1994; Gonzalez de la Rocha and Latapi 1991; Graham 1992; Navarro 1994; Raczynski 1993). Nonetheless, the disagreements reappear over the question "Is this enough?" or "Is it necessary to go beyond safety-nets?"

Organizations such as the World Bank and several of the region's governments advocate safety-nets as the main poverty-alleviating measure. Other organizations and researchers with a different theoretical reference point consider social protection networks to be necessary but insufficient. They contribute to alleviating the situation of the poor, but are in no way efficient tools to eradicate poverty. However, apart from this concept and other general ideas, the 1990s are characterized by an intellectual void regarding the struggle against poverty from a broader economic and social perspective.

Third, policy makers' tendency to work with existing safety-nets reflects the influence of the culture of poverty and the family survival strategies. Although the belief in the presence of an autonomous culture of the poor has been basically discarded, there is a continuing interest in grass-roots networks as strategic actors in the implementation of social programmes. Moreover, the influence of the family survival strategies perspective is reflected in the interest in households both as units of the social reproduction of poor sectors, and as a fundamental setting for microeconomic decision-making.

In addition to these general tendencies, we would like to mention some of the views considered of interest in current regional poverty studies.

The historical causes of poverty are analysed from the political economy perspective in terms of inequitable patterns of development and distribution originating within the domestic economy. This phenomenon emerged at the turn of the century.

Reference is made to political economy rather than to the economy itself. The idea of models of inequitable development and distribution implies the existence of socio-political actors as protagonists of the establishment of such models.

Two paradoxical situations are worth mentioning with regard to poverty studies carried out in the region during the 1980s. The first relates to the current neo-liberal policies dominating the region's governments. This neo-liberalism is extremely pragmatic and tries to base its legitimacy on the idea that the main role of government is to maintain financial equilibrium and stability. This, in fact, has implied a reduction in public expenditures with consequent negative impacts on the poor. It is important to point out that this neo-liberal pragmatism is in many cases widely accepted owing to the underlying recent hyperinflation experience.

Another common characteristic of the research on poverty in the 1980s is the absence of behaviourist views that "blame" the poor for their own situation. In fact, with regard to ethnic factors, even if there is a direct relationship between poverty and indigenous groups and between poverty and Afro-Latin Americans (Brazil), theories establishing causal links between these variables do not exist.

The second significant paradox is that, even though there is general agreement that structural economic factors are the cause of poverty, when it comes to proposing measures to attack poverty the tendency is to seek lines of action such as health issues, education, income-generating projects, etc. that are not targeted at the real causes of the problem.

Certainly, if an international organization centred its work on the causes of poverty it would become involved in domestic political issues, thus exceeding its prescribed role. Nevertheless, it is important to differentiate between: (a) poverty and income distribution inequality; (b) actions to mitigate the situation of the poor; and (c) actions to combat the structural causes of poverty. It is evident that poverty appears as a by-product of income distribution. However, because it is difficult to modify income distribution, poverty is addressed from its social side. Even if many organizations recognize the need to modify patterns of income distribution, this position is not reflected in policy measures. The implication is that it is possible to eliminate poverty while maintaining the distributive model that causes poverty in the first place.

Many agencies disagree about the degree of emphasis that should be placed upon the individual or structural factors in explaining the causes of poverty. This dichotomy appears implicitly in public policy proposals. The World Bank places the most emphasis on the individualistic view. This is evidenced in the importance accorded to educating the poor as a means of increasing their opportunities for entering the labour market. This is the classic liberal image, which considers general welfare to be an aggregate of the opportunities and benefits given to the individual.

The other agencies emphasize structural factors. UNDP, ILO/PREALC, and ECLAC stress the fact that economic growth alone is not sufficient to reduce poverty, and that the implementation of redistributive policies is required to benefit the poor. They agree that the market's role in allocating resources is not sufficient for satisfying the basic needs of the poorest sectors.

The ILO/PREALC states that one of the main causes of poverty and inequality is insufficient and unequal access to employment. It therefore emphasizes the creation of more productive and remunerative jobs. It affirms that this has to be part of a redistributive strategy aimed at completely satisfying basic needs.

Future trends and prospects

Poverty research in Latin America has been oriented mainly to the assessment of public policies. The methods utilized for poverty measurement are the poverty line (PL) and "unsatisfied basic needs" (UBN). International agencies are making special efforts to homogenize data in order to compare the magnitudes and types of poverty. In fact, significant information on the issue is already available. Data comparison has been possible owing to the systematic application of household and consumption surveys.

Furthermore, in the past decade, the debate on state intervention strategies has been intensified as a result of the increase in poverty. As mentioned earlier, a key issue in the debate has been the efficacy and efficiency of targeted policies versus universal coverage policies.

Because current research is clearly oriented towards the quantitative assessment of poverty it does not reflect the heterogeneity of the phenomenon in the region. Furthermore, the utilization of quantitative methods produces homogeneous data. Besides, assessment methods such as PL and UBN measure the situation only at a given moment – they do not reflect the process of pauperization being suffered by most Latin American societies. Neither of these methods is able to assess the growing vulnerability and exclusion affecting the poorest groups of society.

Taking into consideration the efforts undertaken to assess poverty in the region, we believe that now research on other dimensions should be promoted in order to obtain a wider perspective on the phenomenon. Diverse poverty situations should be considered in terms of their temporal dimension and their social dimensions (vulnerability, exclusion). The link between poverty and other economic, social, and political variables should also be analysed. These studies would require an articulation between the quantitative and qualitative approaches. This kind of approach would enhance the comparative perspective and could lead to innovation in the development of public policies. There are, however, some obstacles to future comparative research:

- Insufficient funding sources. It is becoming increasingly difficult to obtain funding for local research, particularly for comparative studies.
- Insufficient academic interchange. There is a lack of interchange between the countries in the region in terms of joint research plans among universities or national research bodies.
- The need to review national assessment tools. Rigorous comparative studies require reliable national data, which will be attainable only through the joint efforts of researchers, public and private agencies, and national governments.
- Weakened academic research support. This hampers the identification of funding sources and discussions centred on poverty assessment or the implementation of social policies. In addition , because of the nature of the poverty problem, emphasis is placed on action-oriented projects rather than academic research on the issue.

References

Abranches, S. (1985) *Crescimento e pobreza no país do milagro.* Rio de Janeiro: Jorge Zahan Editor.

Albanez, T. et al. (1989) *Economic Decline and Child Survival: The Plight of Latin America in the Eighties.* Florence: International Child Development Center, Innocenti Occasional Papers No. 1.

Altimir, O. (1979) *La dimensión de la pobreza en América Latina.* Santiago de Chile: CEPAL.

—— (1982) *The Extent of Poverty in Latin America.* Washington DC: World Bank.

—— (1983) "La distribución del ingreso en México, 1950–1977", in *Distribución del ingreso en México.* Mexico: Banco de México, Serie Análisis Estructural.

—— (1993) "Income distribution and poverty though crisis and adjustment", Paper presented at the ECLAC–UNICEF Workshop on Public Policy and Social Expenditure.

Anaya, R., A. Aguilar and G. Pinto (1984) *Desarrollo y pobreza en Bolivia: Análisis de la situación del niño y la mujer.* La Paz: Mundy Color.

Barbeito, A. and R. Lo Vuolo (1992) *La Modernización Excluyente. Transformación económica y Estado de Bienestar en Argentina.* Buenos Aires: UNICEF/CIEEP/LOSADA.

Beccaria, L. (1993) "Estancamiento y distribución del ingreso", in A. Minujin (ed.), *Desigualdad y exclusión.* Buenos Aires: UNICEF/LOSADA, pp. 115–148.

Beccaria, L. and R. Carcioffi (1993) "Politicas públicas en la provisión y financiamiento de los servicios sociales. Aportes para una agenda de los años 90", in A. Minujin (ed.), *Desigualdad y exclusión social.* Buenos Aires: UNICEF/LOSADA, pp. 193–240

Beccaria, L. and A. Minujin (1991) *Sobre la Medición de la pobreza: enseñanzas a partir de la experiencia argentina.* Buenos Aires: UNICEF-Argentina, Working Paper No. 8.

Beccaria, L. and A. Orsatti (1989) "Argentina 1975–1988: Las nuevas condiciones distributivas desde la crisis", in *La Economía de América Latina.* Mexico: Centro de Economía Transnacional and Centro de Investigación y Docencia Económicas, vols 18 and 19, pp. 57–82.

Bergsman, J. (1980) *Income Distribution and Poverty in Mexico.* Washington DC: World Bank, World Bank Staff Working Paper No. 395.

Berry, A. (1987) "Poverty and inequality in Latin America". *Latin American Research Review,* 22: 202–214.

—— (1990) *Economic Perfomance, Income Distribution, and Poverty in Latin America: The Experience of the 1980s.* Washington DC: World Bank.

Bustelo, E. and E. Isuani (1992) "El Ajuste en su laberinto: Fondos sociales y política social en América Latina". *Comercio Exterior,* 42(5): 428–32.

Camargo, C. and F. Giambiagi (eds) (1991) *Distribuçao da renda no Brasil.* São Paulo: Paz e Terra.

Cardoso, E. and E. Faleto (1970) *Dependenca e desenvolvimento na America Latina*. São Paulo: Zahar Editores.
Cardoso, E. and A. Helwege (1992) "Below the line: Poverty in Latin America". *World Development*, 20: 19–37.
Castañeda, T. (1990) *Para combatir la pobreza: Política social y descentralización en Chile*. Santiago de Chile: Centros de Estudios Públicos.
CEPA (1993) *Evolución reciente de la pobreza en el aglomerado del Gran Buenos Aires 1988–1992*. Buenos Aires: CEPA–INDEC– Secretaria de Programación Económica.
Cortés, R. and A. Minujin (1988) "Argentina: Women's work facing the crisis". Paper presented at the conference on Weathering Economic Crisis: Women's Responses to the Recession in Latin America and the Caribbean.
de Janvry, A. and E. S. Sadoulet (1989) "Rural development in Latin America: Rethinking poverty reduction to growth". Paper presented at the World Bank IFPRI Poverty Research Conference.
Desai, M. (1989) *Methodological Problems in the Measurement of Poverty*. London: London School of Economics and Political Science.
Dos Santos, W. (1987) *Ciudadania e Justica: A políticas Social no ordem Brasileira*. Rio de Janeiro: Editora Campus.
Draibe, S. (1994) "Neoliberalismo y políticas sociales. Reflexiones a partir de las experiencias latinoamericanas". *Desarrollo Económico*, 134: 181–96.
ECLAC (1985) *La pobreza en América Latina: dimensiones y políticas*. Santiago de Chile: CEPAL.
—— (1988) *Determinación de las necesidades de energía y proteínas para la población de nueve países latinoamericanos*. Santiago de Chile: CEPAL.
—— (1989) *Opciones y falsos dilemas para los años noventa: lo nuevo y lo viejo en política social en América Latina*. Santiago de Chile: CEPAL.
—— (1989) *Política macroeconómica y pobreza*. Santiago de Chile: CEPAL.
—— (1990) *Informe social 1990*. Santiago de Chile: CEPAL.
—— (1991a) *El desarrollo sustentable: Transformación productiva, equidad y medio ambiente*. Santiago de Chile: CEPAL.
—— (1991b) *Magnitud de la pobreza en América Latina*. Santiago de Chile: CEPAL.
—— (1992) *El perfil de la pobreza en América Latina a comienzos de los años 90*. Santiago de Chile: CEPAL.
Faria, V. (1994) *Social Exclusion in Latin America. An Annotated Bibliography*. Geneva: International Institute for Labour Studies, Discussion Paper No. 70.
Field, G. 1992 *Crecimiento, distribución del ingreso y pobreza en América Latina: algunos hechos estilizados*. Washington, DC: IDB.
Filgueira, C. (1994) *Heterogeneity and Incidence of Urban Poverty in Uruguay*. Notre Dame, Ind.: Kellogg Institute.

Food and Agriculture Organization (1988) *Rural Poverty in Latin America and the Caribbean.* Rome: FAO.
Galin, P. and M. Novick (ed.) (1990) *La precarización del empleo en Argentina.* Buenos Aires: CEAL–CIAT–OIT–CLACSO.
Galofre, F. (1981) *Pobreza crítica en la niñez. América Latina y el Caribe.* Santiago de Chile: CEPAL/UNICEF, Caderon y Cia.
Germani, G. (1973) *El concepto de marginalidad.* Buenos Aires: Nueva Visión.
Golbert, L. and E. Tenti (1993) *Estructura social y pobreza.* Buenos Aires: Kellogg/CIEPP.
────── (1994) "Nuevas y viejas formas de pobreza en la Argentina". *Sociedad*, 4: 85–103.
Gonzalez de la Rocha, M. and A. Latapi (eds) (1991) *Social Responses to Mexico's Crisis of the 1980s.* San Diego, Calif.: University of California, Center for U.S.–Mexican Studies.
Graham, C. (1992) "The politics of protecting the poor during adjustment: Bolivia's emergency Social Fund". *World Development* 20(9): 1233–51.
Hardy, C. (1987) *Organizarse para vivir. Pobreza urbana y organización popular.* Santiago de Chile: Programa de Economía del Trabajo.
Hernandez, I. (1989) *Algunos efectos de la crisis en la distribución del ingreso en México.* Mexico: UNAM.
ILO/PREALC (1988) *Deuda Social: ¿Qué es, cuánto es, cómo se paga?* Santiago de Chile: OIT/PREALC.
────── (1990) *Empleo y equidad, desafío de los 90.* Santiago de Chile: OIT/PREALC, Working Paper No. 354.
────── (1992) *Empleo y Transformación Productiva en América Latina y el Caribe.* Santiago de Chile: OIT PREALC, Working Paper No. 369.
────── (1993) *Deuda Social: Desafío de la Equidad.* Santiago de Chile: Ricardo Infante.
INDEC (1990) *La pobreza urbana en la Argentina.* Buenos Aires: INDEC.
Jelin, E. (ed.) (1991) *Family, Household and Gender Relations in Latin America.* London: Routledge International.
Jelin, E. and M. Feijoó (1984) *Trabajo y familia en el ciclo de vida femenino. El caso de los sectores populares.* Buenos Aires: Cedes.
Katzman, R. (1989) "La heterogeneidad de la pobreza en Montevideo: una aproximación bidimensional", in *La Economía de América Latina* Mexico: Centro de Economía Transnacional and Centro de Investigación y Docencia Económicas, vols 18 and 19, pp. 99–112.
León, A. (1994) *Urban Poverty in Chile: Its Extent and Diversity.* Notre Dame, Ind.: Kellogg Institute.
Livas, R. (1989) "Dos sexenios de deterioro en el salario: 1977–1988", in *La Economía de América Latina.* Mexico: Centro de Economía Transnacional and Centro de Investigación y Docencia Económicas, vols 18 and 19, pp. 41–56.
Lopes, J. (1990) "Recessào, pobreza e familia: a decada pior do que perdida". *Sao Paulo em Perspectiva*, 4(1): 100–9.

Lopes, J. (1994) "Brazil, 1989: A socioeconomic study of indigency and urban poverty", in: *Democracy and Social Policy Series #7*. Kellogg Institute. Notre Dame (forthcoming).

Lustig, N. (1989) "La desigualdad económica en México", in *La Economía de América Latina*. Mexico: Centro de Economía Transnacional and Centro de Investigación y Docencia Económicas, vols 18 and 19, pp. 35–40.

Melgar, A. (1989) "La distribución del ingreso en la década de los ochenta en Uruguay", in *La Economía de América Latina*. Mexico: Centro de Economía Transnacional and Centro de Investigación y Docencia Económicas, vols 18 and 19, pp. 113–26.

Minujin, A. (1991) "New and old poverty in Argentina: the consequences of the crisis", in *Proceedings of the Invited Papers*, International Statistics Institute, El Cairo, Egypt.

——— (ed) (1992) *Cuesta Abajo. Los Nuevos Pobres: efectos de la crisis en la sociedad argentina*. Buenos Aires: UNICEF/LOSADA.

——— (ed) (1993) *Desigualdad y exclusión. Desafíos para la política social en la Argentina de fin de siglo*. Buenos Aires: UNICEF/LOSADA.

Minujin, A. and G. Kessler (1993) *Del progreso al abandono. Demandas y carencias de la nueva pobreza*. Buenos Aires: UNICEF-Argentina, Working Paper No. 16.

——— (1995) *La nueva pobreza en la Argentina*. Buenos Aires: Temas de Hoy/Planeta.

Monza, A. (1993) "La situación ocupacional en la Argentina", in A. Minujin (ed.), *Desigualdad y Exclusión*. Buenos Aires: UNICEF/LOSADA.

Morley, S. (1992) *Macroconditions and Poverty in Latin America*. Washington D.C.: IDB.

Muñoz, G. and O. Altimir (1979) *Distribución del ingreso en América Latina*. Buenos Aires: CLACSO–CIEAL–El Cid Editor.

Navarro, J. (1994) "Reforming Social Policy in Venezuela: Implementing targeted programmes in the context of a traditional pattern of public intervention". Paper presented at the LASA XVIII International Congress, Atlanta.

Nun, J. (1969) *Marginalidad y Participación social*. Geneva and Buenos Aires: International Institute for Labour Studies and Instituto Torcuato Di Tella, Working Paper.

Pinto de la Piedra, M. (1988) "El componente social del ajuste económico en América Latina". Paper presented to the Seminario de alto nivel: Cómo recuperar el progreso social en América Latina., UNICEF–ILPTES–IDE.

Quijano, A. (1977) *Dependencia, Urbanización y cambio social en Latinoamérica*. Lima: Mosca Azul.

Raczynski, D. (1993) *Social Policies in Chile: Origins, Transformations and Perspectives*. Notre Dame, Ind.: Kellogg Institute.

Redclift, M. (1984) "Urban bias and rural poverty: A Latin American pespective". *Journal of Development Studies* 20: 123–38.

Rocha, S. (1992) *Poor and non-poor in the Brazilian Labor Market.* Rio de Janeiro: IPEA Discussion Paper.
Rodgers, G. (1989) *Urban Poverty and the Labor Market. Access to Jobs in Asia and Latin American Cities.* Geneva: International Institute for Labour Studies/ILO.
Sheahan, J. (1987) *Patterns of Development in Latin America: Poverty, Repression and Economic Strategy.* Princeton, NJ: Princeton University Press.
Souza, P. (1980) *Emprego, salários e pobreza.* São Paulo: Hucitec.
Torrado, S. (1980) *Sobre los conceptos de Estrategia familiares de vida y proceso de reproducción de la fuerza de trabajo: Notas teóricas metodológicas.* Buenos Aires: CEUR.
UNDP (1990) *Desarrollo humano. Informe 1990.* Bogotá: Tercer Mundo Editores.
—— (1993) *Reforma social y pobreza. Hacia una agenda integrada de Desarollo.* Washington, DC: UNDP.
Vergara, P. (1990) *Políticas hacia la extrema pobreza en Chile 1973–1988.* Santiago de Chile: FLACSO.
Wainerman, C. (ed.) (1994) *Vivir en Familia.* Buenos Aires: UNICEF/ LOSADA.
World Bank (1986) *Poverty in Latin America: The Impact of Depression.* Washington, DC: World Bank.
—— (1988) *Targeted Programs for the Poor During Structural Adjustment: A Summary of a Symposium on Poverty and Adjustment.* Washington, DC: World Bank.
—— (1990) *World Development Report, Poverty.* New York: Oxford University Press.
—— (1991) *World Development Report 1991.* New York: Oxford University Press.
—— (1993) *Poverty and Income Distribution in Latin America: The Story of the 1980s.* Washington, DC: World Bank.

Chapter 23

Brazil: Poverty Under Inflation

Sonia Rocha

Introduction

The 1980s in Brazil clearly represented a break from the relatively successful path the country had followed since the 1930s, but especially after the Second World War, to attain the status of a developed country. From 1968 to 1980, per capita GNP grew at an average yearly rate of 6.25 per cent, as a result of a fast rate of investment and modernization. Although the benefits of income growth were unevenly distributed, people were better off at all income levels, which guaranteed social peace. The general awareness in the academic milieu that issues concerning social inequality and poverty were not automatically solved through economic growth (Adelman 1975) did not affect the conduct of economic policy in Brazil. It was taken for granted that growing inequality was a necessary result of productive bottlenecks, especially the scarcity of qualified manpower, and that trickle down effects would soon begin to operate. As a consequence, economic policy was tacitly geared to the attainment of high growth rates as an objective in itself.

High liquidity in international financial markets fuelled domestic investment in the 1970s. As a result, Brazil entered the 1980s as highly dependent on flows of foreign capital and was badly hit by the money shortages and rise in interest rates at the beginning of the decade. The debt crisis and the process of adjustment that followed led to successive short-term economic cycles all through the decade, which resulted in a decline in investment and terrible results in terms of income growth: from 1980 to 1994 GDP grew at a dismal 1.07 per cent annual average. Per capita results were even more adverse, with per capita GDP recording a reduction in the same period. That the outcome was not worse was the result of a big fall in the rate of population growth.

Macroeconomic policy, although highly successful on the foreign front, seemed unable to deal with the monetary and fiscal imbalances that plagued the Brazilian economy. High rates of inflation – the consumer price index reached 1,863.6 per cent in 1989 – penalized individuals on lower incomes and increased income inequality from already intolerable levels (Bonelli and Ramos 1993).

The combination of stagnant incomes and growing inequality placed Brazilian society under great pressure. It caused a sudden break in the pattern of rapid growth and high social mobility that Brazilian society had become used to. Social unrest and urban decay in areas affected by the long period of low and unstable economic growth brought the poverty theme to the centre of national attention. Questions such as "What is the nature of poverty in Brazil?" "How many are poor?" "What are the characteristics of the poor?" "What are the implications of these characteristics for fighting poverty?" became central in a debate that mobilized not only politicians and academics, but the whole society.

One way to determine who is poor in a modern society is to put a money value on the goods and services needed to function in that society. This "poverty line" is the parameter that can be used to distinguish poor from non-poor on the basis of their incomes. In Brazil this income-related approach is the one most commonly used in poverty studies, although many different techniques have been applied to establish poverty lines.

The focus here is on absolute poverty alone, because relative poverty – that is, income inequality – encompasses a specific and rich set of studies. Furthermore, since a large proportion of the Brazilian population still has insufficient income to guarantee access to basic necessities, the priority in social policy is to deal with absolute poverty. Eventually, improving the lot of the absolute poor might also reduce inequality.

Only studies referring explicitly to the use of a poverty line are considered here. This excludes those examining the relationship between low income and certain personal or family characteristics. This is the case, for instance, with studies of the impact of changes in the minimum wage (Ramos and Reis 1994), which is of especial interest because of the widespread use of the minimum wage as the poverty line. Because 27.1 per cent of workers received wages lower than the minimum wage in 1990, wages policy and the growing informal labour market are relevant concerns when considering absolute poverty. Also, since labour income accounts for 84 per cent of family income, the way individuals participate in the labour market is closely related to the incidence of poverty. Studies on the relationship between educational level and income (Lam 1989) demonstrate the high returns of schooling when future income flows are considered and the need for better access to education as a way to reduce poverty. Studies centred on known characteristics of the poor, such as belonging to female-headed households (Barros et al. 1993a), living in the rural Northeast (Jatobá, 1994), or having small children in the family (Camargo and Barros 1991) highlight the need for social policy mechanisms aimed at specially vulnerable groups.

The following section presents studies that use the minimum wage to define the poverty line. I then deal with poverty studies based on poverty lines derived from observed consumption patterns. The third section presents information on the data used in poverty studies. The concluding section synthesizes the main results on poverty in Brazil and their implications for social policy.

The minimum wage as poverty line

Minimum wages were established in Brazil in 1940 as part of a newly created body of labour legislation. The wages, at first defined for fifty different areas, were supposed to correspond to the cost of acquiring the basic necessities for a worker. In fact the wages were from the onset lower than that and, from then on, price inflation and irregular indexation had the effect of further diminishing their value. It is estimated that in 1980, when the number of regional minimum wages had already been reduced to two, the real value in São Paulo corresponded to 62 per cent of its 1940 value; in Rio de Janeiro, the 1980 minimum wage was 21 per cent above its 1940 value (Sabóia 1985).

Despite the fact that the minimum wage does not necessarily correspond to the minimum living costs of a worker, which also vary according to local determinants, the minimum wage, or a multiple of it, has often been used for establishing poverty lines in Brazil.

Pfefferman and Webb (1983) used a two-minimum-wages-per-family poverty line[1] to identify the poorest group. This value corresponded to around US$260 per capita annually, which was roughly double the poverty line then currently used by international agencies in assessing poverty in developing countries. They argued that cost of living in Brazil was substantially higher than that usually found in underdeveloped economies and that the worsening of social indicators for families with incomes below this level gave support to their choice.[2] Using two current minimum wages per family as a poverty line, 62 per cent of the population were identified as poor in 1972, and only 27 per cent in 1974–5.

These results require an explanation. Although the pace of economic growth was rapid in the early 1970s – GDP grew at an average yearly rate of 10 per cent between 1972 and 1975 – an increase in income was not the only cause of the reduction in the proportion of poor people. In fact, the income data for 1972, from the national family survey (Pesquisa Nacional por Amostra de Domicílios – PNAD), are not compatible with the income data from the national study of family expenditure (Estudo Nacional da Despesa Familiar – ENDEF) relating to 1974–5. Since the ENDEF is a more complex survey, which investigated consumption and expenditure in great detail, its records for income are more complete than the ones from PNAD.

It is obvious that analysis of different years cannot be based on data with different characteristics. Additionally, cross-sectional comparison among regions for any given year is necessarily prejudiced when a single poverty line is used for the country as a whole. However, this has been the most frequently adopted procedure. Pfefferman and Webb, for instance, found that the proportions of poor were 9 per cent metropolitan, 25 per cent urban, and 66 per cent rural in 1974–5, ignoring the fact that the cost of living is generally lowest in rural areas and highest in metropolitan areas. Thus, using a single poverty line implies underestimation of metropolitan poverty or overestimation of rural poverty.

The choice of the income variable has a significant impact on the results. Hoffman (1984) argued that global expenditure is a better proxy for permanent income than declared income, and used this variable from ENDEF in conjunction with a two-minimum-wages-per-family poverty line. Nevertheless, the proportion of poor thus obtained for Brazil in 1974 – 56.2 per cent – is almost double Pfefferman's result using declared income.

Pastore et al. (1983) also used a single national poverty line, but they introduced several improvements in relation to previous studies. They defined the value of the poverty line as equivalent to one-quarter of the minimum wage. Though equally arbitrary, it explicitly took into consideration family size, which is known to be larger among the low-income population. Using demographic census income data, they found the proportion of poor had declined from 43.9 per cent in 1970 to 17.7 per cent in 1980. In absolute terms, the number of poor families would have declined from 7.3 million in 1970 to 4.4 million in 1980. Nevertheless, because the poverty line relates to current minimum wages and the real minimum wage was not constant in the period,[3] there are price biases embodied in the results.

Probably the most important contribution by Pastore et al. (1983) was the use of census data to generate a special set of tabulations to compare various characteristics of the poor and non-poor sub-populations, since previous analyses were generally based on published data. Indicators relating to demography, labour market, education, and housing conditions show the impact of the increase in incomes during the 1970s, which occurred simultaneously with rapid productive change and urbanization. It is noteworthy that, if differentiated poverty lines had been used in the study – higher in urban than in rural areas – instead of a single national parameter, the increased proportion of urban population (56 per cent in 1970 and 67 per cent in 1980) would obviously have resulted, *ceteris paribus*, in a smaller reduction in the proportion of the poor than the one obtained in the study.

Fox (1990) presents a very careful analysis of the evolution of poverty in Brazil, considering explicitly the price problem and other conceptual questions. Although a single and arbitrary per capita poverty line is adopted[4] – one-quarter of the highest 1980 minimum wage, which translates into an income of roughly US$200 per year, or about 13 per cent of per capita GDP[5] – it is expressed in real terms for different years. Results based on the 1970 census naturally differ from the ones obtained by Pastore et al. (1983), who used current minimum wages as the basis for the poverty line (see Table 23.1). Nevertheless, it is surprising that different authors arrive at quite different results for 1980 (Pastore et al. 1984; Fox 1990; Tolosa 1991), because the same methodology and the same database were used. The proportions of poor families directly derived from published census results for 1970 and 1980 are 65.6 per cent and 19.1 per cent respectively.

Both Fox (1990) and Rocha and Tolosa (1993) present a set of poverty indicators based not only on census data but also on PNAD data. In both cases results refer to urban and rural strata in different regions.

Poverty rates in the 1980s (Table 23.2) show extreme variation over time: the rates, both in rural and in urban areas, are very sensitive to short-term cycles, whose ups and downs have characterized the Brazilian economy in the last decade. The proportions of poor in 1981 were affected by an unprecedented drop in real GDP (−4.5 per cent), the first since official national accounting began in 1947. The incidence of poverty worsened as

Table 23.1 The proportion of poor in Brazil for census years using poverty lines based on the minimum wage (%)

Authors	1970	1980	Poverty line definition
Pastore et al. (1983)	43.8	17.7	$\frac{1}{4}$ of current minimum wage
Fox (1990)	54.7[a] 47.9[b]	26.2	$\frac{1}{4}$ of the highest 1980 minimum wage
Tolosa (1991)	54.1[a]	34.8	$\frac{1}{4}$ of the highest 1980 minimum wage
Published census data[c]	65.6	19.1	$\frac{1}{4}$ of the current minimum wage

Sources: IBGE, 1970 Demographic Census, Table 10, p. 226; 1980 Demographic Census, Table 1.13, p. 44.
Notes:
[a] General price index (FGV/IGP-DI) used as deflator.
[b] Implicit GDP deflator.
[c] Percentages refer to families and not to individuals as in the other cases. For 1970, the proportion refer to families below the two-minimum-wages poverty line.

the crisis reached its peak in 1983. In 1985, the effects of the export-led growth that had started the previous year were already visible. The poverty reduction process was maintained in 1986, when the anti-inflation shock (Cruzado Plan), followed by significant real wage increases, led to a consumption boom that fuelled the economy until it was checked by the re-eruption of inflation and new short-term cycles in the late 1980s. The decline of GDP in 1990 (−4.4 per cent) contributed to the absence of per capita gains compared with 1981. Economic performance deteriorated further till 1993, when an upturn began. Unfortunately, PNAD data are not available for years later than 1990, but trends in the 1980s suggest that absolute poverty probably increased up to 1993.

The data presented in Table 23.2 highlight other aspects of the incidence of poverty in Brazil. Poverty is higher in rural areas, but, because of rapid urbanization, the rural poverty share is declining. Also, there are significant differences between regions. Poverty in the Northeast is the highest, both in terms of income, as shown here, and from the social indicators point of view. The Southeast region, where the states of Rio de Janeiro and São Paulo are located, has traditionally had the least adverse poverty indicators. Albuquerque (1994) uses social indicators for the poor sub-population to derive a poverty typology using the poverty line based on one-quarter of the 1980 minimum wage per

Table 23.2 The proportion of poor, using a 1/4 minimum wage family per capita poverty line, 1981–90 (%)

	1981 Proportion (%)	1981 Share (%)	1983 Proportion (%)	1985 Proportion (%)	1986 Proportion (%)	1987 Proportion (%)	1990 Proportion (%)	1990 Number ('000)	1990 Share (%)
Urban	14.9	42.5	21.6	17.1	9.6	14.8	17.7	19,057	48.6
Rural	46.8	57.5	54.2	47.1	33.7	46.3	53.4	20,151	51.4
Brazil	24.8	100.0	30.9	25.4	16.1	23.3	27.0	39,208	100.0
Northeast	44.9	54.2	52.5	46.3	32.9	44.2	51.1	21,770	55.5
Southeast	13.5	24.3	19.4	15.5	8.2	13.0	14.9	9,682	12.8

Sources: 1981–7, Fox (1990); 1990, Tolosa and Rocha (1993).
Note: The Northeast is the poorest region and the Southeast is the least poor region in Brazil.

capita. Although the poverty incidence moves in the same direction in all areas, the impact of short-term cycles is stronger in the most developed areas, where the poverty incidence is lowest and least "structural" in nature.

Poverty lines derived from food baskets

Obtaining the poverty line from food basket values and Engel's coefficients has always been the "preferred" procedure as far as international literature on poverty is concerned. Its main advantage is having a basis for defining the minimum food basket that guarantees the satisfaction of nutritional requirements. Deriving non-food consumption in a simplified way is often considered an inevitable shortcoming in the absence of any theoretical basis for defining its minimum adequate level and value.

In a comparative study on poverty in Latin America, Altimir (1979) established poverty lines for each country based on a common methodology: the food basket was derived from per capita consumption of food items known to compose the national diet, adjusted to meet nutritional requirements defined by the Food and Agriculture Organization (FAO). For Brazil, this diet was initially valued on the basis of the available average urban prices. Although recognizing the importance of local specificities in prices and in consumption patterns,[6] Altimir ended up with two poverty lines, one referring to urban areas (US$197), and the other to rural areas (US$130). The national poverty line, obtained as a result of the average rural and urban poverty lines weighted by population shares, corresponded to US$162 in 1970, which was roughly 20 per cent lower than the minimum wage poverty line that was often adopted (see previous section). The most relevant fact about Altimir's study is that, for the first time, different poverty lines were used for sub-areas in the country.[7] Hence, national results for poverty incidence have a different meaning when compared with those from previous studies. Table 23.3 shows the proportions of poor and hard-core poor, the latter having a per capita family income below the value of the food basket (the indigence line). It is noteworthy that the incidence of poverty in rural areas remains much higher than in urban areas, despite the use of a rural poverty line that is considerably lower. Results for the country as a whole are similar to the ones obtained by Fox (Table 23.1) using a single poverty line (implicit deflator variant).

By then the World Bank, according to its 1979 guidelines, was using a relative poverty concept for poverty assessment and policy: the poverty line was estimated as one-third of national

Table 23.3 The proportion of poor and hard-core poor: Altimir's estimates for 1970 (%)

	Poor	Indigent
Urban	35	15
Rural	73	42
National	49	25

Source: Altimir (1979: 63).

per capita income (in Brazil, one-third of 1979 per capita income represented Cr$18,396 annually or Cr$6,745 monthly family income). Considering the specific minimum wages, this represented from 3.2 to 4.1 times the local minimum wage per family.

The arbitrariness and growing confusion that resulted from using different parameters for assessing poverty in Brazil, in international comparisons as well as among sub-areas within the country, motivated the study by Vetter and Hicks (1983) for the World Bank. The Bank needed a parameter to determine to what extent its programmes were correctly targeting the urban poor. Hence, the study was aimed at evaluating the cost of living for the urban poor in different regions, and how an acceptable national poverty line should be established, and at what cutting point. They defined an optimal diet in relation to Rio de Janeiro food preferences and prices, and estimated a set of poverty lines based on the local cost and local Engel's coefficients derived from the ENDEF. Despite using a single food basket, it was found that both food costs and the share of food expenditure in total expenditure differed significantly among regions. Thus the researchers recommended the use of a higher value for the poverty line (four minimum wages per family) in the North, Northeast, and Centre-West, and a lower value (three minimum wages) in the other regions. Although the differences related to urban areas, no recommendation was made concerning urban–rural differentials. Furthermore, no poverty incidence estimates were generated based on these parameters.

Vetter and Hicks' choice was to resort to the ENDEF only for Engel's coefficients, but by then the survey's complete results were already available. Family expenditures – with food consumption as the object of especial emphasis – were published in a very detailed income and regional breakdown. The new data allowed for the application of a wide choice of methodologies for defining poverty lines, relating both to the food basket and other expenditures. Nevertheless, even the poverty studies that made greatest use of the ENDEF had used the basic "food cost–Engel's coefficient–poverty line" approach, that is, the same as Altimir's, although now based on observed low-income consumption. In this sense, conceptual progress was modest, but empirically the gains were important, because it became possible to define specific poverty lines based on low-income consumption patterns according to a quite detailed regional breakdown (twenty-two sampling areas).

Thus, using the ENDEF data, the World Bank Special Report on Brazil (1995) estimated the cost of three variants of twenty-two regional diets that considered low-income consumer's preferences and met the national average calorie requirement (2,242 kcal/day). For the higher-priced diet, typical of families just meeting the calorie requirement, this monthly per capita cost varied from US$10.8 in the rural Northeast to US$29.1 in metropolitan São Paulo. Although these results were presented in terms of an analysis of consumption and nutrition, and were not used to derive poverty lines or to measure poverty incidence in Brazil, it is interesting to relate them to values later used by other authors in order to assess the incidence of poverty in Brazil (see Table 23.4).

Thomas (1982) resorted to the 1979 World Bank Report diets to estimate poverty lines using observed Engel's coefficients. Having a choice among three sets of food baskets, he selected the one embodying exogenous constraints. The more strictly observed diet was rejected because its higher value would necessarily mean a larger proportion of poor than adequate for social policy purposes.

Thomas (1982) and Fava (1984) used practically identical methodologies based on regionalized food costs and Engels coefficients to derive twenty-two poverty lines relating to ENDEF areas of analysis. Nevertheless, their poverty line values differ: Fava's values are generally higher in metropolitan areas, but lower in rural areas.

Some summary poverty incidence results are presented in Table 23.5. Thomas and Fava's poverty rates for the country as a whole are quite different – 29 per cent and 36 per cent, respectively. Although the ranking of sub-areas in Table 23.5 is the same, it is not maintained when the twenty-two areas are considered. Furthermore, for social policy purposes, to have either 16 per cent or 27 per cent of the total number of the poor in metropolitan areas has quite different policy implications. The differences between Thomas's and Fava's parameters and indicators, using essentially the same methodology on the same

Table 23.4 Estimates of minimum monthly per capita food costs and poverty lines based on ENDEF (US$ and % of minimum wage)

	World Bank (1979)		Thomas (1983)				Fava (1984)			
	Indigence[a]		Indigence Line[a]		Poverty Line		Indigence Line		Poverty Line	
	US$	%MW[b]	US$	%MW[b]	US$	%MW[b]	US$	%MW[b]	US$	%MW[b]
Metropolitan São Paulo	29.1	53	20.6	38	40.7	75	18.2	34	53.0	99
Rural Northeast	10.8	20	10.5	19	16.6	30	9.2	17	13.5	25

Notes:
[a] The indigence line corresponds to the cost of meeting food needs.
[b] August 1974 Rio de Janeiro minimum wage (Cr$376.80).

Table 23.5 Poverty incidence estimates using poverty lines derived from ENDEF data, 1974–5

	Thomas			Fava		
	Poor (per cent)	No. of poor*	Share (per cent)	Poor (per cent)	No. of poor*	Share (per cent)
Metropolitan	17.4	4,403	17	34.2	9,488	27
Urban	22.6	6,944	28	34.4	10,562	31
Rural	39.4	13,978	55	38.6	14,664	42
Total	29.4	25,325	100	36.0	34,713	100

Sources: Thomas (1982: 87); Fava (1984: 105).
Note: Thousands. Absolute numbers must be viewed with caution. Thomas's and Fava's results relate to a total population of 93,408 and 96,425, respectively.

database, highlight the difficulties in making comparisons between different periods using empirical results obtained by different authors.

Comparing income distribution based on expenditure surveys with poverty lines, both derived from ENDEF, has an obvious advantage for poverty studies. One reason is that expenditure data reflect permanent income better than income data. Another reason is that expenditure-based distribution guarantees a better coverage of the income of lower-income groups. As a result, a more reliable approximation of the incidence of poverty is obtained. Hence, from a theoretical point of view, the best poverty estimates are the ones derived entirely from expenditure surveys. Using poverty lines based on observed consumption and income from population census or from the PNAD produces some overestimation of poverty because of the income underestimation bias.

This is why the poverty rate for 1974–5 is not comparable with results obtained using the same poverty lines price-adjusted for other years. Rocha (1988) used Fava's food baskets and Engel's coefficients derived from the ENDEF for the nine metropolitan areas together with local product prices from the Consumer's Price System to estimate local and time-specific poverty and indigence lines for the 1980s. This was used as a departure point for generating income-based poverty indicators (proportion of poor, income gap ratio, gap as proportion of non-poor income, Gini coefficients, Sen and Foster–Greer–Thorbecke indexes) for each metropolitan area and the metropolitan stratum as a whole, which accounts for 30 per cent of the Brazilian population. Once the poor sub-population was defined, labour market, housing

Table 23.6 Selected income-based poverty measures and social indicators for the poor sub-population, 1981–90

	Recife		São Paulo		All metropolises	
	1981	1990	1981	1990	1981	1990
Poor ((%) '000)	1,348	1,338	2,902	3,277	10,828	12,260
Proportion (%)	56	48	22	22	29	29
Gap ratio	0.48	0.46	0.38	0.40	0.42	0.42
Squared gap ratio	0.29	0.27	0.22	0.24	0.23	0.25
Children out of school (%)	21	14	19	11	21	15
Inadequate sewerage (%)	88	80	47	30	68	43
Informal employment (%)	41	45	33	30	36	39

Source: Rocha (1992a).
Note: The three social indicators are selected from a much larger set, limited only by the scope of the PNAD. The indicators here refer only to the poor sub-population, but they were also obtained for and non-poor sub-populations.
Definitions: Children out of School – poor children aged 7–14 not attending school, in relation to total number of poor children in this same age group; Inadequate Sewerage – number of poor living in dwellings with inadequate sewerage in relation to the total number of poor; Informal Employment – per cent of poor employees without a labour card, thus without labour legislation guarantees (paid holidays, insurance, retirement, and other benefits), in relation to the total number of poor employees.

conditions, and educational indicators were obtained for the poor, the non-poor, and the total population for all the years using the PNAD database (Table 23.6) (Rocha 1992a).

The set of comparable poverty indicators over several years showed how strongly the incidence of poverty is affected by short-term economic cycles. For all metropolises, the proportion of poor was highest in 1983 (38.2 per cent) and lowest in 1986 (22.8 per cent). Differences in the poverty rate are also notable between metropolises. In 1990, for instance, when the proportion of poor in Brazilian metropolises as a whole was 28.9 per cent, it varied from 47.4 per cent in Recife (located in the less-developed Northeast region) to 12.2 per cent in Curitiba (in the South), reflecting the well-known regional disparities in Brazil. When considering a set of social indicators referring to the poor sub-population, São Paulo performed best among the metropolises, while two metropolises in the Northeast – Recife and Fortaleza – had the worst score (Rocha and Villela 1990). Also, an analysis of the incidence of poverty and the characteristics of the poor in the nucleus and in the periphery of each metropolis offers evidence of a three-stage life cycle of Brazilian metropolises: the three Northeastern metropolises (Fortaleza, Recife, and Salvador) are most backward in terms of economic, social, and, more generally, urban development. São Paulo, with a relatively low poverty rate, the best social indicators for the poor and the non-poor alike, and a periphery that tends to replicate the nucleus social and economic functions, is clearly the most advanced Brazilian metropolis (Rocha and Tolosa 1993).

According to Rocha's studies, the evolution of poverty in Brazilian metropolises in the 1980s presents three basic features. First, income-based indicators reveal remarkable stability, despite adverse economic conditions. Second, social indicators reveal an obvious improvement, for both the poor and the non-poor sub-populations, although in many instances, especially in sanitation, performance has remained critically low. Third, labour market indicators deteriorated for the poor and the non-poor alike.

Taking the metropolitan poverty lines as a point of departure, Rocha (1994) also estimated the incidence of poverty and its characteristics for the country as a whole and for twenty-two sub-areas. Because no consumer price data are available for rural and urban areas, cost relationships between the metropolises and the urban and rural areas in each region, derived from the ENDEF, were used. Results show declining income-based indicators, for both the poor and the hard-core poor, between 1981 and 1990 (Table 23.7 below).

This evidence of declining absolute poverty in the 1980s contradicts the general findings concerning the reduction in average household per capita income in the 1980s (Barros et al. 1993a,b), as well as income-based poverty indicators obtained by Psacharopoulos et al. (1992). There are three important methodological reasons that could explain the disparity in the results. First, if living costs for the poor decline comparatively to income, it is possible to have lower absolute poverty even when incomes are reduced. Second, Psacharopoulos used a single poverty line for the country as a whole, whereas Rocha used twenty-two

Table 23.7 Poverty rates, 1979–90

	Romão (1990)	Cepal (1991)	Psacharo-poulos (1992)	Rocha (1994)	World Bank (1995)
(a) Proportion of poor using expenditure-based poverty lines						
1979			0.45		
1980	0.24		0.34		
1981				0.34	0.20
1983	0.42			0.41	0.27
1985				0.35	0.22
1986	0.28			0.24	
1987	0.35	0.45		0.28	0.18
1988	0.39			0.29	
1989				0.30	0.17
1990			0.41	0.30	0.17

	Cepal (1991)	Peliano (1993)	Rocha (1994)
(b) Proportion of core-poor using expenditure-based indigence lines			
1979	0.22		
1980			
1981			0.14
1983			0.16
1985			0.13
1986			0.11
1987	0.23		0.10
1988			0.11
1989			0.12
1990		0.22	0.12

local and price-specific poverty lines. Third, because poverty increased between 1980 and 1981, part of the disparity can be explained by this difference in the baseline year.

Other studies used poverty lines derived from ENDEF expenditure data to estimate income-based poverty indicators for Brazil, but most of them did not generate a complete series of income indicators for the 1980s. The Economic Commission for Latin America and the Caribbean (ECLAC 1991), considering differentiated poverty lines for metropolitan, urban, and rural areas,[8] found stability in absolute poverty levels between 1979 and 1987. Romão (1990a, b), using poverty lines derived from the 1979 World Bank food baskets, obtained results similar to Rocha's for 1983, but much higher proportions for subsequent years. Peliano (1993), using ECLAC's food baskets, found a rate of 22 per cent hard-core poor in 1990 (see Table 23.7(b)). This last result has served as the basis for a grass-roots national mobilization aimed at fighting malnutrition and poverty, which evolved into a priority under the government of President Cardoso.

A recent report by the World Bank (1995) sums up a series of studies on poverty in Brazil, which were sponsored by the Bank from 1993 to 1995. It encompasses both a complete set of poverty indicators as well as considerations and data on public policies affecting the poor. Income-based poverty indicators and profiles for poor and non-poor were obtained from the PNAD using newly estimated poverty lines (Rocha 1993) derived from the 1987–8 family expenditure survey. Since this new survey investigates expenditures by metropolitan families only, urban and rural poverty lines were generated on the basis of cost relationships between metropolitan, rural, and urban poverty lines from the ENDEF. The studies in this project have the advantage of referring to a single methodological benchmark and, consequently, generating a large set of comparable information on poverty in Brazil in the 1980s and in 1990. Poverty rates for the country as a whole in the 1981–90 period are presented in Table 23.7. It is noteworthy that income-based indicators for 1981 and 1990 show a decline in absolute poverty, although this decline is smaller than the one obtained using higher poverty lines derived from the ENDEF (Rocha 1994).

Data sources for studies on poverty in Brazil

A quite complex statistical system has been developed in Brazil, which covers most relevant economic activity and population characteristics using surveys of varying detail and periodicity. The Instituto Brasileiro de Geografia e Estatística (IBGE) is the federal agency that as well as coordinating the statistical system is also in charge of most national surveys, specifically all those mentioned below.

When considering the incidence of poverty from the income point of view, it is essential to refer to income distribution. For poverty assessment purposes, the most adequate approach is to take the family as the income and consumption unit, and to estimate family per capita income to be compared with the established per capita poverty line. This means taking into account both the sum of all kinds of revenue (labour income, transfers, rent) received by all members in the family and family size.

In Brazil there are two basic data sources for income, where all individual incomes are surveyed in the family context: the Demographic Census and the national family survey (PNAD). The Demographic Census is a universal household-based survey that has taken place regularly every ten years since 1940. It investigates an increasing but essentially comparable set of data, which allows for income estimation at a very detailed level: the statistical unit is a 150 household cluster, making possible an analytical breakdown well below the 5,000 county level. Since results from the 1991 census are not completely processed, the most recent income estimates derive from the 1990 PNAD.

The PNAD, originally a quarterly survey when it was created in the 1960s, has guaranteed a comparable set of annual data since the mid-1980s. Based on a household sample, its results are subject to restrictions: estimates are significant for urban and rural areas separately at state level (twenty-one states) and for the nine metropolitan areas and Brasília. Because PNAD investigates not only income but also characteristics of the family and individuals in relation to demographic, labour market, and dwellings aspects, a poverty profile can be easily derived from a given poverty line. Naturally, this depends on access to the PNAD database. Published data from PNAD present some income results expressed in minimum wage intervals, making it easier to derive proportions of poor based on minimum wage poverty lines directly from them.

Income data are also available from surveys where the main objective is to obtain data on family expenditure. These surveys constitute the essential sources when poverty lines are to be derived from observed consumption patterns. In Brazil, two national expenditure surveys are available, the national study of family expenditure (ENDEF) and the family budget survey (POF).

The ENDEF survey, conducted in 1974–5, is undoubtedly the most complete survey of this kind. It is especially detailed in terms of food expenditure and consumption, but it also investigated a large set of non-food expenditures by income bracket for eight regions, taking into account for each one the urban, rural, and metropolitan breakdown. The ENDEF was used as the basis for establishing the Consumer's Price System, created in 1979 in order to follow monthly consumer prices in metropolitan areas, Goiania, and Brasília. Despite the time-lag, it is still an essential source when deriving poverty lines for Brazil, because it encompasses the only national data on consumption patterns and prices

The POF, conducted in 1987–8, had as its main objective to in non-metropolitan areas.

update product weights in the Consumer's Price System. In contrast to the ENDEF, its scope was limited to the nine metropolitan areas, Goiania, and Brasília. It investigated expenditures and, even in the case of specific food items, prices and quantities have to be derived indirectly using exogenous prices. Because of high inflation rates and the consequent relative price volatility, converting prices to the October 1987 baseline has necessarily introduced some distortions. Consumption and income from POF are significantly above income from the PNAD relating to almost the same period (September 1987). Thus deriving poverty lines from the POF and using them with income data from the PNAD implies some overestimation of income-based poverty indicators.

Concluding remarks

There is enough empirical evidence to show that the incidence of poverty undoubtedly fell in the 1970s, whatever poverty lines are used. In the 1980s, in the face of stagnant per capita income, there was a marked break in this trend. Researchers using different poverty lines to take into account regional and local cost-of-living differences, demonstrated stability or a weak decline in poverty, while those using a single poverty line showed an increase. On the other hand, social indicators for the poor have presented a steady improvement in the postwar period, and even speeded up in the 1980s, despite the adverse economic results in general and the fiscal crisis in particular.

Methodological differences among studies have led to disagreement about the actual numbers of poor. However, this is not the main issue when poverty in Brazil is considered. As a matter of fact, absolute poverty is still widespread and the country is clearly short of resources – financial and others – to procure the basic minimum for all the poor, even considering the most conservative count. Thus, the main issue seems to be to reach agreement on the relative incidence of poverty when sub-areas in the country are considered. This is empirically related to the use of a set of poverty lines in order to take into account differences in the cost of living for the poor in different areas. Once relative values for the poverty lines are defined, there can be a politically agreed absolute number of poor for social policy purposes. To achieve this number from a set of reference poverty lines, it is sufficient to apply percentage variations of the same magnitude and direction to all local specific poverty lines.

There is consensus on the fact that differentiated poverty lines are a must. However, the lack of updated information on expenditure and prices in non-metropolitan areas is a serious hindrance to meeting this objective. Using a single poverty line for the country as a whole, that is, ignoring that the cost of living is generally lower in rural than in urban areas, leads to a relative overestimation of rural poverty and to underestimation of a crucial tendency: poverty in Brazil has become increasingly urban and metropolitan as a result of rapid urbanization. The visible and increasing number of the absolute poor in urban areas, where inequalities of income and wealth are striking, has prompted the general feeling that poverty has increased in the country as a whole.

In spite of rapid urbanization, rural poverty is still critical in Brazil, especially in the Northeast. Some argue that rural poverty is in fact larger than measured because a high percentage of the poor in so-called urban areas are dependent on agricultural activities for a way of living. In the Northeast, for instance, 29 per cent of poor urban household heads work in agriculture (World Bank 1995), making the distinction between rural and urban areas irrelevant. In fact, poverty is more widespread and acute in the Northeast: the poor represent 32 per cent of the total population and account for 55 per cent of the Brazilian poor (World Bank 1995). Fighting poverty in the Northeast means both facing the agrarian problem in particular, and dealing with the general issues of regional economic and social development.

Whereas poverty is widespread in the Northeast, it is highly concentrated in the metropolises of São Paulo (pop. 15.4 million) and Rio de Janeiro (pop. 9.8 million). In these Southeastern metropolises, poverty presents essential features associated both with urban size and density, and with inequality between the individuals. Fighting metropolitan poverty means guaranteeing an adequate urban infrastructure and providing jobs for the poor in an increasingly complex labour market. Recent developments have shown that a new cycle of economic growth may have a much smaller impact in terms of job creation than in the past. Thus, in the short run, the challenge consists in creating a "positive duality" or a way to keep the poor in the labour market, while measures aimed at fighting the roots of poverty – like providing good-quality schooling for all, which normally takes time to produce results – will reduce absolute poverty and inequality in the long run.

Notes

1. Pfefferman and Webb used the Rio de Janeiro minimum wage of August 1974 (Cr376.8), which was the highest minimum wage in Brazil. It corresponded to US$1,300 annually or a US$260 per capita poverty line for a family of five.
2. "There is much direct evidence of the high levels of malnutrition, mortality rates and severely deficient services and living conditions that correspond to income levels in the vicinity of two mirimum wages" (Pfefferman 1978).
3. The real value of the minimum wage fell from Cr69 to Cr62 in São Paulo and from Cr109 to Cr101 in Rio de Janeiro (Sabóia 1985: 34).
4. Fox would have preferred to use a poverty line based on the price of a minimum basket of commodities. Nevertheless, valuing in 1980 prices the cost of regional baskets estimated by Thomas for 1974, the ENDEF data resulted in values that were much too high to be used with the PNAD income data. This incompatibility can be explained by the greater income coverage of the expenditure survey.
5. In purchasing power parity terms, this poverty line is 20 per cent lower than the one established for Venezuela and roughly equal to the one established for Turkey. In the same year the United States poverty line was around $3,000, or 18 per cent of US per capita GDP (Ravallion et al. 1990, as cited by Fox 1994).
6. It was assumed that the cost of the food basket in rural areas was 25 per cent below that estimated for urban areas. It was also assumed that food expenditure represented 25 per cent of total expenditure in rural areas, but 50 per cent in urban areas (Altimir 1979: 55 and 57).
7. In fact Fishlow (1972) conceived that a lower poverty line should apply to the Northeast.
8. Poverty lines in urban and rural areas are, respectively, 90 per cent and 75 per cent of the estimated value for metropolitan areas.

References

Adelman, Irma (1975) "Development economics – A reassessment of goals". *American Economic Review*, May.
Albuquerque, Roberto C. (1994) "Estratégia de desenvolvimento e combate à pobreza". Paper presented at the Seminário Desenvolvimento Social e Pobreza. São Paulo: MRE.
Altimir, O. (1979) *Dimensión de la pobreza en América Latina*. Santiago de Chile: Cuadernos de la Cepal.
Barros, R. P., R. Mendonça, and S. Rocha (1993a) *Welfare, Inequality, Poverty, Social Indicators and Social Programs in Brazil in the 1980s*. Rio de Janeiro: IPEA.
Barros, R. P., L. Fox, and R. Mendonça (1993b) "Female-headed households, poverty and the welfare of children in urban Brazil". The Population Council, Internal Discussion Paper, September.
Bonelli, R. and L. Ramos (1993) *Distribuição de renda no Brasil: Avaliação das Tendências de longo prazo e mudanças na desigualdade*

desde meados dos anos 70. Rio de Janeiro: IPEA, Discussion Paper No. 288, January.
Camargo, J. M. and R. P. Barros (1991) "As causas da pobreza no Brasil: porca miséria!" *Perspectivas da Economia Brasileira – 1994.* Rio de Janeiro: IPEA, pp. 525–44.
ECLAC (1991) *Magnitud de la pobreza en América Latina en los Años ochenta.* Santiago de Chile: Estudios e Informes de la Cepal.
Fava, Vera L. (1984) *Urbanização, custo de vida e pobreza no Brasil.* São Paulo: IPE/USP.
Fishlow, Albert (1972) "Brazilian size distribution of income". *American Economic Review (Paper and Proceedings),* May: 391–408.
Fox, Louise M. (1990) "Poverty alleviation in Brazil, 1970–1987". World Bank, July, mimeo.
Fox, Louise M. and Samuel A. Morley (1990) "Who paid the bill? Adjustment and poverty in Brazil, 1980–1995". World Bank, June, mimeo.
Hoffman, R. (1984) *Pobreza no Brasil.* Piracicaba: ESALQ, Série Pesquisas No. 43.
Jatobà, J. (1994) *Rural Poverty in Brazil's Northeast: A Profile of the Rural Poor.* Recife: World Bank, 1993.
Lam, David (1989) "Declining inequality in schooling in Brazil and its effect on inequality in earnings". October, mimeo.
Pastore, J., H. Zylberstajn, and C. Pagotto. *Mudança Social e Pobreza no Brasil: 1970–1980.* São Paulo: Pioneira, 1983.
Peliano, Anna M. T. M. (1993) *O mapa da fome: Subsídios à formulação de uma política de segurança alimentar.* Rio de Janeiro: IPEA, Documento de Política, No. 14.
Pfefferman, G. and R. Webb (1983) "Pobreza e distribuição de renda no Brasil". *Revista Brasileira de Economia,* 37(2).
Psacharopoulos, G. et al. (1992) *Poverty and Income Distribution in Latin America: The Story of the 1980s.* Washington, DC: World Bank, Latin America and the Caribbean Technical Department, Report No. 27.
Ramos, L. and G. A. Reis (1993) "Quem ganha salário mínimo no Brasil?" *Perspectivas da Economia Brasileira – 1994.* Rio de Janeiro: IPEA, pp. 491–511.
Rocha, S. (1988) "Estabelecimento e comparação de linhas de pobreza para o Brasil". Rio de Janeiro: INPES, Internal Discussion Paper No. 153.
―――― (1992a) "Poverty in Brazil: Basic parameters and empirical results". Paper presented at the International Seminar on Labour Market Roots of Poverty and Inequality in Brasil. Rio de Janeiro: IPEA, August.
―――― (1992b) *Poor and Non-Poor in the Brazilian Labor Market.* Rio de Janeiro: IPEA, Discussion Paper No. 278.
―――― (1993) *Poverty Lines for Brazil: New Estimates from Recent Empirical Evidence.* Report for the World Bank, January.
―――― (1994) "Governbilidade e Pobreza: o Desafio dos Números", Global Urban Research Initiative, Ford Foundation/University of Toronto. Rio de Janeiro.
―――― (1995) *Governabilidade e pobreza : O desafio dos numeros.* Rio de Janeiro: IPEA, Discussion Paper No. 368.

Rocha, S. and H. Tolosa (1993) "Nucleo–periferia metropolitana: Diferenciais de renda e pobreza", in: J. P. do R. Velloso and R. C. Albuquerque (eds), *Pobreza e Mobilidade Social*. São Paulo: Nobel.

Rocha, S. and R. Villela (1990) "Caracterização da subpopulação pobre metropolitana nos anos 80 – Resultados de uma análise multivariada". *Revista Brasileira de Economia*, 44(1): 35–52.

Romão, M. C. (1990a) *Distribuição de renda, pobreza e desigualdades regionais no Brasil*. Recife: UFPE/PIMES, Discussion Paper.

────── (1990b) *Pobreza: Conceito e mensuração*. Rio de Janeiro: IPEA/PNPE.

Saboia, João (1985) *Salário mínimo: A experiência Brasileira*. São Paulo: L&PM.

Thomas, Vinod (1982) *Differences in Income, Nutrition and Poverty within Brazil*. Washington, DC: World Bank, Staff Working Paper No. 505.

Tolosa, H. C. (1991) "Pobreza no Brasil: uma avaliação dos anos oitenta", in: J. P. do R. Velloso (ed.), *A questão social no Brasil*. São Paulo: Nobel.

Tolosa, H. and S. Rocha (1993) "Politicas de Combate à Pobreza: Experiências e Equívocos" in Velloso and Albuquerque (org), *Pobreza e Mobilidade Social*. São Paulo: Nobel.

Vetter, D. and J. Hicks (1983) *Identifying the Urban Poor in Brazil*. Washington, DC: World Bank, Staff Working Paper No. 227.

World Bank (1979) *Brazil: Human Resources Special Report*. Washington DC. Latin America and the Caribbean Regional Office.

────── (1995) *Brazil: A Poverty Assessment*. Washington, DC: Latin America and the Caribbean Department, Report No. 14323-BR.

Chapter 24

Mexico: Poverty as Politics and Academic Disciplines

Agustín Escobar Latapí

This chapter refers to some of the major contributions to poverty research in Mexico in the period 1982–94. As elsewhere in the Third World, poverty research in Mexico has developed in close, sometimes conflicting relation to various forms of state action. As such, most efforts in the field attempt not only to gauge the changing nature and extent of poverty, but also to evaluate state action and to propose policy reform. Research interacts in multiple ways with government policy. Researchers have developed their analyses in a field in which sides are always to some extent political but not always clear cut. There is a multiplicity of positions both within and without the public sector, and collaboration has at times involved opposing theoretical positions. There are some fundamental agreements as well as large differences in the particular biases, sources, methods, and conclusions of the major studies undertaken since 1982. Their common concern, however, is with the process of restructuring affecting Mexico since 1982, and its interaction with poverty.

This common concern is subject, however, to diverse approaches. During the 1980s and early 1990s, national-oriented research based on official figures was usually more prominent than micro-social studies. The first incorporated international quantitative indexes, assessed national trends, and developed original indexes for the measurement of poverty. Micro-social studies, on the other hand, have typically been based on their own regional or local data sets and tend to view the organization, agency, and strategies of the poor, their households, and small-scale enterprises as responding, even modifying, to some extent, the outcome of adjustment and restructuring. For the first type of research, these responses, if at all significant, represent a form of adaptation to existing, given circumstances. For the second, the actions and reactions of the poor are significant in making their livelihood possible, and may impact on the national economic structure. In this sense, the forms in which the poor adapt are not fatal outcomes of macroeconomic developments, but creative solutions to hardship (Escobar and González 1995). Whereas macro-studies lack some of the necessary data to evaluate people's actions and responses, the second often face difficulties of generalization or comparability. There are, however, more meeting points to these approaches than is usually recognized, and bridges have begun to form between them (Cortés forthcoming; García and Oliveira 1994). Both have at times led to simplistic readings and exaggeration: micro-sociological and anthropological studies have been used by policy makers to assert that the poor will make do during restructuring, because there is a "culture of poverty" that teaches them to do so. To some economists engaged in national studies, on the other hand, the focus is on paid employment, which serves to gauge the capacity of the economy to absorb the population in gainful occupations. Clearly, the poor cannot always "get by". If they did there would be no need for a social policy towards the poor. On the other hand, self-employment and unpaid employment matter for a sociological analysis of work, employment, and poverty.

Concepts

The political nature of poverty research is partly responsible for the definition of concepts and measurements developed in the literature. There is a growing number of macro-social studies attempting to provide adequate measurements of poverty (poverty lines, enumeration and aggregation of the poor, income gaps and inequality among the poor). The general aspects of these studies are coined in the mould of internationally accepted concepts of poverty, the most salient of which is the definition of a "poverty line" or, most commonly (Boltvinik 1994; ECLAC-INEGI 1993a,b; COPLAMAR 1983, 1985; Levy 1992) two poverty lines, one defining extreme poverty and another defining absolute, moderate, or relative poverty. But some of these and other analyses (Cortés 1994; Hernández Laos 1992; Levy 1992) calculate other indices developed in the international literature (Sen's various indices, Foster–Greer–Thorbecke's index, Gini's index). Lastly, there are new conceptual and analytical proposals, based on original measurements and indices, most notably Boltvinik's (1992) Integral Measurement of Poverty.

Micro-social studies of poverty define their subject on the basis of a seemingly less strict definition of the poor: there are studies of low-income households that may at times lie above a "poverty line" (González de la Rocha 1986, 1994; Tuirán 1993). There are studies of female-headed households, which are particularly prone to poverty (Chant 1991). Some authors have focused on small enterprises as the basis of subsistence of a large number of poor families (Bueno 1990; Cortés and Rubalcava 1991; Escobar 1988, 1990). Others have devoted their attention to the interaction between families living in irregular settlements and various state programmes, forms of state action, and the political apparatus. These studies also attempt to establish varying levels of welfare for individuals, families, neighbourhoods, and enterprises and to explain their observed differences, but their common interest lies rather in exploring the mechanisms implemented by the poor that make their survival viable. To do so, they depict and explain various patterns of resource allocation and analyse the extent to which household divisions of labour and the various forms of work and work relations lead to some generation of wealth, income, and employment and they pinpoint social-structural factors that make them stay poor or prosper modestly. Some macro-social studies, such as the latest efforts by García and Oliveira (1994), Cortés (1994), and Gordillo (1994), also belong in this group. Although they use large-scale, primary or secondary national official data, they too focus mainly on the actions, reactions, and strategies of the poor in urban or rural settings during restructuring, and at times resort to a dual micro–macro approach.

The point of departure for large-scale studies of poverty during the 1980s and 1990s has been the project undertaken by COPLAMAR (Coordinación Nacional del Plan Nacional de Zonas Deprimidas y Grupos Marginados) at the beginning of the 1980s. This government-sponsored study involved a prominent team of researchers, and its basic aim was to define "social development" policies in the context of relative government affluence. To do so, large data sets were collected and most basic pertinent concepts were redefined or re-operationalized. Extreme poverty was defined as an *income level below the cost of a food basket containing a set level of calories*. After an examination of a number of alternative food baskets that provide this calorie intake, the researchers chose as reference the one based on the food consumption patterns of the seventh decile of the Mexican income distribution structure. Admittedly, it was not the cheapest possible, but it was "real", in the sense that it represented actual consumption patterns in rural and urban

Mexico. A relatively expensive food basket was thus defined, costing 36 per cent more than the minimum possible (Levy 1992). This obviously raised the extreme poverty line and the number of the extreme poor. Researchers justified their choice as one that represented actual consumption patterns and also because the population with incomes below the cost of this basket did not as a rule replace these items with suitable but cheaper food, but were instead undernourished. This was the fundamental object of the study, and this definition of extreme poverty became the key to another research task: the identification of regions within which large proportions of the population earned incomes below this extreme poverty line. These areas were called "marginalized zones", not poor zones, partly because extreme poverty was mostly found in isolated rural areas that lacked jobs and health and educational services. For two or three years, these regions did receive special attention from COPLAMAR. Although the programme subsisted formally, it was somewhat swiftly put into hibernation with the new government, which had to manage a major crisis. Nevertheless, COPLAMAR had a significant impact on federal expenditure. From 1982, states containing many or deeply marginalized zones were in fact privileged by federal expenditure: their participation in federal allotments (*participaciones*) rose faster than their participation in GNP, at times even more rapidly than that of states rapidly gaining population and production (Escobar 1995).

For COPLAMAR, the definition of moderate poverty was much less important, and not a prime object for policy. The demarcation of this line also turned out to be less useful. It also took as reference the patterns of consumption of the seventh decile of the Mexican income distribution, but it included in addition all non-food items of consumption and access to services. These consumption patterns served to construct a "normative basket satisfying essential needs" (CNSE), which comprised a considerable diversity of goods and services, notably housing expenses, domestic appliances, transport, clothes and shoes, education, health care, and recreation (Coplamar 1983; Boltvinik, 1987). Although a diversity of goods and services should unquestionably form part of the definition of poverty, this particular "endogenous" approach to its definition represented a *petitio principii*. It provided neither an evaluation of welfare that accounted for the satisfaction or not of all basic needs, nor an indication of what the welfare shortfall would be when some of those goods and services were inadequate or absent, except via an equivalent income level, which in turn automatically defined 65 per cent of the Mexican population as below this line for the baseline year (1977). Hernández Laos (1992) and others have noted this problem. "Moderate" poverty is conceived in this study as absolute (in terms of this given CNSE), but it also possesses a "relative" aspect: it should identify a segment of the population that receives roughly adequate food and most basic services, *but* does not have access to other goods and services deemed necessary to participate in the production of national development and in the enjoyment of its benefits. As Levy (1992) notes, the consumption patterns of the reference (seventh) decile included – in some of the households – washing and drying machines. It can easily be said that these households were under neither absolute nor relative deprivation, except in comparison with the unquestionably well-off. Later studies discarded this definition, and it had no major effect on policy. Later efforts, most notably Boltvinik's Integrated Measurement of Poverty (detailed below), currently attempt to overcome this concept's deficiencies by means of the provision of a composite index that incorporates a large number of needs whose non-satisfaction can be measured precisely in order to define a global household income gap in relation to a predefined poverty line, independently of a reference group.

During adjustment and restructuring, poverty as a concept gained in public and academic relevance. In 1982, a devaluation of the peso to one-quarter of its US dollar value, coupled with inflation and the stagnation of employment, led to a precipitous rise in poverty levels. In 1986, the sale of state-owned firms was stepped up, Mexico entered the General Agreement on Tariffs and Trade, and at the end of 1987 the first of a series of "pacts" was signed by representatives of major sectors of organized society. This entailed a shock programme of economic reform, which included a prices and incomes policy agreement between the government, employers, peasants, farmers, and worker confederations. In 1988, the government launched its *Solidarity* programme, heralded in Mexico and elsewhere as a model for the struggle against poverty. At the same time, the government's general economic policies adversely affected GNP and individual incomes.

The government carried out household income and expenditure surveys (ENIGH) in 1977, 1984, 1989, and 1992, and a number of analysts base their analyses on them, whether through published tabulations (Boltvinik 1994; Cortés and Rubalcava 1995, Hernández Laos 1992) or through analyses of the corresponding microdata sets (Cortés 1994; Levy 1992). A growing group of academics is interested in the evolution of poverty under restructuring. INEGI, the official census and statistical agency, increases the variety and number of tabulations produced from the survey, and carries out its own analysis of the evolution of poverty, with the endorsement of the UN's Economic Commission for Latin America and the Caribbean (ECLAC; ECLAC/INEGI 1993a,b). Until 1992, however, only the 1984 household survey was available in microdata form to academics. This limited their analyses. Starting in 1993, the microdata from the 1989 and 1992 surveys became available, first very selectively and later to all interested. This unprecedented openness has allowed analysts to pinpoint the shortcomings and biases underlying the government's official position. Although this has naturally led to substantive criticism, it has also fostered a basic agreement on a conceptual groundwork for analysis. A number of analyses define both extreme and moderate poverty and the Gini index of the income distribution structure as a condition for various evaluations of the social implications of the economic crisis. Their research results, however, do not necessarily coincide, either for a given year or for a defined period (Boltvinik 1987; ECLAC/INEGI 1994; Cortés 1994).

Different and contradictory results stem from (a) differing assessments of minimum dietary components and the basic food basket, (b) the composition, size, and value of non-dietary goods and services defining poverty, (c) income adjustments due to inflation, to mismatches between ENIGH and national accounts, and to the monetary equivalent of non-monetary income, and, finally, (d) other indexes defining poverty. These differences are partly conceptual and partly technical and methodological.

The income level required to purchase a minimum food basket has been adjusted in Latin America as a consequence of new estimates of the level of calorie intake required by the population of each country. In Mexico, mean energy needs indexes, as defined by ECLAC/UNDP (1992: 340), fell between 1970 and 1980. In 1970, total energy requirements were set at 2,285 kcal daily and in 1980 at 2,139. High-quality protein needs have, on the contrary, risen from 28.6 to 34.8 grams daily. The drop in total energy requirements resulted from adjustments based on (a) the average national height for men and women, which had been calculated on the assumption of equal average heights throughout Latin America for 1970, and (b) lower energy needs for infants, children, and adolescents. This calorie requirement, however, is higher than that estimated by some authors, who have established minimum requirements closer to 2,000 kcal daily. ECLAC/INEGI (1993b) provides a detailed account of calorie and protein requirements according to age, sex, and rural/urban status.

An income-defined food basket is useful but problematic. It cannot be assumed that people with earnings approaching that cost will in fact consume that basket. This problem may be greater in some regions and countries. In Mexico in 1979, the National Nutrition Institute estimated, on the basis of a nationwide health survey, that 19 million Mexicans, 13 million of whom lived in rural areas, were undernourished. This represented a larger proportion of the population (28.4 per cent) than in other Latin American countries with average incomes below those in Mexico (Lustig 1992). This means that, in order to identify the extreme poor in nutritional terms in Mexico, it is necessary to add a substantial amount to the cost of the food basket. This is in fact the approach used by some authors (Levy 1992), although they have been criticized and the size and method of estimation of this non-dietary component vary from one analyst to another (Hernández Laos 1992).

Internationally used indexes will not be dealt with in detail. Instead, particular attention will be given to Boltvinik's Integral Measurement of Poverty (1992). This index is currently being tested on a specially designed survey in Mexico City, and it is being adapted to analyse other databases. Its fundamental aim is to combine the advantages of the two complementary approaches for the enumeration and aggregation of poverty: those based on an income-based poverty line and those based on an estimation of the satisfaction of basic, or essential, needs. This is not the first attempt to provide such an index. But it is a new approach to an integrated index. Boltvinik proceeds by identifying and weighting aggregate need satisfaction in order to produce all of Sen's indexes. The components for a measurement of need satisfaction are: running water and sewerage, education level and school attendance, electricity, housing, household equipment, and free time. The components of the income-based poverty line are: food, dress, shoes and personal care items, hygiene, essential transport and communications. Among the latter, however, Boltvinik also incorporates the costs involved in the access or acquisition of services required for the satisfaction of essential needs. Health needs, for example, may be satisfied either through social programmes or through private institutions. In some cases, then, they should be identified basically among the first set of indexes, but in others they should be accounted for mostly through the second set. In both instances, however, the cost of accessing the institutions in order actually to receive these services should also be accounted for. This involves both time and money, and Boltvinik pays particular attention to the incorporation of time as an aspect of general deprivation and poverty.

To obviate the limitations of need-non-satisfaction indexes in which non-satisfaction increases with the number of needs established, and deprivation is seen simply as 0 or 1, Boltvinik computes a continuous variable for each need, and estimates the satisfaction of each need into an index in which the distance separating the household from the satisfaction of each need is aggregated. The resulting index varies from +1 (complete deprivation of every need) to −1, after rescaling each need, in order to normalize the distribution and withdraw the effect of improvements that have negligible effects on need satisfaction, for example less than one person per room. Households at the norm (those whose average of satisfaction is equal to the norm) therefore have a value 0. Households can be classified into three groups: those with all their needs unsatisfied, those with all needs satisfied, and those with mixed satisfaction of needs. Boltvinik proposes to use a range of 0.1 to −0.1 to define mixed households on the *threshold* of poverty. Other mixed households, if their average departed more significantly from the norm, could be allotted less equivocally to groups above and below. The problem of the time necessary to fulfil some of the needs is met by adding another weighting factor, rather than by computing income lost in securing those services.

After weighting the importance of the non-satisfaction of each need *according to the general profile of need satisfaction of each country* (or region), Bolvinik arrives at a poverty line. He then proceeds to aggregate the distance to this line for every individual below it, which produces a measure of the intensity of poverty. From this, he computes what he calls a "Sen poverty index based on the non-satisfaction of basic needs", which is sensitive to inequality of need non-satisfaction among the poor.

Lastly, Boltvinik incorporates income and time availability (time worked beyond the norm, children's work-time, and time devoted to the satisfaction of non-income-related needs) into his index. This is important because the reason most poor households cannot satisfy their education, health, and other needs is the extra amount of time they have to devote to work and to the satisfaction of other more essential needs, such as clean water and fuel for the household. Therefore, households above the extreme poverty line that are forced to devote a large amount of extra working time to securing that income are classified as extreme poor according to his index, because, as is known, extra work-time bars them from schooling their children or from overcoming the education gap of the adults. Boltvinik's method for an integral measurement of poverty calls for the improvement or development of new databases. A large local (Mexico City) survey especially designed to calculate these indexes has however been carried out, and its results are currently under preparation.

Other concepts that have been subject to considerable research and debate in Mexico have to do with the household and with individual and household cycles and their impact on wellbeing and poverty. A pioneering effort in this regard was carried out by García et al. (1982), who analysed the relevance of the household and the household cycle among the working class in Mexico City. Social anthropologists had traditionally based their analysis of the peasantry on the household. This explains why, once they turned their attention to the cities, they did a large amount of household-based research. This is the case of González de la Rocha's research in Guadalajara (1986, 1994), which stated that the basic social unit acting to ensure the survival of the poor is the household. Although official sources collect information on households, Selby et al. (1990), Chant (1991), and González de la Rocha (1986, 1994) place considerably more emphasis on the household as a crucial unit in individual and collective decision-making by the poor. According to them, household dynamics lie at the basis of the reproduction of urban poverty. González de la Rocha places special emphasis on the household cycle. Stratification of poor urban households according to their per capita income is closely related to the stage of the household cycle. As this cycle progresses, the number of household workers changes, and so do their occupations. Welfare and per capita incomes, therefore, vary quite substantially along this cycle, and the local working class cannot be divided into strata that remain above or below. This variation does not change poor households into middle-class or affluent households: at times their income may match or exceed that of non-manual workers, but their patterns of survival and reproduction usually entail the reproduction of their condition as an urban working class. González de la Rocha views the working class as a single social aggregate, with internal differences explained mostly by the availability of workers in the household.

Similarly, the work of Escobar (1986) showed that Guadalajara workers crossed the boundaries between formal and informal work and enterprises during their working lives, and that this crossing was patterned on their life cycles. This meant, according to him, that there were no separate formal and informal working classes, but rather a single working class, moving from one type of workplace and work relations to another. The two concepts used (household and life cycles) matter for an evaluation of urban poverty, because jobs, income levels, and need satisfaction are dependent upon the individual and the household cycles. Although the use of these concepts has been criticized by academics using a life-course perspective, the notion that household stages and the phases of the life cycle matter for an analysis of poverty and well-being is now widespread in Mexico.

Hypotheses and theoretical frameworks

Whether from a critical or a "collaborative" standpoint, it is recognized that adjustment and restructuring are changing the levels of poverty and the pattern of income distribution. Debate in Mexico does not in general question the need for economic reform, although the direction of reform is the subject of wide discussion. It is centred instead on whether these changes are resulting in increased or lessened poverty and on whether "short-term" increases in poverty will be reversed in the medium to long term, when and if Mexican restructuring succeeds. The government's position can be summarized as follows: (a) although restructuring depresses wages, the poor find creative ways to counteract lessened employment and pay, with informal work compensating to some extent for the downfall; (b) the depression of incomes is short lived; (c) by 1992, incomes had increased, with poverty and inequality dropping. This position finds support in the official publication discussed above (ECLAC/INEGI 1993a, b). Most independent efforts do not explicitly reject this position by means of a contrary set of hypotheses. They tend instead to "deconstruct" official findings and to show contrary results. These can, however, be stated as a hypothetical construct stating that poverty has increased. This is due to a sharp short-term decline in GNP (1982–84) and a consistent, long-term fall in real wages and in the participation of wage income in the national economy, owing to falling salaries (main cause) and the stagnation of formal employment (secondary cause). Informal employment has led to a rise in household income from non-wage sources, mostly self-employment. This rise, however, by no means offsets the fall in wages. The falling participation of wage income is concomitant with a rise in profit and rent income, which has also led to an increase in socioeconomic inequality. The mediate cause of these changes lies, according to these analysts, in the specific policies of adjustment and restructuring implemented in Mexico.

Other hypothetical statements concern the role of added work or effort on the part of the working classes and the poor in general. A group of anthropologists, socio-demographers, and human geographers have focused on the household as the significant social unit defining the amount of extra work performed by individuals, as well as who, in a household, is "assigned" to paid work, market-oriented unpaid work, and housework (Chant 1991; González de la Rocha 1988, 1990, 1994; González de la Rocha and Escobar 1986; Selby et al. 1990). To some (González de la Rocha, Escobar, Tuirán, Cortés), additional work is countercyclical: the economically active population (EAP) tends to grow under crisis and restructuring. To others (Boltvinik), the EAP is procyclical: it grows and falls with the economy. Although support for either of these theses really depends on the definition of the EAP (on the inclusion of the underemployed, the self-employed, and unpaid workers) and on the data sources (censuses vs. employment surveys, which show contrary trends), what matters, in my opinion, is (1) whether or not increased effort on the part of the poor lessens poverty and inequality (see the Major Results section below) and (2) whether it creates wealth or merely redistributes a given GNP among underproductive, immiserated workers. This discussion attempts to establish the nature of informal work during restructuring, which is related to various approaches to informality. The approach closest to most Latin American governments since the mid-1970s is derived from the classic International Labour Organization (ILO) formulation, according to which most informal activities are easy entry, low capital, small scale, underproductive, and therefore providing low income. This approach does not see formal–informal exchanges as significant. According to De Soto (1987), the poor are economic actors who would generate wealth were it not for a repressive, "mercantilist" state. The emphasis here is on the political, not the economic, constraints. If the poor's shops and micro-businesses were allowed to operate freely, they would invest more, pay better wages, and become a pillar of development.

For others the informal economy is a product of the particular political economy of peripheral capitalism, and the wealth it generates is appropriated by the formal economy. In a crisis of the formal economy, the informal economy will suffer too, because demand from the formal economy drops (Portes et al. 1994). This is, admittedly, a simplification: these approaches could be compatible with different outcomes, depending on whether the state and the capitalist sector increase or decrease their exploitation of informal work with restructuring. For example, capitalist firms may attempt to increase their market share and decrease their investment levels and labour costs by resorting to more subcontracting, which would lead to a growth of informality and informal work. Formal employers, also, may be happy to allow informal goods and services to form the basis of the subsistence of their workers if this results in lower wage demands in their own firms. As has been noted, this is counterproductive in a fairly closed economy (because it reduces aggregate demand for the goods of formal firms) but makes sense both for individual firms and for an open economy. But the opposite may also be true. Formal employers may try to maximize their use of existing capital stocks by increasing in-shop production. State action may also affect informal work: the government could become more lenient towards informal work for economic, political, and social reasons, or it may try to compensate for revenue problems by increasing or developing new forms of taxation reaching otherwise illegal enterprises.

These two theoretical frameworks are based on the *posited* relevance of the articulation of the state, the capitalist economy, and informal work. However, because both society and economy are undergoing restructuring, the nature of informality since 1982 in Mexico is open to question, since restructuring could affect precisely this articulation. In other words, a political economy approach could be consistent with a rise in a productive informal sector during restructuring and not only, as Portes et al. (1994) assert, with a decrease in this sector as a consequence of falling formal demand for their goods and services.

Studies of gender and poverty, lastly, explore two main problems: first, to what extent and in what ways gender segregation and discrimination in the labour market produce greater levels of poverty among women; second, the various interactions between women's household roles and power positions and poverty. Because gender has in fact been shown to make a very significant difference for poverty, whether through the inequality of poverty within a household or via labour market discrimination, it has become widely incorporated into the discussion, but mainly into the discussion most interested in the logic of the making and reproduction of poverty. Thus, analyses based mostly on aggregate, secondary data sources tend to complement gender analyses of those sources with in-depth interviews and case studies (García and Oliveira 1994), while microsociological studies likewise resort to aggregate figures to buttress their findings within households and workplaces (González de la Rocha, Chant). There is now general agreement on the existence of a particular approach that may be called a "gender perspective", although what exactly constitutes this perspective is far from agreed.

Data sources

The large-scale studies depicted above have one major common source: the national household income and expenditure survey (ENIGH), which has been carried out at intervals of between three and seven years during the past forty years. This survey is national in scope. Although INEGI maintains that its validity is for the national level of aggregation only, it is carried out in every state (Mexico comprises thirty-two states and a Federal District), and currently it is being tested for consistency and fit with census data at the state level. This implies aggregating the forty categories of household expenditure into a smaller number, because the forty are valid only for the national sample. Microdata analysis of the 1984 survey (Levy 1992), however, shows that, in spite of a relatively large sample size (19,000 households, 65 per cent urban and 35 per cent rural), rural sub-samples are extremely small and even nil in some states.[1] This implies that state-by-state analysis of the rural sub-samples is not always possible. In addition, the number of households in the survey has systematically dropped since 1984. The 1992 sample consisted 10,000 households, 57 per cent urban and 43 per cent rural (ECLAC/INEGI 1993b). The proportion of rural households in the latter sample is higher, and rural coverage seems to have improved. However, this raises comparability problems that may or may not be counteracted by weighting procedures (see the Major Results section below). The (long and detailed) questionnaire explores: dwelling and basic services; main and secondary occupations for those aged 12 and over; credit card use; actual consumption of food, alcohol, and tobacco, including consumption of self-produced food; gifts received and payment in kind of food; transport expenses; business income; agriculture, husbandry, and forestry expenses and production; housework; personal expenses; education; culture and recreation; communication and vehicle servicing; dwelling expenses; consumption of non-food items; gifts received and payment in kind (later translated into their income equivalent); clothing, shoes, and accessories; domestic equipment; health care; recreational goods; and capital increases, earnings, withdrawals, and losses.

Deriving national income from this survey is not automatic. Owing to differential under-reporting (capital earnings are particularly under-reported and such households under-sampled, and non-monetary income is under-reported by poor households) its results do not match national accounts. A number of analysts (Boltvinik 1994; Cortés 1994; Hernández Laos 1992) correct for under-reporting in the survey by means of income/expenditure adjustments based on the "System of National Accounts". Other analysts do not carry out this adjustment, and this operation alone is responsible for some differences in their outcomes. Income and expenditure under-reporting in the ENIGH seems to be a major problem: even the 1990 population census, which asked only one income question, reported 1 per cent more GNP than ENIGH. The usual assumption (that under-reporting is not a major obstacle as long as it can be assumed to be roughly constant) does not hold, because households in Mexico have changed their income sources significantly during the past thirteen years.

Also, the fortunes of a small number of Mexican dollar billionaires have increased considerably (*Forbes magazine* reported twenty-four of them in 1994). Their aggregate income was estimated as equivalent to the income of the poorest 25 *million* Mexicans.[2] It is obvious that none of these families formed part of the survey, or, if they did, they grossly under-reported their income. If income concentration estimations could be based on a sample containing an adequate number of households *in pre-defined* income brackets, the survey would report a remarkable rise in the concentration of income (but only if it could be comparable to previous ENIGHs).

Additionally, the survey calculates a rent income equivalent to every owner-occupier household. Although this seems common sense, the scarcity and high cost of capital, together with high inflation rates in Mexico during the 1980s, meant that rental housing costs rose faster than inflation. Also, more than half of Mexico's poor are owner-occupiers. Adding a rent equivalent thus meant that the total income reported for the sample, and particularly for poor owner-occupied households, grew far more than money income. If the rent equivalent is subtracted or reduced to an index equal to the change in the real value of housing, *total income drops perceptibly for Mexico's poor*, and income concentration grows simultaneously (Boltvinik 1994).

Lastly, the survey pays close attention to gifts received. During prolonged economic hardship, some of the poor increase their gift exchanges. Because the survey reports only gifts received, this results in a net non-monetary income increase for Mexican households. But, because the survey does not report gifts given to others, it is impossible to estimate expenditures thus incurred. This produces an optimistic bias in income assessments *as restructuring progresses* (Boltvinik 1994). Some analysts typically subtract gift income from their studies of *trends* in poverty (ibid. Cortés 1994). If analysis disregards gifts received, the incidence and intensity of Mexican poverty, as well as income concentration, rise.

A number of other data sources are regularly employed by macro-poverty analysts. These include national population censuses, employment surveys (ENEU, ENE, Encuesta Industrial Mensual), and economic surveys of production and employment. The last two are regularly included in the government's "System of National Accounts", whose main concern is providing adequate economic information. The first source, the national population censuses of 1980 and 1990, provides a good basis on which to evaluate the findings of ENIGH and the employment surveys. The censuses are subject, however, to mutually inconsistent biases that make changes very hard to establish. Most census-using scholars agree that the 1980 census significantly over-enumerated the economically active population and that the 1990 census significantly under-enumerated the EAP – particularly women's work. Matching census results to the quarterly employment survey (ENEU) is impossible, except in one regard: the number of *waged* occupations. Whereas the surveys report large increases in the numbers and proportions of self-employed and unpaid family workers, the 1990 census reports a relative drop in both, compared with 1980. For this reason, some analysts prefer to use the results of national employment surveys as a basis for studying trends in work-derived income during the 1980s. An obstacle to this is that quarterly surveys are carried out only in the main thirty-seven cities, with national (rural-inclusive) surveys carried out at variable intervals of two to four years. Others have decided to use census results at their face value (Boltvinik 1994) in view of the match just described. This has consequences for their results.

Micro-sociological analysts use a variety of other sources for their analyses. Individual and household histories, migration, values and attitudes, internal power arrangements and organization are all integrated into questionnaires and case studies, which can therefore relate employment, income, poverty, and interaction to government programmes. In 1982, González de la Rocha carried out fourteen family case studies that served to define the issues and categories for a survey of 100 poor families. In 1985 she re-interviewed sixty-eight households in her initial sample and replaced those not found with households containing main workers in the same industries as those lost, only younger, to compensate for the sample's ageing. She followed the same strategy again in 1987. Chant (1991) has also systematically returned to the households she studied during the 1980s in three Mexican cities. The National Consumer Institute, on the other hand, began a panel survey of household structure, income, and expenditure in 1985 in Mexico City and later extended it to other cities.

Major results

Most analysts agree that poverty and extreme poverty dropped as a percentage of total households and total population during 1957–77. Those analysing income inequality, however, point out that the lowest decile of the Mexican income structure consistently lost ground, relatively speaking, during the period. Whereas in 1957 it captured 2.4 per cent of GNP, in 1977 it received only 1.1 per cent of GNP. This is nevertheless consistent with a systematic improvement in their income levels, granted that economic growth was high and constant throughout the period (Escobar and González de la Rocha 1995; Reyes Heroles 1985; Tello 1991). More significant differences appear when restructuring is analysed, however.

Analysts of the 1977 and 1984 ENIGH, as well as other data from that time, agree on several major points. There is virtually no disagreement on rural poverty. Both COPLAMAR, using 1977 data, and Levy, using 1984 data, agree. Levy (1992: 44–48) characterizes the major traits of poverty in Mexico in 1984 as follows:

- between 10.0 per cent and 19.5 per cent of the Mexican population can be considered as extremely poor;
- they are mostly located in rural areas
- the poorest among these are even more heavily rural;
- the extreme poor have large families, a greater proportion of children in the household, greater dependency ratios, and lower schooling;
- not even the extreme poor devote more than 60 per cent of their income to food;
- most of them work in agriculture; and
- those in urban areas are better off independently of income, in spite of similarities regarding household composition, expenditure, and schooling levels.

The results from several major studies of the 1984 ENIGH are summarized in Table 24.1. As mentioned before, differences result from (a) the definition of dietary intakes, (b) the amount

Table 24.1 Mexico: absolute rates of poverty according to various sources, 1984 (% of population)

	ECLAC1	ECLAC2	SPP/ILO/ UNDP[a]	Hernández Laos	Levy
Extreme poverty					
Rural	30.0	24.0	19.5	52.9	37.2
Urban	19.0	8.0	4.9	20.0	10.0
National	22.0	13.0	8.7	29.9	19.5
Poverty[b]					
Rural	61.0	51.0	54.2	76.1	96.7
Urban	47.0	30.0	15.2	49.6	72.8
National	51.0	37.0	24.7	58.5	81.2

Source: Hernández Laos (1992), abridged by the author. ECLAC2 was adjusted to match national accounts.

Notes:
[a] Joint research by the Ministry of the Budget and Planning, the International Labour Organization, and the United Nations Development Programme.
[b] Includes extreme and moderate or absolute poverty.

and nature of non-dietary goods and services and their income equivalent, and (c) adjustments made, whether for inflation or to correct mismatches with national accounts. All use income levels to estimate the population's ability to purchase a given food basket, and some add certain amounts to this basket to allow for other basic goods and services. Relative to the lowest estimate of a poverty line (SPP/ILO/UNDP), the others apply income levels 70 per cent above this mark (ECLAC), 319 per cent above (Hernández Laos), and 43 per cent above (Levy 1992). These differences are then compounded or lessened by adjustment to national accounts (Hernández Laos 1992).[3]

As can be seen, there are large differences among the studies, although they agree on the rural nature of poverty for 1984. Most of them could be used as a basis for a poverty alleviation programme, except perhaps for the lowest estimation, which would leave out of the programme a large number of undernourished, unschooled children and adults. COPLAMAR and other sources have produced reliable figures that indicate that the proportions of undernourished, unschooled children and adults are considerably larger than the number of extreme poor estimated by SPP/ILO/UNDP.

Differences among the studies widen during the period of crisis and restructuring. The studies differ not only on the definition of levels of poverty but also on the nature of the trends found.

Table 24.2 Mexico: Official estimates of the evolution of poverty, 1984–92

	1984 Million	%	1989 Million	%	1992 Million	%
Individuals in extreme poverty	11.0	15.4	14.9	18.8	13.6	18.1
Households in extreme poverty	1.6	11.4	2.3	14.1	2.1	11.8
Poor individuals[a]	30.4	42.5	37.8	47.7	37.2	44.0
Poor households[a]	4.7	34.2	6.3	39.4	6.4	35.9

Source: ECLAC/INEGI (1993b: 110–11).
Note:
[a] Poor = extreme poor + "intermediate poor".

Official estimates on the basis of ENIGH on the extent of extreme and "intermediate" poverty for 1984, 1989, and 1992 point to a rapid increase in the incidence of both kinds of poverty from 1984 to 1989 and a later slight decline (Table 24.2).

Boltvinik, Cortés, Rubalcava, and others challenge these findings. Boltvinik (1994) provides the most thorough macrosociological analysis of poverty. He first uses national economic statistics to conclude that wages and waged employment dropped systematically from 1980 to 1990. This agrees with most other studies (Rendón and Salas 1993).[4] Boltvinik then deflates rent equivalent income from their 1992 levels to 1989 values according to *rent price indexes, and not general price indexes*. This results in a larger amount of deflation of rent income than the official one. In addition, he subtracts gift income, because the survey does not account for gifts given. As a result, total household income in deciles 5, 6, and 7 *dropped* by 3.1, 2.7, and 1.6 per cent between 1989 and 1992. Since households in lower deciles remain poor, poverty should have increased, albeit moderately, from 64 per cent to 66 per cent during the period (Boltvinik 1994: 126).

Boltvinik also provides assessments of changes in schooling, overcrowding, public services and access to health care and social security (ibid: 126–43). These assessments are based on censuses and sources other than ENIGH. He concludes that, during the decade of crisis (1980–90), adjustment and restructuring policies brought about a *significant slowdown in the rate of improvement of all these goods and services*. At the same time, however, he adds that the provision of these services seems to have had a significant impact on the alleviation of poverty. The services may be inefficient, but their coverage and actual delivery have improved. The obvious risk here is that the proposed privatization of these services may withdraw their benefits from large segments of the poor. His conclusion is consistent with analyses dealing with the evolution of infant and child mortality rates from 1980 to 1987–8, which on the whole *slowed their rate of improvement of the 1970s but did not worsen* (Langer et al. 1991). This latter analysis also concludes that the gap in mortality rates widened during the period between the poorer and the richer states of Mexico, and that some poverty-related infant and child diseases account for a growing number of deaths (tuberculosis, gastrointestinal diseases, and other malnutrition- and poverty-related illnesses such as pneumonia).

There are reasons to believe that this increase in poverty – during a period in which the government claims general income improvement – may be still larger. According to Cortés (1994), 1992 income levels may have been overestimated by *increasing the proportion of households reportedly living in "low density" or rural areas.* The survey referred to assigns a lower cost to the food basket in rural areas. As explained in the previous section, the rural sub-sample of ENIGH has increased as a proportion of the total sample. Apparently, this was done by reclassifying households in semi-urban areas as "rural" and therefore as able to survive on lower incomes. The result is that Mexico, according to the survey, is more rural now than in 1984, and Mexico's low-income households are therefore able to buy more food on lower incomes than before. This is contrary to reality. Mexico is becoming still more urban. If these households were reassigned, as seems natural, to urban areas and to urban costs of living, the results would show that their ability to purchase the food basket has dropped, and the resulting poverty levels are greater for 1992. But it seems this adjustment cannot be done on the basis of the existing microdata sets, except by a case-by-case evaluation, which is very time-consuming.

A further difference between official and other analyses lies in the year taken as a baseline. Average wages and salaries fell by 19.2 per cent from 1982 to 1984. This latter year is therefore a *low* reference point for 1989 and 1992, and one that can easily provide optimistic evaluations of later dates. Both Cortés and Boltvinik use 1977 as a baseline, because this corresponds to the last survey before the 1982 crisis. This is then a *high* point of reference, but not as high as 1981, when average pay set record levels.

The evolution of poverty in Mexico during restructuring cannot be explained on the basis of GNP performance alone. A large number of analyses have shown that wages fell in Mexico during 1989–92 in spite of moderate economic growth, and that income concentration rose. Unemployment was not considered a major factor in Mexican restructuring up to 1994. Although it rose significantly in 1983, it has never reached 10 per cent in any major city. This is due to the fact that adjustment with inflation meant that the public and private sectors enjoyed a rapidly falling wage bill and had no need to resort to massive lay-offs (Lustig 1992), to the inability of the poor to remain unemployed, because there are no unemployment benefits in Mexico, and to the relative openness and acceptable incomes provided by work in the informal economy. Income inequality therefore is related not to unemployment levels, but rather to the rewards of people who work.

Cortés and Rubalcava (1991) provided the first evaluation of changes in the income structure from 1977 to 1984. In their words, during this period Mexico underwent "equalization through impoverishment". The Gini index dropped from 1977 to 1984, but since economic performance was negative this meant that the number and proportion of the poor rose. Cortés (1994) carried out an analysis of income inequality from 1977 to 1992 that controls for number of earners in the household and for changes in the number of households. According to him, from 1977 to 1984, the households most affected by adjustments were those in the cities. This brought about a fall in their income, and a relative "equalization" of their income to rural incomes, which make up the lowest three deciles. Per worker income in deciles 6 to 10 fell during this period. This produced less inequality. From 1984 to 1989, however, 70 per cent of the gains in the national economy were captured by the tenth decile. Other gains were explained by an expansion in the number of earners per household. This produced more inequality, because most gains went to the top. During the last period (1989–92), there was a further gain of the top deciles, explained mostly by a rise in earnings per worker in the tenth decile and a rise in the number of workers per household in the middle deciles. This again increases inequality, because most gains go to the top.

In summary, from 1977 to 1992 there was growing income inequality explained by increasing incomes per worker for the tenth decile and increasing numbers of workers for the "middle" deciles (deciles 6–9, which comprise a part of the poor). The latter finding coincides with previous micro-sociological analyses (Cortés 1994: 15). On the basis of a simulated income structure in which the number of household workers remains fixed, Cortés also concluded, again in agreement with micro-sociological analyses (González de la Rocha 1986), that *inequality – and poverty – would have been considerably greater in Mexico in 1992 if households had not increased their number of workers*.

Cortés's and Boltvinik's analyses are complementary in most respects, and they do not contradict official results for 1977–84 and 1984–9. They do contradict, however, the official results concerning 1989–92: poverty and inequality increased in Mexico at a time of moderate but constant growth. A "comprehensive" approach to the understanding of poverty should also stress that the components *partially* alleviating this worsening of poverty came from the satisfaction of other, mostly non-income, needs, such as education, health, less overcrowding and some additional public services provided to poor households. The main difference between Cortés and Boltvinik lies in their appreciation of the changes in the size of the labour force, and in the sociological significance of this change.

There are no recent analyses of the question posed above, i.e. whether the growing workload of the poor produces some actual wealth among them or merely redistributes existing GNP. This is obviously related to the role of the informal economy and its changes with restructuring. Lustig (1987, 1992) has provided two analyses of this question. Simply put, she showed that most of the added labour producing non-wage returns after 1977 did not produce much added income to wage-based households; in other words, although labour participation is countercyclical, non-wage earnings (including earnings from self-employment) are procyclical. This would modify Cortés's findings to some extent, because this would mean that the poor have had to place more and more members in a race that is increasingly competitive and whose total rewards are mostly fixed. Those not entering the race may in fact lose income, but those "winning" the race are only taking what is available, not generating any more wealth. In my opinion, this must be increasingly the case, as the informal economy becomes saturated, formal demand for goods and labour stagnates after 1994, and capital is no easier to get (which would improve the productivity of the labour of the poor in small economic units). In other words, increased labour invested in non-formal work may have been very useful to the household up to approximately 1987, but it is less and less so.

Another aspect of the results of the above analyses has to do with the rural/urban divide. As said, there is agreement that most extreme poverty and the poorest among the poor were found in rural areas at the onset of adjustment and restructuring. But these policies affected, initially, mostly urban workers. This meant that the urban component of poverty rose from 1977 to

1984. Official results (ECLAC/INEGI 1993b) indicate that the number of extremely poor individuals in rural areas rose from 6.7 to 8.4 million from 1984 to 1989, and still increased slightly to 8.8 in 1992. Those in urban areas rose from 4.3 to 6.5 million and then dropped to 4.8. But comparative trends in rural and urban poverty and inequality resulting from this analysis may not be entirely reliable, owing to the above-described changes in the rural/urban allocation of a part of the sample and for the other reasons noted by Boltvinik and Cortés.

Gender, as said in the previous section, is increasingly salient, although so far this has meant mostly that women's studies have become increasingly relevant. There are no specific studies of male unemployment or of the marginalization of middle-aged men from formal employment in gender terms, although this phenomenon is increasingly important. Studies on gender and poverty develop in two main areas: (a) whether women's increasing participation in the labour market has produced less or more discrimination and segregation in the market and an improvement or not in their position in the household; (b) the interaction between women's household roles and poverty, which itself may be divided into two main areas of discussion – first, whether female-headed households are poorer or not, and whether they tend to change or reproduce societal gender roles; second, whether women's positions in the household require poverty to be defined on an intra-household basis (as said before, intra-household divisions of labour and differential consumption may lead to greater deprivation among women).

García and Oliveira (1994) found that increased female participation in the labour market, before restructuring, was due to the increasing participation of young, educated, childless women (whether married or not). This was a period of steady but slow rise in their participation rates. The longer-term analysis of trends, which included the period 1982–7, however, showed that increased participation was due to the incorporation of women in their thirties, with little or no schooling, with a marriage history, and with small children. *The factors that had inhibited the participation of these women in the labour market before 1982 (low schooling, young children) were no longer important.* In other words, falling domestic incomes forced poor women to seek employment or other money-making activities, and their added income was the key element in cushioning the household from the worst impact of restructuring (González de la Rocha 1988, 1990). However, González de la Rocha, García and Oliveira (1994), and Escobar (1992) also found that these women were mainly working informally, via domestic employment or other personal services. This meant that their incomes were low, and that their incomes worsened as more and more of these women entered the market. The rise in *maquiladora* or in-bond export production, which still employs mostly women (approximately 360,000 in 1992), does not seem to have altered this situation substantially. This is still a very small fraction of national employment, and wages in these plants are lower than average in Mexican manufacturing, which does not significantly improve the total income of these women's households.

Roberts (1992) found women earned, on average, 23.6 per cent less than men in the border cities and 27.0 per cent less in the principal Mexican cities in 1987–8. In the border area, women who owned small firms equalled men's earnings, while in the main cities they were still at a disadvantage of 32.4 per cent in relation to men's earnings. Discrimination in the labour market is important for analyses exploring the impact of women's income-producing work on their households and their ability to overcome intra-household authoritarianism and inequality. González de la Rocha (1994) asserts that labour market discrimination makes for the reproduction of authoritarianism, because women's incomes are below those necessary to threaten men's economic dominance in the household, in spite of the fact that women's income may be used up entirely in securing household basics. In summary, women are participating much more in the labour force now than at the onset of restructuring. This, however, has not yet improved their household position.

González de la Rocha (1988) has asserted that female-headed households, which have increased as a proportion of total households in Mexico, show lower total and per capita income levels than male-headed households. This is due, in her view, to labour market discrimination against and segregation of the main household earner (a woman) and to a lower availability of other household members for money-earning work. This entails higher dependency ratios. Lower availability results from the age structure of the household (female-headed households are overwhelmingly made up of women in their thirties and young children) and the need for one of the other members to replace the household head in housework. Chant (1988, 1990) countered that, although total and per capita consumption levels are lower, female-headed households produce greater well-being among their members for two reasons – the absence of male violence and authoritarianism, and a more egalitarian division of work and consumption. In more recent research (1994), González de la Rocha has found that female-headed households allot a greater proportion of total expenditure to items fundamental for well-being, such as food and education, and therefore less to alcohol and high-cost items that in other households are given preferably to men (tobacco, meat). Per capita food consumption in female-headed households is in fact higher than in comparable working-class male-headed households (ibid.).

The question of women's intra-household deprivation is a crucial one, because it calls for special kinds of targeted programmes as opposed to general price or "family" subsidies. It also means that women may be extremely poor in households that do not seem to be so, which has long-term consequences for these women and their offspring (who would show the effects of extreme poverty even though the household income may lie above that line). This finding, which is often repeated in the literature, calls for a redefinition of vulnerable groups and the policies directed at them. Although gender researchers' results agree on this point, it would be necessary to explore whether differential food consumption affects the household by creating a gender barrier to nourishment, as they assert, or whether the expensive and prestigious items reserved for men affect them by creating other health problems, associated with meat, animal fats, and alcohol. If the second tends to be the case more often than the first this would not call for complacency, because it would mean that a sizeable portion of the household budget is devoted to items that could be better spent on basics, and that this bias is still responsible for some of the malnutrition and morbidity/mortality rates found.

However, it seems that the amounts of time worked and the income received are not the only changes resulting from restructuring in Mexican households. Several other occurrences are serving to turn households into units that more efficiently organize the survival of the poor. First, there is a rise in the number and proportion of non-nuclear households, explained by the inability of newly weds to afford a new house and the advantages they and their parents derive from their continued residence in the home. The same result (a complex household structure) is produced by the incorporation of persons who provide additional incomes or perform housework while others previously tied to house chores seek paid work. Second, results differ on the extension of mutual help and inter-household cooperation. Mexican research into the survival of the urban poor has always stressed inter-household cooperation (Lomnitz 1975, 1977). But whereas González de la Rocha has found that inter-household gift and help exchanges increase with restructuring, Selby et al. (1990), on the one hand, and Benería, on the other, found that co-operation tends to become internal to the household, with inter-household exchanges losing importance or becoming less flexible. Less inter-household cooperation would seem to be at odds with the general finding from ENIGH discussed above, i.e. that gift income has increased significantly among Mexican households.

NOTES

1. It is understandable that no rural populations were interviewed in the Federal District in 1984; it is more than 99 per cent urban. The absence of rural households in the samples of partly rural states (Yucatán and Guerrero), however, is less easily understood.
2. This is an unadjusted estimate of this income equivalent and, since the fortunes of these billionaires and the incomes of the poor come from entirely different sources, they are not strictly comparable.
3. The line defining extreme poverty lies at a per capita monthly income of 1,803 pesos at (1st quarter) 1984 prices according to SPP/ILO/UNDP. ECLAC places it at 3,069, H. Laos at 7,560, and Levy at 2,580.
4. The only source stating that wages have risen since 1987–8 is the presidential state of the nation address, which is based on the Encuesta Industrial Mensual, a fairly small sample of large enterprises. A breakdown of these figures shows that income rose only for non-manual employees in these firms (Rendón and Salas 1993).

REFERENCES

Boltvinik, Julio (1987) "Ciudadanos de la pobreza y la marginación" *El cotidiano*, September-October: 305–26.
────── (1992) "El método de medición integrada de la pobreza. Una propuesta para su desarrollo". *Comercio Exterior*, 42(4): 354–65.
────── (1994) "La satisfacción de las necesidades esenciales en México en los setenta y ochenta", in P. P. Moncayo and J. Woldenberg (eds), *Desarrollo, desigualdad y medio ambiente*. Mexico City: Cal y Arena.
Bueno, Carmen (1990) "Es la venta de comida una actividad marginal en la dinámica de la ciudad de México?", in G. De la Peña et al. (eds), *Crisis, conflicto y sobrevivencia. Estudios sobre la sociedad urbana en México*. Guadalajara: Universidad de Guadalajara/CIESAS.
Chávez Galindo, Ana María, David Moctezuma, and Francisco Rodríguez (1994) *El combate a la pobreza en Morelos. Aciertos y desaciertos de Solidaridad*. Cuernavaca: CRIM.
COPLAMAR (1982) *Vivienda*. Vol. III in *Necesidades esenciales de México*. Mexico City: Siglo XXI.
────── (1983) *Macroeconomía de las necesidades esenciales*. Mexico City: Siglo XXI.
Chant, Sylvia (1988) "Mitos y realidades de la formación de familias encabezadas por mujeres", in L. Gabayet et al. (eds), *Mujeres y*

sociedad: Salario, hogar y acción social en el occidente de México. Guadalajara: El Colegio de Jalisco.

────── 1991 *Women and Survival in Mexican Cities: Perspectives on Gender, Labour Markets and Low-Income Households.* Manchester: Manchester University Press.

Cortés, Fernando (1994) "La evolución en la desigualdad del ingreso familiar durante la década de los ochenta". Centro de Estudios Sociológicos, El Colegio de México, mimeo.

────── (forthcoming) "Procesos sociales y demográficos en auxilio de la economía neoliberal. Un análisis de la distribución del ingreso en México durante los ochenta". El Colegio de México

Cortés, Fernando and Rosa María Rubalcava (1991) *Autoexplotación forzada y equidad por empobrecimiento: la distribución del ingreso familiar en México (1977–1984).* El Colegio de México, Serie Jornadas. México D.F.

──────1995 *El Ingreso de los hogares.* Aguascalientes: INEGI/El Colegio de México/UNAM.

De Soto, Hernando (1987) *El otro sendero.* México, D.F.: Ed. Diana.

ECLAC/INEGI (1993a) *La pobreza en México.* Aguascalientes: ECLAC/INEGI.

────── (1993b) *La pobreza en México. Apéndice Metodológico.* Aguascalientes: ECLAC/INEGI.

Escobar Latapí, Agustín (1988) "The rise and fall of an urban labour market: Economic crisis and the fate of small-scale workshops in Guadalajara, Mexico". *Bulletin of Latin American Research* 7(2): 183–206.

────── (1990) "Estado, orden político e informalidad: notas para una discusión". *Nueva Antropología,* 37.

────── (1991) "El nuevo Estado mexicano y el trabajo informal", in J. Alonso, A. Aziz, and J. Tamayo, *El nuevo Estado mexicano. 1. Estado y economía.* México D.F.: Nueva Imagen.

────── (1992) "Cambio ocupacional y movilidad individual en Guadalajara, 1982–1990", in *Ajusteestructural, mércados laborales y TLC.* Mexico City: El Colegio de México, Fundacion Friedrich Ebert and El Colegio de la Frontera Norte.

────── (1995) "La reestructuracion, la produccion de lasclases y el genero". *Estudios Sociológicos,* 38.

Escobar Latapí, Agustín and Mercedes González de la Rocha (1995) "Crisis, restructuring and urban poverty in Mexico". *Environment and Urbanization,* 7(1): 57–75.

García, Brígida and Orlandina de Oliveira (1994) *Trabajo y vida familiar en México.* Mexico City: El Colegio de México.

García, Brígida, Humberto Muñoz, and Orlandina de Oliveira (1982) *Hogares y trabajadores en la ciudad de México.* Mexico City: El Colegio de México/UNAM.

González de la Rocha, Mercedes (1986) *Los recursos de la pobreza. Familias de bajos ingresos de Guadalajara.* Guadalajara: El Colegio de Jalisco/SPP/CIESAS.

—— (1988) "Economic crisis, domestic reorganisation and women's work in Guadalajara, Mexico". *Bulletin of Latin American Research,* 7(2): 207–23.

—— (1990) "Crisis económica, organización doméstica y trabajo femenino", in O. de Oliveira (ed.), *Trabajo, poder y sexualidad.* Mexico City: El Colegio de México.

—— (1994) *The Resources of Poverty. Women and Survival in a Mexican City.* Oxford and New York: Blackwell.

González de la Rocha, Mercedes and Agustín Escobar (1986) "Crisis y adaptación: hogares de Guadalajara". Paper presented at the III Encuentro de investigación demográfica en México (SOMEDE), El Colegio de México, November.

Gordillo, Gustavo (coord.) (1994) "Tipología de los productores agrícolas de los ejidos y comunidades de México". Document prepared for ECLAC (CEPAL), Mexico City.

Hernández Laos, Enrique (1992) "La pobreza en México". *Comercio Exterior* 42 (4).

INEGI (Instituto Nacional de Estadística, Geografía e Informática) (various dates) *Encuesta nacional de ingresos y gastos de los hogares.* Mexico City and Aguascalientes: INEGI.

—— (1995) *Encuesta nacional de ingresos y gastos de los hogares,* 2 vols, CD-ROM. Aguascalientes: INEGI.

Langer, Ana, Rafael Lozano, and José Luis Bobadilla (1991) "Effects of Mexico's economic crisis on the health of women and children", in M. González de la Rocha and A. Escobar (eds), *Social Responses to Mexico's Economic Crisis of the 1980's.* San Diego, La Jolla: Center for US–Mexican Studies, University of California.

Levy, Santiago (1992) "La pobreza en México". Unidad de Desregulación Económica, Secretaría de Comercio y Fomento Industrial, Mexico City, mimeo.

Lustig, Nora (1987) "Crisis económica y niveles de vida en México: 1982–1985". *Estudios económicos* 2(2).

—— (1992) *Mexico: The Remaking of an Economy.* Washington, DC: The Brookings Institution.

Portes, Alejandro, José Itzigsohn, and Carlos Dore-Cabral (1994) "Urbanization in the Caribbean Basin: Social change during the years of the crisis". *Latin American Research Review,* 29(2): 3–38.

Reyes Heroles G. G., Jesús (1985) "Política económica y desigualdad social: Elementos de una estrategia para redistribuir el ingreso en México", in *Igualdad, desigualdad y equidad en España y México.* Madrid: Instituto de Cooperación Económica, and Mexico City: El Colegio de México.

Roberts, Bryan (1992) *Enterprise and Labor Markets. The Border and the Metropolitan Areas.* Russell Sage Foundation Working Paper No. 32.

Selby, Henry, Arthur Murphy, and Stephen Lorenzen (1990) *The Mexican Urban Household. Organizing for Self-defense.* Austin: Texas University Press.

Tello, Carlos (1991) "Combatting poverty in Mexico", in M. González de la Rocha and A. Escobar (eds), *Social Responses to Mexico's Economic Crisis of the 1980s*. San Diego, La Jolla: Center for US–Mexican Studies, University of California.

Tuirán, Rodolfo (1993) "Las respuestas de los hogares de sectores populares urbanos frente a la crisis: El caso de la Ciudad de México", in R. Béjar Navarro and H. Hernández Bringas (coords.), *Población y desigualdad social en México*. Cuernavaca: CRIM–UNAM.

Vélez, Félix (ed.) (1994) *La pobreza en México: Causas y políticas para combatirla*. Mexico: ITAM/Fondo de Cultura Económica, Series Lecturas No. 78.

Part VI
An Overview

Chapter 25
The Great Chain of Poverty Explanations
S. M. Miller

In some high-income countries, such as the United States, the causes of poverty are restricted to two opposing and highly politicized frameworks. One emphasizes "the culture of the poor", characterized by inadequacies in personal behaviour that lead to poverty. The other stresses "structures", whether of inadequate employment opportunities or of discrimination, as poverty inducing. Discussions of poverty causes in lower-income nations provide a much broader agenda of explanations, many of which are also used in highly political debates. This chapter builds on both sets of national outlooks and is deeply indebted to the discussions at the CROP meeting in Paris in 1994, which led to the chapters in this volume.

Poverty hypotheses, explanations, and frameworks can be about its causes and processes as well as about policies that would be effective in reducing poverty rates and gaps. The Great Chain of Explanation is composed of many clashing as well as complementary beads.

The methodology of poverty explanations

Two contrasting tendencies afflict poverty discussions. On one side, these analyses are usually under-theorized. On the other, poverty has too many causal explanations. Causal associations are not necessarily theories that explain the processes that lead to outcomes. Despite many assertions about what causes poverty, few are stated with a precision that can be empirically (or even logically) tested. Broad frameworks rather than bounded hypotheses prevail. Some explanations call for experimental designs that may not be achievable. For example, it is argued that if such and such experiences had not occurred in the past, poverty rates in a nation would not be what they are today. "As if" rewriting of history is hard to measure.

In the absence of focused theory, methodology dominates. The methods and the problems chosen (a methodological issue as well as a political one) direct the understanding of poverty dynamics. Sometimes, this is because of Type III error: asking the wrong question. That misstep is often due to the cultural, financial, and political embedding of poverty research. For a time, certain issues are to the fore and favoured in research attention while others are ignored or neglected (for example, in the United States research on public assistance use is much more studied than the specific obstacles experienced by poor households).

Methodologies can attenuate The Great Chain of Explanation, stopping with a confirmable, acceptable conclusion (frequently a correlation) that should demand further exploration. Many empirical generalizations are unexamined and their causes not pursued.

The classic case in poverty explanations is deploying the characteristics of the poor as the causes of poverty. If the aged or immigrants or female-headed households have a higher incidence of poverty than do other social categories, then poverty is seen as caused by these particular social attributes. Explanation stops at that point rather than seeking to understand the processes that result in a social category's high poverty risk.

Although one wants to avoid demanding infinite regress to deeper, less obvious, or veiled causes, it is important for both theory and practice to understand what produces high poverty risks for, say, female-headed families or the low educated. After all, these are (somewhat) convenient social (and sometimes political) labels rather than revealing dynamic processes. "Why" is usually more important than only "who". Gunnar Myrdal's methodological contribution of "cumulative causation" cautions that correlational and other more static methods may obscure feedback and interacting effects (Myrdal 1944: Appendix 3).

The Great Chain of Explanation has important background assumptions and requirements. At one level, the task is to uncover empirical generalizations. At a second, the need is to clarify the contexts in which they occur – or not. That is, the recurring research and policy question of "under what conditions" has to be explored. The third level is the explaining of the finding, what forces and processes produce that result, and what its consequences are. Calculating poverty risks is not the same as interpreting the meanings and effects of poverty.

The great problem in poverty research is that explanations imply a policy or direction. At one level, this is the problem of for whom one is creating knowledge: politicans, administrators, the voting public, other researchers – or the poor. Different questions come to the fore depending on the constituency for research. The other is how this knowledge is used or misused, understood or interpreted.

A largely unexamined question is whether better explanations (better politically or scientifically) result in different and more effective policies. The answer will probably be different in different nations.

The political embedding of poverty discourses led to a strong division between so-called structural or cultural explanations. The structural level focuses on "basic" (usually economic) forces outside the household's control, while the cultural level points to the traditional or chosen behaviour of households as leading to their poverty. The structural is regarded as a radical outlook; the cultural as a conservative one. As we shall see, the division is not sharp, and structural interpretations can be in the service of conservative positives that advocate reduced social spending.

The following report on current explanations of poverty only occasionally attempts to phrase explanations so that they might be testable hypotheses. That could be a follow-up step.

Locality and demography

An important distinction is made between urban and rural areas. In nations with large rural populations and usually low incomes, the hypothesis is that the poverty rate and the poverty gap per poor person are higher in rural than in urban areas. In higher-income nations with smaller rural populations, the hypothesis is that rural–urban differences in poverty rates are not as great, though the poverty gap per poor person may be larger in rural areas. Urban and rural poverty may require different modes of explanation.

Regional differences, which often are associated with rural conditions, affect poverty risks. Those living in areas that have long-term economic difficulties (e.g. poor soil, broad swings in the prices of and demand for its products, low productivity) experience high rates of chronic poverty. The structural conditions of production and marketing keep people in poverty, often leading to high rates of migration to cities and to highly populated zones of poverty within them. Where one lives may determine one's poverty history.

The hypothesis of regional differences in producing differential rates of poverty is not restricted to low-income countries or to rural areas. William Julius Wilson's emphasis on the dwindling job opportunities available to people living in particular areas is an urban phenomenon (Wilson 1987). Douglas Massey and Nancy Denton (1993) make a somewhat different point. Their hypothesis is that segregation in a locality of a stigmatized group (which could be extended to poor people generally) maintains or worsens their poverty.

The underclass hypothesis, at least as developed in the United States by poverty researchers, is a locality-based analysis. It counts in the underclass those poor persons who live in areas "impacted" by poverty (e.g. high percentages of welfare and poverty households). Although the underclass concept connotes disturbing personal behaviour, its measurement is based on an evaluation of localities.

The general underlying hypothesis of locality is that where one lives affects the likelihood of moving into, staying in or moving out of poverty. A derivative hypothesis is that a majority of those who are counted as poor live in localities that have many poor people in them. This is the concentration of poverty argument. In contrast, several studies show that in high-income societies a majority of the poor live outside high-poverty areas. (Such generalizations are obviously affected by the definition of concentration.)

On the demographic (and biological) side is the easy assumption that the poor are poor because of mental deficiency and illness – that in somewhat meritocratic societies, the more fit persevere and manage an above-poverty experience, while those left behind are mentally incompetent or at least less competent. This thesis raises once again the heredity–environment split, which, more and more, biologists contend is not a useful formulation. In any case, this hardy perennial of explanations of poverty is hard to study.

Large household size, which may be associated with ruralness, is often cited as a high poverty risk. Because household arrangements vary within as well as among nations, differing definitions of a household may be involved in this generalization. The explanations of why particular nations or localities have large families include an intra-family social security pattern of the younger generation supporting the older in the latter's late years, the fears of early deaths of children, and cultural and religious preferences for large families.

Economic structures and policies

Economic explanations range from the very broad (macro) and historical to specific instances of labour market imperfections. Later, what might be regarded as more meso and micro approaches are discussed.

In many low-income nations a widely accepted analysis is that their present poverty is the continuing effect of their weak position in international markets in earlier (and later) years. This situation usually resulted from imperialist control of the economy. This view has many variants, such as world systems analysis and dependency and dedevelopment theories, all of which are not easy to test without making major assumptions.

A common form of the explanation is that the imperial power forced the colony to pursue mono-crop or raw material production as the basis of its economy. The now-independent nation cannot escape from the long-term economic distortions inflicted on it, particularly with unfavourable terms of trade harming the economy. The results are a high level of chronic poverty as well as periods of crisis poverty. In this perspective, political independence does not overcome economic dependence, particularly in unstable world markets that are heavily influenced by the actions of richer countries. The inevitable result, then, is high levels of poverty.

A second historical–contemporary view is that particular economic growth paths doom large sections of a society to poverty. Although this analysis is usually applied to low-income nations, high-income countries may have similar experiences. The content or composition of gross domestic product (GDP) and the way that it is produced affect not only who wins and loses but which people and regions are thrust into or cannot escape from poverty. It is not only the rate of growth in GDP but what produces that growth that determines the fate of people. For many who espouse this perspective, international agencies have fostered the wrong kind of growth, one that enriches a few and impoverishes the many. Low wages and high rates of unemployment may result from a growth path that also enlarges an urban middle class or swells great wealth among a few.

Affluence and poverty are not incompatible events; the latter may produce the former. The poor are not just left behind as others advance but are the victims of the affluence of the few. The difficult question that follows is whether economic growth can occur without increasing inequalities and poverty. Do growth paths vary in their inequality consequences? The World Bank did studies along these lines in the 1970s (Chenery et al. 1974); they might be updated for more recent periods.

A general proposition is that a slowing of the rate of growth in many nations is causing or maintaining poverty levels. This is partly a result of policy decisions to limit inflationary pressures and of structural changes occurring in the world economy. The heightened importance of international financial factors as well as stronger global competition constrict growth rates.

A new element is seen as worsening the situation. Worldwide transformations in modes of production have the consequence in many countries that a percentage increase in economic growth has less employment-promotion and poverty-alleviating effects than it did in earlier periods. Nations have to grow more rapidly than before just to stay at the same level of poverty. If they falter, the thesis contends, poverty rates will increase rapidly.

Price levels can be important. Inflation frequently causes poverty. As prices rise, especially for basic commodities, vulnerable sectors and groups that cannot adjust suffer decline in their level of living. Although inflation can be a pressure in all nations, it is particularly threatening in lower-income societies that may have very high inflationary rates. On the other hand, these societies may provide subsidies to consumers of basic commodities (e.g. bread) in order to lower the price and maintain levels of living. The general point is that price levels as well as incomes affect poverty rates (and definitions).

Meso interpretations assume the central importance of low wages and unemployment in the production of poverty. It is important to understand that in many low-income, rural, highly seasonal economies, the concept of "out of the labour market", an important concept in the United States and the Netherlands as well as in other nations, is not an appropriate term. People can be continually in and out of the labour market. Dichotomies do not work in these situations.

Depressed regions and sectors in a nation, which may or may not be connected to world markets, can be causes of poverty. Regions that have low value-added industries and industrial sectors that have low value-added production are likely to have workers who receive low wages. (High value-added sectors can also have low-paid workers but the latter's percentage of the sectoral labour force is likely to be lower than in low value-added regions and industries.) Regional and industrial distributions affect the poverty rate and gap. The general point is that what is happening in industries affects the poverty situation.

Whether low wages or unemployment are the more important determinant of poverty rates is controversial. An important factor is that the number of hours worked during the year affects income and that (full or partial) unemployment occurs among many more people than those listed as unemployed at a particular time of year. The annual average unemployment rate is an inadequate indicator of the income impact of unemployment.

Adding to the difficulty of assessing the impact of unemployment in high-income countries is that social policies regarding unemployment and disability benefits may affect unemployment rates. High benefits may encourage labour market departures. How the household is constructed and counted may affect poverty rates resulting from either low wages or unemployment.

At what might be considered a micro level, a variety of interpretations are adduced. A favourite of neoclassical economists and many political figures is that poverty results from the low human capital of the poor. They cannot gain higher wages or have the chance of more secure employment because they offer little to employers. Their basic factor income is stunted though a nation may (expensively) attempt to supplement it with transfer income. The policy implication is that they should add to their human capital if they are to improve their prospects.

One difficulty with this approach is that it assumes that, if those with low human capital were to improve their capacities, better paid and more secure positions would be forthcoming. In effect, it proposes a Say's Law of employment: higher capacities produce their own demand. The question is whether this interpretation would hold for the many rather than for a few.

Another difficulty is that the human capital approach usually fails to examine why so many have low human capital. In many nations, spending on education is low and frequently misdirected. Obtaining usable education and training can be a difficult road. In this critical perspective based on The Great Chain of Explanation, low human capital is a symptom more than a cause.

Discrimination in labour markets is discussed in the following section.

Social structural explanations

The socially vulnerable become the economically vulnerable. They suffer discrimination in the labour market because of prejudice and stereotyping. Marginalized people, whether they are demarcated as women, minority groups, or recent immigrants, may have difficult in getting jobs (indeed, may be barred by law or custom from seeking paid work or working in certain protected activities) and may receive low wages when they are employed. Usually, they are concentrated in particular, low-wage industries or localities. It is being "different" in some socially disapproved way that causes their poverty. This differentness carries over in the social realm where they experience the social exclusion that is ignored in this chapter on economic poverty.

Migration has additional negative consequences because it disrupts long-time ties and networks that connect people to access to economic resources and that yield social support. In the new place, migrants have trouble getting an economic foothold and are frequently relegated to minimum subsistence work. Worsening the prospects of migrants is the psychological damage that migration can inflict as the familiar and secure are lost to uncertainty and threat.

"Minorities", even when very large in number, long in residence in the nation, and whether defined by race or ethnicity, frequently suffer employment and social discrimination. They are barred by embedded practices from the better jobs, have difficulties in securing public benefits, and receive few public services. In terms of poverty as social exclusion, prejudice may force them into restricted and poor-quality housing areas and isolate them from mainstream life. Like other excluded or marginalized groups, they are both socially and economically deprived.

The emphasis on households in poverty obscures their gender structures. The sharing of work and economic resources may not be equal. Women may receive fewer resources than male members of the household and may be exploited. As employees or as entrepreneurs, they are likely to receive low incomes. They may not be fully or at all covered by social programmes. Even in some relatively well-off nations, married women were not counted as unemployed and eligible for unemployment benefits.

Turbulence rather than economic and political stability is the usual condition of many nations. The turbulence can be due to ethnic fighting, attempts to maintain or overthrow undemocratic or democratic governments, struggles over sharing the economic product of the nation. Whatever the cause, the result may be a devastated economy and widespread poverty.

Regions, ethnic groups, and migrants may suffer from inadequate infrastructures, whether of schools, roads to markets, or basic facilities of life. These deprivations reduce their economic opportunities and their social integration.

Social exclusion is not a linear effect of income inadequacy. In this hypothesis, activity deprivation (an indicator or measure of poverty) can decidely decline at a threshold income point rather than experience a gradual reduction with each lowering of the income level. What might be regarded as an extreme poverty line produces the social exclusion that some regard as a main characteristic of poverty. This seems a testable hypothesis.

Culture and individual behaviour

Cultural explanations of poverty have a strong vogue. At the present time, "agency" is a key word. It is used to convey that the poor do things that make them poor or keep them in a condition of poverty. The poor are not passive victims but engage in activities that promote or maintain poverty. They are the leading actors in the poverty drama. It is not mainly or only what is done to them, but what they do as personal agents, an active force, in their fates. In this perspective, choice and therefore individual responsibility are involved in the production of poverty.

Earlier, the culture of poverty had considerable social science and political play and is still important in discussions of poverty. The cultural emphasis is usually on practices and outlooks that are transmitted from one generation to another and limit possibilities of escaping from poverty. A cultural explanation need not involve intergenerational transmission; people's survival or coping or response strategies may be dysfunctional or ineffectual responses to their present difficult situations. In one version, if poor people's incomes move above the poverty line, their behaviour will prevent them from maintaining their improved position. They lack the discipline, responsibility, or ability to defer gratification that are needed to sustain economic inclusion. Until their survival processes are challenged and changed, governmental and other aid will fail to improve their life conditions and chances.

At one level, it often appears obvious that poor people are often not doing things that would help them and indeed may be engaged in behaviours that harm them in economic and everyday life. A frequent assumption is that if non-poor persons were in the same situation as poor persons, they would cope more effectively than do poor people. This assumption cannot be put to the test because the non-poor cannot be forced into serving as a comparison group and the non-poor who might volunteer for such a test would be a biased sample of the non-poor. A somewhat different slant is that the poor have to do more to cope with difficult situations than the non-poor who have faced less strained and continuing challenges.

The experience of poverty can be considered a cause of poverty; for living poorly for some time makes it difficult to accumulate the economic, political, social, and psychological resources to overcome poverty conditions. Poverty creates the obstacles to its overcoming. It may discourage the poor from having confidence that great effort would lead to improved outcomes.

The biographies of poor persons do not add up to an analysis of the causes of poverty. One does not have to be an adherent of the "Annales" school of history to believe that individual history may have to be "explained" at least in part by forces beyond the ken of the biographee or the biographer. Individual biographies do not simply add up to a social or macro analysis.

What may work for some poor individuals may not be effective for most of the poor. Exemplars and models of how to rise from destitution are by definition exceptions. Extrapolation from individual poverty escapes can be misleading in developing poverty policies.

Despite the difficulty of formulating testable propositions about the culture or behaviour of the poor as causative agents in their poverty, such explanations have some role – *at some level*. That formulation brings in once again The Great Chain of Explanation. At what point does one go beyond the immediately phenomenological to examine other conditions implicated in the processes that end up as poverty? One way of thinking about the issue is: if aid is given to the poor, what behaviours and actions do they have to take to gain from the aid?

That formulation also rests on the the way aid is forthcoming. Is aid that attempts to build on traditional community ways of behaving more effective than aid that attempts to depart from embedded practices? This question could be researched: do different ways of providing help have different positive effects for the poor? For example, some argue that it is the sense of powerlessness that reduces the positive impact of public transfers and other kinds of aid. The urgent need is for the participation of the poor and the mobilization of their communities if the poor are to benefit from outside help. Or, that giving the poor a more powerful role in society would enhance their effectiveness in moving out of poverty conditions. In principle, it should not be too difficult to set up aid projects in similar communities that differ in the degree and kind of participation of the poor in programmes aimed at overcoming the inertia resulting from past defeats.

A way of reconciling structural and cultural explanations of poverty is to pose a somewhat researchable question along these lines: what changes in structures, opportunities, outside help or living conditions would elicit behaviour that would bring and keep people out of poverty?

Contrary to the offering of the culture of the poor as the causative agent in poverty is the contention that it is the culture of the non-poor that keeps the poor in their poverty place. The culture of the non-poor denies economic opportunities to the marginalized (the discrimination mentioned earlier), isolates them socially so that they cannot participate effectively in the larger society, and encourages their political, economic, and social exploitation. This position argues that the non-poor exert themselves to keep the poor in traditional places in order to transmit advantages to their families; or that their everyday behaviour (such as in job networks) bars the poor from improving their position. This outlook would require the study of the impact on the poor of the intended and unintended behaviour of the non-poor.

Underlying causative approaches that emphasize the culture of the poor or the culture of the non-poor is the notion of the social construction of poverty. One implication is that poverty and its causes are viewed quite differently by the poor and the non-poor. That is clearly a researchable hypothesis and might be extended to consider what the effects of these different views are on the prospects of reducing poverty.

Poverty policies as causative agents

A widely accepted hypothesis is that nations that rely on means-testing in their social policies will have higher rates of poverty than countries that rely mainly on near-universalistic policies. Some testing of that hypothesis has occurred in comparative studies of welfare state spending patterns.

A somewhat parallel proposition is that economic growth and unemployment rates are more determining of the poverty rate than is social spending. The assumption is that social policies cannot adequately offset the impact of economic structures and policies. Holding other influences constant would be a difficulty in evaluating this hypothesis; also, some argue that social policies affect the measured unemployment rate. Nonetheless, this postulate is open to comparative evidence.

In many low-income nations, it is conjectured that the demands on aided nations by international agencies, particularly but not only the International Monetary Fund (IMF), produce poverty. The IMF usually requires that countries seeking its funds reduce government deficits, the supply of money, and subsidies to consumers, as well as to devalue their currencies. The contention is that, as a result, levels of living deteriorate. Many are plunged into poverty while conditions worsen for those already poor. Poverty rates and gaps increase. It is difficult to study this position carefully because nations may not maintain IMF policies for long or may carry them out only partially and because many other factors influence economic functioning and poverty conditions. Some contend that analyses of IMF interventions support this negative appraisal of the organization's effects.

They would extend the conclusion to other public and private aid agencies. The World Bank, especially in the past, has been somewhat similarly indicted. Its emphasis on big projects may have harmed people in rural areas, widened inequalities, and distorted the economy by enriching a few.

National poverty policies could have similar negative effects. In the American case it has been contended that public assistance policies provide incentives to the poor not to seek to improve their conditions. In this conservative structural version, an unusual use of structural analysis, the poor behave as rational actors. They are responding in a calculated, conscious way to the incentives and rewards available to them and therefore do not attempt to change their situations.

Although this position, espoused by Charles Murray (1984), lost the scientific debate, it won the political debate and is having a deep influence on the reconstruction of social policies, at least in the United States.

That political debate raises the contentious question of the relationship between research and policy. Among the issues involved is who decides what is a policy success and failure. In some circumstances, a small gain from an intervention might be considered a great success while a large gain might not be so evaluated because of the (monetary, political, or social) costs involved in its achievements. Cost–benefit analyses are not free of such issues because what is to be counted as cost and as benefit are often contentious issues that divide evaluators and their interpretors.

A neglected contention is that the administration of policies, not just their design or intentions, is fateful for its poverty-reduction effects. Poor management can fell many a well-designed programme. Some policies experience considerable corruption and waste so that little aid is actually received by the target population. Such occurrences may contribute to a sense of powerlessness and helplessness among the poor. This view could be investigated by case studies of communities at the moment of announcement of poverty policies and some time later when few funds or services filtered through to them.

The inconstancy of policies may weaken their policy effects. A turbulent policy setting – short-lived programmes; shifting from one programme design to another; uncertainty about funding – blocks cumulative gain from programmes. Officials and legislators frequently exhibit an inability to delay gratification and expect rapid results. They use policy succession as an indicator of a commitment to rational policy-making: if a programme does not seem to "work" in a short time, substitute some other policy.

Another issue concerns the effects of participation or its absence in the conduct of poverty programmes. Some argue that programmes that do not involve the poor in their design, or at least, in their implementation, are inevitably limited in their effectiveness and indeed may be inappropriate. They may actually hurt the poor by deepening their feelings of powerlessness. This perspective usually regards participation of the poor as an end in itself rather than only a means. One difficulty in evaluating this outlook is that "participation" has many forms and qualities that are not easily measurable. It would be useful to study some forms of participation in different countries to see if specific settings are crucial in the impact of participation.

In this general perspective, the position of an increasing number of poverty analysts is that it is important to concentrate poverty programmes on women. By improving their social conditions, educational possibilities, and economic activities, particularly as "penny capitalists", communities and households are enabled to improve their situations. In particular, aiding female-headed households would make a major difference in containing current and future poverty rates. The hypothesis is that poverty programmes would be more effective in reducing poverty rates if they were not gender-neutral, which usually means male-centred, but attempted to be women-centred or women-friendly. Some beginning studies along these lines have been made.

Power and poverty

A broad thesis is that it is not economic markets of themselves that determine the distributions of income and wealth and the rates of poverty. Rather, it is the concentration of economic and political power in the hands of narrow privileged groups that produces inequalities and poverties. This standpoint regards market explanations of poverty as inherently limited, if not misleading; for such interpretations treat the market as unaffected by economic blocs and power elites. The power perspective does not regard markets as neutral floors where supply and demand rationally dance into equilibrium. Powerful groups press markets in preferred directions. Low wages or agricultural producers' prices are not "natural" market results. Power dictates their level.

In this view the poor are poor because they lack the political power to challenge prevailing practices of economic and social exploitation. Consequently, economic improvements require power shifts. If oppressed groups do not gain power, market biases and distortions that force poverty upon the many cannot be remedied. Such contentions require historical as well as difficult contemporary analyses and may have to investigate the impact of foreign power groups on internal poverty situations.

In some countries, reductions in infrastructure and social policy spending are singled out as the cause of increased poverty rates. Political decisions to rein in expenditures to reduce government deficits are identified as the agents leading to heightened poverty rates.

This perspective again raises the question of the role of power in determining poverty rates and conditions. Dominant economic, political, and/or social elites, not abstract market forces, may determine the fate of others. A political and psychological result is that the power of the few engenders the powerlessness of the many – a broad hypothesis about the barriers to action of the poor.

Indeed, some analysts regard analyses of discrimination as obscuring or avoiding the basic causative agent – power. Exclusion does not just happen; it is usually made to happen. The concentration of power in the hands of particular groups, wielded through their control of key economic and political institutions as well as by their maleness and ethnic status, determines the fate of the majority of the population. In this version of The Great Chain of Explanation, power is the force that keeps or pushes people into poverty; discrimination and prejudice are mainly means.

The implication is that only a deep shift in power relationships would make reductions in poverty rates possible. Without a dramatic transfer of power, poverty-alleviating efforts are unlikely to be initiated. If initiated, they will not be backed by resources and conducted by administrations that could make them effective. In this explanation, the route to poverty remedy is through power transfer or, better, power transformation where the (majority) poor gain their rightful influence.

Less sweeping than the power explanation of poverty is the view that in many societies there is little political or societal interest in attenuating poverty. It is just not on the political agenda. Other issues gain attention and precedence. Combating inflationary possibilities is a strong competitor for national action; that concern often leads to limiting wage increases. Or the drive for increasing productivity (and poverty) by employment reductions has precedence over poverty reduction.

In contrast to this concern with neglect and inattention are situations where the poor are centre stage but in negative contexts. In some nations poverty-bashing is a rewarding political action. The poor or immigrants are kept in their place or pushed into an even more disadvantaged position because politicians feel that they gain support by doing so. Poverty-bashing creates political advantages that lead to worsening poverty.

A sampling of implications

This chapter's emphasis on the economic measure of poverty has neglected the social dimensions of poverty in terms of definition, processes and causes (Miller and Roby 1970; Townsend 1979). Undoubtedly, the understanding of what causes poverty would be expanded by utilizing a more social perspective. Also, this chapter has treated those in poverty as a single group, ignoring the enormous variations among the poor. For example, the extremely poor, the poorest of the poor, the Fourth World in the lexicon of the international poverty organization Aide à Toute Détresse, may have had quite different experiences from those who only occasionally are poor, or who have been poor for a relatively short time, or whose resources hover around the poverty line. Variations among the poor as well as variations in the causes and processes of poverty require attention.

The testing of many poverty hypotheses or beliefs about causes may not be easy. Because much thinking about what to do about poverty is clouded by unthought-through notions of what causes or perpetuates or alleviates poverty, some advance in evaluating explanations and processes is an important step. Further development of hypotheses and theories would do well to apply this volume's arrays of hypotheses and frameworks to a large number of countries. The questions are not only which points hold up for many countries and which do not but the conditions under which they may be sustained as clarifying explanations. Because *poverty is a name for many varied situations*, we should not expect one all-encompassing explanation.

The Great Chain of Explanation is subject to three contrasting inferences. One is that the great range of causative analyses reveal that social scientists and policy makers do not understand what causes poverty – that the response to most explanations is the Scottish verdict "not proven" – and do not know what is effective. Such agnosticism can lead to a decision not to act. Not acting is an important policy that assumes that poverty will not worsen and that its damage can be ignored. A different way of regarding social science uncertainty is to look upon policy interventions as a way of testing explanations. That requires a deeper approach to understanding programme effects than is usually employed in evaluation studies.

Second is the view that all explanations are implicated and have to be dealt with in order to have a deep effect on poverty rates and rates. With the great diversity among most nations' poor, that proposition cannot be ignored. In most nations, however, one or two measures (e.g. an income "floor" to prevent poverty, the experience of rather than a "safety-net" that operates only after one has plunged into distress) are likely to be important for many.

Third, many regard more "fundamental" or "basic" explanations, such as the power thesis, as compelling. In this view, anything short of root transformation is a waste of time and energy, an avoidance of the difficult steps that must be undertaken if poverty is to be eradicated. Certainly, policy makers and administrators need to recognize the limited poverty-eliminating possibilities of less basic measures. These are limitations in terms of how much poverty can be reduced for how many people and for how long.

So-called "bandaid" measures may protect the damage of a poverty wound only to some extent. Nonetheless, bandaids may be useful for some poor persons in overcoming obstacles or simply in alleviating difficult conditions. Denying or delaying the use of bandaids in the hope of producing a revolution or transformation raises ethical questions about treating people as means not ends. Political questions also emerge about what conditions produce the possibilities of deep changes. Does bandaid reform lower pressures for deeper shifts or does it promote desires for more encompassing transformation?

The danger in short-term, limited policies occurs when they impede the understanding of and the need for broader and deeper actions or they lead to under-attention to poverty issues because of over-confidence in what narrow policies can accomplish. That situation is likely when political rhetoric to win support outruns any reasonable assessment of possible achievement of an anti-poverty programme.

A different view of The Great Chain of Explanation is that the importance of different causes of poverty varies among nations. In some countries, a particular explanation explains little whereas in another it may have an important role. To some extent, cross-national borrowing of poverty concepts and analyses from the United States has clouded the understanding of poverty dynamics in particular countries.

Within a nation, poverty has diverse sources. It can result because many in a group are left behind in deteriorating circumstances as other members emerge, or because a locality's economic opportunities decline. Some are poor because of deliberate policies to repress them economically, politically, and/or socially. Others may be the victims of Zsuzsa Ferge's "quasi-intentionality" or "unanticipated anticipatable consequences" where the effects of policy would clearly push people into poverty but no attention was paid to this result (Ferge 1987).

The Great Chain of Explanation does not have one final point. It is a circle or necklace, with each link possibly important. Which is crucial in a particular place at a particular time is not fore-ordained. On the other hand, the many routes into poverty and the many obstacles to moving beyond it do not mean that one policy may not be effective in changing the prospects for a large number of poor persons.

The understanding of the "causes" of poverty is blocked by the conventional separation and isolation of academic divisions into economics, sociology, psychology, anthropology, political science, and, some would say, biology and genetics. In society, the influences ensconced in these academic boxes interact with one another. It is their interpenetration that is the important question. For example, what are the effects of a rise or decline in income of a poor family on its work effort, family constellations, educational efforts, political behaviour, or social interactions?

Issues of interaction raise questions about the correlational methodology that is almost standard in poverty and other sociological analyses: holding some influences (variables) "constant" in order to estimate the "independent" effect of a particular influence. When the issue is interactional effects that may not be the best strategy for getting at "causes". This is particularly so when the concern is with the policy implications of a causation accounting: would an important independent variable have the same effect in real conditions when influences with which it customarily interacts are absent or of high or low significance

(Lieberson 1985: chs 7 and 10: 146–51). Certainly, the order in which interventions should occur is important. Perhaps the most general point is that explanation does not simply and mechanically lead to policy formulation. Policy is a leap from causative statements.

The Great Chain of Explanation is more a worry bead than a secure fastener. It directs analysts to "why" and "how" questions, not to comfortable answers. However, it should not lead us to declare that a cause is a cause, is a cause, is a cause. Rather, it should awaken us to the range of possible answers and interventions.

REFERENCES

Chenery, Hollis, Montek S. Ahluwalia, C. L. G. Bell, John H. Duloy, and Richard Jolly (1974) *Redistribution with Growth*. New York: Oxford University Press.

Ferge, Zsuzsa (1987) "Study poverty", in Zsuzsa Ferge and S. M. Miller (eds), *Dynamics of Deprivation*. Aldershot: Gower, pp. 9–31.

Lieberson, Stanley (1985) *Making It Count*. Berkeley: University of California Press.

Massey, Douglas S. and Nancy A. Denton (1993) *American Apartheid: Segregation and the Making of the Underclass*. Cambridge, Mass.: Harvard University Press.

Miller, S. M. and Pamela A. Roby (1970) *The Future of Inequality*. New York: Basic Books.

Murray, Charles (1984) *Losing Ground: American Social Policy, 1950–1980*. New York: Basic Books.

Myrdal, Gunnar (1944) *An American Dilemma*, vol. 2. New York: Harper & Brothers.

Townsend, Peter (1979) *Poverty in the United Kingdom: A Survey of Household Resources and Standards of Living*. Harmondsworth, Middx.: Penguin Books.

Wilson, William Julius (1987) *The Truly Disadvantaged: The Inner City, the Underclass, and Public Policy*. Chicago: University of Chicago Press.

About the Contributors

Dayo Akeredolu-Ale, Professor, read sociology at Ibadan (Nigeria), the London School of Economics (LSE) and the University of London. He is currently Director of the Centre for Social Policy, Ibadan, and an international consultant in social policy and human resources development. Formerly, he taught sociology at the University of Ibadan and was Research Professor of Social Policy at the Nigerian Institute of Social and Economic Research (NISER), Ibadan. He was twice Visiting Fellow at the Institute of Development Studies, Brighton, UK, and has been consultant to several government institutions in Nigeria as well as to many United Nations agencies. His research interest is comparative social policy, with more specific reference to the history and evolution of social policy systems; poverty; democratic development; and the monitoring of social-sector programmes. He has several publications in these areas as well as on issues in the sociology of development.

Karunatissa Athukorala, Sociologist, in the Department of Sociology, University of Peradeniya, Sri Lanka. He has been working as a lecturer, trainer and researcher in the fields of rural sociology, urban and rural poverty, health and sanitation. He has undertaken a number of academic policy studies, monitoring and evaluation studies on behalf of national and international organizations. He acts as a resource person of a national monitoring committee of "Samurdi", the national poverty eradication programme launched by the Sri Lankan government recently. He has submitted more than 60 consultancy reports to various clients and has written more than 20 publications, both national and international. At present he is a director and advisor of a large-scale local NGO (Integrated Development Association, Kandy), working in the environment and energy sector.

Soon-Il Bark, Senior Fellow, at the Korea Institute for Health and Social Affairs, has been interested for many years in poverty problems in Korea. He has actively participated in such studies as the welfare needs of the lower income class, causes of poverty, and estimation of minimum living costs. He recently published *Poverty Realities and Social Security in Korea* (Ilshin-sa Press, 1994). He has been advisor to several advisory committees for the Ministry of Health and Social Affairs in preparing long-term development plans in social welfare in Korea.

Rivka Bar-Yosef is Professor of Sociology at the Hebrew University of Jerusalem. Her main research work and publications are in the field of social policy, family sociology and women's issues. She has served on various public committees, and as advisor and consultant to Government bodies. She is currently involved in a large research project dealing with occupational and welfare problems of immigrant engineers from the former Soviet Union.

Hakchung Choo, Senior Fellow and Director, Center for Economic Education at the Korea Development Institute, has been engaged in policy research on social development since he joined the institute as a founding member in 1972. He authored two volumes on *Income Distribution and Its Determinants in Korea* (KDI Press, 1979 and 1982). He also coordinated a project on Korea Year 2000 (KDI Press, 1985). The official version of Korean social indicators published since 1979 is based on the recommendation of a project where he served as the principle investigator. He was also Chief Economist and Director, EDRC, Asian Development Bank, Manila, Philippines, 1988-1991, and has been a member of the Academic Advisory Board, International Center for Economic Growth, since 1989.

Bhaskar Dutta is Professor of Economics at the Indian Statistical Institute, Delhi. He obtained his PhD, from the University of Delhi in 1978. His research interests include game theory, welfare economics and social choice theory. He is on the editorial board of *Social Choice and Welfare, Mathematical Social Sciences, Economic Design* and *Journal of Quantitative Economics*.

Ludmila Dziewiecka-Bokun, studied music, law and political science, and is now Associate Professor at the Institute of Political Science of the Wroclaw University. M.A. in Law 1969 with distinction. PhD in Political Science 1983 with distinction. She specializes in social policy, theory of the state and politics and has contributed numerous essays, articles and books in these fields both in Poland and abroad. She was a Visiting Fellow at Oxford University (1989), Heidelberg University (1990/1991), Leiden University (1992 and 1994).

Paul Frater is an economist and Executive Director of Business Economic Research Limited (BERL), Wellington, New Zealand. He has specialized in economic studies and analyses, industry surveys, project formulation and evaluation, market research and forecasting surveys, income distribution, social analysis and poverty measurement. He is a research leader along with Charles Waldegrave (The Family Centre) and Bob Stephens (Public Policy, Victoria University) of the New Zealand Poverty Measurement Project. He undertakes numerous domestic and international social policy projects for both government and non-government organizations.

Laura Golbert, Professor, sociologist, researcher, CIEPP (Interdisciplinary Research Center on Public Policies). Consultant of international organizations. Adviser to the Chamber of Deputies, National Parliament. Latest publications: *New and Old Ways of Poverty in Argentina: the Experience of the '80s* (1994), *Food Support: a New Problem for the Argentinians* (1993), *Social Structure and Poverty in Argentina: the Scenario of the '90s* (1993).

Björn Halleröd is Senior Research Fellow in Sociology at the University of Umeå, Sweden. His principal research interests are in the study of distribution of economic resources and poverty. In several works he has discussed different theoretical concepts of poverty. He has also explored how the choice of definition influences the outcomes from empirical analysis and, hence, the conclusions that are to be drawn. In the last few years he has been working on a study of consensual poverty in Sweden.

Matti Heikkilä has a PhD in Sociology and is Head of the Social Research Unit of the National Research and Development Centre for Welfare and Health (STAKES) in Helsinki, Finland. His main research interest has been issues of poverty and deprivation in the welfare state context. Recently he headed a research project exploring the consequences of economic stagnation for welfare policies in Finland.

Gabriel Kessler is Master of Sociology, and has had fellowships from CONICET (National Council for Science and Technology Research) and the Buenos Aires University. He is now working as a consultant of international organizations. Co-author of *The New Poverty in Argentina* (1995).

Jürgen Kohl is Professor of Sociology at the University of Heidelberg, Germany. He has been senior researcher at the Mannheim Centre for European Social Research, 1994–95, Visiting Professor at Northwestern University, Evanson, Ill., USA, 1991–93, and Jean Monnet Research Fellow at the European University of Florence, Italy, 1989–90. He is the author of *Staatsausgaben in Westeuropa* (Public Expenditure Development in Western Europe), 1985, and *Alterssicherung im international Vergleich* (Old Age Security in Comparative Perspective), 1994, and has published numerous articles on comparative social policy, especially in the fields of public pensions and poverty policy.

Karima Korayem, Professor and Chairperson of the Economics Department, Faculty of Commerce, El-Azhar University, (Women Branch), Cairo, Egypt. PhD (Economics), McMaster University, Canada, 1974. She has worked as a consultant to several international, foreign, regional, and national organizations. Among them: UNESCWA, UNDP, UNICEF, World Scientific Center, the General Electric Center for Advanced Studies (TEMPO), Industrial Development Center for the Arab States (IDCAS), the League of Arab States, the Minister of Finance (Egypt), and the National Bank of Egypt.

Agustín Escobar Latapí is Professor-Researcher at CIESAS Occidente in Guadalajara, Mexico. He holds degrees in Social Anthropology and Sociology from Universidad Iberoamericana in Mexico and the University of Manchester, respectively. He deals mostly with labour markets, informality, migration, urban poverty and social mobility. Together with Mercedes González de la Rocha, he edited *Social Responses to Mexico's Economic Crisis*, published by the Center for U.S.–Mexican Studies at the University of California, San Diego. Recently, they published "Crisis, Restructuring and Urban Poverty in Mexico" (*Environment and Urbanization*, Vol. 7, No. 1). Mercedes and Agustín were jointly awarded the 1994 Prize for Scientific Research in the Social Sciences, granted by the Academy of Scientific Research in Mexico.

Mikko Mäntysaari is Head of Research and Development in STAKES (National Research and Development Center for Welfare and Health) in Helsinki, Finland. He is also Docent in social work at the Universities of Tampere and Kuopio. Following graduation from the University of Tampere, he was a social worker for two years, and after that researcher at the University of Tampere. His doctoral thesis was published in 1991. In 1993–94 he was Professor of Social Work at the University of Tampere. He is currently doing research on quality control of social work.

Alastair McAuley, Professor, is a Reader in Economics at the University of Essex. He has been studying the economics of the Soviet Union and the ex-communist countries of Eastern Europe since the mid-1960s. He has been interested in questions of inequality and poverty in the region since the end of the 1970s. His best known book on the subject is *Economic Welfare in the Soviet Union* (London, 1979). His recent articles and discussion papers include "Poverty and Anti-poverty Policy in a Quasi-developed Society: the Case of Uzbekistan", *Communist Economics and Economic Transformation*, vol. 6, no. 2 (1994); Social Welfare in Transition: what happened in Russia, Research Paper no. 6, World Bank, 1994; "opredelenie i izmerenie bednosti" Bednost': vzgliad uchennykh na problem (Demografia i sotsiologia no. 10) IESPN pri RAN, Moscow, 1994.

S. M. Miller, Senior Fellow, Commonwealth Institute, Cambridge, USA. Formerly Professor of Sociology and Economics and Chair of Sociology at Boston University. At New York University: Professor of Sociology and Education, Director, Urban Institute, advisor to the President on urban affairs and Senior Fellow, Center for International Studies. Professor of Sociology and Senior Fellow, Syracuse University. Advisor on poverty and minorities, Ford Foundation; executive committee, Field Foundation. Advisor to poverty and community action programmes in Ireland, Britain, France and the European Community as well as in the US. Worked with George Wiley and Martin Luther King, Jr. Author of books on social mobility, inequality, social policy and deprivation.

Ramesh Mishra studied sociology and social policy in England, receiving his PhD from the London School of Economics and Political Science. He has taught in universities in England and Canada and is currently Professor of Social Policy at York University, Ontario, Canada. Mishra's special interest is in the theory of welfare state development and in the comparative study of social welfare. His books include *Society and Social Policy* (Macmillan) and *The Welfare State in Capitalist Society* (Harvester-Wheatsheaf).

Mojca Novak is Assistant Professor of Sociology at the University of Ljubljana, Slovenia. Her publications in the field of modernization studies and poverty studies include also *Late Coming Pattern Mix: Slovenia at the European Periphery* (1991), and *Good Morning, Poverty: Evidence, Approaches, Policies* (1994). Recently she has been involved in poverty studies and level of living studies.

Charlott Nyman has been a graduate student at the Department of Sociology since June 1994 after completing her BSc in Human Resources Development and Labor Relations at Umeå University, Sweden. Since then she has been involved in researching intra-family consumption patterns from a gender perspective. Nyman is currently involved in a qualitative research project on the sharing of income, consumption and power within families. Related research interests include women, poverty and the welfare state.

Else Øyen has been Professor of Social Policy at the University of Bergen, Norway, since 1975. She is a former Vice-President of the International Sociological Association, and has been Chair of the ISA Research Council. She is now Vice-President of the International Social Science Council, with special responsibility for scientific affairs. Øyen is Chair of CROP (Comparative Research Programme on Poverty), an international and interdisciplinary research programme under ISSC. Her research interests span from theory of the welfare state and comparative studies of health and social policy programmes in industrialized countries, to analyses of poverty phenomena in developed and developing countries, and comparative methodology. She is the author of several books and numerous articles in these areas.

Maria Petmesidou is Associate Professor of Sociology, University of Crete. She was Acting Head of the Department of Sociology in the period 1986–89. Her research concerns social transformation in southern Europe, industrial restructuring, technological innovation and changes in labor markets, social exclusion and welfare policies. She has participated in many EC-financed research programmes and is responsible, on the part of the University of Crete, for the coordination of a number of teaching programmes in cooperation with European Universities. Her more recent publications are: (1) *Social Inequalities and Social Policy in Greece* (Exantas, Athens, 1992) (in Greek), (2) Statism, Social Policy and the Middle Classes, *Journal of European Social Policy*, 1, 1991, 31–48, (3) (with L. Tsoulouvis),

Aspects of the Changing Political Economy of Europe: Welfare State, Class Segmentation and Planning in the Postmodern Era, *Sociology*, 28, 1994, 499–519.

Veli-Matti Ritakallio, PhD, is Senior Research Associate at the University of Turku, Finland. He is the author of *Finnish Poverty: A Cross-National Comparison* and *From Marginalism to Institutionalism: Distributional Consequences of the Transformation of the Finnish Pension Regime* (with Markus Jäntti and Olli Kangas). He has published several books and articles on various forms of poverty in Finland. Ritakallio is recipient of the "Aldi J.M. Hagenaars Luxembourg Income Study Memorial Award 1994".

Sonia Rocha has a Bachelor's Degree in Economics from the Catholic University, Rio de Janeiro, Brazil, and has done her graduate studies in economics planning in the United States (Master of Arts Degree, Bucknell University, Pennsylvania) and in France (Docteur, University of Paris I). She worked in the Brazilian statistical agency – IBGE – in the planning and analysis of a wide range of economic and demographic surveys, as well as in the elaboration of synthesis statistics, such as the input–output matrix and national accounts. Since 1988, Rocha has been a researcher on poverty measurement and analysis based on data from national household surveys at the Institute for Applied Economic Research, Ministry of Planning. She is a consultant with the World Bank on poverty in Brazil, and has published around seventy articles in Brazil and abroad.

Syed Abdus Samad, Professor, is at present Executive Secretary, Association of Development Research and Training Institutes of Asia and the Pacific (ADIPA), and Coordinator, Information Technology and Economic Management Programme, Asian and Pacific Development Centre (APDC), Kuala Lumpur, Malaysia. In 1996 he returns to his chair as Professor of Economics, Bangladesh Administrative Staff College. His areas of research cover public policies, economic reforms, poverty, information technology, privatization, and urban and regional economics.

Kalinga Tudor Silva, Professor, holds a BA from the University of Peradeniya, Sri Lanka and a PhD from Monash University, Australia. At present he is serving as Associate Professor, Department of Sociology, University of Peradeniya and Chair, Center for Intersectoral Community Health Studies (CICHS). He is the senior author of *The Watta-Dwellers: A Sociological*

Study of Selected Urban Low-Income Communities in Sri Lanka (Lanham, MD, University Press of America, 1991). He has published on a variety of subjects, including the relationship between poverty and ill-health in the developing world. He served as a Senior Fulbright Scholar and distinguished Visiting Professor in the US from 1992 to 1993.

Ewa Toczyska has a PhD in economics and is at present Lecturer in Socioeconomics at the University of Gdansk, Poland. She is editor in chief of the journal for NGOs in North Poland. The journal supports the organizations which fight against poverty. She works in cooperation with the Regional Information and Support Center for NGOs in the Gdansk region. Toczyska is a Consultant in the Regional Office of Social Welfare in Gdansk.

Witold Toczyski has a PhD in Economics, and is a Lecturer in socioeconomics at the University of Gdansk, Poland. He is author of *The Nature and a Question of Poverty*, and has recently edited a book entitled *The Family Policy Report in the Gdansk Region*. Toczyski participates in the activity of the local authority in the Gdansk region.

Luzviminda B. Valencia, Professor, is a faculty member of the Department of Sociology, College of Social Sciences and Philosophy, University of the Philippines, Diliman, Quezon City. She did postgraduate studies at the University of Chicago, and at Harvard University. Her pioneering works on tropical diseases, especially on leprosy, have earned her international recognition. She was a Visiting Faculty/Scientist in the Department of Social Medicine, Harvard Medical School in Boston (1988–90) and a Visiting Professor in the Department of Sociology, California State University at Harvard (1992–93). Professor Valencia is also an active ecologist/environmentalist consultant with the Department of Environment and Natural Resources, the Philippines.

Charles Waldegrave leads the Social Policy Research Unit at The Family Centre, Lower Hutt (Wellington), New Zealand. The Family Centre is a community-based agency that works in the fields of family therapy, community development and social policy research, in three distinct cultural sections (Maori, Pacific Island and European). He is a research leader along with Paul Frater (Business Economic Research Limited) and Bob Stephens (Public Policy, Victoria University) of the New Zealand Poverty Measurement Project. The Family Centre has developed an international reputation and is regularly contracted in social policy work in most continents. Waldegrave has published extensively in all of the above mentioned fields.

Francis Wilson, Professor, has been teaching at the School of Economics of the University of Cape Town since 1967. During the 1980s he directed the second Carnegie Inquiry into Poverty and Development in Southern Africa out of which came his most recent book (co-authored with Mamphela Ramphele) *Uprooting Poverty: The South African Challenge*. Subsequently, the research unit (SALDRU) of which he is director has been responsible for coordinating, in collaboration with the World Bank, a project for statistics on living standards and development. The first collection of tables drawn from these data and released into the public domain was published in 1994 as *South Africans Rich & Poor: Baseline Household Statistics*. Since 1990 he has been chairman of the Council of the University of Fort Hare, South Africa.

Ruizhen Yan, Professor, Director of the Institute for Rural Development, People's University of China, Beijing, China. Yan is Vice-Chairman of the Association of Agricultural Economics and advisor to the Asian Society of Agricultural Economists. His PhD postgraduate work was in Agricultural Economics at the People's University of China 1955. Since the 1950s Yan has been actively engaged in academic work through participating in international conferences, giving lectures at universities abroad, joining international research projects and making field trips in rural areas in more than 20 countries. Yan has published extensively in the areas of economic reform and poverty research in rural China, including 10 books and more than 90 papers. Recently, he established a Development Support and Poverty Shedding Experimental Zone in Tai-Huan Mountain, with financial support from the German NGO - EZE.

Wang Yuan, Professor, in the Institute for Rural Development, People's University of China, Beijing, China, with particular emphasis on agronomy and ecological economics. She has published several books, including *An Introduction of Modern Agricultural China. Poverty and Development – A Study of China's Poor Areas*, and *Facing the Cross-Ways of Black and Green*. Her recent research work is in the field of sustainable agriculture in the poor areas.

Suk Bum Yoon, Professor of Economics at Yonsei University, has conducted research in the area of measuring poverty lines with applications of quantitative methods based on individual utility functions. His current research has established empirically that a utility-function-based subjective poverty line is highly correlated with degrees of inequality in income distribution. His most recent book published in Korean, *Poverty in Korea* (Sekyung-sa Press, 1994), is a comprehensive survey on poverty studies in Korea based on both historical and quantitative approaches.

Index

Absolute/relative poverty. *See also*
Relative poverty
absolute poverty line (defined), 259
Brazil, 518, 534
Canada, 478, 480
China, 146, 147–50
Cyprus, 312, 313, 314
Czechoslovakia (former), 396
Eastern Europe, 387, 391
Egypt, 202, 204. *See also* Egypt: relative poverty
Ghana, 219, 220
Greece, 295–96
growing popularity of distinction, 47
Israel, 430, 433, 448
Korea, 86–87, 88, 89, 90, 98
Latin America, 504
lines, 259–62
New Zealand, 164, 175–76, 181
Nordic countries, 328, 340
Philippines, 125, 128, 140
Poland, 422–23
South Asia, 68, 80
South-East Asia, 140
Soviet Union (former), 360
United States, 455, 458–60, 482
Africa, 187–247. *See also* Anglophone West Africa; Egypt; South Africa; Southern Africa
African Development Bank, 217, 218, 224
concepts of poverty, 56–57
data (need for improved), 188, 222–23, 224
Data Research Africa, 231
definition of poverty, 187
Economic Commission for Africa, 218, 222, 224

electricity shortage, 239–40
failure of the state, 18
lack of resources, 56
malnutrition as concept of poverty, 48–49, 56
overview of research, 37–38, 187–88
role of outside agencies, 187
subsistence concept, 56
Aged, the
Australia, 28–29, 334
Canada, 480
compared with children, 484
Cyprus, 313, 314, 315
Czechoslovakia (former), 397
Greece, 292, 294, 295, 297, 299
Hungary, 390, 395, 404
Israel, 448
Poland, 411, 414
South-East Asia (lack of study in), 124
Soviet Union (former), 361, 381
Sweden, 339
United States, 458, 460, 471, 472, 483–84
Western Europe, 271, 272
Yugoslavia (former), 404
"Agency" concept, 577
Ahluwalia, M. S., 110–11, 112
Altimir, Oscar, 500, 524
Analysis
conflict as analytical framework, 14–16
vs. fact-finding, 20–22
need for macro analysis, 34
Anglophone West Africa, 210–26
data (poor quality of), 222–23, 224
dearth of studies, 222–23
evaluation of research, 222–24

Anglophone West Africa, *cont.*
  Ghana. *See* Ghana
  Liberia, 210, 221
  Nigeria. *See* Nigeria
  policy relevance of studies, 223–24
  pre- and post-1983 research, 210–11
  Sierra Leone, 210, 221, 222 (Table 12.2)
  The Gambia, 210, 221
  theoretical framework, 27, 223
Anglo-Saxon concept, 50, 51, 253
Angola, 244 (Table 13.2)
Anti-poverty programmes
  "bandaid" measures, 584–85
  as causative agents, 579–81
  effectiveness of (overview), 27–30
  Egypt, 202–3
  European Community, 267–69
  failure of (overview), 29–30
  importance of monitoring, 265
  India, 113–19
  sensitivity required of, 578
  social insurance vs. means-tested, 483–84
  South Asia, 78–79
  Soviet Union (former), 356–57
  United States, 456, 462–63, 483–84
  weaknesses of, 36–37, 579–81
  for whites only (apartheid), 229
Approach(es). *See also* Causes/explanations of poverty; Hypotheses; Methodologies; Research; Theories/theoretical frameworks
  Consensual Poverty, 52, 263–64, 334, 341–42
  culture of poverty. *See* Culture of poverty approach
  Egypt, 191–93, 194, 197
  holistic, 59–60, 218
  multi-dimensional. *See* Multi-dimensional approach(es)
  "net earnings capacity", 51, 460–62
  New Zealand, 164–82
  overview of, 35
  qualitative. *See* Qualitative research
  quantitative. *See* Quantitative research
  resource, 253–54
  social engineering, 485–86
  social structural, 485–86, 575–77
  South Asia, 68–73
Argentina, 497, 506. *See also* Latin America

Armenia, 368, 382
Asia, 63–186. *See also individual countries;* South Asia; South-East Asia
Asian Development Bank, 66, 75, 140
Asian and Pacific Development Centre (APDC), 75, 80
Asian Regional Team for Employment Promotion (ARTEP), 66, 69, 74–75, 80
  concepts of poverty, 53–56
  effectiveness/failure of anti-poverty programmes, 28, 29–30
  feminization of poverty, 123–24, 126–27
  lack of resources, 54
  malnutrition as concept of poverty, 48–49
  overview of research, 38–40, 63–64
  social exclusion concept, 56
Atkinson, A. B., 173, 387, 388, 389, 391
Australia
  the aged (poverty mainly among), 28–29, 334
  children, 271
  compared with Sweden, 334
  compared with United States, 473, 483
  effectiveness of anti-poverty programmes, 28
  incidence of poverty, 271
  income equality and distribution study, 170
  influence of research on New Zealand, 162
  Luxembourg Income Study, 270, 271
Austria, 269
Azerbaijan, 368, 382

Baltic republics, 375–77, 379 (Table 17.7). *See also* Estonia; Latvia; Lithuania; Soviet Union (former)
Bangladesh. *See also* South Asia
  ARTEP studies on, 74–75
  Bureau of Statistics, 66
  effectiveness of anti-poverty programmes, 27
  Food for Works Programme, 79
  Grameen Bank (programme), 45, 67, 78, 79, 80

Infrastructure Development
  Projects, 79
  poverty level in, 76
  rural poverty, 70–71
  SAARC report, 73–74
Basic (human) needs concept. *See
  also* Lack of resources
  China, 148–49
  compared with poverty line, 506–7
  as concept of poverty, 48, 50, 53,
  500
  Cyprus, 312
  Egypt, 189, 191–92
  food-energy intake, 103–4
  lack of consensus regarding, 97
  Latin America, 499, 500, 505–6,
  507
  Mexico, 542, 545, 546
  Poland, 417–19
  problems of, 506–7
  Russia, 363
  Slovenia, 400–1
  South Africa, 239–41
  Turkey, 320n.15
  United States, 455, 462
  Yugoslavia (former), 401
Belarus, 369 (Table 17.3), 370, 382
Belgium, 269, 273, 274
Bhutan, 73–74. *See also* South Asia
Blank, R., 470–71
Botswana, 244
Brazil, 517–38. *See also* Latin
  America
  absolute vs. relative poverty, 518,
  534
  Afro-Latin Americans (poverty
  among), 509
  children, 519, 529 (Table 23.6)
  comparative research, 524
  data sources, 532–34
  Economic Commission for Latin
  America and the Caribbean, 531
  education level and poverty, 519
  Engel's coefficients, 524, 525, 526,
  528
  female-headed households, 519
  implications of results, 534–35
  indigence line (defined), 524
  malnutrition, 536n.2
  minimum wage (as poverty line),
  518, 519–24
  poverty lines, 518, 519–32, 535
  poverty rates (1979–90), 531 (Table
  23.7)
  recent economic history, 517–18
  Rio de Janeiro, 519, 522, 525, 535,
  536nn., 1, 3
  rural/urban poverty, 519–33
  passim, 535, 536nn., 6, 8
  São Paulo, 519, 522, 526, 527, 529
  (Table 23.6), 530, 535, 536n.3
  World Bank reports/studies, 525,
  526, 527, 531, 532
Burton, L., 460, 461

Canada, 477–82. *See also* North
  America
  absolute vs. relative poverty, 478,
  480
  the aged, 480
  basic needs approach, 481
  Canadian Council on Social
  Development, 478–79, 480, 481
  children, 271
  compared with United States, 477,
  479–80, 481
  concepts of poverty, 478–82
  data sources, 490n.1
  incidence of poverty, 271
  "low income cut off", 478, 480, 481
  Luxembourg Income Study, 170,
  270, 271, 479–80
  overview of research, 44
  as pioneer of income-tested
  programmes, 484
  poverty lines, 478–81
  rediscovery of poverty, 18
  re-evaluation of social policies,
  249–50, 481
  research trends, 480–81
  "Social Assistance Dynamics"
  study, 275
  Toronto (Social Planning Council),
  479
Categorizing poverty (methods of),
  19–20
Causes/explanations of poverty, 569–
  86. *See also* Concept(s) of
  poverty; Hypotheses; Theories/
  theoretical frameworks
  anti-poverty policies as, 579–81
  characteristics of the poor as, 570
  cultural vs. structural, 569, 571
  culture and individual behaviour,
  14, 577–79
  "cumulative causation", 570
  difficulty of testing, 583–84
  economic structures and policies,
  18, 573–77, 581–83
  human capital approach, 575

Causes/explanations of poverty, *cont.*
    implications of, 583–86
    international organizations:
        harmful effects of, 573, 579–80
    international organizations: views
        of, 510
    international variation, 585
    large household size, 572
    in Latin America, 509–10
    locality and demography, 571–72
    mental deficiency and illness, 572
    methodology and problems of,
        569–71
    migration and minorities, 576
    multi-faceted, 34. *See also* Multi-
        dimensional approach(es)
    in Nigeria, 214
    vs. outcomes, 50, 54, 57, 58
    overview of recent research, 265,
        266
    poverty-bashing (political),
        583
    in Russia/Soviet Union, 360, 377–
        80
    social exclusion, 26, 575–77, 579
    social/political apathy, 14, 583
    in South Africa, 236
    underclass hypothesis (USA), 473–
        77, 572
    unemployment, 574, 575
Central Europe, 57–58
Children
    Brazil, 519, 529 (Table 23.6)
    Canada, 271
    compared with the aged, 484
    Cyprus, 313
    Egypt, 200, 205n.17
    Greece, 294, 295, 296
    Hungary, 393, 395, 396, 404
    Israel, 438–40, 444, 445, 448 (Table
        20.2)
    large household size as cause of
        poverty, 572
    Latin America, 505
    Luxembourg Income Study
        findings, 271–72
    Mexico, 554, 555, 557
    Nordic countries, 347
    Poland, 411, 412–13, 414, 419
    Russia and former Soviet Union,
        361, 377, 381
    South Africa, 243
    United States, 460, 472, 484
    Yugoslavia (former), 402, 404
China, 145–59
    absolute and relative poverty, 146,
        147–50
    alternative poverty standards, 148–
        50
    concepts of poverty, 55, 146–50
    Engel's coefficient, 148, 150
    goals for growth, 152
    history of research, 145–46
    hypotheses, 150–52
    mountain regions and rural
        poverty, 18, 31, 145, 146, 148,
        150, 151–52, 153, 154
    peripheral areas, 151, 154, 155
    policy miscarriage, 152
    poverty lines (official), 150
    proposed economic reforms, 154–
        56
    suggested research initiatives, 156–
        57
    theoretical systems, 152–54
    urban poverty, 146
Comparative research
    absolute poverty line, 259–60
    Eastern Europe, 387–90, 406
    equivalence scales, 262–63
    ex ante vs. *ex post* studies, 252–53
    Latin America, 505, 511, 524
    Luxembourg Income Study. *See*
        Luxembourg Income Study
    major Western projects, 264–77
    measures and indicators needed
        for, 278–79
    need for increased, 30–31
    Nordic countries, 334, 335, 338
    poverty definition recommended
        for, 277–78
    problems of, 5–7, 257–58, 338
    recommendations for future, 156–
        57, 277–79
    relative poverty line, 260–61,
        278
    to overcome dominance of
        Western thought, 16
    United States, 472–73
    Western Europe, 251–81
Comparative Research Programme
    on Poverty (CROP), 3, 23, 157,
    569
"Composition of the poor"
    (indicator), 279
Concept(s) of poverty, 47–60. *See
    also* Approach(es); Causes/
    explanations of poverty;
    Definition(s) of poverty;
    Measure(s) of poverty

INDEX 601

absolute poverty. *See* Absolute/
 relative poverty
Africa, 56–57
"agency", 577
Anglo-Saxon, 50, 51, 253
Asia, 53–56
basic needs. *See* Basic (human)
 needs concept
Canada, 478–82
"causes" vs. "outcomes", 50
China, 55, 146–50
classic: regional variations of, 53–
 58
classic (Western), 49–53
"consensual poverty approach",
 52, 263–64, 334, 341–42
Continental, 50, 51, 253
cultural preferences in, 47
"cumulative long term", 55
direct, 50, 51, 253–56, 281n.15
disposable income, 278
Egypt, 189–91
"emulation hypothesis", 52
feminization of poverty, 123–24,
 126–27
Ghana, 56, 219–21
inadequacy of current, 59
indirect, 50, 51, 253–56, 281n.15
Latin America, 58, 499–501
malnutrition, 48–49, 54, 56, 58
material poverty, 54
Mexico, 540–48
"net earnings capacity", 51, 460–62
Nigeria, 56, 213–15
in non-producing West, 57–58
Nordic contributions, 48, 51–52,
 53, 58
outcome-based. *See* Outcomes of
 poverty
pauperization, 463, 473
persistence of poverty. *See*
 Persistence of poverty
Philippines, 124–25
Poland, 416–24
poverty line. *See* Poverty line(s)
"regionalization", 55
relative deprivation, 50, 51, 255,
 256, 257, 259
relative poverty. *See* Absolute/
 relative poverty; Relative
 poverty
Russia, 361–65
social exclusion. *See* Social
 exclusion/marginalization
social minimum. *See* Social minima

South Africa, 56–57, 232–33
South Asia, 54, 67–68
Soviet Union (former), 359–61,
 364–65
"standard of living" (Ringen),
 254
subsistence minimum. *See*
 Subsistence (minimum) concept
"time-adjusted", 51
underclass (USA), 473–77, 572
United States, 454–77
welfare state concept, 57–58
Western Europe, 251–64
Conflict (as analytical framework),
 14–16
Consensual (Subjective) Poverty
 Line/approach, 52, 263–64, 274,
 334, 341–42, 360
Consequences of poverty, 265–67
Consumer price index/indices
India, 102–3, 108
Israel, 447
Korea, 91, 93
Continental concept of poverty, 50,
 51, 253
Croatia, 401, 402. *See also*
 Yugoslavia (former)
CROP (Comparative Research
 Programme on Poverty), 3, 23,
 157, 569
Culture of poverty approach, 71–72,
 577–79
Israel, 436
Mexico, 540
South Asia, 71–72
United States, 473, 569
"Cumulative long term" concept of
 poverty, 55
Cut-off points, 9–10. *See also* Poverty
 line(s)
Cyprus, 312–15
absolute deprivation/poverty, 312,
 313, 314
the aged, 313, 314, 315
children, 313
compared with Greece and
 Turkey, 287–88, 316
concepts of poverty, 57
data availability, 316
degree of poverty, 315
economic characteristics and
 development, 287–88
education level and poverty, 314
equivalence scales, 313, 320n.18
feminization of poverty, 314

Cyprus, *cont.*
  household income and expenditure survey, 312
  possible elimination of poverty, 319
  poverty line(s), 312, 313, 314, 315
  rural and urban poverty, 313, 314, 315, 320n.18
Czechoslovakia (former), 396–99. *See also* Eastern Europe
  comparative research, 387–90, 406
  concepts of poverty, 57
  economic status, 386
  historical perspective approach, 398–99, 405
  major findings, 399
  pensioners, 397
  poverty estimates, 397
  poverty lines, 388, 389, 391, 396–98
  theoretical frameworks, 396–99 passim
Czech Republic, 270

Data
  Africa (need for improved data), 188, 222–23, 224
  on living standards (growth of), 22
  need for primary, 46, 52, 87
  poor quality of, 34–35, 87, 90–91
  vulnerability to misuse, 22
Data Research Africa, 231
Data sources
  Brazil, 532–34
  Canada, 490n.1
  Cyprus, 316
  Ghana, 218–19
  Greece, 315–16
  Hungary, 396
  India, 101–3
  Indonesia, 140
  Israel, 431
  Korea, 95–97
  Latin America, 505
  Malaysia, 140
  Mexico, 551–54
  Nigeria, 211–13
  Nordic countries, 346
  Philippines, 128–29
  Poland, 415–16
  Singapore, 139–40
  South Africa, 236–37
  South Asia, 73–76, 80
  Soviet Union (former), 365–66
  Turkey, 303–4, 315–16
  United States, 490n.1

Definition(s) of poverty. *See also* Concept(s) of poverty
  Africa, 187
  in comparative research (recommended), 277–78
  consensual poverty, 341
  Denmark, 344–45
  Egypt, 189–91, 193, 204n.1
  European Community, 255
  generality of, 86
  Ghana, 219
  individual lack of resources, 15
  lack of universal, 34
  Mack and Lansley's, 52
  Malaysia, 139
  minimum level of well-being, 103
  New Zealand (official), 161, 162
  Nigeria, 213
  OECD, 296
  poverty line. *See* Poverty line(s)
  "registered poverty" (Norway), 337
  relative deprivation (Israel), 433
  Ringen's, 254
  social assistance, 335, 336
  South Africa, 232–33
  Townsend's, 255
  United Nations Development Programme, 500
  weaknesses of, 21, 86
  World Bank, 500
Denmark. *See also* Nordic countries; Welfare state/system
  contrasted with Nordic neighbours, 346, 348
  Copenhagen, 345
  definition of poverty, 344–45
  economic poverty, 330–31
  EU membership (significance of), 328, 330–31, 346, 348
  Luxembourg Income Study, 269
  marginalization, 345
  Ministry of Social Affairs, 328
  persistence of poverty, 331
  poverty line (use of EU's), 331
  recent history, 325–27
  rediscovery of poverty, 327, 328, 346
  social assistance research, 337
  unemployment, 326, 328, 344, 345, 348
Development
  approach (proposed), 60
  relation to poverty, 24–25
  vs. underdevelopment, 37

Direct concept of poverty, 50, 51, 253–56, 281n.15
Direct measures of poverty, 21, 254 (Figure 14.1), 256
Disease, poverty related
  Egypt, 200
  Mexico, 557
  Philippines, 126, 127
  South Africa, 233, 240
  Douthitt, R. A., 51, 52

Eastern Europe, 385–408
  absolute vs. relative poverty, 387, 391
  comparative research, 387–90, 406
  concepts of poverty, 57–58
  economic status, 249, 386
  equivalence scales, 389
  failure of the state, 18
  incidence of poverty, 386
  limitations of research, 249
  poverty lines, 388–89
  research weaknesses, 405
  social policy, 385–86, 390–92, 404–5
  subsistence concept, 387, 389
  theoretical frameworks, 387–88, 389–90, 391–92
  welfare state (relation to poverty trends), 57–58
Easton, Brian, 174–75
Economic Commission for Latin America and the Caribbean (ECLAC), 498–503 passim, 510, 531, 544, 555
Economic and Social Commission for Asia and the Pacific (ESCAP), 66, 75, 80
Education/(il)literacy
  Brazil, 519
  Cyprus, 314
  Egypt, 197, 198, 200, 202
  Greece, 292–93, 295, 296, 297, 299, 300
  Israel, 439, 440, 442, 443, 445, 450
  low spending on, 575
  Turkey, 310, 312
Egypt, 189–209
  adaptation to poverty, 198–200
  anti-poverty measures, 202–3
  basic needs approach, 189, 191–92
  Cairo, 197
  children, 200, 205n.17
  concepts of poverty, 189–91
  data (non-availability), 203

definitions of poverty, 189–91, 193, 204n.1
disease and health risks, 200
education levels and illiteracy, 197, 198, 200, 202
effects of poverty, 200
extreme poverty, 193–95
food and (mal)nutrition, 189, 190, 191, 192, 196, 199, 200, 201, 202, 204n.1, 205n.8
gaps in research, 203–4
Institute of National Planning, 190, 192, 194, 205nn., 6, 11
main features of poverty and the poor, 196–200
Ministry of Social Affairs, 190, 192–93, 198, 201, 205n.10
non-governmental organizations, 198
poverty estimates compared, 193–95
poverty gap, 195, 205n.14
poverty line, 189–91, 204nn. 1, 2, 4, 5, 205nn., 8, 9, 12, 15
relative income approach, 190, 192, 194
relative poverty (head-count index), 193, 195, 204, 205n.9
rural poverty, 191–201 passim, 204nn. 3, 4, 205nn., 8, 9, 12, 13
sociological definition/approach, 190, 192–93, 197
structural adjustment and stabilization, 201–3
subjective definition/approach, 190–91
urban poverty, 192, 193, 194, 195, 197, 199, 204n.4, 205nn., 8, 9, 12, 13
women's status, 196, 197, 198, 199
Elderly people. See Aged, the
Electricity. See also Housing
  shortages in Africa, 239–40
"Emulation hypothesis" concept of poverty, 52
Engel's coefficient
  Brazil, 524, 525, 526, 528
  China, 148, 150
  defined, 148
  Korea, 91, 92, 93
"Engel's law", 260, 403
England. See United Kingdom
Equivalence scales, 262–63
  consensual, 263–64
  Cyprus, 313, 320n.18

Equivalence scales, *cont.*
  Eastern Europe, 389
  EUROPASS project, 274
  Finland, 332
  Greece, 291, 293, 294, 298, 299, 319n.3
  Jensen (New Zealand), 177
  OECD, 263, 264, 274, 374, 403, 410, 418
  Poland, 410, 418–19
  Russia and former Soviet Union, 360, 363, 374
  Western Europe, 263
  Yugoslavia (former), 403
Estonia, 369 (Table 17.3), 375–76, 382
Ethnographic research (South Asia), 67
Europe. *See also* Eastern Europe; Western Europe
  children and poverty, 271–72
  overview of research, 40–41
  theoretical framework overview, 25–26
European Community/Union, 251–86. *See also* Western Europe
  Community Action Programmes to Combat Poverty, 267–69, 281n.18
  conceptual and methodological issues, 251–64
  definition of poverty, 255
  European Community Household Panel, 268
  Eurostat, 40, 177, 178, 268
  former Soviet Union (research funding in), 359
  Greece (initiatives in), 290, 293, 298, 300, 317
  impact of integration, 318, 348
  measures of poverty, 249
  overview of research, 40–41
  research sponsored by, 267–69
  social exclusion, 267, 269
  Working Group on Indicators of Poverty, 268
European Research on Poverty and Social Inequality (EUROPASS), 41, 268, 273–75
Explanations of poverty. *See* Causes/ explanations of poverty

Fact-finding vs. analysis, 20–22
Feminization of poverty, 123–24, 126–27. *See also* Women's status

Cyprus, 314
Nordic countries, 342
Finland. *See also* Nordic countries; Welfare state/system
  economic poverty, 331–32
  equivalence scales, 332
  Helsinki, 337
  housing, 348n.3
  hunger, 344
  Jyväskylä, 343
  Luxembourg Income Study, 270, 332, 334
  marginalization, 336, 343
  persistent poverty, 336
  poverty gap, 332
  poverty lines, 332
  poverty reduction, 332
  recent history, 325–27
  rediscovery of poverty, 327, 329, 347
  social assistance research, 335, 336
  unemployment, 326, 329, 336, 347
  women's status, 336
Food
  baskets. *See* Basic (human) needs concept; Poverty line(s)
  expenditures: "Engel's law" (defined), 260
  food-energy intake, 103–4
Food, lack of
  in Africa, 56
  as concept of poverty, 48–49
  in India, 54
Food, lack of. *See also* Basic (human) needs concept; Malnutrition/ hunger
Foster–Greer–Thorbecke indexes, 195, 319n.8, 528, 540
France, 270, 273, 275, 281n.20

Gambia. *See* The Gambia
Gans, Herbert, 52
Gender. *See* Feminization of poverty; Women's status
Georgia (Asia), 368, 382
Germany, 170, 270, 271, 272, 275–76
Ghana, 215–21. *See also* Anglophone West Africa
  absolute poverty, 219, 220
  Ayirebi, 217–18
  concepts of poverty, 56, 219–21
  data situation, 218–19
  definition of poverty, 219
  major findings, 219–21
  marginalization, 216, 220

INDEX 605

poverty line, 216, 219–20
programmes and surveys, 216–17, 218–19
regional differences, 216
rural poverty, 220–21
theoretical orientations, 219–21
Gini coefficient, 20
Greece, 290, 292, 298
Israel, 437, 438
Kyrgyzstan, 374, 383 (Table 17A.3)
Mexico, 540, 544, 558
New Zealand (use in), 172, 173
Russia, 378, 383 (Table 17A.2)
South Africa, 238
Turkey, 311
GNP/GDP
effect of growth on jobs, 28
per capita (categorization issues), 19–20
role in poverty causation, 28, 573
Great Britain. *See* United Kingdom
Greece, 289–303
absolute poverty, 295
the aged, 292, 294, 295, 297, 299
Athens (Greater Athens Area), 291, 292, 298–301 passim
border regions, 293, 295
characteristics of the poor, 293–94
children, 294, 295, 296
concepts of poverty, 57
data sources, 315–16
EC initiatives, 290, 293, 298, 300, 317
economic characteristics and development, 287, 288–89, 302–3
education, 292–93, 295, 296, 297, 299, 300
equivalence scales, 291, 293, 294, 298, 299, 319n.3
EUROPASS project, 273
findings (summary), 317–19
Gini coefficients, 290, 292, 298
household expenditure surveys, 291–97 passim, 302
housing conditions, 296
impact of European restructuring on, 318–19
income inequality studies, 290–91
lack of social benefits, 29
multidimensional approach, 300
paternalistic structures, 289
poverty gap, 293–99 passim
poverty line, 290–96 passim, 298, 299, 300, 319n.7

redistribution programme, 298
relative poverty, 295–96
research deficiencies, 289–90, 315–17
rural poverty, 289–97 passim
Sen indices, 292, 299
social exclusion, 289, 318–19, 319n.2
social policy, 289, 301–3, 318
Theil coefficient, 298
unemployment, 290, 294, 300, 319n.11
urban poverty, 290–96 passim, 298–301, 319n.11
women's status, 294

Haveman, R., 460, 461, 462
Head-count ratio
defined, 141
Egypt, 193, 195, 204, 205n.9
India, 105
Soviet Union (former), 368–76 passim, 380, 382
Health. *See also* Disease, poverty-related
Israel, 439, 441, 443, 444–45
Hirschmanite tunnel effect, 86
Holistic approach, 59–60, 218
Housing
Argentina (indicator of poverty), 506
Finland, 348n.3
Greece, 296
Israel, 439, 440, 441, 442, 443–44, 450
Mexico, 552
Poland, 417
Turkey, 310
Human capital approach, 575
Human Development Index, 9, 63, 221
Hungary, 392–96. *See also* Eastern Europe
the aged, 390, 395, 404
changing structure of prosperity, 392–93
childhood poverty, 393, 395, 396, 404
comparative research, 387–90, 406
concepts of poverty, 57, 389, 393, 394
data sources, 396
economic status, 386
Luxembourg Income Study, 270
major findings, 396

Hungary, *cont.*
    persistence of poverty, 395
    poverty line, 388, 389, 391, 393–95
    poverty rates, 390, 395
    research characteristics, 395–96
    rural poverty, 390, 404
    theoretical frameworks, 392–96 passim
    urban poverty, 395, 404
Hunger. *See* Malnutrition/hunger
Hypotheses. *See also* Approach(es); Causes/explanations of poverty; Theories/theoretical frameworks
    China, 150–52
    difficulty of testing, 583–84
    "emulation hypothesis", 52
    Mexico, 548–51
    Philippines, 126–28
    South Africa, 234–35
    underclass (USA), 473–77, 572
    United States, 462–65
    weaknesses of current, 36

Illiteracy. *See* Education/(il)literacy
Income
    disposable (as measure of poverty), 278
    as indirect evidence of poverty, 52
    Israeli study of inequality, 436–38
    lack of (as indirect conceptualization of poverty), 51
    Latin America (insufficiency), 58
    limitations as measure of poverty, 34, 48
    as measure of poverty, 258–59
    South Africa, 238
    study of (contribution to poverty analysis), 168
India, 100–22. *See also* South Asia
    anti-poverty programmes, 27, 67, 72, 78, 79, 109, 110, 113–19
    ARTEP studies on, 74–75
    concepts of poverty, 55
    consumer price indices, 102–3, 108
    database for research, 101–3
    decomposition, 109–10
    estimation procedures, 105–6
    green revolution in Panjab, 69
    head-count ratio (use of), 105
    malnutrition and lack of resources, 54
    measurement issues, 103–5
    National Planning Commission, 67
    National Sample Survey Organization, 67, 101
    1956/57 to 1988/89: trends, 105–6
    1956/57 to 1973/74: incidence, 106–7
    1970/71 and 1987/88: experience between, 108–10
    per capita total consumption expenditure (PCTE), 104
    poverty levels, 76, 110–13
    poverty line, 103–9, 114, 116, 117
    rural poverty, 18, 26–27, 102–19 passim
    SAARC report, 73–74
    trickle-down mechanism, 100–1, 110–12
    urban poverty, 102–10 passim
Indicators of poverty. *See also* Measure(s) of poverty
    "composition of the poor", 279
    Gini coefficient. *See* Gini coefficient
    K ratio (Turkey), 307
    objective and subjective, 424
    poverty gap. *See* Poverty gap
    poverty/relative poverty risk, 279
    schematic overview, 266
    social assistance as, 335–36
    Working Group on Indicators of Poverty (EC), 268
Indirect concept of poverty, 50, 51, 253–56, 281n.15
Indirect measures of poverty, 21, 254 (Figure 14.1), 256
Indonesia, 130–41. *See also* South-East Asia
    absolute poverty, 140
    ARTEP studies on, 74
    data sources, 140
    effectiveness of anti-poverty programmes, 28
    findings, 140–41
    malnutrition, 141
    measures of poverty, 139, 140–41
    poverty line, 139
Inequality: analysis in relation to poverty, 262
International Food Policy Research Institute, 204n.3
International Labour Organization (ILO)
    Asian Employment Programme. *See* Asia: Asian Regional Team for Employment Promotion (ARTEP)
    Egypt (1977 survey), 191, 196, 197, 204n.3

INDEX 607

Latin America (PREALC), 499, 501, 502, 504, 510
necessary biases of, 22–23
Philippines, 128
publications of, 66
Sierra Leone study, 221
South Asian initiatives, 69, 80
studies compared with those in Western countries, 230
view of causes of poverty, 510
International Monetary Fund
as cause of poverty, 579–80
Egypt, 202, 203
Soviet Union (former), 359, 361, 362, 364
International organizations. *See also* Non-governmental organizations (NGOs)
as causes of poverty, 573, 579–80
importance in Latin America, 22–23, 499
necessary biases of, 22–23
role in Africa, 187
views on causes of poverty, 510
International studies. *See* Comparative research
Ireland, 270, 273, 275
Israel, 429–52
absolute vs. relative poverty, 430, 433, 448
the aged, 448
children, 438–40, 444, 445, 448 (Table 20.2)
concepts of poverty, 57, 58, 429–36
consumer price index, 447
data sources, 431
education, 439, 440, 442, 443, 445, 450
equality/inequality issues, 431–32, 436–38
Gini coefficients, 437, 438
growth of research, 431
health issues, 439, 441, 443, 444–45
historical context, 429–31
housing, 439, 440, 441, 442, 443–44, 450
Income Distribution Committee, 436–38
income issues (other than distribution), 443
integration (immigration) issues, 434–36, 443–44, 445
Jerusalem, 442
longitudinal studies, 440–43

National Insurance Institute, 429, 431, 440, 446, 447, 448, 450
persistence of poverty, 443, 449
poverty culture theory, 436
poverty issues, 432–34
poverty line, 433, 439, 448, 449, 450
poverty rates/gap, 448–49
Prime Minister's Committee on Distressed Children and Youth, 438–40
recommendations, 450
relative deprivation (as definition of poverty), 433
rural poverty, 434
selected studies, 436–49
social policy, 29, 446–49
state denial of poverty, 432
subsidies, 446–47
transfer payments, 447–49
unemployment, 450
women's status, 438, 441, 445
Italy, 270

Jencks, C., 52, 462, 476–77

Katzman, Ruben, 500
Kazakhstan, 368, 369 (Table 17.3), 382
Korea, 86–99
absolute/relative poverty, 86–87, 88, 89, 90, 98
concepts of poverty, 54, 55
consumer price index (CPI), 91, 93
data (inadequacy of), 90–91, 95–97
effectiveness of anti-poverty programmes, 28
estimation methods, 91–95
Hirschmanite tunnel effect, 86
historical background, 86–87
inconclusiveness of studies, 98
Korea Development Institute, 88
Livelihood Protection Law, 93, 94
major findings, 87–91
methodological problems, 90–91
poverty line, 87, 88, 91, 93, 95, 97
recommendations for further study, 97
rural poverty, 88–90, 93, 96, 97
sample surveys (independent), 96–97
urban poverty, 87, 88–90, 92, 93, 95, 96, 97
K ratio (Turkey), 307

Kyrgyzstan. *See also* Soviet Union (former)
  data sources, 366
  determinants of poverty, 379–80
  incidence of poverty, 369 (Table 17.3), 373–75, 382
  Kyrghyz Multipurpose Poverty Survey, 380
  measures and indicators, 374–75, 380, 383 (Table 17A.3)
  rural/urban poverty, 380

Lack of resources. *See also* Basic (human) needs concept; Subsistence (minimum) concept
  Africa, 56
  Anglo-Saxon concept, 50, 51, 253
  Asia, 54
  as definition/concept of poverty, 15, 50, 51, 59, 255, 328
  Egypt, 196–97
  India, 54
  in non-producing West, 57
  Philippines, 124, 127
Lansley, S., 52, 53, 280n.8, 341, 342
Latin America, 495–566
  absolute and relative poverty, 504
  adjustment policies, 501–2
  basic (human) needs concept, 499, 500, 505–6, 507
  causes of poverty, 18, 509–10
  child poverty, 505
  comparative research, 505, 511, 524
  compared with Soviet Union, 370
  concepts of poverty, 58, 499–501
  data sources (comparative research), 505
  Economic Commission for Latin America and the Caribbean, 498–503 passim, 510, 531
  ethnic factors, 509
  future trends and prospects, 510–11
  international organizations: leading role of, 22–23, 499
  lack of poverty reduction in, 28, 495
  Latin American Social Science Council, 42
  measurement of poverty, 504–7
  non-governmental organizations (role of), 504
  pauperization, 511
  poverty debate in, 498–99
  poverty line, 500–1, 505, 506–7

quantitative vs. qualitative approaches, 511
recent economic history, 495, 497–98
Regional Employment Programmes for Latin America and the Caribbean, 501, 502, 504, 510
research overview, 41–42, 495–96
rural poverty, 495, 497
social policies, 503–4
structural poverty, 507
theories/theoretical frameworks, 498, 507–10
(un)employment, 498, 502–3, 510
urban poverty, 495, 498, 502, 505
Latvia, 369 (Table 17.3), 370, 376, 382
Lesotho, 31, 243, 244 (Table 13.2)
Lewis, Oscar, 52, 71
Leyden Poverty Line, 91 (Table 6.4), 92, 397, 398, 421
Liberia, 210, 221. *See also* Anglophone West Africa
Life expectancy
  Israel, 444
  Turkey, 312
Literacy. *See* Education/(il)literacy
Literary descriptions of poverty, 16
Lithuania, 369 (Table 17.3), 376–77, 382
Lorenz indices, 437
Luxembourg, 273
Luxembourg Income Study, 269–73
  Canada and USA compared, 479–80
  findings, 271–72
  Finland, 270, 332, 334
  income measure (use of), 177
  limitations of, 41, 272–73
  LIS scale, 280n.14
  New Zealand (compared with), 170, 178, 179
  Norway and Sweden, 170, 270, 271, 272, 334
  usefulness of, 40–41, 488–89
  working papers, 270–71

Mack, J., 52, 53, 280n.8, 341, 342
Macmillan, W. M., 229
Macro level perspective
  advantages of, 48, 55, 56
  vs. micro in South Africa, 235
  in proposed holistic approach, 60
Malawi, 244 (Table 13.2)

INDEX 609

Malaysia, 130–41. *See also* South-East Asia
  absolute poverty, 140
  data sources, 140
  definition, measures and terms, 139
  effectiveness of anti-poverty programmes, 27–28
  New Economic Policy, 45
  pattern of growth as cause of poverty, 18
  training of researchers in England, 123
Maldives, 73–74
Malnutrition/hunger. *See also* Food, lack of
  Africa, 56
  Brazil, 536n.2
  as concept of poverty, 48–49, 54, 56, 58
  Egypt, 196, 204n.1
  Finland, 344
  India, 54
  Indonesia, 141
  Israel, 444
  Latin America, 58
  Mexico, 542, 545, 555, 557, 562
  Philippines, 124, 125, 126, 127
  South Africa, 243
  Sri Lanka, 76
  Turkey, 312
Marginalization. *See* Social exclusion/marginalization
Material poverty (defined), 54
Mayer, S. E., 52, 462
Mead,, Lawrence, 466–67, 473
Mean Welfare Index (Ghana), 220
Measure(s) of poverty. *See also* Concept(s) of poverty; Indicators of poverty
  Canada, 478–81
  cut-off points, 9–10. *See also* Poverty line(s)
  direct and indirect, 21, 254 (Figure 14.1), 256
  "duration of poverty spells", 279
  economic vs. sociological, 255–56
  "Engel's law", 260
  equivalence scales. *See* Equivalence scales
  European Community, 249
  Gini coefficient. *See* Gini coefficient
  GNP per capita, 19–20
  head-count ratio. *See* Head-count ratio

Human Development Index, 9, 63, 221
  income as, 258–59, 278
  Indonesia, 139, 140–41
  lack of agreement on, 34
  Latin America, 504–7
  limitations of income as, 34, 48
  Lorenz indices (Israel), 437
  Malaysia, 139
  Mean Welfare Index, 220
  methodological issues, 256–59
  Nelson Inequality Index, 172
  "Orchansky" index, 396
  overall, 103
  poverty gap. *See* Poverty gap
  poverty line. *See* Poverty line(s)
  shortcomings of, 8–11
  Singapore, 138–39
  strong influence on results (Israel), 449–50
  Theil coefficient, 298
  Western Europe, 249
Mediterranean countries. *See also* Cyprus; Greece; Turkey
  concepts of poverty, 57
  paternalistic structures of, 289
Methodologies. *See also* Approach(es); Research
  estimation of cut-off points (Korea), 91–95
  overview of, 35
  Western Europe, 251–64
Mexico, 539–66. *See also* Latin America
  children, 554, 555, 557
  concepts and measures, 540–48
  COPLAMAR project, 541–43, 554, 555
  data sources, 551–54
  diseases, 557
  Gini index, 540, 544, 558
  Guadalajara, 547
  household income and expenditure surveys (ENIGH), 543–44, 551–53, 554, 556, 557, 563
  household restructuring, 560–63
  housing costs, 552
  hypotheses and theoretical frameworks, 548–51
  Integral Measurement of Poverty (Boltvinik), 540, 543, 545–47
  major results, 554–63
  malnutrition, 542, 545, 555, 557, 562
  Mexico City, 545, 547, 554

Mexico, cont.
  poverty lines, 540–48 passim, 563n.3
  research characteristics, 539–40
  rural poverty, 542, 545, 551, 554, 555, 557, 559–60
  (un)employment issues, 540, 548–50, 556, 558, 559
  urban poverty, 547–48, 551, 554, 555 (Table 24.1), 557, 558, 559–60, 562
  women's status, 550–51, 560–62
Micklewright, J., 387, 388, 389, 391
Micro level perspective
  focus on individual, 48, 54
  vs. macro in South Africa, 235
  in proposed holistic approach, 59
Milanovic, B., 387, 389
Miller, S. M., 22, 26, 30, 43, 53, 569, 583, 591
Minorities
  in Israel (integration), 434–36, 443–44, 445
  in New Zealand, 167
  in Nordic countries, 342–43
  social exclusion of, 576
  in South Asia, 73, 81
  in United States, 463, 464, 466, 467, 468, 473–77
Moldova, 369 (Table 17.3), 382
Mozambique, 31, 243, 244 (Table 13.2)
Multi-dimensional approach(es), 34
  Greece, 300
  Nordic countries, 340, 341, 347
  Poland, 420–21
  South Africa, 233
  Western Europe, 256–59
Murray, Charles, 465–70 passim, 473, 580
Myrdal, Gunnar, 570

Namibia, 244 (Table 13.2)
Nelson Inequality Index, 172
Neoclassical approach (South Asia), 68–69
Nepal, 67, 73–74, 75, 76, 78. *See also* South Asia
"Net earnings capacity" concept of poverty, 51, 460–62
Netherlands, the, 270, 271, 273, 274, 275, 334, 574
New Zealand, 160–86
  absolute vs. relative poverty, 164, 175–76, 181
  Christchurch Child Development Study, 165
  concepts of poverty, 57
  definitions of poverty (official), 161, 162
  Department of Social Welfare, 166, 174, 175, 182
  Department of Statistics, 168, 169, 170, 172, 174, 175, 177, 178, 182
  descriptive and self-report approaches, 164–68
  dismantling of anti-poverty programmes, 18–19
  early studies, 164
  economic decline, 160, 162–63
  equivalence scales (Jensen), 177
  Eurostat and Luxembourg Income Study comparisons, 170, 178, 179
  food costs, 176
  household surveys, 168–77 passim, 182
  income distribution and equality approaches, 168–73
  influential books, 167, 168
  Maori/minorities, 167, 171, 172, 173, 181
  Ministry of Finance, 175
  national wealth and poverty survey, 166–67
  New Zealand Poverty Measurement Project, 177–82
  poverty line: lack of official, 182
  poverty line approaches, 173–82
  Real Disposable Income Index, 169
  Royal Commission on Social Security (1972), 162, 163, 164, 168, 174
  Royal Commission on Social Security (1988), 163–64
  social policy history, 160–64
  The Statistics of Incomes and Income Taxes, 172
  universities (involvement of), 172, 173, 176
  women's status, 167, 169, 171, 172, 173
Nigeria, 211–15. *See also* Anglophone West Africa
  concepts/causes of poverty, 56, 213–15
  data situation, 211–13
  failure of the state, 18
  major findings, 213–15
  poverty line (lack of emphasis on), 214

theoretical orientations, 213–15
urban poverty, 214
Non-governmental organizations. *See also* International organizations
Africa (role in), 187
Egypt, 198
Latin America, 504
Non-poor people: relationship to the poor, 11–16
Nordic countries, 325–53. *See also* Denmark; Finland; Norway; Sweden; Welfare state/system
absolute vs. relative poverty, 328, 340
accumulation of deprivation, 337–42
alcoholics/substance abusers, 343–44
children, 347
comparative research, 334, 335, 338
contributions to poverty concepts, 48, 51–52, 53, 58
data sources, 346
differences and similarities (summarized), 345–48
direct and indirect measures of poverty, 21
economic poverty, 330–34
effectiveness of anti-poverty programmes, 28
ethnic minorities, 342–43
feminization of poverty, 342
impact of European integration on, 348
inequality emphasized over poverty, 327, 346
level-of-living surveys/approach, 327, 343, 346
major results, 347
marginalization, 336, 342, 343, 345, 346
new research trends, 348
Nordic Council of Ministers, 335
Nordic Welfare State model, 325–26
On Social Assistance in the Nordic Capitals, 335
qualitative research, 330, 342–45
quantitative research, 330–42
rediscovery of poverty, 249–50, 327–29, 346, 347
resource approach, 253
social assistance research tradition, 334–37

theoretical frameworks, 26
young people, 334, 344, 347
North America, 453–93. *See also* Canada; United States
absolute vs. relative poverty, 482
comments and suggestions, 482–90
culture of poverty approach, 71–72, 473, 569
effectiveness of anti-poverty programmes, 28
feminization of poverty, 123–24, 127
influence in Philippines, 123–24
need for comparative research, 484–85, 488–89
overview of research, 42–45
poverty line: emphasis on, 482
research roles of various disciplines, 487–88
social insurance: relative success of, 483–84
Norway. *See also* Nordic countries; Welfare state/system
the aged, 271
atypical poverty demographics, 272
contrasts with Nordic neighbours, 329, 347, 348
EU membership (rejection of), 348
incidence of poverty, 271
lack of research/rediscovery, 329, 347, 348
Luxembourg Income Study, 170, 270, 271, 272, 334
Oslo, 337
recent history, 325–27
"registered poverty", 337
social assistance research, 337

OECD
definition of poverty, 296
equivalence scales, 263, 264, 274, 374, 403, 410, 418
"List of Social Indicators", 263
Luxembourg Income Study. *See* Luxembourg Income Study
Social Assistance Dynamics Panel Study, 41
Soviet Union (research in), 362
Old people. *See* Aged, the
"Orchansky" index, 396
Outcomes of poverty
basic human needs concept, 48, 50, 53
vs. causes, 50, 54, 57, 58
continental concept, 50, 51

Outcomes of poverty, *cont.*
  direct concept, 50, 51
  welfare deprivation as, 338
Øyen, E., 3, 5, 6, 11, 265, 267, 592

Pakistan. *See also* South Asia
  Aga Khan Rural Support
    Programme, 45, 72
  ARTEP studies on, 74–75
  green revolution in, 69
  People's Work Programme, 79
  poverty level in, 76
  SAARC report, 73–74
Panjab (green revolution), 69
Participatory approach (South Asia),
    72–73, 78
Persistence of poverty
  Denmark, 331
  Finland, 336
  Hungary, 395
  Israel, 443, 449
  United States, 454, 476, 486
Philippines, 123–40. *See also* South-
    East Asia
  absolute poverty, 125, 128, 140
  American research influence in,
    123–24
  compared with Indonesia, Malaysia
    and Singapore, 130–38, 139
  concepts and definitions, 124–25,
    129
  data sources, 128–29
  disease and poverty, 126, 127
  economic orientation predominant,
    124, 130
  evaluation, 129–30
  failure of government, 125, 127,
    129
  family income and expenditure
    survey (FIES), 128
  hypotheses, 126–28
  lack of resources, 124, 127
  "learned helplessness", 127–28
  malnutrition, 124, 125, 126, 127
  "mass poverty", 125
  national agencies, 125, 128
  number of poor (1975) in, 140
  Philippines Business for Social
    Progress, 45–46
  poverty level, 123
  rural poverty, 124, 126, 127, 129,
    130
  urban poverty, 124, 129
  Western training of researchers,
    123

Philosophy of poverty research, 8–11
Piachaud, D., 47, 50, 53
Poland, 409–28
  absolute and relative deprivation,
    422–23
  the aged, 411, 414
  Central Statistical Office, 409–20
    passim
  Chief Census Bureau, 421
  children, 411, 412–13, 414, 419
  concepts of poverty, 57, 416–24
  current research, 412–16
  data (from surveys), 415–16
  equivalence scales, 410, 418–19
  history of research and concepts,
    409–11, 416–17
  household budget surveys, 409,
    410, 413, 414–15
  "individual income functions of
    welfare", 422
  Institute of Labour and Social
    Welfare, 416, 417
  Institute of Social Economy, 409,
    411, 412, 413
  low incomes, 419–21
  Luxembourg Income Study, 270
  measuring of poverty, 424–25
  multidimensional approaches, 420–
    21
  poor housing, 417
  poverty lines, 410, 416–19, 421–22
  social dysfunctions (researchers
    of), 411
  social minima, 416–19, 421–22
  "spheres of indigence", 410
  state censorship, 411, 424
  subjective measures, 421–22, 423–
    24
  unemployment, 412, 413
  women's status, 411, 412, 414
Political economy approach, 18–20,
    70–71
Political environment, 19–20
Poor people
  as an economic burden, 12
  heterogeneity of, 583
  isolation of, 11. *See also* Social
    exclusion/marginalization
  relationship to the non-poor, 11–16
Poverty alleviation programmes. *See*
    Anti-poverty programmes
Poverty gap
  aggregate, 279
  average, 279
  defined, 274

Egypt, 195, 205n.14
Finland, 332
Greece, 293–99 passim
Israel, 448
Soviet Union (former), 369–75 passim, 380
United States, 460
Poverty line(s)
absolute vs. relative, 259–62
Brazil, 518, 519–32, 535
Canada, 478–81
China, 149–50
in comparative research, 259–60, 261, 278
compared with basic needs approach, 506–7
Consensual (Subjective), 263–64, 274, 334, 341–42
critique of official US, 456–58
CSP (Centre for Social Policy, Antwerp), 274
Cyprus, 312, 313, 314, 315
Czechoslovakia (former), 388, 389, 391, 396–98
Denmark (use of EU's), 331
Eastern Europe (similarities in), 388
Egypt, 189–91, 204nn. 1, 2, 4, 5, 205nn., 8, 9, 12, 15
Engel's. *See* Engel's coefficient
Estonia, 375
EUROPASS project, 274
European Union, 331
Finland, 332
Ghana, 216
Greece, 290–96 passim, 298, 299, 300, 319n.7
Hungary, 388, 389, 391, 393–95
India, 103–9, 114, 116, 117
Indonesia, 139
Israel, 433, 439, 448, 449, 450
Korea, 87, 88, 91, 93, 95, 97
Kyrgyzstan, 375
Latin America, 500–1, 505, 506–7
Latvia, 376
Leyden's. *See* Leyden Poverty Line
Lithuania, 376
Luxembourg Income Study, 271
Mexico, 540–48 passim, 563n.3
multiple, 261
New Zealand (approaches), 173–82
Nigeria (de-emphasis in), 214
Philippines, 123
Poland, 410, 416–19, 421–22
relative (defined), 259

Russia, 358, 362–64, 370 (Table 17.4), 382 (Table 17A.1)
Sierra Leone, 221, 222 (Table 12.2)
Singapore, 139
South Africa, 232, 238
South Asia, 76, 80
Soviet Union. *See* Soviet Union (former): MMS budget
Subjective. *See* Consensual (Subjective) Poverty Line/ approach
Sweden, 333, 334
Turkey, 304, 308, 311, 536n.5
Ukraine, 365, 372
United States, 123, 454–60, 482–83, 536n.5
Venezuela, 536n.5
weaknesses of, 21, 34, 97, 506–7
World Bank's (1979), 524–25
"Poverty risk", 279
Programmes. *See* Anti-poverty programmes

Qualitative research
central task of, 330
Latin America (needed in), 511
limitations of, 330, 342
Nordic countries, 342–45
Quantitative research
Latin America (predominance in), 511
Nordic countries, 330–42

Rainwater, Lee, 255–56, 261
Rediscovery of poverty
Canada, 18
Nordic countries, 250, 327–29, 347
Western Europe, 18, 250
"Regionalization" concept of poverty, 55
Regional overview, 18–19
Relative deprivation concept, 50, 51, 255, 256, 257, 259
Relative poverty. *See also* Absolute/ relative poverty
Egypt, 193, 195, 204, 205n.9
Greece, 295–96
line, 259, 260–61, 271, 278
Soviet Union (former), 360
Yugoslavia (former), 402–4
"Relative poverty risk", 279
Research. *See also* Approach(es); Comparative research; Methodologies
analysis vs. fact-finding, 20–22

Research, *cont.*
empirical, 258
growth of, 20–21
overview of continents, 37–45
overview of recent, 266
positive aspects of current, 37, 45–46
qualitative. *See* Qualitative research
quantitative. *See* Quantitative research
relationship of poverty to occurrence of, 187
relationship to policy, 580
weaknesses of current, 22–23, 33–37, 45, 87, 571
Resource(s)
approach/concept, 253–54, 259
defined, 15
disposable income as measure of, 48
inadequate internal, 18
lack of. *See* Lack of resources
transfers of, 15–16
Rimashevskaia, N. M., 356
Ringen, Stein, 51, 52, 253–55, 256, 257, 280n.3, 340, 401
Room, Graham, 253, 280n.3
Rostow, W. W., 55, 153
Rowntree
evolution of research, 47
method, 91 (Table 6.4), 92
subsistence minimum concept, 255
Ruggles, Patricia, 455–60 passim, 476
Rural poverty
Brazil, 519–28 passim, 530–33 passim, 535, 536nn., 6, 8
China, 18, 31, 145, 146, 148, 150, 151, 151–52, 153, 154
Cyprus, 313, 314, 315, 320n.18
Egypt, 191–201 passim, 204nn. 3, 4, 205nn., 8, 9, 12, 13
Ghana, 220–21
Greece, 289–97 passim
Hungary, 390, 404
India, 102–19 passim
Israel, 434
Korea, 88–90, 93, 96, 97
Kyrgyzstan, 380
Latin America, 495, 497
Mexico, 542, 545, 551, 554, 555, 557, 559–60
Philippines, 124, 126, 127, 129, 130
Sierra Leone, 222 (Table 12.2)

South Africa, 26, 237, 238–39, 240, 241, 242
South Asia, 70–78 passim, 81
Turkey, 289, 307–11 passim, 320n.14
urban/rural distinction, 19–20, 571–72
Yugoslavia (former), 390, 404
Russia, 354–84. *See also* Soviet Union (former)
basic-needs concept, 363
children, 377
consensual definition, 360
data sources, 366
equivalence scales, 363
explanations of poverty, 377–80
failure of the state, 18
Gini coefficient, 378, 383 (Table 17A.2)
head-count ratio, 370 (Table 17.4), 371, 382
incidence of poverty, 368, 369 (Table 17.3), 370–72, 377–78, 379 (Table 17.7), 382
income distribution, 383 (Table 17A.2)
inequality and growth of poverty, 378–79
Institute for the Study of Socio-economic Problems of the Population, 356, 358, 362
MMS budget, 363
poverty gap, 370 (Table 17.4), 371–72
poverty line, 358, 362–64, 370 (Table 17.4), 382 (Table 17A.1)
subsistence minimum concept, 361–65
transition in research, 357–59, 380
women's status, 377
working poor, 377–78, 381
Rwanda, 18

Saharan African Programme, 217
Samad, S. A., 29, 30, 33, 593
Scale of equivalency. *See* Equivalence scales
Scandinavia. *See* Nordic countries
Sen, A. K.
concepts, 47, 50
indices, 195, 292, 299, 528, 540, 545, 546
Serbia, 403–4. *See also* Yugoslavia (former)

Sierra Leone, 210, 221, 222 (Table 12.2). *See also* Anglophone West Africa
Singapore, 130–41. *See also* South-East Asia
 data sources, 139–40
 effectiveness of anti-poverty programmes, 28
 findings, 141
 measures and poverty line, 138–39
 training of researchers in England, 123
Slovenia, 400–1, 402, 403, 406. *See also* Yugoslavia (former)
Social Assistance Dynamics Panel Study, 41
"Social Assistance Dynamics" study, 275–77
Social exclusion/marginalization
 Asia, 56
 as cause or theoretical framework, 26, 575–77, 579
 European Community, 267, 269
 Finland, 329
 Ghana, 216, 220
 Greece, 289, 318–19, 319n.2
 Nordic countries, 336, 342, 343, 345, 346
 scope and significance of, 14
 Turkey, 289, 318–19
 United States, 475, 476
Social features (as concepts of poverty), 53
Social minima
 Poland, 416–19, 421–22
 Slovenia, 400–1
South Africa, 227–47
 African National Congress, 227, 231
 apartheid and race relations, 19, 187, 227–28, 229, 234–35, 236, 239
 basic indicators, 244 (Table 13.2)
 Carnegie Commission (first), 229, 232, 235, 244n.5
 Carnegie Inquiry (second), 230, 231, 232–33, 235, 236, 237, 239, 240, 241, 243, 245nn., 7, 15
 causes of poverty, 18, 236
 children (nutritional status), 243
 concepts and definitions, 56–57, 232–33
 current research and lacunae, 242–44
 data, 22, 230, 231, 236–37, 245n.16

disease, 233, 240
Gini coefficient, 238
historical context, 228–30, 234–35
hypotheses and theoretical framework, 234–35
impact on neighbouring countries, 31, 243–44
income data, 238
independent black enclaves, 236, 239, 243, 245n.10
lack of poverty reduction in, 28
macro vs. micro perspectives, 235
major results, 237–41
multiple characteristics of poverty, 233
poor living conditions, 239–40
poverty line, 232, 238
Project for Statistics on Living Standards and Development, 230–31, 237, 238, 239, 242, 245n.16
Reconstruction and Development Programme, 30, 227, 230
rural poverty, 26, 237, 238–39, 240, 241, 242
South Africa Living Standards Survey, 238, 245n.8
Transvaal, 228–29, 242
unemployment, 241
urban poverty, 241
women's status, 240, 241
South Asia, 65–85
 absolute/relative poverty, 68, 80
 anti-poverty policies and programmes (progress of), 27, 28, 78–79
 classifying poverty research in, 66–67
 concepts of poverty in, 54, 67–68
 culture of poverty approach, 71–72
 data sources, 73–76, 80
 defined, 65
 empowerment of the disadvantaged, 73, 81
 evaluation of research in, 79–82
 factors affecting recent trends, 76–78
 green revolution, 69, 71
 historical context of poverty in, 70
 Independent South Asian Commission on Poverty Alleviation, 65, 73–74, 76
 labour migration, 82
 neoclassical approach, 68–69
 participatory approach, 72–73

South Asia, *cont.*
  plantation economy, 70
  political economy approach, 70–71
  poverty incidence and trends, 76, 80
  rural poverty, 70–71, 72–73, 74–75, 76, 77, 78, 81
  significance of (in poverty research), 65–66
  South Asian Association for Regional Cooperation (SAARC), 65, 66, 73–74, 76, 77, 80
  theoretical frameworks, 25, 26, 68–73
  United Nations University South Asian Perspective Project, 75
  urban poverty, 71–72, 76, 78, 81
  weaknesses of externally driven research in, 23
  women's status, 73, 75, 81
South-East Asia, 123–44. *See also* Indonesia; Malaysia; Philippines; Singapore
  absolute poverty, 140
  ARTEP studies on, 74–75
Southern Africa, 31, 243–44
Soviet Union (former), 354–84. *See also individual republics*
  the aged, 361, 381
  anti-poverty measures, 356–57
  cause of poverty, 360, 377–80
  children, 361, 377, 381
  compared with Latin America, 370
  concepts of poverty, 57, 359–61, 364–65
  data problems and sources, 357–58, 365–66
  equivalence scales, 360
  head-count ratios, 368–76 passim, 380, 382
  incidence of poverty, 367–70, 377–79, 381, 382
  inequality and growth of poverty, 378–79, 381
  isolation (problems of), 356
  lack of research, 355–56, 357, 358
  limitations of research, 249
  MMS budget, 359–61, 363–65, 367, 368, 369, 375, 380
  poverty gaps, 369–75 passim, 380
  poverty line. *See* Soviet Union (former): MMS budget
  relative poverty approach, 360
  socialism and poverty, 354–57
  transition in research, 357–59, 381
  women's status, 377, 381
  working poor, 377–78, 381
Spain, 270, 273, 281n.20
Sri Lanka. *See also* South Asia
  ARTEP studies on, 74–75
  concepts of poverty, 55
  culture of poverty approach, 71–72
  effectiveness of anti-poverty programmes, 27
  Food Stamp Scheme, 79
  Janasaviya Programme, 46, 67, 78
  malnutrition, 76
  national institutions, 66, 75–76
  national poverty databases, 75–76
  poverty level, 76
  rural poverty, 72–73, 74, 75
  SAARC report, 73–74
  urban poverty, 75
Structural poverty
  distinguished from culture of poverty, 569
  Latin America, 507
Subjective Poverty Line. *See* Consensual (Subjective) Poverty Line/approach
Subsistence (minimum) concept, 50, 51, 53, 59
  Africa, 56
  distinguished from relative deprivation, 255
  Eastern Europe, 387, 389
  as indirect concept, 256
  re non-producing West, 57
  Russia, 361–65
  Yugoslavia (former), 389, 400–1, 402, 403
Swaziland, 244 (Table 13.2)
Sweden. *See also* Nordic countries; Welfare state/system
  A Book About Poverty, 333
  accumulation of deprivation, 339–42
  the aged (poverty among), 271, 339
  atypical poverty demographics, 272
  compared with Australia, 334
  compared with other Western countries, 333
  Consensual Poverty Line/approach, 52, 334, 341–42
  construction of welfare state, 325–26
  economic poverty, 333–34
  EU membership, 348
  incidence of poverty, 271

level-of-living standard surveys, 327
Luxembourg Income Study, 170, 270, 271, 272, 334
poverty lines, 333, 334
recent history, 325–27
rediscovery of poverty, 327, 328–29, 347
"Social Assistance Dynamics" study, 275
social assistance research, 335, 336–37
Stockholm, 337
unemployment, 326, 329, 347
women's status, 339
young people (poverty mainly among), 28–29, 334
Switzerland, 270, 271

TACIS programme, 359
Tadjikistan, 382
Tanzania, 244 (Table 13.2)
Thailand, 28, 74
The Gambia, 210, 221. *See also* Anglophone West Africa
Theil coefficient, 298
Theories/theoretical frameworks. *See also* Approach(es); Causes/explanations of poverty; Hypotheses
Anglophone West Africa, 27, 223
China, 152–54
culture of poverty. *See* Culture of poverty approach
Czechoslovakia (former), 396–99 passim
Eastern Europe, 387–88, 389–90, 391–92
Ghana, 219–21
Hungary, 392–96 passim
Latin America, 498, 507–10
Mexico, 548–51
Nigeria, 213–15
overview of, 25–27
place of (in research), 487–88
social exclusion. *See* Social exclusion/marginalization
South Africa, 235–36
South Asia, 25, 26, 68–73
United States, 462–65, 487–88
weaknesses of current, 36, 130
Yugoslavia (former), 401, 402, 403
Third World: studies compared with those in West, 230

"Time-adjusted" concept of poverty, 51
Townsend, Peter, 47, 50, 51, 52, 56, 255, 256, 259, 280nn., 3, 5, 328, 344
Training programmes (futility of), 30
Turkey, 303–12
concepts of poverty, 57
data sources and quality, 303–4, 310–11, 315–16
economic characteristics and development, 25, 287, 288, 304–10
education, 310, 312
estimates (1970s, 1980s), 310
extent of poverty, 308
findings (summary), 317–19
Gini coefficient, 311
Hacettepe University survey (1973), 304, 308, 311
impact of European restructuring on, 318–19
interregional inequalities, 309
K ratio, 307
modernization, 304–10, 318
nutrition and life expectancy, 312
paternalistic structures, 289, 305
poverty line, 304, 308, 311, 536n.5
research deficiencies, 289, 315–17
rural poverty, 289, 307–11 passim, 320n.14
social exclusion, 289, 318–19
socioeconomic inequalities, 304–10, 318
squatter housing, 310
State Planning Organization (SPO), 306, 308, 309
unemployment, 310
urbanization (effects of), 309
urban poverty, 307–8, 309, 310
Turkmenistan, 369 (Table 17.3), 382

Ukraine. *See also* Soviet Union (former)
data sources, 366
incidence of poverty, 368, 369 (Table 17.3), 372–73, 382
poverty gap, 373
poverty line, 365, 372
shift away from MMS budget, 365
working poor, 378
Underclass hypothesis (USA), 473–77, 572
Underdevelopment: poverty as problem of, 37

Unemployment
  as causation factor, 574, 575
  chronic throughout OECD, 489
  Denmark, 326, 328, 344, 345, 348
  Finland, 326, 329, 336, 347
  Greece, 290, 294, 300, 319n.11
  Israel, 450
  Latin America, 498, 502–3, 510
  Mexico, 548–50, 556, 558
  Poland, 412, 413
  South Africa, 241
  Sweden, 326, 329, 347
  Turkey, 310
  United States, 469, 470, 474, 475
UNICEF
  data used in the Philippines, 128
  Eastern Europe/former Soviet Union (research in), 361
  Latin America, 505
  nutrition research, 243
  Russia (research in), 361
  support in South Asia, 80
United Kingdom
  the aged (poverty among), 271, 272
  children and poverty, 272
  dismantling of anti-poverty programmes, 18–19
  incidence of poverty, 271
  Luxembourg Income Study, 170, 270, 271, 272
  "Social Assistance Dynamics" study, 275
  training of South-East Asian researchers, 123
United Nations
  Africa (predictions re), 187
  data used in the Philippines, 128
  Economic Commission for Africa, 218, 222, 224
United Nations Development Programme
  Africa, 217, 218, 221, 223, 224
  basic human needs concept, 500
  Human Development Index, 9, 63, 221
  Latin America, 499, 500, 501
  policies of, 503, 504
  view of causes of poverty, 510
United Nations Protein-Calorie Advisory Group, 140
United Nations University South Asian Perspective Project, 75
United States, 453–77. *See also* North America
  absolute vs. relative poverty, 455, 458–60, 482
  the aged, 458, 460, 471, 472, 483–84
  alternative (non-income-based) concepts, 460–62
  basic needs concept, 455, 462
  Boston, 469
  children, 271, 460, 472, 484
  comparative research, 472–73
  compared with Canada, 477, 479–80, 481
  concepts of poverty, 454–77
  culture of poverty approach, 71–72, 473, 569
  data sources, 490n.1
  Department of Agriculture (surveys), 123
  dismantling of anti-poverty programmes, 18–19, 29
  effectiveness of anti-poverty programmes, 28
  Family Support Act (1988), 467–68
  female-headed households, 461, 464–69 passim, 474, 475, 476
  feminization of poverty, 123–24, 127
  growth of research, 454
  incidence of poverty, 123, 271, 455
  Institute for Research on Poverty, 454, 487
  international influence of, 123–24, 585
  Luxembourg Income Study, 170, 270, 271
  "net earnings capacity", 460–62
  overview of research, 42–44
  Panel Study of Income Dynamics, 454
  pauperization, 463, 473
  persistent poverty, 454, 476, 486
  poverty gap, 460
  poverty level (defined), 123
  poverty lines, 123, 454–60, 482–83, 536n.5
  racial issues, 463, 464, 466, 467, 468, 473–77
  social assistance, 275, 456, 462–63, 483–84
  social isolation, 475, 476
  social policy shifts, 453–54
  subsistence concept (official use of), 255
  theories and hypotheses, 26, 462–65, 487–88, 569

underclass, 464, 467, 473–77, 572
unemployment, 469, 470, 474, 475
War on Poverty/Great Society, 44, 453, 455, 462, 464, 465, 467, 477, 486, 488
welfare state: conservative attack, 463–68, 580
welfare state: liberal defence, 468–73
"workfare", 467, 473
Urban poverty
 Brazil, 520, 521, 523–33 passim, 535, 536nn., 6, 8
 China, 146
 Cyprus, 313, 314, 315, 320n.18
 Egypt, 192, 193, 194, 195, 197, 199, 204n.4, 205nn., 8, 9, 12, 13
 Greece, 290–96 passim, 298–301, 319n.11
 Hungary, 395, 404
 importance of culture of poverty approach, 71–72
 India, 102–10 passim
 Korea, 87, 88–90, 92, 93, 95, 96, 97
 Kyrgyzstan, 380
 Latin America, 495, 498, 502, 505
 Mexico, 547–48, 551, 554, 555 (Table 24.1), 557, 558, 559–60, 562
 Nigeria, 214
 Philippines, 124, 129
 Sierra Leone, 222 (Table 12.2)
 South Africa, 241
 South Asia, 71–72, 76, 81
 Turkey, 307–8, 309, 310
 urban/rural distinction, 19–20, 571–72
 Yugoslavia (former), 390, 403, 404
Uruguay, 497
USSR. *See* Soviet Union (former)
Uzbekistan, 366, 368, 369 (Table 17.3), 380, 382

Venezuela, 536n.5

Water. *See also* Basic (human) needs concept
 Egypt (unsafe water), 200
 omission from African poverty definitions, 187
 South Africa (poor quality in), 240–41
Welfare state/system. *See also* Nordic countries
 attacked and defended in USA, 463–73
 attempts to modify, 18
 bifurcated (USA), 477
 experience of being poor in a, 344–45
 as model for assessing poverty, 249–50
 New Zealand, 160–64
 Nordic (development and future of), 325–26, 348
 poverty-alleviating effects of, 332, 334, 347
 relation to poverty trends in Central/Eastern Europe, 57–58
 research affected by type of, 265
 task of, 489
Wentzel, Wilfred, 238, 239
Western Europe, 251–86. *See also* European Community/Union
 the aged (poverty among), 271
 conceptual and methodological issues, 251–64
 equivalence scales used in, 263
 growth of data on living standards, 22
 major research projects, 267–77
 measures of poverty, 249
 multi-dimensional approaches, 256–59
 as policy model for Eastern Europe, 385–86
 rediscovery of poverty, 18, 250
 three-fold shift in perspective, 23–24
Western world
 children and poverty, 271–72
 classic concepts of poverty, 49–53
 common poverty pattern in advanced, 272
 conceptual focus on, 48, 49
 dominance in research training, 123
 overview, 249–50
 rediscovery of poverty, 18, 250
 studies compared with those in Third World, 230
Wilson, W. J., 474–75, 487
Women's status
 Brazil (female-headed households), 519
 Cyprus, 314
 Egypt, 196, 197, 198, 199
 feminization of poverty. *See* Feminization of poverty

Women's status, *cont.*
  Finland, 336
  Greece, 294
  Israel, 438, 441, 445
  Mexico, 550–51, 560–62
  New Zealand, 167, 169, 171, 172, 173
  Poland, 411, 412, 414
  social exclusion, 576
  South Africa, 240, 241
  South Asia, 73, 75, 81
  Soviet Union (former), 377, 381
  suggested concentration on, 581
  Sweden, 339
  United States (female-headed households), 461, 464–69 passim, 474, 475, 476
World Bank
  Africa, 187
  Brazil, 525, 526, 527, 531, 532
  as cause of poverty, 580
  definition of poverty, 500
  Egypt (estimates, findings re), 191–98 passim, 201, 203, 204nn., 2, 4
  estimate (1990) of world poor, 63
  Ghana (projects in), 217, 218
  Indonesia, 140
  Latin America, 499, 501, 508
  necessary biases of, 22–23
  Philippines, 128, 140
  policies of, 503, 504
  poverty line used by, 524–25
  publications of, 66
  relative poverty concept, 524–25
  Russia/Soviet Union, 354, 358, 359, 361, 362, 364, 365, 366, 368, 372 (Table 17.5), 373, 376, 377, 380
  South Africa, 231, 236, 238
  South Asia, 68, 75
  Sri Lanka research, 68–69, 77
  studies compared with those in Western countries, 230
  studies of growth patterns, 574
  target system for evaluating impoverished countries, 149
  view of causes of poverty, 510
World Development Report
  South Africa (ranking of), 237
  use of GNP per capita, 19, 20
  use in the Philippines, 128

Young people. *See also* Children
  Israel, 438–40
  Nordic countries, 28–29, 334, 344, 347
Yugoslavia (former), 400–4. *See also* Eastern Europe
  the aged, 404
  children, 402, 404
  comparative research, 387–90, 406
  concepts of poverty, 57
  Croatia, 401, 402
  economic status, 386
  equivalence scales, 403
  food ratio, 403
  major findings, 402–4
  poverty rates, 390
  relative poverty estimations, 402–4
  rural poverty, 390, 404
  Serbia, 403–4
  Slovenia, 400–1, 402, 403, 406
  subsistence concept, 389, 402, 403
  surveys of well-being, 401–2
  theoretical frameworks, 401, 402, 403
  urban poverty, 390, 403, 404

Zambia, 244 (Table 13.2)
Zimbabwe, 244 (Table 13.2)

international social science council/conceil international des sciences sociales

CROP

Comparative Research Programme on Poverty

CROP publications

1. **Poverty: Research Projects, Institutes, Persons**, Tinka Ewoldt-Leicher and Arnaud F. Marks (eds.), Tilburg Bergen, Amsterdam 1995, 248 pp. (will also be published on Internet).

2. **Urban Poverty: Characteristics, Causes and Consequences**, David Satterthwaite (ed.), special issue of *Environment and Urbanization*. Volume 7 No. 1 April 1995, 283 pp.

3. **Urban Poverty II: From Understanding to Action**, David Satterthwaite (ed.), special issue of *Environment and Urbanization*. Volume 7 No. 2 October 1995, 266 pp.

4. **Women and Poverty – The Feminization of Poverty**, The Norwegian National Commission for UNESCO and CROP, Oslo and Bergen, 1995. (Published in Norwegian only)

5. **Poverty: A Global Review. Handbook on International Poverty Research**, Else Øyen, S. M. Miller, Syed Abdus Samad (eds.), Scandinavian University Press, 1996.

CROP Secretariat
Fosswinckelsgate 7
N-5007 Bergen
NORWAY

Tel: +47 55 58 97 39
Fax: +47 55 58 97 45
E-mail: crop@uib.no
www: http://www.uib.no./svf/helsos/crop